Living Like Crazy

Paul Gilbert

First published in Great Britain in 2017 by Annwyn House

Second Edition
Published in 2018 by Annwyn House
York, YO24 1AW

Proofer: Dom Egan
Indexer: Dr Laurence Errington
Typesetter: Dr Hannah Gilbert
Book Cover by Angela House
Cover image by Romolo Tavani, © Shutterstock
ISBN: 978-1-9998683-0-7

In memory of John S. Price

(1930-2017)

Mentor and inspiration

Living Like Crazy

Paul Gilbert

Annwyn House

Contents

Acknowledgements

For any work of this kind there are a huge number of people that contribute. We are a species that loves to pass on information and teach; our minds are vehicles for the flow of information. Indeed, from generation to generation human culture is completely and utterly dependent on it. I have been fortunate indeed to have many teachers who themselves have been containers of knowledge generated over the eons. Some of them have now passed away and are remembered fondly.

The 1970s was a fortunate time when you could study for free and I took full advantage. After my economics degree I realised my true wish was to study psychology, and almost by accident I was lucky enough to do so at Sussex. From there I was able to go to Edinburgh, where Ivy Blackburn expertly and gently guided me in my PhD studies and cognitive therapy. Clinical psychology training followed in Norwich and here again were some fantastic teachers. My supervisor over many years was Kitty Lawrence, who was brilliantly insightful and wonderfully supportive. I remember her with considerable gratitude and fondness. One of the leading psychiatrists in Norwich was Roy Divine, an ex-lecturer in neurology, whose ward rounds were run like teaching seminars. Another psychiatrist who I worked closely with was Bill Hughes. He was keen on Jung, and later went on to do Jungian training. In the meantime, in the early 1980s he instigated for us trainee psychologists to undertake joint psychiatry and psychology training, empathy training with actors, person-centred training, and also a couple of years of Kleinian group therapy training, which was fascinating (if at times bizarre). That was Wednesday nights in the hospital library. Nothing like this exists today, tragically. For his friendship, enthusiasm and guidance, a great debt. Elspeth McAdam was for a few years a psychiatrist in training and then consultant; she became a wonderful friend, mentor, discussant, and a passionate family therapist. These were wonderful days for learning.

But the 1980s was also a time when the government was interfering more and more in the running of the Health Service, and doing it badly. In Norwich all promotions were frozen for years, and so I had to move to Derby, having been invited to run the adult mental health specialty by my long-term friend from Edinburgh, Chris Gillespie. Once again, many generous people educated me. I was able to spend four years in a Jungian day hospital, with supervision. Chris Cullen helped me to link with Derby University and set up the mental health research centre, linking university and hospital. This functioned well for many years until the trust closed us down because of cuts. From the early 1990s Steve Allan was one of our first research colleagues, who was a wizard at statistics and other things, and we published much together before he moved to Leicester. Karl Olsson followed wonderfully, and then Chris Irons, who subsequently did a PhD with me and has moved on to become an amazing compassion focused therapist and trainer. In recent years Kirsten McEwan and Francisca Catarino have both brought fantastic dedication, brilliance and support of the research to the project.

The late 1980s and 1990s was also a time when evolutionary approaches to psychopathology were growing, and in this country we had a small group of thinkers that included the eminent John Price, well known for his work on social hierarchies and depression, Brian Lake and Dorothy Heard, whose expertise was in attachment, and Anthony Stevens, one of the leading Jungian UK therapists and evolutionary focused thinkers, who did a lot of work on combining Jung's concept of archetypes with Bowlby's concepts of attachment and who encouraged me to read Bowlby. The late Michael Chance was an ethologist and primatologist well known for his concepts of variation in attention structure in hierarchical organisations. He edited a book that I provided a chapter for called *Social Fabrics of the Mind*. Also in our group was Dave Stevens, who was a Buddhist psychologist interested in evolution, and Dennis Trent, an American psychologist who was working with us. We would try to meet on a regular basis around the country for discussions about how to advance evolutionary approaches to psychopathology and therapy. One of the consequences was a 1994 paper in the British Journal of Psychiatry on social competition and mental health problems. Also, we had colleagues in America such as Michael McGuire, and Russ Gardner, a wonderfully original thinker who devised the concept of mental states also being a communication state. Another wonderful thinker was Leon Sloman of the Clark Institute in Canada; we ended up editing the book *Subordination and Defeat* together in 2000. To this group of people I owe a huge debt for their excitement, enthusiasm and just wonderful knowledge they were all so eager to share.

In 2006 we set up the Compassion Mind Foundation, a charity to support compassion research and implementation around the world as best we could. People like Deborah Lee, Ken Goss, Chris Irons, Mary Welford, and Jean Gilbert, who were all (in the 1990s) part of the shame discussion group, worked diligently to get the foundation established and the training organised. Diane Woollands was, at the time of my research, a medical secretary and threw herself tirelessly into the business of getting things through approved by the Charities Commission and then taking us through the first few years of conference and workshop training to establish our financial footing. Fantastic efforts, and after Diane left the Foundation was managed by Mary Welford with Jane Redford, and then later on Leanne Culson took over the administrative reigns until she left earlier this year. Much has happened since then, and we now have the most incredible people working in the foundation.: Jaskaran Basran actually started with me as a voluntary researcher with Francisca, and later stepped into the role of foundation administrator, and she has just been the most extraordinary person. Nothing is too much for her, and her brilliance in sorting out all kinds of computer and or organisation problems is extraordinary. Immense gratitude to her. Binita Shah joined us recently and has been the most fantastic accounts manager. Angela Wright has become my PA and tries to keep my written English readable. Angela House is our foundation promoter and guiding strategic developments. My wife Jean, as a Trustee, works tirelessly in the background, ensuring that training runs smoothly. Recently, my daughter Hannah has come on board, bringing with her experiences in anthropology, therapy training and compassion- focused wellbeing organisation.

Compassion Focused Therapy has now spread all over the world, slightly leapfrogging evidence of its effectiveness - although that is catching up rapidly now. So, I couldn't finish these acknowledgements without recognition for our international colleagues and close friends. A vast number of people have been very supportive and contributed to the development of compassion focused therapy. In this country, to mention just a few are: Deborah Lee, Ken Goss, Chris Irons, Mary Welford, Wendy Wood, Andrew Rayner, Michelle Cree, and Kate Lucre. In Portugal Jose Pinot-Gouveia Marcela Matos and Daniel Rijo have pioneered great CFT research. In the USA, there is Russell Kolts, Yotam Heineberg, Dan Martin and Dennis Tirch. Dennis set up a Compassionate Mind Foundation in New York and is a fellow guitar player. Nico Petrocchi, set up a Compassionate Mind Foundation in Rome and with whom I've run some personal retreats and practices in an amazing monastery on the outskirts of Rome. He is also a brilliant researcher and singer. Francis Gheysen and Pascal Delamillieure have established a Compassionate Mind Foundation in France. James Bennett Levy established a Compassionate Mind Foundation in Australia. James Kirby from the University of Queensland has now established a compassion research centre and is also a brilliant researcher, and great fun (although I'm not sure about his singing or guitar playing… yet!). He also helped to get me invited as a visiting professorship at the University.

I am hugely thankful for the help and assistance of our proof-reader, Dom Egan, and expert indexer, Dr Laurence Errington, who have helped to remove errors and improved the quality of the text.

Finally, as mentioned many times I am deeply indebted to my family – Jean, Hannah, James and Lucy, for all their love and support Hannah has been especially enthusiastic and encouraging, and has spent many hours trying to ensure that this book is in reasonable order. Without her, it would never have seen the light of day.

PREFACE TO SECOND EDITION

Hannah and I must confess we were not anticipating a second edition quite so soon. It has come about because the copies we originally produced sold very quickly. We also became aware of some my linguistic difficulties (poor spelling and grammar) which we had missed first time. We wanted to resolve these and with the help of a wonderful copy editor, Dom Egan, we hope we have. Dom also suggested work on the footnotes to make them more consistent, and in a couple of places just make things clearer. We hope your reading experience will be smoother.

I haven't added very much to this edition other than in the postscript. These address the issues of how we might think about the different levels of our minds to better consider some of the social problems we have. Basically, human minds are in a constant battle between different emotions and motives that have their origins in reproductive strategies. Ever since the advent of agriculture there's been a battle between those who follow self-focused accumulator strategies, of having more and more, and those who would wish to focus on accumulating less and sharing more. The former strategies became advantaged with the invention of agriculture and we are still perplexed with what to do about them. The strategies are simple in themselves: Seek as much control as you can over resources, hold onto those resources and exploit your power for your own self (and kin) benefit where you can. Gain and maintain power and privilege. Today the strategies operating in high wealth environments are finding new ways to exert their power in processes like dark money and so on. These are minds out of balance which could only prosper in this modern environment, where wealth has been accumulated over many generations in the hands of the few, and by the efforts of the many. These strategies would have been unhelpful in our original hunter gatherer societies, where accumulators and non-sharers were shunned. Today it is quite the opposite. Privilege and honours are bestowed on the wealthy. These self-focused competitive strategies are driving us crazy. In spite of living, in the West at least, with comforts and wealth beyond the wildest dreams of people a thousand years ago, we are easily frustrated - often in a rage - over limitations, traffic jams, work demands, no time for fun. To some extent the very wealthy can buy themselves out of this, but in order to do it they create the conditions to keep us working harder and faster because the money has to flow upwards. These strategies are not designed for slowing, appreciating and sharing.

Humanity is struggling to find ways to balance our minds and create schools, workplaces, cultures and societies that enable us to balance our minds and where wealth is created for human benefit. Wealth should be created to improve humanity; our time and our efforts are not to create Ferraris for the rich but solar panels for the poor. We are struggling to know how to create the social conditions that will enable us to stimulate cooperative sharing psychology. Be it with use of taxation or creation of the welfare state, those following self-focused accumulator strategies have done a good job in gaining power and ridiculing such efforts. But the fact is that caring and sharing are not simply moral issues because they are what makes us human. This is easily demonstrated. There is considerable research now that shows that sharing and caring have profound effects on our mental states, a whole range of physiological processes (even genetic expressions), the quality of our social relationships, the goods and services we choose to create, the cultures we choose to build. If you think of humanity as a set of interconnected minds then caring and sharing psychology that flows in that field of shared minds has profound effects on the well-being that flows between all minds. As we begin to understand our minds and the ways in which the content of our minds are full of evolved dispositions, we are but one step away from recognising a need to take more control over how our minds are nourished, educated and asked to operate in different facets of life.

The fact that is we all just find ourselves here and hang around for around 25,000 days. We are bubbles of consciousness that experience the playing out of different archetypal themes, to survive, to thrive, have friends, to form sexual relationships and families, grow old, decay and die. The challenge now is to wake up to the dramas that have been written for us by our genes and by our cultures, and think about whether we would like to write some new scripts. In terms of programs like *Westworld* it is about waking up and seeking to break out from the programming and conditioning that has been so neatly created behind the scenes by our genes and our social conditions.

We can think of our minds, cities, business activities and societies like gardens. They will grow according to a whole range of random factors that impinge on them. There is no deliberate cultivation or aim. But, like a garden left to grow by itself, you may not like the outcome. Randomness alone is not a reliable process for the advancement of humanity. Wise cultivation maybe.

FOREWORD

Some history

From the time of being a teenager, and being introduced to Jung's concepts of archetypes, I've felt a fascination with the evolution of the mind and the nature of its internal potential. This potential has both a positive but also a (very) dark side, which obviously has been known for a long time. Reaching back thousands of years, it was mainly spiritual and contemplative pursuits that sought to tame the dark side in favour of morality and compassion. Some religions, however, such as the Aztecs, accentuated the dark side with horrific human sacrifices, torture and social control. Even religions which were supposedly compassion-orientated have instigated atrocities such as the Crusades and the Inquisition.

A lot of Freudian and early psychodynamic writing was concerned with the dark sides of the mind: monsters from the id, to quote the classic 1950s science-fiction movie *Forbidden Planet*. With the advent of the counselling and cognitive behaviour therapies, issues regarding the fundamental nature of our minds gradually passed into the shadows. Concern was focused on consciously available thoughts and changeable behaviours. Metaphors for the mind increasingly utilised concepts from the computer world of information processing and data analysis. Exploration of the conscious and non-conscious dark sides were left to the writers of fiction. Our foreboding archetypal patterns that scare us, and figure so largely in human history, in our wars, tortures, slavery and general nastiness, turn up in the storylines of *Game of Thrones* and *Westworld*. My own explorations into this territory, however, were difficult and had to wait until I had some psychodynamic training.

My interest was always in evolutionary models of the mind, and my first book in 1984 on depression, called *Depression: From Psychology to Brain State*, touched on these to the extent that one can understand why certain environments trigger certain mental health problems by understanding the way the mind evolved. In those days, psychologists were battling with organic psychiatrists, who argued that a lot of mental suffering was the result of mischievous neurochemistry and disordered synapses. The idea that the source of these physiological changes could be in the environment, rather than a flaw in the person, was an emerging paradigm linked to the studies of how stress, learned helplessness and attachment disruption change our bodies and brains. This emergence occurred along with the development of what was called biopsychosocial medicine and psychosomatic medicine.

It's difficult to know where the studies of the linkage between environment and physiology started. For psychology, it was probably the famous Russian physiologist Ivan Pavlov, who showed that physiological changes occur according to stimulus contingencies. For example, you could get dogs to salivate to a bell if you paired the bell with food often enough. The environment changes the physiology. Experiences change us physiologically, and once changed those physiological patterns have powerful effects on how we think and feel and are motivated. We can get caught in loops between physiological change, cognitive change, and back to physiological change. *Depression: From...* almost didn't see the light of day, though, because it was rejected by quite a few publishers. I was immensely grateful, therefore, to Michael Forster, who in 1982 saw the book and thought it worth pursuing. Michael went on to create Psychology Press, which would later merge with Routledge and others. He was extremely enthusiastic and helpful to me.

During the late 1970s and early 1980s, I was exposed to psychodynamic models from both my supervisor Kitty Lawrence, who was a wonderful early guide and mentor, and trainer psychiatrist Bill Hughes. He brought training psychologists and psychiatrists together to do things like drama training for empathy awareness and also set up some psychodynamic Kleinian object relations training, which is focused on the dark side in many ways. He went on to do his own Jungian training. My good friend, psychiatrist Elspeth McAdam, introduced me to family therapy and the work of Humberto Maturana and Francisco Varela, and their book *The Tree of Knowledge*. In addition, I was lucky to develop close relations with people like John Price (UK evolutionary psychiatrist), Russell Gardner (US evolutionary psychiatrist), Anthony Stevens (UK psychiatrist and Jungian analyst) and Michael Chance (UK primatologist). Brian Lake (psychiatrist and analyst) and also Dorothy Heard (psychologist and attachment theorist) joined us with wonderful insight and discussions (see their book *The Challenge of Attachment for Care Giving*). We would meet regularly, although Russell was in the United States. Occasionally, we would have international meetings and chat with people like Randolph Ness and Dan Wilson (evolutionary psychiatrists). Another highly influential figure was Professor of Psychiatry Michael McGuire, who studied primates and wrote on evolutionary approaches to mental health problems. Unfortunately, there was no such thing as Skype or Zoom in those days. Some of us, mostly under the direction of Russell Gardner, formed a society called Across Species Comparison in Psychopathology. This was primarily to develop evolutionary models of mental health problems – a key aim was to de-pathologise. There is nothing in evolution that requires happiness, and quite a lot that permits and even creates suffering. We had a newsletter and about a hundred members, but like many things, it gradually faded out. My relationship with Anthony Stevens fostered even more interest in archetypal psychology, and I was very influenced by his book *Archetype: A Natural History of the Self*. I was also lucky to be able to work for four years in a Jungian-run day hospital, where we had regular supervision. As a result, I had the fortune to be exposed to these themes that gelled very much with my evolutionary approach.

What these discussions did was to highlight the fact that evolution progresses mostly from challenges to survival, reproduction, and ensuring one's offspring survive to become breeding members of the community. These resulting motivational systems, of sex, power, status, belonging and attachment, have been evolving over many millions of years, and although we have the capacity for thinking and self-awareness, they are still our basic drivers. Moreover, these are the motivational systems that can be the source for our well-being but also create the demons within. As the Emperor suggests to Luke Skywalker in *Star Wars*, "you have no idea of the power of the dark side"; we can see this is often true, as we act out various archetypal patterns without realising their powerful and harmful effects.

I remained fascinated in trying to understand how our evolved mind sets us up for suffering and also to be pretty demonic to each other at times. In 1989, supported again by the wonderful publisher Michael Foster, came my next book, *Human Nature and Suffering*. Even though Michael thought the book was too big, he published it as it was. The title tells the story, that there are aspects to our basic nature that set us up for suffering through no fault of our own. What might not have been captured well enough, however, is that while we do have archetypal minds, many inherent tensions and conflicts within us are shaped by our environments. Unless we understand these innate orientations and processes, and take steps to engage and regulate them, we are in trouble. This was also part of the movement of evolutionary psychology in general, and there was an increasing push by psychologists to develop alternative models to the medical pathology model. Aside from those developments, this was a book that explored basic motivational and emotional organising systems relating to how we deal with threat and how we feel safe. Central ideas were that that different motivational systems are linked to particular survival and reproductive (sexual competition) strategies, and these guide us in conscious and unconscious ways. As I was writing *Human Nature and Suffering*, it became obvious that there were different ways to think about depression. Along with a number of evolutionary thinkers, what we were discussing was a need for richer, evolutionarily rooted models of mental health difficulties like depression. This would help to offset the pathologising models of medicine and to root some of them in understandable adaptations to particular environmental contexts. These could also offset some of the sketchy heuristic models that were arising increasingly often. In 1992 Michael and Psychology Press published my third book, *Depression: The Evolution of Powerlessness*. This book sought to highlight the fact that depression, as psychiatrists Akiskal and McKinney had argued back in 1973, is a final common pathway of a number of different processes. It is not one 'thing'. What could these multiple processes be from an evolutionary point of view? What could be the natural conditions that drive down positive feelings, suck out confidence and leave us feeling exhausted? A number of theories presented themselves: such as, stress without control; (learned) helplessness; and arrested defences, such as being in situations where the fight and flight defensive responses are highly stimulated, but cannot be executed appropriately. One example would be being trapped with a bully more powerful than oneself. You can't express anger or fight, and you can't escape, so you are in a blocked and trapped position. Other conditions that can trigger depression and loss of positive, confident emotion might be those of isolation and abandonment separation. One of the models I did my early research on, was based on the way in which being subordinated, threatened and defeated turns off positive emotion. Then self-evaluation focuses on a sense of worthlessness and inferiority, submissive and inhibited assertive behaviour, and self-criticism. Gradually, evolutionary theorists were beginning to articulate ways our evolved brain sets us up for suffering. Both *Human Nature and Suffering* and *Depression: The Evolution of Powerlessness* have recently been reissued as classics by Routledge (in 2016). This is obviously delightful, and although they are old, I still like them.

As the 1990s began to unfold, as well as writing my *Overcoming Depression* book and books on counselling, I was working on a project for a book that I was going to call *Living Like Crazy*. I wanted to come back again and again to the issue that, outside of the cinema, we are paying insufficient attention to the archetypal in us, not only in terms of basic human needs, but also of dispositions to create suffering for self and others. Therefore, the title again tells the story that the way that cultures have emerged – from the hunter gatherers into agriculturally sustained larger villages, and then the emergence of the tribes, and the tribes into empires, from the Assyrian, Egyptian, Greek, Roman, Viking, Mongol, Chinese, Japanese, European, British, American, etc. – have all created serious disparities of wealth and health. We are the inheritors of cultures that utilised slaves to build their power bases, waged horrific wars and created social contexts of inequalities that we are in some ways still trapped within. We are all born to live in cultures that formed from complex histories; every moment emerges from the preceding moment (to quote a Buddhist insight). Therefore, we have to adopt the living practices of our culture, whether or not those living practices are conducive to our well-being. In fact, very little thought has been given to how to create societies that are conducive to human peacefulness and well-being; rather more is given to the military for weapons development in defence against other tribes and to entrepreneurs to compete with each other in any way they wish, regardless of the damage they do to the environment and to us, who have to work to earn a living. It's difficult to look back on much of recent history and find societies that were specifically focused on improving the wellbeing of all. The Industrial Revolution, with its grimy, miserable, dark factories and mines, created places people would not choose to spend much of their lives in, but of course they had no choice.

At its core, this book is about how we have inadvertently created cultures that are in some ways grossly abnormal. Some of this abnormality is wonderful – for example, modern medicine, sanitation, and the ability, in the West, generally to enjoy freedom from famines - but some of it forces us to live in very crazy and destructive ways. Here, I will simply say that crazy is the way in which we are wilfully destructive and use our intelligence harmfully and irrationally. The speed at which we are destroying the planet in ecological terms, or filling our seas with plastic bottles, or fishing the oceans to emptiness, the monies we spend on wars and developing weapons, the allowance of huge disparities of wealth and health, are only a few examples. This book is not going to focus on these themes so much as the underlying archetypal processes that have given rise to them. We use a lot of dissociation to cope with the reality of our craziness, and to keep the awareness of the depth of our potential suffering out of our minds as much and as often as we can. This way of defending ourselves, however, is very costly.

It's not our fault! Dissociation and denial are part of our natural defence systems when we run up against overwhelming pain. But it is crazy. Not many people will look back on our human history of wars, tortures, the Roman gladiatorial games, the Holocaust, ethnic cleansing, slavery, etc., and think that it is anything other than a type of psychopathic madness. Part of our craziness is coming to terms with the fact that as biological beings we are embedded in a rather unpleasant process called the flow of life. Why does all moving life have to eat other life? Why is predation so vicious? Why is life so short? Why are disease and decay our final exit routes? How come physical bodies are so fragile and so vulnerable to infection, bacteria, parasites and internal invaders? How come we must all face the death of those we love most? For some people, life is simply an accident, an absurdity. For others, they either refuse to see the reality or believe that a loving Creator has some mysterious plan in all this. Both are rather frightening. Ideas of reincarnation – that somehow we are born and grow, decay and die, over and over again, maybe remembering all our diseases, pains and deaths at some point – are an absolute horror show. (This has been brilliantly depicted, incidentally, in the recent television series *Westworld*.) Here we are, not asking to be here, and like Frankenstein's monster, not asking to be created in the way that we are. In this quite painful existence, we try and work out what to do to cope with our anger, fear and sadness at finding it like this. Therefore, we need our dissociations and distractions from the suffering of life. My distraction is, or used to be (until I put on too much weight), red wine. One thing that becomes clear for many is that it is our connectedness with, and care for each other, that makes the whole thing bearable and at times even inspiring. When we feel loved and safe, we are able to enjoy the many sensual pleasures in the world, from the smell of the forest to the sharpness of our first swim in the early morning.

This book

In many ways this is an old book, but the themes and archetypes are not. Much was written between 1990 and 1995. The book was a sort of working-out process and became part of the journey that inspired the later focus on compassion. Indeed, there is a chapter on compassion at the end of the book. However, I never really thought I had captured the essence of what I wanted to. I wasn't particularly self-critical, but not really happy that I had nailed it. Nonetheless, I sent it off to a few publishers, and their general view was that it was interesting but there was probably no market for it. Again, too big, and covering too many themes. Good advice was offered, and I made some adjustments, but I had other things I needed to do, and other books to write under contract. I parked it on my computer with the intention of coming back to it, but knowing that it would take some work. And then the months turned to years, and I began to think about updating it. But as the 2000s emerged, so did an increasing clinical workload and other work requirements; in addition, we were getting heavily into developing a therapy that could recruit specific motivational systems to help people in mental distress. This would become known as Compassion Focused Therapy (CFT), and you can see its beginnings in the first edition of *Overcoming Depression*, which came out in 1997. I then contributed a chapter to a book called *Genes on the Couch* (2000), which I had co-authored with Kent Bailey, about the importance of inner conflict and warmth. Then, from 2002 I worked on an edited book on compassion which was published by Routledge in 2005 with the title *Compassion: Conceptualisations, Research and Use in Psychotherapy*. Subsequently, more books on compassion came: most notably, *The Compassionate Mind* in 2010 and *Mindful Compassion* in 2013, the latter of which was co-written with a former Tibetan Buddhist monk called Choden. Compassion was now well and truly my personal research focus and passion. The most recent edited book is *Compassion: Concepts Research and Applications*, again published by Routledge.

Living Like Crazy, therefore, started to gather dust, and although I had some chapters available on the *Compassionate Mind Foundation* website, and had received some nice comments about them, I didn't think they would ever be published. That was until my beloved daughter discovered the manuscript and started to read it, and rather than accept the glum head shaking of my "not good enough, let's just open a bottle of wine and forget about it" approach, she said "definitely not!", and decided that she wanted this to be the first book for her new publishing company. She explained patiently and clearly why she thought this would still be useful for people and that some of the themes were worth putting out there. I was tempted to start rewriting the book, updating many of the references and so forth, but upon reflection I realised that I would lose many of the textures and historical feel of the book, and of course there was the probability that I would never finish it. In any case, as my daughter noted, she felt many of the themes were useful and still very fresh, and in some ways even more relevant for a contemporary audience.

And here it is, two months after our original discussion, the products of her encouragement, enthusiasm and support. Many hours have gone into rewriting certain areas and Hannah's careful reading and fine tuning. We hope it will provide a useful travel map around the archetypal mind as well as sketching in some of the stepping stones and issues that underpin the development of Compassion Focused Therapy. It is also a book that is underpinned by a basic philosophy of compassionate humanism. So, with thanks to my daughter, here we are.

Prof Paul Gilbert, OBE
Derby, UK
September 2017

1: SOCIAL CRAZINESS

It is increasingly recognised that people can behave in highly destructive ways when their social relationships and environments take certain forms. When we reflect on the huge-scale atrocities of the twentieth century's world wars and those of previous millennia, of the history of slavery and torture and general abuse, we can see extreme examples of this. There is increasing agreement that violence, crime, rape, depression, anxiety and paranoia all increase in certain environments and are reduced in others. Moreover, people can be severely traumatised by their environments. For example, we now know that many people who are caught up in major traumas such as wars, be it with the Nazis, in Vietnam or Bosnia, will come to suffer major risks of forms of post-traumatic stress disorder. There is a significant increase in the risk of suicide, alcoholism, depression, self-harm and domestic violence. Despite the crazy way we often turn violence into entertainment, it is very destructive to the human mind. Our environments affect our risk of health and disease. Life expectancy, rates of non-violent death and illness vary according to the group one studies, even within the same country. Unsurprisingly, the poor always do less well than the wealthy.[1] Persons and social environments are locked together and each affects the other. Some social environments are crazy-making.

Our identities and values are shaped by the groups we live in.[2] If we are brought up in, say, an Islamic society, we will come to endorse a different set of values and take on different self-identities, then if we are brought up in a Christian or secular society. Our sense of ourselves and our values are (in part, at least) created *through* our relationships.[3] Even the way our brain matures, the kinds of connections nerve cells make in the brain, are affected by the quality of our

---

[1] Alder, N.E., Boyce, T., Chesney, M.A., Folkman, S., Kahn, R.L. and Syme, S.L. (1994)
[2] Abrams, D., Cochrane, S., Hogg, M.A. and Turner, J.C. (1990)
[3] Fogel, A. (1993)

relationships.[4] Indeed, relationships often regulate our biological selves.[5] There is now good evidence that we are psychologically, socially and physiologically patterned by our childhoods but also throughout life, for good or for worse. All this has implications for how we see ourselves. For example, imagine I had been kidnapped as a very young baby into a violent drug gang. This version of Paul Gilbert would not exist. My brain would be patterned differently; my values would be patterned differently; my very sense of myself would be different. Moreover, that version of Paul 'drug baron' Gilbert may not like this version of a somewhat cowardly prof writing this book. For sure, the person writing this book would not like the aggressive version from that other life. We are all versions of ourselves, biological beings of whom there is no real me, only a version choreographed from our genes and our environments. Yet despite this variation, there is also a commonality in humanity. We share basic motives and emotions. We all need secure attachments and to be cared for and about; we all seek to belong and can become tribal; we all mature more or less at the same time and begin looking for sexual partners and opportunities to reproduce; we all would prefer status rather than to be rejected and marginalised. If our loved one(s) die we can be thrown into the biological and mental turmoil of grief. If we suddenly discover our lover is having an affair with someone else, our sense of security might be lost and we become generally anxious and/or angry. As I wrote in *Human Nature and Suffering* back in the 1980s, we are short-lived biological beings doing our best to meet our evolved biosocial goals, for supportive relationships, sexuality and status. We are 'driven' by such motives and choreographed by our genes and our environments. Depending on that pattern we can have meaningful, even joyful lives, or ones of sheer misery; ones of moral integrity or moral neglect.

---

[4] Schore, A. (1994) reviews considerable work on how the brain is affected in a maturation via different social relationships, especially those between child and caregiver. Henry, J.P. and Stephens, P.M. (1977) explore the biological consequences of different early histories of animals.

[5] Hofer, M.A. (1984) shows how much relationships regulate our biologies and how we often we become biologically attuned to others in relationships. For example, women who live together tend to menstruate together.

The Myth of the Autonomous Individual

We often see craziness as a problem of the individual. We might label it as depression, anxiety, neurosis or psychosis. This book will suggest, however, that we need to look beyond the individual and consider that groups and societies can also be crazy, to the extent that social behaviour and values lead to much suffering and destructiveness. Indeed, applying the criteria of psychological disorder to social groups suggests some interesting similarities. Consider the problems of those given labels of neurosis: they might feel out of control; suffer symptoms of distress; seem to experience higher than 'normal' levels of conflict and tension; cause suffering to themselves and others even if they do not wish to; lack insight into the nature of their difficulties; or be highly resistant to change, even if logically they know it is in their own long-term self-interest to change. Could these types of problems and processes be seen to exist in groups, societies and nations? I think the answer is yes.

We have turned a blind eye to the 'social creation of suffering' by our fascination with individual craziness – for which we hope to find a cure 'for the individual'. The reason for this lies partly in our history, and the nature of our scientific endeavours that focused our thoughts away from social craziness and onto internal mechanisms. Before exploring how social relationships can create destructive patterns of behaviour and intense suffering, we should note how we came to focus only on individuals. It is in the Western cultural Age of Enlightenment that we find the origins of this scientific focus.

The Origins of the Mechanistic Approach to Human Suffering

The Age of Enlightenment was, according to Gay[6], the age when humans regained their nerve in their own abilities. Via reason, education, individual efforts and inventions, by the accumulation of human knowledge and understanding, the world and the people in it could be changed. It was an age that saw a decline in religious autonomy as the accepted means to understand the workings of the world, and a commitment to science and social reform with

---

[6] Gay, P. (1977)

a renewed belief in the value of human effort to improve things – an ideal that humans could be the masters of their own fate. This renewed optimism was captured by Descartes when he claimed that science would enable men to become "masters and possessors of nature" and that science was "to be desired not only for the invention of an infinite number of devices that would enable us to enjoy without any labor the fruits of the earth and all its comforts, but above all for the preservation of health, which is doubtless the first of all goods and the foundation of all other goods of this life".[7]

But this renewed scientific confidence did not emerge alone for it was a cousin and aid to the Industrial Revolution by which it was also influenced. The inventions of new mechanisms, from trains and industrial machines to clocks and mechanical toys, were seen as offering a path to a better life. The type of science adopted was classical Newtonian science, as the Industrial Revolution dictated it should be – focused on mechanisms and inventions. And so it became natural to think that almost everything could be understood by understanding how 'mechanisms work'. This mechanical vision was to pervade not only much of science, but also medicine and psychology. The understanding of the 'mechanisms of the body' was to offer great rewards, and a small step takes us to, "if things go wrong then it must be something 'in' the mechanism (the body)". Along with the industrial changes, medical sciences were at the forefront of the Age of Enlightenment[6], promising freedom from some of nature's crueller tricks of disease and famine. Although some feminists point to the masculine language of the time, noting Bacon's famous phrase that nature should be "put to the rack" and made to give up her secrets, this was not mere masculine posturing, but an angry reflection on the suffering inherent in nature.

Indeed, perhaps one of the most important problems we face is that we dissociate from the underlying fear and anger, even rage, we have at finding life such a horror show of fragility, impermanence and suffering, Yes, I know some people find life joyful too, as we can all do at times – but humans have been plagued by life-changing injuries, diseases and famines, by wars, tsunamis and other disasters. And not all families are full of love and singing Mary Poppins songs.

---

[7] Descartes, quoted in Gay, P. (1977)

Many grow up in the context of poverty, community crime, alcohol abuse, domestic violence and emotional neglect. The slums of the world probably harbour many more children than exist in white middle-class suburbs. And of course, we all know that we will die, and while we hope for a quick and painless departure at the end of a meaningful life, many will die slowly, losing faculties and in pain. Nor are we free from watching our loved ones stumble painfully to the exits. It would be a nightmare to hold these in mind all the time, so we dissociate from these realities or create various religious fantasies to help us cope.

The point is that without awareness of the historical contexts in which the Age of Enlightenment was born, it is easy to see such sentiments as arrogant and misguided. The great hope of the Enlightenment was healing, to make things better, and indeed medicine became one of its champions, known as *the great art of healing*[6]. It promised considerable relief to human suffering. In a way, as Gay[6] points out, there was also a shimmering of compassionate sentiments because of increasing discussion and insight about the suffering of humanity and the wish to address it. From around 1750 onwards, it seemed we were well on course. And it is difficult not to be deeply impressed by – not to mention immensely grateful for – the many cures: from simple tooth ache (can you imagine having to knock your own teeth out, or surgery without anaesthetics?), to vaccinations for small pox and polio. The vision that 'things are fixable and improvable if you know how' is something many have cause to be grateful for. If today we are losing our nerve, and we recognise that we can have science and inventions which create more misery than they relieve, that take us closer to Armageddon not away from it, that depersonalise the human soul, then this is the benefit of hindsight. But in truth, this calls us not to abandon science but to *reappraise* it. And this reappraisal comes from loosening our faith in a strict 'science of things' and challenging our belief that suffering comes from faulty mechanisms alone. More than anything, the Enlightenment focused on humans as the creators of their new world and on production, whereas a new science asks us to look inwards and to create new values. In the late nineteenth century, new ideas about the nature of humanity were introduced by figures like Freud and Nietzsche, who offered up new versions of human nature, of dark forces up to mischief out of sight, and the first glimmerings of our disquiet resounded. The shimmer of doubt was not only for our creations but for the creators themselves: perhaps it is ourselves we should know better, before we project ourselves onto the world as inventors and improvers.

Yet even here, the mechanistic vision and ideals were powerfully set. The ideas that more is better and that suffering comes from faulty mechanisms (the body) to be cured with new inventions (drugs) is still with us. Even Freud's theories were basically mechanistic, focusing on 'energies' dammed and repressed, and he believed that one day neurosis would be understood in terms of its chemical substrates. As we shall see later, the Jungian alternative saw human nature as formed from a collection of archetypal possibilities that are essentially meaning-creating and task-performing devices, orientated to a social life. However, the emergence of a new evolutionary approach to human behaviour would reinvent the concept of archetypes and call them "adaptive strategies", and this propelled the significance of understanding the evolved mind.

In the meantime, psychology, although abandoning the energy transfer models of Freud, was not without its mechanistic triumphs. As to the psychologists and philosophers of the Enlightenment, whom Gay[8] has called the "Newtons of the mind", the concern was with the mind's inner operations. Psychologists, in their efforts to be seen as scientific, came also to study internal 'mechanisms' and to do for psychology what physiology had done for medicine: to discover the basic structures and workings of the mind. They developed experiments, came to use statistical tests and studied such things as attitudes, personal beliefs and attributions, perception, memory and emotion. They broke up the human psyche into different functional components without too much concern for how these operate as a system, or how the mind functions in its natural habitats. Emotions, cognitions, memories and life goals could be considered as separate functional components of the mind subject to independent variations, located in specific places or brain processes, compartmentalised and dissected out for microscopic study of their inner workings, separate from higher order laws of organisation and functional utility. Like medicine, and true to the spirit of the enlightenment,

---

[8] Gay, P. (1977)

the focus was (and is) on understanding the mechanism, and this approach has spawned many therapeutic approaches, from psychoanalysis to cognitive therapy. The focus is on the internal workings of individuals – or should we say 'bits' of individuals?

The Age of Enlightenment was also the beginning of the age of the splits. Biology, philosophy, psychology, sociology and ethology came to exist as separate disciplines with their own theories and methods, their own texts and heroes, and their own truths. Like blind men touching the elephant, their new information at times seemed to contradict that which was found by other groups. But 'real science' was always mechanistic. To peer into biology, to study genes and neurochemistry, has always seemed to many more like real science than the study of social attitudes or political beliefs. Efforts at an integration of 'the sciences' are usually met with challenges from those whose territory one had encroached upon. And there were no good careers to be found here, because science and research monies followed specific methodologies and the discovery of specific mechanisms. So serious has the split in our understanding of human behaviour become that in 1986 Eisenberg[9] would criticise psychiatry and psychology for developing two sciences: a brainless one and a mindless one and never the twain should meet. The social scientists would add that the study of mental suffering is also, more often than not, 'socially decontextualised'. In this context the medicalising, dissecting into smaller units for study, and seeing these smaller units as the focus of troubleshooting, was to undermine our understanding of how systems work as wholes and the concept of the *emergence of patterns* from interacting processes both within minds and within social environments. Again, (and as discussed in my book *Human Nature and Suffering*) the concept of pattern generation, and what is now called autopoiesis, disappeared into the shadows. The crucial issue of emergence was that new patterns and completely new phenomena could emerge from how different elements organise and relate to each other. For example, if you split hydrogen and oxygen you do not get water, water can only come from the way those atoms are related. Only slowly are we beginning to see minds as contextualised in

---

[9] Eisenberg, L. (1986)

evolutionary functions, as contextualised in relationships, as contextualised in culture, as contextualised in history – as providing the depth of insight we need to address the problems of humanity. The way your mind and my mind are organised is a result of evolutionary forces, but it is also the history of the world. You and I might be very different had the Nazis won the war and we lived in very different cultures. This combination of genes that make up you and me might not even be here at all! We are patterns that have come into being, into existence as a result of a past that can actually be followed back to the dawn of time. We come into existence and we go out of existence like a breath.

Back to the core points. As the road of time stretches forward, we have become able to see that our problems and the sources of our suffering, turn out to be far more complex than the philosopher-medics of the eighteenth century could ever have anticipated. Today the over-medicalisation of suffering with its mechanistic approach, rooted in Newtonian science, threatens to darken rather than enlighten our visions. When it comes to mental suffering, some even see medicine as a toxic exercise, creating far more problems than it solves[10]. The hope that if you understand the 'internal workings of the mind machine' then you can fix it has been shaken. The problem with this view is that it focuses only, or mainly, on internal workings of individuals and their (supposedly) aberrant or disordered biologies or psychologies. We believe that by studying humans in isolation, socially naked, and focusing only on their internal workings, we will find answers for personal suffering. We hope to reveal the sources of our suffering by peering deeper into internal mechanisms, into our beliefs, or into our genes. Our craziness and destructiveness lie in malfunctions of the mechanisms – we suffer because we are sick, repressed, or distorted in our thinking – we are not working right. Drugs or personal therapies (it is hoped) can alter or mend our problematic internal workings.

Although understanding internal mechanisms will always play an essential role in how we come to understand ourselves, in this book our problems are seen to lie in other places. This book explores the *interaction* of the social with the internal workings of the evolved mind. And it is to social changes that we must

---

[10] Breggin, P. (1993)

look to create a world that is more 'fit' to live in. I shall argue that it is in our allocation of resources, the competitive motives we stimulate and allow between each other and also between groups; the creation of haves, have-nots and have-lots, in our segregated lifestyles; in our shaming and status-giving; in our patterns of leadership, subordination and group identity, that we will find the sources and prevention of much suffering. It is in social changes that we can impact and regulate these basic motives, so that we can have the most impact on human misery.

Social Questions

The mechanistic approaches of science tell us little about our more serious craziness, which threatens us as a species. Why do we pollute and exploit our environments? Why do we engage in short-term self-interest that turns out to be so destructive? Why do we cure the sick on one day but are keen to blow-up and maim others on another? Why do we invest thousands in healing one baby, yet abandon millions in the wars, famines and ghettos of the world? Why do we like to think of ourselves as moral and caring and yet behave so often immorally? Why do we follow leaders like Hitler? Why do we fear, shame and humiliate others so often and yet will do almost anything to avoid it? Why are we so cruel to some people, yet will sacrifice ourselves to save others? Why is human history so full of atrocities? Why do rational people behave in such crazy, destructive ways and why do we accept it? When we ask these questions the mechanistic, socially de-contextualised approach struggles for answers.

We may have learnt a lot about the internal workings of the brain, but we have not yet focused sufficiently on its adaptive functions. Nor do we always appreciate the biological reasons for why so many of our most important life goals and motivations are orientated to the social. Social psychologists can take it for granted that we are highly social beings, and nothing resembling human behaviour can exist outside of the social, yet they do not always ask why this should be so. Evolutionary psychology starts by asking, why is the social so important? Why do we feel bad when we are rejected or not loved? Why are we so jealous when our sexual partners defect to other mates? Why is grief so painful when our children die before us? Why is shame so powerful when to be shamed may have no major impact on our chances of survival and no physical injury has been delivered? Why do we create such weapons of mass destruction? Why is violence and mental anguish so rife in our inner cities? Do we really suffer only because our mechanisms have gone wrong?

This book suggests that the more serious forms of our craziness cannot be understood as (just) the actions of autonomous individuals, or the effects of brain chemicals that do not know their place, but are patterns of social relationships. What we do in groups can be far more crazy and destructive than what we do alone. Much of our craziness is something that happens between people, in their interactions, as much as it does inside people. In fact, our suffering and crazy behaviour often comes not from errors in the clockwork but from the activation of (previously) adaptive social strategies. Most, if not all, of our potential social strategies (e.g., to care for our children, form alliances and friends, be hostile to outsiders, exert control via violence, select certain types of sexual partners etc.) evolved long ago, and it is social relationships and social contexts that recruit, amplify, modify or restrain certain strategies. Indeed, many of the behaviours that are now turning out to be so destructive and rather crazy, may at one time have been adaptive in certain social contexts. It is only in our modern life, which in many ways is hardly recognisable compared to the small groups we evolved within, that we now have to lift our eyes and see that at times doing what comes naturally is not only immoral but also highly destructive. It is one thing to be xenophobic if living in isolated groups on the African plains, but quite another once we have atomic weapons in our hands. And never in our evolved history have we had to cope with such large disparities of resources and status. We, once struggling to survive as hunter-gatherers, are not a species who evolved to cope with huge surplus and resources. The advent of agriculture and the ability to accumulate vast resources has played havoc with our hunter-gatherer minds which we have not recovered from or worked out what to do about. We have just allowed humans to do what comes naturally in these abnormal environments which, unfortunately in the context of huge resources where sharing is irrelevant is often greed, tribalism and nepotism. It is crazy – agriculture saved us from starvation and formed the foundation for some wonderful cultural advances, but it has also contributed to driving us crazy.

The key view of evolutionary theory is that if we find behaviours that we do not like or cause suffering to self and others, we should not automatically assume that something has gone wrong 'in the machine' (the brain), in the sense that there is a pathological process going on inside it, but rather ask, in what social contexts are these behaviours prevalent? What function are they serving? What is their adaptive evolved linkage? We may behave destructively because in the past (over millions of years) it was adaptive to do so. For example, the rates of violence of inner cities, although highly undesirable, cannot be taken as evidence of mass individual pathologies, a problem in the genes. Rather it should be suggested that in situations of relative deprivation, where opportunities are few and social restraints absent, violence becomes a strategy to acquire resources and status and to protect oneself. It is a better bet to forego (relatively) altruistic strategies and settle for aggressive ones.

The social and psychobiological nature of our development, however, offers a caution to the evolutionary view that certain forms of destructive behaviour are simply the result of adaptive strategies operating in certain contexts. As I will explore further in Chapter 4, much depends on what one sees as normal adaptive processes and strategies. There is increasing evidence, for example, that a neglectful, stressful and, of course, violent and abusive upbringing affects the maturation of the brain. Early life experiences do affect how the frontal lobes of the brain (the areas involved in empathy and altruistic feelings) mature and how they become 'wired up' with other brain areas.[11] A tendency towards aggressive behaviour may indeed be related to adaptive strategies, but the brain of the loved child and the brain of the abused child turn out to be different. The problem is that if (say) an abused person suddenly finds themselves in a highly supportive and loving context, it does not automatically follow that they will find it as easy to operate in this context and build supportive alliances (be able to trust, feel secure) in the same way as a child who has matured within a loving context. Their minds and brains are patterned for a different social context, and this

---

[11] Schore, A. (1994)

understanding – that it is not just beliefs or even unconscious conflicts; it is actually a different mind/brain pattern for a different context – is the issue here. If we are to help people change, then we must help them change in quite fundamental ways in terms of how their minds are literally organised. And we need to move beyond thinking about individuals and about changing social contexts. Tricky.

Some Basic Themes

This book is not primarily about 'anxiety', 'depression' or other 'mental disorders'. Rather, it explores the more everyday kinds of craziness which we often do not even recognise as crazy. It is the destructiveness of our socially shared values, our need for recognition and status, our fear of shame, our tendencies to dominate others or submit to them – these are to be our focus. A basic theme of this book is that we are the products of both biological and cultural evolution. We have inside of ourselves many different potentials: to create pacifist societies or Nazi death camps; to fly to the moon or develop atomic weapons; to be compassionate and tolerant of each other, or to hate and inflict violence on each other. Although we cannot decouple ourselves from our evolutionary past, neither are we merely programmed robots or simple vehicles for genes. Our genes are not the modern-day equivalent of the Fates. The quality of our relationships and the social values and ideals we adopt are the salient, mediating factors between our basic human nature, and our actions and experiences in and of the world. These values are shaped by the social contexts of our lives.

Commentators and psychotherapists alike see the source of many of our problems as arising from what is called *narcissism*. This is a troublesome concept that defies clear definition, and pathologises and locates the issue in individual malfunction. Yet it is not a purely individual concept, for as Lasch[12] made clear, it can be applied to whole societies. In brief, narcissism refers to a self-focused orientation with a disregard for the feelings or needs of others – in

---

[12] Lasch, C. (1979/1991)

lay terms, it is a kind of selfishness or egocentricity. Narcissism tends to go with various other traits such as a sense of entitlement and superiority, a tendency to be easily frustrated if one does not get what one wants, and an acute vulnerability to shame, humiliation and envy. This can lead to a highly exploitative lifestyle. Alternatively, I suggest that it is a competitive self-promoting orientation to life which is not balanced by altruism that is the basis of narcissism. Whether one is promoting one's own superiority, or that of one's group (e.g., white supremacy), the vigorous pursuit of status, and the personal ownership of resources in some contexts, can result in highly narcissistic lifestyles and ideals. Indeed, it is these narcissistic ideals, reflected in capitalist economics and certain religions, which have done much to permit and amplify these tendencies within us. But narcissism lives more strongly within us when it is socially endorsed and rewarded. When narcissism brings no rewards, it may over time subside, and new ways to obtain status and resources are sought.

The second theme is that, traditionally, evolutionary ideas have often been used by the right wing to foster support for their ideas of the innate supremacy of some groups and individuals over others. As we will see in later chapters, this is captured in ideas such as social dominance orientation. However, in this book I will suggest that this is to misunderstand evolution. For example, altruism and attachment behaviour, and the enormous importance of love in our social relationships for our maturation into confident, happy, mentally healthy and caring people, has been the real challenge of evolutionary biology in recent years. Indeed, it is possible that left-wing political ideals can be equally supported with a recognition of the power of human evolution, and explorations of the early forms of egalitarian hunter-gatherer life styles. Altruism and compassion are not precluded from evolutionary explorations. Indeed, if we have the view that people have basic needs for social support and care, and should be treated with respect and fairness, then these basic needs are to do with the kind of species we are. Therefore, it comes down to context. Prosocial behaviour tends to be functional and therefore bonded around friends and relations. It is much easier to be charitable and forgiving to those we like than those we do not, to those we know than those we do not, to those we share our values with than those with whom we do not. Therefore, we need to use our newly evolved intelligence to begin to dissolve these boundaries, continue to develop systems of law and moral regulation to avoid the strong exploiting the weak. It helps to think of ourselves as a common humanity rather than a local tribe or kin group. We need to start practising doing things that do not necessarily come naturally and can be difficult because they run up against deeper motivational pushes. We can decide which evolved part of us will run our show.

So, the third theme of this book follows from this and is concerned with why compassion, although often seen as a high ideal, is often so hard for us. We will note that altruistic motives were originally evolved to advance genetic reproduction and replication; therefore, the mechanisms for it are sensitive to those contexts. We will see that we are a multi-mind with lots of different motivations, which are constantly seeking competition for expression and often operating below our conscious awareness. The more we understand our minds, the greater the chance we can see what our biological minds are up to; we can peer into their tricks and deceptions, the source of our inner demons and angels. We will look closely into the origins and forms of our 'archetypal minds' and explore how they are shaped via their social contexts. From there, I will consider our needs for recognition and status; explore the power of shame and subordination; note how leaders so easily manipulate the less pleasant sides of our characters; look in on the darker side of religion; explore our acceptance of, and support for, cruelty; and investigate some of the social conflicts engendered by modern economics. In the final chapter, I shall explore altruism and compassion and see if we can learn how to treat each other better. By looking into the shadows, we might be better able to leave them. To know what we are capable of, or even where our genetic self-interest may lead us, is not to withdraw from moral debate but quite the opposite: to advance the view that without social restraint and social fairness, without respect for our environments, without awareness of our evolved archetypal potentials which can 'impassion' us, we are at risk of becoming crazier. Our genetically built motives may well entice us to favour family, friend and tribe over others, or in a mega-world of strangers, to grab as much of the cake for ourselves as we can, but if this behaviour leads to ecological destruction, social conflict, and devastating wars, it is not serving our interests. Importantly, we do not need to throw up our hands and abandon steering this evolved mind through potentially dark seas. Evolution has also created in us a new type of extraordinary mind that can think, reason and plan, and gain insight, do science and be able to write books like this. We have shown that we can use this mind in the most amazing ways for good but also for some terrible horrors for ourselves but also other (e.g. factory-farmed) animals. The challenge now is to come together as a species – recognising our common humanity, that we all of us just found ourselves here, neither choosing to be born nor the dispositions, needs, wants and cravings we were born with, nor how we were shaped by our backgrounds and so become one version of countless possibilities. We can work out how to come together (or get a critical mass of folk working together) to try to create the necessary conditions so that all minds can be born into a world that offers opportunities for cultivating particular versions (mind-body patterns) conducive to the wellbeing of self and others. Obviously, many of us would like to see conditions that maximise the chances of physical and mental health, and social morality for all.

Just as centuries before we recognised that in order to avoid the spreading of disease and infection we needed sanitation, the same is true with our minds. In order to avoid continually stimulating our darker sides or lives of misery, we need to work out how to create non-toxic mental environments. When we consider this, we immediately focus on *motivation competition*, because our minds are full of so many different motives for pleasures, resources, and avoiding threats and harms, as well as following a moral life. These give us different urges with different priorities and involve different competencies and ways of seeing the world. Promoting compassionate behaviour and rational morality in this sea of competing motives is easily shipwrecked by naïveté. Therefore, this book is not primarily about the evolution of love and compassion but the blocks to it. It concerns our hidden, socially shared craziness. We will see how culture rather than pure nature leads us into the horrors of our selfish exploitations.

Conclusion

Most of us, no less than for the many generations before us, wish to live a life free from persecution and fear, to have hope and feel supported in our communities. We wish for a life both joyful and meaningful. On the whole, peace is preferable to war, and social fairness and low crime preferable to high crime and social segregation, mental wellbeing and confidence preferable to distress and self-dislike. The dreams of the Enlightenment are with us still, but we have moved on and can no longer look for answers in only our disturbed biologies and new inventions. We will continue to invent things and change the face of the world, but this may not make us happy or protect us from social disintegration. Our answers are both in ourselves and our collective relationships. Our solutions may turn out to be educational and political. We have had an industrial revolution that was energised by scientific and technological understanding into how to make objects, mechanisms and engines but which featured less interest in morality, social justice or ecological respect. We need a new entrepreneurial revolution, which will use our new sciences of the mind to create contexts for human wellbeing – not just profit regardless. We need our economies and businesses to continue to make and provide the goods and services that support us and give comfort to life, but to do so in a way that advances human wellbeing on all levels rather than detract from it. When the intelligence and creativity of our entrepreneurs are contextualised and they view themselves as members of the human race with responsibilities, like those in medicine, to try to avoid doing harm and not allow the means of production to drive us into a crazy making world, the world will change. Throughout history, business and trade have changed the world. When we have insight into how we are driving ourselves crazy in so many ways, and really choose to put our minds to finding solutions, I have faith in our human abilities. It would help if we could discover how to harness and cultivate prosocial motives rather than the 'grab more' ones. That is some challenge because, as this book will outline, there are many obstacles and challenges to our path to compassion and liberation from some of nature's trickier design features and cultural traditions.

2: FROM WHENCE WE CAME

Our troubles......arise from the fact that we do not know what we are and cannot agree on what we want to be. The primary cause of this intellectual failure is ignorance of our origins. We did not arrive on this planet as aliens. Humanity is part of nature, a species that evolved among other species. The more closely we identify ourselves with the rest of life, the more quickly we will be able to discover the sources of humans' sensibility and acquire the knowledge on which an enduring ethic, a sense of preferred direction, can be built.[13]

There has long been the view that humans are basically a flawed species who carry the seeds of their own destruction within them. According to this view, our brains are jerry-built devices, cobbled together over millions of years as we plodded the troubled road from DNA sludge to upright primate. Although this journey would result in a complex organ with many billions of brain cells, this organ was going to struggle to cope with the advent of culture. The brisk pace of change that would be forced upon us once humans could speak, ask questions, share ideas, become self-conscious, would also give rise to the development of agriculture, which would make possible resource accumulation and allow vast numbers to live together. From this point, cultures grew – with language, simple technologies, writing, and then onto science and the modern era. All these developments would not only change the world but change the nature of our minds. Multiple personality disorder would not be simply a psychiatric oddity, but a way of life. We would cry and grieve on leaving our own children as we went off to war to drop bombs on someone else's. We would appeal for others to be rational and restrained while following pure self-interest ourselves. The friction between our inherited natures and the demands of complex social living would, to quote Dixon, make us "our own worst enemy".[14] Human nature as

---

[13] Wilson, E.O. (1992), p. 332
[14] Dixon, N.F. (1987)

evolved and human nature as socially and culturally constructed would form a great divide within us. Try as we might to be rational and reasonable in facing our social and ecological problems, our animal nature would constantly overrule common sense. Good intentions would commonly be sacrificed on the altar of innate dictates that place self, kin and tribe above all others.

As a eusocial species, we are unique amongst the mammals in that we have clear divisions of labour, cooperate in particular ways around these divisions (and will even sacrifice ourselves for our tribes and groups), and more to the point expect others to do so too. In this view, our emotional brains evolved for reasons to do with survival (of genes), not rationality. Rationality, so this view goes, falters in the face of human passion, be it for love, power, sex or revenge, and of course tribal loyalties.

Of course, the inherent contradictions of human life and behaviour have been the source of puzzlement for many centuries. Until recently, though, these contradictions have been neatly framed in moral terms, as battles between good and evil, not biological ones or ones of basic brain design. Having said that, it is interesting to note that, through the ages, evil and irrationality have often been associated with the past – the animal within. The pre-postmodernist Devil(s) always appeared animal-like, of cloven hoof, or reptilian. The linkage of animal nature as bad nature was also highly influential in the immediate post-Darwinian period of the 1880s. The birth of psychoanalysis came with various assumptions regarding the human's animal heritage. Their writings were efforts to illuminate how our evolved, basic natures can be hidden beneath a veneer of socialisation.

As Ellenberger[15] points out

> Psychoanalysis evidently belongs to that "unmasking" trend, that search for hidden unconscious motivations characteristic of the 1880s and 1890s. In Freud as in Nietzsche, words and deeds are viewed as manifestations of unconscious motivations, mainly of instincts and conflicts of instincts. For both men the unconscious is the realm of the

---

[15] Ellenberger, H.F. (1970) offers an excellent historical review of the development of psychoanalytic ideas through the centuries.

wild, brutish instincts that cannot find permissible outlets, derived from earlier stages of the individual and of mankind, and find expression in passion, dreams, and mental illness. [16]

This was also the age of Dr Jekyll and Mr Hyde, of Frankenstein and Count Dracula. Such explorations in literature showed a fascination for 'the beast within' – based on some certainty that what nature had prepared us for was little more than a selfish, aggressive, brutish, pleasure-seeking, self-promoting life, whose deceptions, tricks and illusions knew few bounds. Such ideas echo religious ones, that left to our own devices we are basically not so nice. It's Adam's curse; we are a Lord of the Flies. Only society and social control can (it is argued) contain our passions away from such self-centredness.

But there is another view. True, we have the capacity for rage, violence, envy, sadism and so forth, but we have also evolved the capacity for altruism, compassion, healing and nurturing. To exclude our prosocial potentials from an understanding of the evolved nature of the mind is to exclude some of our most distinguishing features. Even war can be seen less as a problem of our innate aggressiveness (a hunger for fighting and violence) but more as complex problems of group loyalty and conformity, fear, obedience to authority, and searching for prestige. It is part of being a eusocial species which is distinct from other mammals in many ways. Indeed, at his talks in Wembley in 1993, the Dalai Lama insisted that compassion is the distinguishing nature of humans – not violence. In this view, society can be as much a source of human craziness as a container of it.

Those endorsing this view see violence and rage not as a basic part of our nature struggling to get out. Rather, they may represent the under-development of empathy, care and interest in others, a turning away from intimacy and relationship in favour of a grandiose, devouring self, who cannot tolerate frustration and limitation. A kind of acquired craziness. The brutishness of humanity comprises strategies that are recruited in certain contexts. If you put a person against a wall and threaten him/her, then do not be surprised if they try to kill you. Perhaps Mary Shelley had the measure of humanity when she

---

[16] Ellenberger, H.F. (1970), p. 277

depicted Frankenstein's 'monster' as a forlorn creature, abandoned by its creator and in despair of finding acceptance. Many saw in Shelley's depiction an image of ourselves: of beings created against our will, vulnerable to disease, decay and eventual (often painful and frightening) death with the only question to God in our minds of 'why did you create me this way?' So, the pursuit of answers to the sources of our craziness leads us into the space between our innate nature and culture, to the place where self-identities are created and strategies are chosen. The questions then become, how do we come to play on our human natures? Under what conditions and in what contexts do we play the notes of rage, power, and violence, and under what conditions are we more able and more likely to play the notes of altruism and compassion? Considering the split between a biological nature as bad and a socially constructed identity as good is to start off on the wrong foot. As I shall argue throughout this book, different social values and social contexts recruit our biologies in different ways – some helpful, some not. One cannot explore the reasons for our social problems without reflection on the *interaction* between human nature and human social values.

To engage on this journey of exploration into the interactions between biology and society, we must first look back and ponder how we got to be us, from whence we came. Before we think about *how* culture shapes our identities, we need to fathom *from what* basic stuff of our humanity, cultures weave their creations – namely, us. As we look back in time we find that human nature is itself a mosaic of different possibilities. Human nature is not one thing but a complex array of potentials – a theme explored in the next chapter.

Darwin's Legacy

Insights into the basic nature of living organisms begin once it becomes clear that neither animals nor humans were created as set entities by a creator. In fact, it is only just over 150 years since, in 1839, Charles Darwin set sail on the Beagle. It was this voyage that set in motion a radical set of ideas about nature and its designs – organisms are not static but evolve and change. Darwin's job, as the natural historian for the voyage, was to record and study the various species encountered along the way. What struck Darwin, as it had many natural historians, was the great variety of species he saw. This diversity posed questions of how such variations could arise. But these questions had been around for some time.

The big idea of evolution had actually been intuited many centuries before: it may have been a sixth-century Chinese philosopher, Tson-Tse, who first suggested that all organisms are originated from a single species. This single species, he suggested, had undergone gradual and continual change, generation by generation, resulting in the diversity of lifeforms that are now all around us.[15] This is exactly what Darwin came to believe, which is of interest because it demonstrates the importance of the climate of cultural values and beliefs into which a new idea and paradigm are born. Darwin proposed his ideas in a climate that was ready and able to appreciate them; in this, Tson-Tse had been less lucky.

In 1798 the clergyman T.R Malthus painted a rather pessimistic prediction of what happens when population growth outstrips resources. Malthus had a view that as things improve, particularly (but not only) through agriculture, so the population will expand. This will increase conflict and vulnerability to disease and poverty. This was sometimes referred to as the Malthusian catastrophe. Darwin was influenced by such ideas on competition conflict, and by the time he published the *Origin of Species* in 1859, Europe was at the height of the industrial revolution, celebrated a few years earlier in the Great Exhibition of 1851. Capitalist economics, invoking ideas of survival of the fittest as survival of the best, were well established alongside key social beliefs about change and progress. Capitalist economics had little concern for those losers pushed out of the game by being outcompeted. The downside of the Malthusian idea - that competition generated winners and *losers* - was neatly forgotten. At the same time, the working class organisation of the Chartist movement, which was at its height in the 1840s, tried to address the disappointments of the Reform Act (1832), which had withheld voting and democracy from working class people and kept it in the hands of property owners and politicians – many of them seen as corrupt. The point is that Darwin was formulating his ideas at the same time that social groups were grappling with the whole issue of competitive self-interest and conflict. In biology, questions had arisen regarding the extinction of some creatures, the origin of variation and complexity of species, and doubt about 'God as designer'. The issue of competing for survival, and the reality of 'survival of the fittest', was an economic concept that had preoccupied people like Adam Smith, and textured the background to Darwin's thinking.

Life in the Harsh Lane

Although Darwin flirted with the Church as a possible career, he lost such sympathies with the death of his daughter, Annie. Moreover, as the extent of the cruelty, suffering and hardship that is so much part of nature became more apparent, there were many who felt (and many who still feel) that if God did create life, it was a bad idea. It was clear that all life has to feed off other life to survive. With phylogenetic change, this became pretty savage. Before life arrived on land, the sea was a turmoil of eat or be eaten. Some million years later came the dinosaurs, which were either carnivore or omnivore. The carnivores were pretty savage flesh-rippers. Although they are nothing like they were, predators today are still pretty vicious. Becoming prey is a not a nice way to die. It can take lions up to an hour to kill a buffalo, and many predators seek out the young. Parents can only watch as their newly arrived offspring are ripped to pieces. Hunting dogs and hyenas will eat their prey as they flee in terror. But the need and search for food is endless, with many predators and prey often existing at the edges of starvation, particularly at certain times of the year. Many offspring do not make it to adulthood. The struggle for survival that nature has set up is truly a horror show. We too as predators are pretty awful, the way we kill sentient creatures, grossly overfish the oceans, farm other mammals and eat their young. Few species are free from the predatory intent of humans – slices of flesh adorn all our high streets.

And what happens to what we ingest? Organic matter goes in one end, and a rather toxic, nasty product called 'shit' comes out of the other. Indeed, some viruses like the rubella virus, which causes cholera, use our digestive systems, causing diarrhoea which enables it to spread more easily into the soil, rivers or wherever. In fact, viruses and bacterial infections have evolved to use mammalian digestive systems and other bodily processes to reproduce themselves and flourish. Viruses need hosts and often harm or cause great suffering to them. In addition, they force them (e.g. you and me) not only to be carrying agents, but to infect each other with suffering. It is always sad when I feel I have picked up flu and passed it on to my family – and that's a relatively mild condition. Our vulnerability to these sources of suffering also greatly increase when we began husbandry and farming animals. There are some rather nasty parasites, flies and malaria-carrying mosquitoes that I could easily live without. Animals grazing the savannas of Africa are hounded by flies, tics and parasites. There are even worms that can travel through our systems and eat away at our eyes, making us blind. Anyone who speaks of the 'miracle' of creation has one eye closed. Viruses can also cause changes in DNA, which then become a source of selection. In fact, a lot of our DNA looks as if it is junk, a leftover from previous virus infiltrations.

The horror show continues, because some species' breeding patterns are rather horrific. Darwin especially noted the parasitoid wasp group, where the female lays her eggs in a host through a process called ovipositing. As the eggs hatch, the larvae eat the host from the inside out. This basic idea was particularly utilised by the directors Ridley Scott and James Cameron in the first two instalments of the *Alien* movie series. As noted previously, Darwin was deeply affected by some of the horrors of nature, and by the death of his second daughter, Annie, in 1851 from scarlet fever. Any remnants of a belief in a loving God faded. This was to cause some distress between him and his beloved wife, Emma, who remained a devoted Christian.

This is also the time, of course, when medicine was revealing more and more of the causes of our diseases and the viral, bacterial and parasitic horrors of creation. The Gnostics, who were not aware of these things many centuries earlier, believed that the creation of the material world, and what they called 'the desires of the flesh', was a mistake, possibly created by a narcissistic or even evil deity! Again, this idea, that there is something not terribly wonderful about Creation, had been part of human thought for many centuries. Even the Buddhists were not terribly keen on the 'desires of the flesh'. So, not surprisingly, it was always recognised that evolutionary theory (though Darwin never used the word evolution, but rather the term natural selection) could dethrone God. In doing so, this would cause very serious emotional distress to many people whose only respite from a life of suffering were such religious beliefs, or what Marx was to call "the opium of the masses". Indeed, Captain Fitzroy, who skippered the Beagle on Darwin's first voyage (and was himself a devoted Christian), was known to have turned up at public meetings with Bible in hand to denounce Darwin. It is believed he felt guilty for his part in bringing Darwin's ideas into the world, which may have contributed to his depression and eventual suicide by cutting his throat with a razor in 1865 (although there were many other personal and financial reasons too). It is a story, though, that speaks to the potential collapse into despair when we look into the reality of biological life and have to let go certain religious ideas. After all, we created many of our Gods out of fear, and built them into traditions and cultures which now give us a sense of meaning, hope and belonging.

The problem of 'humans as evolved animals' and the desire for a moral, just society were then, as they are now, of major significance. These issues apart, it was also clear that if God did create the world and its lifeforms, he did not create fixed species once and for all – they had a tendency to change. Nor could the biblical timescales be correct. The earth had existed far longer than the 4,004 or so years suggested biblically. Thus, the origins of the world, humans and other species needed new explanations. The days when the church could impose its views under threat of death or torture were over, and science would now not be subdued by dogma. Even before Darwin set sail, these debating positions and questions had been building for fifty years or more.

Darwin certainly wasn't the first, nor the last, to see the idea of a creator as a pretty terrifying idea, given the way life actually is. Indeed, it is exactly due to this implications that the religious minded can be so resistant to evolution – not just because they wish to believe in a creator, sidle up to him to win his favour and avoid his wrath, but because they don't want to acknowledge the horrors of life and the despair that may follow. For some of us though, *this* denial is frightening, and it supports religious and tribal conflicts that can get in the way of genuine compassion. Whether you look at the Aztecs and their horrific mass human sacrifices to their gods or some modern-day terrorists who believe they can win a place somewhere better than this existence by savagery, the fact is that some forms of religious belief that deny evolution are crazy-making.

This might all seem rather joyless, and with one eye closed to some of the wondrous beauties and pure pleasures of living: the beauty of a wonderful sunset, the stunning enormity of the Himalayas, sharp sensations of the first swim in the sea, the crisp sweet smell of spring air, the fun and joyfulness of friends, the tender touch of a lover. Balance is important, but this book is more about the darker side of humanity because the pleasures take care of themselves. The point is that prosocial behaviour and compassion addresses the harmful things we do to each other, our craziness. If we are to cultivate compassionate minds we have to address the reality of what biological, vulnerable, short-lived lives we have – and how our minds evolved against this backdrop; how they have been made and the functions that they are consciously and unconsciously supporting.

But let's get back to Darwin and evolution, because it was into this climate of searching for answers to these issues and problems that Darwin was able to go further than our Chinese philosopher, Tson-Tse, and suggest that changes in species came from their interactions with the environment: that a process or processes of *selection* were at work. What do we mean by this? How were the selections made, and what was being selected?

Natural Selection

Let us start with an example. Think of a population of fat and thin rabbits. In hot times, thin rabbits might do better than fatter ones, because they are faster when running away from predators, more agile and eat less. Therefore, fatter rabbits tend to become (easier) prey for predators, and therefore there are fewer of them to breed, and thus fewer to leave their genes (for fatness) around.[17] Gradually,

---

[17] Darwin had no idea about genes, of course. How traits were passed on was a mystery. It was a Moravian Monk, Gregor Mendel, who had a particular interest in peas, and published a paper in 1865 (ignored for 35 years) on the inheritance of traits that was to offer the first clues on inheritance. Christopher Wills (1991) gives an easy and clear exposition of this history and more technical details. For those interested in what we now

the population of rabbits would have more thins than fats. However, suppose that for some reason the climate suddenly changes; it gets cold. Predators die off and food becomes more difficult to find. Now it may be that the fatter rabbits are better able to withstand the cold and thus survive better. Over time, they get more of the breeding opportunities, and so fatter rabbits come to replace the thinner ones. Gradually, the average weight of the population increases.

One can use the same kind of thinking to understand many traits. For example, why are rabbits who live in cold, snow-bound conditions white, while those who life on grass-lands, brown? Darwin called this process *natural selection* – that is, those who had attributes that help them survive will do better than those who are less gifted with these attributes. Natural selection theory was a way of understanding how species are transformed over time. Modern biologists have now added considerably to both the theory and evidence for natural selection, incorporating recently discovered findings on the nature of DNA and genes[4].

---

know about DNA, RNA, and chromosomes, etc. see his book and also Wilson, E.O. (1992). Another beautifully written and accessible book is Steve Jones' (1993) *The Language of the Genes,* based on the Reith lectures he gave on Radio 4. If you want to get really technical, try Gardner, E.J., Simmons, M.J. and Snustad, D.P. (1991). Here, we are less interested in the details of the mechanics of genes, as fascinating as they are, but more with the fact of genes. What has become important in recent times is the degree to which psychosocial factors (e.g., stress in early life) can affect how genes work (see Post, R.M., 1992). One of the difficulties for many of us interested in this area is that knowledge is expanding so fast and becoming so technical, it is impossible to keep up. I am not keen on imputing human values to genes, such as wisdom or selfishness. However, the distinction between genotype (genetic structure) and phenotype is fascinating. The phenotype is the expressed behaviour, or actual working, of a trait which will be affected by its developmental history. Genes and environment mix together (environment effects neural circuits and pathways) forming gene-neural structures and giving rise to phenotypes. Genes share complex relations with psychological traits, however. Some traits are influenced by many genes (called polygenic) and a single gene may influence a variety of traits (called pleiotropic). Although the genotype constrains to some degree the variability allowed by the phenotype, the greater the flexibility for learning, the more variable phenotypes will be. Environments which provide poor quality in nourishment/diet, or social factors (e.g., availability of caring others/mother) result in major disturbances in the maturation of the nervous system, i.e., disturbances of the phenotype. This is now called epigenetics.

The key to natural selection is how animals deal generally with threats to their existence and also seek out the resources they need for survival and reproduction. It's fairly straightforward to recognise that many of the emotions that we have in our threat system, such as anger or anxiety, are there because evolution built them as defences. Generally, ethologists and others have identified the four *f*s: feeding, fighting, fleeing, and having a good time on a Saturday night. As discussed in my books *Human Nature and Suffering* and *Depression: The Evolution of Powerlessness*, a lot of these basic defence systems can become the source for quite a lot of mental distress in the form of depression, anxiety and paranoia. In addition, our inner defence immune system, which can protect us from bacteria and viruses, can also become the source for inflammatory immune diseases – it attacks its own tissue, as in arthritis. All defences need appropriate regulation, and if they become too intense, too easily triggered, and last too long they can become a liability. When we encounter evolved design features like this, it is called a trade-off. That means some of our traits can be advantageous to us in some contexts and at some level of intensity, but not others.

Sexual Selection

Key to understanding how evolution has created *social motives and styles* of social relating is that, added to natural selection, are those factors that impinge on actual breeding behaviour. Darwin also noted that advantage in breeding, and thus leaving offspring behind to succeed one, is influenced by how successful one is in competing for mates and producing viable offspring. Having competencies to help you survive is well and good, but not if you don't leave genes behind. Why sex evolved at all is a matter of debate. Indeed, there are some species that do not reproduce via sex. Certainly, all the creation myths that see male and female diversity to have been there from the start are wrong. The evolution of sex differences was not part of life in the beginning. Its evolution, its coming into existence, has to do with the benefits of recombination of DNA and error correction. This is a complex point and we must leave the issue here.

What we do know is that animals who reproduce sexually have to get together and they have evolved all kinds of ways of attracting each other, with scents, calls, colours, plumage and body displays. The peacock tail is an attractor, although something of a nuisance in getting away from predators. The concept of *intersexual selection* means that those animals who are (relatively) good at selecting and attracting mates (breeding partners) and mating will do better at leaving offspring than those who are rather less popular and able. Humans, too, are attracted to certain qualities and displays in each other and find them sexually desirable and inviting of relationship. But culture and learning can modify the exact form of attraction, or its phenotype. The fact is that intersexual selection has played a significant hand in shaping our psychologies.[18]

Many forms of courting ritual and display have been beautifully captured on film by makers of nature films: the most obvious example being David Attenborough and his team. Many have seen his trilogy of nature documentaries: *Life on Earth*, *The Living Planet*, and *The Trials of Life*.[19] The role of sexual selection was also beautifully brought to our screens recently with the Channel 4 documentary series, *The Sexual Imperative*. Thanks to the skill of such programme-makers, it is no longer only the scientist who can see these behaviours.

Mate Selection

One of the major developments in our understanding of human psychology has been the realisation that 'mate selection' is a powerful aspect of human psychology. First, a general point: sexual preference will be to mate with individuals who show signals of health (good genes); that is, physically healthy people are more desirable than those with signs of poor health (e.g. spotty), the sick, deformed or decrepit. After that, men and women have psychologies that equip them to follow different strategies. The argument goes like this: in the case of women, they can be sure that any infant they give birth to is their own, but

---

[18] Ridley, M. (1994) Ridley sees sexual selection as key to many human dispositions and this is a point of view expressed in this book.

[19] Attenborough, D. (1992) Three volumes following the BBC series.

males cannot. Females, unlike males, do not have to worry about being cuckolded. Rather females have other concerns. These are to mate with the high(er) status males and choose males who will help in rearing offspring and provide resources, i.e., males that are altruistic and capable of controlling resources. Women who obtain these pairings will be more successful in leaving genes behind them than those who do not select their men for those qualities. Thus, women evolved to be coy and choosy. This means that females will be attracted to two types of signal – status and altruism.[20] Research using pencil and paper measures of attitudes basically confirms this.[21] However, such pencil and paper tests are only a first step. More recent work suggests that the relationship between traits of status/dominance and altruism/agreeableness with female preference are complex.[22] For example, agreeableness/altruism seems more important than dominance/status in some contexts, and indeed when men are non-altruistic (disagreeable), dominance may have little effect on attraction. It is as if women search first for altruistic tendencies and only then are concerned with status – echoing the view that for women personality is important in attraction.[23]

---

[20] Trivers, R. (1985) discusses his own theories about the role of differences in parental investment on mate choice.

[21] See Buss, D.M. (1989), who reports on his huge cross-cultural study exploring differences in mate preferences. See also Ridley, who discusses this work. In section 111 of Barkow, J.H., Cosmides, L. and Tooby, J. (1992, eds.) are a series of chapters dedicated to the evolved psychology of sex differences and behaviour. A particularly accessible account is given by Buss, D.M (1994). He discusses differences in behaviour when men and women are seeking short- (more commonly men) versus long-term (more commonly women) sexual relationships; and the roles of sexual jealousy and physical attractiveness. I hope I can be forgiven for giving a rather impoverished review here, but sufficient to give the basis for what is to follow.

[22] Jensen-Campbell, L.A., Graziano, W.G. and West, S.G. (1995) have developed important research methodologies in this area.

[23] One consequence (and one I don't think has been researched) is that women will lose sexual interest in partners in contexts when investment is expected but not given. Certainly, in the case of depressed women one common reason that they say they have lost (sexual) interest in their partners is that their partners are not investing time or energy in their children, or themselves. Interestingly, however, in women who have been abused in early life there may be a distortion in the ability to detect altruism in men. It is not uncommon to find women who have been physically and/or sexually abused to make

For men, the story is rather different, in part because they invest less in offspring and can leave more genes behind by seeking many partners. At most, women can give birth only once a year or so, whereas theoretically men could sire over a hundred in the same period. Another key issue is that males can be cuckolded and end up caring for offspring that are not their own.[24] They are attracted to women who are younger rather than older and, say Wilson and Daly,[25] men have a tendency to treat women as property that must be guarded from other males to avoid them being cuckolded. This psychology shows up in the rights bestowed in marriage, the value of female chastity and virginity, codes of honour, issues of adultery and the provocation to violence.

These psychologies are so important that we shall meet them often throughout this book, particularly when we explore shame and pride in Chapter 6. The battle of the sexes is, in a way, the battle of reproductive strategies. However, as I shall discuss in Chapter 5, different ecologies may bring out slightly different reproductive strategies (e.g., high versus low investing relationships) in both males and females.

Beating and Suppressing Competitors

In addition to intersexual competition, reproductive success is not just about advertising oneself as a good breeding partner. The problem is that others have similar desires. We come to what is called intra-sexual competition: competing with members of your own gender to get yourself into a privileged position for intersexual attraction and prevent competitors from breeding. In some species there is not much advertising, but rather a lot of group sex (e.g., squid), and even gang rapes. Sex is a frenzy of attempted fertilisations. Indeed, in some mammals, sex is not always a cooperative venture. Importantly, though, in many species there can be serious conflict between same-gender competitors *before*

---

liaisons with rather disagreeable males. This is an extremely complex area that needs more research. I touched on this aspect elsewhere; Gilbert, P. 1989).

[24] As Ridley, M. (1994) points out, much depends on whether females are sought out for a one night fling or to raise children.

[25] Wilson, M. and Daly, M. (1992)

sex takes place. Indeed, far more energy can go into dealing with competitors than actually finding mates.

Imagine this situation: there you are as, say, a crab on the sea bed, happily advertising yourself as a good breeding partner. You have got a nice place to stay (your territory) and are advertising it. Then another crab of the same sex happens by and recognises that you do indeed have a good place to advertise. The key idea for the intruder is to get you out and take over your territory. Not particularly neighbourly, but now much will depend on how good you are at defending your spot. If you can beat off challengers and send them packing, then you will be able to stay and be more successful in attracting mates. If you lose, you'll have to vacate your spot and go find somewhere else, maybe not so good. Of course, if you are the challenger, then the reverse situation is the case; i.e., much will depend on how good you are at capturing another's territory and/or defending it when it is captured. Access to mates is therefore not assured; it has to be won – this especially true for males. This is a theme we will meet again when we explore the issue of how cultures bestow manhood – that, too, often has to be won and proved.

Via this type of process, arising from direct and open contests, there will be a tendency for those who are good at competing and wining contests (gaining, then holding onto good territories or resources) to be more successful than fellow competitors. This process, by which breeding success is determined according to how successful you are at beating challengers, is called *intrasexual selection* (intra means 'within' and 'the same as', which in this case means the same gender).[26]

---

[26] Gilbert, P., Price, J.S. and Allan, S. (1995) have pointed out that much of sexual selection requires various psychological competencies for social comparison. This allows animals to work out their likely chances of winning or being defeated in any contest. It turns out that social comparison is important for many forms of social behaviour; such as fitting in with a group and reciprocal altruism. Caryl, P.G. (1988) gives easy access to modern evolutionary ideas and games theory on the wars of attrition, and different strategies for escalating threat and attack and deescalating and backing off.

Dominance and Superiority

While earning territory is one way of advertising one's suitability as a partner, most mammals, including humans, form into free-ranging groups. Here, ranked hierarchies are a key way in which social relationships are organised within such groups: there are those who are more dominant and those who are subordinate.[27] The way these ranks form within groups has been studied by ethologists and depicted by many natural history films, giving us wonderful access to this information. We can all watch the contests of fish, birds, seals, walruses, the rutting of the deer, the boxing of the hares, the threat displays of the gorilla and chimpanzee – these contests are called *ritual agonistic behaviour*. Often, they involve particular types of (threat) display, such as standing erect, tense posture and meeting eye gaze. These postures allow each contestant to weigh up the other. This weighing up uses some form of social comparison. Being good at it means that an animal will tend to take on those he/she thinks they can beat and back off or submit to those judged to be superior. This has the effect of avoiding fights over every resource.

Paul MacLean[28] has noted that the displays of human armies on parade, as they goose step and display their combative confidence, is not that dissimilar to the lizard threat display. It involves very similar postures and use of muscles. Staring and direct eye contact is used as a threat signal in animals and humans. Boxers and wrestlers can stand almost nose to nose trying to stare each other out. Ritualised threats can also be given by groups, and some writers have suggested that a country's testing of weapons, military parades and exercises are forms of threat displays, signalling combative competence.

The evolution of fighting ability purely to gain access to opportunities to reproduce is a source of considerable nastiness. Consider for example the bighorn sheep up in the Rockies. During the breeding season, the females issue

---

[27] There are new ideas on how the psychological competencies that evolved for coping with sexual selection can be recruited into various forms of pathology; see for example Price et al., (1994) and Gilbert, P. (1989, 1992a, 1992b).

[28] MacLean, P.D. (1985, 1990). Probably one of the foremost neurophysiologists, who has charted the basic structures of the brain.

scents that stimulate a change in the males, who then start fighting for access. They have evolved huge horns and thick heads that crash into each other at around 35 km an hour with horrendous force. The muskox is the same. The antlers of the deer that can get stuck in trees (meaning that they will die of starvation) are purely for sex attraction and fighting. In species after species, nature has created animals capable of gladiatorial contests using hormones and other neurochemicals to force then to behave in such harmful ways. Unlike us, they have no way of understanding why.

Clearly gaining dominance, or some rank equivalent (one way of which involves the power to push others out of a territory and/or subdue and inhibit competitors from gaining control over resources), has been so important in the control of breeding opportunities (and the resources that go with them). Consequently, many traits which help it along will have become deeply entrenched within the gene pool and within us. This awareness of, attention to, and concern with one's relative social rank or standing has become a *basic archetype* for construing relationships (see next chapter). The *rank archetype*, as I will call it, is an internal energy control system, that signals to self and others the readiness (confidence) to challenge (be assertive if you like) and seek resources. This sense of readiness is often derived from social comparisons (inferior-superior), for both animals and humans. When we feel confident of winning (or not being put down) we may be full of energy, but when losing (we are put down, shamed, feel inferior, or attacked in a way we can't defend) we can become angry, depressed or anxious and lose confidence. The most obvious personal experience of the rank archetype at work in oneself is through our self-esteem (e.g., low self-esteem is often associated with feeling inferior to others, inhibited, lacking confidence and so on).[29]

Human competitive motives are, as you would expect, more complex. One is *up rank,* competing where one wants to go higher and higher and have more and more. Feeling superior to others and more in control is the point. A second motive for striving for status and power is to be free of the control of others; the more power and freedom I have, the less I have to obey the orders or wishes of

---

[29] See Wilson, E.O. (1992); Dixon, N.F. (1987)

others. Yet another rank motivation is competing to *avoid being inferior*. These individuals are really trying to avoid rejection, or being 'unchosen'. If they have too much status, power or resources, and feel they will be envied or ostracised because of this, they can become anxious. Of course these motives can overlap in that some individuals seek power because they have a very fragile sense of themselves and their connectedness to others. No doubt there are others too.

Nonetheless, the point is that striving for status, power and social control (for oneself but also over others) has been noted as a key motivation by psychotherapists, philosophers, ethologists, anthropologists and sociologists. True, the way status is achieved in human groups varies and is highly dependent on cultural approval and recognition. But humans are also extremely concerned with rank and status – their image and self-presentations. These are mostly to gain esteem, prestige and some relative power to influence others and secure good outcomes for themselves.[30] In fact, all these underpin the very fabric of political life as we negotiate our place in the world. Politics is, in a way, the management of our rank psychology.

A caveat to this is that some female primates rely more on their kinship networks for gaining status, and far less on their fighting ability. Infants often inherit the status of their mothers, and dominant females can offer more protection than subordinate females. Nonetheless, females of various species can try to suppress the mating chances of competitors. They can also try to form alliances with males who have the power to defend them. It is also now recognised that females can exert an influence on male reproduction by their choosiness – they can reject matings, especially from highly aggressive males and those who may be poor when it comes to investing in offspring. It is also clear that female power-

---

[30] Barkow, J.H. (1989) has developed many important ideas about how early, evolved rank mechanisms (e.g., fighting it out) have changed and adapted as we move closer to humans. One of the key changes is that status and rank are now linked to prestige. We seek to be chosen and accepted for roles. (See also Gilbert, P., 1989 and the next chapter). Feminists point to another level in this prestige system and note that those with power (e.g., males) can define which roles are worthy of prestige, and thus status and privilege, and which are not. Their analysis is linked to that of power: see, for example, Radtke, H.L. and Stam, H.J. (1994). We will be meeting these ideas throughout the book.

seeking is often about promoting their genes; that is, the social position of their offspring. History is replete with females in competition, promoting their sons and daughters into positions of power in Machiavellian ways.

There are a lot of subroutines and emotions that can go with these forms of competition. For example, envy and jealousy are emotions that are centred on feeling that others are doing better than we are or that they have things that we want. Evolution has constructed minds that in some contexts, particularly when there is intense competition, can be very sensitive to how competitors are doing and even at times seek to undermine them.

Males and females influence each other's evolution. For example, as previously noted, the scent secreted by the bighorn sheep is what activates the hormonal changes for aggression in males. Females are sexually receptive for very short periods of time – sometimes just a few days. After it is all over, you wonder what the males were thinking about ('I've got such a headache, what the hell happened to me'). Humans, of course, are very different and potentially sexually active 24/7. This requires a different type of competition. One form of competition is called sperm competition, and is linked to the type of sperm produced and the human male's penis size. Compared to other primates the human penis is very large. One view is that it could be used to scoop out other male sperm, which indicates that early humanity was somewhat promiscuous. The point is that if we step back and look at the struggles for reproduction – from the preening and fighting, to the at-times raping, to the turmoil of emotions that are centred on sexuality, such as jealousy, anger, anxiety and possessiveness – we can see that evolution has created minds easily manipulated by signals and the release of hormones and neurochemicals into crazy behaviour. We like to think we were free of this biological manipulation of our minds, but, of course, this is not so.

Prosocial Behaviour

Let us look on the bright side. There are other aspects of evolution that can actually orientate us towards more prosocial behaviour. We are a multi-mind that has evolved different motives and competencies to do different things in different contexts. Once we get to the point of actually fertilising eggs and producing offspring, then all attention has to be directed to ensuring their survival. It's no good having personal survival and getting to reproduce, if one then forgets about the kids and they die of starvation under a tree. This takes us to what is called parental investment and the ways in which caring for others, paying attention to them and doing things to protect them, addressing their distress and enabling them to flourish, can evolve as basic motives.

It seems likely that many forms of prosocial behaviour (caring, helping, loving) have evolved in this way. Let us begin with care of children and attachment to them. Suppose that here is a population of squeens. Most reproduce, but some spend a longer time with their offspring. The time spent with offspring is a randomly distributed trait, meaning that within any population of squeens there will be some who spend no time at all and some who hang around for a short while after birth. In so far as the presence of parents acts to deter predators, then those squeens born to parents who stay close to them at birth get a slightly better chance of survival and of going on to reproduce more squeens, compared to those who do not carry the genetic trait for 'staying with their offspring'. Gradually, more and more squeens will evolve who spend time with their children, because time-spending squeens leave more offspring to reproduce the gene spread through the population at the time.

In fact, recognising one's kin and not cannibalising them, and later caring for offspring, were major adaptations. Many of us may have seen the videos of the poor baby turtles struggling out of their sand nests only to become a meal for a gull or waiting fish. For animals who do not invest time with their offspring, there is a tendency to reproduce in high numbers (hundreds and sometimes thousands), but as few as only 1 or 2 percent will survive to reproduce. Turtles lay hundreds of eggs and then leave the beach immediately, and that's the last they see of their creations, most of which are food for waiting predators. What was to evolve in mammals was a very different strategy for post-birth survival that invests in protection and provisioning. Birds use it, of course, but for most mammals, offspring mature within a womb followed by live birth, followed by caring. The scientific name for selecting good partners and caring for offspring is called *parental investment*.[31]

Something else of interest happens here, though. Let's think again about our squeens who stay around after childbirth. Now in the first generations, although physically present, the parent squeens may have no interest in their offspring; they are just hanging about the place. Then a small genetic variation leads a parent to stay near to the nest. From the baby squeens' point of view, their chances of survival may increase further if they positively interact and attract the parent and elicit care from them. What we see here is an evolutionary process that is operating on both the offspring and the parent. They are influencing each other's evolution. When ducks are born they are predisposed to follow objects, and in this way stay close to their mother. Without this, baby ducks could not use the preparedness of the mother to care for them; they'd simply wander off anywhere and get lost. Therefore, those baby ducks who are good at staying close to Mum are going to increase their chances of survival (and thus of passing on their genes) compared to those who are poor at it.

But there is a question that we have not addressed. Once one is alive, why bother looking after the kids, or indeed anyone else? If it doesn't bring immediate rewards, why do to it? The answer to this is that it is *inclusive reproductive fitness* – meaning the success in leaving one's genes behind in succeeding generations is what drives evolution along. To some extent this answer is implied in this section, but we need to look at it in a little more detail. Given that it is not really the 'individuals' that are of interest, but the genes that build them, the caring will also be extended to kin relations.

The Benefits of Altruism

That we help each other and make sacrifices is clearly the case, although perhaps not as much the case as many would like. But how could altruism have evolved? If all individuals are trying to maximise their individual success, why would

---

[31] Trivers, R. (1985) gives as easily accessible an insight into the biological details of parental investment as any. He also gives a clear account of kin and reciprocal altruism.

anyone care for anyone? Part of the answer is in inclusive reproductive fitness, and the roles of kin selection and altruism. Exploration of how these could evolve was first put forward by Haldane in 1955, and by Hamilton in 1964[32]. Put simply, it is in our *genetic* self-interest to help those who share our genes. The more genes we share in common, the more helpful we may be. And, of course, the more effective our help, the more those shared genes are likely to be passed on to succeeding generations. Some say this sounds more like nepotism than altruism, and there are problems with this approach.[33] Still, at least it is caring behaviour to some degree. When mothers leave hospital with their babies, they want *their* babies and not any baby. If mistakes are made and it is subsequently discovered, when the child is older, it can cause enormous distress – we are highly motivated to care for our own children. This is called *kin altruism*, or basically the evolution of caring for our kin.

In some species, males do not want to be burdened with caring for another male's offspring, so they will kill the resident offspring when taking over a harem. This both reduces the burden on caring, and brings the female into a reproductive state. However, it all depends on the species. For example, although in most non-human primates orphans rarely survive, among bonobos (our closest relatives) orphaned infants are looked after by both males and females, and often do survive.[34] Much has been written on these aspects, and we will not explore

---

[32] Trivers, R. (1985) gives as easily and accessible insight to the biological details of parental investment as any. He also gives a clear account of kin and reciprocal altruism.

[33] This model is not without its detractors. Some suggest that only individuals can select each other, not genes. Others make the point that since chimpanzees share nearly 99% of our genes, the genetic variation between chimp and humans is small and therefore between any two humans is so small as to make selection difficult and of dubious value. It is highly misleading, therefore, to say that a child shares 50% of its genes with a parent or that siblings has 25% genes in common, etc. - when nearly 100% of genes are common to the human race! (see Eibl-Eibesfeldt, I., 1989). Also, of course, some very intense caring behaviour is directed at our pets - with whom we are not very genetically related – although, come to think of it, my wife has compared me to a Labrador at times! Attachment and familiarity are equally likely to be powerful influences on caring behaviour simply because one does not want to lose the sources of positive attachment feelings.

[34] de Waal, F. (1995)

the genetic and biological implications here.[35] It is worth nothing, however, that psychologically we are adapted for certain types of caring behaviour and thus have the evolved psychology – feelings and motivations – for it.[36]

Trivers[37] also pointed out that we might well help others with whom we have less genetic relatedness if the costs of helping are less than the benefits of possible reciprocation in the future. Others have argued that friends are more likely to help each other, and that friendships are more likely to develop between similar rather than dissimilar others. This similarity in tastes and personalities may well reflect genes with more similarities. This is called *reciprocal altruism*: we will be helpful to others who are likely to be helpful to us.

Following the Rules: The Strategists

It is now clear that evolution gives rise *to a psychology (a mind) that can make certain kinds of evaluations, and will follow rules*. In competitive situations, the rule might be 'submit to those stronger, challenge those weaker'. This goes with competencies for social comparison and having some sense of oneself in relationship to another, being able to work out who is stronger and who is weaker. For infants, rules might be proximity maintenance, 'stay close to Mum'. The rules for altruism are a little more complex, but recently some researchers[38] have given a more concise overview. They point out that in humans some forms of help are given according to what is deemed polite or admirable, or gains prestige. As we shall see in later chapters, helping, compassion and behaving peacefully are very much controlled by social learning rather than purely genetic rules. However, much depends on the cost and nature of the threat that requires help. As both the threats and costs increase, Burnstein, Crandall and Kitayama note:

---

[35] See Archer, J. (1992) and Trivers, R. (1985)

[36] Kriegman, D. (1990), Slavin, M.O. and Kriegman, D. (1992), and Glantz, K. and Pearce, J.K. (1989)

[37] Trivers, R. (1985)

[38] Burnstein, E., Crandall, C. and Kitayama, S. (1994). In regard to altruism and prestige, see Hill, J. (1984)

a) Natural selection favors those who are prone to help others as a function of the latter's relatedness, potential fecundity, or other features indicating a recipient's capacity to enhance the donors inclusive fitness, and b) this effect is especially strong when help is biologically significant (e.g., the recipient will not survive otherwise). Such a heuristic is demonstrated in several studies involving hypothetical decisions to help: In life-or-death situations, people chose to aid close kin over distant kin, the young over the old, the healthy over the sick, the wealthy over the poor and the premenopausal woman over the postmenopausal woman; whereas when it is a matter of an everyday favor, they gave less weight to kinship and opted to help either the very young or the very old over those of intermediate age, the sick over the healthy, and the poor over the wealthy.[39]

So, it seems caring and helping depend on the cost and the nature (seriousness) of the threat. But what is crucial is that we have an evolved psychology for helping and acting compassionately. In so far as our future survival may well depend on how caring and helpful we can be to each other then we need to study the social conditions and developmental trajectories that will privilege compassionate and non-exploitative behaviour. A Buddhist monastery is likely to be different in this regard, compared with a Nazi, xenophobic state.[40] So

---

[39] Burnstein, Crandall and Kitayama, p. 773

[40] We will have more to say about this in Chapter 4, but we can note here that there are, in fact, various models of human psychology that take radically different approaches to the problem of the bio-cultural linkage(s). The first is a kind of *plasticine model* which suggests that all our values, emotions and social dispositions are social constructions. Everything that is fundamentally social is learnt. The brain is only a vehicle for the transposing of social inputs into meaning and meanings are purely in the social domain and not the biological. To be concerned with the biological, this argument suggests, is like thinking we can discover anything meaningful about a written text by understanding the way a word-processing program works. This is a cold, passionless, approach, denuded of the body, with a profound dislike of any linkage of us to animals.

The opposite view is reductionism. Here the biological is seen as primary – and it shapes the cultural. The cultural is simply a complex interplay of social relations for the enactment of reproductive strategies. True, reproduction is not the primary focus, but the things that will lead to it (e.g., attachment, care of children, gaining sexual access) are. Nonetheless, the real control is with the genes and gene-neural structures. Social

whatever the evolved root to caring behaviour, as we shall see in the next chapter, there are many rearing and socialisation experiences that can increase or reduce it.

Social Success or Reproductive Success?

Our social fears and pleasures are in fact related to those things that in the past have reduced or increased our reproductive chances. Thus, for example, being

---

meanings are complex effects of a particular set of genetic dispositions (humans) and must fit with evolved dispositions, otherwise they are meaningless. Culture then is merely a surface texture. Such a view sees the mind like an onion with multiple layers. As one peels back the layers and gets more deeply into the biology, one is moving closer to the real nature of mind – the real science of mind.

Many theorists are not happy with either extreme position and feel that we have been thrown off course by our fascination and analogies with computers. The brain itself is a socially responsive organ that changes its structure, its actual hardware, with social experience. Computers are not like this at all. They can certainly learn new things, but they don't change their hardware; they have neither feelings nor consciousness; they don't care what others think of them, nor if they are cared for, although they might be programmed to act *as if* they do. The process of becoming a particular human being involves both the interplay of genetic disposition and the biological alteration induced by socio-cultural experience, plus the social contexts in which social performances will be enacted.

To those who favour interactional explorations, causation does not lay at any particular level, but in the connections and interplays between levels. It is mostly 'the betweens' that are interesting and exciting. Complex patterns are always built from simple ones. Molecules are built from atoms, compounds and proteins from molecules, and organisms from proteins. It is simple and complex. Complex patterns are built from simpler patterns and complex systems from simpler systems. One cannot regress or necessarily infer the complex from the simple. If this were so, everything would be an epiphenomena of everything else, only simpler. For example, minds would be epiphenomena of biology, and biology epiphenomena of molecules and molecules epiphenomena of atoms and so on, down to sub-atomic particles. You end up explaining everything with next to nothing. At every higher level of organisation, the new patterns produced have properties of their own and these properties have organising effects on the smaller components from which they are constructed. Thus, humans are not simply the sum of a determined biology, for biology is responsive to the social. Yet at the same time, one cannot ignore the simple components from which complexity emerges. Houses are not just a collection of bricks, but if you remove the bricks the house falls in.

rejected, being left out or made an outsider, losing a mate to a competitor, being put down, shamed and generally subordinated, or made to feel that one has lost status, feeling inferior or worthless: these are the kind of things that can really upset us. While having our status boosted, being desired by a mate, accepted within one's group, having friends who accept and help us: these are all things that help us feel relaxed and good. In fact, if we lose the signals of acceptance, we can become pretty miserable, angry or anxious. When it comes to sexual relationships, some of our most intense feelings come from being in them (in love) and losing them (jealousy and grief).

That these experiences are universal in humans speaks of their evolved nature. On the whole, reproductive success has become secured by social success. Humans and animals are not focused on maximising their genes in succeeding populations; rather, they are orientated to social outcomes, gaining access to mates, forming helpful relationships, gaining status and access to resources, and caring for children - if all goes well, reproductive success may follow, *but gene maximisation is not a motive, only the social outcomes that might lead to it*. Thus, in the pursuit of status some might be so fixated on this social goal that they actually forego having children. Indeed, although it is rich Westerners who could afford to have more children, it is here that birth rates are declining rapidly, while they are increasing in other, poorer parts of the world. The motive for having many children can be religious (aversion to birth control), social and ecological. Having large numbers of children in poor countries offsets high infant mortality. Also, having many children will add to economic advantage and offer care for parents in their old age.

It follows, therefore, that social success depends on competent *social strategies that are appropriate to the social ecology*. This has major implications for understanding our psychology, because pursuing the goals that might have led to social and reproductive success in the distant past (e.g., hostility to, or excluding of, strangers) will become a serious craziness once we have nuclear bombs in our hands.

The Evolution of Social Relating

We have seen that evolution theory can explain the origins of various innate dispositions for social behaviour. One key aspect is that many of these dispositions have to be translated into specific behaviours and social signals. Suppose a peacock, via a mutation, developed a fluorescent pink tail, but this was an absolute turn-off and females avoided it. The genes for pink fluorescent tails would not make much headway. If it was a real bird-puller though, if it drove them wild with excitement, things would be different. Think of language. If the capacity to make some kind of auditory signal evolved in one animal, but others could not decode it, then it is, in effect, useless and gives no advantage. Be it squawks or the blackbird's song, any kind of change of social signal must not be too dissimilar from what already exists; it has to be able to be decoded by those receiving it. In animals who interact, the decoding and signalling systems must be co-ordinated. To put this another way, there is a need to have both sender and receiver decoder devices. It turns out that many social signals are like this. Not only can most humans automatically *express*, facially, certain emotions if aroused (e.g., anger and anxiety), but most humans can also *recognise* facial expressions. An angry face is recognised as such, for example, regardless of culture. Some of these expressions and non-verbal signals are very old. Staring and maintaining eye gaze can be a threat signal for both animals and humans. This bears on what have been called display rules, which can be both innate and socially defined. Eye gaze avoidance (looking down) is a signal of subordination in many species; bowing to the queen only happens in countries who have queens. In some cultures, displays of subordination are highly ritualised and embellished with cultural meanings – but are still displays of subordination.

By the process of co-evolution operating over many millions of years, we humans are able to interact and can now send complex messages to each other. Moreover, not only can we signal threat to competitors and come-on signals to potential mates, but we can also signal our preparedness to enter into all kinds of relationships by using social signals such as smiles, body postures and verbal statements of desire or intent. These include caring for each other (as in parent and child, or friends), cooperating, signalling status as we stand erect and confident, or signalling our subordinate status as we stay quiet with our head down. Motives that depend upon the sending and decoding of social signals, and that give rise to the dances and reciprocal interactions of relating, are called *social mentalities*. More of this later.

The Environment of Evolutionary Adaptation (EEA)

Some critics of evolution theory say the role of the environment is not stressed enough. However, evolutionists are very concerned with the environment, because they recognise that many of our social behaviours and strategies evolved in (mostly) stable contexts and are designed to fit, or work, in those certain environments. This is called the environment of evolutionary adaptation (EEA).[41] If the environment moves too far away from the EEA, then problems arise. For example, humans have a preference for sweet things, which on the plains of Africa is an advantage (e.g., we reject things that taste bitter). However, in the modern sweet shop, it is a source of dental decay and if taken to an extreme, diabetes. We are suffering an epidemic of obesity because our environment of 10,000 years ago meant there was a natural limitation on food intake and availability. Tesco was not even the dream. Our pets too can suffer from obesity because high-fat, high-salt, high-sugar foods are in abundance. Our basic psychology is constantly running up against our environments. Some of the features of our environments are fantastic, such as that created by modern medicine, clean running water and central heating, but other aspects are a disaster and cultivate the worst in us.

There is little question that in some major ways we are now way outside our EEA. Of course, in many areas modern life has brought many benefits – from simple home comforts to helping to reduce pain and disease. However, modern life has introduced entirely new social contexts that require us to use a

---

[41] Barkow, J.H., Cosmides, L. and Tooby, J. (1992). This is a wonderful edited book in many ways, covering many of these issues. Although Tooby and Cosmides in their early chapter take an unnecessarily hostile and combative attitude to the social sciences, and to some extent set up straw men, they cover in-depth many of these themes of how an evolutionary approach can help the social sciences. The interaction between culture and biology is also well laid out by Hinde, R.A. (1987, 1989).

psychology for which it was not designed. For example, the preferred group size is between 50-150 and stable over time. This allows for relationships to be negotiated and adaptive rank and altruistic strategies to work. If groups get much bigger than this, then these strategies begin to break down, simply because they need to be worked out in consistent relationships. Violence and exploitation of unknown others increases in large amorous groups, and one cannot depend on others coming to one's aid. The days of hunting and fishing, of close-knit isolated groups, of children roaming freely (and not tied to the small boxes of the modern home with a fraught, isolated mum) are gone. In their place, we have the mega-groups, the highly structured work day, the constant fear of loss of employment, the availability of drugs and alcohol, the high rises and run-down estates, the pollution, the lack of exercise, the enormous segregation of society, the television that beams us pictures of what everyone else has and we do not, and the disturbing and pacifying nature of our entertainment on our social relationships. More of this later.

In fact, the effects of television, or mass communication in general, on our adapted minds are odd and not well understood. Television offers new forms of relating not existent in nature, which utilises out innate strategies in some rather bizarre ways. When executives tell us that television reflects real life, it is well to remember that by the age of ten many children have seen in excess of 5000 murders and acts of extreme violence on the box. I have to say (thankfully) I have never actually seen any one murdered in 'real life' yet. Television feeds off an innate need for newness and excitement, but as the Romans found in their games, once violence is the source of this entertainment, one is pushed to be more inventive in maintaining interest. Television also feeds off needs for consistent relationships – hence the popularity of soap operas. Even in sports, it is the relationships, getting to know about the players etc., this is crucial to developing a following. However, the media also makes these relationships more distant, beyond human touch, embrace, interaction, mutual dependency or reciprocation. For some people, real interactions become frightening, and much of their needs for 'relating' are sought through the contrived scripts of the soaps. While we can watch and may fantasise, we can never really participate. So, we are confronted with real oddities in how we live today compared with how are brains were 'expecting' to live. We can also think of many opportunities for criminal, callous and cruel behaviour that are a direct result of our environments. For example, in hunter-gatherer societies, people were as interested in sex as they are today, but they did not have sex traffickers and pornography; later, came war raids and sex slaves, of course, but not in the small groups. Hunter-gatherer people may have had an interest in smoking the odd weed, but they did not have drug barons and protection money. It would have been inconceivable for individuals to break into other individual's huts and steal from them.

The mismatches between EEA and our current social contexts can produce considerable stress. Not surprising then that there is evidence of increasing vulnerability to stress-related disorders, e.g., depression (which has been steadily increasing this century). Even in major disorders like schizophrenia, a person may do better in a small, close-knit community than in our current depersonalised ones.[42] As Jung has said, "everything casts a shadow". I personally would not like to go back to the Ice Age. However, in order not to be burdened with the disturbances caused by an ill fit between innate psychology and social change, it may be necessary to be more aware of our basic evolved psychology: not just our potential for deception and savagery, but also of our needs for belonging and community. The greatest challenge today is how to produce fair, peaceful and open societies given that our evolved psychology was designed for working with close-knit, familiar others. In designing social and economic living environs it might be interesting to start with a thought about our evolved nature.

---

[42] Eisenthal, S. (1989) gives a good overview of socio-cultural approaches to psychiatric illnesses. It is very clear that social environment (e.g., social status, unemployment poverty social isolation and disintegration, family structure etc.) plays an important role on people's states of mind. Even Freud noted how his mood was affected by his money worries! For an evolutionary approach to psychiatry McGuire and his colleagues have developed important ideas the most recent is McGuire, M.T., Marks, I., Nesse, R.M. and Trosi, A. (1992). This is far more technical than we can explore here. See also the special issue of the Journal, Ethology and Sociobiology, vol. 15, no 4. See also Glantz, K. and Pearce, J.K. (1989).

Evolution and the Brain

The Triune Brain

If evolution has given rise to various abilities and desires to attach ourselves to parents/caregivers, care for our children, find sexual partners, etc., how do we do all these? In order to engage in our courting rituals, status acquisition behaviours, care for others and so on, we need the brains for it. When it comes to basic brain design we can again turn to evolution for clues. Our evolutionary history has created our basic forms. Humans evolved from primate stock some five or more million years ago, and we share about 98.5% of our genes with chimpanzees. The primate line in turn evolved from earlier evolved species reaching back to the stem reptiles (and beyond) that first appeared some 250 million years ago.

Evolution is very conservative in how it changes things. For example, most vertebrates have four limbs, similar internal organs (heart, liver, kidneys, lungs) and so forth. The basic design of the nervous system, with the spinal cord along the dorsal surface and sensory organs (eyes, ears, olfaction, mouth, etc.) in the head, find its beginnings in changes occurring in the sea some 400 million years ago. We can refer to this as the conservation of form. Because evolution proceeds like this, adapting and adding on as it goes, we can see ourselves as 'emerging beings', cobbled together over millions of years.

Paul MacLean,[43] along with many other neurophysiologists who have studied basic brain architecture, have found that the brain has evolved in a series of stages and levels to some degree representing its phylogenetic history; we actually have reptilian and mammalian vestiges. In fact, the brain evolved in a gradual way, in a kind of adapt and add-on process. In fact, it is rather jerry-built. Some adaptations, such as live birth and care for children, had to inhibit other behaviours such as a tendency to return to foraging and forget all about the

---

[43] MacLean, P. (1985)

kids back home (as might a turtle) or even eat them! Indeed, MacLean[44] has suggested we have three (or possibly four) brains in one. This is depicted below.

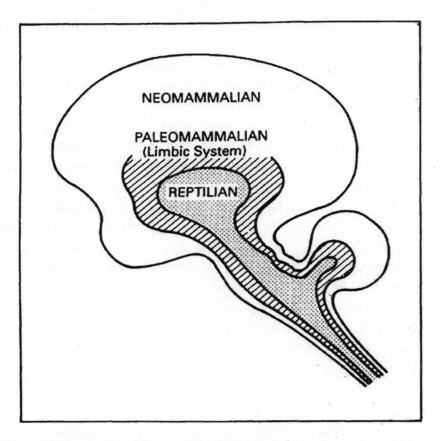

Figure 2.1 Components of the human brain. The forebrain evolves and expands along lines of three basic formations that anatomically and biochemically reflect ancestral commonalities with reptiles, early mammals and late mammals (From MacLean, P., 1985).

---

[44] MacLean, P.D. (1985)

The reptilian complex is the oldest part of the brain, and amongst other things is concerned with routines, territorialities, fighting/challenging, guarding, hunting/predation, grooming and sex. The mammalian brain moved us from cold to warm bloodedness, and modifies reptilian forms of behaviour to fit group living, foraging and the family. The cortex is the most significant change for the purely human. It is the site of our most important inhibitions and social awareness – such as empathy and sense of self. It is the source of our symbolic and systemic thinking, and our capacity to plan and anticipate. Of course, empathy can be used to help in one's deceptions. Many a villain has gained status by knowing what makes others tick. A non-empathic torturer puts the gun to your head, an empathic one to the heads of your children.

The early simian primates, who appeared over 10 million years ago had a brain capacity of about 500 cc or less. Around two million years ago, early humanoids called *Homo habilis* first appeared on Earth. They had a brain capacity of 650-700 cc, about half that of modern humans. They walked upright, lived in family groups, had developed simple tool use, followed a hunter-gatherer way of life and may also have built shelters. Over the subsequent two million years, evolution was to come up with *Homo erectus*, Neanderthals and *Homo sapiens*. Today our brain capacity is around 1660 cc. In just two million years the expansion of the brain, and especially the cortex, has been rapid and dramatic. As Bailey[45] points out, "the proportion of the neocortex to total brain size is estimated at 50% in prosimians, 67% in monkeys, 75% in apes, and 80% in humans..."[46]. Much of this cortical mass is represented in motor areas and the frontal cortex, the seat of the empathic abilities – abilities we shall explore in Chapter 12.

These three 'brains' do different things, have different priorities and can conflict with each other. It may be, for example, my reptilian brain which encourages

---

[45] Bailey, K. (1987). This is a fascinating text which tries to explore the implications of our evolved brains on our psychology. I am not sure I agree with all the tenets of his progression-regression approach since so much of our behaviour depends on ecology on the one hand and the 'patterning' of internal potential on the others, rather than just up-down, forward-backward notions. Still, a major and important text.
[46] Bailey, K. (1987), p.103

me to focus on possessiveness, ownership and control over the territory around me. My more purely human brain, however, may see these desires and impulses as evidence of a poor moral character, and so I suppress them and become more altruistic.[47] It may be my reptilian brain that produces arousal in me if a conflict starts to get heated and/or nonverbal signals appear aggressive. On the role that the reptilian brain has in our everyday life, Bailey says this:

> We must acknowledge that our species possesses the neural hardware and many of the motivational-emotional proclivities ... of our reptilian ancestors, and, thus our drives, inner subjective feelings, fantasies and thoughts are thoroughly conditioned by emanations from the R-complex. The reptilian carry-overs provide the automatic, compulsive urgency to much human behaviour, where free will steps aside and persons act as they have to act, often despising themselves in the process for their hatreds, prejudices, compulsions, conformity, deceptiveness and guile.[48]

On the other hand, some of our prejudices are not a source of self-hatred but pride, and we all too eagerly throw ourselves into the fight. The problem is that it is the pre-human adaptions in the brain that supply the emotions of our lives, the sense of pleasure and pain, the passion and the conviction. All too often the reasoning, intelligent talents of the cortex, can be recruited to fill in the gaps of logic and offer justification for the worst prejudices (reptilian dictates) and calls to violence. Moreover 'states of mind' have a major effect on how the cortex (and its various talents) are used. The reasoning of the defeated, frightened and depressed is different from the reasoning of the victor, secure or happy; the reasoning of the neurotic is different from the reasoning of the psychotic. As MacLean notes,

> It is one thing to have such an animalistic brain to ensure us of the authenticity of food or a mate, but where does confidence lie if we must

---

[47] Gardner, R. (1988) has developed calls for a science of `basic plans'. Basic plans are gene-neural structures which are concerned with specific forms of behaviour, such as mating, care for offspring, gaining access to the higher ranks and so forth.
[48] Bailey, K. (1987), p.63

rely on this same brain to supply the feelings of belief and conviction in regard to neo-cortically derived ideas, concepts and theories?[49]

The more our convictions involve relationships (with Gods, lovers or enemies), the more we may be reliant on the feelings emanating from our more primitive brain structures. It is understandable then why Buddhists stress education in mindfulness, and why one Zen master was moved to say "great doubt great enlightenment, little doubt little enlightenment, no doubt no enlightenment." Of all the religious-based groups, Buddhists seem closest to intuiting that the brain is an unruly entity, and training is needed to bring it under control. Without training it is taken to flights of fancy and emotional urgency which are sources of suffering to self and others.

While evolution is a process of selection, the medium through which behaviours are expressed is via the physiological. The fact that we need evolved brains to do certain things can be ignored by those who only focus on culture as the determining influence on behaviour. If there are things that damage our brains, then we become less competent at various social behaviours – or even less interested. There are now many studies of individuals who tragically have had damage to different parts of the brain and this produces specific changes in their competencies, be it for memory, emotion recognition or emotion regulation. Damage to the frontal cortex, for example, can render people impulsive, aggressive and fearful, or disinterested and apathetic. If there are genetic problems, then our brains may be affected so that the coordination of emotions, thoughts and behaviour become especially problematic. Moreover, personality traits are also part regulated by the effects of genes on the organisation of the CNS.[50]

---

[49] MacLean, P.D. (1985), p.412

[50] The role of genes on personality is a hotly debated area and often gets political, but I think most agree that at birth we are not exact copies of each other. There are many ways of classifying personality types. Americans researchers are keen on what they call the big five. These include *neuroticism* (the ease by which you can be aroused and disturbed by negative emotions, such as anger and anxiety), *agreeableness* (how friendly, caring empathic and helpful you are), *extroversion* (how social and outgoing you are), *conscientious* (how reliable, responsible and disciplined you are), and *openness to*

Culture certainly educates our brains into what behaviours we develop and enact. Thus, some cultures are far more concerned with possessiveness, ownership and self-centredness than others (we might call this narcissism – old brain education). Some cultures are war-like, others are more peaceful. In fact, this point is crucial when we come to thinking about how we behave in such crazy ways. Some of our behaviours might be okay if we were still reptiles fighting for territories, but to encourage certain kinds of possessive aggressiveness in humans, given the world as it now is, is to risk serious and counter-productive conflicts.

Defending Ourselves

As we discussed above, natural and sexual selection has provided us with a whole range of threat detection and responding mechanisms. Many of these can be switched on very quickly because threats often turn up out of the blue and require rapid action. So, like all other animals, we have to be able to defend ourselves from harms and hurts. There are two basic harms and hurts. The first is a direct harm. Interestingly, it is the things that were threatening in the distant past that most easily arouse our anxieties now. For example, fear of cars or electric light sockets are rarely the stuff of phobias. Phobias of spiders, snakes and other creepy crawly things are much more common. Yet in our society cars

---

experience (how open and flexible you are to new ideas and situations). This gives a flavour of the kinds of traits psychologists are interested in, although there are many other ways of exploring personality and classifying basic traits. Although genes may favour a particular pattern of traits in a particular person (some estimates are that around 50% of variation of personality is genetically related, but studies vary), genes can only offer tendencies. For example, if you are abused and live in a hostile environment, this is not going to help mature an openness to experience. If on the other hand you are by nature rather rigid, then a non-threatening, supportive environment might soften this and help you loosen up. More complex is the idea that our personality may actually help to shape our social environments. For example, if you are not very agreeable, then others may find it difficult to be pleasant and agreeable to you. So, you tend to elicit more disagreeable interactions from others compared to a very agreeable person. Then, because others are not very agreeable with you, this tends to increase your tendency to be disagreeable back.

and electric light sockets kill far more people. A spider does not have to be in any way dangerous, and the person may rationally know this, still the experience of panic at the sight of one can be intense. In other words, we are biologically set up to develop fears of such things, because in our distant past those who developed fear quickly survived better (and left more offspring) than those who were more laid back about such creepies.

By being overly sensitive to spiders and not cars or electric light sockets, the brain is in effect making a mistake, because the probabilities of dying from cars and electric light sockets is far higher than from spiders. To put this another way, at times the brain jumps to conclusions and gets us to react quickly, without worrying too much about the details of the data. Today, such behaviour is irrational, but our rational minds can have difficulty controlling it. It is one thing when this is about phobias for spiders, but quite another when we have the same emotionally focused reaction to social stimuli such as prejudice, paranoia and tribalism.

This raises a key issue that *when we are called on to defend ourselves we can jump to conclusions, because it is better to be safe than sorry.* Our brains and bodies are reacting before our rational mind gets into any kind of gear, and then it can be recruited to accentuate rather than ameliorate. In fact, this *better safe than* sorry principle probably accounts for why some fears and prejudices are so easily activated. In terms of the types of things we find it easy to be threatened by, these are a mixture of social and non-social. For children, the separation from the mother can activate defensiveness and anxiety. At the age of nine months, anxiety toward strangers arrives just at the time the child is becoming mobile. The child may never have experienced a hostile stranger, but often by nine months a child can easily become wary of them, although much may depend on how commonly the infant encounters strangers, their typical reactions to the child, and their parents' attitude to them. Emotions, such as jealousy, arise from perceived threats of one's mate(s) defecting or being unfaithful; paranoia arises from threats from up-rank members or alien groups and of being pursued by them; hypochondriasis arises from perceived threats of disease – we could develop quite a long list.

While it is true that we have all kinds of ways of dealing with social and other threats, it is also the case that some of the ways we respond are fairly primitive. In terms of our emotions, threats can arouse in us anxiety and anger; no different in principle to many other animals. We may not wish to feel these things; they just seem to come over us. Indeed we, like other animals, have a menu of possible ways of defending ourselves from various threats. If we thought we were entering a situation that could threaten our status, we might avoid it or run away. We might say as little as possible to avoid attracting attention to ourselves. At times, we may find it difficult to speak, as if some internal brake has come on. In groups of people (especially if they are strangers to each other), some will speak up and others seem more inhibited. Mostly, the inhibited ones do not wish to stay silent; they just find it difficult, as if a part of them is holding them back. The capacity to be inhibited in the face of possible down-hierarchy threat is almost certainly not of human origin but evolved much earlier.

We can list the possible defensive responses to threats. None of them are specifically human:

Fight, attack and threaten and subdue or control the other – in humans this includes not only violence and threats of violence but also attacks on others sense of self by shaming and criticising, either face to face or behind their backs.

Take flight, runaway, putting distance between self and that which threatens. It includes any kind of escape behaviour.

Concealment as in camouflage, hiding, deception and denial. Whereas animals have ways of camouflaging and concealing themselves in the physical environment we have ways of concealing what's going on in our minds - sometimes even from ourselves.

Inhibit certain types of signals – such as freezing, fainting and playing dead, or when in social situations submitting, sending no-challenge signals and not counter-attacking.

Help seeking or running back to the group or supportive other(s) for help or protection. Help seeking is a very central part of human behaviour and has soothing qualities when it is available.

If threats are anticipated in the future then we have two basic ways of dealing with them:

Avoid the situation altogether by predicting threats in advance, i.e., avoiding closeness to that which threatens, keeping away from it. There are many psychotherapies that highlight the fact that avoidance of emotions and situations can underpin a lot of emotional difficulty and mental health problems. Hence, many psychotherapies try to help people expose themselves to that which they are frightened of.

Preparation, planning and developing the skills, knowledge, alliances, tactics etc. that will make the threats surmountable if and when they are encountered. Making sure you have a safe burrow, or (in humans) enough weapons, or that you are skilled enough in your self-presentations either to subdue threats or to have learned how to disarm their impact. One can work on making oneself sufficiently attractive so that one is less likely to be rejected or threatened.

The fact that the brain tends to work on a better-safe-than-sorry basis may mean that some of these responses are activated inappropriately, too intensely or last for too long, but the important point is that they are common, central ways of dealing with threats. Often, these are associated with quick changes in arousal (anger and anxiety) that make their enactment more urgent. At other times, especially with preparation, people can spend long periods of time planning and developing themselves to be able to cope with predicted threats.

Elsewhere[51] I, and others, have argued that when the threat system is activated, our brains tend to operate in a highly segregated way; that is, the urgency of our

---

[51] Gilbert, P. (1992a, 1992b, 1993, 1995). In these writings, I made clear distinctions between defence and safeness systems. Unfortunately, space does not allow me to go into the details here. See also Bailey, K. (1987) for a more complex analysis of how,

defensive responses tend to take control and the higher rational and (perhaps) compassionate side of ourselves gets put on hold. *When we feel safe*, however, we are more relaxed and can be more rational and compassionate. So, for example, people tend to be kinder and more helpful when they are in good moods then anxious or depressed.

cf: Iranians coming to the UK & becoming xians

Safety and Safeness

— Not surprising that refugees are Safety-Seeking:

We can also make a distinction between safety and safeness. For example, in psychotherapy, safety is often referred to as safety seeking. These are the behaviours that are basically preventive, because they are focused on stopping bad things happening: for example, getting into a car and putting on your safety seatbelt; or when going on holiday checking that you have your passport and enough money. We may feel safe when our safety checks are done. Crucially though, the state of being safe means that we can now attend to other things such as explorative behaviour or undertaking tasks. Once we have put on our safety seat belt, we can choose to drive to where we want to go. Or when we feel safe, we can just relax and go to sleep. The point is that safety is about focusing our attention on preventing threats, and safeness is focusing our attention on engaging the environment in a safe way. The safer we feel generally, the more confident we are. Not surprisingly, some of that sense of safeness is taken from early life experiences. For people with mental health difficulties that safety seeking may stay turned on, and they remain very vigilant to possibilities of harm. Part of mental health problems is that our safety seeking fails to turn off, and we constantly feel threatened in one way or another.

Elsewhere,[52] I have argued that when we feel safe (compared to when we feel threatened) our brains tend to work in a more holistic and coordinated (less stereotyped and segregated) way. Positive affect dominates, and we are more open (less defensive), explorative and trusting. Research suggests that when children feel safe in their social environments, they play more cooperatively, are

---

under stress, we regress to the primitive and automatic. Marks, I. (1985) also explores the evolution of basic defensive behaviours.

[52] Gilbert, P. (1989, 1993, 1995)

more open to new experiences and are more creative in their problem-solving. Indeed, it may have been through the ability to provide highly secure (trusting) environments that early humans were able to liberate themselves from constant needs for defensive processing and so become more explorative and able to develop their intelligence. As we shall note in Chapter 12, Buddhist meditation appears to activate the brain and body systems underpinning these capacities for safeness, relax the self and deactivate the defence system. Individuals who are safety-focused tend to be very vigilant and sensitive to certain kinds of threats, whereas individuals who feel safely connected to others are more open.

Frustration

There is another whole class of threats, apart from direct ones that can be activated in ways that are unhelpful and destructive. These are called frustrations and they tend to recruit the same types of response noted above (although freezing and fainting rarely, if ever, are used to cope with frustration).[53] Under threat of losing something we want or value we can act in fairly automatic ways, often with frustration and anger. Now logically we might know this is not a good idea, it does absolutely nothing to help us, and occasionally we can end up doing exactly the opposite of what we want, but the feelings just take us over.

The Dalai Lama, at his 1993 talks in Britain, gave one of his own examples: as a boy he loved to fix watches. He would sit for hours trying to get them to work. One day a particular watch just wouldn't go right. He felt the frustration building in him until finally it broke through. He picked up the hammer and smashed it. No more watch. He used this as an example of how important it is that we learn to control these impulses and not act in such crazy ways that are simply destructive. More importantly though was that his intention had been to make a beautiful, operating watch and by losing control (in his view becoming mindless rather than mindful) he had done exactly the opposite of his intention. Part of training the mind for mindfulness or compassion is to help us to notice when we

---

[53] Berkowitz, L. (1989) makes the point that competitive situations increase susceptibility to frustration and aggression.

are being pulled away from our intention and not simply reacting because our primitive brains are pushing buttons all over the place inside us.

Smashing watches is one thing, but sadly it does not stop there. Many of our frustrations arise from our interactions with other people. As we shall see later, some individuals believe, or are educated to believe, that other people should be for them as they wish; they should admire them and send them lots of acceptance signals. When relating to a sexual partner, they think that the partner should be like a Duracell battery, ever ready, willing and able, and if they are not it can engender such rage and frustration that violence can follow. We are not educated to expect frustration and disappointment in our basic relationships and how to deal with it. Learning how to tone down impulsivity and improve frustration tolerance would certainly help many people. Turning other people simply into objects for our own satisfaction and gratification, and being frustrated when they do not function as we want them to, is one of the ways we drive ourselves crazy. It's *the objectification of the individual*. So much misery is caused in intimate relationships because people are not able to work together on how they disappoint each other.

To cut a long story short, we can say that we are predisposed to find things threatening and these include certain social relationships (those sending signals of put-downs and shame, rejections, defections to other sexual partners, or exclusion). When we are not receiving enough good signals from others, we can feel frustrated. When feeling frustrated and disappointed, we have stored within our brains an evolved set of potentials for rage, dysphoria and anxiety; even if we would wish for these not to be able to take us over, they can and do. Living in cultures which promote 'me first' competitiveness, which see it as acceptable to treat others as objects, does not help us deal with frustration, accept our limitations and loses; all these ideas can seriously influence our responses and attitudes to being frustrated and not having our own way. To avoid our frustrations, driving ourselves and others crazy, to avoid becoming a victim to the inner, earlier evolved adaptive responses, we should learn how to deal with disappointment and frustrative rage. We will return to this theme in Chapter 12.

Conflicts of Interest

Frustration in social relationships is going to arise particularly at points where there are conflicts of interest. In modern societies, it is how conflicts of interest are created and (not) resolved that causes so many problems. Various political systems not only help resolve or suppress conflicts of interest in individual members, via laws and traditions, but they can also create them. In understanding our contemporary conflicts of interest, we can also see that we are well beyond the EEA.

Conflicts themselves are complex, and there are many different types. In one type, person A and person B are in conflict over resource Z. Both want the same thing and the loser may leave the field. A only threatens B in so far as B seems in a position to get Z. Provided B does not challenge for the resource, A does not act aggressively and conflict is avoided. Fighting for a territory or food are examples. In a second type of conflict, A wants something that B has or is in a position to give or share: A wants something from, or of, B. This may be labour (as in slavery), attention, help, closeness, sex etc. The purpose here is to coerce B to act in a certain way in relation to A. Here, B cannot simply get away (and de-escalate the conflict) since they actually are the source of the wanted resource. The key issue is that there is no external resource that they are in conflict over, but it is the behaviour of one to another that is the source of conflict. Many of our more serious conflicts are of this type and to do with exerting control over the behaviour of others.

As evolution theory makes clear, conflicts of interest are salient factors in how members of the same species relate.[54] Sometimes these conflicts of interest arise from different reproductive strategies, such as a woman being choosy and wishing to relate to males who will invest in her and their offspring. Men might prefer having more than one sexual partner and investing less heavily than the female desires. Conflicts of interest can arise between child and parent, in that

---

[54] Such ideas have been well explored by Slavin, M.O. and Kreigman, D. (1992) and Glantz, K. and Pearce, J.K. (1989). Both sets of authors give very useful (although different) views and models of how evolutionary psychology can help us understand psychopathology in relation to conflicts of interest.

the child often wants more time, energy, attention and goodies than the parent is able or willing to give. Conflict can arise between siblings, and while some siblings can do extremely well, others do not. And of course, rivalries can grow in triangles, between mother-child and father, or between siblings or friends or groups and nations.

At times, conflicts of interest arise from wanting the same thing as someone else. Sometimes, conflicts of interest arise from gross inequalities, where one party wishes to hang on to what they have and another feels that this is to be deprived. But because humans also have the capacity for compassionate relating, it is not inevitable that someone's gain need be experienced as another's disappointing, frustrating loss. Once we recognise that at times voluntarily accepting, giving-in, sharing and giving up things (and not just being forced into it – which breeds resentment) is helpful, then, although it may be difficult, it too can be a source of feeling good about oneself. Moreover, a recognition that in giving to others we may reduce the number of enemies, and increase the number of friends, may be useful. The trouble is that cultural mottos that assert 'giving in is weakness, and self-sacrifice only for the naïve' do not actually facilitate altruistic means of resolving conflicts of interest.

When groups and nations seem only interested in protecting their own interests, then although these strategies may well have been laid down in an earlier age, and perhaps were adaptive for small, close-knit groups, to act so automatically and xenophobically in the world as it exists now is problematic. The poor will not wait forever for their share of the world's resources, and the world is not an un-emptiable well. If, for example, the world was serious about helping the Israel-Palestinian conflict, it would launch a massive programme to defeat poverty and deprivation. Even given the last world war, it seems we have not yet learnt the lesson that the most serious unrest and violence is seeded in communities of the deprived. In many ways, we must learn to control some aspects of our evolved nature rather than letting it control us.

Conclusion

We started with a concern of 'who are we' and 'where did we come from' – simple questions, perhaps, but with rather strange answers. We, as a species, came from a long history of gradual changes, beginning with DNA fragments that gradually became single cell organisms and arriving at us. Along the way there were a countless number of accidents, sudden shifts of climate, meteorites wiping out most of life and goodness knows what else. En route, biological forms have been changing and adapting, this way and that, 99% of them now extinct. But the changes have left their mark and design in our biological forms, rooted deep in our motives and emotions that are the guiding and steering mechanisms of our lives. As we began to recognise how we got to be here, through a process of evolution, we start to appreciate some of the real tragedies and horrors of life: the reality that all life has to eat other life; the realities of the horrors of viruses, diseases and parasites and the painful ways they kill us and those we love; the realities of our decay into old age, decrepitude and, sometimes, painful slow deaths; the realities of the horrors of predation; or the reality of nature's violent and rivalrous breeding strategies, including sexual competition.

Although we have a new intelligence which can gain insight and create the cultures around us, we are still locked into the evolutionary struggles that underpin the very struggles of life itself. To move forward with an agenda to try to improve the wellbeing of all living things, clear insight into what is driving us crazy offers opportunities for remediation and prevention. At least we know that the dark side is not about evil, but about nature itself. Nonetheless, as the Emperor in Star Wars says to Luke Skywalker, "you have no idea of the power of the dark side". Looked at through an evolutionary lens, he is probably right.

3: THE ARCHETYPAL MIND

You are a universe, a collection of worlds within worlds. Your brain is possibly the most complicated and amazing device in existence. Through its action you are capable of music, art, science, and war. Your potential for love and compassion coexists with your potential for aggression, hatred......Murder?[55]

The above quote is taken from a modern introductory textbook on psychology, and sets the tone of this chapter. We are indeed worlds within worlds, a mosaic of possibilities. As we saw in the last chapter, we have lots of different motivations: for self-focused competing for resources and recognition; for sex, to find long-term breeding partner(s); for caring for our offspring; for seeking care, help and support; for co-operative building of alliances and friendships; for belonging to a group/tribe; or for harm avoidance. The means to secure these biosocial goals are not always easy, and at times they can conflict. For example, when is it useful to be narcissistically self-focused and when to be gentle, kind and build close relationships? When should one act on a motive/desire and when should one resist? We also have many different emotions: being angry, anxious, sad, and joyful, as well as loving and hating, and these too can be in conflict. Humans have a kind of awareness which allows us to have some insight into these conflicts. This enables us to choose to act or not, but sometimes we do not exercise this very wisely. As the quote above states, we are a mosaic of possibilities, which at times can create inner chaos and confusion. Of course, given the way our genes and backgrounds create and shape us, there are many different potential versions of ourselves, many ways in which the different potentials within us get organised and patterned. It follows then that some of these patterns we will live to the full, while we may never encounter others until, or unless, the conditions exist to bring them out of us. Only in war, or following the murder of a loved one, may we experience the savagery of our capacity for

---

[55] Coon, D. (1992) p. 1.

sadistic rage and violence; only in the grief of a lost child or partner may we know the deep darkness and pining of our mind.

If all animal life on Earth was wiped out tomorrow, what are the chances that some new species would come to reproduce sexually, develop ways of communicating with each other, care for their young, cluster in groups and form dominance hierarchies, so that they too would become 'worlds within worlds'? Difficult to know, but it is possible. And would they develop the insightful intelligence and knowing awareness that we have – which is, considering the longevity of our planet, very recent? These new species may be different to us in many ways, and may look far more alien than those making guest appearances on *Star Trek*. Yet there could well be many similarities at the behavioural level – given time. When we see common patterns of behaviour (of sexual selection, care for young, dominance hierarchies etc.) all over the earth and in the sea (in whales and dolphins), it does look as if, on this planet anyway, certain patterns of social behaviour might emerge in more or less the same form, given certain contexts and conditions.[56]

The story of evolution also suggests that the brains and minds of these new species, just like ours, would not come into existence all in one go, but rather would evolve slowly, bit by bit. To get close to being like us, they would need many millions of years of gradual change and adaptation. This, of course, is a radically different story to that in the Bible and other religious myths, which favour our origins in terms of complete wholes or beings (e.g. Adam and Eve). Depending on which story you believe, you end up with very different ideas

---

[56] In fact, sexual reproduction and selection would be the key to any subsequent behavioural and psychological evolution. Much would then depend on what is called r and K selection. r selection involves short life spans, producing large numbers with low parental investment. K involves long(er) life spans, fewer offspring and more parental investment. If K-selected species started to get a foothold, then it is possible that many of the behavioural patterns common to mammals would emerge and with them the psychological competencies to exploit such behavioural strategies (i.e., motivations and algorithms). An excellent overview of r and K selection is given by Chisholm, J.S. (1988). He also makes the point, one that will be emphasised here, that K-selection (which is typical for humans) involves inner potential, maturing in social contexts, and that *life history* is crucial to understanding the development of any individual mind.

about the nature of mind. The story we shall follow, however, is the evolutionary one.

The Bits and Pieces Mind

It is the evolution of brain and mind 'bit by bit' that is really central to understanding the nature of our minds. A recurrent debate in the psychological and social sciences has been on the question of whether evolution produces animals who have just a few general competencies for learning, or whether it gives rise to a large number of specialised or *modular systems* that are relatively context-specific. The former theorists look to concepts such as intelligence, and how we learn, in support of their claim of us having relatively few specialised systems. Those advocating specialist systems look to our varied, context-dependent behaviours (e.g., cooperation, courting behaviour and care of offspring) to support their claim. They point out that there are specific mechanisms that orientate us to seek out *certain kinds* of sexual partner and that we are kin-sensitive in our caring. This is not a new debate. For example, at the turn of the last century, Spearman argued strongly in favour of a general factor 'g' that underwrites intelligence and which could be applied to a large variety of different problems. Opposing him was Thorndike. He asked,

> Are not our minds made up of an enormous number of highly specialized capacities to operate with particular kinds of problems? Do we have a mind with a capital M that can operate with any kind of material, and on any kind of problem, or are we a bundle of specialized capacities to do particular things?[57]

---

[57] As quoted by Reisman, J.M. (1991), p. 105. In fact, recently this whole idea of specialist mechanisms in the brain – or modules – has been experimentally studied and advanced by two researchers, Cosmides, L. and Tooby, J. (1992). They point out that the way we reason about social events is often less on the basis of logic and more on safety-first and adaptive criteria. This allows us to process information fast. They have been particularly interested in the detection of deception. Their views and research findings are well laid out in Cosmides, L. and Tooby, J. (1992).

In many ways this has turned out to be false argument, because both are true. We do have general abilities such as intelligence and competencies for reasoning, insight and self-awareness, although they depend on how the brain works as a system (e.g., they depend on memory and the capacity for abstract thinking, amongst other things). But we also have specialised systems. For example, there are a number of different and specific emotions; there are specific types of defence, (e.g., to run away, freeze or fight)[58]; and there are specific talents (e.g., drawing, music and empathy). It is possible to be very a brilliant physicist but hopeless at drawing, be tone deaf and not very empathic. Ornstein put it this way:

> The long progression in our self-understanding has been from a simple and usually 'intellectual' view to the view that the mind is a mixed structure, for it contains a complex set of 'talents', 'modules' and 'policies' within... All these general components of the mind can act independently of each other, they may well have different priories... The discovery of increased complexity and differentiation has occurred in many different areas of research... in the study of brain functions and localisation; in the conceptions of the nature of intelligence; in personality testing; and in theories of the general characteristics of the mind. [59]

Although we often think of ourselves as somehow whole and integrated individuals, this is an illusion. We are made up of many different talents, abilities, social motives, emotions, and so on. Not only are we 'worlds within worlds', but *we are something of a jerry-built species*. It is these internal

---

[58] And, as we saw in the last chapter, many of our anxieties tend to be about things that were dangerous in our earlier environments rather than our cultural ones. We tend to develop phobias about snakes and creepies rather than guns, carbon monoxide gas or radiation, even though guns, carbon monoxide gas and radiation today kill far more people. The films *Jaws* and *Predator* taped into archetypal fears of predation (and the predator), while monster movies often have monsters who have many reptilian features, e.g., claws and spiked teeth, etc.

[59] Ornstein, R. (1986), p.9. See also Cosmides, L. and Tooby, J. (1992).

modules that give us our sense of meaning, but meanings change according to which module operates.

The Jerry-Built Archetypes

There is a long history in philosophy, reaching back to the Greek philosopher Plato and found in the works of Kant, Schopenhauer and many others, which suggests we cannot know reality directly but only our internal constructions of it. These philosophers suggested that meaning is given by the mind to things and events, not the other way around. Although, this is not true in all cases, and the environment can carry much of the information that guides decision-making, as a general principle it still holds good. We know that the brain is very selective in its sensitivities. We only see a very narrow band of light frequencies, cannot see ultraviolet or infrared, and this is the same for our experience of sound.

Carl Gustav Jung (1875-1961) followed in this tradition. He first met Freud (who was 19 years his senior) in Vienna in the winter of 1907. Both men were interested in developing new theories of the mind, and with these theories they hoped to be better placed to understand psychopathology. Their first meeting was a long and enthusiastic one, and very shortly afterwards Jung joined the inner circle and became one of Freud's favourites. But a long and prosperous relationship was not to be, and by 1913 serious differences of opinion had emerged. The reasons for the break-up of their relationship were various, but a crucial difference was Jung's rejection of Freud's libido theory and his growing belief that the psyche was not made up of competing drives, as Freud insisted, but rather of various, internal meaning-making and action-directed systems. These systems, which he called *archetypes*, influence the unfolding of development, e.g., to seek care, to become a member of a group, to impress and excel (hero archetype), to find a sexual partner(s) and become a parent, to find meaning and wisdom, and to come to terms with death. These are the sources of our passions and dreams and are enacted in the rituals and myths of all societies.

Jung's work has sometimes been dismissed as too mystical and obscure for serious study. Certainly, he was concerned with the spiritual aspects of life, but it would be wrong to dismiss his ideas on this score. Although his ideas on the inheritance of archetypal forms, via repeated experience over generations, were misguided, many suggest the concept of 'archetype' remains valid and appropriate from the Darwinian perspective.[60] Jung postulated that humans, as an evolved species, inherit specific predispositions for thought, feeling and action. They are also innate attention-directors: e.g., the young baby attends to the nipple, is soothed by touch, and adults are attentive to, and excited by, certain sexual stimuli. These predispositions exist as foci within the collective unconscious, capable of guiding behaviour, thoughts and emotions. Jung distinguished the *collective unconscious* from the personal by suggesting that the *personal unconscious* represented those aspects of personal experience that were rooted in real events. They had at one time been conscious but were either forgotten of repressed. The collective unconscious, however, was the realm of the inherited universal predispositions: the internal motivating systems that form the bedrock of species' typical behaviours. He said,

> The archetype in itself is empty and purely formal, nothing but a *facultas praeformandi*, a possibility of representation which is given a priori. The representations themselves are not inherited, only the forms, and in that respect they correspond in every way to the instincts, which are also determined in form only. The existence of instincts can no more be proved than the existence of the archetypes, so long as they do not manifest themselves concretely. With regard to the definiteness of the form, our comparison with the crystal is illuminating inasmuch as the axial system determines only the stereometric structure but not the concrete form of the individual crystal. This may be either large or small, and it may vary endlessly by reason of the different size of its planes or by the growing together of two crystals. The only thing that remains constant is the axial system, or rather, the invariable geometric proportions underlying it. The same is true of the archetype. In principle, it can be named and has an invariable nucleus of meaning but

---

[60] See Wenegrat, B. (1984, 1990). Also Hall, C.S. and Nordby, V.J. (1973).

always only in principle, never as regards its concrete manifestation...
(pp. 13-14) [61]

Jung was first and foremost concerned with those various universals common to humanity. He attempted to articulate the internal psychic mechanisms that (across various cultures and time) brought into existence (into relationship) various universal life themes, myths, rituals and stories. These life themes (for attachments, seeking sexual partners, joining groups, forming social ranks, worshipping gods, etc.) arise, he argued, from some kind of pre-wiring, or preparation of our psychology: i.e., our pre-wiring is part of our jerry-built brains, with its different modules, policies and talents. Thus, as we do today, Jung saw the mind as a mixed structure, made up of various motives and modules. But he stressed the innate nature of these modules which allow us to do certain things (e.g., to form sexual relationships, attachments to our children). Crucial too was that they matured, unfolded and interacted, creating patterns of experience leading to individuation. Because these are evolved predispositions, they are shared with all human beings and, in this sense, are collective and our innate predispositions are largely unconscious. [62]

---

[61] Jung, C.G. (1972).

[62] Jung can be quite difficult to read in the original but there have been many clear expositions of his work. I would recommend Hall, C.S. and Nordby, V.J. (1973). Ellenberger, H.F. (1970) places Jung's work in its historical context alongside many other thinkers on the nature of the mind and the unconscious, and Stevens, A. (1982) has explored the relationship between the concept of archetype and the behaviours of attachment. Wenegrat, B. (1990) has also given a very helpful exploration of the relationship of the concept of archetypes to modern sociobiological theory that is well written and highly accessible. Although Slavin, M.O. and Kreigman, D. (1992) never really recognised they were dealing with archetypes in their use of evolutionary psychology, nonetheless, they give a very useful view of how evolutionary psychology helps us understand many facets of the archetypal mind. See also Buss, D.M. (1991). Jung did not emphasise the idea that our archetypes were laid down at different times in evolution and therefore each new adaptation had to accommodate itself to what went before. However, the idea that humans could as it were regress to more primitive forms of behaviour and feeling is implicit in his work. This idea of regression to the primitive in us has been developed with some force by Bailey, K. (1987). In his view, when we are under stress or maturation difficulties there can be: a) reduced control of behaviour via neocortical structures in preference to "lower limbic and reptilian structure" control, thereby inhibiting language and rationality; b) responses that become more stereotyped

The Social Archetypes

In many ways, we are the species we are because we have travelled a certain road and have been subjected to evolutionary pressures. Focusing on evolved social motives, roles and patterns of relating offers better insight into why certain patterns tend to emerge constantly, and how our cultures can lead us to act in destructive ways, especially to each other.

What the concept of archetype does is to offer a bridge between the biological concepts of natural and sexual selection, and the internal psychology of ourselves. As Jung made clear, in a way, the repeated returns of salmon to their place of origin, the building of nests, the rutting of the deer, the burrowing of rabbits, our fear of spiders – all these represent the legacies of generation upon generation repeating archetypal forms of the species. Archetypes connect us with our biological heritage. And, with the risk of repeating myself, they show themselves in the hero's quest, the search for the sexual partner(s), the care of offspring, the belonging to a group and the submergence of the individual identity and morality to group identity and conformity. Archetypes speak with the familiar tunes of love, sacrifice, deception, rage, envy, betrayal and shame, to name some of the most common. They operate in our dreams, fantasies and ambitions, in our hopes and fears. They are a source of the repetitive themes in social living reflected in our narratives and storytelling.

Jung's friend and Nobel-prize-winning author, Hermann Hesse, never really understood all the controversy over archetypes. He said that as far as humans are concerned, writers had known about them for centuries, and if they could not feel them within themselves and connect with them, they could not write stories. In fact, storytelling is an interesting human activity for we can learn much from it. For example, despite thousands of years and many differences in cultural styles and language, from the ancient Egyptian, Greek, Indian and Chinese cultures, we are able to understand the themes of all the stories humans

---

and less flexible; and c) the reduction in control of higher cortical centres, through which sex differences are maximally accentuated.

have ever written! Whatever the textures of culture, these are surface textures, and do not ultimately cover over the deeper meanings of human life.

Pathways for evolved dispositions

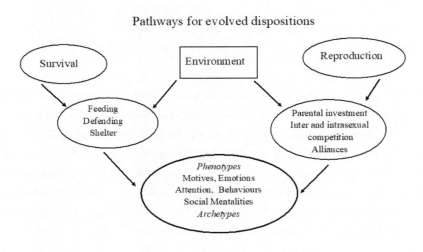

Figure 3.1

Figure 3.1 shows a rough scheme by which survival and reproductive strategies operate, and highlights different evolved motivational patterns associated with each stream. The phenotypes are environmentally choreographed patterns of our motives, emotions, ways of attending and behaviour. They also give rise to the specific social mentalities by which we process social information for the purpose of pursuing specific social goals such as caring for offspring, mating and building alliances. Another term we can use that might be easier to hold in mind is *archetypal* or *archetypes*. These are not exactly equivalent terms scientifically but close enough for our purposes – basically, evolved dispositions.

Sociobiologists talk of distal (things that have shaped genotypes over the long term – like millions of years) and proximate causes (things that operate on the phenotype: that is, things that influence an individual's life, e.g., rearing practices and current social-environmental triggers of behaviour). It is important to neither underestimate the power of distal forces as they have shaped reproductive strategies, nor underestimate the power of socialisation and development.

For example, if we think about survival for many of us today: we no longer have to defend ourselves against predators, and are actually more likely to be knocked over by a bus. If you think of feeding behaviour, then those in the West are generally no longer at the point of starvation. In fact we face an epidemic of obesity that is clearly environmentally caused. We no longer live in caves or build mud huts, but rather in high-rises and densely packed cities. And in terms of reproductive strategies, these too have been greatly changed by our environments. We now have contraception, and online dating, a fashion industry and multiple sports for people to show off their athletic prowess and compete. Even the number and timing of offspring any one individual will have is related to social factors. In the wealthier sections of the West, birth rates are falling, but they continue to rise in the poorer areas of the world.

The environment also plays a huge role in cultivating (or not) our dark sides. Crimes of all kinds are greatly enhanced in certain environments, particularly in poorer, more economically deprived environments and ghettos. Mental and physical health problems are also greatly affected by our environment. The introduction by Walter Raleigh of smoking was an environmental change that has drastically elevated the risk of cancer. Our modern diet greatly elevates our potential for obesity, diabetes, heart disease and much more. Not only this, but the quality of our environments has a major impact on our brains. We literally mature different types of brain and different physiologies in different types of environment.

So, the internal, archetypal life is *only at the level of potential*. What emerges in the inner world of a person is the way these inner potentials for complex social behaviours are nurtured and matured within primary social and cultural relationships.[63] This is what makes us so human: the crucial role of relationship(s) in our becoming. Jung, of course, had no way of organising, or naming the structures of archetypal forms other than how they seemed to appear in the minds of his patients, in his own, and in his reading of history. Evolutionary biology, psychology and ethology, concerned as they are with the naturally evolved designs of minds, were in the future. It would not be surprising if today we were able to take the fundamental idea of 'archetypes' as valid but organise, name and study them in different ways. This is what is attempted below.

Archetypes and Social Behaviour

From an evolutionary point of view, archetypes evolved because they solved problems, especially those of social living; that is, they help us in our social lives and increase our social success. Being good at detecting deception, or caring for offspring, or making it to the top, or getting support from allies - all these have, in the past, given reproductive advantage (although the person enacting them may lack insight into their innate nature). As we noted in the last chapter, our recently evolved competencies for feelings, fantasies and thoughts can be very much focused by these things. We feel good when we are loved, find a mate(s), are accepted by friends, gain status and prestige. We feel bad when we are not loved or accepted, lose prestige, are disrespected, marginalised or rejected. Using modern evolutionary ideas, it seems that some of the key themes of our social archetypes are concerned with particular types of social relations. These include

1.   *Care providing.* As discussed previously, the evolution of care providing is a selected strategy for survival of offspring. The motivation to care requires mechanisms for stimulus awareness, when to care and to some degree how to care. Different species will do this in different ways: for example, the

---

[63] I have explored some of these ideas in detail elsewhere; e.g., Gilbert, P. (1989, 1992a, 1992b). Recently, Slavin, M.O. and Kreigman, D. (1992) have written a fascinating book on similar ideas using evolutionary psychology to inform self-psychology.

chirping of chicks or the flash of a throat will stimulate 'go find worms' in the parent. In humans, caring motivations organise our minds to be thinking about the needs of the other in order to promote their welfare or protect them. Hence, signals of need and distress activate a range of emotions and desires in the care provider. If signals of distress or need do not activate these motivational systems then the individual may simply ignore the person in need of care. But, as with all of these social mentalities discussed, the key is getting the idea that these are built-in, biologically evolved systems, which can be regulated by the environment and also our capacities for insightful and knowing reasoning.

2.   *Care seeking and receiving.* There would not be a lot of point in evolving capacities to be caring if targets of caring were not influenced or affected at all by the signals of care coming in. Therefore, as I discussed in *Human Nature and Suffering*, mammals – and particularly humans – have biological systems that are very sensitive to caring signals from others and will biologically be affected and organised by the signals. Distressed infants, for example, can be soothed by a caring touch or voice from their parent, and this happens because the signals result in very real physiological effects in the infant's brain. We also know that if children do not get certain types of signals, particularly affectionate ones, this can affect the maturation of the brain and particular emotion regulation systems. We also know that many problems of mental health are linked with early-life difficulties and to feeling not cared for or cared about. These social mentalities of caregiving and care eliciting have obviously evolved as dynamic reciprocal relating systems. Jung called them a parent-child archetype. The desire to seek care from someone wiser and stronger will change with age, but the strong motive remains throughout our lives and can even power some religions.

3.   *Cooperation and alliances.* Forming alliances requires that individuals experience each other as safe in some ways. Alliance building often involves aggression inhibition, conformity, sharing, cooperation, affiliation, friendships, group living and reciprocal behaviour. Our ability to cooperate begins very early, in the shared joys and attuned interactions between the child and caregiver. Later, it matures into experiences of friendship and companionable relating based on mutual pleasure, desire to be with, respect and valuing. That

we have preferences for group identity with 'like/similar others' also relates to this archetype or set of archetypes. Evolutionary theorists highlight that this cooperative living together in close-knit groups probably also underpins the evolution of morality and moral thinking. There are of course forms of Machiavellian cooperation where it is in our interests to cooperate whether or not we like people who we cooperate with. The downside of this social mentality, however, is that it also underpins tribalism to some degree. This is partly because the numbers that we can feel alliances for, or with, are linked to what we feel we share. Our morality can be quite different to an out-group than in-group members. Indeed, the underpinning of morality is probably linked to reciprocal altruism. This is why we see killing in-group members as a crime, but out-group members, as in war, as heroic. It is not the action but the context of the action that defines its social approval or sanction. Nonetheless, the point is that having friends or individuals around that one feels one can rely on or be supported by is important for mental wellbeing and feelings of belonging.

4.   *Competing for resources and social place: ranking ourselves*. Competition can be a 'scramble' where one's success does not affect another's gain, or a loss, or 'contest' where one's gain does affect another's loss. This is where the sexual reproduction strategies come into their own. Competition can involve direct competition for resources, gaining and maintaining rank/status (dominance/leader) and accommodation to those of higher rank (submission/follower). Social comparison is one of the core competencies of who, when, how and over what to compete for. In humans, the rank archetype tends to be involved with proving self to others. It is represented in heroic ideals, avoidance of shame and inferiority, and exerting certain types of control. As we shall note later, unhindered by compassion and care for others, it can be a destructive archetype. It can underpin narcissistic self-interest, Machiavellianism, and even psychopathic pursuits. It is the archetype that highlights the fact that when not integrated to other aspects of mind, be it caring or even morality, it can take us into difficult places.

5.   *Mate selection and sexual behaviour*. This involves attracting, being attracted to, courting, conception and mate retention. This archetype(s) gets going around sexual maturity when we begin to experience new feelings and

desires for physical relating. Some will be coy and choosy, while others are free and sexually promiscuous. The mate selection archetype affects (but not determines) the preferences for numbers, types (those showing signals of altruism-status), fantasises and mechanisms of control over breeding partners.[64] In bonobos, sex can begin at an early age and is often a very short encounter, can be bisexual, and is often used as a greeting as well as a way of reducing tensions. We are not quite so liberal, but human sexuality too can be used for different reasons other than reproduction, including pleasure, calming and pair bonding. Tragically, human sexual desires can also be, and often are, exploited.

Internal Psychology

Underpinning our archetypal life are two basic orientations: to self and to others. We have the psychological means to engage in either self-promotion and defending our own interests (which in Chapter 1 was called narcissistic) and promoting others and defending their interests, e.g., altruistic.[65] In regard to the latter, these evolved (probably) because of the benefits of altruism. We will meet these two basic psychologies many times as we go through this book.

The psychological (archetypal) mechanisms that have evolved within us can be seen to comprise at least four aspects. Firstly, there must be some kind of *motive system(s)* to make these kinds of relationship matter: i.e., it matters that our parents love and care for us; it matters that we are accepted by peers; it matters that we find a sexual relationship(s). Because these are social goals which have emerged via evolution, they can be called *biosocial goals*.

---

[64] As we noted in the last chapter, the archetypes of mate selection and choice effect the types of people we are attracted to: why males tend to choose younger sexual partners than themselves (and want more of them); why beauty is such a big thing for men; why females tend to choose status and altruism and may be less influenced by youth, or looks. (See Buss, D.M., 1989; Ridley, M., 1994 and section 111 of Barkow, J.H., Cosmides, L. and Tooby, J. (1992). Wilson, M. and Daly, M. (1992) also explore why men tend to treat women like property.

[65] Shott, S. (1979) offers sociological explorations, but ones which also fit with an evolutionary ones that see it in terms of altruistic and non-altruistic strategies.

Secondly, there must be *strategies* for securing these goals (e.g., how to be sexually attractive, how to detect deception, how to express a threat display, or how to signal distress). The more conscious we are of our strategies and goals, the more we can lay plans and develop our preparations for securing our goals, and the more we can adapt plans and styles to social contexts (cultural styles and traditions). For example, when wanting to form a sexual relationship, we will adapt our plans and strategies to fit with the socially acceptable means of courting and self-presentation.

Thirdly, there must be ways of evaluating how well or poorly we are doing in relationship to our efforts. In other words, there must be some feedback to allow correction (improvement or abandonment) of specific strategies. Emotions seem important here for they inform us with some urgency if plans and goals are threatened or need to be ditched.[66]

Fourthly, many of these social behaviours can be played out in domains of *varying closeness*. These can be loosely labelled as variations in: *intimate, personal, social* and *public*. For example, intimate care-giving might involve looking after one's child or soothing an upset lover. Public caring may be charity work where one may not even see the recipient of one's giving. The motives and feelings will obviously be different according to the domain of intimate - public. Moreover, one may be skilled at public caring, doing lots of good works for others, but be much less skilled at intimate caring. It is also possible that one's actual behaviours are not an exact reflection of an archetype. For example, public caring may, in some cases, have as much to do with gaining respect and prestige as with any genuine feeling for the targets of one's giving.

Armed with these observations we can now explore in more detail some of our most salient, social archetypal forms, and from here explore in the subsequent

---

[66] Keith Oatley and his colleague Johnson-Laird have developed important ideas about the nature of emotion as aids to our plans and goals. For example, happiness arises when we reach goals or subgoals, fear when we are threatened, anger when we are frustrated, sadness when we lose access to the means to secure goals. I believe that their view fits well with the ideas expressed here, and regret that it would take us too far away from my primary concerns to explore this here. See Oatley, K. (1992)

chapters of this book how these forms can become amplified (inflated), distorted, reduced (deflated) and/or come to have destructive effects. Using the classification noted above, social archetypal forms can be outlined as *care-eliciting; care-giving; alliance formation and cooperation-conformity;* and *social rank (dominant-subordinate).*

The Care-Eliciting Archetype(s) and the Importance of Investment

Our early attachment relationships between us and our primary caregivers have major effects on our psychological and biological selves.[67] In the *care-eliciting* situation, the self (or group) targets behaviours towards another who is seen as capable of providing what is needed. Basically, the individual attempts to elicit *altruistic-type investments* from others. These can vary from food, comfort and protection, to needs for approval, recognition, and support. Later in life, many forms of relationship will be based on the degree to which people feel that they are investing in others and others are investing in them: i.e., making and accepting commitments. Some forms of love, for example, are very much based on this notion of people investing in each other and people will monitor the degree and levels of reciprocal investments.[68] When we feel that people don't care for us, we are also feeling that they don't want to invest in us. So, we often judge how much someone cares (or even how much a society cares for us and others) by the level of investments they are prepared to make, the degree of their

---

[67] See Schore, A.N. (1994). Some see attachment as the child archetype. However, this is not an evolutionary but a developmental concept. I much prefer to think in terms of archetypal forms that evolve both phylogenetically and ontogenetically. Thus, I would make distinctions between care-eliciting, playfulness, exploration and so on and not wrap them all into one archetypal form of the child. I think this allows a better linkage with evolution theory, and in the case of care-eliciting allows one to explore the issue of social investment. It follows, of course, that there will be many archetypal forms of relating that I do not touch on here.

[68] Elsewhere, I have argued that if a person perceives that investments from others are dropping below a certain level, this can activate the defence system and produce feelings of dysphoria, anger and so on. Gilbert, P. (1993). In R.J. Sternberg's (1986) theory of love, he suggests that love consists of three components: commitment, passion and intimacy. Various forms of love exist according to the strength of each component (see Coon, D. 1992).

commitment. Again, what's central here is the ability to evaluate people's intentionality and motivation.

As a rule of thumb, the child feels secure and content on receiving parental care (investment of time and energy), and the parent feels happy at seeing his/her offspring react positively to their input. This, in essence, forms the basic (archetypal) dynamic of attachment behaviour between parent and offspring. When the parental investment, as elicited or needed, is not forthcoming or punitiveness dominates the relationship, the child may suffer in various ways. In addition to suffering negative emotions, s/he may develop the view that other people's investment, care and love in them is precarious or dangerous. This failure may be attributed to the self (i.e., there is something about me that makes me unlovable - not worth investing in) or the other person(s) (i.e., they are untrustworthy, unhelpful or bad). If the person defensively turns away from care-eliciting, due (perhaps) to a failure in *trust* (i.e., not feeling safe with care eliciting behaviour), then this archetype and social mentality may become blocked or inhibited. Alternatively, it might become emotionally amplified, and the child moves into adulthood in a state of feeling that is seeking satisfaction of unmet needs for closeness and needs constant signals of intimate investments. It is the conditions by which the child experiences the investments and care of others that lays down the styles of attachment behaviour and capabilities for intimacy and care of others which manifest later in life. These in turn can have long-term effects on subsequent relating styles and mental health.[69] Years of research into patterns of attachment and intimacy have suggested three or four archetypal forms of attachment and closeness-seeking behaviour. In exploring adult patterns of relating style, Collins and Read, and also Holmes, give the following overview of these forms.[70]

Secure attachment. These individuals like to be close to others but can cope with distance. They are comfortable with mutually dependent relationships and rarely worry, in the normal course of events, about abandonment. They have a basic

---

[69] Bowlby, J. (1969, 1973, 1980, 1988). Much of the recent theorising about attachment and research evidence has been excellently outlined and discussed by Holmes, J. (1993). In regard to attachment as an archetype, see Stevens, A. (1982).
[70] Collins, N.L. and Read, S.J. (1990) and Holmes, J. (1993)

trust (feel safe) in themselves and in others. Closeness tends to be joyful, respectful and mutually valuing.

Anxious ambivalent attachment. These individuals feel that they can't get close enough to others, and are very sensitive to cues of rejection or abandonment. Thus, they operate their attachments not via safeness but defensiveness. Their threat system is highly tuned to cues signalling withdrawal of others' support, care, etc., and these are experienced as intense frustrations and threats. They often worry that their partners and friends may leave or ignore them. Their needs for constant reassurance of their loveability and acceptance sometimes drives others away, and can show up as clinginess, possessiveness, jealousy and other anxious forms of attachment and relating. Being more fearful and defensive, they are prone to various negative emotional states, especially anxiety and dysphoria.

Avoidant attachment. These individuals prefer distance and can appear relatively detached, aloof and emotionally cold. Again, this is not safe relating but defensive; avoidance is their chosen, defensive response. They do not like to be dependent on others. Their partners often wish them to be closer, but this call to intimacy is frightening. They may be distrustful of others' motives and are sensitive to being hurt and/or controlled in relationships. They are the least emotionally expressive and are most likely to endorse self-sufficiency or self-reliance. Attempts to control others with various threats may also be noted.[71]

Ambivalent/disorganised attachment. These individuals show mixtures and oscillations of anxious and avoidant. If others get too close they are worried about being controlled and 'swamped' and they show avoidant patterns. If others are too distant, they are worried about abandonment and aloneness and show anxious dysphoric patterns. In some troubled personalities, this oscillation can be marked.

---

[71] There may be various types of avoidant. For example, some people seem distant, schizoid loners without any real desire to relate, but are not necessarily hurtful to others. (A few) others of this type can become sadistic killers. A different type, however, avoid genuine, warm, caring intimacy (although they do not seek aloneness). They can be socially skilled but also hurtful, shaming and highly controlling in condensing ways.

We see here how the archetypal patterns for care-eliciting, closeness and attachment can be associated with different emotional patterns, according to how they operate in the threat or safeness systems. In other words, although altruistic, investment goals and strategies may well have certain preferences or a natural course – i.e., to mature into secure attachments, though it is not inevitable they will.[72] Nevertheless, even though some people have insecure attachments early in life, they may still develop secure attachments later in life – as if there is some pull towards secure (mutually investing) attachment(s), especially if there are good corrective experiences. It may be that in the 'correct' context the biosocial goals and strategies for (eliciting and giving) altruism can become established because these are innate potentials. However, many researchers agree that these patterns of social relating are not the result of direct genetic-behaviour linkages, but are significantly shaped by experiences of the early social environment interacting with an innate temperament. It is not an active environment shaping a passive child, for the influence is both ways.[73]

---

[72] Moreover, different attachment styles may reflect different reproductive strategies (see Belsky et al., 1991). For example, exciting new work by Shaver and his colleagues found that these attachment styles affected care-giving (with the avoidant attachers being less invested in their relationships than the other attachment types) and sexual behaviour (the avoidant more likely to engage in one night stands and be interested in 'sex without love'). Anxious attachers, apparently look for high investments but are less interested in sex – as if their care-eliciting system is still child-like. Thus, a combination of genes and early life might be shaping reproductive strategies. This work was reported by DeAngelis, T. (1994).

[73] Some theorists suggest that males are particularly vulnerable to develop avoidant patterns of relating, causing problems with the latter capacity for closeness and intimacy, because it is the nature of the maturation of boys that they must psychologically separate from mother and identify with (often) a more distant, less available father, who may be poor at intimacy. Moreover, culturally the role models for males may be for toughness and self-promotion, rather than softness, intimacy and care of others. Due to this separation and switch in identification from mother to father, the boy develops a need to be overly controlling of others especially females – continually re-enacting the traumas of the early psychological separation from the feminine-female. Although interesting, these ideas have never being tested and other explanations of the male tendency to have more difficulties with intimacy and care for others exist. The sociobiological view of why men tend, in certain ecologies, to treat women like property can be found in Wilson, M. and Daly, M. (1992) in the aptly named chapter, 'The man who mistook his wife for a chattel'.

When early relationships work well, and there is good enough parental investment, the parent not only protects the child from dangers, answers distress calls, offers help, fulfils the material needs for food, shelter and warmth, and does not overly bully or attack the child, but also provides the child with many *psychologically* important signals of the child's 'pleasure to be with'. The psychoanalyst Kohut,[74] called such signals *mirroring*, or 'the gleam in the mother's eye'. All those behaviours, such as listening to, emphasising with, showing pleasure in, rewarding and mirroring, enable the child to internalise a sense of his/her attractiveness and acceptability to others. Via the approval and joy a parent offers the child, the child comes to feel safe in their interpersonal worlds, and to see him/herself as a person of value with status in relationships. Such signals play a powerful role in how the brain develops. Not only does a child learn they are loved, but they learn they are *lovable*. Without these signals, or where there may be shaming, *de-valuing*, ignoring or rejecting behaviour, the child may fail to internalise a sense of their value and attractiveness, and learns instead that their power to elicit investment from others may be weak and fragile. In such contexts, the strategies for altruism may not develop, for it may be more adaptive to be distrustful and/or self-reliant. We might say that the person is constantly on the defensive, vigilant to where the next threat is coming from.

The Care-Giving Archetype(s)

Although we often concentrate our attention on the receiver of care, the archetypal psychology of caregiving has sometimes been overlooked. This is extraordinary, because the psychology of caring is perhaps the most important psychology that we must understand and develop.[75] We will return to it in Chapter 12. Some feminists believe that the neglect of caring is because psychology has been dominated by males and male agendas which have focused on self-assertiveness and self-promotion, achievement, (and its sub-straits e.g.,

---

[74] Kohut, H. (1977)

[75] Our capacity to care for others, especially the sick and needy, is one area in which we are well in advance of our chimpanzee relatives. For example, no chimpanzee has been seen to comfort another in grief, and if animals are sick and look odd they are often avoided. See Goodall, J. (1990).

IQ), justice, aggression and so forth.[76] It is certainly the case that the psychology of compassion, peace-making, and caring have, until recently, been less explored areas of our functioning than many others.[77] And, moreover, these are often seen (sadly) as roles only appropriate for women. So, what do we mean by caring? Fogal, Melson, and Mistry define caring giving as

> The provision of guidance, protection and care for the purpose of fostering developmental change congruent with the expected potential for change of the object of nurturance.[78]

The orientation of the care-giving archetype(s) may be expressed to other humans, animals, inanimate objects (e.g., the family car) or the self. It takes in the concept of 'looking after'. Fogal et al. also note four dimensions of caring: 1) choice of object (as noted above); 2) expression of caring and nurturant feelings; 3) motivation to care and nurture; and 4) awareness of the role and need for caring. Because caring is not overly modularised, we can use our psychology to care for the garden, our vegetables, or a favoured musical instrument or car. The ability to use specific skills in many insightful and 'knowing' ways is what marks human intelligence.

Humans often gain a sense of wellbeing and purpose in life from giving to others. This may involve helping relatives or neighbours, taking careers in the helping professions, or charity work. Many individuals state that helping others is a source of personal meaning and purpose. It can feel good to be seen (and see oneself) as wanted and helpful to others (especially to kin and friends). Eisenberg and Mussen[79] have reviewed much of the work which explores the promotion of care giving and prosocial behaviour in children and note a number of factors: including experiences of personal competency and general well-being; having role models that attend to, value and reward caring behaviour; experiencing the benefits of sharing and caring; having opportunities to practice; and having models for developing prosocial forms of conflict resolution.

---

[76] Gilligan, C. (1982)
[77] This point is made vividly by Hinde, R.A and Groebel, J. (1991).
[78] Fogel, A., Melson, G.F., & Mistry, J. (1986), p.45
[79] Eisenberg, N. and Mussen, P.N. (1989)

Experiences with punitive and neglectful parenting have detrimental effects on the development of caring behaviour. It is as if having to be highly self-focused and self-protective reduces the opportunity to develop empathic concern for others. Furthermore, parental competitive behaviour which is focused on their child getting ahead and 'beating others' may reduce caring behaviour.

Care-giving can be conducted defensively, however, when a person needs to be needed almost irrespective of the other persons' actual needs. In this situation, the carer can be overprotective and intrusive, or they might suffer serious problems of guilt when there is a conflict between their own needs and that of another(s). Sometimes caring for disabled relatives can place significant burdens on individuals leading to stress, guilt, resentment and feeling trapped by one's obligations. At the other extreme, problems in care-giving can arise in situations of abuse and neglect, where the abuser does not seem able to construe the object of nurturance in terms of developmental needs and protection. It is the absence of caring that can lead to exploitation, where the other(s) is rendered little more than an object to satisfy personal desires.[80]

Although not all forms of caring behaviour require empathy, some forms of caring do. Empathic awareness begins early and matures into complex competencies, given the right opportunities.[81] When empathy blends with caring and sympathy and is guided by our intelligence, it becomes *compassion* and kindness. It is a mark of our craziness that if you explore how much compassion has been researched, you'll find it is surprisingly little. Yet compassion is probably one of our most important characteristics and certainly the one that really distinguishes us from other animals. It is the caring archetype(s) we need

---

[80] As we saw in the last chapter, sociobiologists argue that genetic relatedness is an important factor in caring of many kinds. This is why abuse is more common in step-relationships. While the research supports the idea that step-children are indeed more likely to be abused, there are other not mutually exclusive explanations, e.g., some divorced people may have had problems maintaining relationships (thus the reason for divorce in the first place and creating subsequent step relationships) and be a poorer caring group anyway (Belsky et al., 1991). Or it may be women with children are less choosy and pick poorer quality males.

[81] Goldstein, A.P. and Michaels, G.Y. (1985)

most in order to heal our potential for exploitation and craziness.[82] It is not only caring and compassion for others; we also need to develop compassion for ourselves – which many of my patients' often lack, filled as they are with self-loathing, self-dislike or arrogance which passes as caring. It is a tragedy that our competitive culture often devalues compassion, self-sacrifice and care for others in the way it does.

It is likely that the adult competency and valuing of caring and compassion relate to similar factors as in children: namely, experiences of being cared for; having role models that attend to, value and reward caring behaviour both at the intimate level through to the public level (rather than pure capitalist self-interest); experiencing benefits of sharing and caring (e.g., security and reciprocation); being socially rewarded for caring (e.g., seeing others prosper from one's input or feeling appreciated, having a warm glow); having opportunities to practise; having models for developing prosocial forms of conflict resolution; and where giving to (and accepting from) others is not always seen as personal weakness.

The Archetype(s) of Alliance Formation: Cooperation and Conformity

Cooperation and group conformity probably evolved from the need for, and due to the benefits of, forming alliances. Very few male primates make it to the top without allies, and in females, alliances are essential for gaining rank and protection. In humans, cooperation and competition have long been contrasted as two very different ways people secure goals. They require quite different motives and skills.[83] There is no clear dividing line between cooperation and

---

[82] Smail, D. (1987). See also Kreigman, D. (1990).
[83] See Johnson, D.W. and Johnson, F.P. (1991). Argyle, M. (1991). Many sociobiologists have pointed out that genetic relatedness is important in cooperation. Trivers, R.L. (1985) summarises this work well. Axelrod, R. (1990) has written a very accessible book based on his 'tit for tat' model. This was a model that won most gains in a computer simulation. Basically, your first move should be friendly and thereafter do what the other does. If they cooperate you cooperate, but if they compete you should compete. In regard to motives, McClelland, D. (1987) has distinguished between power and affiliative motives. Affiliative motives are to do with getting close to others and include caring and cooperation.

care-eliciting/giving, although not all cooperative relationships necessarily involve caring or desire for affiliation. In fact, in the cooperative relationship the motivation and cognitive competence is one of *sharing and mutual gain*. People thrive best in mutually supportive networks of familiar and friendly others, rather than amongst hostile strangers. Positive social relationships are a key to happiness and mental health.[84] But in order to develop these networks, certain judgements are necessary. One of these uses our innate evaluative ability for social comparison that allows judgements of *same-different and reciprocity*.[85] The same-different, social comparison allows for in-group/out-group identification – we are more likely to join groups and cooperate with others who seem like ourselves. Bailey and his colleagues[86] have suggested that what is happening here is that via social comparison we can come to relate to others 'as if' they are kin. Indeed, the more intimate our cooperation, the more we want to be treated like kin, gaining the same degree of commitment and feelings of being valued.

In cooperation, there is also a pressure (and desire) to *conform*. This conformity may arise from following fashion, working on the same research, sharing religious beliefs and so forth. There can be an archetypal pressure to reduce differences and to become more wary of others the more different from us they appear to be. Evaluations of conformity, reciprocity and sharing are key social concerns and convey to people that they are (and will be) accepted, valued and appreciated. Finding a place within a group and gaining a sense of belonging allows for the self to feel reassured by their fellows and benefit from a *mutuality of reciprocating investments*. Caring and affiliative cooperation also depend on social skills of acting friendly. Some forms of cooperation often involve the positive emotions of affiliation, liking and pleasure with avoidance of hostility. The affiliative style is particularly relevant to intimate and personal cooperation.

However, there are other forms of cooperation that arise from rather non-affiliative emotions. Aggressive-dominant styles might give rise to rigid,

---

[84] Argyle, M. (1987)

[85] Gilbert, P., Price, J.S. and Allan, S. (1995). In this paper, we explore evolution theory and social comparison and give a fuller overview of these issues than I can here.

[86] Bailey, K.G. (1988) and Bailey et al. (1992)

authoritarian (social and public) cooperative activity and groups that are disciplined and obey orders (e.g., armies). Since this form of cooperation does not depend on empathy or morality, one can expect that compassion will be inhibited under the pressure to obey orders without question. Thus, the dark side of cooperation and conformity arises from how our archetypes work once we are in a group. We can behave immorally to out-group members because we seek the security of in-group membership, and in-group membership is another facet of our self-identity, and/or we wish to see our group as superior.[87] Sometimes we have such needs to belong, and avoid causing offence to others by challenging their immoral behaviour, that we completely give up our individuality.[88] As Milgram demonstrated some years ago, when he got subjects to deliver what they believed to be painful electric shocks to others, we can cooperate with authority as a form of submissive behaviour (see Chapter 8). In such situations, although submissive behaviour appears cooperative, it should be seen for what it is – submissive compliance. When people behave immorally, the point at which they feel they are willingly cooperating rather than just submitting to immoral group law, or an aggressive leader, is sometimes difficult to know. Fear of being made the outsider (especially to a group we see as having power) can inhibit moral behaviour, and we may identify with values that are immoral and anti-social (e.g., sexism, racism). People will conform and go along with things (even against their 'better judgements') in order not to be expelled, ostracised or rendered 'not one of us'.[89]

This archetype plays out also in mental health problems. Many patients speak of feeling like *outsiders*, never having had much of an experience of fitting in

---

[87] See Abrams, D., Cochrane, S., Hogg, M.A. and Turner, J.C. (1990) for a discussion of group belonging and self-identity, and Pratto et al., (1994) for a discussion and research evidence of how, once in a group, individuals may try to privilege their group, to make it superior to other groups. Hence, their work explores how the rank archetype (although they don't use this term) is reflected in how people operate in groups. We will explore their ideas in a later chapter.

[88] Sabini, J. and Silver, M. (1982)

[89] Sabini, J. and Silver, M. (1982)

and belonging. Feeling a member of the out-group can be associated with paranoid anxieties, depression and envy. Much may depend on whether one feels an inferior or superior outsider.

Non reciprocation: A different type of adult problem can be activated by feeling exploited or unappreciated. Some people attempt to form cooperative and caring relations with rejecting and punitive individuals under the false belief that there must come a point when, if they give (invest) enough, they will reciprocate (the other will increase their investment in the relationship). Rarely does this happen. Some therapists believe that the issue of reciprocity lies at the heart of many neurotic difficulties.

There have been all kinds of problems created when allies in war do not keep their promises afterwards. Many of the tensions of the Middle East (including their intense distrust of the West) can be traced back to the many broken promises given to the Arabs by the Allies in the First and Second World Wars. Like the other social archetypes, the role of emotion and feeling in cooperation is crucial to an understanding of how it works. Not all cooperation is affiliative or particularly voluntarily. Some of it is fearful and submissive (to avoid punishment and rejection), sometimes it is based on guilt, and sometimes there is very little choice. Failures in reciprocation can unleash much anger and resentment.

The Competing and 'Ranking' Archetype(s)

There are two types of competition. The first is called scramble, where everyone goes for the most they can but individuals are not in direct competition, and where one person's gain is not another person's loss. The second is contest, where if one wins, the other(s) loses. This type of competitive behaviour results in ranks of (relative) winners and losers.[90]

---

[90] The right wing have invented a new form of competition which they call 'trickle down'. The idea here is that if everyone is allowed to compete to their fullest, then the benefits in terms of the resources produced will 'trickle down' to the less able. Judging on the evidence of the last 15 years, this looks like a fallacy. The disadvantaged tend to

Competitive behaviour that results in some kind of hierarchy or organisation of greater and lesser is, in many ways, a fulcrum around which much craziness turns. This is partly because competitive behaviour can involve *social control and power*. Our concern with, and awareness of, our rank, relational status or social position is an archetypal concern. Even amongst friends, individuals can be interested in whether they are a special friend or just any friend. For this archetype, the basic ways of thinking (and experiencing the self) are in terms of *greater-lesser, superior-inferior, winner-loser* and *dominant-subordinate*.[91] Unfortunately, as we shall see later (especially in Chapter 11), some cultures purposefully create conditions where people construct themselves in terms of winners-losers, weak-strong, worthy-unworthy, and so forth, which inflates the competitive motives and social mentalities within us. Yet there is increasing evidence that societies which produce these values, and have wide discrepancies in the distribution of economic resources, are suffering deteriorating standards of mental and physical health and rising crime compared to more egalitarian societies.[92] This is irrespective of GNP in industrialised countries. Thus, public forms of competitiveness and the creation of a *'culture of rivals'* can have serious consequences leading to non-caring societies and craziness. Of course, you will be aware that what sits behind the scenes are none other than our sexual competitive reproductive strategies guiding the motives and the phenotypes.

Sex. The social mentality for sexuality requires a system sensitive to certain signals which then stimulate physiological patterns to prepare the body for sexual activity. From here, there is an instigating of a set of interactions with a potential partner. As discussed previously, different genders have different orientations to sexuality, though altruism and trustworthiness remain important attributes for long-term partnerships. We are, however, seeing major social changes in sexuality in a relatively short time brought about by greater freedom. There is a greater preparedness for short-term relationships, and recently homosexuality and bisexuality have become more accepted as important and

---

get poorer and the disparity between rich and poor increases and the values of society become more cynical and ruthless.
[91] Gilbert, P., Price, J.S. and Allan, S. (1995)
[92] Wilkinson, R.G. (1992)

valid expressions of desire. The role of social contexts can be seen by noting that in certain conservative or 'traditionalist' groups, homosexuality can be seen as shameful, while in Sparta 2000 years ago it was the higher form of sexuality. Sexuality has also given rise to a terrible dark side of humanity, which of course is sexual exploitation, abuse and so forth. Sexual desire is multi-textured and socially choreographed. Many researchers highlight how sexual stimuli are used in all kinds of ways: for example, in advertising and fashion. So again, we see the operation of these underlying competitive sexual strategies guiding motives and phenotypes.

Resource holding potential (RHP) aggressive ways to the top: Humans have two major ways of ranking themselves and working out where they stand (or their social place) in a relationship. We can label these *aggression* and *attractiveness*. These judgements may be made very rapidly and have powerful effects on our emotional lives.[93] The most primitive form of ranking is derived from *threat-aggression, intimation* and *non-affiliation*. If anyone threatens your control or pursuit of resources, territory or status, you may respond to this *threat* by threatening them in various ways. Aggressive men tend to be very rank sensitive, quick to see put downs, even in facial glances, and defend their status with violence or the threat of it. This way of gaining (and defending) rank, by using the strategies of aggression, involves displays of one's fighting ability. In technical terms, this is called *resource holding potential or power* (RHP).[94] It is the most common way animals make it to the top. To signal favourable RHP is to signal the ability to fight and win. In many situations, animals work out their relative RHP in contests of ritual agonistic behaviour (e.g., the rutting of the deer, the charge displays of the gorilla etc.), and these are made as much from bluff and threats as from actual fighting. In humans, a country putting its

---

[93] Clark, C. (1990)

[94] The term was first introduced by Parker, G.A. (1974, 1984). A good review of how RHP works is given in Caryl, P.G. (1988). It involves the ability to signal to others that one is stronger than they are and that one can inflict a defeat on them. See also Price, J.S. and Sloman, L. (1987) for an exploration of RHP in depression. For how this relates to social comparison see Gilbert, P., Price, J.S. and Allan, S. (1995).

weapons on display and marching armies through the streets is an RHP display. It can also highlight a leader signalling to its people 'I can protect you; aren't we powerful?' Crude, primitive and horrendously expensive, but often effective.

Human ranks often involve elements of RHP. Indeed, a different system of classification of child relational styles to that of attachment, which is based on the rank archetype, has been derived from the study of *peer group relationships* by Montagner and his colleagues.[95] They distinguished children's social relationship styles in terms of *affiliative, aggressive* and *fearful* (and their various combinations). Their classification includes children who show the following characteristics: 1) leader (affiliative); 2) dominant aggressive; 3) fluctuating; 4) dominated fearful; 5) dominated aggressive; 6) dominated leader; and 7) isolated. I suspect that a similar classification could be used to explore various forms of social relationships, from families to work organisations.

At the present time, the work on peer group classification and attachment has not been integrated, but preliminary data by Troy and Sroufe[96] suggests that avoidant types are more likely to be either aggressive (victimizer) or subordinate (victim), the anxious attached child more easily becomes subordinate (fearful-victim), while the secure child more generally becomes affiliative.

In humans, defence of rank/status is often more subtle than with crude physical aggression or aggressive displays, and takes the form of shaming, where the focus is on putting down the other by verbal jibes and ridicule – destroying the self-presentation of the other and showing them up to be not as good as they are trying to portray themselves. These are attacks on the other person's attractiveness. Shaming can also be used as a form of social control (see Chapter 6).

Social attention holding power: using attractiveness to move up: The second form of gaining rank involves status and respect via *the demonstration of attractiveness to others, such that others willingly choose to bestow rank upon*

---

[95] Montagner, H., Restoin, A., Rodriguez, D., Ullman, V., Viala, M., Laurent, D. and Godard, D. (1988)
[96] Troy, M. and Sroufe, L.A. (1987)

us.[97] Significant parts of our lives are spent trying to elicit signals of value, status and recognition from others. Body image, dress sense, passing exams, showing our sporting ability, demonstrating our wit or intelligence are all examples where we recognise that our rank, status and sense of worth depends on being approved of, recognised and chosen by another individual or group – it is aimed at *impressing others* so that they will invest in us. I have referred to this as social attention holding power (SAHP), and first introduced[98] the idea of SAHP to contrast it with RHP (resource holding power), which is based more on fighting ability. SAHP relates to things like popularity, charisma and the ability to manipulate people's attentions, not via threat, but via attractiveness. The signal is less to do with 'do as I say because I am more powerful than you and a potential threat' (as in RHP) but 'select me and I will be useful to you'. Thus, SAHP often involves displays of altruism, talent and/or the ability to protect. When we chose our mates, or presidents, or select people for jobs, mostly we are operating on SAHP signals. SAHP therefore depends on social signals and judgements of others; it is not something one can easily impose. My colleague Dr Nicholas Allen at the University of Melbourne suggested that SAHP operates like the stock market. Qualities are given SAHP (and hence status or prestige) depending on what others are judging to be valuable. An obvious example of this would be a film star.

The qualities to which a group gives high SAHP (e.g., intelligence, forms of beauty, being a rock musician or poet, toughness or bravery) tends to lead to mimicry. Individual members of the group will try to be like those who have high SAHP. If, for example, body thinness (especially in females) is given high SAHP, then others will start to copy it – even to the point of it being maladaptive (as in anorexia). *The SAHP system shows clearly that our craziness can be*

---

[97] This distinction between rank via aggressiveness and rank via attractiveness/prestige has been made for some years by Barkow, J.H. (1980 and 1989) and Kemper, T.D. (1990). The role of prestige on status has been well recognised throughout history.

[98] Gilbert, P. (1989) is where I first introduced this idea and it came from many discussions with John Price and Michael Chance. Barkow, J.H. (1989) talks of prestige and so does Kemper, T.D. (1990). In 1989 I used the idea that attention directing and eliciting resources from others in the form of praise, admiration and approval were the central ways human try to gain status.

created as much between individuals as within individuals. Clearly, there is far less risk of violence involved – unless you stir up aggressive envy, of course.

Being seen as altruistic and helpful can also win one SAHP, and research suggests that females make mate choices on SAHP-type traits rather than RHP ones.[99] Unlike the aggressive tactics of gaining and maintaining rank and status (via intimidating and forcing the other(s) into involuntary subordinate compliance) ranking via attractiveness attempts to produce a voluntary giving to, and bestowing of, status by others. In that sense, there must be concern with conformity to some degree, because if one does not conform to the socially proscribed judgements (e.g., what constitutes attractive qualities), then status is unlikely to be bestowed. Many a composer has suffered this fate. Having produced a masterpiece (by the standards of subsequent generations), their innovations were too new to gain credit at their first performances. Thus, ranking via attractiveness is often a tricky business of trying to be better than and different (original even) from others, but also conforming.[100] Competitors may look at such efforts with envy or attempt shaming: claiming, for example, that the performances are too outside the accepted norms or are faked. Signals of put down, indicating that we are not attractive or not chosen (not chosen as the lover, not getting the promotion or the favours/investments we hoped for) can activate many of our defences (outlined in Chapter 2), and are common to both types of rank.

To bring these ideas together, the two ways of gaining and maintaining our rank are outlined in Table 3.1.

---

[99] Jensen-Campbell, L.A., Graziano, W.G. and West, S.G. (1995)
[100] Wolfe, R.N., Lennox, R.D. and Cutler, B.L. (1986)

Table 3.1 Types and Tactics of Ranking Behaviour

RANKING

SELF   OTHER

Inferior-Superior
Controlled-Controller

RANKING SYSTEMS
(TACTICS)

AGGRESSION	ATTRACTIVENESS
Cohesion	Talent
Threat	Role Competence
Authoritarian	Democratic-authoritative
To be obeyed	To be valued
To be reckoned with	To be chosen

IF SELF IS CONSTRUED AS LOSING/INFERIOR
(Possible Defensive Responses)

Envy

Shame

Revenge

Defeated

Depression

Social Anxiety

Hostile Resentment

Controlled by others

Involuntary subordinate

Self-criticism (self attack)

In the SAHP system, as with care-eliciting, what is at stake here is *potential investments from others* (mutual support of others). Seeking status via attractiveness is to seek the investments of others. Thus, the drive for self-expression and positive self-presentation can be derived from our needs to gain rank, to be valued, accepted and seen in a positive light. But these behaviours are affected by our need to conform to certain standards – that is, we try to excel in the domains the group has decided are worth excelling at and rewarding. These standards may relate to gender behaviours, appearances, intellect etc. As Table 3.2 above shows, to receive put downs from others (things which reduce our SAHP) can activate the defence system, and have many different effects. We can become anxious, feel resentful, seek revenge, criticise ourselves and so forth. To be shamed – to lose SAHP – is to carry the label that we are not worth investing in – not esteemed, have negative rather than positive SAHP. So powerful is shame that Chapter 6 is devoted to it.

Many therapists believe that our need to impress others (or, at least, excessive needs to) relates to our hero-ideals and rather grandiose selves. They suggest that many of the ideals of the young child are grandiose but that with positive mirroring and love, these gradually mature into realistic ideals, aspirations and care for others. The self is neither carried away (inflated) by success nor devastated by failure and defeats. However, without good enough mirroring and an internalisation of a sense of one's own worth, the grandiose, heroic and up-rank motivated self can get out of hand. Either the person gives up on competing in the world and lives as a shamed, subordinate self, preoccupied with self-doubt and social fear, or the person becomes highly competitive, easily frustrated and angry and filled with fantasises of revenge and/or being really great. Evolutionary theorists suggest that aggressive forms of ranking are more likely when the opportunities for SAHP (status) are few and social restraints absent. This can be the common situation for males without jobs who live in inner cities.

Deception: As we shall see in the chapter on leadership, the SAHP system carries one big disadvantage – it is highly open to deception. RHP is less open to deception for at the end of the day, one might be called to account. The SAHP system, however, can involve multiple signals (e.g., to be able to do a job, to be able to protect, to be altruistic, to be faithful to a cause, to have talent, to be sexy, etc.) – indeed, anything that can be deemed attractive. All these are open to deceptive displays (not necessarily consciously). People may think they are more competent than they are.[101] Sexual relationships can fall by the wayside because, after a certain time, one or both partners discover that the promises of the courting period turned out to be deceptions. Many leaders in democratic societies probably could not stay in office without some ability to deceive. However, as we shall note in Chapters 7 and 8, this is rather complex and leaders can be kept in power even when they are known to be frauds.

SAHP Social Roles and social mentalities

As a reminder: a social mentality is a motivational system to create a certain kind of role relationship and pursue a biosocial goal. In order to do that, individuals need to be competent at sending and decoding social signals that allow them to form a kind of dance of reciprocal interactions. This makes them very different to motives, for example, to eat or avoid falling off a cliff. The idea of a social mentality, first introduced in *Human Nature and Suffering*, is to depict the nature in which our minds mature, enabling us to acquire the competencies for complex patterns of interaction. In addition, social mentalities create a social field, in that it is the interaction between minds that give rise to patterns within minds: that is, a field of mutually interacting changing and influencing minds. Thus, social mentalities can only be understood as a relational concept.

With these thoughts in mind, and taking all five types of social behaviour together, leaving aside the issue of fulfilments of relating obtained via fantasy,

---

[101] There is now quite a sizable literature that suggests in Western society people tend to overestimate their abilities and see themselves as more competent than others see them (see Taylor, S.E. and Brown, J.D. 1988). This may be adaptive given how the SAHP system works. The more one is slightly, personally deceptive with oneself, the more confidence one can display – and confidence, up to a point that it does not become arrogance, gains SAHP (see Gilbert, P. 1992). Displaying a lack confidence can be a thumbs down for SAHP, unless it is seen as modesty. Indeed the balance between displays of modesty and arrogance can be difficult at times.

archetypes can usually only manifest in social interactions and social roles. Thus, *we can focus on evolutionarily meaningful, core (archetypal) self-other relationships in terms of how the self and other(s) are construed and engaged.* These are basic social mentalities, and are listed in Table 3.2 below:

Table 3.2 A Brief Guide to Social Mentalities

	Self as	Other as	Fears
Caring eliciting/ seeking	Needing input from other(s): care, protection safeness, reassurance, stimulation, guidance	Source of: care nurturance protection, safeness reassurance stimulus and guidance	Unavailable withdrawn withholding exploitation threatening harmful
Care-giving	Provider of: care, protection safeness, reassurance, stimulation, guidance	Recipient of: care, protection safeness, reassurance, stimulation, guidance	Overwhelmed, unable to provide, threat focused guilt
Corporation	Of value to others, sharing, appreciating contributing, helping	Valuing one's contribution, sharing, reciprocating appreciating	Cheating, non-appreciating or non-reciprocating, rejecting/shame
Competitive	Inferior-superior, more-less powerful harmful/benevolent	Inferior superior, more-less powerful harmful/benevolent	Involuntary subordination, shame, marginalisation, abused
Sexual	Attractive/desirable	Attractive desirable	Unattractive rejected

Adapted from Gilbert, P. (1992). *The Evolution of Powerlessness*. London Psychology Press

The inner world is thus made up of various models and ideals concerning self-other relationships (e.g., wanting to be cared for, loved, be accepted by a group, nurture others, obtain status, find a sexual partner who will not defect, etc.), and thus indicating needs, and potential threats, frustrations and disappointments. But as I have stressed, this is a highly relational psychology which comes to life in and through relationships.

All these social roles are potential SAHP enhancers or losers. For example, suppose we try to elicit help, support and/or care from another and find that the other(s) does not wish to give it. This sends a signal that our social standing in their eyes is not high enough for them to want to invest time and effort in us. By refusing help, we judge that they are thinking that the cost of helping us outweighs the benefits.

Caring for one's children is to raise their SAHP and to help them internalise confidence in (high) SAHP strategies. That is, they will come to feel confident in forming supportive relationships and have an internal sense of their own goodness and (SAHP) worth. For the parent, the child's confidence and ability to form good supportive relationships will make them more successful in relationships where non-aggressive forms of status are prevalent. Caring can also raise one's own SAHP through the process of gratitude. By helping others, we may think that we are creating a good impression on others. Hence, some aspects of caring are (perhaps unconsciously) aimed at increasing our SAHP though altruism, by creating relationships such that others will see us as helpful, agreeable and desirable as partners and colleagues. As we saw earlier in this chapter, women can make mate choices on the basis of male signals of status and altruism. Men can raise their SAHP by attracting attractive women.

In the cooperative situation, SAHP goes up when we are seen to belong to a particular group. The group's SAHP reflects on our own. To be a member of a high SAHP or prestigious group is to have high personal SAHP. Indeed, many may try to raise their individual SAHP via group membership. *Within* the group, SAHP goes up by the demonstrating abilities to advance group goals and this can include hostility to outsiders. In sports (e.g., cricket) one's SAHP goes up by being good at defeating opponents (e.g., as a fast bowler). In the street gang, one's SAHP is raised if the group is aggressive to outsiders and one is known to be fearless. In an academic environment one's SAHP goes up by being seen as bright and well published, and bringing prestige to one's department or university. Thus, conformity to group values and demonstrated ability to support and advance those values and goals brings SAHP. The group decides it is in their interests (the costs outweigh the benefits) to invest time and energy in those individuals who can perform well in terms of the group's goals. Thus, those who are (judged to be) poor performers will loss SAHP and may even be rejected. SAHP is also given for helping others (altruism), for mutually helpful internal alliances can advance the goals of the group – from which all may gain.

In competitive situations, individuals compete for various positions within the group by demonstrating their usefulness to others. It is a 'select me signal' and it shows up in various forms of leadership-type behaviours and charisma. In leadership, there is often a subtle mixture of affiliation and aggression. If subordinates become too challenging, then they can be reminded of their subordinate position with a little threat in the form of shame or put-downs.

In regard to sexuality, SAHP is pretty straightforward. It is linked to inter- and intra-sexual selection and competition, and it relates to the degree to which we are able to attract partners. It also links to the degree to which we feel that we are 'a turn on' for them, that we are 'desired', that we can stimulate their pituitary to launch a cascade of arousing hormones! People may spend many hours at the gym trying to hone their bodies not just for fitness, or as a signal to members of the same gender, but as a sexual attractor. Once again, culture plays a huge impact here, because going to the gym to get a *six pack* wasn't really that much of an issue in Europe until relatively recently (mine is a one pack now!). For women, however, they have been under social pressure to appear attractive for a long time and sometimes the means of doing so have not been beneficial to them, such as wearing stiletto heels or corsets and all kinds of plastic surgery.

The Big Two: Caring-Altruism versus Contest Competition?

Psychologists and scientists tend to classify things and put them into categories when in reality they are better viewed as dimensions. Nonetheless, it is true that classifying things can help us understand them better and this is also the case for basic human motivation. Over the last 40 years, therefore, there have been numerous attempts to try to identify basic patterns of human motivation. Different workers have come up with different systems: for example, the motives for meaning, or mastery, or security are very important for humans once we have achieved some degree of stability, e.g. in food-seeking and relating. However, I am going to be selective here and focus on two particular social motives and social mentalities that tend to crop up time and again as particularly important players in the human mind. In fact, many have argued that caring and individualistic ranking (the 'big two') represent the basic sources of differences between people.

Back in the 1940s, Maslow[102] distinguished democratic from authoritarian persons. The authoritarian person is very much motivated through the rank system and is concerned with control, status and obedience to authority. The democrat is concerned with social freedom, with an interest in the welfare of others. More recently, McClelland[103] distinguished the affiliative from the power orientated (amongst others). The affiliative person is concerned with closeness, cooperation and caring, while the power-orientated person is concerned with rank, status, prestige and gaining control over others. The feminist anthropologist Eisler[104] distinguishes dominator (masculine) from partnership (feminine) styles. Again, the dominator style is about rank, control and status, whereas partnership is about cooperation, caring and freedom. The ethologist Michael Chance[105] has argued that there are two mental modes which are represented in in-group behaviour and in us. The hedonic mode operates when we feel safe, our attention is open and there is a general enjoyment in the company of others that is free from threats to one's status. The agonic mode,

---

[102] Maslow, A.H. (1943)
[103] McClelland, D.C. (1987)
[104] Eisler, R. (1990)
[105] Chance, M.R.A. (1980, 1984, 1988)

however, operates when we are preoccupied with social threats, are not relaxed and are concerned to either assert our power over others, or engage in various defensive behaviours to reduce, head-off or avoid social threats. In the hedonic mode, our attention is open and orientated towards positive emotion, whereas in the agonic mode it is threat-focused and safety-seeking. The interpersonal theorists[106] have argued that dominance-submission is a central dimension of behaviour, and this can be associated with either love or hating forms of behaviour giving rise to loving/friendly dominance, controlling/aggressive dominance, friendly submission, and aggressive/resentful submission. This interpersonal system allows us to think about how caring-altruistic and competitive (contest) goals and strategies interact and are blended together.

These are just a few approaches that seem to distinguish caring-altruism from competitive rank contest-competition. In my view, most of these are describing the predominance of different biosocial goals and their strategies.[107] For example, those with altruistic biosocial goals have the desire to create a network of supporting and enjoyable *mutually investing* relationships and to minimise conflicts and fights (SAHP via altruism). They may or may not be sexually promiscuous (a bit like bonobos) but if they are, other people will be attracted to them as friendly/agreeable personalities, and their sexuality is playful rather than aggressive or dominating (of course this may not be the case for partners, who might think them immoral and untrustworthy). But sexual adventurism does not of itself point to a non-altruist. They can, of course, be deceptive (men can flirt from relationship to relationship and avoid long term commitments) but on the whole, they are neither highly fearful nor aggressive. In conflict situations, they try to reconcile quickly and have an interest in the welfare of

---

[106] Leary, T. (1957) was one of the first to systematise these ideas. Since then there have been changes to the basic model e.g., Kiesler, D.J. (1983); Horowtiz, L.M. and Vitkus, J. (1986) and also reformulations and critiques. Birtchnell, J. (1993) has developed a new approach which replaces the dominant-subordinate dimension with upperness-lowerness and the horizontal dimension with closeness distance.
[107] Gilbert, P. (1989)

others – at least up to a point. Michael Chance would call this a hedonic personality (personal communication).

Those with the rank (competitive contest) goals more developed, and altruistic strategies and goals very much in the background, focus on gaining rank and prestige as their central concern. They are preoccupied with their relative rank (and on improving it). They are not interested particularly in developing mutually investing and enjoyable relationships. Any altruism that is used is not (on the whole) to create a *pleasurable* and relaxed social climate (nor are they much concerned with the welfare of others, though they may pretend to be so). Their main concerns are to advance their path to the top and/or maintain control over others by threats. It is easy to see this as the more primitive or earlier evolved strategy.

Now, of course, these are no more than rules of thumb and all of us can operate in various domains and with various combinations of biosocial goals and strategies. We can all be rank-focused, socially aggressive, cooperative and so forth. It is *the patterns* of these archetypal potentials that make for individual differences – no two people will be exactly the same. However, as we shall see in the next chapter, it probably does make a difference if someone has an interest in developing mutually investing supportive relationships or not, whether they can take an interest in others and their environments, and take pleasure from investing and nurturing others (and their environments). Moreover, cultural and social contextual factors can make each strategy more or less likely to emerge in people. If the environment is mutually supportive and trustworthy, then altruistic strategies are more likely to come to the fore because this is an adaptive way to behave. If on the other hand the social climate is one of 'dog eat dog', and we constantly create a 'culture of rivals', or a changing chaotic storm of winners and losers, haves and have-nots, this may not gel well with the human brain. It is conducive to stress craziness. So, a key issue will be whether the social context, in which we are born and grow, can make a difference to whether our altruistic tendencies can come to the fore, or whether we become more selfish, self-centred, and narcissistic, and grabbing whatever we can. With a better understanding of our minds, we can to start to think about how to create social contexts conducive to human wellbeing, rather than to allow historically created contexts to sculpture toxic environments and 'infect' our minds. Tricky. It's understandable why some people would love to change our genes, make us less aggressive, less tribal, less narcissistically self-focused and more prosocial, but in reality, before we do that we need to change our environments.

Conclusion

There is increasing recognition that the potential for certain patterns of relating exist by virtue of our evolved history. But the cultures that shape them have taken the forms they have through history, and are equally subject to a whole range of arbitrary processes. Our general phenotypic patterns can be detected and described in various cultures and times, but as Jung said, at the archetypal level, they are only potentials and never actual forms. In this chapter, we have explored five basic forms of relating although many others are possible.

Many of the current debates between evolutionists and social constructionists are not whether or not socialisation makes a difference, for clearly it does, but the *degree to which it can* make a difference. All cultures operate constraints, be this of sexual behaviour or laws on killing and murder. All cultures have ways of giving or withholding prestige. In all cultures, parents prefer to care for their own offspring, rather than any child. Young and healthy folk are seen as more attractive and desirable than the old and unhealthy. And in all cultures, stories of betrayal, alliances, love, envy, disgrace and jealousy make monotonous appearances on the stage of human history. Cultures shape us for sure, but there are only so many themes to work with. This makes socialisation and cultural values more, not less, important, for as I shall continue to argue throughout this book, there are some cultural contexts that bring out the worst in us – and drive many of us rather crazy.

4: THE BIO-SOCIAL MIND

Contemporary culture theory is, for the most part, a form of sensory deprivation. Those who proclaim culture to be a "system of symbols and meanings" make an uncritical assumption that culture, symbols, and meanings neither touch nor are deeply touched by organic life. Indeed the ideologues of culture theory tend to regard any concern with the relations between culture and organic nature or evolution as a threat to the hegemony of the cultural system over meaning.[108]

Man's nervous system does not merely enable him to acquire culture, it positively demands that he do if it is going to function at all. Rather than culture acting only to supplement, develop and extend organically based capacities logically and genetically prior to it, it would seem to be ingredient to those capacities themselves. A cultureless human being would probably turn out to be not only an intrinsically talented though unfulfilled ape, but a wholly mindless and consequently unworkable monstrosity.[109]

In 1925 London Zoo set up a small baboon enclosure and introduced 100 hamadryas baboons. Most of these animals were strangers to each other, taken from different troops. At first there were only six females, but others were introduced later. By 1931, 64% of the males and 92% of the females were dead. Only one infant survived. The cause of these deaths were savage fights resulting in severe wounding. Broken bones, including skull fractures, became common. Moreover, the sexual behaviour was often not far short of rape, and even when females were killed, the males dragged their bodies around trying to copulate with the dead female. Nothing like this is ever encountered in their natural

---

[108] Halton, E. (1992) p.36

[109] Taken from Geertz, C. (1993) As Quoted by Halton, E. (1992) p.36. Halton adds, 'By implication, one can also say that a natureless human being could not be considered "civilized" but a similarly unworkable monstrosity' (p.36).

habitat – baboons would never have survived as a species if it were.[110] The idea that the archetypes which facilitate ranked social structures, or supportive alliances, will work effectively regardless of the social context is simply not true. The social confinement in a non-cohesive group, which was so far outside of their environment of evolutionary adaptiveness (EEA)[111], brought about these baboons' tragic craziness.

In many non-human primates, social cohesion depends on complex social structures that arise through the history and stability of the group. Because of these established patterns, most animals will know each other; infants are born into established hierarchies and family networks and gradually find their place as they mature (or go off to form bachelor groups). Foraging ranges are large enough to enable some degree of avoidance and dispersion (i.e., there is not overcrowding), and territories/ranges are often passed on from generation to generation. Stability and consistency is the basis of the primate EEA, in which so much of theirs and our evolution took place. When these social parameters are not in place all hell can break loose, as London Zoo found to its cost.

Social Archetypes Need Social Relationships

Whether it is ants, bees, rats, tigers or primates, infants are born into pre-stabilised patterns of social relationships, such as styles of parenting and group activity (i.e., their EEA). Hence, each individual member of a species will have evolved (and comes equipped with) the behavioural competencies to make sense of the species-typical social ways of its own kind. Thus, it is impossible to separate out the biological evolution of many of our psychological abilities from the stable social contexts in which they evolved. Care-eliciting behaviour, for example, and the long periods of dependency of the child on parent(s) could only evolve because over many millions of years these patterns of caring were consistent. This means that we have to appreciate just how important the social

---

[110] This event is discussed both by Sagan, C. and Druyan, A. (1992), and by Stevens, A. (1982).

[111] For a discussion of EEA, see Barkow, J.H., Cosmides L. and Tooby, J. (1992, eds.).

context is for our maturation and competent enactment of our human psychologies.

The EEA for humans is for parents and extended kin to give high levels of investment to infants; peers to give the opportunities for play and practising social skills, and act as 'familiar others' with whom alliances can be built; and elders to pass on the traditions of (until recently) hunter-gathering life. Although humans have an innate capacity to learn language and symbolic representations, they cannot develop these in any coherent way without others who speak to them and communicate. These 'socialisations' allow the child to develop the knowledge necessary to run their archetypal programmes competently. The archetypal forms we explored in the last chapter will be shaped by the social knowledge acquired during maturation. It is not their exact form that is inherited, only the potential. This means that different social contexts will shape and train us in different ways.

Shaping the Person

Brain Education

Although genes (and the archetypal possibilities they contain) are necessary for maturation and the timing of maturational changes (e.g., entry into sexual maturity, developing the ability for symbolic and abstract thought, and so on), the archetypal brain is not a closed system simply following a pre-set pattern irrespective of what is happening in the outside world. *The quality and forms of our relationships actually help to shape the various types of connections that nerve cells make in the brain.* In fact, we now know that the brain is very 'plastic' in this regard. In a major review, Allan Schore[112] has charted the way

---

[112] Schore, A.N. (1994) See also Bailey, K. (1987). Both make clear that in the absence of adequate frontal lobe development, behaviour is controlled by our more primitive brain areas. Social behaviour, therefore, can be seen in terms of a dimension of

the brain matures during infancy and early childhood, and has shown just how much various areas of the brain are dependent on social input. For example, the frontal lobes of the brain (which have major regulating effects on lower and reptilian brain areas) are very important for the development of affiliative and prosocial behaviour, and abilities like empathy. The availability of care and the quality of emotional attunement of the infant with the caregiver(s) sets the basic system for trust, a sense of security and shapes our social emotions. Empathic potential is partly innate (reptiles don't have it, but humans do), but it also develops and matures considerably after birth – at least in contexts where empathy is valued and will be useful (see Chapter 12). Many prosocial archetypal roles depend on the early experiences of a loving, caring environment.[113]

Put another way, the goals and strategies for altruism, including the motivation and capacity to enact competent affiliative behaviours, depend on the experiences of social contexts and relationships which coordinate brain development, especially in the frontal cortex. It must also give opportunities to practise these behaviours and be rewarded for doing so. The maturation of altruistic strategies is thus neither solely hardware (biology) nor software (learning), but each interpenetrate the other. Moreover, the maturation of a self that is able to love and be loved acts as a buffer to the more segregated functioning of the primitive brain with its defensive and aggressive passions and emotions.

---

progression (towards altruism, caring, love, compassion) and regression (towards violence, anxiety, impulsiveness, rage and greedy self-promotion).

[113] This is important because if you were to find (for example) that very aggressive people have poor frontal lobe functions, it is not clear that this is genetic. It could be the result poor early environments that affected their maturation. Indeed, the more we recognise the role played by relationships in early life in *actually shaping the way our brains work* the more urgent it becomes to ensure that people are given every opportunity to provide loving environments for their children. Nevertheless, it is also not the case that every abused child will turn into an unfeeling psychopathic type – though the chances are greatly increased. It is still possible that the innate competencies for empathy are strong enough, or have just enough education to mature, allowing even the most abused person to become a relaxed and loving adult, although the chances (without corrective emotional experiences) are sadly reduced.

The brain and the outside world are linked right from birth. There are various types of experience that shape the brain and link what happens outside of us with what happens inside our heads and bodies. A crucial one comes from the social activation of *our emotions* and the direct, emotion-generating experiences (such as joy, love, fear and anger) that we encounter as we grow up. The capacity to have these emotions arises from our genetic endowment; they are part of our archetypal minds, but repeated stimulation of these emotions influences what happens in the brain, how the brain matures and comes to lay down complex rules and guidance for emotional processing. If a parent interacts with a child such that s/he continually activates anxiety or frustration in the child, then this will affect the ease of activation of these emotions later. To give one example: if we are stressed, hormones such as cortisol, and chemicals in the brain, are released. Over time these hormones and brain chemicals will change the way transmission takes place in the brain; they affect what are called receptors, and the types of connection one nerve cell (neurone) makes with another.[114]

The Education of Emotions

Implicit in a lot of what has been said in this and earlier chapters is the idea that social roles are often enacted with *feelings*. We need to spend a little time exploring feelings, because it is feelings and emotions that get us acting in such crazy ways: whether this be the murderous passions of the jealous lover, the savage warring and loyalties of the territorial group, or the pride and fear of shame of the warrior male. Indeed, emotions allow us to act relatively automatically in many social roles: we love our children, are sexually aroused by a potential lover, are enraged by unjustified put-downs, feel contempt for those we devalue, feel guilt when we have failed to help others and grief when

---

[114] Now the exact details need not concern us here (see Schore, A.N. 1994, for a superb overview). One can very crudely think of what happens to a muscle. If you exercise it over and over it gets bigger; that is, the biology is changed by how it is used. Similarly for emotions, the biology of the emotions are changed by how they are used and activated. The brain is altered by emotional experiences, sometimes permanently. Of course, emotions are not muscles.

we lose loved ones. Thus, feelings and emotions are (mostly) adaptive and important for the social roles we function in. However, although there is an evolved tendency for different feelings to be aroused in certain social contexts, one of the central characteristics of humans is the education of our social-emotional selves. From these we shape our identities.

Upon our evolved basic emotion-frameworks, the social world has a great impact. There are a variety of ways emotions 'mature', or become refined and blend together during development. First, emotions can be paired, or associated with certain outcomes. For example, the parent says, "don't touch the kettle", and delivers a smack if the child does. Subsequently, what was an object of interest to the child is now one of fear because exploring kettles can result in a smack. The child will have an emotional reaction to the kettle via learning. Another form of association is when one emotion (social role or behaviour) is paired with another. For example, the child shows anger and father says, "if you do that again I'll hit you, or I won't love you". If repeated over time the child may learn that anger (and expressing their displeasure) is bad and brings frightening consequences. So, the internal experience of anger may trigger fear or guilt. Anger may be suppressed and not worked through or matured into the capacity for healthy assertion and competitiveness. Sometimes this is technically referred to as classical conditioning.

Emotions and feelings about things can also be changed by simple exposure to them. Exposure to what a person finds threatening can help reduce the fear and, indeed, exposure is a most powerful therapeutic technique. Equally, this desensitisation from repeated exposure can have negative effects. For example, constant exposure to violence can reduce our sensitivity to it. But this is not always the case. Exposure to intense fear over which we may have little control can lead to being highly traumatised and a worsening of it through what is called incubation.

A third way that emotions are 'educated' is by what we call social referencing. The young child goes to the fireworks and is at first frightened by the lights and sounds, but Mum picks her up and says, "Oh look, aren't they pretty?" In effect mother is instructing the child what to feel about the fireworks. Social referencing is when we learn to feel what others appear to be feeling – to mimic their feelings. Fighting men often have to be taught to kill and t=o 'hate' the enemy – it does not come nearly as naturally as some might think. Social referencing allows us to develop conformity of feelings and values at a deep level.

Beliefs and Archetypes

Some cognitive therapists suggest that it is our beliefs and interpretations that lead us to feel strong emotions. This may well be true but a belief itself gives no indication of why certain types of belief tend to activate certain types of feeling. Hence, as some have suggested, beliefs can powerfully arouse our negative emotions, like fear and anger, when they tap evolved, defensive programmes (e.g., such as fight/flight).[115] Therefore, it is important to recognise that beliefs themselves can be partly archetypal – and certainly our fantasises often are (e.g., of sex, revenge, love, belonging, reunion, adoration). Indeed, the most distressing beliefs, those which really connect to our emotions, are often related to archetypal themes: being rejected; death of loved others; finding no one to love or share one's life with; threats of death and injury to self; being shamed and subordinated; being a loser or defeated; loss of allies; defection by sexual partners, and so forth. So, beliefs can take archetypal forms. Moreover, these beliefs, which are so common in psychological states of distress, do not always respond to logical reasoning alone.

When beliefs are highly archetypal and enthused with passion, they can take control of us for good and for bad. We act out their scripts because of the power and the emotion. We can be passionate about social justice and fairness, but we can also be passionate about tribalism and justification for violence. Hence, emotionally archetypal charged beliefs can be extremely dangerous, and often not much influenced by logical arguments. If we connect beliefs and emotions together with the idea of the archetype, we have a more powerful understanding

---

[115] Beck, A.T., Emery, G. and Greenberg, L. (1985); Gilbert, P. (1993)

of the passion that so often infects our beliefs, their biological and social origins, and what can make them so resistant to change.

Beliefs are of course transmitted socially, and we can acquire them even if at times they are complete nonsense and harmful. For example, people have believed in some gods demanding sacrifice. Once infected with this belief, people can be tormented with the fear that they might be upsetting the gods. Today we live in a world not just transmitting beliefs between small closed groups, but via a media whose intentions are not always moral or simply to inform. They can seek to manipulate us for a particular cause, be it political or otherwise. We need to be particularly attuned to the acquisition of beliefs through our media, because they intuitively understand that if they can tap archetypal fears they can manipulate their audience, leading us to distorted forms of truth, and activating the less savoury aspects of our minds. When our archetypal minds are fused with passion it may be more difficult to think rationally or change.

Archetypes and Values

Learning by association and social referencing have an enormous impact on our *values*. We learn to place value on things by giving them emotional textures, especially textures of good-bad, desirable-undesirable, shame-pride. It is our emotions that make things matter to us.[116] Values are often communicated by direct experiences, copying others, and via instructions which are emotionally toned: "You should work hard, be tough, brave, care for people, love God, join your tribal political party". Thus, we learn what is good and what is bad, what to aspire to and what to avoid; what archetypal aspects to value or devalue, turn towards or away from, in ourselves and others (e.g., sexuality, caring, toughness). Hence, a most important aspect of early life is the way it provides

[116] Tomkins, S.S. (1981)

the environments and contexts for the maturation and experiences of *emotions and values*.[117]

This education of values is partly to help conformity to the group and to ensure that the group, more or less, acts as a coherent whole following the same values, goals, social practices and traditions. Moreover, this education is preparing the child for the type of social world s/he will inhabit. In very competitive cultures, parents are likely to endorse competitive values and role-behaviours based on achievement, self-promotion and need for specialness.

Values and emotions are also used not only as aides to conformity/sameness, but to demarcate *differences* between self and other(s). One learns what it means to be a Christian, a Jew, a particular ethnicity, a communist, etc. by infusing these differences with feelings (and historical narratives). Obviously to facilitate identification we have to make clear that our group is in some way better than the other group. You can stop defections by highlighting your superiority, specialness or tradition, and excite a sense of belonging. The moment these differences are no longer *felt to matter*, they fade away. Thus, the fracture points of difference between self and others rely on feelings and emotions. It is these passions, to positively endorse differences and defend them, that can cause so much conflict and intergroup craziness. To lose the sense of difference, can, for some, be experienced as a loss of self-identity. In many ways, the social archetypes focus the emotions and give then a particular organisation. Armed with these thoughts on emotion, especially the fact that the social archetypes are fuelled by our emotions, we can now explore the 'education' of the social archetypes in more detail.

Turning On and Turning Off

Archetypal roles and their passions are linked to values. Values are usually reflections of a deeper connection to our archetypal world than just being

---

[117] Some researchers believe that it is emotions that give rise to consciousness and that purely rational systems cannot be conscious. Consciousness, they argue, is all about feelings and textures. There is some dispute about this, however.

cognitively based. The internal organisation of values has a huge effect on meanings and behaviours. For example, if one has strong beliefs that sexual relations outside marriage are wrong, then no matter how sexually aroused one is by another, there may be no effort to explore extra-marital opportunities. However, even though a person may turn away from such possibilities, they may still be troubled by *fantasies* of extra-marital sex. As the psychoanalysts recognise, our internal fantasies can reflect the activation of various archetypal possibilities and these fantasies can be pleasurable or fearful depending on our attitudes to them.[118] It is also possible that some of them are kept well out of consciousness.

This brings us to the role of the group culture in providing the contexts, proscriptions and prohibitions for feelings and actions. Many a religious person has found themselves in torment over their fantasies because they have internalised values and judgements of prohibition about them. The group culture offers up social roles which require a certain orientation to our archetypal lives. This means that the cultural proscriptions and prohibitions can introduce into us serious conflicts between what we feel we ought to do, what we feel and think in contrast with what our internal fantasies and feelings are inviting us to do. Indeed, this conflict between the different parts of ourselves (whether to be aggressive or forgiving, whether to have sex with the secretary or stay faithful to our partner) is not only the source of much neurosis, but is at the heart of psychoanalytic theory. These potential conflicts are socialised in different ways.

In the study of gender differences in emotional awareness and expression, there is increasing evidence that girls are related to differently than boys in the home, at school and by peers. This is partly archetypal, and partly to educate them for different roles in society. Any biological differences between them can be amplified. Boys may end up with more difficulties in understanding and coping with feelings of vulnerability (care-eliciting roles) or problems in being empathic to the expression of other's feelings (care-giving roles). Instead, they are, compared to girls, more familiar with anger and self-assertion (competitive roles). Girls, on the other hand, experience the reverse socialisation. What this

---

[118] See Halton, E. (1992) for a fascinating discussion of this in relation to dreaming.

means is that socialisation itself may track various archetypal themes – but the group is selecting which to activate (and develop) and which to inhibit in specific sub-groups.

These values change and as they do, so do a great deal of other things, including self-identity, motives, emotional orientations and behaviours. For example, Brody[119] refers to research that has explored the attitudes expressed in women's magazines from 1900-1970. She points out that

> In the early part of the century, the magazines advised traditional values, including the ideas of self-sacrifice, avoiding conflict, and minimising anger, whereas in more recent times, they promote self-development and open communication of negative and positive feelings including anger. Even in modern times, however, women are seen as responsible for maintaining intimate relationships, a role that has remained invariant all through the 20th century.[120]

During the 1980s, more emphasis had been put on developing the archetypal possibilities of greater exploration of female sexuality and enjoyment (sometimes with the help of artificial aids). Also, more women have gone out to work and now see themselves as trying to push back privileges enjoyed for so long by the male club alone. Some estimates suggest that one in five women are either postponing childbirth or avoiding it all together. These are real cultural differences. Clearly, the way women are treated in different societies varies. Although, there are still obvious differences between the sexes (as they follow different reproductive strategies), social context is crucial, for it is social values and economic conditions that lead societies to differ. There is considerable unfairness, for example, in the pay differential between men and women for the same job. Cultural differences are not small either. They account for the drop in Western birth rates, differences in child-rearing practices, differences in social laws, differences in how men compete in the market place for jobs, and even big

---

[119] Brody, L.R. (1993). In regard to the issue of gender differences in the socialisation of emotions and roles, see also Gilligan, C. (1982) and Radtke, H.L. and Stam, H.J. (1994, eds.). For a historical-cultural overview, see Eisler, R. (1990).

[120] Brody, L.R. (1993), p.103

differences in health and life expectancy. How we respond to different social behaviours also varies. For example, although adultery may be common, it arouses strong feelings, and societies deal with it in very different ways. There are many historical contexts where women have suffered very badly. Although it may be relatively easy to stimulate the desires for male dominance over women, understanding this and how culture can tap and inflame an unsavoury archetypal potential are exactly the reasons we need to learn to stop this from being acted out.

So, anthropological and sociological explorations of emotion and social roles show that there is wide variation in them from culture to culture.[121] However, this is more to do with the amplification or inhibition of archetypal potential, rather than the creation of new archetypal possibilities. A culture may devalue and shame competitive self-promotion and pride, or it may value them and reward them. But what it cannot do is delete the possibility of this competitive behaviour, any more that it can delete the archetype of sexuality from the gene pool. Hence, the moment an egalitarian culture changes and becomes more Westernised and competitive, so that the contexts and advantages of self-promotion change, then this archetypal form begins to take hold of individuals, and their fantasises begin to revolve around getting ahead and gaining material possessions. The culture and archetype are locked together and feed off each other. If there were no archetypal possibilities for such behaviour, it would never get off the ground. The danger is that some forms (such as competitiveness) seem to take hold more easily than others (e.g., open egalitarianism).

Archetypal Inflation

No archetypal form lives by itself. In other words, we need to think of a person in terms of the internal patterns of his/her archetypal lives – or as some say, a collection of possible selves.[122] Indeed, because our jerry-built brains have so

---

[121] Shott, E. (1979). See also Kemper, T.D. (1990, eds.) and Howell, S. & Willis, R. (1989)

[122] Rowan, J. (1990) gives a fascinating discussion of how many of our internal archetypal forms can appear to us *like separate selves or personalities*. In therapy, we

many different modules, motives and emotions, which evolved over many millions of years, we are riddled with internal conflicts and possibilities. What happens when some of these get over developed? Jung used the idea of inflation to refer to the situation where a person (the conscious ego) becomes over-identified with one or a few aspects of the archetypes.

For example, a person who is (emotionally) carried away with ideas of grandeur and feels themselves to be superior to others can be said to have an *inflated* view of themselves, or an inflated sense of dominance. It's called hubris. This inflation is like a balloon in the psyche that inhibits but can also deflate other archetypal forms. Jung and other analysts have spoken of 'psychic energy' that can be allocated to various archetypal forms. Thus, at the same time a person has an inflated sense of grandeur, they may also have a deflated (reduced motivation for) sense for empathy, caring and compassion, and thus a tendency to be exploitative and feel entitled. This inflated archetype can cause problems because of the underdevelopment of other archetypal potentials. This considerably reduces response flexibility, and can throw the person into chaos, if they can't use that basic archetype to deal with life issues.

Just about any archetypal possibility can get inflated and others deflated. For example, an inflated care-seeking archetype might lead to anxious attachment, an inflated sexual archetype might lead to infatuations and constant ruminations and fantasises about the 'object(s)' of sexual desire, an inflated concern with appearances (persona or looks) might lead to a constant need to look (or be) acceptable to others – in fashion. The point about archetypal inflations is that they are highly emotionally charged and the person may feel compelled to pursue certain goals and feels deeply frustrated (and thus activates the defence system) if they are thwarted in pursuing them. The central idea here is that if inflation is archetypal, it will be associated with some passion and urgency. In

---

can be trained to enter into dialogues with them. For example, we can identify the bully (the part of ourselves that is very critical when we do poorly and comes out at times of disappointment), the carer (the part of ourselves which wants to reach out and help others), the show-off (the part of ourselves that wants admiration), and so forth. In some ways, the evolutionary approach points logically to this way of therapeutic working. As yet, the research on its effectiveness is not far progressed.

these situations, two things can happen. First, the person falls victim to the emotions attached to the social archetype (e.g., feels compelled to seek attachment objects, seek sexual patterns, become dominant). Second, there can be an arrested development, for as Jung pointed out, it is the integration of the psyche and its various archetypal forms that allows us to not over- or under-identify with any one particular archetypal possibility.

Inflations can occur for many reasons. Some might relate to genes.[123] For example, a recent view of manic (bipolar) depression is that there is inflation of the rank archetype.[124] What happens is that the normal changes that take place with winning and losing competitive situations have become inflated and dysfunctional. Hence, the person swings from feeling a great success, dominant, a winner and full of their own importance with boundless energy into the defeated, low-rank state associated with feeling low in energy, inferior, incapable of facing the world and worthless. Most of us have the archetypal possibilities to feel elated by success and deflated and defeated by failure – these are adaptive. However, for those with bipolar depression, this normal energy regulation mechanism is poorly controlled, as if the thermostat has gone and so it is not working correctly.

Other inflations relate to maturation and the experiences of development (e.g., a punitive early family life might lead to inflation of aggressive dominance and low frustration tolerance). In many cases, inflations do show up in attitudes (e.g., "I have to be the best; I must be a winner; I must be loved"), but if it were only at the level of attitudes or values, then they would be relatively easy to change – often they are not. It is because our attitudes often *reflect* patterns of archetypal organisation that they are so emotionally powerful and compelling, and in a sense without caution we can get trapped in them.

---

[123] There is increasing evidence the genes play an important role in the susceptibility to major mental illness. This research has come from work on twins who were adopted and reared apart.

[124] See Price et al., (1994) and Gilbert, P. (1992a). This theory might suggest that in cultures which are highly competitive, rates of bipolar disorder will be higher (at least the milder forms) than in those non-competitive egalitarian cultures. However, I do not know of any research on this.

Inventiveness

We should also note that amplification on a theme is very common for humans. For example, humans did not evolve with musical instruments. There were no grand pianos or guitars in the cave homes of our earlier ancestors. Yet playing and listening to music is a salient emotional experience. Using this example, we can see that many of our competencies may be recruited to understand and be deeply emotionally moved by music (films get their most powerful effects by pairing music with actions – get the wrong music and the impact of a scene is reduced); moreover, we can play instruments that require a dexterity and memory probably never recognised in earlier times. How, we might ask, did humans evolve so that they could write and play a Rachmaninov piano concerto or jazz guitar like Pat Metheny? It seems that we can take certain abilities and talents, amplify them, and put them to new uses. We are highly inventive and creative, and this probably depends on our basic exploratory abilities, and also a biological property of the cortex to bring such talents and abilities together in the brain. It is as if the cortex allows for an enormous mix and match of internal abilities – which reduces rigidity and increases blending of talents and archetypal forms. This inventiveness also allows for archetypal inflation and amplification. Indeed, many cultural forms, such as religious structures or the complex self-presentational forms we now have, reflect our inventiveness and creativity – the ability to do something new with archetypal possibilities.

When used in the service of caring, this inventiveness gives rise to medicine. However, when recruited into competitiveness or territorial defence, it gives rise to the arms trade, and when used to subdue others, it gives rise to torture. Inventive we may be, but archetypal forms of relating are never far away. It is clear then that what makes us the species we are is not only our personal inventiveness, but that we can store and improve on others' inventiveness. Our sciences have been built up generation by generation. Yet despite this, when it comes to the social, we want much the same we always did: love, acceptance, sex, status and freedom from persecution.

Social Shaping

Social and Economic Sources of Inflation

We noted above that the way our internal world matures (which reflects our orientation to our archetypal possibilities) gives us our emotional sense of who we are. This maturation takes place in specific social contexts and rearing practices. The contexts in which people grow, and the values they aspire to, will set out the domains of aspirations, opportunities and conflicts they will encounter. A gardener from Scunthorpe is unlikely to become a Tibetan Buddhist because s/he was/is not exposed to those practices and philosophies. Becoming a terrorist requires that we live in a certain place, are encased in certain values and world views, are engaged in the frustrations, aspirations and conflicts of our group, have the means of conducting terrorist acts, and so forth.

So cultural values and practices define domains of opportunity, our aspirations and frustrations and also our identities. Here, economics plays a key role, and I shall explore this more fully in Chapter 11. Patterns of resource distribution (economic relations) create certain types of conflict. Indeed, there is now evidence that ecological factors (shortages and intense competition) can have major effects on intra-group and family relationships for both human and non-human primates.[125] How do the ecological factors affect our archetypal minds?

Ecological factors (the availability of resources) will have a 'pull' on either the archetypes of competitiveness or the more altruistic goals and strategies of cooperation and caring (egalitarian). Economic and political practices can do much to create ranked social structures of haves, have-nots and have-lots, open or close down opportunities, and alter vulnerabilities to physical and mental health at different socially ranked positions. This is because economic values and practices do two things. First, they influence the aspirations of people by shaping people's wants (for cars, TVs, fashion clothing, jeans, or freedom to

---

[125] MacDonald, K.B. (1998) has written a very scholarly and important book on how evolution and culture/socialisation combine to produce personality. See also Power, M. (1991).

travel, etc.). These wants are partly to satisfy biological needs (like having one's own place, food and shelter) and partly to satisfy social needs (to have what others have, to keep up with the Joneses, to feel that one is the same as others or maybe a little superior) - i.e., conformity and rank.

Second, economic practices operate a kind of invisible hand in advantaging some and disadvantaging others. Associated with the creation of wants, economic arenas also create the conditions of frustration of wants and aspiration. The manipulation of frustration is a fuel of capitalism. We are educated – not as the Buddhist would have us be, i.e. encouraged to detach ourselves for the material world – but to engage it more fully and want, want, want. And frustration is, of course, a powerful emotional experience.[126] It almost goes without saying that if people don't aspire to want, or value the things available, then they will not be frustrated by not having them. If we explore this a little further, we can see that capitalist economics are designed to produce winners and losers.[127] The dark side of capitalism is, therefore, a system forged from needing personal accumulations and an amplification of individualistic competitiveness rather than cooperation and sharing. It is, therefore, a kind of reptilian territoriality, of ownership, possessiveness and defence.

Thus, the economic culture of capitalism shapes the internal archetypal psychology of its members – leading them further and further into a psychology of striving, possessiveness and frustration of aspiration. Stirring up the archetype for competitive possessiveness can also stir up all the other emotions that go with it, not only susceptibility to frustration but also envy, shame, anger and the narcissistic needs to outdo others, 'me first and sod the rest'. Without the right education, one does not get the good job; without the good job, one does not get the car, the house, the holidays or the status (SAHP). Without any job, one is left in a limbo of aimlessness, unsatisfied wants, boredom and watching television portrayals of all those who have done better than you. Excessive

---

[126] Berkowitz, L. (1989). He makes the point that competitive situations increase susceptibility to frustration and aggression.
[127] Galbraith, J.K. (1987); Keegan, W. (1993). Both these writers give powerful insights into economic organisations and social attitudes.

competition may be good for business, but not for mental health (see Chapter 11).

In this competitive arena, it is always the weak/subordinate (those without the power to accumulate) who will lose out to the strong/dominant, for the weak have fewer options to protect themselves. The breakdown of family life, and the increases in social tension under the stresses of economic change as jobs disappear, communities fragment and houses are repossessed, constitute major sources of threat/harm. These threats/harms and reductions in personal control will not be equally distributed throughout society, but will often fall more heavily on those who have been subordinated. As Brody[128] notes, fear and anger are greater in groups who have been subordinated. These include groups such as the ethnically marginalised, the young, the unemployed, women, and the less educated. It may be this that accounts, at least in part, for some of the class differences in psychopathology. Interestingly, it does not seem to be so much the absolute levels of poverty that are associated with health indices but the distribution of inequality (i.e., degree of variation in the ranks).[129]

Growing up to Fit One's Group

Parenting is not an enclosed system, but is highly influenced by the social contexts in which it happens. MacDonald[130] has pointed out that rearing practices are influenced by the social contexts of groups; in other words, the kind of upbringing one has will be significantly influenced by the kind of group one's family exists within.[131] To explore this we can note his comparison of the African Gusii and !Kung tribes, who have very different social structures and

[128] Brody, L.R. (1993)
[129] Wilkinson, R.G. (1992)
[130] MacDonald, K.B. (1998)
[131] Belsky et al. (1990) give a very clear outline of the theory and evidence for the idea that certain families create different contexts for reproductive strategies. The paper is followed by two commentaries: one by Hinde, the other by Maccoby – the later offering alternative explanations for some of Belsky et al.'s observations: especially the fact that evolution has made possible wide variations in reproductive behaviour.

hence very different rearing practices. The Gusii have moved away from the more traditional egalitarian hunter-gatherer styles of living and are more competitive and aggressive. They foster individual self-interest, are male-dominated, (sexually) competitive, hierarchical, war-like and territorial. Their rearing practices seem to prepare children to enter this type of group. They are often punitive (beatings are common, even of very young children), low on warmth, have aversive initiation rituals, and are highly controlling of female sexuality. When the children become adults, they are suspicious, distrustful, prone to paranoia and envious, and are aggressive (rape is not infrequent).

The !Kung, however, are different in many ways. They are egalitarian, with strong family and group ties, where meanness and non-sharing are considered shameful. Many researchers believe that this is the more typical EEA for humans. The !Kung are non- territorial, (mostly) monogamous and affectionate to each other, and mutual support is crucial to their survival. Murder and rape are extremely rare, and violence is regarded as the worst possible thing. Their rearing practices help the child to fit this type of life style, which will depend on developing mutually supportive, investing networks. Thus, rearing is affectionate with much physical closeness by mothers and fathers, playful and non-aggressive. When children become adults, they are trusting, warm and keen to reduce conflicts rather than aggressively dominate others.

We see here not two different races or set of genes, but two different social groups recruiting different social and sexual strategies. If we accept that our brains are affected by our early experiences, then one would anticipate that the brains of the Gusii and the brains of the !Kung will have matured (and operate as adults) in slightly different ways.

It is a sad fact that in many ways the history of our Western rearing practices shows that we have been more inclined to follow Gusii practices than those of the !Kung. In her book, *For Our Own Good*, Alice Miller[132] has collected much historical evidence to suggest that the models prescribed for bringing up children in Western society in past centuries were hostile. The child was seen to be full

---

[132] Miller, A. (1983)

of wilfulness or even sin (a paranoid or perhaps envious view of childhood), someone who must be made to submit to the power of the parents by threats and punishments. In previous centuries, little was written on the need for love, playfulness, father involvement, physical closeness and tenderness, and rather more on the need to bring about a basically subordinate attitude in the child ready to fit with the religious, military and economic hierarchical and authoritarian structures of the time. Gone too was the need for extensive kin helpers in child rearing. Single mothers' coping alone is a gross abnormality.

To a society that was waging wars and developing an empire, relying on exploitation and child labour with the threat of hell for disobedience, such rearing patterns were in tune with the needs of the society – needs for there to be a mass of subordinates obeying orders, working in factories and securely wedded to, or at least prepared for, hierarchical control. Life was cheap. But even if people wish to provide loving, caring environments, the social circumstances of their lives may make this extremely difficult. Consider the fate of a baby born in the battle zones of Bosnia, the backstreets of Delhi, a deprived estate in Brixton, or into a depressed family who have recently lost their home. One might also add in the availability of drugs and alcohol. These social contexts can in no way be seen as neutral on those who are to act as the baby's carers. The parents' experiences and 'states of mind' will shape the babies' experiences of their social world and psychobiological maturation. Social contexts which are threatening or frustrate the aspirations of people will impinge on the relationship between carer and cared-for. The parent who has become depressed or aggressive because of their social circumstances may be less available and more easily stressed by the child's demands than those for whom intense frustration is not a major part of life.

Moreover, beyond the confines of the home environment, the baby (and later, child) will encounter others (peers, siblings and adults) who share the same social reality, values and social experiences. In Bosnia in the 1990s (and other war areas), there was considerable worry that many children were growing up severely traumatised and prone to serious mental health problems – not to mention needs for revenge. We can only ponder how much of our war-torn history has rendered many millions of people the same – and the effect this traumatisation has had on shaping our cultural values and paranoias. Only now are we beginning to realise the extent of it.

It follows, therefore, that the emergence of the child's sense of self, and whether they grow with rage and contempt in their hearts or will come to follow a more altruistic path, will be effected by several factors: a) the philosophies of child rearing a parent follows (e.g., on physical punishment or the degree of protection/control exercised, or gendered attitudes, etc.); b) the basic interpersonal style of the parents towards them (e.g., warmth); c) the tensions between the parents (which themselves may be affected by money problems); and d) by the social contexts and ecologies which impinge both on the parents and the child. [133]

Two Types of Reproductive Environment?

Some commentators worry that in our increasingly divided societies we are creating two groups who are following different reproductive strategies. [134] In one group are the so-called 'middle classes', who, freed from major economic hassle, try to provide a loving, warm and highly investing environment for a small number of offspring. They promote both the importance of hard work and education, and the development of social bonds to secure goals. Their children are likely to be highly educated and socially skilled at developing and maintaining affectionate bonds, and they will defer breeding until they have established themselves in their groups. Current government policy privileges them, because consumer choice of good schools, for example, goes with where one lives (in an inner city or suburb) and having the resources to exercise choice. In contrast are the marginalised groups who suffer serious economic hardships, are more likely to live in families fraught with tensions, are less well educated, less socially skilled or able to maintain social bonds or unable to use them to

---

[133] There is now clear evidence that the quality of early child-rearing has a major impact on susceptibility to psychopathology (e.g., see Brewin, C.R. Andrews, B. and Gotlib, I.H., 1993). It is also the case that disturbed patterns of attachment and child rearing tend to pass from generation to generation; see Diamond, D. and Donane, J.A. (1994).

[134] See Belsky et al. (1990)

advance themselves (i.e., they don't develop helpful alliances and connections), and are far more vulnerable to early pregnancies, criminality, psychopathology and general ill-health.

Although stereotypes are always dangerous, we should note that in some inner cities, now often deserted by the police and social services, there is a collapse of the social structures built up after the Second World War to offset the destructiveness of wide variation in the ranks of social opportunity and privilege. Study after study shows that children in deprived inner-city areas do more poorly in education and social relationships, and are more vulnerable to physical and mental ill-health.

When one considers the differences between groups like the Gusii and !Kung, it is clear that their differences in social behaviour and personality are not genetic. Although genes may play a role in individual cases, when looked at from the society as a whole, what we see is social contexts ascribing different reproductive and social strategies (archetypal forms of behaviour) to certain groups.

Two Types of Social Group?

Michael Chance[135] has suggested that there are three basic types of social mode, or patterns of social interaction, two of which I briefly mentioned in the previous chapter. These are called the agonistic, agonic and hedonic mode. The first, agonistic mode is unstable and rarely lasts long. Individuals are engaged in conflicts and are actually fighting, about to fight, or escaping. In the agonic mode, fighting and escaping are inhibited to some degree. This is because the

---

[135] Chance, M.R.A. (1980, 1984, 1988) argues that the hedonic and agonic modes reflect patterns of attention and in this way have a coordinating effect on our inner archetypal minds. Thus, it is possible to speak of a hedonic state of mind or even a hedonic personality. The hedonic personality might relate to the dimension of personality the personality theorist have labelled agreeableness (see note 21, from Chapter 2 of this book). Some of the issues around the notion of hedonic and agonic were discussed in a special edition of *World Futures: The Journal of General Evolution (Special Edition)*, 1992 35, 1-172: 'The Socio-Mental Bimodality'.

subordinates are submitting sufficiently to prevent it, or if they can't escape or submit they become depressed. The attentions of the subordinates are fearfully directed to the dominant members and much of their behaviour is to avoid punishment – that is it is self-protective. In some human groups, excessive submission or appeasement is common in the agonic mode. These behaviours are to calm the potential aggression of the dominant. However, subordinates will fight (and rebel) once they think they have the power to win. The agonic mode can fester rebellions.

The hedonic mode is not derived from needs or fears to calm an aggressive dominant, nor concern with either escaping, submitting or waiting one's chance to aggressively move up the ranks. Rather, the interactions are primarily explorative, open and affiliative-affectionate, and the social structure is flexible. Members in these groups are neither orientated to fighting nor escaping/submitting, but rather on developing mutually supportive and pleasure bonds.

These may not be clear-cut categories but dimensional and various, changing mixtures are possible. But just as different social structures seem to recruit different reproductive strategies (e.g., high investment in few offspring or low investment in many), so the predominant modes one finds oneself in tend to recruit different aspects of our archetypal minds. It is easier to feel and be caring with some people rather than others. Nevertheless, the modes idea is important, because it suggest types of social organisation around the nature, degree and type of interpersonal threats. These threats in turn may be linked to the group structure – whether it is egalitarian, as in the !Kung, or competitive/aggressive as in the Gusii.[136] The modes are important also because they indicate what

---

[136] In our Western societies, which have various mixtures of egalitarian and competitive structures, the agonic mode can be difficult to spot and may be superimposed on a more hedonic one. The agonic mode is primarily defensive and non-trusting – fitting for the competitive group. In such groups, there is always a threat around what will happen if one does not conform, submit to the hierarchy, or if one tries to defect. In some groups, such as harsh disciplinarian groups, the agonic structure is clear to see, and there can be a good deal of down-hierarchy aggressiveness. In our chapter on cruelty, we will note just how common this was in British society in days gone by. However, even in some religious cults, where the social structure looks friendly and hedonic, it is in fact fake,

might be necessary to create hedonic modes, be this in families, companies or health services. The important research questions are how can we create hedonic contexts that enable people to feel safe, be sharing and caring, able to be creative, want to make a contribution and feel appreciated for doing so.

One of the key factors that may influence whether a social group has taken up an agonic or hedonic structure is not only the mutual support it offers, but the degree of freedoms it allows and accepts. These freedoms include the ability to come and go, and where boundaries between sub-groups are permeable. Mann[137] suggests that in early human times, groups were highly permeable and people would indeed come and go as they wished. They had much greater choice of associates. The focus of the groups were mostly on mutual support and interest (like the !Kung today). This type of social organisation was known in the early days of Crete, for example.[138] However, as groups expanded in size and developed agriculture, material possessions and defence of territory become more important to the social organisation. From there on existed increasing pressures on humans to stay within the group. We were, to use Mann's terms, caged and trapped. It was neither easy (because of few alternatives, a dependence on food grown locally, and/or the nature of the local terrain) nor socially acceptable to leave and defect out. Moreover, social sanctions against internal rebellion and non-conformity were necessary. As today, being seen as a traitor or betrayer were serious crimes.

We cannot truly explore the history of these changes, from our comparatively early egalitarian origins to the more competitive and highly ranked structures of

---

because the moment a person wants to pull out, the sheer vindictiveness of the group can be appalling (as we will see later). Moreover, many of these groups/cults ask for a major switch of allegiances by giving up ties to old friends and family. These kinds of request should always been seen as a deceptive form of a hedonic mode. There can also be sexual privileges for the higher (usually male) ranks.

[137] Mann, M. (1986)

[138] There is now clear evidence that the quality of early child rearing has a major impact on susceptibility to psychopathology (e.g, see Brewin, C.R. Andrews, B. and Gotlib, I.H. 1993). It is also the case that disturbed patterns of attachment and child rearing tend to pass one generation to generation see Diamond, D. and Donane, J.A. (1994).

today, but we should add two things.[139] According to Michael Chance, and many others, early humans, like the bonobos, lived in predominantly hedonic-egalitarian groups, and it was this that freed our attention for positive social relating, which in turn fuelled the evolution of our intelligence. Freed from the fear of constant down-hierarchy attacks and the needs to make up hierarchy challenges, our attention was turned to more explorative prosocial pursuits. The benefits of helpful social relationships meant that the more rewarding one could be to others, and the more rewarding one felt others to be, operated a different evolutionary pressure. This was to be socially skilled, empathic and motivated to forming close-knit affectionate alliances, and to communicate and share with others. We can see how this would have made gaining positive social attention (SAHP) highly adaptive – including the various ways to manipulate it (see Chapters 5 and 6). Indeed, it is difficult to imagine how language could have evolved in an agonic mode which did not encourage sharing and closeness. If, as MacDonald[140] points out, it is our social reward system (i.e., social rewards are now the most important type of reward to humans) that has greatly expanded in humans, it may well have been the emergence of hedonic-type modes, based around kin-networks, that fuelled it.

The Two Modes and Mental Health

Two of the modes that Michael Chance has outlined – hedonic and agonic – loosely overlap with caring/altruistic and aggressive competitive. Different psychologies are brought out in us according to which we find ourselves in and mature within. Chance believes that we actually have, in our heads, the potential to organise our understanding of, and orientation to, social relationships in the two modes. Our biosocial goals, motivations and strategies vary according to which mode we are in, and thus our personalities, identities and states of mind can be shaped by these modes. For example, if we live in poverty in the inner

---

[139] Eisler, R. (1990). This is an anthropological and feminist exploration of the shift from basically hedonic, egalitarian social structures to the more, male-rank-dominated cultures of the last few thousand years.
[140] MacDonald, K.B. (1998)

city, surrounded by violence, then we will tend to operate in the agonic mode. On the whole, it is adaptive for people to forgo high levels of altruism, become sexually segregated (with males becoming more violent and territorial), to be distrustful (especially of strangers), and highly threat-sensitive. Most male violence, and what we call psychopathology (e.g., some forms of anxiety, milder depressions and violence), are really the activation of *adaptive strategies for living in the agonic mode*. In so far as the brain chemical serotonin may be low in both those who are violent, and those who are depressed or socially anxious, then this low serotonin reflects not a pathology as such, but more the mode the brain is attuned to.

Anthony Stevens[141], a Jungian analyst, has pointed out that even if people (currently) live in a hedonic community, they can still have various agonic and aggressive fantasies and ideals, as if the *potential* for agonic relationships is still there. It may be that whatever archetypal tendency we have for forming agonic-type orientations in our heads, it is increased by punitive parenting early in life.

In the hedonic mode, however, our psychologies are quite different, and we seek more altruistic relationships. Indeed, we know that when people feel safe and supported in their social environments, their brains work in different ways from when they feel threatened. There is increasing evidence, for example, that children and adults learn and function differently in contexts of threat compared to contexts where the environment is non-threatening and safe. Creativity, cooperative behaviour, affiliative behaviour, exploration, risk-taking, and the integration of various psychological abilities may be enhanced in non-threatening (safe) environments.[142] In socially threatening environments, one may find less flexible, open and explorative behaviour, less prosocial behaviour, and more stereotyped, automatic defensive (aggressive, anxious or appeasement) responses. It may well be that the brain works differently in the two modes, and certainly the archetypal patterns recruited (caring/altruistic versus competitive) are different. The relative safeness of the hedonic mode may have affected the evolution of our brain – if it is true that safeness was a hallmark

---

[141] Personal communication

[142] Eisenberg, L. and Mussen, P.N. (1989); Isen, A.M. (1990)

of early human groups. Moreover, evolving in supportive networks may well have advanced the evolution of the cortical competencies for inventiveness. Undoubtedly deception and manipulation played a role here (e.g., getting others to invest more in you than you do in them), but the key thing was that the social structure is far more relaxed and explorative in the hedonic mode compared to the agonic mode.

The hedonic group is also the ideal for most people. Indeed, as Scott[143] points out, in times of oppression people through the centuries have craved, theorised and sought egalitarian relationships. Some have been attempted, as in the early Christian gnostic and Buddhist-inspired movements. For example,

> In the fifteenth century the Toborites anticipated both radical equality and the labor theory of value: "Princes, ecclesiastical and secular alike, and counts and knights should only possess as much as common folk, then everyone would have enough. The time will come when princes and lords will work for their daily bread."[144]

One of the sources of archetypal inflation (and deflation) is culture, and the way socio-cultural forms impinge on our personal relationships. It is our groups and societies that structure the patterns of many forms of social relating and offer up the values we should endorse. For example, if (as we shall discuss in the next chapter) manhood is construed on the need to be dominant, assertive, independent and avoid expressing caring and compassionate feelings, then there will be a tendency for certain types of dispositions to become inflated (or privileged) in males. Moreover, such males will tend to create agonic modes as part of their social organisation, and this will involve the subordination of many groups of people and their values. This helps their gene-built strategies for aggressiveness to survive and reproduce.

---

[143] Scott, J.C. (1990)
[144] Scott, J.C. (1990), p.91

More Than Two Modes?

There have been various attempts to try to show how our internal psychology fits with the social context. Fiske[145] has drawn on a wide cross-cultural literature, which suggests four basic forms of socio-culture patterns of organisation:

1) *Communal sharing*, which is similar to egalitarianism: people are treated as equals and social caring and help-giving is important. This may have overlap with Chance's hedonic mode and reflects mostly a caring archetypal pattern.

2) *Authority ranking*, where people are attentive to where they are in the social ranks and have rights or powers increased or reduced according to their ranks. Ranks tend to be rigid. This seems close to the agonic mode, although there may be strong laws to inhibit violence in the lower ranks. Its core seems to be around the rank archetype.

3) *Equality matching*, where people keep track of favours and obligations. This looks like a cooperative archetypal pattern derived from reciprocal altruism, perhaps.

4) *Market pricing*, where forms of social behaviour are made from economic exchanges and the values placed on commodities and attributes (money or special skills can buy you up the ranks).

The central idea to both Chance and Fiske is that we are not autonomous persons acting regardless of the social context we exist within, but that different psychologies (beliefs and values) are needed and recruited in the different social modes. This, of course, makes much evolutionary sense and moves us some way from the Newtonian mechanistic psychological theories of old.

---

[145] Fiske, A.T. (1992). I am very grateful to my colleague Dr Nicholas Allan for alerting me to this literature.

Social Life and the Control of Tension

Whatever social pattern or culture we exist within, however, all cultures attempt to resolve salient conflicts that can bubble from the various archetypal possibilities in us. Solutions to various inherent conflicts can include monogamous marriage laws, which restrict breeding partners, to major social stratifications (e.g. a caste system) and gender role prescriptions. Eisenstadt[146] has given an excellent summary of the types of conflicts, frustrations, tensions and protests that are so much part of our social lives, and for which culture(s) attempt to offer meanings and solutions. He suggests these tensions and protests revolve around four motives:

1. The search to overcome the tension between the complexity and fragmentation of human relations inherent in any institutional division of labor and the possibility of some total, unconditional, unmediated participation in social and cultural order.

2. The search to overcome the tensions inherent in the temporal dimension of the human and social condition, especially the search for immortality; the tension between the deferment of gratification in the present and the possibility of its attainment in the future; and the tension between an emphasis on productivity and labor and the distribution and the accompanying stress of visions of unlimited goods.

3. The quest to suspend the tension in the model of the ideal society: the principles of distributive justice upheld within it on the one hand and the reality of institutional life on the other.

4. The quest to suspend the tension between the personal and the autonomous self and the social role, that is, the possibility of finding full expression of the internal self in social and cultural life as opposed to the retreat from it.[147]

---

[146] Eisenstadt, S.N. (1992)

[147] Eisenstadt, S.N. (1992), pp.73-74

Tensions are also created from our inherent conflicts of interest (e.g. status pursuits, reproductive strategies, demands of child rearing, etc.). That social life, of which most wish to participate in, is fraught with tensions, conflicts and paradoxes should not lead us to assume that the postmodernist view that 'anything goes' offers adequate solutions. On the contrary, there are certain basic needs and requirements that a society must furnish its people with to avoid a collapse into more 'primitive' competitive and exploitative arenas. As I shall argue in Chapter 11, political theory and politicians cannot simply make up human psychology as they go along. Nor can they abnegate their responsibilities for social fairness, justice and promoting a mutually supportive community infrastructure. To do so is to end up where we are heading now, with increasing social tensions born from basic unfairness, reduced hope and serious exploitation.

Integration: Bringing Things Together

If we follow the argument put forward so far, we see that humans evolved (at least for some of the time) in egalitarian groups that promoted the importance of prosocial relationships – at least in close knit groups. This probably had a major effect on the evolution of the brain, especially the cortex. Today, we no longer live quite like this, because population size has overrun us, although we are often trying to get back to it. But most importantly, we can see that gene-behaviour linkages are fraught with problems, because behaviour, indeed the very sense of ourselves and values, will depend on many social contexts and early life patterns. So, there is a link *between cultural values, economic relationships, sources of threat, construction of self-identities, archetypal roles and biology.* There are many models describing these relations, including those of Robert Hinde.[148]

Neither biology nor social contexts alone can explain our behaviour and our craziness. Rather, we need to understand their interaction in the context of our jerry-built, archetypal minds. Although it is difficult to be precise about the exact

---

[148] Hinde, R.S. (1992)

mechanisms that shape people, it is clear that there are some complex interactions going on between cultural forms of relating, the coming into existence of personhood, and biology. It follows then that it is not just genes that drive us crazy (although for some this is sadly true), but the social domains that inflate certain biological tendencies in our jerry-built minds. It is because of inflations of the archetypal in us that our goals, motivations and inner fantasies (to ourselves and others) can become so destructive.

Conclusion

As Eisenstadt[149] says, "culture does not free us (or deprive us) of biology but has co-evolved as an intrinsic aspect of human biology" (p. 37.). It is not possible to understand the passions that infuse many of our destructive behaviours toward ourselves and others without acknowledgement of the archetypal in us. If we wish to build societies that at least make some attempt at social justice, then we need to consider how certain types of environments create certain types of people. Those who look after the checks and balances of society should keep an eye on the archetypal. Political discourses are not freed from the realities of our evolved brains.

On the whole, much of our evolution took part in close-knit, stable groups of 50-150 individuals. This advantaged a proliferation of altruistic strategies requiring complex social intelligence that could communicate, feel love and friendship, be explorative and via trust in others (jointly) explorative of the environment. Not only do most of us function best (in regards to our mental health) when we feel loved and valued, egalitarian (hedonic) ideals have been common throughout history and in all cultures. Why these never seem to last long may be connected with how the more individualistic reptilian parts of ourselves were advantaged once we became trapped in increasing large numbers with agriculture. In such large and expanding groups, one could not keep track of altruistic favours, nor develop close relationship with more than a few others. Gaining control over others proved more advantageous to those so inclined. It

---

[149] Eisenstadt, S.N. (1992)

may be also that certain ecologies advantage more agonic type relationships[150] – but it is unlikely that intra-group aggressive competition was the driving force of our intelligence and large brains (although it was never fully banished either). But regardless of these speculations, the point seems to be unless we address ourselves to the social dimensions of life then our efforts to reduce crime and human misery may run into the sand.

---

[150] Power, M. (1991)

5: THE DESIRE FOR RECOGNITION, IDENTITY, STATUS AND SUPERIORITY

> *Micropolitics, like all politics, has to do with the creation and negotiation of hierarchy: getting and keeping power, rank and standing, or what I call "social place".... In everyday, face-to-face encounters and relationships, we constantly monitor the shifting micropolitical balance. We want to know where we stand, relative to others, at a given moment. And we want to have a say in negotiating our standing. (Clark, 1990)[151]*

> *We do not content ourselves with the life we have in ourselves and in our being, we desire to live an imaginary life in the minds of others, and for this purpose we endeavour to shine.[152]*

Status is a big issue for humans. Throughout the ages, many observers of human behaviour (especially male behaviour) have noted that a concern "to shine" (to use Pascal's term) can manifest itself in heroic deeds and the pursuit of glory, fame and recognition. Indeed, the desire to create a good impression, gain recognition and even distinction, is not only the stuff of social psychology and psychotherapy, but also underpins much of our philosophy and political lives.[153] To a large extent, social life is also political, because we are in a constant process of negotiating our social place and where we stand in relation to others. We seek

---

[151] Clark, C. (1990), p.305
[152] Pascal, B. [1670], p.45
[153] Two researchers, Barkow, J.H. (1989) and Kemper, T.D. (1990), have developed important and very insightful ideas and theories of how human ranks are very much based on prestige and attractiveness. This is the basis of status which, as I pointed out in the last chapter, is about attracting allies who will invest in us and in whom we can trust. The concern with socially attractive self-presentations as a way of gaining status has been known for long time, however, and Fukuyama, F. (1992) has plotted this history and the political implications. Also as the historian Gay, P. (1995) makes clear, the drive for prestige, status and superiority has been wrapped around gender identities, and various struggles of class, race and religious denominations.

approval of our talents and abilities, our looks, our opinions, our worth. We seek, in effect, positive social attention, from which we shape our identities. Much of the emotional colour of our lives is shaded by our perceptions of, and changes in, our social place. The loss of positive attention and recognition can fuel our social rages, anxieties and depressions. Without approval and recognition, we can feel devalued, inferior, subordinated and excluded. The need for approval and recognition reflects both the archetypes of rank/status and also cooperation-conformity, and because these are archetypal they can be pursued with passion.

The German philosopher Frederick Hegel (whose dialectic theories were to have a great impact on Marx) thought that humans were different from animals because they alone had this need for recognition. Hegel argued that humans are prepared to go to war and sacrifice themselves, to face a "violent death", for no more than recognition, honour and prestige. It is this, he argued, that marks their nobility: they will lay down their lives for an idea and a cause. Indeed, as a eusocial species, we are the only mammal that does this. The problem here is that nobility is a subjective, group-informed judgement. While many might see nobility in the fight for human rights, other defences of (male) honour might not be so noble, particularly retaliatory vengeance or face-saving violence. In many cases, the drive for recognition and prestige that Hegel placed so central to humanness is none other than the desire for rank and status. To suggest that this drive is what separates human from animal, or master from slave, as Hegel apparently believed, is misguided.[154]

---

[154] Chimpanzees have been found to engage in war-like behaviours (Goodall, J., 1990). Bonobos, or pygmy chimps, who may be closer to us than common chimps, engage in far more sex and have never been seen to kill one of their one kind. Sociobiologists suggest that war-like behaviours directed towards out-group members may still have effects on genetic representation. In other words, even though you may die in a war, there could still be a genetic pay-off in the survival of your relatives. See Reynolds, V., Falger, V. and Vine, I. (1986, eds.) for detailed explorations of the evolutionary approach to war. Barkow, J.H. (1989) believes that early humans went in for what he calls "autopredation", and this had a major effect on our evolution. This is contentious, although clearly war-like behaviours are all too common in humans (see Barkow, J.H., 1991, and peer discussion).

Hegel could not have known about sexual selection theory and the importance of display behaviour. He chose, understandably, to root his ideas in the theories of human history. While it is true that history has been shaped by (mostly) males trying to gain recognition and assert themselves over others, the forces at work here are not purely social, but archetypal. We now know that the whole sexual selection process depends on displays and *recognition of those displays* – being able to influence, attract, subdue or repel others via one's display. Indeed, territorial marking, displays of strength, displays to the opposite sex or allies, and all kinds of general showing off, are common in animals. Confident displays from dominant animals can have the effect of suppressing certain behaviours of the more subordinate. Indeed, research has shown that confident displays can even affect the biology of the more subordinate.[155] Displays are the way animals advertise things about themselves (e.g., as strong, sexual, available, dominant-subordinate). They are sending messages of competence and intent. And behind such displays and needs for recognition are needs for social success (derived from reproductive strategies). What humans have done is to amplify and weave these functions of display behaviour into complex needs for recognition and approval. These in turn are mediated and incorporated into a symbolic sense of self. But we have not created new archetypes, stripped of their primitive roots. Human needs for approval and recognition are related to many things: to be loved and wanted; to be admired, chosen and esteemed; to create relationships with others so that others will invest in oneself; to avoid losing out to competitors; to avoid abandonment, exclusion – and being shamed, subordinated and losing one's freedom. That so many writers have seen the human need for recognition for so long tells us how powerfully archetypal it is. Fukuyama gives this concise overview of the issue when he writes:

> The concept underlying "recognition" was not invented by Hegel. It is as old as Western political philosophy itself, and refers to a thoroughly familiar part of the human personality. Over the millennia, there has been no consistent word used to refer to the psychological phenomenon of the 'desires for recognition': Plato spoke of thymos, or 'spiritedness',

---

[155] Discussed in Price et al., (1994)

Machiavelli of man's desire for glory, Hobbes, of his pride or vainglory, Rousseau, of his amour propre, Alexander Hamilton of the love of fame, and James Madison of ambition, Hegel of recognition, and Nietzsche, of man as the "beast with red cheeks". All of these terms refer to that part of man which feels the need to place value on things – himself in the first instance, but on the people, actions, or things around him as well. It is the part of the personality which is the fundamental source of the emotions of pride, anger, and shame, and is not reducible to desire, on the one hand, or reason on the other. The desire for recognition, is the most specially political part of the human personality because it is what drives men to want to assert themselves over other men and therefore into Kant's condition of "asocial sociability". It is not surprising that so many political philosophers have seen the central problem of politics as one of taming or harnessing the desire for recognition in a way that would serve the political community as a whole. Indeed, the project of taming the desire for recognition has been so successful in the hands of modern political philosophy that we citizens of modern egalitarian democracies often fail to see the desire for recognition in ourselves for what it is.[156]

The forms and expression of the rank and cooperation-conformity archetypes as they blend and interact may be complex, but they are still rooted in a brain which evolved within the context of hierarchical and kin-based social structures. In some ways, the biological linkage may seem unimportant, but the failure to see the desire for recognition as closely tied to the very old, evolved issues of rank and the need to secure interpersonal investments from others causes problems. It can allow us to see it as something specifically human and noble, as did Hegel. More importantly, as argued in Chapters 3 and 4, if you feed something which is archetypal and biologically prepared, it can grow with a passion, pushing aside the rational mind. We may become intoxicated by it, and it can control us rather than we control it. The charismatic leader depends on finding something archetypal in us upon which to fuel his/her own ambitions as leader. It may be

---

[156] Fukuyama, F. (1992), pp.162-163

offering us an identity, opportunity for superiority, to be loved, to belong (conformity) or a place in heaven. When we are touched by the archetypal, we are at risk of being taken over by passion and emotion. Only later may we discover that some archetypal forms can be dangerous inflations, and we have been led down a blind alley. An intoxication with pride, status, recognition and the need for superiority can be like this.

So, like Hobbes and his ilk, we now see the desire for recognition as having the potential to cast dark shadows: for indeed, it can be a source of our anxieties, depressions and violence, and our need to demean others and distinguish ourselves from them. Fukuyama says of Hobbes, who took the opposite view to Hegel, that he saw little which was noble in recognition; he was not intoxicated by it as was Hegel:

> Hobbes demands... that men give up their struggle to be recognized, in particular, their struggle to be recognized as superior on the basis of their willingness to risk their lives in a prestige battle. The side of man that seeks to show himself superior to other men, to dominate other men, on the basis of superior virtue, the noble character who struggles against his "human all too human" limitations, is to be persuaded of the *folly of his pride*... Contrary to Hegel, Hobbes believes that the desire for recognition and the noble *contempt, for "mere" life* is not the beginning of man's freedom but the source of his misery[157]. (italics added)

This takes us to the heart of the issue, because it makes clear the potential folly of pride and that it can so easily hold within it contemptuousness – a destroyer of self and others. As feminist writers have stated, sexual prowess and the idea of conquering women or 'bedding them' has in some cultures been seen as the essence of pride in one's manhood. Not only have men attempted to assert themselves over other men, but also over women. The nobility of men can also be framed as a toughness which seeks to banish so-called feminine values and traits from their psyche. That is the problem with an inflated archetype – one ends up doing too much of one thing and too little of another – but our

---

[157] Fukuyama, F. (1992)

intoxication with it does not allow us to see this; our values become distorted and one-sided. That is a form of craziness. Essentially too, the drive for recognition can underpin a kind of narcissistic focus on the self, and how the self exists in the minds of others. Hence, the need and drive for recognition can be fuelled by a deep uncertainty in the self, which then becomes a narcissistic preoccupation.

Prove Yourself

The Personal

As Hobbes saw, an excessive desire for recognition is a cause of both our own craziness, and the craziness we force on others. It can be associated with harmful competitiveness and a need to constantly prove the self as worthy, able and strong. It has many faces – fame, glory, vanity and narcissistic self-promotion. Excessive desires for recognition often go with a certain self-centredness and lack of interest in others. One cannot easily care or give to others if it detracts from one's own need for recognition or status (specialness). The narcissistic pursuit of fame, glory and recognition can lead to poorer abilities for cooperation, and a lack of care, compassion, and empathy for others.

Hobbes, unlike Hegel, might have felt more at ease with a modern psychotherapist view, which suggests that excessive needs for recognition arise from a failure to mature our heroic and grandiose selves (which we have as children) into healthy ideals and realistic aspirations.[158] It can represent a narcissistic problem, a certain craziness, a need to compensate for an underlying sense of worthlessness or a terror of being ordinary or subordinated. This (hidden) sense of worthlessness, they argue, arises from a lack of being valued, or excessive devaluing/shaming and rejection, in childhood. I certainly go along with that, but I don't think this is only a problem of childhood. Rather, I believe

---

[158] Kohut, H. (1977), see also Slavin, M.O. and Kreigman, D. (1992).

that societies can be highly manipulative of people and use the desire for recognition, and to find a secure sense of social place, to shape themselves. The social definitions of worth and the opportunities given to gain respect, prestige and recognition of worth are key factors in this process. Nowhere is this more vividly displayed than in an exploration of gender. The way many societies treat the two sexes brings this out clearly, as we shall note shortly[159]. But first, let us attend to the importance of the audience from whom we seek recognition.

Audience Comparisons

Our human needs for recognition, approval and status show themselves in ways that are difficult to test in animals. It involves much more than the pair-wise comparisons and contests of animals who fight over a territory. It often involves triangular relationships and larger audiences. In sexual relationships, a person may be concerned that their lover is comparing them unfavourably with another (potential lover/competitor). Thus, we hear questions like, 'do you love me *more than* John/Sue?'[160] In other words, the person may not only compare themselves directly with John/Sue but be concerned about how the other (the lover) compares them with John/Sue. They are competing for preferential status in the eyes of the other. If the person is able to believe that indeed they are preferred to the other, then all may be well, but if not, things might switch to anxiety, deception and/or aggression. The fear that these comparisons are going badly (one is not a preferred or valued person) can be the source of envy, rage and depression. To some extent, mental wellbeing depends on our ability to tolerate and accept these social judgements on us. However, certainly in our intimate relationships, we need to have at least some sense that we are special to the other.

In many domains of life, when we compare ourselves to others and search for recognition, we have in mind a larger audience rather than a specific other. Thus, in the beauty contest or boxing ring, passing exams, and in various forms of

---

[159] In Chapter 4, we noted work on the socialisation of emotion and how this varies between males and females. See Brody, L.R. (1993).

[160] See Gilbert, P., Price, J.S. and Allan, S. (1995) for a more extensive exploration of these themes.

showing off, we are not only giving an audience an opportunity to compare us with others, but rather, depending on the audience and our desired relationships to the audience, we are attempting to win preferential recognition (be chosen, admired, selected) from the larger audience. When we win, our mood goes up. When we lose, it goes down. If our self-presentations vary too much from the average, then we may appear odd. Therefore, there is a fair degree of conforming to the standards of judgement set by the audience.

In this context, social comparison plays a major role, for by comparing the self with others one is able to estimate what others will find attractive in the self (i.e., noting who is getting the attention and for what) and in comparison with others, how one should change one's behaviour to obtain positive attention (e.g., work harder, pass exams, wear certain make-up and clothes). Thus, fashion, fitting in, various forms of competition to win approval and positive attention, and showing off etc., are influenced by such comparative processes. Often, of course, one wants to fit in, yet also be a little individual and better than others, a dilemma between 'getting along' and 'getting ahead'.[161] And if not getting ahead, then certainly a little different or original. To be regarded as 'just' ordinary and unoriginal, nothing special, etc. are not normally judgments people enthuse over. It would be regarded as quite impolite to tell your host after the dinner, "Well, thanks for your very ordinary meal", or to tell your new lover, "you are okay, I've had better I've had worse". In both cases, you want some enthusiasm. Here, some degree of recognition of value offers ways of building relationships. People prefer judgements that they have done well and their efforts are appreciated and esteemed. There are all kinds of ways we seek to impress.

Once one removes the aggressive tactics of ranking in favour of attracting and being chosen, then the difference between men and women disappear, at least within same gender competition. Women, like men, can be equally concerned with their appearance (their displays), and the way others judge them. Indeed, in terms of appearance, women can be as competitive as men. Little seems free from competitive social comparison, even loving relationships. New evidence

---

[161] Wolfe, R.N., Lennox, R.D. and Cutler, B.L. (1986)

suggests the people compare their (sexual and romantic) relationship with others and tend to see their own as superior.[162] We like others to admire our sexual partners. And those of us who have children will know that we often compare our children to those of others and (on the whole) think ours are better. We take pride from their public performances at the Christmas panto, for example. Indeed, some parents are highly competitive where their children are concerned – especially in obtaining approval and success.

It is clear, however, that we can't socially compare only with up-rank people, because we will always feel inferior to them. Indeed, one of the sources of depression is when people put their social comparison levels too high and therefore experience a sense of deficit and inferiority. Downward comparison is probably better for you, if you are depressed. Or sometimes depressed people compare the non-depressed state with what they can do in their depressed state, which is again not helpful: "I used to be able to do so much more but now look at me, a shadow of my former self". What drives us crazy, however, is that our media is constantly inviting us to make upward, completely unrealistic comparisons that leave us feeling constantly not only 'wanting' rather than experiencing content, but also that 'they' (those on the TV) can be, can do, and can have things we never can. We will always be a 'lesser than'. This doesn't fit well with our hunter-gatherer minds.

On the Nature of Gendered Male Identities

In his book, *Manhood in the Making*, David Gilmour[163] pointed out that in very many societies manhood is not something that exists by virtue of growing into it, *it is something that must be won and proved*. We saw the same theme, this need to win one's place, when exploring intrasexual selection in animals in

---

[162] Van Lange, P.A.M. and Rusbult, C.E. (1995). This is, they point out, part of a general tendency to the self as better than others. Indeed, there is now quite a large literature on what is called overconfidence. Positive biases (called warm glow) seem helpful to mental health (Taylor, S.E. and Brown, J.D., 1988). We cannot go it into this here as it would take us too far from our main themes.

[163] Gilmour, D.D. (1990)

Chapter 2. But in humans, winning one's spurs is, of course, more complex. One example Gilmour offers is of the fishermen of the Truk Islands.

> Trukese men are obsessed with their masculinity, which they regard as chancy. To maintain a manly image, the men are encouraged to take risks with life and limb and to think "manly" thoughts... Accordingly, they challenge fate by going on deep-sea fishing expeditions in tiny dugouts and spearfishing with foolhardy abandon in shark infested waters. If any men shrink from such challenges, their fellows, male and female, laugh at them, calling them effeminate and child-like. When on land Trukese youths fight in weekend brawls, drink to excess, and seek sexual conquests to attain a manly image. Should a man fail in any of these efforts, another will taunt him; "Are you a man? Come, I will take your life now...[164]

Gilmour has given many examples to demonstrate that recognition of manhood is given or taken away by the group, it is not genetically given but depends on cultural signals. Moreover, in some societies recognition of manhood is bestowed only if there is also a disavowal of compassion, softness, tenderness and (and what we might see as) higher moral codes. Indeed, as Goldner and her colleagues[165] point out in their exploration of violence and gender, in many cultures the division of labour makes gender a pervasive construct. It permeates language, religion and socio-economic life. In cultures that require men to be strong, dominant and competitive, any personal attribute such as fear and vulnerability, must be projected if men are to cope and show themselves up to the business of 'doing the job'. Once women have become the holders of such projections, so that it is they who are the vulnerable ones (but not men – who are fearless), and it is women who are viewed as inadequate and not 'up to it', there operates a "taboo against similarity and the dread of collapse of gender difference operates silently and powerfully in all relations between men and women."[166] Indeed, throughout the world, one of the judgments men fear is

[164] Gilmour, D.D. (1992) p.12
[165] Goldner et al. (1990) give a very interesting and insightful feminist analysis.
[166] Goldner et al. (1990), p.348

being called 'effeminate'. And this label, which is essentially aimed to shame, is used not only for individuals but also whole social movements that have had a desire to become more compassionate, peaceful and 'soft'.[167]

By the nineteenth century, views and social definitions of manhood and womanhood were well entrenched in European culture. Many of these were informed by recourse to biblical, and later supposedly 'scientific', truths. It was common to see men as essentially aggressive and competitive, as the breadwinner, while women were created or best suited for domesticity. As Gay notes,

> Just after 1900, in his massive treatise on adolescence, the American psychologist G Stanley Hall took the same track. Boys must train their capacities in "wrestling, fighting, boxing, duelling and in some sense hunting," thus emulating in their lives the animal world "which is full of struggle." He welcomed schooling in "man-making" as a defense against "degeneration, the essential feature of which is weakening of will and loss of honour. Real virtue requires enemies, and women and effeminate and old men want placid, comfortable peace, while a real man rejoices in noble strife which sanctifies all great causes, casts out fear, and is the chief school of courage."[168]

Although there were feminist texts, even before the seventeenth century, critical of such masculine ideals (which often included the subordination of women), these were largely suppressed. In various societies, proving one's manhood requires endorsement of these narcissistic, self-promoting pursuits, and a view that social life is primarily agonic, i.e., brutish, competitive and one of struggle. Thus, masculine identities are often infused with anti-social, competitive ideals of struggle rather than cooperative or caring ones. Caring, compassion and 'looking after is women's business – at home.

Women have suffered too from this male-on-male competition. When resources are at stake, competitors do what they can to undermine each other, and women

---

[167] Gay, P. (1995) offers a fascinating discussion of these issues.
[168] Gay, P. (1995), p.97

were easy targets. There was always the view that to allow women into the enclaves of power would weaken those enclaves, for it was thought that women lacked the aggression and stamina, even the intelligence, for gaining competitive advantage. They had not, nor could not, work their way up the ranks via their fighting ability and proving their combative/competitive talents. Thus, no woman could be powerful without a man behind her, whom she controlled with her sexual favours. And the fear was/is, that to allow her to start on the rungs of access to power would change the social status, respectability and power of that profession. And further, she would comprise or distract males from the tasks of beating other males. The inherent deceitfulness of women and the problems they cause men goes back to Adam and Eve. Thus, as Gay[169] points out, the paradox was, and is, that women are both feared for their (imagined) weakness and their (sexual) power! Not surprisingly, still today women are not on an equal footing either for opportunity or salary.

But we need to return to our main theme, which is that, unlike womanhood, manhood is often based on recognition in overcoming ordeals set by cultural tests. In some societies, it requires the (usually young) male to leave the safe confines of the group/family and go forth, to fish, hunt, or plunder some other place, bring back trophies, make one's fortune, gain glory and fame, get a job or career, or in various ways prove their courage and ability. This is rarely seen as an issue for females. Greek and Nordic myths (the Sagas) both engage this mythology. It is an unwritten text that if one's tribe is threatened, then men are expected to go to war to kill other men, and of course be prepared to die (perhaps horribly). Not to accept this contract for being part of this group is to lose any claim that one is a true man. Pretty crazy stuff, and the world has suffered immensely from it for thousands of years. It's very tough to break free of these historical and archetypal patterns. But when you stand back and just think of billions of babies born with hope and potential, only to find themselves years later ripped apart because of human tribal archetypal horrors that we neither understand nor seem able to do anything about, it is nothing short of crazy and deeply tragic. Is this all 100s of millions of years can accomplish! Of course, the

---

[169] Gay, P. (1995)

archetypes are clever. At no point did they allow us to see the brutality and the stupidity of it, but rather feed our heads with razzmatazz, glitzy dopamine, approval seeking, a genuine wish to be a protector, and hero dreams; dreams that become deceptions as you lay on the battlefield with your guts spread out before you. What we need is for our armies to form an international profession and not allow themselves to be utilised by any tribal tyrant; to lock our politicians up together until they do their jobs properly. One day, we might get our international act together so that no country can own an army, or all armies are under international control. This is how to defeat the archetypal mind, but the archetypal tribal mind will not give up easily, and there will be massive resistance to it.

At other times, recognition of manhood arises from facing ordeals within a group, such as initiation, which can involve ritual beatings, painful circumcisions from which one must not cry out, being separated from the group and family, fighting, defending one's honour, and so forth. Thus, in some societies, having the status of manhood recognised means showing scorn for personal risk, a cavalier or even contemptuous attitude to life and death, a preparedness to engage in struggle, to face injury and pain, a concern with glory and winning, and more often than not a lack of feeling for others, especially one's enemies. Moreover, compassion, caring, fear and vulnerability is, as we noted above, projected onto females. These are often captured by terms like 'warrior attitudes'.[170] As Sam Keen notes in his book on manhood, *Fire in the Belly*,[171] "Perhaps the greatest price men have paid for their obsession with

---

[170] McCarthy, B. (1994) gives a slightly more positive view of warrior male values which he sees as follows: *Physical courage* and the preparedness to face death and injury; *Endurance*, the ability to keep going despite hardships; *Strength and Skill*; and *Honour*. While honour can lead to protecting the weak and showing mercy to weaker individuals, it can also lead to more destructive things, including blood feuds that can last many generations and the right of a man to kill his wife if she commits adultery. For *Star Trek* fans, the warrior values are supposed to be the basis of the Klingon culture! Warrior values remain intact in a society because of the privileges bestowed on those who follow them competently.

[171] Keen, S. (1992), p.139

fearlessness is to have become tough on the outside and empty on the inside. We are hollow men".[172]

Cross-cultural work, however, shows that despite the commonality of these shapes for gendered identities, they are social constructions – not a biological or unchanging fact. Such identities require education, training, and the group reinforcement and endorsement of certain values. Overing[173] has compared two very different Amazonian groups, shaped by different ecologies and hunter-gathering patterns: the Shavante and the Piaroa. These vary in similar ways to the African Gusii and !Kung tribes, which we noted in the last chapter. The Shavante value hunting and warrior values. Children are gender segregated from an early age. Males are brought up to be aggressive and 'bellicose', to recognise male-superiority in terms of the products of their contributions to the group and political decision-making. Women are excluded from political decision-making and many of the rituals of manhood involved demonstrations of fearlessness and an aggressive control over females. Females are trained to value certain attributes in males and be shaming of fearful males. The Piaroa, however, are quite different. They are not gender-segregated, and the kind of male behaviour valued by the Shavante would be considered as evidence of 'lack of control' and as sub-human; something to be pitied. Tranquillity, emotional control and the rights of individual members (male and female) are valued equally. Warrior values are seen as highly disruptive to the group and shunned. The ability to be social and tranquilly cooperative are considered to be the most important (and thus valued) characteristics of being human.

So then, despite our evolved biology, there is nothing fixed and determined in the psyche, but rather we have a set of potentials that are open to be matured into some form according to the environmental contexts. Moreover, as we noted in the last chapter, rearing styles are not neutral on brain biology. If we look

---

[172] Keen, S. (1992), p.139

[173] Overing, J. (1989). This chapter is one of a number of chapters on the theme of peace. These authors make clear that peaceful living depends on both the ecologies of groups and the values they endorse. Following a feminist approach, Eisler, R. (1990) has classified groups into dominator and partnership. We shall note this in the next chapter.

back in time, across the centuries of European culture for example, it is sad how much of our own history has been shaped with the (mostly male) endorsement of ideals involving warrior values – seeking of fame, glory, being the best, beating opponents and not being 'effeminate'. It is also well to note that the more competitive the culture, both internally and externally, the greater the shift towards warrior values. Capitalism, as an ideal and theory, has never understood, nor come to terms with, the psychology that must be ignited if it is to work 'efficiently'. Capitalism is underpinned by these warrior values in subtle and sometimes not so subtle ways.

In our own current context of the West, if one's manhood is only recognised by one's fellows in the number of pints one can down, the women one can lay, the money one can make, the fights one does not walk away from, the eloquence of one's put-downs, the ruthlessness with which one seeks to achieve things, or the need to see the self (or one's group) as superior, then indeed we have allowed ourselves to become a trifle mad. Yet for some young men these are the only cultural stereotypes offered to them.

The Manipulation of Identity

Our identities are socially created, and of course very much shaped by those we look up to and whose approval we seek. Our need for approval and acceptance – particularly up-rank related – makes us very vulnerable to manipulation. We often seek to impress those who have superior power and status. The young man can feel pride and his status boosted when older men chose him for some favoured role or position. Therefore, we try to impress our parents, leaders, teachers, bosses, etc., those in positions to make decisions about our future. We may seek not only to gain their favour, feel close and chosen by them, but to gain similar positions and power as they have. Those more powerful can therefore use us for their own enhancement.

When Mike Tyson was imprisoned for rape, it turned out that he had shown serious emotional problems throughout his adolescence. However, according to a report by Rendall,[174] he was given clear messages that once he was champion of the world he could have any female he wanted. However, his rape and aggressions were not explained by the failures of his guardians, nor the expectations and values he had been given, but by his blackness, maleness, and early life experiences. Newspapers were replete with ideas that you can take the man out of the ghetto, but not the ghetto out of the man. In speaking of one of his managers, Rendall suggests that:

> The only thing Cus D'Amato wanted before he died was another world champion. Nothing was to stand in the way of that goal, least of all any problems at school that Tyson might have, in which D'Amato professed himself to be utterly disinterested.[175]

In case we think that we have now put space between ourselves and the fishermen of the Truk Islands, or the ideals of early psychologists like G. Stanley Hall (noted above), the treatment of Tyson should be a mirror to our own society. Interest in individuals is notably absent provided they can deliver and show themselves as able to get results. If, in their struggle for recognition, some behave badly, then either we turn a blind eye to it or blame and punish them (not the system), labelling them as bad or mad. Under this system of values, people become agents for others to manipulate, objects for the creation of material wealth and fame. They become preoccupied with showing that they can meet challenges and beat opponents, be this on the street, football field, stock market, workplace or even in acquiring sexual partners.[18] We are in a constant struggle to show ourselves worthy to be chosen. It is, of course, not only males who get caught up in this. When Virginia Bottomley took over as Health Secretary, and proceeded to continue with reforms of the NHS, newspapers saw in her actions none other than the motive to prove that she was as tough as her male colleagues, that she had 'the balls' for the job.

The attribute of beating opponents remains highly valued by capitalism.[176] The more ruthless and single-minded people are in pursuing their ambition, their

---

[174] Rendall, J. (1992)

[175] Rendall, J. (1992), p.4

[176] Keegan, W. (1993), p.4. See also Gay, P. (1995).

cause, or profits for shareholders, the more they may be valued. It shows itself in many ways and comes over as toughness, determination, 'having bottle', the 'right stuff', and more specifically, the ability to create profit (wealth). A major cultural script for males (and now any who wish to enter the marketplace) is showing that they are 'up to the job'. When this becomes the focus, capitalism abandons morality. The point is never whether we have toughness, resilience, courage and fortitude – it should go without saying these are useful talents. It all depends how they are used; what is the motivation and goals that drive them; how to use them wisely and keep them on moral track. If profit maximisation *is the only goal*, then these potentially admirable qualities become spades to our more destructive sides. Courage becomes recklessness, toughness becomes callousness, and resilience and fortitude become stubbornness. Often when governments talk about making tough decisions (and voters may like the idea of toughness, but not always the consequence) related to cost-cutting, what they really mean is callous decisions, because mostly those decisions will affect the poor and not the rich. Tough decisions would force those to pay who are best able to pay. The reasons they do not do that are well known.

Male Violence. A Problem in the Ranks?

If one has any doubts about the undercurrent of male competitive behaviour (and women can get pulled into this too of course), how it ripples just below the surface of our culture, and how often it involves male-male conflicts and sexual conquest, one only has to visit the local video shop. Shelf after shelf is filled with so-called 'tough guys' displaying their competency to beat opponents (and often with slinky women at their sides). There's always the setup whereby bad guys do nasty things that then sanctions the good guys to come in and engage in vengeful violence. But that's okay (we tell ourselves), because it's violence in the service of justified vengeance, and so we can take excitement from it. Many who work therapeutically with males note how these scripts become incorporated into gender identities. Such scripts exclude concern about *stereotypical feminine* attributes of self, such as fear, sadness, grief, acknowledgement of vulnerability, care and compassion.[177]

John Archer recently edited a large tome on the very serious problems of violence.[178] There are no simple reasons nor easy solutions, of course, but increasing recognition of the psychology and social contexts for violence is a necessary start if we are to reduce it. And there must be a political will to do so. Dobash and Dobash[179] analysed police records from Glasgow and Edinburgh of 3,000 cases of violence. Men were offenders in 91.4%. The victim was a woman in 39.5% and another man in 51.8% of cases. Daly and Wilson,[180] and others, who have looked into violence and murder and also bullying,[181] show that one motive is status, image and face-saving, proving oneself as strong and a 'force to be reckoned with'. Young males are far more likely to be both the victims and perpetrators of violence. This is not to demote the enormous violence against women and children in the home, of course. Although women are much less likely to use violence, they can still be extremely vindictive and down-putting in their verbal attacks on each other, and enjoy watching it.

Regardless of our evolved dispositions, there are many social factors that can increase violence. These include early backgrounds where violence (and abuse) is part of family life, poor frustration tolerance, social attitudes to proving the self, codes of honour, personality, polarised attitudes to males and females, poverty, the availability of guns and weapons, drugs and alcohol, social contexts that increase conflicts (e.g., at the boundaries of gang territories), having few conflict resolution skills or role models promoting anti-violent behaviour, feelings of hopelessness and alienation from the wider culture, joblessness, lack of moral role models, etc. Many, many factors. However, in a sense, when the

---

[177] Meth, R.L. and Pasick, R.S. (1990) explore the socialisation of the male psychology and the problems and ways of working with males in therapy. Many males whose problem is acting out (violence and aggression) do not come for therapy – and unlike people with depression, they may not see that there is much wrong with them. The power of denial is great indeed.

[178] Archer, J. (1994)

[179] As quoted in Archer, J. (1994, ed.), p.122.

[180] Daly, M. and Wilson, M. (1994)

[181] Ahmad, Y. and Smith, P.K. (1994)

poorer members of a society regress into primitive territorial gangs, they have accepted their subordinate position. Their violence is then less directed as a protest at the elite but to each other, as if they accept this is all they can do in their limited domains – for no other choices are open.

It is very clear that the inner areas of some American cities are far more violent than rural Britain. When a society is split into the haves, have-nots and have-lots, those who are seriously disadvantaged can collapse into more primitive and aggressive male-dominated and segregated social structures. The societal norms for good conduct (which may be derived from history and tradition) break down. A disadvantaged person may feel neither part of the society nor bound to it. They may even be contemptuous of society, its laws, and those who try to enforce them. In these contexts, violence is pronounced in young men at the margins of society. In some of these groups, drugs become the only means of gaining advantage. In commenting on the massive violence in a Colombian city, Medellin, Salazar says,

> Drug trafficking has become the major means of social and economic advancement, and the youth of the city consider it the only way to achieve wealth and status. In the hope of eventually breaking into the cartels, boys form contract killing gangs. Almost invariably they end up dead themselves.[182]

In addition, of course, these young juveniles can be persecuted by the police rather than helped, thus pushing them further into their criminal gangs. When we encounter them grabbing our bags and wallets on holidays, our fear, anger and contempt descend as a justifiable indignation and annoyance. Yet we don't ask or worry about the conditions of their life. Our anger and sense of threat can make us callous – it's how our minds automatically react, unless we choose to notice and reflect.

---

[182] Salazar, A. (1992), p.12

The Benefits of Rank as Privilege

The problems of masculine identity and warrior values can be played out on the streets of our inner cities or other 'wars'. Violence is but one tragic face of the need for recognition and status. Our identities are not freely given, for the need to prove oneself and fit social definitions stalks all the shadows of our social life. We send our children to school, against their protests of separation, to ensure that in this competitive and workaholic culture of ours they will obtain the skills necessary to prove themselves and find a place. Examination upon examination follows not only of intelligence and ability but also social competence. The losers are dumped in a meaningless world of unemployment and lost hope, contemptuous of the society that judged them as losers. The winners are privileged, and the social construction and automatic acceptance of this privilege is at the very centre of how human dominance hierarchies work. In non-human primates and other animals, the dominant maintains his/her position via displays. S/he does not have to fight over every resource for the rest come to accept his/her rank and are deferential and submissive – they know their place. This is adaptive because it greatly reduces fighting and being in a state of a constant free-for-all. Indeed, ranks could not be established at all without subordinates being prepared to inhibit their claims on resources – this is archetypal. James C Scott quotes from Horschild on the advantages of status in humans:

> To have high status is to have a stronger claim on rewards, including emotional rewards. It is also to have greater access to the means of enforcing claims. The deferential behaviour of servants and women— the encouraging smiles, the attentive listening, the appreciative laughter, the comments of affirmation, or concern—comes to seem normal, even built into the personality rather than inherent in the kinds of exchange that low-status people enter into.[183]

As Michael Chance[184] has noted, for non-human primates and humans, dominance and status hierarchies are not only hierarchies of deferential

---

[183] Scott, J.C. (1990), p.28
[184] Chance, M.R.A. (1984, 1988)

behaviour, but ones of attention and display. In many animals, the dominant receives more of a certain type of attention, as well as having more control over resources. But it is the control of attention that aids him/her, helping to keep his/her dominant position constantly in the minds of the others. Moreover, the manipulation of attention, especially attention to the self (or avoiding attracting shaming attention), is controlled by confidence – which is in part an internal judgement and in part a consequence of the rank position a person is in. As Scott says

> More of the public life of subordinates than of the dominant is devoted to "command" performances. The change in the posture, demeanour, and apparent activity of an office work force when the supervisor suddenly appears is an obvious case. The supervisor, though she too is constrained, can typically be more relaxed about her manner, less on guard, for it is the supervisor, after all who sets the tone of the encounter. Power means not having to act or, more accurately, the capacity to be more negligent and casual about any single performance. [185]

Status goes with increased freedom to act and the choice of one's actions. In capitalism, a degree of freedom can be purchased with success in the market place – or lottery. Nevertheless, in order to maintain the rank, and the privileges of it, a person must 'keep up appearances' and behave as expected of his/her position. Not to do so is to display the wrong signals, invalidate the performance, and thus bring one's status under threat. So, from time to time the rights and worthiness of having that rank must be demonstrated, not only to subordinates but to superiors. And one can demean oneself with actions not in accord with one's rank and socially sanctioned role.

Thus, rank is about control: control over resources and access to the goodies of society, and control over others. This control also allows the subordination of ideas, values, lifestyles and other people. *We can see then that such control also plays powerfully on the archetypal mind, bringing to the fore certain things and suppressing others – both in the self and in those with whom one relates.* Indeed,

---

[185] Scott, J.C. (1990), p.29

although class, caste, religious, racist and sexist structures can operate beyond the confines of individual choice, one is born into them, and with the increasing commercialisation of public life it becomes possible to win or buy access to privilege. Thus, students operate a cost-benefit analysis of which qualifications will give the best access to the labour market, higher status and better paid jobs. Beating opponents is via examinations and getting results for the organisation. Nobleness and hard work is not a virtue, it is self-interest. The concern is more "can one obtain the skills to make oneself into a saleable object and climb, via one's talents, up the rank?" If along the way there are the means to reduce the number of competitors for these roles and privileged positions – especially if competitors threaten to undermine the very system of values on which ranks are based – then there exists the silent and hidden hand of racism and sexism.

Status and Cultural Change

Thus, cultures can engage in a collective collusion in the creation of narcissistic heroes. The young are enticed with possible prestige and status by the older members to 'follow in their footsteps', and compare themselves not only with current, but also past, heroes. This is because the managers of the young control the status of the young (and thereby render it less threatening to them) by giving or withholding approval. In this way, older members can also feed off the success of the junior members. The general wins the battle because the young soldiers fight well for him; the business or sports manager gains because their workforce or team work well for him, etc. Thus, the old(er) and the young(er) cannot (usually) afford to alienate each other, but rather must collude in status-seeking pursuits. The young must follow in the footsteps of the old, although age cohorts and peers will gradually try to change the surface textures. If the young refuse to take part, there are all kinds of sanctions to get them back on track. Like our genes, values and traditions have a tendency to keep replicating themselves because the young tend to be dependent on the old(er) members for their status and prestige. Once a group or culture has developed a certain value system (be this for fighting ability, fearlessness, honour, body image or intellect), it changes slowly, no matter how destructive it is. In the next chapter on shame, I will give clear examples of this.

What is interesting about the rank archetypes is that for humans, with our highly developed social and cultural forms, those with status also become the controllers and bestowers of status. One tends to look up-rank not down-rank for approval. And obtaining status is organised in socially shared tests and standards (strength, fighting ability, body image, intellect). We must prove ourselves to others and agree to *conform* to being tested. One is clearly aware of what happens to others if they pass the test and what happens if they don't. Simple, individual efforts to gain rank (fighting with the ones above and below you) are not enough: at least, not outside violent groups. The problem is that if one has gained status/recognition via passing the tests set, then one is hardly going to change the nature of such tests and trials. To do so would be to invalidate one's own status and hard-won rank.

However, if we are to seek to bring new social discourses and styles of living, to shift to a more caring, compassionate and nurturing reality, then we must think how best to 'break ranks', and use our privileged positions to undermine the very system of values that gave us our privileges.

Superiority in Groups

Superiority of One's Group

It was implicit in the above discussion that gaining recognition and status is not only achieved via personal efforts but by group membership.[186] Groups, like individuals, rank themselves and defend their interests. Research has shown that one's feeling of belonging to a group also effects one's sense of personal identity

---

[186] Ahmad, Y. and Smith, P.K. (1994)

and status.[187] One can feel personal pride or shame from the successes or failures of one's group or team, feel it as a personal affront or attack if a member of one's group is threatened and so forth. Some commentators suggested that the good feeling generated in England when we won the football World Cup in 1966 helped to re-elect the Labour government. Remember the song by the rock group Queen – 'We are the Champions'?

Animals, like humans, will often work together to defend a territory. In predators, like hunting dogs, should a stranger wander into the territory, they can be attacked by many members of the defending group. Their distress calls in turn may bring the stranger's group to its defence, resulting in group threat displays and skirmishes. Chimpanzees have even been reported to engage in war-like behaviour and systematically wipe up out another group.[188] Group defence of a 'position' (a territory or set of privileges) is not purely human.

However, in humans such group behaviours, often fuelled by the ideals of charismatic leaders, are taken to new highs (or lows). Group-based conflict has been endemic to human history. It is unclear if this has always been so, or whether early humans lived relatively peacefully by groups avoiding each other or co-existited.[4] But once humans began to settle into territories and exerted control over those territories, some groups developed expansionist and paranoid tendencies. It was as if the reptilian in us got a face lift and made a comeback. The other group, over the hill, become potential enemies who could invade, capture and steal resources and take over the territory – unless one had become strong enough or big enough to defeat them. Like animals, human group-based conflicts can be about territories, claimed on the basis of historical precedent.

The biological reasons people combine in groups, and the socio-psychological factors impinging on them to excite ethnocentrism, discrimination, xenophobia and inter-group violence are, not surprisingly, complex. But certainly, defence of a group's own interests, and especially those of a ruling elite, is one of them. When individuals in groups seek to expand or defend their self-interests and control (be this for territory, economic resources, professional boundaries, or

---

[187] Abrams et al., (1990)
[188] Goodall, J. (1990)

exporting values – as in religion), there can be a collective change in the psychology of individual members. Van der Dennen has given a concise summary of these:

> Within the group members close ranks; there is an increase in group cohesiveness and solidarity; the own group is considered superior to the other group; each group becomes hierarchically organised; theirs is a greater willingness to accept centralised leadership; deviating opinions are barely tolerated; the group demands more loyalty and conformity from its members. Between groups negative stereotypes tend to develop; communication between groups decreases, preventing the correction of negative stereotypes; during intergroup negotiations, members pay more attention to points of disagreement than they do to agreement; distrust and hostility towards the other group rises, sometimes erupting in open aggression; tactics and strategy for winning are emphasised at the expense of concern about the merits of the problem negotiated.[189]

The most serious conflicts are, therefore, inter-group conflicts. Preparation for such conflicts, both to avoid them and to win them, has sucked off huge amounts of resources in the manufacture of weapons and the maintenance of armies. At one time, it was estimated that a third of all the world's research resources were directed to military purposes. Of course, all those who take it upon themselves to use aggression to reach goals are not without well-articulated self-justifications, be they religiously based, pitting class against class or ethnic group against ethnic group. Superiority, both moral, religious and racist, together with notions of threats posed by other groups, or simply desires for greatness, expansions of power and masculine ideals are all used to offer, what Gay[190] has called alibis for aggression in the cultivation of hatred.

Although wars are often with neighbouring groups, the same psychological processes can be seen to operate when groups within states are in conflict (e.g.,

---

[189] Van der Dennen, J.M.G. (1986), p.36
[190] Gay, P. (1995)

the miner's strike of 1984). As we shall see in our chapter on leadership, group leaders can do much to either amplify or quell these tendencies. Moreover, it is not a biological given that group conflicts will always escalate into violence, for if groups value peaceful co-existence and work to resolve rather than win conflicts, peaceful solutions are more likely.

Groups within Groups

Most modern nation states contain within them large numbers of subsidiary groups, following their own traditions, values and religions. If the cohesiveness which binds them together breaks down then civil war can break out. But in societies based on intra-group competition (and advantaging individual possessiveness), there comes into existence the same archetypal psychological forces that shape in-group/out-group differentiations. Once again, there can be a drive for superiority of one's own (sub)group. Pratto, Sindanius and their colleagues[191] have researched this motivation which they call *group social dominance orientation*: a desire to make and see the group one belongs to as superior to others. This is the psychology of the league (be it football, business or country). Groups often strive to be in the 'higher leagues', and so attract supporters in increasing numbers. But when the internal socio-political fabric of life is also wrapped in these desires, it can be most destructive. This is because there operates a need to define the sub-group and its boundaries. The boundaries that define and separate in-group from out-group or high- from low-status (sub)groups can therefore be various. They may be made on the basis of race,

---

[191] Pratto et al. (1994). In a subsequent study by Sidanius et al., (1994), exploring gender and individual differences in SDO, there was some support for a weak effect of gender, and for males to be marginally more SDO that females. But it was very small and it is unclear the degree to which such differences are innate, the result of socialisation or the result of the fact that males have more status in the work environment and, therefore, are more sensitive to losing jobs and privileges. Nevertheless, SDO tended to go with racist attitudes, negative feelings to ethnic minorities, people of colour seen as inferior, seeing civil disturbance as criminal rather than social protest, political conservatism, support for military spending, opposition to spending on the poor, and support of the death penalty. Such a combination of effects suggests that these attitudes are linked – to some underlying archetypal orientation, perhaps.

gender, age, profession, economics, locality, or religion. Since superiority is the aim, *group practices must discriminate to avoid a collapse into equality.*

Pratto and colleagues argue that:

> Ideologies that promote or maintain group inequality are the tools that legitimize discrimination. To work smoothly, these ideologies must be widely accepted within a society, appearing as self-apparent truths; hence we call them *hierarchy-legitimizing myths.* By contributing to consensual or normalized group-based inequality, legitimizing myths help to stabilize oppression. That is, they minimize conflict among groups by indicating how individuals and institutions should allocate things of positive or negative social value, such as jobs, gold, blankets, government appointments, prison terms, and disease. For example, the ideology of anti-black racism has been instantiated in personal acts of discrimination, but also in institutional discrimination against African-Americans by banks, public transit authorities, schools, churches, marriage laws, and the penal system. Social Darwinism and meritocracy are examples of other ideologies that imply that some people are not as "good" as others and therefore should be allocated less positive social values than others.[192]

Those who have lived through the recent Thatcherite era might take exception to Pratto and colleagues on one point: that elites often seek to minimise conflict. It was in the nature of the leadership of the Conservative government that they sought to maximise not minimise conflict. In every domain of life nothing was given, everything had to be won. In the NHS 'reforms', hospital was set against hospital, profession against profession, and even patient against patient. Thus, it became a government that presided over the most dramatic segregation and rank-divisive period of recent times. That the old philosophy of 'some are better than others' was present is in no doubt; this was not a time for the minimisation of conflicts. It was more that elite groups harnessed, created and used conflicts for their own ends – all, of course, under the banner of 'efficiency'.

---

[192] Pratto et al. (1994), p.741

When marginalised groups and people who have lost out, act badly or look at us with threat in their eyes, we see not the hurt of an injured, frustrated, subordinated self, but confirmation of our belief in the importance of maintaining our superiority – and that the threat from them is real. Having created the threat by the legitimisation of inequality, we now use threat to maintain ourselves. For example, one source of religious fundamentalism and terrorism springs from the minds of those who experience and feel that their group has been subordinated, deprived of recognition and access to resources, from a sense of social injustice. We know this perfectly well, but it is a measure of our craziness that we seek not to correct this injustice but to defend ourselves against their rage by increasing our power over them, by strengthening ourselves and depriving them more, hoping they will wither away. Rarely do we address the origins of their humiliation. The movement away from egalitarian efforts will produce enemies in the subordinated groups, while movement towards egalitarianism will produce enemies in those who wish to maintain their superiority and privilege. As was common in the nineteenth century[193], the privileged will have many justifications for calling into question the nature, wisdom and foundations of a compassionate psychology to the less fortunate.

Conclusion

We started by thinking about what our invention of human culture, especially since agriculture, has done with our sexual competitive strategies. It has given them quite a makeover! The human need for recognition can be plotted from the primitive reproductive strategies that set us up for various kinds of social display, through to the harnessing of these archetypal processes in group behaviour. We noted that this need for recognition will shape behaviour in different ways depending on a group's primary values, and these are often highly gendered. Recognition can be given for tranquil sociability as in the Piaroa, or aggressive, warrior-like competitiveness, as in the Shavante. In some ways this reflects different modes of living which Michael Chance called agonic and hedonic. But what is clear is that we cannot decontextualise the biological basis

---

[193] Gay, P. (1995)

of many of our emotions and values from the social domain. We are both biological animals whose primary, overriding desires are to fit in, be recognised, appreciated and seen as an agent of value. Underneath this, the basic reproductive strategies tick away. Exactly what this 'value' will be depends on the social reinforcement of our potential attributes.

Evolution, nature and culture have handed us quite a nightmare set of problems. Although we are potentially a very cooperative and altruistic species, this is often (but not by any means always, as the compassion chapter will show) kin- and family-bounded. Our brains were not really ready for the massive changes agriculture brought. Becoming a eusocial species with a division of labour that would be exploited by the wealth holders, and preparedness to go to war for our tribe, has been absolutely tragic for humanity; tribalism is a curse even though it will also give us a sense of belonging. Narcissistic fighting for control of resources within groups is a nightmare. The challenge is how to work with these processes. Tricky.

6: SHAME, PRIDE AND FREEDOM

If distress is the affect of suffering, shame is the affect of indignity, of defeat, of transgression and of alienation. Though terror speaks to life and death and distress makes of the world a vale of tears, yet shame strikes deepest into the heart of man. While terror and distress hurt, they are wounds inflicted from outside which penetrate the smooth surface of the ego; but shame is felt as an inner torment, a sickness of the soul. It does not matter whether the humiliated one has been shamed by derisive laughter or whether he mocks himself. In either event he feels himself naked, defeated, alienated, lacking in dignity or worth.[194]

It is generally agreed that shame is one of the most powerful, painful and potentially destructive experiences known to humans.[195] This chapter explores why this is so, the extraordinary lengths we will go to avoid it, and how destructive shame – and also pride - can be. It will be suggested that shame and pride relate to our sense of status, and in particular our *social attention holding potential* or SAHP (see Chapter 3), being intimately linked to our need for recognition. Indeed, shame and pride can be viewed as 'status regulators'. This chapter explores how shame and pride are both archetypal and yet socially created and related to social control. The latter part of the chapter considers the nature of personal freedom, given that shame avoidance is so powerful a motivation.

---

[194] Tomkins, S.S. (1963), p.118

[195] In recent years, there has been an explosion in research and theorising about shame. Key texts are Harper, J.M. and Hoopes, M.H. (1990), Lewis, H.B. (1987); Lewis, M. (1992); Kaufman, G. (1989), and Nathanson, D.L. (1994). For those who like psychoanalytic approaches, see Lansky, M.R. (1992), who articulates some of the complex psychologies of shame. Fossum, M.A. and Mason, M.J. (1986) explore family dynamics of shame and how to recover. Scheff, T.J. (1988) explores shame in relationship to approval and conformity.

The Experiences of Shame

The word shame comes from the Indo-European word '*skam*', meaning 'to hide'. The story of Adam and Eve is a story of shame. Knowledge brings self-awareness (and the need for fig leaves); transgression to authority can bring the punishment of exclusion and expulsion. In general shame, like embarrassment, pride, prestige, status and honour, are all experiences that are part archetypal and part socially constructed and contextualised. What is shaming in one culture may not be in another. But the potential for shame is universal. Shame is often considered a self-conscious emotion. A self-conscious emotion can recruit any of the primary emotions such as anxiety, fear or disgust, but fuse it with a sense of self. There is not one emotion for shame, it can take different textures. There can also be a sense of deflation that is common to shame, like heart sink or a feeling of dread which can suck the energy out of us. Shame is not just a self-conscious emotion, though, because it is also a socially conscious emotion and often depends on *social comparison*. A failure in the context of everyone succeeding can have different effects if you know others have failed. The most powerful experiences of shame often arise from feeling there is something that is both *different and inferior* to others.

We have seen that, from an evolutionary point of view, display and creating impressions on others (attracting, repelling, subduing, or preventing attacks) are the salient features of all social, sexually reproducing animals. Shame is the experience associated with a subordinated status; being seen as weak, worthless, bad and inferior, not up to the mark. Indeed, shame is sometimes known as the affect of inferiority.[196] Shame displays are often similar to subordinate and defeated animals with gaze aversion, curling the body to look smaller, reduced outputs and seeking to hide. Over millions of years, being subordinated and rejected seriously reduced reproductive success as well as increasing the threats and vulnerabilities associated with having been allocated a low rank. Subordinate animals that exist on the periphery are often easier prey. Because human ranks are so concerned with SAHP, gaining and losing respect have moved from violence to shaming, ridiculing and general putting-down. Shaming

---

[196] Kaufman, G. (1989)

and humiliating can be alternatives to physical violence. A person's status can be ruined by being shamed without a blow being struck. Whether or not violence is accepted as a tactic of gaining and defending status depends on the group. Violence might be accepted in a street gang but beating up opponents might lose SAHP in an academic conference, even if you felt like it!

The emotions and feelings of shame are varied and included feeling inferior, self-conscious, angry, confused, lost, defeated, inhibited and frightened.[197] Shame is not only an experience which taps directly into the competitive rank archetype (and our sense of inferiority), but also threatens a *loss of investing relationships* – of care, affiliation, cooperative alliances, sexual partners and friends. It is an experience that gives rise to feelings of separateness and loss of positive-relating, because it is associated with a loss of value and feelings of badness and not being wanted (a loss of SAHP). Personal shame can operate over different domains. For example, we might be ashamed of our behaviour such as stealing, or getting drunk and having a one-night stand. We might feel shame for things we struggle with, such as obesity. But we can also have a sense of shame for the things that clearly are not our fault, such as a birthmark or by a disease; some people can feel a sense of shame over their memory and intellectual loss, or loss of physical functions and appearance with cancer. This can be so intense that individuals may not even want their partners to see their bodies. Shame is very much about 'being seen'.

We might feel shame because, try as we might, we are intellectually inferior to classmates and hover at the bottom of the class. We might feel ashamed because we find ourselves in a stigmatised group, such as the untouchables caste in India. People who have been abused often carry a sense of shame that clearly was not their fault (although not uncommonly self-blame and self-dislike can be an issue), but they feel they have been contaminated or ruined, sometimes with a

---

[197] In some of our own research (Gilbert, P., Pehl, J. and Allan, S. 1994), we found shame was associated with a number of feelings, including heightened self-consciousness, inferiority, helplessness, anger at self and others. Nathanson, D.L. (1994) who follows the affect theory of Tomkins, suggests four types of response for dealing with shame, withdrawal-avoidance and attack self-attack others. My classification of defensive responses is taken from behavioural and evolution theory.

sense of body disgust for themselves. They may have unrealistic beliefs that they could have done something to stop it.

Groups can have reflected shame, such as families feeling shame due to the actions of their children, and in some cultures, many engage in extreme acts, such as 'honour killings' to heal shame. Groups can be ashamed of the action of members of their group, such as football hooligan violence, or even actions from the past, such as the Crusades. We recognise issues of shame when, in our international relations and attempts to solve conflicts, we talk in terms of 'face saving', which implies concern that each party to a conflict should not feel shamed or humiliated.

Shame is not defined by whether we feel we have caused our shame or not. It is very much a judgement, particularly of how we think we exist for others, whether we feel diminished in their eyes, and how we want to exist in our own minds. Shame is a self-conscious *and* social conscious emotion at the same time.

Developmental Origins

Because personal and collective shame are so linked, let's explore briefly the development of personal shame. There are now many ideas and theories about the origins of shame[198]. Some believe that the capacity for shame exists from birth and arises when there is a major interruption in pleasure or the capacity for pleasure. For example, the mother is in playful contact with the infant then turns away, creating an interruption of positive emotion and disappointment. Some think this 'deflation' and interruption in the child's positive feelings is the beginning of the sense of shame. Others highlight the facial expressions (disapproval or disgust) from the other as activating different emotions within

---

[198] See Harper, J.M. and Hoopes, M.H. (1990), Lewis, H.B. (1987); Lewis, M. (1992); Kaufman, G. (1989) Nathanson, D.L. (1994), Lansky, M.R. (1992), Fossum, M.A. and Mason, M.J. (1986) and Scheff, T.J. (1988)

the infant.[199] Other writers focus on shame as a purely social experience. It arises in the context of disappointment, put-down and ridicule where one's claims and efforts for status, value, worth and goodness are invalidated or ridiculed. Other writers like Michael Lewis suggest that shame can't really arise until the infant has some self-awareness, a sense of themselves as an object for the other.[200]

Evolution has equipped children to enter the world as social, interacting beings. Their entry is marked by enormous needs for relating, care, joyfully shared interactions and recognition. How they experience their caregivers will have a major effect on whether they move forward with confidence (taken from the many positive mirroring experiences encountered whilst growing up) or with a sense of shame: a sense of being flawed, not good enough and lacking value or worth. Research has shown that the way the caregiver and infant interact has a major effect on the infant's nervous system, emotions and sense of self.[201] When the non-verbal communication is attuned (baby smiles, mother smiles; baby gestures, mother gestures), the infant experiences positive emotions. Miss-attuned behaviours (e.g., baby smiles but mother presents a blank face) produces negative emotions. The reciprocal interactions between child and parent, as the child seeks recognition for his/her talent, abilities, lovability and general sense of goodness, are crucial for developing a non-shamed experience of self. Shame can arise from at least three types of social outcome: thwarted efforts to be recognised as good and able, pressure to conform, and direct attacks and puts-downs. If we stay with the concepts we've been developing, such as those for the importance of social attention holding power (SAHP), then we can say that *failed efforts to be recognised as good and able that act as thwarted social*

---

[199] Nathanson, D.L. (1994). This is a very insightful book and shows just how strongly shame and pride are linked. Personally, I am not so sure about the affect theory of Nathanson's approach, but clearly this has much to contribute. I am grateful to conversations with David Cooke for illuminating some aspects of this approach.

[200] Lewis, H.B. (1987); Lewis, M. (1992)

[201] Schore, A.N. (1994) not only gives a very in-depth review of the neurobiology of development, but also has a clear focus on shame and the way shame can inhibit maturation of the frontal cortex, on which later empathic abilities will depend. See Shreve, B.W. and Kunkel, M.A. (1991) 'Self-Psychology, Shame, and Adolescent Suicide: Theoretical and Practical' in *Journal of Counseling & Development*, March 1991.

attractiveness (SAHP), or being a source of attention with negative evaluation, underpins shame. This highlights again the social agency of shame. Consider the following scenario: Sue, a three-year-old, sits quietly doing one of her drawings. Then suddenly she jumps up, rushes to Mum and proudly holds up the drawing. Mum responds by kneeing down and saying, "Wow - that's wonderful. Did you do that? (Sue nods proudly). What a clever girl". Now in this encounter Sue not only experiences her mother as proud of her, she also has emotions *in herself about herself* – she feels good about herself (psychoanalysts would call that a good self-object experience). Sue gets positive mirroring. No shame here. But suppose that when Sue goes to Mum with her drawing Mum responds with, "Oh God, not another of those drawings! Look I'm busy right now. Can't you go off and play?" Clearly, the way Sue will experience both her mother, the interaction between them and the feelings in herself, about herself, will be quite different. In this case Sue is unlikely to have good feelings in herself and will have a sense of disappointment and probably shame. Her head goes down and she slinks away. Thus, the lack of recognition and dismissal of the self, when the self tries to display something attractive to others, can be shaming. Experiences like this happen in the most loving of homes and the child learns to cope, but if they are common and arise against a background of insecurity and low parental warmth, they can, over time, be quite damaging.

The failure of an excited and hopeful display can cut deeply into the child's (and adult's) internal experiences. A less painful experience perhaps, closer to embarrassment, is when, at a party, we think we have a really good joke. We tell it carefully, waiting for others to laugh with us and recognise our joke-telling ability. But instead the others groan and show clearly that they do not share our sense of humour – it falls completely flat and there is an awkward silence. Frustration of hoped-for admiration and approval can be embarrassing and shaming. We remember that awful sinking feeling when the end of term results came out and there, on the list for all to see, is your name, in last place, with an F by it. One can do all kinds of things to recover – deny the importance of it, or even try to create a positive identity with one's peers by one's cavalier not-caring attitude. As we shall note below, physical appearance and unattractiveness (being scared, spotty, burnt, losing one's hair, fat, or suffering from some physical deformity) can be experienced as intensely shaming. It is important to note, however, that embarrassment is different to shame in the sense that there is more humour around embarrassment and we are often happy to later talk humorously about our embarrassments. We don't think embarrassment marks us as bad or inferior, and it focuses on our behaviour rather than our global sense of self. Shame is not about humour, it is about that which we wish to conceal, and it is about a sense of self.

In regard to the social dynamics of shame, shame is partly an issue of balance. When shame-prone, we want others to neither be too distant nor too close. If we are too distant from people, if people look at us with disinterest, if we are not chosen because we're not good or attractive enough, if we are the kid that is always not chosen to be on the team, etc., that in itself is a source of isolating shame. Yet on the other hand, if people get too close to us and connect to us in-depth and with intimacy, we can be frightened of what they may discover about all those secrets we keep locked away; frightened they may see that we are not as emotionally regulated as we publicly portrayed ourselves to be; frightened that they will see we are not as confident as we pretended to be; frightened that when the make-up comes off they may not like what they see. How can we be close yet private? And so, we yo-yo between finding a middle ground that never quite works until we are honest with healing shame. It can help when we realise that we are basically a consciousness filled with all kinds of stuff because evolution put it there. We do not need to own it, nor claim it and see it as a mark of badness – just take responsibility for how it acts in the world. What is obvious is that as we become closer to others, we trust them. As we trust them, we reveal more of our personalities, and still being accepted we feel safe and loved. Love is not just for the nice things, it helps us to work with the darker sides that we all have. And if you think about it, it is clear that compassion is one of the most important de-shaming of processes.

Conforming: We can also try to avoid shame by going along with others, showing we are the right stuff – even if, in the quietness of our own being, we know our behaviour is immoral. An ex-solider in therapy told me that getting into fights was often more to do with avoiding the shame of not fighting than any real enjoyment or desire to fight. No one wanted to 'break ranks' and point this out. Conforming to cultural values to avoid shame operates powerfully: as we shall see below, when we discuss destructive practices that harm the body. Here again, even physical appearance can be influenced by group judgements. For example, to have facial scars gained SAHP in the duelling groups of young men (especially in Germany) in the eighteenth century. Whereas facial scars from say an illness or car accident, tends to reduce SAHP.

Direct attacks: We also know, of course, that children and adults are put down and shamed directly by being told they are stupid, bad, don't fit, are unwanted and physically attacked. Indeed, some people will deliberately use the threat of, and our aversion to, shame to control others. It is not just frustration of approval and admiration of a performance that shames, but direct attacks can shame. The most extreme forms are in places like boot-strap camps, aggressive fights to demand or gain respect (rank), and torture.

Culture and Shame

If we only focus on the family we will miss the wider cultural contexts in which the role of shaming does its harm. As we have noted in the last chapter, even if children come through childhood with a sense of self relatively intact, they still have to find their place in the outside world. It is then (at school and onwards) they will encounter further the narcissistic ideals (e.g., of manhood, womanhood) that their cultures live by. Thus, the culture, via the values and behaviours of those previously subjected to it, will start to mould the emerging adult to it. Be it communism or capitalism, or a particular religious belief system, among the key means of control used will be those of giving or withholding recognition, status (SAHP) and shaming. Some societies are known to be more shaming and less accepting of individuality than others. There is a cultural confinement of variation. For example, sexual confinements require people to follow exclusively heterosexual lifestyles and alternatives, so that bisexuality or homosexuality is shamed. Gender definitions are hemmed into narrow spaces by the cultural lack of acceptances of variations.

When I gave a presentation on shame at one academic institution, over lunch there were a number of comments that their institution had a highly shaming culture, maintained by some high-status males. Students gave presentations in some anxiety for fear of ridicule. Some of the academics seemed to thrive on point-scoring and shaming – not on open debate. An evolutionary view might be that those who go in for ridiculing others, especially publicly, are taking opportunities to demonstrate their 'fighting ability' and wish to create uncertainty and anxiety in the minds of others (especially subordinates). Consciously, of course, they would say they are interested in good science. Shame and scorn can be used to keep less orthodox (competing) theories and ideas out of the debating arena. Heresy in academia is a feared event.

Kaufman, in his classic book on shame, suggests:

> Three central cultural scripts in contemporary American society that continue to activate shame, and thereby mould the self, are *to compete for success, to be independent and self-sufficient,* and *to be popular and conform.*[202]

This leads to three basic shame-based fears: the fear of failure, the fear of needing others, and the fear of being different and not fitting in. Since achieving all three is near impossible, avoiding shame is impossible. If culture needs winners, it must also create losers. As Kaufman[203] notes, shame is a central, organising cultural fear, although it is hidden – *it is shameful to acknowledge our shame*. To feel shame is to acknowledge a failure. Thus, shame is the underside of all those tactics we saw in the last chapter – to gain recognition and acceptance. Indeed, it may not only be the desires for honour and prestige that drives the needs for acceptance and recognition, but also the avoidance of shame. Thus, these are as much fear-based pursuits as they are positive acclaims.

Group Shame

Shame is usually considered a personal or family experience but, in fact, given that various groups try to privilege themselves over other groups, then those

---

[202] Kaufman, G. (1989), p.46
[203] Kaufman, G. (1989)

groups (defined by ethnicity, religion or even gender) who are subordinated can become shamed as a group. Groups who feel marginalised, shamed and deprived by more dominant groups often foster resentment and desires for revenge. It has been noted by many writers that the origins of the Second World War lay in the reparations for the First. The shame and humiliation of Germany was so great that it was a seedbed waiting for a hero whose own narcissistic self would resonate with the group's narcissistic injury. Hitler's rise to power arose from his direct, anti-shame and pride-building approach to the German people. All his speeches where charismatic displays aimed at inspiring Germans with a grandiose sense of their own greatness and superiority. It is, therefore, not surprising that scapegoating and grandiose needs to win a superior position were part of his rise. Nor is it surprising that it was the working class, the most shamed and humiliated group, who would support him. Oppressors who come from the ranks of the oppressed can be filled with sadistic, vengeful fantasies.

In many societies, personal shame and family and group shame are linked. To shame oneself by a failure in (say) courage, sexual acts, or other actions that break the social taboos is to bring shame or disgrace to one's associates. Thus, the family or group (e.g., a political party) or even a country can be shamed by the actions of any of its member(s), and we speak of a damaged reputation that can be both personal and group-based. A family may feel shamed by their child's revelation of homosexuality or teenage pregnancy. In these contexts, the self is publicly shamed, rendered inferior or disgraced and often stigmatised. In some ethnic groups, there can be more concern not to shame the family or traditions as much as not to shame the self.

Stigma refers to the group's judgement of SAHP. Thus, to be stigmatised is to receive a judgement of unfavourable SAHP from others. In effect, the group is making social comparisons and defining which attributes gain and which lose SAHP. In groups, we often talk about shunning. As Goffman[204] points out, it is the avoidance of stigma (and being shunned) that often controls an identity and social roles. Goffman also notes that whole groups of people – such as ethnic minorities, the mentally ill, the obese and the disfigured – can be given labels of

---

[204] Goffman, E. (1968). A classic text on stigma.

stigma which influence the types and amounts of attention paid to them. These labels do not come from personal actions, but simply because one has been placed within a certain class of person. Hence, shame and stigma can be felt for other reasons apart from personal actions.

Even those who could not have had any part in the actions of another can feel shamed and stigmatised. A politician on television revealing what his country had done during the war said, "you know, I still feel a deep sense of shame about all that. It is something I can't get rid of, I suppose. It's just there, a reminder". (He was two years old when the war broke out). As Serney noted[205], children of parents found guilty of war crimes have also suffered much shame. In the modern climate, as men begin to see the damage of some patriarchal practices and identify with feminist agendas, even though they themselves may not see themselves as destructive or power-mad, they can have a sense of shame from being seen as male.

Gender and Shame

Work with my colleague, Steven Allan, has found that women score higher on various self-report measures of shame. Another colleague, Mia Gregory[206], has also noted that men and women are socialised to feel shame about different things (e.g., running away from a fight is more potentially shaming for men than women, whilst sex before marriage tends to be more shaming for women but can be a source of pride for men). Many situations, she suggests, used to measure shame, are loaded towards female scripts and this may account for females scoring higher on such scales. She is currently researching this and has some preliminary, supporting evidence.

In the previous chapter, we noted the sources of culturally constructed male shame as it arises in judgements of weakness, fearfulness, not having 'the bottle', being soft, and so forth. We noted how many of these attributes are projected onto women. Derived in part for patriarchal religions, stretching back

[205] Serney, G. (1990)
[206] Personal communication

to *Genesis* and Adam and Eve, men have often blamed women for igniting the wrath of the dominate male in the sky over the 'apple affair' (see Chapter 10), and so have wrapped female identity in highly shame-based definitions. As Gay notes,

> the Bible more than once paid wry tribute to woman, depraved woman. "All wickedness," as Ecclesiasticus has it, "is but little to the wickedness of a woman." Had she not prevailed in the Garden of Eden? Had she not brought about mankind's fall? The Church Fathers had taken up the refrain, inveighing against woman, the vessel of corruption, the source of sin, the sly submissive Eve.[207]

Not very nice, but what is going on here? What fear do such gender discourses hide? Well, it's our old friend sexual competition, the control and regulation of sexual behaviour of one gender by another, spruced up with a bit of social makeover. Shame is often about *social control*, so we have to think of the whys and wherefores of control. If we start to think why shaming, especially of sexuality, is so important, then we can see it as a form of coercion. But why?

A good outline of an evolutionary explanation is given by Wilson and Daly[208] in their aptly named chapter, 'The man who mistook his wife for a chattel'. Basically, men can treat women as *property* and recruit the psychology of entitlement, ownership and control. There are four central ideas about why this is:

> 1) Men (unlike women) cannot guarantee their mates' offspring are their own. Thus, they have to be careful not to invest in a female(s) and her offspring, which may actually be sired by someone else.

> 2) Human males do invest in their offspring – at least, more than many other primates – and females tend to select for (signals of) high- rather than low-investing males. So being cuckolded could be costly.

---

[207] Gay, P. (1995), p 293

[208] Wilson, M. and Daly, M. (1992). They offer a much fuller exploration that I can do here. Anyone interested in the Battle of the Sexes (as the battle of reproductive strategies) would do well to read it.

3) However, male reproductive interests can be served by cuckolding other males, or at least gaining 'control' over (or inseminating) more than one female.

4) Therefore, shaming female sexual behaviour allows some control over it by being openly solicitous.

There are other reasons why women tend to be shamed and excluded by males. Intense intra-male contests for access to females could be highly disruptive of in-group cohesion – and costly. At some level, men intuited that their own desires for breeding partners could set one against another (the Helen of Troy story). In an effort to contain such male intra-group aggressions, and their possible distracting qualities, women are often kept away from all-male groups. For example, until recently many sports teams were not allowed to take their wives on tour, men-only clubs were common, and women have never been allowed into units of fighting men. Also, shame of women can arise from efforts to control women, to stop them using their sexuality to form alliances and breeding with whomever they liked, and therefore reducing the risk of getting cuckolded. Yet another reason to shame female sexuality and thus control it might be to stop women exploring their own sexuality and, like the bonobo chimpanzees, finding same-sex pleasures rather engaging and giving men the push. For these and other reasons, solutions had to be found. One was the subordinating structure of marriage (and the harem), which in effect rendered women into property and domain over them given to men. They were domesticated and made safe. Indeed, although moral, compassionate, caring and 'love-based' psychologies would soften these proprietorial aspects, Wilson and Daly suggest that 'women as property' is a core mind-set of men:

> ... whose operation can be discerned from numerous phenomena which are culturally diverse in their details but monotonously alike in the abstract. These phenomena include socially recognised marriage, the concept of adultery as a property violation, the valuation of female chastity (and virginity), the equation of the protection of women with

protection from sexual contact, and the special potency of infidelity as a provocation for violence.[209] (brackets added)

Even in so called love songs, the issue of property and jealousy are often clear. In the Beatles song 'Run for your Life' (from their album *Rubber Soul*) are the immortal words, "I'd rather see you dead, little girl, than to be with another man". If you listen to songs, ideas of 'you belong to me; you are mine; I will never let you go', etc. speak to the issue of possession. What Wilson and Daly do not touch on is how this mind-set of the evolved mind became recruited into highly shaming scripts and identities. We should also mention the fact that it is, at times, in women's interests to stop other women from 'flaunting it' and attracting men (and their resources) away from them to give to other women. So, for both men and women (although for different reasons), obvious sexual advertising (and in the extreme, even enjoyment) needed to be constrained. And further, non-threatening roles (such as domesticity) found shame is another effective way of constraining women. As Ussher points out,

> Women are objectified, associated with danger and temptation, with impurity, with uncontrolled sexuality. They are at the same time to be worshipped and defiled, evoking horror and desire, temptation and repugnance, fear and fascination: The Madonna/whore dichotomy is evident throughout misogynistic discourse... Women are presented as labile, fickle, defective. They must be kept down, and kept outside the corridors of power. It is through the misogynistic practices that women are re-formed, reinvented, in a different guise: our bodies distorted, reshaped in a form pleasing to men; our minds controlled, ordered, altered; any threat of independent thought neutralized. Is it surprising that we were made mad?[210]

Unfortunately, misogyny may be too tricky an explanation here, and misses the real issues of the psychology of property (in men), and the reasons women sometimes collude with shaming other females, especially highly sexual ones. Because it is a psychology of property, women can be idealised yet also

---

[209] Wilson, M. and Daly, M. (1985), p. 291
[210] Ussher, J. (1991), p.21

controlled and shamed. The upshot is that female identity is one filled with potential shame: shame of sex; shame of sexual organs; shame of menstruation; shame of 'flaunting it'. Shame is an agent of social control, and the more an individual internalises it and believes it, the greater the control. To put this another way, to shame sexuality is to control and inhibit its free expression.

Some feminists may not have helped the fight against these male dominating strategies by arguing that men are misogynist. There is a problem with this word, because in addition to superiority beliefs misogyny also implies a distaste and hatred for women. To introduce the emotion of hatred when we're talking about the dynamic of power is to confuse process. This problem is about power. This is about objectification of people. Men can treat women like objects for their own satisfaction; it is a sort of master slave relationship. But masters do not hate their slaves: they may beat them and treat them as objects, or even kill them out of narcissistic rage, but they don't hate them. It is the slave who hates the master, so it is understanding how hate actually flows in the other direction. Hatred goes up-rank, rarely down-rank. In calling men misogynist, we risk creating a mis-attunement and causing confusion in men that would wish to align themselves with the feminist agenda. This is partly because of confusion over the definition of the word, and because men do not recognise feelings of hatred. It just doesn't ring true in the male psyche, therefore it's difficult to form an alliance. What does ring true in the male psyche (if somewhat ashamedly) is not hatred but callousness indifference in pursuit of objective narcissistic self-gratification. That is part of what misogyny can also imply. It's pretty bad, but it's not rooted in hatred (although obviously there will be individual cases). This is what is captured in religion, right from the beginning – Eve was created from Adam for Adam. It is this psychology that also allows us to rip the heart out of nature and treat any other lifeform the way we want: not because we hate, but because we feel entitled to callously use whatever we want no matter the damage. It's not (only) that some men think they are superior to women; they think they are superior *to everything* and *almost everyone* and will try to assert themselves over other men and enslave or treat them with callous indifference too. After all, it was the appalling callous conditions in the factories of the Industrial Revolution that impassioned Marx and Engels to call for revolution. The question is not hatred but the objectification for self-gratification which is a serious problem, not just regarding men with women, but in general.

But let's get back to shame. One way of overcoming shame is projection. As women woke up to the tricks of identity played on them (and their subjugation to male reproductive strategies), some became angry: an anger that was a kind of humiliated fury. Not surprisingly, some women have sought to turn the tables - to shame the shamers. Thus, some accounts of patriarchy are deeply shaming of men. The problem is, this produces serious conflicts, because although the messages of feminism are often about increasing care and compassion in the world, the experience of men is that they (as men) are hated and despised. It is very difficult to see love and compassion in the eyes of the other if at the same time they seem filled with vengeful hate and ridicule. Given the abuse women have suffered, it's understandable of course; hatred goes from the injured to the injuring, but it's problematic. Gender shaming (which males and females can do to each other: "all men are rapists, all women are tarts") gets in the way of mutual valuing. And hatreds operate in the spaces of these shaming and counter-shaming exchanges. Many feminists are well aware of this and recognise that simply projecting all badness onto men may feel good but is not in the end helpful.[211] To heal our awful splits and conflicts, feminism, and psychology in general, needs to reveal shaming narratives (and the reasons for them) not add to them. One way we can come together is to recognise evolution has made us all the way we are. We chose none of this, and if reincarnation is correct (one hopes it is not) then who knows, maybe I have been a woman many times and maybe my wife has been a man many times. But what we can all agree on though is we have a problem with *objectification of people for narcissistic self-gratification*. This has power to create serious harm in the world.

---

[211] hooks, b. (1984) This is a heartfelt and compassionate approach to feminism, that is not about shaming and finger-pointing but trying to move freedom and fairness in new directions. Ussher, J. (1991) has written a powerful critique of some radical feminist views (especially in the last third of her book). Although she does not talk in the language of shame, she does speak of elitism and contempt.

Shame and Humiliation: Private and Public

In understanding the cultural aspects of shame, it is useful to distinguish shame from humiliation. Their similarities and differences are outlined in table 6.1 below:

Table 6.1: Similarities between shame and humiliation

SHAME	HUMILIATION
HAVE IN COMMON	
Sensitivity to put down/injury	
Desire to protect self	
Increase in arousal	
Complex emotions	
Rumination	
ARE DIFFERENT IN	
Internal Attribution	External attribution
Self bad	Other bad
Inferiority	Not necessarily inferior
Acceptance	Unjust

Shame and humiliation both involve put-downs and rejections, increase arousal, activate complex emotions (e.g., anger-rage and fear) and lead to rumination on a damaged self or attacks on the self. In a way, their differences reflect different ways of coping with attacks on one's SAHP. Humiliation focuses more on what another is *trying* to do to us and ignites vigorous defence. We see them as the bad. The attack on our SAHP can be seen as unjust. If we feel we have the power (dominance) to enact this defence then we may do so, with attacks or counter put-downs. Humiliation is a source of narcissistic rage. In shame, however, there is the feeling that in truth there is something flawed, bad or worthless about oneself. One cannot defend oneself against the attacks on one's SAHP because one agrees with the negative judgement of the other. This does not mean, however, that when we are humiliated we will always act out our counter-attacks. One may be humiliated by others but not shamed (e.g., in torture you may be humiliated but may not feel shame, even though you are in no position to fight back). The reasons for not fighting back can be complex. A Buddhist monk told how he held onto his compassion for his torturers; another victim was determined that his spirit should not be broken. Neither experienced shame, but their resistance was internal. One may even deal with humiliation by taking a morally superior position, as when the crucified Jesus, appeals to God to, "forgive them for they know not what they do". It is unlikely that Jesus felt ashamed, even though he was severely humiliated. So, fear and subordination themselves do not necessarily result in shame. There is an old saying that goes something like, "the lord and master rides by on his horse and the peasant bows lowly and silently farts".

In James C. Scott's book, *Domination and the Arts of Resistance*[212] he makes clear (as did Goffman[213]) that there is a public and private face to acts of subordination. What is said and agreed in public may be very different in private. Compliance to authority, even public acts of (involuntary) subordination, do not suggest shame but social fear. I may be humiliated in public and fear it, but in my mind I remain good, and it is the other who has turned bad. In shame *I am privately and publicly bad*. I might feel shamed by my lack of courage to resist the public humiliation and defend myself, but not the focus (accusation) of the humiliation itself. Thus, humiliation and shame are different, although, of course, they often coexist and are not mutually exclusive. *What turns humiliation into shame is often self-blame, personal identification with the shamer and/or a sense of internal damage.* The key issue in shame is the internalisation of being bad, damaged, no good, etc.

To date, we are not entirely sure what determines whether judgements of externally delivered unfavourable SAHP are internalised or not. It may be we

---

[212] Scott, J.C. (1990)
[213] Goffman, E. (1968)

are more vulnerable to shame when we have no power to fight back, especially if it occurs in childhood, or in the context of a marriage that one cannot get away from. Clearly shame and self-blame tend to inhibit counter-attacks. Aggressive counter-attacks from a child or abused spouse could be costly. It may be to do with one's subordinate status. Steven Allan and I have recently found some evidence (in our current ongoing research) that anger to those seen as more dominant and powerful is inhibited, but rage is more likely to be expressed if the other is seen as subordinate.

Shame, Humiliation, Revenge

When a person (or group) is not paralysed with self-blame, one of the effects of humiliation is revenge. The capacity for revenge, to be motivated to get back at others who harm us, and to be known as capable of doing so, clearly has a long evolutionary history. It is to be motivated to have and express a credible counter-attack. Nonetheless, as Alice Miller[214] points out, many of our sadistic and revenge fantasies are first encountered in childhood. Broucek[215] notes a painful recognition of the film director Ingmar Bergman that makes clear their early origins. Bergman wrote:

> One of the strongest feelings I remember from my childhood is precisely of being humiliated; of being knocked about by words, acts and situations. Isn't it a fact that children are always feeling deeply humiliated in their relationships with grownups and each other? ... Our whole education is just one long humiliation, and it was even more so when I was a child. One of the wounds I've found hardest to bear in my adult life has been the fear of humiliation and the ease of being humiliated. Every time I read a review, for instance – whether laudatory or not – this feeling awakes...to humiliate and be humiliated, I think, is a crucial element in our whole social structure... When someone has been humiliated he's sure to try to figure out how the devil he can get

---

[214] Miller, A. (1983)
[215] Broucek, F.J. (1991)

his own back, humiliate someone else in turn, until, maybe the other feels so humiliated that he's broken, can't humiliate back again, or doesn't even bother to figure out how he can do it.[216]

Looking at the various differences in the socialisations of men and women, which we noted in Chapters 4 and 5, a case could be made for believing that males are socialised into the avoidance of shame via focusing on humiliation – to not internalise attacks on their honour but act out their aggression in defence of honour – while women are socialised to internalise their critics as a form of social (sexual) control, to inhibit their aggressive counter-attacks and thus accept a more submissive position.[217]

As Bergman indicates, the constant battle to avoid humiliation or force it on someone else is a source of much of our craziness. The moment we lose our compassion and respect for others, we can enter a world where humiliating each other is possible and even desired. All those whose pride is vengeful and contemptuous are likely to have experienced intense humiliation – often as children. If we allow so many arenas in which humiliation and shaming are accepted social currency, be it in the creation of poverty, at school or work, or in our ethnic and gender relations, there is not much hope for respectful, open relationships. If so many people have contempt for the social order and institutions of modern life, then maybe it is because they have felt so humiliated and excluded by them. Even if we forget our humiliation, our desire for revenge can tick away out of conscious awareness. It can texture some of our behaviours or even the enjoyment of our fantasies and entertainments. We can certainly note just how much of entertainment (particularly that which claims to be exciting) is currently focusing on males taking revenge on other males.

The problem with humiliated fury and revenge, of course, is that it can fester for years and be a source of bitterness, both for individuals and groups. In some societies, it can lead to blood feuds and generation after generation can be caught

---

[216] Broucek, F.J. (1991), p.72

[217] Lewis, M. (1992) notes that during growing up criticism of girls are often global and directed at the self, whilst for boys it is more focused on behaviour. This means that girls are more likely to self-blame in a global sense if things go wrong.

up in them. When leaders try to move the political on to reconciliation, as Nelson Mandala is doing in South Africa, there will be many who will feel resentful if robbed of their opportunities for revenge. This is why non-vengeful leaders, be they political or religious, are our most important assets, because many humans, in the ghettos of the world, have good reason to feel vengeful.

Shame, Humiliation and Rank

Although shame and humiliation are experiences associated with inferiority and badness, it has no clear relation to *socially constructed* ranks – if this were so, the lowest ranks in society would be the most vulnerable. On the contrary, higher ranks can also be vulnerable to it, for they have much to lose by a damaged presentation. Scott[218] gives an example from George Orwell's essay 'Shooting the Elephant'. As a sub-inspector in India in the 1920s, Orwell was called to shoot an elephant who had been in heat, broken its tether and killed a man. When they caught up with the elephant, it was grazing peacefully and no longer a threat. Even though Orwell is clearly in the dominant position his choice is not a free one:

> And suddenly I realised that I should have to shoot the elephant after all. The people expected it of me and I had got to do it; I could feel their two thousand wills pressing me forward, irresistibly. And it was at that moment, as I stood there with the rifle in my hands, that I first grasped the hollowness, the futility of the white man's domain in the East. Here was I, the white man with his gun, standing in front of the unarmed native crowd – seemingly the leading actor of the piece; but in reality I was only an absurd puppet pushed to and fro by the will of those ... faces behind. I perceived in this moment that when the white man turns tyrant it is his own freedom that he destroys. He becomes a sort of hollow posing dummy, the conventionalized figure of sahib. For it is the condition of his rule that he shall spend his life in trying to impress the "natives", and so in every crises he has to do what the "natives" expect

---

[218] Scott, J.C. (1990)

of him. He wears a mask and his face grows to fit it ... A sahib has got to act like a sahib; he has got to appear resolute to know his own mind and do definite things. To come all that way, rifle in hand, with two thousand people marching at my heels, and then to trail feebly away, having done nothing – no, that was impossible. The crowd would laugh at me. And my whole life, every white man's life in the East, was one long struggle not to be laughed at.[219]

He did shoot the elephant. Sadly, this was not done cleanly, and the poor creature took over half an hour to die causing great distress, but delight to those who had been threatened by the elephant. This, of course, is a source of our craziness: for how often do we find ourselves posing as hollow dummies, doing what is expected of us from fear of being laughed at? "A man has got to do what a man has got to do." How many young men in street gangs have acted out many harmful behaviours because his (gang) audience expected this of him? How often do we feel the need to carry out threats, or risk ourselves, or compromise our own values, to show we are of 'the right stuff'? Once one has placed oneself in a superior position, although this might be a privileged position, it is as well to know its limits, to know the point at which we become hollow dummies whose face has become distorted by the mask of acceptability.

Group *conformity* can rely on this – on our preparedness to make of ourselves hollow dummies, mouthing the party line. We want to be accepted into the bosom of defined groups – as good Christians, strong men, as scientists, communists, feminists, and other 'ists'. Those who bestow authority upon themselves, who take the privilege of defining what is and is not good group behaviour and values, know well how to use our fear of shame, ridicule and exclusion to bring about our conformity. And when not, we hear the cry, "traitor, betrayer - you are not really one of us".

---

[219] Scott, J.C. (1990), pp.10-11

The Body

Shame, Conformity and the Body

Shame is about being seen – and judged. We become aware that we (especially our bodies) are 'an object' to others, and our sense of ourselves can come from the judgements of others made of us as objects. The existentialist philosopher, Sartre wrote

> To see oneself blushing and to feel oneself sweating, etc., are inaccurate expressions which the shy person uses to describe his state; what he really means is that he is physically and constantly conscious of his body, not as it is for him but as it is for the Other. This constant uneasiness which the apprehension of my body's alienation as irredeemable can determine ... a pathological fear of blushing; these are nothing but a horrified metaphysical apprehension of the existence of my body for the Other. We often say that the shy man is embarrassed by his own body. Actually, this is incorrect; I cannot be embarrassed by my own body as I exist in it. It is my body as it is for the Other which embarrasses me.[220]

What both Adam and Eve, and Sartre, indicate is that shame is intimately linked to our bodies, how we are seen, observed and judged. We might call this body or physical appearance SAHP, and it is particularly linked to our sexuality. Humans are the only animals to have sex in private, and cover the body's sexual parts. The control of sexual self-presentation and actions is often via shame. We are not at all like bonobos in this regard, who have sex openly with anyone in the group, and use it to calm arousal and foster good relationships. It may be that the more men are able to control women's sexual behaviour, the more covered the body. In some Islamic societies, for example, female sexuality is often linked to the honour of males in the family, and this is an environment in which females are most covered up.

---

[220] Mollon, P. (1984), p.212

The role of the body in the construction and experience of ourselves has recently become a major focus in sociology. A good review of this work is in Chris Shilling's book, *The Body and Social Theory*[221]. As Shilling makes clear, ours is a time when the body is more under the spotlight than at any other. This may be partly because we know so much more about how our bodies work, and partly because we have so many ways of changing its shape and appearance, via dieting, steroids, hormones, plastic surgery, exercise, make-up, hair dyes and so forth. Fashion, and the desire to exert control over our looks, is about our desire for recognition and the avoidance of an unattractive self-presentation. The number of animals subjected to immense suffering to satisfy our vanities is horrendous.

The body is also the physical basis of gender distinction. In nearly all societies, past and present, ornamentation, decoration and adornments of the body have been noted. In some societies, facial markings, tattoos, scarrings and piercings are used to advertise things about the self. These can be used to accentuate gender differences. For example, during maturity boys and girls are socialised into taking different attitudes to their bodies via exercise and display – girls to make their bodies smaller or thinner, and boys to make them bigger and more muscular. Dress also tends to be gender specific. As we noted above from early societies onwards, there has often been something intrinsically shameful constructed in the female body, contaminating even, as in menstruation, while for men, the athletic body (and indeed the phallus) was one for adoration.

As we grow older, we have to accommodate our changing bodies and may respond with some alarm, or pleasure. The first is growing into sexual maturity, changing shape and getting 'more hairy'. The feelings from the sexual organs become a source of pleasure or shame, a source of social comparison and social labelling. We may think we own our own bodies, but in reality our experiences of our bodies are controlled by the attentions, judgements and social discourses we share with others. Our comfort or dis-ease with our bodies comes from others' treatment and regard of them, and how we are educated into the various meanings of bodily feelings and their varied performances. Moreover, we are

---

[221] Shilling, C. (1993)

aware of the stereotype of the 'good body' – the body of status and positive attentions – and may seek to shape ourselves to it.

The second is growing old. As one patient said to me, "I don't worry about aging and dying, but of aging and just looking old, becoming decrepit". It is through our bodies and faces that we advertise ourselves and display ourselves. And it is on such appearances that the most shame threats can be aimed.

Shame, the Body and Illness

Another area where shame and the body play a large part is in medicine. Lazare[222] notes that patients are often at high risk of experiencing shame and humiliation in the medical encounter. This is because they are presenting parts of themselves not normally shown to 'strangers', and because in illness these parts can be abnormal, in smell, shape and texture, or potential contagion. Some may actually avoid medical help (e.g., for bowel cancer) out of shame. Moreover, some illnesses are stigmatising (e.g., venereal disease), and as he says,

> As if humiliation of disease, treatment and dying were not enough, there are medical and lay terms assigned to various conditions that may be intrinsically shaming: hyper*tension,* heart *failure*, coronary *insufficiency*, *failed* back, *lazy* eye, Mongolian, *idiocy*, and *incompetent* cervix.[223]

As for mental illness, nearly all forms are felt to be stigmatising and speak to a failure in character or personal weakness. Many patients dread the word 'neurotic' being ascribed to their conditions, because it speaks (socially) of dismissal of their suffering (it is *only* neurotic, or *just* in the mind) and shame. Once we assume that their experiences are somehow inferior ones, speaking of illness, deficiency or internal failures (diseases), we are able to dismiss them and try to 'cure' them with drugs, therapy, and social constraints of choice. We wish to force them to become like us – for we are healthy and superior. Even

---

[222] Lazare, A. (1986) Every medic could gain insight from reading this paper.
[223] Lazare, A. (1986), p.1645

professionals dread themselves being found out as suffering from a mental illness.[224]

Lazare notes the role of 'doctor' is filled with potential shame, for they must be respected and wise. Indeed, a common complaint by doctors these days is that they are less respected than they used to be. The fear of being shamed from medical errors can haunt some doctors, especially in today's increasingly litigious approach. Moreover, the increasing industrialisation of medicine may simply reduce the time for sensitivities to patient feelings. In the process of dying, our insensitivities can be a problem. Even death can be seen as a medical and/or personal failure. Medics have assumed more and more control over our bodies and can now keep one alive even against one's stated wishes. The problem here is one of shame and dignity. As Lazare says,

> When patients discuss the importance of "dying with dignity" the indignities they refer to are the altered appearance (edema, emaciation, deformities, etc.), diminished awareness, incontinence, the need to be washed and fed, the need to ask or beg for medicine to relieve pain, the need to use a bed pan, and the perceived loss of meaningful social roles and social value.[225]

Although euthanasia is a complex problem, as medicine becomes more proficient in keeping bodies alive and assumes more control over them, it is a problem that will not go away. Many, including myself, might be alarmed to know that if one loses one's mental faculties, then a living will may not be worth the paper it is written on. While one recognises the potential abuse for euthanasia, there is also a hidden cruelty in its prevention. There is of course the old argument we wouldn't treat our pets like this. It is an area where we have become wise at helping disease, but not wise in helping death. Therefore, death

---

[224] Rippere, V. and Williams, R. (1985, eds.). Although in our macho Western societies having (had) a mental illness can be a mark of inferiority, in many other societies having come though it is seen a major contribution to becoming a good healer (see Ellenberger, H.F. (1970). Many regard Jung's insights and theories as coming from his own breakdown. A common motto is "nobody can walk the road with another they have not walked themselves". Still, I do not wish to idealise mental suffering, but de-shame it.
[225] Lazare, A. (1986), p.1645

continues to hold our self-aware minds in terror with that underlying sense of shame that maybe we won't be able to face it, maybe we will be rendered a panicking wreck - which we would prefer neither to experience nor others to see. This is not to undermine the wonderful work of the hospice movement, but the vast majority of people will never have access to such end-of-life care. Some of us think it's kind of crazy that the medical profession, the law profession and politicians can't get together to think about the most compassionate way(s) for our lives can encounter the inevitable. I was very sensitised to this when I took a holiday job as a porter on a psychogeriatric unit in the early 1970s.

Shame and the Destruction of the Body

Amongst the most tragic and powerful demonstrations of a culture's abilities to manipulate behaviour against the body via shame was Chinese foot-binding. If Mao was to be thanked for one thing then surely it was the outlawing of this practice. If there is any doubt that cultural shaming cannot drive us crazy, then I hope this example will dispel it. It is graphically depicted in Jung Chang's autobiography, *Wild Swans*[226]:

> My Grandmother's feet had been bound when she was two years old. Her mother, who herself had bound feet, first wound a piece of white cloth about twenty feet long round her feet bending all the toes except the big toe, inward and under the sole. Then she placed a large stone on top to crush the arch. My grandmother screamed in agony and begged her to stop. Her mother had to stick a cloth into her mouth to gag her. My grandmother passed out repeatedly from the pain.
>
> The process lasted several years. Even after her bones had been broken, the feet had to be bound day and night in thick cloth because the moment they were released they would try to recover. For years my grandmother lived in relentless, excruciating pain. When she pleaded with her mother to untie the bindings, her mother would weep and tell

---

[226] Chang, J. (1991)

her that unbound feet would ruin her entire life, and that she was doing it for her own future happiness.

In those days, when a woman was married, the first thing the bridegroom's family did was to examine her feet. Large feet, meaning normal feet, were considered to bring shame on the husband's household. The mother-in-law would lift the hem of the bride's long skirt, and if the feet were more than four inches long, she would throw down the skirt in a demonstrative gesture of contempt and stalk off, leaving the bride to the critical gaze of the wedding guests, who would stare at her feet and insultingly mutter their disdain. Sometimes the mother would take pity on her daughter and remove the binding cloth; but when the child grew up and had to endure the contempt of her husband's family and the disapproval of society, she would blame her mother for having been too weak.[227]

Chang suggests that the practice was actually started by a concubine of an Emperor many hundreds of years earlier. It is believed that the object of foot-binding was to make women seem fragile, weak and increase their dependency. That was originally supposed to signal sexual attractiveness *and high status (SAHP)*. Even in our society, the use of stiletto heels, which are known to damage not only floors but women's feet and increase the risk of falling and breaking ankles, are seen as fashionable and desirable. It is very unclear how far men find these attractive and how far this is a female-fuelled competitive strategy. More likely in the case of foot binding it renders females helpless and less able to take flight. Indeed, Mao didn't ban foot-binding for some compassionate reason but because women couldn't be fighters or work the fields.

In case we think that we in the West would not engage in this type of behaviour we should recall that during the eighteenth-century girls as young as three were put into corsets and bound tightly so that their ribs could not expand. It was designed to create the 18" waist. These corsets were often left on until they fell

---

[227] Chang, J. (1991), pp.31-32

off. The lungs could not grow properly, the ribs remained soft and easily broken causing considering pain, and the effect in childbirth was a higher risk of death.

Another complex example of shame and the mutilation of the body is via circumcision. In some societies, male circumcision is a ritual that is believed to give males an opportunity to prove themselves by undergoing the ordeal without screaming. This is not the case for female circumcision. Although the reasons for female mutilations are more complex than just those of shame, the fear of shame, being laughed at and rejected for not being mutilated is a key factor. The World Health Organisation estimated that around 90 million women have been subjected to circumcision, mostly in Africa. Children from seven days to fifteen years can be subjected to it. There are various forms, done without anaesthetic, from removal of the hood of the clitoris to far more invasive removals, and subsequent stitching closed of the vagina. Many are at risk of dying from loss of blood and infections, and none are without pain for the rest of their lives, not to mention the robbing of their sexual feelings. Again, although some have suggested that these practices are related to male sexual jealousy and control, it is also the case as Barkow[228] points out, that it is predominantly carried out by older women who use the practices to exert power over younger females. However, other evolutionary theorists would agree with the feminists that it derived from male-based reproductive strategies to control female sexuality.[10]

In a recent exploration that links these practices to shame and honour, Geraldine Brooks suggests

> In most Muslim countries women are the custodians of their male relatives' honour. If a woman commits adultery or a daughter has sex before marriage, or is even suspected of doing so, they dishonour their father, their brothers and sometimes the whole family that bears their name. To lessen or destroy sexual pleasure is to lessen temptation; a

---

[228] Barkow, J.H. (1989)

fallback in case the religious injunctions on veiling and seclusion fail to do the job.[229]

Such practices, it must be added, are not in the Koran, nor is the idea that women's pleasure should be lessened. Indeed, husbands had a duty to ensure it. Tragically, related to the issue of honour-shame and genital mutilation is also honour killings. Here, a husband or father can take it upon himself to murder his daughter or wife if, by having sex outside proscribed relationships, they bring shame on the family name.[230] In the West, we may not kill the daughter if she becomes pregnant, but many have been thrown out on the streets or their lives made miseries.

Circumcision is also fuelled by (highly erroneous) beliefs about normal physiology.[231] Indeed, there are many cultural practices that are highly

---

[229] Brooks, G. (1995), p.15. This is taken from an extract published by the Guardian. At the time of writing the book is not yet published, but it's called *Nine Parts of Desire* and will be published by Hamilton later this year.

[230] Ussher, J. (1991). This is, for the most part, a deeply moving and scholarly book. But it gives the impression of a change in understanding as it was written. Given what Ussher says later in her book, I was surprised that she accepted misogyny explanations so easily. Some feminists see these practices as deriving from misogyny. But there are reasons to be troubled by this explanation. It may not be hatred that powers these practices, but the drive for status, superiority, control and fear. It is fear, exploitation and the need to control that give life to social values and practices. Hatred comes from transgression of those values – to those who will not obey. Indeed, it is because women have been made *objects of desire not hatred* that the terrors of attempts to control what is desired is so powerful. Group hatred leads to things like ethnic cleansing, not such practices based on the control of that which is desired. Thus, misogyny (hatred) is a secondary effect. As another example, Western forms of slavery did not arise from hatred or from enslaving defeated peoples in war, but from exploitation, ownership and profit. Slavery did not begin with hatred but greed. Hatred comes when those so subordinated rebel or refuse the inferior positions they have been put into. See Wilson, M. and Daly, M. (1992) for other explanations to do with the psychology of property – not hatred. Hatred is a consequence not a cause.

[231] In some societies, it is believed that the female sexual organs will grow and "hang to the ground" if not removed. My own circumcision had nothing to do with shame or hatred but more my parents' beliefs about later health problems (we were living in Africa at the time) if I weren't. I read somewhere that there was now a society advocating treatment to help men to get their foreskins back! I wonder whether Freud's castration anxiety had anything to do with these practices and not some innate fear he proposed.

destructive due to ignorance. For example, as Barkow[232] notes, the value of colostrum obtained in the first days of suckling after birth was known since the 1920s. It provides many important nutrients and aids the child's immune system. However, some societies have come to see it as unhelpful, and can refrain from breastfeeding for up to a week, thus putting the child at considerable risk. They have various beliefs that it is bad for the child or will contaminate the child – thus robbing the child of one of the most important sources of early food.

Clearly, change is essential and a matter of education and support, with great caution to avoid shaming. Men could do much more to support women against these tragic and horrendous human practices. It is easy to see why women are enraged by such practices. One of the reasons people are unwilling to tackle the problem, as Brooks[233] notes, is that in bringing it to light it gives opportunities for outsiders to look in and shame or ridicule a community, and render them as no more than barbaric. Kaufman[3] has noted it is *shameful to acknowledge our shame* for in effect we are acknowledging our badness – so we keep it hidden. Our collusion in silence is one reason we do not challenge values and rebel (see Chapter 8). As Brookes notes, a nation trying to lift itself from so much external shaming and humiliation is thus highly ambivalent about tackling the problem. Indeed, as for all of us, the last thing we want when we are trying to regain our dignity is for someone to point out our potential shame.

These examples should leave us in no doubt whatsoever that shame and honour *at a cultural level* can be terrifying and extraordinarily destructive. Moreover, these are, quite obviously, not genetically determined behaviours, but (perhaps) rather gross and tragic amplifications of certain reproductive sexual competitive strategies which depend on group values. It is extremely unlikely that (say) a woman with bound feet or a woman who has been circumcised would be found attractive by a man from a Western society – indeed it would probably be the reverse. So, both men and women have to be socialised into finding these attractive or desirable qualities. We should remind ourselves that, as discussed in the last chapter, once a system of values (for gaining or losing SAHP) gets

---

[232] Barkow, J.H. (1989)
[233] Brooks, G. (1995)

going it can be very difficult to change it. Some kind of 'face-saving' is nearly always necessary to allow those who have to change their values and practices, to change them without feeling shamed and marginalised. They may also need to be given new (SAHP-confirming) roles and learn to value different attributes and qualities.

Intense, personal shame can also be the source of complete self-destruction. Most of us will know of a person, perhaps someone famous, who has been driven to kill themselves from being shamed. There are many whose self-destructive acts are derived from the pain of living with a sense of shame, inferiority and failure. In some societies, ritual suicide (as in Japan) is a way to salvage some honour (for self, family and group) from a shamed identity. We can be shamed to death.

Shame and Abuse

There is increasing evidence that sexual abuse greatly increases vulnerability to shame (low SAHP) and psychopathology. Bernice Andrews[234] has reviewed some of this literature and recently explored the role 'shame of one's body' plays in depression. She developed an interview to tap and explore body shame and history of abuse in women. Sexually abused women had high body shame and depression. Abuse seems to destroy the capacity to take pleasure in one's body; one's sexuality is not something to be enjoyed or advertised (or gain SAHP from), but something that can bring the unwanted attentions of a dominant. It would be adaptive therefore to take a negative attitude to one's body and sexuality to reduce the risk of eliciting the unwanted attentions of a dominant. *In both rape and abuse, one has lost control over one's reproductive strategies.* Sexuality becomes frightening and associated with trauma, not something to take pleasure from. To anticipate sex as pleasurable, one must anticipate the reaction and behaviour of the other and the control one will have during the

---

[234] Andrews, B. (1995)

encounter. Clearly, for an abused person neither personal control nor positive reactions can be anticipated.

A patient who had been abused and hated her sexuality explained it this way to me. Although her experience of her abuse was of humiliation, and she blamed her father not herself, the consequence was to leave her feeling contaminated and rendered her feeling inferior and tainted: the soiled and spoiled experience. This is sometimes felt as having some of 'the good self' stolen from one. "I can now," she said, "never be like others. I have lost my self-respect. I don't belong to myself. My body is not *my* body. He took all that away."

Abuse is the extreme experience of being made an object: a subordinate without power. To be unable to resist the attentions of a dominant is to be completely defeated in a struggle for control. In evolutionary theory, control over one's own reproductive behaviour is a central form of control. People who have been physically and sexually abused are vulnerable to strong shame experiences, in part, because they learn they have no power to stop others from violating and intruding into and onto them. This sense of intrusion into the self is often experienced as deep shame-proneness. The self loses its sense of personal boundaries and is merely an object, a thing, for others to use. To have become an object is to have completely lost one's claim on dignity (claim on SAHP). The more the person feels bound to a drama of violation that is culturally shunned, and the more they feel they may have been in some way responsible, the greater the potential for shame.

Paradoxically, the idea that one has been damaged, ruined or rendered inferior by the unwanted sexual intrusions of a male(s) is actually a male strategy for controlling women – for it is men who see such outcomes (rape and abuse) as rendering women into 'inferior goods'.[10] Thus, although self-blame in a causal sense is not necessary for shame (as in the example given above of the politician shamed by the war crimes of his parents), it is a common mark of shame that the person feels there is something wrong or bad about them – and this involves an internalisation of social judgements. It may also seem paradoxical that the more a woman is injured in a rape, the more others (e.g., a husband) may feel sympathy and be less shaming. To be injured is to prove one has struggled.[235]

So, abuse damages us in various ways. These include, first, that it focuses us on the limits of our power and ability to defend ourselves – we are subordinated and defeated; second, it is a highly traumatic experience, often involving intense fear and being trapped (one can't get away from the abuser); third, it destroys trust and security; fourth, we may be forced (threatened) to keep the abuse secret or even blame ourselves for it; and fifth, by having been abused we lose SAHP – we become inferior 'goods'. These experiences and their various combinations will increase susceptibility to a depressed, subordinated self. There is also increasing evidence that a history of abuse has a major effect on the psychobiological maturation of the brain.

There is much that we could say on the development of shame due to sexual and physical abuse, emotional coldness, rejection and controlling, critical parenting. All these can do much to damage a person's sense of self and belief that they are basically good (have favourable SAHP). It tends to close down the development of altruistic strategies (of seeking pleasurable, affiliative relationships – suitable for the hedonic mode, see Chapter 4) and orientate us instead to a highly defensive self-focused set of strategies to either dominate others or to avoid being dominated (e.g., via social avoidance of various kinds – that is to live in the agonic mode). It is the rule rather than the exception that in the pathologies of both depression and aggression the backgrounds of patients often involve shame, rejection, emotional coldness, and/or abuse. More often than not, our clinics are full of people whose craziness has been created for them.

Avoiding and Facing Shame

So far, this chapter has explored various sources of shame. A key concern has been to focus on the social and external aspects of shame, and how shame (the gains and losses of SAHP) can shape so much of our behaviour. We can now give some thought to the many tactics and strategies people use to enhance or

---

[235] Wilson, M. and Daly, M. (1992)

protect their status and SAHP – to avoid shame. In regard to the behaviours used to avoid or overcome shame, the whole range of defensive responses noted in Chapter 2 are open to us. We may become angry or anxious, feel inhibited and acutely self-conscious, conceal ourselves, or (wish to) run away and hide[236]. If we can anticipate shame as a future possibility, we may avoid situations where it might occur or we can become deceptive. If shame threatens, we can feel the automatic emotional arousal of the defence system. It is often outside conscious control.

Nathanson[237] suggests four strategies for dealing with shame: attack self, attack other(s), withdraw, and avoid. Commonly, we often *make good our preparations to avoid shame as a possibility*. Indeed, the preparations we take to avoid shame (including deception and concealment) can be numerous, and although many of our social efforts are aimed at recognition and acceptance, they are equally about avoiding shame. In my view, there are a range of strategies to deal with shame. Each can be used individually or collectively.

1. *Compensation* involves efforts to make up for or prove that the self (or group) is good and able, and to avoid at all costs being located in an inferior position. This can involve vigorous competition. As we will note below, pride can be a typical form of compensation for (potential) shame.

2. *Concealment* occurs when individuals or groups hide or avoid that which is potentially shameful. For example, a person may find it difficult to show off, initiate things, or get close to others. In therapy, they may find it very hard to reveal the sources of their suffering, such as an abuse. Body shame (including shame of disease) may lead to various forms of body concealment. Other people are always seen as potential shamers, who should not be allowed to peer too closely into the person. In groups there can be a collective agreement 'to remain silent' on certain things or avoid exposure. The group may have secrets that they do not want revealed. When we look shortly at how groups avoid too close an inspection of destructive practices, we will note this as concealment.

---

[236] Gilbert, P., Pehl, J. and Allan, S. 1994
[237] Nathanson, D.L. (1994)

3. *Distractions* are used to keep things out of mind. For example, at a point of potential shame, individuals may change the subject or even be humorous as a diversion. If shame thoughts come to mind, the person immediately distracts themselves and tries to avoid thinking about the issues.

4. *Projection* involves seeing in the minds of others what is in our own mind. In the case of shame, it is believing that others see us as inferior/bad if that's our own personal view. We believe others judge us as we judge ourselves. It is defensive to the extent that doing so gives us an opportunity to take defensive actions, such as concealment or compensation. People can react very badly to criticism which was designed to be helpful because of projection, assuming that it's a putdown, rather than a genuine attempt to be supportive, and that the other sees us as inferior or flawed. When we use projection, it can make us very touchy, even when people are not thinking negatively about us or are trying to be helpful. Sometimes patients are not aware of unconscious fears of their own inferiority or flawedness. This is why in supervision, particularly with young therapists, one has to be very careful in offering them corrective feedback.

5. *Projection identification* involves seeing the other as the weak, inferior shameful - not the self. Shaming homosexual desire, for example, is a way of avoiding such feelings in oneself (which are feared) – seeing the weaknesses you feel in yourself only in others who may then be attacked is projective identification. As we noted in the last chapter, men can project onto women their feelings of vulnerability and weakness, and then ridicule them for it. Shaming humour can be used by an individual, or groups to shame other groups. We project those aspects that we see as inferior in ourselves. Racist and sexist jokes can be like this.

6. *Violence/attack*: 'If you shame me, I will hit/hurt you', and if not in regards to direct violence, then to be seen to have a credible counter-attack; this may be retaliatory shaming/humiliating, withdrawal of resources, etc. Subordinates (usually) cannot afford to openly shame dominants for dominants can counter-attack – which might be costly. As we noted in the last chapter, violence, especially between men, often arises as a shame-avoidant (status-reducing) strategy – face-saving.

7. *Direct engagement* involves acknowledgement of one's personal shame or that of the group: facing it and working through it. Digby Tantum,[238] a professor of psychotherapy at Warwick University, notes that in many cases recovery from shame is more likely if people explore its boundaries. In group psychotherapy, the group might take a movement forward when one or more members owns their feelings of shame and shares them with others. Groups can become stuck if all members remain defensive and shame avoidant and are unprepared to take risks. Thus, confronting and healing shame, rather than avoiding or compensating for it, may be a source of personal growth.

Loneliness and Shame

At the heart of shame is desperate loneliness, because shame is an isolating experience. It is the experience that tells us we are disconnected, the unwanted, the undesired. Individuals who are concealers and have secrets, and believe they would be rejected if their secrets were discovered, may never really feel connected; there is always that worry that if people get too close to them they will discover things about them they don't like. Shame is the experience of wanting the ground to open up and disappear so as to be removed from the sight of others. This is what makes it such a painful and difficult experience to work with therapeutically – we desperately want to hide. Unhealed though, shame can be responsible for a lot of destructive behaviour, especially if it gets turned into humiliation, need for face-saving, and retaliation against the shamer.

---

[238] Personal communication

Pride

Social and Personal Pride

Many writers note that we can experience pleasure from our own personal achievements.[5] Even very young children seem to experience pleasure from achieving things, e.g. building a castle of blocks, etc. I felt very pleased with myself when I managed to grow my own vegetables one year. Pleasure from accomplishment is often talked of as 'pride in oneself' without regard to a social audience. I shall not focus too much on this form of pride, and in any case it is more complex than is sometimes thought. For example, we can accomplish things with expert skill but take little pleasure from doing so. Personal pride is not related purely to accomplishments, but to personal, moral values of what we decide has worth, and what we have put effort into.

My concern here is mainly with *social pride, the pride we experience when we think we have achieved something that boosts our SAHP and prestige.* It is true, of course, that personal pride (in accomplishments) and social pride (SAHP) often overlap, but my concern is to highlight the social aspects of pride, especially its potential destructive effects. There are many aspects to social pride. It can relate to material possessions (e.g., pride in our new car) and we can show these off to others; it can relate to personal attributes (e.g., our good looks, a new hairdo) and to talents (e.g., at tennis or solving an academic puzzle). What all these have in common is that they are prestige boosters, and as such are obviously related to one's social group bestowing SAHP. This type of pride is concerned with recognition and status. The two responses (from others) that can destroy social pride are contempt and envious attack.

Pride, Shame and the Values of the Elite

Social pride is seen most clearly when we make favourable social comparisons. We do things that suggest we have gained favourable SAHP. More often than not, this involves copying the values and behaviour of an elite (those who already have SAHP). The elite (be they in science, the military, work, religion, etc.) do not always force others to join them and adopt their values (although they can do – as in religious and political persecutions), but rather hold themselves up as an ideal, a superior type of group with superior values – *something to aspire to*. Social pride increases as we come closer to such ideals. Usually, the elite will have some control over key resources (e.g., wealth) or occupy high-rank positions. The more others are excluded, the more selective and distinguished their group may appear to be, and the greater the hold they exert on social and personal values. The same principles hold for the golf club as the political party. To join and be accepted is to make one a 'special kind of person' - to raise one's SAHP. The problem is that if elite's values are destructive, then social groups can actually try to mimic destructive and divisive behaviour.

Shame and Self-Destructive Pride

Pride, I believe, like honour, is a two-edged sword. Getting recognition from one's fellows gives a certain buzz; we feel good, uplifted. I like good reviews – who doesn't. And like others, I tend to down rate those who give bad ones – to protect my pride. But pride is dependent on social recognition and therefore on conformity to group values. If any of these values, such as the masculine ideals we saw in the last chapter, are crazy then we are in deep trouble, because we can only gain pride by obeying the rules for gaining recognition – and of course, social approval can collapse at a moment's notice.[239] The Dalai Lama[240] made the interesting observation that pride was always potentially destructive. Social pride depends on displays and proofs, and this should be contrasted with self-confidence, which he argued was preferable to social pride. Confidence does not depend on so fragile a thing as approval. When we feel internally confident, we can tolerate failure, uncertainty and differences between ourselves, but these can threaten those whose pride is SAHP-focused.

---

[239] Scheff, T.J. (1988) gives a very good account of how we are all so dependent on social approval – often without realising it until it suddenly isn't there.

[240] Dalai Lama (1993). Taken from his tapes of lectures given at Wembley in 1993.

In a society like ours that bases status and prestige on achievement, pride and status-seeking based on such values can become a problem. Indeed, in science, for example, whole careers can be ruined if an institution loses status and thus research monies. This invites fraud and deception. The need to gain prestige, to be the first, etc., clearly means that some will not always follow the rules. Obviously, cheating and deception in science or in business is of course problematic, particularly if people are falsifying information to promote their own prestige. There is a similar situation in sport, which can be plagued by drug cheating by participants to advance their status.

In fact, there are many examples where social pride is terribly destructive. When the *Guardian* newspaper[241] recently interviewed some young males who had been involved in football violence, they all spontaneously said it was a matter of pride. They were proud to be English – and, of course, were contemptuous of foreigners. For them their violence was a virtue, but one that was very much aimed at gaining status in their groups (e.g., who could be more fearless). When xenophobia and inter-group aggression become virtues, the more one harms the other, the more one's fellows may increase one's SAHP and the greater one's pride. During the war, pilots would paint the number of 'kills' on their aircraft; the more kills, the more SAHP.

In all the examples given in this and the previous chapter, be it seeking ones gender identity, needing recognition, feeling wanted or body mutilations, we see how incredibly dependent we are on social contexts and social relationships – on patterns of and the discourses for connectedness, and the fear of disconnectedness. Another issue is the degree to which, without realising it, we can voluntarily adopt self-destructive, crazy values and behaviours. However, it is sometimes thought that if people volunteer to subject themselves to certain ordeals then this is acceptable. To some extent, we can see that because it is children who are involved in foot-binding and genital mutilation then they were, at the time of the injury, quite involuntary victims. But a belief in voluntariness can be overplayed. How free were the parents to not perform these practices? Boxers, for example, often come from the poorer sections of society. Because

---

[241] *The Guardian*, 17 February 1995, p.2

they appear to choose this route to fame and proving their manhood, we allow it to continue, despite the clear evidence of potential brain damage. And what should we think of those whose shame is turned into self-destructive pride? Here personal and social pride have become very inter-linked.

The abuse of steroids is well known to cause long term damage to liver, kidneys, bones and the immune system, yet people risk it to build bodies and competitive performance and present themselves in certain ways; no one forces them into it. Even when knowing the risks that they are taking, some say that the buzz of success and the feelings of pride from winning are such that it is worth it. A patient explained to me how his muscular body was the most important source of his self-esteem. It gave him his confidence with women and with other men. He felt it inconceivable to feel confident with a body like mine (and I didn't think mine was so bad). The whole tone of his emotional life was shaped by his personal and (guessed at) image to others of his body.

Excessive drinking when used to impress others is similar. A patient's drinking started at university, when he began to enjoy the prestige of having the reputation of being the best drinker in the team. If he'd had a bad day on the field, he would drink more. His friends cheered him on as he burnt out more brain cells and crippled his liver. Yard-of-ales, you name it, he did it. Others turn to drink because their inner shame makes it difficult for them to relate and feel comfortable – and in time, some will become biologically dependent, compounding their shame.

There are a host of pathologies where shame (or the fear of shame and humiliation) has turned to pride. The most notable of these is anorexia. Although they can have some ambivalence about their thinness (e.g., by wearing baggy clothes), people suffering from anorexia are proud to be thin. One of my patients said it was the only thing she was good at: what else, she said, was there for her to achieve? The feelings of emptiness/hunger were a source of personal pride and conquest. Getting on the scales and seeing that she had lost weight gave her a buzz of pride and sense of achievement. The social aspects of this pride is that anorexic women can be highly competitive with other women, and take many of their images from the media. Although the psychology of this sad disorder is quite complex and involves rage, fear and a very lost and frightened sense of self, it can be their competitive social pride that makes it so difficult to shift. The therapist may be trying to remove the only good thing they feel about themselves. The question is, at what level in the social scheme of things is it decided that certain body shapes are worth esteeming? Why are so many models *so* thin? Why would social cultures create that kind of competition and how is that related to sexual competition? Why the fascination with almost pre-puberty body shapes? The unconscious is tricky.

Some forms of perfectionism involve the problem of shame turned to pride. Perfectionists can make their own and other peoples' lives a misery. I struggled a long time with a patient who was highly autocratic and perfectionist, but it was difficult for him to change his values. He felt that if only the world was like him then all his problems would be over. His perfectionistic autocracy gave him a sense of superiority. His difficulty was that when he could not match his perfectionistic ideals, that others might see his mistakes, or others did not acknowledge his talents, he become extremely angry with himself and others and depressed. But instead of seeing how he was setting himself up for disappointment and a sense of failure, he only wanted to cure the depression via drugs – so he could be even better.

Disorders like perfectionism and anorexia are quite different disorders than panic attacks, for example, which of course no one takes pride in or wants. Another way to think of this is to distinguish disorders of loss of control, such as depression and panic where the efforts of the therapist match those of the patient – to regain control – from disorders of over-control (which involve pride) where, by contrast, the efforts of the therapist are often at odds with those of the patient. People rarely wish to give up things they feel *increase* their sense of control. Although some values (e.g., excessive thinness, toughness or perfectionism) can be highly destructive, they have become a source of pride and control. Shame (or fear of it) turned to pride is not just a problem of the inversion of values that produce individual craziness and suffering, it is a cultural craziness. Whole cultures and groups can adopt values that are intensely destructive but are proud of doing it! The masculine contempt for life and pain that we saw in the previous chapter is one obvious example. At times, of course, violence might be unavoidable, but this is not something to be proud about; rather, it should be seen as a human tragedy. We were all once one day old, babies full of hope not asking to be here. We are acting out what we are acting out because of our archetypal minds that we've lost (or maybe never had much) control over.

If cultural values and practices where simply a matter of asking "do they work, are they useful, or what are their advantages and disadvantages?", if we were only rational about them, then it would be easier to change them. But we are not rational. If it were only at the level of public discourse that certain values are held, but in private people knew these values (e.g., those of manhood when it is contemptuous of life and death, or striving for success and independence, or to be thin) were crazy-making, then social values could be changed relatively quickly. But we often don't, and the reason is that we often hide our shame and fear of humiliation with the internalisation of destructive values. These values become our values operative in the private domain – at the very core of our being and sense of personhood. The real damage is when people internalise the (SAHP-giving) values of their culture and primary relationships, be it of manhood, toughness, extreme right-wing white supremacy, religious bigotry, and so forth. These values take hold more easily when they touch the archetypal in us or in some way connect with evolved strategies.

This suggests there is an enormous problem in our understanding of human freedom. If so much of our internalisation of values is to gain recognition, stay in contact with our fellows, avoid rejection and shame, then where is our freedom? And if, in order to do this, we have to go crazy, what then?

Freedom

The Problem of Freedom

Although it may appear that we have chosen to seek recognition in certain ways, how free are we? Clearly, unless we follow the values laid down by our culture, then social recognition is unlikely to come our way. Once we have internalised values from our parents and cultures, to speak of freedom and voluntary behaviour seems to deal in cosy illusions. The boxer chooses to box, but would he if other options were available; how many boxers are the sons of millionaires? And how often is ignorance the basis of our choices? Yet we are obsessed with the idea of freedom and free choice, despite our recognition that the most subtle forms of control are those where we can get people to internalise values and act them out as if they were their own. To what extent are we being robbed of our sexual explorations by cultural insistence on heterosexuality, for example?

This case is reported in Mark Tully's[242] personal book on India. In 1987, Roop Kanwar, an 18 year old newly married Indian women, was living in the village of Decorla. In that year on the unexpected death of her husband, she burnt with him on his funeral pyre (sati). This highly published case brought much attention in the Indian press. In order to gain the prestige of a saint, which satis apparently do, this has to be a voluntary act. Clearly, proof of voluntariness is difficult and claims were made for Roop Kanwar and other such satis that their choices were not voluntary, they were shamed into it, drugged or simply thrown on the pyre. But whether sati is forced, a pathological response to grief, a seeking for status and admiration even in death, or realising that a widowed woman may have poor status, the question of voluntariness is far from the whole issue. But that was, apparently, the key theme which occupied the press. Tully quotes the feminist Indian writer, Sharada Jain's argument:

> The climax of the horror story in fact lies not in Decorla... It lies in the elitist 'distanced' quarters. It is from the urban educated elite that the oft repeated question came: `Did Roop Kanwar commit sati of her own

---

[242] Tully, M. (1992)

will or was she forced?' If, even at this level, the utter irrelevance of the question is not clear and if, even here, the condemnation or approval of the event depends on the answer to this question, then the focus of action has to be deliberated on with great care.[243]

Of course, as Tully points out, for the others involved there is a difference as to whether people are forced into things or choose them. However, to stop here is to miss the far more disquieting questions about the whole nature of freedom of choice set within cultural contexts. We so often think of being forced to do something in terms of direct threats. But this is to miss the more subtle, hidden level at which force can be applied. It works on the limitations of opportunities, the social constructions and definitions for gaining a sense of worth and value, and the socially shared discourses of shaming and exclusion.

The Problems of External Freedom

It is sometimes difficult to separate external from internal freedom. *External freedom* can be listed with things, like freedom from oppression, freedom from being injured by others, economic freedoms and freedoms of opportunities, although even here we have difficulties because people are not equal and thus there are limits to their freedoms. I wanted to be a pilot when I was a young lad, but trouble with my eye sight ruled that out. Later, I wanted to be a heavy rock guitarist, but musically I was not so hot. I still dream about it though. A patient had, for a long time, wanted to be a doctor, but sadly he simply was not bright enough to pass the exams, despite a lot of effort.

External freedoms also require that the social contexts of shaming are few. Political correctness has attempted to move this along, but sadly it also, far too often, uses the old tactics of shaming. A policeman told me how on an 'anti-racist day' there was a general effort to shame racist attitudes and people were left feeling awkward and angry. I have been on similar such days. This, of course, does little except change the public face but not the private value system. This is why some involved with political correctness are accused of authoritarian

---

[243] Tully, M. (1992), p.224

tendencies. It not so much the ideas, but the tone and manner in which they are expressed that causes problems. Those on a crusade can be the most shaming without even realising it! Behaviourists have argued for a long time that punishment- and fear-based control is very inferior to reward, because while people may seek to avoid punishment, they won't necessarily do it in the way intended. An appreciation of the pain and suffering caused to others by our views, a learning to value others, seem more likely to change attitudes than simply complying out of shame avoidance. What is needed is an empathic training and empathic engagement, and for this, one has to create a secure and safe base where we can allow ourselves to feel and acknowledge a sadness for the plight of others rather than shame.

When trying to help people who have committed various crimes that have harmed people, it is very easy to be pulled into desires to shame them and make them confront their bad behaviour. This is sometimes regarded as retributive type justice. The problem with shame is you are also going to run into the shame defences – this may be a determination to continue but be more efficient, not get caught or even stimulate humiliated fury. So, the issue is how you create opportunities for people to gradually discover empathic potentials within themselves which then give an insight into the harmfulness of their crimes.

When it comes to being free to do as one wants to oneself, such as in bodily mutilations[244], it may seem that we are gradually freeing people from following

---

[244] Grant, L. and Norfolk, S. (1995) in an article called 'Written on the Body', in *The Guardian Weekend*, (April 1, pp.12-20) explore body mutilations, piercings, scarrings, etc. – some of which seem quite horrific. Understandably, various therapists believe that such desires (and need for pain) are derived from previous sexual abuse, lack of love and denial of emotional pain, etc. – and understandably, many mutilators are angered by this "we are right and you are wrong; we know what you are *really* suffering from" attitude of some therapists. As in all things, the reasons are complex and not uni-dimensional. I think Grant and Norfolk sum it up well when they admit we don't really know – but many do have a growing sense of unease and recognise that apparent freedoms may be quite illusory, no matter how good they may feel. I guess that is part of it – the attitude of "if it feels good, do it". If mutilating oneself makes you feel better, more normal or more special, more powerful or more sexual, then it must be good. The cult of individuality is all about how something feels. Submitting to one's god in acts of

uni-dimensional life styles. But we should be cautious. It may also be the case that it is somewhere in the social dimensions of our 'culture of meaningless' that render so many without identity, a cause or values, and a sense of what they do matters, that the body becomes the canvass to play out confusions and pain. And, of course, freedom to exploit the world and others (to accumulate as much wealth as we can) many turn out to be no freedom at all for we end up living in chaos and intense conflicts. My freedom may only be assured if I work for your freedom.

The Problems of Internal Freedom

Hermann Hesse writes,

> If I were to reduce all my feelings and their painful conflicts to a single name, I can think of no other word but: dread. It was dread and uncertainty that I felt in all those hours of shattered childhood felicity: dread of punishment, dread of my own conscience, dread of the stirrings in my soul which I considered forbidden and criminal.[245]

A key ingredient of psychotherapy is to give a person greater freedom to move within themselves. This freedom comes from recognising that what is in us, is not, in an odd sense, us at all. What I have inside me is the temperament I was born with, a set of archetypal potentials reaching back to the reptiles and a host of memories, emotional experiences, at times rather odd fantasises, and values that have been given to me. In large measure I (as I feel myself to be) created few of these things. Given this, freedom seems a most perplexing thing. If I am depressed or anxious, my state (reflecting the arousal of some biological inner programme) controls my thoughts as much as my thoughts control my state.

From our earliest experiences we will develop a tendency to *rate ourselves* in social rank and conformity terms. When individuals are depressed they often think of themselves as inferior compared to others. A depressed person may

---

confession may feel good but may not be freeing. Submitting to pleasures, likewise, may be.
[245] Hesse, H. (1971)

label or judge him/herself and/or has judgements made by others that are not only negative but also suggest they have been allocated a low rank and/or low status position. Personal and social judgements such as unlovable, worthless, bad, weak, inadequate, useless, etc. are in effect assignments of low status, rank and worth. In contrast, when people feel confident, they often think of themselves as equal or superior to others and do not use such negative status labels to describe themselves. But, of course, as archetypal and powerful as these labels are, they are used according to social discourses.

Internal freedom may be increased by a reduction in internal shaming and fearful self-criticism. In my view, it is dependent on the development of *compassion to self and others*, the subject of a later chapter. We can begin to remove the global labels on self and others of bad, weak, worthless and so forth. We can learn to loosen the tight control we put on ourselves and others so that our inner lives are not full of dread. In this way, we can face ourselves and others as mosaics of complex, not simple, possibilities: to come to know ourselves, both the bright side and the dark side and others without shame. Then we no longer experience certain things inside us with dread. We are not ashamed to be frightened, not ashamed to give in, not ashamed of our sexual feelings, not shamed by our gender or ethnicity, not shamed by our limitations and mistakes, not shamed by our needs for others' affection. As the cognitive therapists say, a mistake is just a mistake, a sexual feeling is just a sexual feeling. Things are what they are, but it is our judgements of them that make them shaming. And although our judgments of these inner things often come from the cultures we live in, still we can reclaim our right to be complex and refuse the one-dimensional spaces on offer. If we don't self-down and attack ourselves, we can move within our minds without 'off limits' signs cropping up all over place. We learn to face what we need to face. And when we are more familiar with ourselves and more accepting of the complexity of our different 'possibilities of being', we can be less shaming of others and aware of how shame constrains, inviting concealment and deception. The most shaming people (e.g., men of other men) can be those who fear shame the most. There is a reciprocal interaction between facing our own shame and helping others accept theirs. When cultures reduce shaming, the less is the need to compensate by seeking power and the avoidance of weakness. The less we interact with shame, the more compassion can exist. And compassion is crucial, for we are not talking of training in psychopathic indifference. What should ultimately reduce freedom is a recognition of responsibility; we reduce our freedoms because we do not wish to be harmful.

Freedom in the Healing of Shame

Healing shame is a great source of freedom. We are no longer frightened of our inner worlds of memories, fantasies and emotions that they may indicate something bad about us, or that we had become lost in them. We are free to explore many potentials within. But healing shame is not easy, because as we encounter shame we realise just how isolating and disconnecting shame has kept us. It is a risk. At times, acknowledging our shame and our drive for approval, social esteem and pride can mean acknowledging what sits behind these drives, noticing perhaps that without them are feelings of emptiness and cutoffness, which, as Kaufman[3] notes, are extraordinarily painful. We may not be free to face our pain without others to hold us as we go. The incredible thing about healing shame is the recognition that forgiveness, acceptance for the darker sides, and connectedness, changes the relationships we have with ourselves and others. Many times, I have worked with people who felt that as they dealt with shame, and grieved for the sadness behind it, they felt a sense of release and inner freedom.

Groups too who acknowledge their shame (in say, atrocities of war) and enable guilt might take a first step to healing, although this is often a painful thing to do. If they are unable to acknowledge their bad behaviour, they may conceal and deny it or seek to justify it, then they can get stuck and the risk of repeating it increases. But as seems to be in the efforts being made in South Africa, acknowledging harmful acts can also be freeing and healing.

Conclusion

Shame is all about status and self-presentations to the outside and inner worlds. In humans, the sexual reproductive strategies of competing for status have given way to more complex status management strategies based on attractiveness and social attention. We can lose status (SAHP) not from physical attack but more often from attacks on our self-presentations and effects to present the self as attractive, able and competent. As Nicholas Allen[246] has noted, social attractiveness (SAHP) can be like the stock market. What is valued depends on what others think is valuable. No self-presentation has value in itself without social agreement of its value. This is what opens the possibility that some social behaviours become highly valued but also highly destructive. Indeed, we have seen just how destructive the collusions in shame can be.

Shame and pride are cousins in the creation of identities, but they can rob us of many of our potentials and hold us in highly constrained lives, frightened to be other than that which the social culture ordains we should be. To avoid shame, we learn to wear the mask of conformity, behind which we become the hollow dummies of the tough and non-feeling, the hyper-heterosexual, achievement orientated. In our proud presentations we see that in reality, sometimes perhaps, we are masking a submissive compliant self. We hide from the realities of our shadows, confusions, pain and loneliness, and from the alienation within ourselves, for we fear that revelation will once more mark us down. It is our shame and shaming that can drive us really quite crazy. But with courage and compassion we don't have to be trapped here. We can see this is a common human experience because we will be made the same way – we just need the courage to address it.

---

[246] Personal communication

7: POWER AND LEADERSHIP

Those who want to lead are not fit to and those who are fit to, don't want to! (an old proverb)

Greatness is a transitory experience. It is never constant. It depends on the myth-making imagination of humankind. The person who experiences greatness must have a feeling for the myth he is in. He must reflect what is projected on to him. And he must have a strong sense of the sardonic. The sardonic is all that permits him to move within himself. Without this quality, even occasional greatness will destroy a man.[247]

Leadership is a form of social dominance, and leaders can exert powerful influences on the behaviours, ideals and feelings of the led. This chapter is concerned with rank and how, in humans, dominance expresses itself through the use of various forms of power. We will note that leaders can use their power in many different ways. They can use it to gain recognition, status and superiority for themselves and in so doing can act to suppress, intimidate, subordinate and structuralise the hierarchy and make sharper the boundaries between insider and outsider (the good and the bad). On the other hand, leaders can act to relax, encourage and nurture subordinates, helping them to reduce their dependence on leaders, to de-structuralise the hierarchy and soften boundaries. To obtain a leadership position obviously requires some type of power. However, what this and the next chapter will try to explore is that styles of leadership do not exist in a vacuum, but are influenced by social contexts, external and internal stresses, and by the demands of followers.

---

[247] Herbert, F. (1978) p.123

Notes on Power

In evolutionary theory, power is defined by reproductive success – for a sociobiologist, that is the ultimate in power. Mostly, however, social power is explored in the contexts of the relationships and motivations of people. When we explore the social origins of power, which followed the advent of agriculture,[248] we can see this as a history of the changing forms of dominant-subordinate relationships, and the different social patterns of living it spawned. Feminists,[249] philosophers,[250] sociologists[251] and psychologists[252] have been among the many to have placed power central to their explorations. Apart from the interpersonal theorists,[253] dominant-subordinate relationships have been in the background, not the foreground, of these explorations.

Power is usually defined as the ability to influence or `make happen'. The concept of power can be used in a scientific, non-social way as energy – an electric company calls itself Powergen – clearly no social dimension here. In relationships, however, we might speak of constructive power (e.g., to build, create, give life, save life and nurture) or destructive power (to tear down, destroy). Usually the former is slow-working over time, whereas destructive power can be quick and immediate. What might have taken years to build can be destroyed in seconds. The immediacy of destructive power can give a person

---

[248] Mann, M. (1986). See also Chapter 4 of this volume.

[249] There have been many good feminist works on power; although at times confusing gender with forms of power is not always helpful or revealing. A good recent edited text is Radtke, H.L. and Stram, H.J. (1994). See also hooks, b. (1984).

[250] Steven Lukes' (1986) edited volume contains many key papers written over the last few decades by philosophers, economists, sociologists and psychologists. The one person who does not appear in this volume but who did much to reveal social-historical roots of power is Foucault.

[251] The textbook by Anthony Giddens (1989) gives a very thorough overview of the sociological approaches. Kemper, T.D. (1990) and Barkow, J.H. (1989) also offer major ideas of the nature of social power.

[252] See Gross, R.D. (1992) chapter on Social Influence. Also, Podsakoff, P.M. and Schriesheim, C.A. (1985).

[253] The first person to derive a model of the dimensions of dominance-submission and its interaction with love-hate was Leary, T. (1957). Since then there have been changes to it: e.g., Kiesler, D.J. (1983) and also reformulations and critiques, see Birtchnell, J. (1994).

a very strong sense of their influence and energy – even their aliveness. The child builds the tower of blocks and then smashes it – with a smile. In all of us there exist impulses to create and destroy. And these can share complex relationships. We might create armies and weapons of destruction in order to destroy – but they can also be used to protect.

Types of Power

Hollander and Offerman[254] suggest three types of power: *Power over others*, the power to make or entice others to do things a leader wants; *Power to*, involving the degree of freedom to do as one wishes, also called empowerment; and *Power from*, involving the ability/power to resist the wishes/demands of others. As they point out, high status involves all three forms of power, whilst subordinates have at best one or two, and sometimes practically no such powers at all.

When it comes to considering the forms of power psychologists have suggested five main forms: *Reward power* is the ability to provide something that others want and will work for (e.g., controlling access to wages, food, love, approval etc.). *Coercive/punishment power* is the ability to control others through actual or threatened aversive outcomes (e.g., to injure the other or remove/withhold something of value to others). Both of these are fairly direct, used by animals, and require little psychological capacity. The other three however require more complex psychologies. *Legitimate power* is linked to rights and obligations which require an understanding and recognition of rights and obligations. It is used as a basis of law and socially defined roles (e.g., the power of the captain, teacher, president, etc.). *Expert power* relates to an awareness of the superiority of another's knowledge or skill, and is linked with respect and at times admiration (e.g., doctors, priests, scientists). *Referent power* refers more to attractiveness, liking and a person's charm or charisma.[255] Many forms of power

---

[254] Hollander, E.P. and Offerman, L.R. (1990)
[255] This formulation was put forward by French, J. and Ravens, B.H. back in 1959. It has stood the test of time pretty well, although it not without its problems; see, for example, Podsakoff, P.M. and Schriesheim, C.A. (1985).

and indeed leadership requires that the dominant has access to and can control *the attention* of subordinates.

As we noted in Chapter 3, interpersonal theorists[256] have argued that dominance-subordination is a vertical dimension of relating while love-hate is a horizontal dimension. So, therefore, it is possible to have both loving and hating/aggressive forms of dominance. These are all helpful ways of explaining the complexities of power and leadership, but at times they can hide those complexities rather than reveal them. So, in what follows, armed with these notes on the nature of power and social influence, we will now explore leadership in greater detail.

Leadership

In his study of charisma, Lindholm[257] notes that we do not always behave in our own genetic self-interest when it comes to following leaders. There has been more than one leader who has taken us on a trip into mass destruction. In 1978 the world was shocked by the Jonestown community's suicide of men, women and children. Some, who were not present at the time, killed themselves later. This was not the first, nor will it be the last, time that followers have killed others and themselves in devotion to a cause, manipulated by a leader. It is our rank psychology that courts so much craziness.

Leaders vary in style and basic psychology (e.g., in terms of their charisma, skills/knowledge, tendency to punish or reward). But they are also shaped and given access to leadership positions/roles via their cultures and social relationships.[258] Some leaders are elected by those they will lead, others are

---

[256] The interpersonal school is derived from the work of the social psychiatrist Harry Stack Sullivan and the psychologist Timothy Leary. See note 7 above.

[257] Lindholm, C. (1993)

[258] The research on leadership has advanced greatly in the last 50 years, with many changes of emphasis. It is not the intention here to give a review of this work, but we can note various differences of approach. These include those which have focused leadership in terms of personality style and social skills of leaders, task-focused leadership styles, transactional (between leader and follower) leadership, attributions followers make of leaders, projections of follower aspirations onto leaders, motivating and inspiring qualities of leader behaviour, and cultural role-structuring of leader

imposed (as in the military) by superiors. Some leaders are encouraged to adopt certain styles and do certain things because of what is expected of (and projected onto) them. In the preceding chapter, we noted how George Orwell had to shoot an elephant, not from any personal desire to do so, but because of the expectations of the crowd and his concern to maintain his image of himself and of his 'white-man' group. In his book, *On the Psychology of Military Incompetence*, Norman Dixon[259] notes that preferred leadership style varies according to the context. For example, in low-stress times soldiers prefer democratic leaders, but in stressful situations, like war, they prefer autocratic, strong leadership which tells them what to do and on whom they can depend. Thus, subordinate preferences for styles of leaders are affected by personal and social stresses and the potentially saving, protective qualities the leader seems to provide. Given this, some individuals are able to manipulate group values for their own ends and farm support. Authoritarian leaders can, for example, exaggerate threats, especially from outsiders, and thus increase their appeal by offering themselves as strong, protective and decisive leaders. In low-stress times, leaders may rely more on their intelligence and less on experience, but the reverse is the case in stressful times.[260] Thus, there is a complex interaction between leadership behaviour, the psychology of followers, and social context which allows, encourages or even demands certain actions.

Leadership behaviours can be expressed in many contexts and at many different social positions. It involves various combinations of power, such as directing the attention of others and the ability/power to control, guide, influence, encourage or coerce the behaviour and values of others. Nearly all humans have the ability to adopt leadership behaviours. Even in simple twosomes, one may be more the leader than the other, although they may swap roles from time to time. Thus, leadership behaviours can emerge in just about any social relationship: e.g., playground, street gang, terrorist group, church fete society,

---

behaviour. Good reviews of this work can be found in Hollander, E.P. and Offerman, L.R. (1990) Fielder, F.E. and House, R.J. (1988) An interest evolutionary approach to leadership can be found in Crook, J.H. (1986).

[259] Dixon, N.F. (1987)

[260] Fielder, F.E. and House, R.J. (1988)

local cricket team, the hospital ward, business organisation, and government. Leadership research also makes the distinction between task (target) focused leadership and person (process) orientated leadership. Task leaders tend to focus on the outputs and how to get the job done, often target-focused. The person-orientated leader tries to create the conditions to enable the task to happen. They tend to be more process- rather than outcome-focused. Hence, they work with subordinates to support and guide them. These two styles have started to appear in the National Health Service with concerns on targets, rather than finding resources staff feel they need, and attending to process. Although leader-follower relationships are to some degree archetypal potentials (and this is what can give them their passion and emotion distorting qualities), we should note that our first experiences of leaders are our parents.

The Family

Target-focused versus process-focused shows up in many styles of leadership in which leaders don't pay much attention to *how* things are done (just that they're done), whereas person-focused leaders are interested in the 'how' of the doing. Same styles can show up in families. Researchers over many years have identified different parenting styles, such as authoritative, disengaged permissive and authoritarian. These are also likely to be leadership styles, although I don't know of any research that has yet connected them. Authoritarian styles seem task-focused on behaviours that are expected and required. So, for the most part children need to obey their parents and detailed emotional exploration may not be a particular focus. Person- and process-orientated parents are probably concerned with the process of the child's growth and development, and they're interested in how children learn and grow, not just that they obey the rules.

Family structures are also authoritarian, hierarchical structures. Human family relationships, however, are highly contextualised within their cultures. Cultures legitimise the use of power within the family. They may not only amplify gender differences in the power exercised within families (men as head of the household) but bestow rights. In some societies, men are (more or less) bestowed the right of sexual access to their wives, and even today in some cultures there are issues around whether rape can occur inside marriage. In the middle ages, wife-beating was allowed, provided the stick was no thicker than a thumb. In modern societies, noted for their highly segregated and privatised families, power is exercised by the limitation of freedom of choice and rights. Thus, for example, women and children who are locked into abusive relationships may lack the resources or opportunities to move away. Male dominance of the family is thus encased in socially bestowed privileges and values.

For all animals, parents are automatically positioned to control the behaviour of their offspring. Thus, the parent-child relationship is also a dominant-subordinate one. In childhood, the experience of being subordinate to one's parents is also associated with enormous needs for care and acceptance from them. This combination of care-eliciting and care-giving with subordination has the effect of blending different archetypal potentials together. *It is not surprising, therefore, that humans can learn and develop their attitudes and emotional sensitivity 'to authority' from the experiences they have with, and of, their parents.* Parenting is, in many ways, a leadership role because it involves differences in power and demands for obedience. And our attitudes to leadership and authority (seeking it, subordinating ourselves to it, or hating it) can be shaped during our formative years.

Society bestows and accepts the rights of parents to behave in certain ways to their children. Children are automatically assumed to come under the power and control of their parents. The use of physical punishment (and types of punishment in general), religious indoctrination, diet, indeed the right to impose various forms of lifestyle, are seen as parental rights. The state may intervene at times, as with laws on education, and there can be conflicts over the exact limits of power that can be exercised with families, e.g., the state may intervene in cases of sexual abuse or if parents refuse to send their children to school or to allow blood transfusions, on religious grounds. Generally though, children are indoctrinated to adopt the prevailing attitudes and values of their group, be these religious, political, or gender based. Young children can be taken on political marches, made to read the Bible or Koran, forced to view history through a particular lens, and so forth. If any of these practices are crazy, then we can easily pass them on.[261] What remains troubling is that parents can indoctrinate their children with a lot of religious fear and anxiety perfectly legally. In decades to come, this may be seen as emotional abuse. It is odd that we allow religious-based schools, because children are not in the position to choose if they want to be indoctrinated this way, and may carry a fear of God through their lives, as numerous testimonies of people who have been through religious-based education institutions have testified. The state should provide freedom from fear, indoctrination and dogma as much possible.

Leadership Roles

Once out of the family there are other groups and social relationships in which we must find our place. Leadership roles can be ascribed and defined by social groups and one passes some entrance test or exam to enter them (e.g., lawyer, doctor) which legitimises the use of power. As we saw in Chapter 5, in some societies obtaining the recognition of manhood legitimises the use of certain types of power and authority (e.g., over women). Historically, leaders could be given their roles 'as of right' (e.g., by an institutionalised class or caste system). In fact, many leadership positions (kings, emperors, and so forth) were family determined. Even today, the family origins and its social rank can significantly influence a person's chances and aspirations to leadership positions. Top leaders of social institutions are rarely those who have risen through the ranks, but usually they begin their claims from class-bestowed privileged positions. The importance of the rank of one's family is also noted in many non-human primates. Females especially, usually obtain their rank from their mother's and

---

[261] As we have said many times, not only are children indoctrinated to view the outside world and their own roles and places in it in certain ways, but they are also indoctrinated in how they should view and treat themselves (internal archetypal potential), what to make of their sexual feelings (masturbation and homosexuality are sins against God), their fears, and their needs for intimacy. From an early age, they are taught what is good about themselves and what is bad, what they should affirm and what they should negate, what they should be proud of and what they should be ashamed of.

aunt's rank. As it has been for millions of years, we mature, leave the family and emerge into the social world where rank is everywhere.

Exercising Power

Even though a social group may legitimise the use of power, and select an individual(s) for leadership roles, the way power is exercised depends on complex interactions between the person exercising it and those on whom it is exercised. Some may become leaders even against their wishes, via their popularity or the personal values they express. John Lennon, for example, along with other pop groups of the time, had an enormous effect on the values of the young. However, he consistently denied that he wished to be seen as any kind of leader. He wanted fame for his music.

Psychotherapists note that the acts of being attended and looked to, or treated as a leader (saviour, guru, etc.) can ignite leadership desires. Indeed, these kinds of attention can stimulate physiological processes such as serotonin and testosterone. Indeed, without caution one can be intoxicated by it, becoming grandiose and carried away by it. There is an inflation of the up-rank archetype. We become vulnerable to hubris. For example, therapists have to be very careful of the idealisations, admirations and needs projected onto them, so as to avoid getting inflated ideas about themselves. Whether one is a doctor, lawyer or psychotherapist, it is very easy to fall victim to inflations of one's own rank and power, one's own importance.

One may never know how a person is going to behave until they are given or find themselves in positions of power: e.g., when they put on the uniform. Some years ago, Zimbardo and his colleagues[262] took a group of students and arbitrarily divided them into guards and prisoners. Before the week was out the experiment had to be stopped because about a third of the guards had become vindictive and authoritarian, devising various punishments for disobedient

---

[262] Zimbardo et al. (1973). See also the discussion by Gross, R.D. (1992) pp. 583-584. For a recent discussion of the research problems and importance of such research see McDermott, M. (1993).

prisoners. The simmering of a Gestapo mentality was not hard to see. This was a shock to the researchers. So, positions of power can inflate and excite underlying archetypal tendencies in a person.

Secure and Insecure Dominance

Styles of leadership have been studied in animals as styles of dominance. In most non-human primate studies to date, subordinates show greater activation of stress hormones than dominant animals, especially higher levels of circulating cortisol. However, in unstable groups dominant animals can show almost as high levels as subordinates. The work of Sapolsky[263], who has studied free ranging baboons in Africa, suggests that secure, dominant baboons in stable groups share many characteristics: they have low-stress cortisol levels; they differentiate well between a threatening rival and other animals; when threatened, they escalate fights and usually win; if they lose, they displace aggression onto a third party; and they have high levels of non-sexual interactions with infants and females and are generally relaxed and affiliative.

High-ranking but insecure baboons (especially if the group is unstable) share different qualities: they have high levels of stress hormones; they tend to be more aggressive (generally and sexually); they are more likely to pick fights (rather than just respond to threats); they appear more suspicious; and they are generally less relaxed and less affiliative. These differences can have huge effects on the whole group, including their stress hormones. While these differences in leadership/dominance style reflect the stability of the group they also reflect individual differences. Thus, we see that security of the position may be important for the kinds of behaviour that dominants express. This leads us to the idea of differences between *secure* and *insecure dominance*.

Some human leaders certainly seem to show forms of insecure dominance. This insecurity is mediated through both the social context and personality. It is possible that in humans insecurity may be, in part, a general personality trait (as it seems to be for baboons and chimpanzees). The combination of strong needs

---

[263] Sapolsky, R.M. (1989, 1990a,b, 1992); Ray, J.C. and Sapolsky, R.M. (1992)

for power in humans (to control others) compensates, perhaps, for basic personal insecurities, quite possibly of an insecure, avoidant attachment style (see Chapter 3). Many researchers have argued that aggressive leaders have often had disturbed backgrounds with low parental warmth. There is a basic view in psychotherapy that 'the absence of love is replaced by power and fear'.

It will be recalled from Chapter 3 that we noted many researchers draw distinctions between *threat/aggression-based dominance* and *affiliation-based dominance styles*. Insecure dominance, we can suggest, shows itself in the readiness to adopt threat-based leadership styles: that is leadership is primarily organised via the threat system (see Chapter 2). In humans, the interaction between threat and affiliation is complex because humans can be far more manipulative of their social-presentation and image, i.e., presenting themselves as affiliative when in fact they are not. As we shall now see, insecure patterns of dominance show up quite commonly in leadership styles.

Personality

Although this book has tried to veer away from being overly focused on traits within individuals (and research on leadership suggests that personality is only one facet of leadership, for it is always the interaction that is important), our exploration of leadership does require some consideration of personality. It seems to be the case that some leaders are more likely to have particular traits and personality styles which reflect quite serious insecurities. These may include narcissistic, obsessional, autocratic, authoritarian, psychopathic and hypomanic (or manic-depressive) traits. The definition of narcissistic, which underpins many of them, is captured by Adler[264]:

> These patients tend to be extremely self-centred, often needing praise and constant recognition in order to feel momentarily good about themselves. Rather than feeling a sense of their own worth or value, they require repeated bolstering from the outside. In their relationships

---

[264] Adler, G. (1986)

with people, they tend to be exploitative and insensitive to the feelings and needs of others. Their behaviour can be superficially charming on the one hand and arrogant on the other. They expect special privileges from those around them without giving anything in return, yet they can feel easily humiliated or shamed and respond with rage at what they perceive to be criticisms or failure of people to react in the way they wish... Many can elaborate active fantasies about magnificent success in love, sex, beauty, wealth or power. They often devalue people they have previously idolised and tend to split, i.e. see people as either all good or all bad, or alternate between these extremes.[265]

Adler's description highlights status evaluative and power-hostility components, the use of others for self-valuing purposes, tendency for exploitation and sense of entitlement, and a comparative lack of the more prosocial aspects of human nature such as empathy, moral thinking, and care-giving. They can have the motto, "if you're not with us, you're against us". They can be strident in emphasising the importance of their own vision and truck little disagreement. They can be envious, grandiose and expect allegiance. They can maintain this allegiance by a mixture of threats, shaming and offering favours and prestige to allies and followers. Yet for all this, at times their style may inspire devotion.

The psychopathic person has many narcissistic traits, but in addition is generally more callous, sadistic, distrustful, amoral, exploitative, ruthless and can be easily activated into violent fights. Their compassion for others is notable by its absence; this lack of a caring motivation is what marks them out.

Autocratic and authoritarian personalities are similar to the narcissist but they are extremely rank-focused. Dixon[266] used psychoanalytic theory to argue that these personality styles are a defence against uncertainty and anxiety: i.e., insecurity. They must know their place and can be incredibly deferential and submissive to those ranking above them and controlling of those ranking below.

---

[265] Adler, G. (1986), pp.430-431
[266] Dixon, N.F. (1974/1994)

They have strong beliefs in the value of the ranked authority system and the importance of obeying orders, and they are not so keen on democracy.

The manic-depressive traits, from which some leaders suffer, are believed to relate more to a mood disorder. Winston Churchill was a classic example. This leads them to swing between grandiose ideas about their self-importance, have marked needs for power, low frustration tolerance but high energy, be charismatic, take risks and be creative. However, when depressed they are riddled with self-doubt and feelings of worthlessness, with a tendency to hide away and feel suicidal. They usually lack the sadistic and callousness of the psychopath, but can be paranoid to some degree and are very sensitive to threats and challenges to their own (and their group's) status. People with narcissistic traits (and these can be present in any of the above types) may not have full blown manic-depressive illnesses, but nonetheless they can show marked swings of mood and confidence.

Although these are usually regarded as personality or mood disorders, it is quite wrong to think that having a disorder consigns one to the backstreets of history. Indeed, some are not satisfied with simply being psychopathic and narcissistic in their own limited social domains. Their drive for leadership and greatness marks them out from other less leadership-focused personalities. In such a pursuit, these traits can be a positive advantage in making it big. Unfortunately, in the past, and to some degree still, these individuals can take hold of whole cultures, societies, groups and organisations, with a terrible cost. More worryingly, once in power their poor emotional and/or physical health can have very serious consequences.[267] They can hard to depose too.

Anti-Social, Divisive and Prosocial Leadership Style

Running alongside explorations of personality have been many efforts to distinguish leadership styles using different constructs. For example, Maslow distinguished democratic from authoritarian leaders; McClelland distinguishes

---

[267] Freeman, H. (1991). This is a superb paper and anyone interested in how political actions can be influenced by dysfunctional brains would find much food for thought.

the affiliative from the power-orientated; Eisler distinguishes dominator (masculine) from partnership (feminine) styles; Kalma et al. distinguish between sociable and aggressive leaders. Elsewhere, I have distinguished the prosocial from the anti-social and divisive leader.[268]

So, there is no single system of understanding, and all have their insights and limitations. Much may depend on where you look of course, i.e., whether you focus on the tasks, results or on interpersonal style. The types of leaders we will note shortly may well get results, but they tend towards the authoritarian, dominator, aggressive, divisive leadership styles. I will refer to these collectively as anti-social because their style can have very negative effects on and for others.

Anti-social and divisive leaders tend to come from insecure backgrounds with a history of abusive, emotionally cold, rigid/authoritarian or neglectful parenting, which leads them to develop various mixtures of the above-mentioned traits. Judged through the lens of the last two chapters, we could see these individuals as being highly shame-prone, sensitive to humiliation, extraordinarily status conscious, and in need of defending against humiliation at all costs. The way this is done, as in the Hitler complex, is not just via defence of self but an active promotion of one's superiority – in other words, heightened activity of a primitive up-rank, archetypal mentality. To be superior promises the power to defeat any who would make claims on one's status or position. Although one can certainly link such psychologies to reproductive strategies – and genes – these distal explanations do not always help us understand the complex of forces which bring these archetypes to such prominence within any one person at a point in history. We should always consider family background and social context.

Divisive leaders have particular philosophies, motives and tendencies which include the following: a perception of the world as competitive and that the strongest wins; a belief in the superiority of one's social group, often with a fear,

---

[268] Maslow, A.H. (1943); McClelland, D.C. (1987); Eisler, R. (1990) Kalma, A.P., Visser, L. and Peeters, A. (1993); Gilbert, P. (1989). See Snodgrass, S.E. (1992) for a discussion and some evidence that social role rather than gender differences account for differences in leader-subordinate/follower behaviour.

dislike or even contempt for outsiders; a belief in the importance of strength and pride; a belief in the importance of close in-group loyalties as a protection against external badness (us against them); a need for control and power over others; a fear of losing status; a belief that their own way (vision) is superior; a simple right versus wrong moral system, or no moral system at all; a tendency to use people to meet their own ends; and often a lack of care for others.

Prosocial leaders tend to have very different backgrounds, coming generally from a secure and warm family life, and have developed the archetypal abilities to empathise and care for others. Thus, there are far more *altruistic strategies* in their styles. Compared with anti-social leaders, they have different philosophies, motives and tendencies which include the following: a preference for cooperative over competitive behaviour; a preference for partnership and peaceful solutions to conflicts rather than winning; a belief in the importance of valuing and nurturing others as people rather than as a means to an end; a complex moral system; an opening up of groups and dissolving boundaries ("we are all the same under the skin"); and a sardonic sense of the heroic.

These are dimensions rather than absolute categories. One could compare (say) Nelson Mandala with Hitler to get a feel of the differences. But, in general, it is probably preferable to think of the style rather than 'the individual' because at times a person may show one face of leadership but at other times another. They may have mild tendencies towards either prosocial or divisive styles, or these styles may be marked and rigid. They may appear highly prosocial to in-group members who show allegiance but anti-social to outsiders and defectors. They may be intuitively inclined towards (for example) prosocial leadership, but the social group (electorate) which supports them demands another style and invalidates their prosocial efforts – telling them they need to be tough-minded. The ease (and degree) by which a leader will compromise their own values in order to get elected or chosen suggests that for some, gaining leadership roles is more important that pursuing personal principles. Personal principles can be too costly. On the other hand, the group might encourage an amplification of a preferred personal style. Some who are mildly aggressive become more so with being encouraged to go further and be more ruthless. As we noted above, insecurity can affect style, but this insecurity may come from stresses in the environment.

People who are groomed for leadership by virtue of their families' social position, i.e., they are placed in leadership positions, need not be socially skilled. However, some divisive leaders are highly socially skilled, good orators and good at manipulating the values and (usually) needs for superiority, certainty, and strength in their followers.

Fear-Based Patterns

Sometimes those with anti-social leadership styles can inspire devotion. At other times, as in China and the old USSR, they bring to life social patterns of fear and suspicion. Such regimes usually only survive with the support of a hidden class of 'secret police' henchmen and women who are ruthless and vicious and can create the fear of 'the knock on the door in the middle of the night'. Societies never seem to have had much problem in finding such folk and such 'police forces' can include a fair number of both narcissistic and sadistic personalities, who can colour the whole police force. Anti-social leaders, protected by the young men of the secret police and other arms of enforcement, may slowly age and can in fact be quite old before they are deposed or simply die in post. However, it's not always so secret a force, and such activities can indeed be quite open. The point is that these leaders preside over their armed forces, murdering and torturing their own populations. Occasionally, the armed forces will stage a coup, but often they are willing accomplices. It has been so for thousands of years. It was soldiers, at least as commonly depicted, who beat and then crucified Christ. Once powerful leaders can get their armies to instigate 'a rule of terror', the population has no chance.

For some supporters, appeasement and compliance is used to reduce the potential aggression of the leader(s) and/or his/her supporters. That is, the primary internal psychological organisation in both leaders and subordinates is *defensive* (see Chapter 2) rather than relaxed and open. The fear-based anti-social leadership style and its effects are the most easily detected. Even if the leader appears friendly, fear and apprehension can be common experiences. The psychology of their subordinates is to make sure they know where the threat might be (and for what) and take necessary appeasing and ingratiating steps to reduce it. Behaviourists would call this 'punishment'-based control. Michael Chance[269] called this pattern of social behaviour agonic – meaning that the defensive aspects of fight/threaten (in the dominant) and appeasement/submit or flight/escape (in the subordinate) are primed (see Chapter 4). The group remains cohesive and functioning because subordinates play the game of appeasing the dominant. This leads to constrictions on the patterns of attention, reduces open exploration and may reduce the development of compassionate values.

If you watch members of a group interact when the leader is out of the room and compare this to when s/he is present, you can sometimes have a feel for whether an anti-social style is operating. When an anti-social or frightening leader enters, the previous fun and jokey exchanges may cease, as does the free exploration of ideas. There is a switch in attention. Everyone watches their backs to ensure they are not the next to be attacked and they are preoccupied with the mood the leader is in. Bad moods signal hard times, and times to watch yourself. Everything is done to avoid putting the leader in a bad mood – even withholding important information about 'bad news' or mistakes. The poor folk who do put the leader in a bad mood can be blamed by other subordinates for causing them a hard time. At one meeting, a subordinate said to another "why did you say that? You know what he's like. Now we are all going to suffer. Why couldn't just keep your mouth shut?" My housemaster at boarding school was like this and it was well known that the other masters (we called them masters then, not teachers) were wary, if not frightened, of him. He was a cane-happy sod.

Of course, at times anti-social styles are unintended and reflect poor social skills, or stress, but at other times these divisive leaders enjoy the idea that others are apprehensive of them and believe this ensures them respect. Indeed, a belief in, and even admiration of, fear-based respect probably marks the divisive leader. Industry is just beginning to recognise that some leadership styles are disastrous,

---

[269] Chance, M.R.A. (1984; 1988)

that there is a dark side to charisma.[270] Perhaps in our modern age there is a gradual fading in the valuing of tough leadership (but it is gradual and at times I doubt it). Those who do well at interview and present themselves with confidence, keenness and are socially skilled (often being male helps too) have often appeared the preferred choice to place in positions of power and leadership. However, unless you observe them working with their team, you have little idea how they will perform as leaders. Some turn out to be narcissistic, who value themselves but not others, are competitive with subordinates and shaming. They create such poor morale and inhibit other's creativity that they can cost an organisation dearly. They hate critical feedback and can behave very aggressively ensuring that it is shutdown. Nearly all of us will have had some experience of having to work with these characters. So, management training is all the vogue right now, teaching people how to be socially rewarding and supportive, able to appreciate subordinate feedback and build a cooperative-friendly team spirit.

The thing to watch out for is those who can mimic such behaviours in 'training workshops' but do not really (privately) value these behaviours. There can be slippage in their non-verbal behaviour and style. They may say 'the right things' but not feel or act friendly. At the slightest conflict, they become aggressive/shaming, threatening to escalate such conflict unless the other backs down. Non-verbal behaviour is so important because it taps right into the ancient emotional brain, and this, in interpersonal interactions, is what can set the emotional tone of the relationship(s). Indeed, we know that people monitor nonverbal communication at least as much as verbal. The way leaders deal with conflicts (of interest) both verbally and non-verbally is crucial to the skill of a leader. Good prosocial leaders have the ability to keep conflicts serious but also playful. People don't feel personally attacked; they play the ball not the player. Leaders like the Dalai Lama, Nelson Mandela and Gandhi are well known for such abilities.

Prosocial leaders are rarely feared. They encourage free exploration and affiliative styles. They are easy to approach and open to the opinions of others.

---

[270] Hogan et al. (1988)

Subordinates do not fear them, because as leaders they do not use shame and humiliation as a means of control. Generally, subordinates enjoy working with and for them, and do not feel patronised or looked down on. Prosocial leaders are concerned to see others mature, grow and pass on. They are not envious of others' success. Their dark side is that they may not perform well in conflict situations – or at least can be very stressed by it and indecisive. Their needs for affiliation can interfere with tough decision-making.

Leadership and Deception

As mentioned above, a prosocial style can be superficial – it is a con and deception devised to be attractive to others. It is often seen in cults, but not uncommonly in politics where self-presentation to win votes may hide a dark, scheming and manipulative style. That the prosocial style is a deception is revealed at times of conflicts of view or doubt, or if a member of the group desires to leave and defect. Everything changes for the potential defector. Where before they were wanted and esteemed, now they are degraded (e.g., called scab, traitor, heretic, weak, or made fun of, etc.). They can be threatened with fear of permanent expulsion, loss of status and prestige, loss of support, or outright persecution from the previously supportive group and its leader. To put this another way, when a subordinate looks for the exit they find they are trapped – it is hard to leave, or if they do, impossible to return. Many religious-based groups use this threat of course. No one can love you like God can love you – if you leave the clan, the religion, you will put yourself beyond God and his love. Don't defect. You can always tell a genuine spiritual group from an antisocial one simply by how free you are to come and go.

So, the superficial prosocial leader knows how to play the game. They can stay prosocial as long as they receive sufficient subordinate, compliant, loving, or devotional signals. As we shall see later, Jim Jones was almost certainly one of these types. They are among the most dangerous because of their skilful manipulation of needs for love, acceptance and conformity in subordinates, and their ability to create a sense of protection and belonging for in-group members, with subtle (and sometimes not so subtle) undercurrents of fear.

Most of our history has not been shaped by leaders who have been on management training courses. It is alarming how much human history, not to mention our value systems, have been shaped by people who seem rather crazy and certainly anti-social. Our civilisation, culture and even our self-identities, have been significantly shaped by our leaders and the mimicry of their values. Even now we don't take nearly enough care in choosing our leaders (see next chapter). But through most of our history we have not had that much choice. In fact, human history is the history of the tragedy of the power of the narcissistic antisocial leader. Let's look at a few of them

An Historical Legacy of Anti-Social and Divisive Leaders

Gaius Julius Caesar was born around 100 BC. He was a man of extraordinary personal ambition. According to Grabsky's recent study, Caesar was a great commander.[271] And well he might have been, but he was an archetypal, anti-social leader. From a very early age he was fixated on the desire for power and status in Rome. He, like many with anti-social leadership styles, was quite willing to take subordinate positions and ingratiate or grovel if it suited his purpose. He was known as a good orator and a ruthless manipulator. He also bore grudges. Once, when he was captured by pirates off the island of Rhodes, he joked with them that he would hunt them down and crucify them. When his ransom was paid and he was released, he did exactly that.

Caesar worked out that the only way to gain power back in Rome was via developing his reputation as a military commander. His conquests had no other purpose as far as we can tell except to impress and give him power. For this, he was prepared to wage wars that would kill and enslave very many thousands. Among his many campaigns was the invasion of Gaul, which at the time was most of Northern Europe. He regarded the Gauls as semi-barbaric: a typical out-

---

[271] Grabsky, P. (1993)

group perception for the anti-social leader. In fact, they were developing an interesting culture of their own that he pretty much wiped out. There is no doubt that he was a courageous commander and gained the loyalty of his men by fighting with them, often shoulder to shoulder. Not all anti-social and divisive leaders are like this. But he also succeeded in stifling the growing culture and civilisation that was emerging in Gaul and changing the course of Western history for ever: all for personal ambition. Roman emperors however could be more prosocial and articulate, such as Marcus Aurelius, who waged many wars in Northern Europe and supported the games, but was also a Stoic, following the teachings of Epictetus (to whom cognitive therapists often refer today). He had some interesting, almost compassionate, personal philosophies and values including believing in the practice of self-restraint. But there are also some horrors such as Nero and Caligula. In the end Rome was torn apart through warring factions and power struggles.

Grabsky's book is full of descriptions of people who can be described, to a degree at least, as having anti-social and divisive leadership styles. For Napoleon, Grabsky's narrative tells us of another ruthlessly ambitious man, who appeared to fear passing into history without trace. New looks at history suggest that Richard the Lionheart was actually a thug, and the Crusades pretty barbaric affairs. Francis Drake was a plunderer and slaver - facts not commonly taught in our idealised history books. Genghis Khan was horrific. And much of the Viking Empire which stretched down to the Mediterranean and beyond was based on slavery, savage raids on settlements and pretty ruthless kings. British history too is soaked in the wars and battles of rival kings and queens with their hangings, burnings and torturing of opponents.

Hitler is the most obvious, recent and extreme form of anti-social leader. He was moody and unpredictable, and full of ideas of the need for conquest and the creation of the super-race. Unlike Caesar, who from the outset was interested in personal power, Hitler always linked his greatness and that of the German people together. Caesar did not see himself as a rescuing hero. Hitler did - the chosen one to act out the vengeance for the First World War.[25] Indeed, the *rescuing hero* type of leader is also potentially dangerous for he (it is usually is he) can inflame the insecurities of people, work on their grievances and offer himself as a saviour. As Lindholm notes, Hitler was devastated by the defeat of the First World War:

> But Hitler did not disintegrate. His experiences had altered him, so that at this hopeless moment he received the call that reformulated his identity. Voices, like Joan of Arc, told him to rescue the motherland from the Jews. His blindness miraculously vanished as Hitler suddenly knew himself to be the saviour of his adopted nation. Henceforth, he and Germany were, he felt, mystically merged and he could act from his inner feelings with absolute certainty.[272]

A seriously inflated archetype if ever there was one. There is another fact that is not well known. According to psychiatrist Hugh Freeman[273], one-time President of the Royal College of Psychiatry, Dr Morrell, the personal doctor to Hitler from 1936, was giving him large quantities of medication including sedatives, narcotics and amphetamine – often on demand. These may well have increased his tendency to psychosis and paranoia. Towards the end Hitler was not only showing the signs of syphilis but also Parkinson's disease, probably the consequence of such drug abuse and a burnt-out dopamine system. Undoubtedly, his judgement would have been very clouded.

Throughout history, the drives for power, dominance, saviourhood and rescuing heroes have been linked - and they can make a very unsavoury mixture. Indeed, one of the great tales of leadership, represented in many religious groups, is of a leader's belief in saviourhood together with the subordinates need to feel saved, restored and reunited as a group. In Hitler, the need for high dominance was obviously amplified as was a clear paranoid orientation to outsiders. The sheer scale of human suffering he brought to the world probably bears few equals, although Stalin comes to mind. Like many effective leaders he was clever, manipulative, ruthless and a good orator, capable of arousing strong feelings of power, national pride and devotion to the cause. He was able to deceive Chamberlain that he was trustworthy. Like many, he was a complex character,

---

[272] Lindholm, C. (1993), p.109
[273] Freeman, H. (1991)

however, because, as Lindholm[274] notes, he had strong needs to be loved and cared for. At the time he was persecuting Jews, he passed a decree that lobsters should be given a painless death. He was also a vegetarian!

His contemporary, Stalin, was not much different. He cleverly outmanoeuvred Trotsky after Lenin's death and hounded him into exile, where in Mexico in 1949 Trotsky was murdered with an ice pick in the head. Trotsky was not that pleasant himself and was quite able to shoot deserters, but he was a rival of Stalin's and possibly Lenin's preferred choice of successor. Stalin could not tolerate dissent, bore grudges and had no qualms in sending millions to the death camps. His will and vision were imposed with a terrible cost to the Russian people. Socialist ideals became a nightmare in his hands. Even now, the power vacuum in this totalitarian state leaves room for new anti-social leaders to come through, peddling their paranoid messages, and appeal to greatness to the oppressed.

It is a harrowing realisation that at the time of the Second World War, the main leaders of the conflict all had very serious problems. In Germany was a highly disturbed personality and drug addict, the leader of Italy not a lot better, Stalin was a clear paranoid and psychopath, and as gifted as he was, Churchill suffered from manic-depression.

As noted above, some individuals can appear to be prosocial leaders, even offering love and compassion, but such outward appearances actually hide, or overlay, a cauldron of hate and fear. This can be most deceptive – at least to some people. The cult leader Jim Jones gained his following by preaching a lot about love and offering saviourhood. He told his followers that no one could love them like he could – all else was a pale shadow. He told people how much they could find love through him, and preached an idealistic and simplistic morality. Yet he was a loner who from an early age said, "I was ready to kill by the third grade. I mean I was so fucking aggressive and hostile, I was ready to kill. Nobody gave me any love, any understanding.... I'm standing there alone. Alone. Always alone..." [275]

---

[274] Lindholm, C. (1993)
[275] Lindholm, C. (1993), p.140

Moreover, like some anti-social and divisive leaders, he focused sexuality and sexual values on himself. David Koresh was the same. For Jones,

> Those who showed an interest in the opposite sex – and were therefore "compensating" for their homosexuality – were humiliated, or sometimes sodomised by Jones to prove their homosexuality... Jones' sexual contact with men generated tremendous sexual conflict within some of them. He made his lessons in buggery all the more humiliating by always assuming the dominant position. As he conquered his partners, he told them again and again that it was for their own good. He derived no pleasure at all from the act, he told them, but made sure they did.[276]

In the next chapter, we shall look at 'followership' and ponder why these kinds of people get the attention they do. Hitler and similar others can only get power because there are many willing to support them. For Hitler, these were vast numbers in the military, police, academia, businesses right through to the clerks on the shop floor. Unless we understand the social, economic and political conditions that allow these individuals to come through – with their messages of strong leadership, power and pride – then we will not understand how such terrors can be brought to life. It is comforting to think that they, and the people who follow them, are crazy in a psychiatric sense – and maybe some are. But even though these are extreme anti-social and divisive styles of leadership, they have impacted on our history substantially. Crazy it may be, but in a common and tragic rather than pathological sense.

Problematic in another way are those who have these styles to a mild degree, and by their commitment to dogmas and ideologies are impassioned for what they believe to be a moral crusade. As Dixon[277] points out, unfortunately virtue and crusades can be highly destructive. We might hope that such leadership styles are unlikely in democracies, and certainly the excesses are constrained, but not completely.

---

[276] Lindholm, C. (1993), p.145
[277] Dixon, N.F. (1987)

Autocracy and Democracy

Autocratic forms of leadership are represented at both extremes of political activity, but the right and left wing have different concerns in regard to rank. The right wing is concerned with competition and the emergence of ranks and differences, protecting privilege, and with gaining, maintaining or identifying with a superior position. The left dislike competition and any form of ranks (at least that is what they say publicly, but we know the warnings in *Animal Farm*). They often identify themselves with the low(er) ranks – the workers. The two wings can see themselves in complete opposition although the leadership styles can be similar. Many noted similarities of interpersonal style between Scargill and Thatcher at the time of the miner's strike in 1984.

In many ways, various leaders arise because they seem to offer solutions to the various social tensions inherent in our modern institutional life styles. We explored what these tensions were in Chapter 4, with recourse to the ideas of Eisenstadt.[278] A potential threat to society comes from a failure to tackle these social tensions and find compassionate solutions for those who feel outsiders and are disadvantaged. The left has been labelled as a party of envy, fighting for the subordinates, the underdog, and is identified by the rich as a potentially inhibiting and grasping party concerned more with the distribution of wealth rather than its creation. The right is derived from a sense of superiority and fear of subordinate attack. Both, in different ways, can reflect authoritarian rather than compassionate values; both support the politics of conflict rather than consensus; and both think in terms of strong government to impose their own system of values (which are seen as threatening either to one or other ends of the hierarchy).

Do we really only have a choice between the politics of greed and fragmentation versus the politics of envy and corporatism? Without a clear psychological understanding of the dynamics of rank, these polarised conflicts will continue, and although winners and losers may change places, overall nothing changes.

---

[278] Eisenstadt, S.N. (1992), pp.73-74

Within the friction between competing groups, one or other may gain the ascendency. But as Milgram noted,

> Some dismiss the Nazi example because we live in a democracy and not an authoritarian state. But, in reality, this does not eliminate the problem. For the problem is not "authoritarianism" as a mode of political organisation or a set of psychological attitudes but authority itself. Authoritarianism may give way to democratic practice, but authority cannot be eliminated as long as society is to continue in the form we know. [279]

As I write, this it is the fiftieth anniversary of the liberation of the Nazi concentration camps. For all the television programmes that there have been, all the stories sadly told, there was not one programme that I saw which had any in-depth analysis of the social-psychological forces that brought the Nazi state to life, and nothing on our vulnerability as a species to such tribal violence because of the evolutionary archetypes in our brain The superficiality was, to my mind, interesting because I doubt it was deliberate, and speaks to the denial and dissociation we have about the nature of our crazy brains, but also frighteningly that we don't have an in-depth explanation for the horrors that our evolved human brains can create. We can defeat it, but we need some enlightenment.

Western democracies suffer other flaws, one of which, not surprisingly, is wealth and money. Behind the scenes, particularly in America, wealth buys political access. Huge funds are needed to support political parties and people running for election. For most of us, it's very difficult to have any inkling of what's actually going on, who's actually pulling the strings, who's actually paying for papers to peddle right-wing (or left-wing) propaganda. Occasionally, brilliant journalists are able to peel back the curtains on the behind-scenes deals and lobbying. The problem for democracy then is the whole game: the thinking up of the policies, who they are designed to privilege, who funds political parties and helps to propagate those policies, who can use the media to promote and sell those policies and so on. Democracy is a complex multi-textured mechanism for

---

[279] Milgram, S. (1974), p.179

the manipulation of minds – that sometimes does manage to improve human well-being – but as current history shows, tends to privilege the wealthy elites. Leadership in these shifting grounds of power is tricky. When politicians speak of "we are a democracy", they rely on the fact that most have not had the opportunity to understand just how complex and multi-textured that concept is. We need to be careful that we don't assume a voting system is a democracy – which is tending to be what is happening now.

Recent Leaders

Although we now live in a democracy, it is in the very nature of the manipulation of power that democracy often fails to provide prosocial leaders. Hugh Freeman[280] has given a powerful and frightening review of how psychological and physical health problems have plagued many of our recent leaders in Europe and America. His review highlights many concerns, some of which are noted here. Woodrow Wilson suffered a number of mini-strokes that led to a personality change. In 1945, at the time of the Yalta conference, Roosevelt was so terminally ill he may not have really understood what was going on. J.F. Kennedy used amphetamine and steroids, both of which could have affected his judgement. Lyndon Johnson has been described as highly narcissistic with feelings of insecurity and grandiosity. In 1966-67, when the Vietnam War was becoming preoccupied with carpet bombing and defoliation, Johnson viewed his critics as 'enemies and traitors'. Nixon was known to have many narcissistic traits, to be exploitative and untrustworthy. At the time of the Watergate scandal he was drinking to such an extent, "that his aids thought him incapable of dealing with any business - however urgent - at these times."[281] Ronald Reagan, towards the end, was known to be suffering from dementia, now sadly well advanced. Yet it was believed that if he could have stood again, he would have won. It is true of course that the personalities of leaders do not exclude them from bringing social advances. Johnson did introduce important polices of social reform and a "new deal." But the pressures of modern leadership can still play havoc with a

---

[280] Freeman, H. (1991)
[281] Freeman, H. (1991), p.24

person and while they may be helpful to insiders, they can be highly destructive to outsiders.

In Britain, Anthony Eden, at the time of the Suez crisis, was abusing drugs and alcohol, and was described by some to be "quite simply mad."[282] As the history books are written on Margaret Thatcher and the upsurge of the right in the 1980's, we get clear evidence of the autocratic leadership style. Ian Gilmour's book *Dancing with Dogma*[283] leaves little doubt that at least some of the elements that go to making an autocrat were present in Thatcher's style. For example, Gilmour (who was one of her ministers in the early years) writes,

> Mrs Thatcher regarded her first cabinet (and, I suspect, also her other cabinets) not as an aid to good government but as an obstacle to be surmounted. Her belief that dialogue was a waste of time rather than a means of arriving at an agreed course of action was a part of her rejection of consensus politics. Consensus, the Prime Minster later proclaimed, was achieved only by 'abandoning all beliefs, principles and values. Whoever won a battle,' she asked, 'under the banner of, "I stand for consensus"?' In her mind, of course, 'conviction' was diametrically opposed to consensus.[284]

As the years passed, and more and more cabinet colleagues defected, speaking of her autocratic treatment of them, we began to get more insight into the psychology that controlled her. Rank and dominance and the need for greatness were written everywhere. And for whom was this greatness desired? Not for the poor who became poorer still, but for an elite: for an ideal of being British. Her obsession with enemies was revealed clearly when she said at the time of the miner's strike in 1984, "We had to fight the enemy without in the Falklands. We always have to be aware of the enemy within, which is more difficult to fight and more dangerous to liberty" (quoted by Gilmour). So, the miners were not just ordinary people fighting, often vigorously, for their jobs (manipulated by their own leader to a degree), but were potential enemies of the cause. This was

---

[282] Freeman, H. (1991)
[283] Gilmour, I.I. (1993)
[284] Gilmour, I.I. (1993), pp.4-5

a time when a Prime Minister openly talked about ninnies and wimps, and efforts at shaming. It was a time that ideology and causes mattered more than people. It was a time when there was no such thing as society only a collection of individuals, until that is, Brussels threatened British interests, then the idea of Britishness and society made a comeback.

When her end came it was shabby, marred by back-stabbing and retribution for the failures in the courage and loyalty of her subordinates (colleagues). Such an old story and somewhat typical of a person who has little ability to reflect on the self, and see the sources of her difficulties as coming from within. To be fair to Thatcher though, it is less clear how much she was motivated by a personal ambition to be great, or more to rescue an identity for family and country. Certainly, her stated intent was to free people from government control, although in this quango-ised state of ours even this is doubtful. It is now estimated there are 7,700 quangos of various sorts, often staffed by Conservative appointees and costing the state £54 billion.[285] She was certainly a strong leader and enjoyed the title of the 'Iron Lady'. But, outside of competitive sport perhaps, why would anybody be pleased with the title of being an iron person - cold and inflexible? We must leave it to the historians to decide. She changed Britain significantly. Who knows what we may now be like without her. But it is her style that marks her as being the autocratic in divisive type.

We can see that some divisive leaders have a number of qualities: a need for power; a belief in their own way; a focus on the importance of strength; a tendency to talk in terms of fighting, conquering, pride and becoming great; a need to stress the importance of being more powerful than competitors; paranoid or contemptuous attitudes to those who are not in-group members; a preparedness to subdue subordinates not with argument but with fear or shame – the language of wimps and ninnies. They will also constantly talk up the greatness of their own country and nation. Of course, we don't need to do that because we've called ourselves Great (Britain) anyway, just in case other people didn't realise that.

---

[285] As quoted by Hutton, W. (1995a)

In whatever context leadership arises, the lack of compassion for followers and subordinates can lead to appalling abuses of power; the First World War being a most tragic example. As Dixon[286] makes clear, at times military leaders have seen their subordinates as no more than cannon-fodder. But even democratically elected leaders can show a complete lack of interest in certain sections of the groups they lead, except to keep them in check. Many leaders in the West appear to have a view of the "workers" as manoeuvrable production units whose value depends on whether they can be fitted in with wealth-creating; i.e., production fodder. Rebellions can be ruthlessly put down (e.g., the Miners' Strike of 1984).

If we are becoming increasing cynical about, and distrusting of, our leaders, religious and political, and even democracy, we might remember our history and what has gone before. There is no way to avoid leadership. Sure, some will try to manipulate us to get our vote and sure they will have the various human failings, but we can still insist on compassionate values once we sort out in our own minds the issue of how we want the world to look for our children and grandchildren. Do we want them to live in a polluted, highly competitive, 'dump the losers' world?[287]

As Freeman[288] makes clear, some of our problems with leadership arise because our jerry-built brains were never designed to cope with the leadership of the mega-groups we now live within, nor the mass of information leaders have to cope with, nor the uncertainties of positions that can change rapidly, nor the complexity of the competing interests of all the subgroups that exist within the modern state, nor indeed with the grandiosity and scale of power that is so much

---

[286] Dixon, N.F. (1974/1994)

[287] We don't have to go with the message of a need to be special or great or if we do we can be great for other reasons apart from beating opponents or competitors. We may need strong leaders but they need to be chosen by us to tell the truth and advise us of the reality – a reality that in our hearts we all know. Sociobiologists might say, "so what did you expect of a jumped-up clump of DNA that only got to where it is today by looking after self-interest." You can't argue with that, I guess, but this does not mean we are completely powerless either. The more we understand ourselves and the cultural values we adopt, the leaders we support and why, the more we are given some freedoms to choose. It's worth a hope anyway.

[288] Freeman, H. (1991)

part of a modern nation state. To say that political leadership, with its hands on nuclear buttons and the arms trade, is in crisis, is an understatement.

Selecting for the Best or Worst?

Democracy, as many realise, has a number of serious flaws. It requires potential leaders to be bright, but also it entices them to be manipulative and even deceptive, prepared to engineer information and statistics, or at least cherry-pick, to make themselves look good. To play to the media, and to increasingly develop a debate which is designed to undermine the opposition rather than create visions of a better world. Very few people are sufficiently 'in the know' to make informed judgements, and so our dependency on leader/party rhetoric is ensured. Many democracies currently operate in a highly competitive, adversarial domain, where point scoring is a mark of good leadership. For sure, a lot of excellent work goes on in the select committees, but the pantomime of our adversarial Question Time is not such a good advert for democracy. Most developed societies operate a first-past-the-post system, and when there are only two major parties, the number of minor ones might split the vote. There is no other profession that depends so much on manipulation of attention.

Moreover, typical of the divisive leadership style are appeals to *national pride*. These presentations can be filled with rhetoric and nonverbal displays of power as they glower down from their podiums. As we have seen, pride and the appeal to superiority can be a powerful appeal indeed, but also terribly destructive. Thatcher's messages were full of restoring British pride. But the origins at least of some of our industrial wealth are in slavery, which is hardly a source of pride. Also, democratic leaders (and the media who might support them), to get votes, can pander to the worse in us – to our xenophobic tendencies and fears (and desires for retribution) of crime. Groups like the unemployed, immigrants, those on welfare, single parents or those on death row are marginalised and shamed to boost the prestige of the potential leader. Leaders may grossly mislead people and, to quote George Orwell, the political can become a matter of `defending the indefensible', a reality Gilmour[289] would see all too readily in the Britain of the 1980s.

Leadership and Alliances

Our animal-primate psychology is revealed in other ways when it comes to leadership and flaws in democracy. One of the most serious problems facing us is that both primate and human leadership/dominance are always derived from alliances. So indeed, over many centuries human leaders have built around themselves a system of alliances (reaching back to simple serfdoms and chiefdoms) that ensure a continuation of elitist values and institutions. Because leaders need support they have to build in a potential reward system for followers and supporters, enabling them to gain power in the higher echelons of the group and protect their privileges. There is always a complex interaction between leaders and alliances. The use of favouritism and patronage to alliances is as powerful a mechanism in humans as it is in non-human primates. No chimpanzee can make it to the top without offering favours to alliances.

As Hutton points out, this has been achieved in Britain via the continuance of an old system of favours and mutual supports, operated through the institutionalisation of the peerage, honour and patronage system:

> the incapacity of the constitution to offer any check to discretionary executive government has even corrupted the Conservative Party, with the contagion spreading to the state. Honours are routinely awarded to party contributors; funds are accepted from foreign donors of questionable character and motive in return for undeclared favours; defence contracts and flotation of privatised utilities are awarded to government supporters in industry and city. What has been constructed in Britain, using the ancient and unfettered state, is a form of conservative hegemony in the literal meaning of that word: a system of supremacy over others.[290]

---

[289] Gilmour, I.I. (1993)
[290] Hutton, W. (1995a), p.4

And moreover,

> The Lord Chancellor, a member of the cabinet appoints the judges who come from the same milieu as his party colleagues while the government's chief officer, the Attorney General is also drawn from the ranks of the governing party... Judges appoint other judges in their own image, while the criminal justice system is increasingly involved in maintaining order.[291]

In whatever social milieu we explore, be it patriarchy[3], or the establishment of academic and scientific hegemonies, or the political institutions we inhabit, or even the rise of tyrants like Hitler, we see that leaders and alliances are wrapped around each other to protect their own interests and shape the values and pursuits of privilege – supremacy. Barkow's[292] recognition of the role of status and prestige in forming and maintaining human ranks, is, in our current human society, the primate mind advanced by its skilful manipulation of favours. Until these psychological aspects of our minds are addressed and confronted, as they work themselves out in our traditions, values and institutions, it is unlikely that we will be free from creating a certain craziness in our social spaces. This is because, as we saw in Chapter 5, such archetypal forces are designed to create inequality, specialness, privilege and unfairness, not the reverse.

Self-Interest on the World Stage

It seems clear that many positions of power rely on forming alliances and various trades of favours to support mutual self-interest. Internationally, this has had many tragic consequences. In the first place, the growth of the arms trade and the power of Western armies has led many Western governments to support foreign groups and governments that were not far short of barbaric. They did so from pure self-interest and xenophobia, but their actions were clothed in the

---

[291] Hutton, W. (1995a), p.36
[292] Barkow, J.H. (1989)

language of moral crusades and freedom. Chomsky's[293] book *Deterring Democracy* leaves no doubt that the West has been involved in a fairly systematic process of propping up many two-bit dictators provided they leave open the door to Western influence (and access to their resources), with tragic consequences for the people. In the history of modern wars, we can see time after time the meddling hand of the West. Not only do they arm one, and at times both sides, but the conflicts of the lands fought over are often due to Western influence. Some of the problems in the Middle East can be traced back to the European countries making poorly thought-out deals after the First World War. Some of Africa is split up into unrealistic nation states disrespectful of tribal boundaries with arbitrary borders due to the legacy of colonialism.

Time after time, the desire to support alliances rather than stick to moral principles has been to our shame. The history of Vietnam is a history of broken promises. Hồ Chí Minh had helped the Americans against the Japanese and were promised that the Americans would do what they could to keep the French (whose colony it was before the war) out. In the six months of 1945, when they briefly had independence, Hồ Chí Minh actually quoted from the American constitution. In the end, the alliance to France was stronger than to Vietnam, and the French recolonised the south, creating a new rebel group in the north. Understandably the sense of anger and betrayal was immense. The rest, as they say, is history. Turning a blind eye to our own, and our allies', immoral behaviour has been the source of much suffering.

Democracies then do not liberate us from pursuing self-interest and exploitation. We just do it in different ways, hiding our historical immoral behaviours and using appeals to national pride and self-interest with a little xenophobia thrown in for good measure. This gets votes. As we shall see in our chapter on economics, once a society begins to loosen the restraints on self-interest, and anything goes in the pursuit of profit and wealth accumulations, societies begin to fragment and we end up with the worst economic and social depravities. A

---

[293] Chomsky, N. (1992). This is a detailed exploration of (mostly) American foreign policy and how in reality much of it has hindered rather than helped democracies in other parts of the world.

civilised society becomes civilised by the restraints it imposes on self-interest and exploitation, not by deregulation and removing restraints.

Leading Change?

If we are honest, for most of us in the West life is a good deal better than it was 200 years ago. It's better to be a woman now than then, to be homosexual, to be educated, and to be sick and old. It is, of course true that Western societies, indeed the world, are undergoing rapid change. We need leaders who are managers of this change. These managers and leaders are going to have to address themselves to the increasing conflicts and tensions of competing groups, wealth disparities and social injustices. If our psychological health, both nationally and internationally, were put more on the agenda as a salient concern in managing this change, then I suspect we might have a very different orientation of how we go about things. But sadly, we don't. The pursuit of wealth and self-interest rule today. The creation of short-term employment contracts, and increasing part-time work (which has far fewer rights than full-time) and the increasing insecurities gradually proliferating, as our cultures and communities fragment, suggests times of increasing violence, depression and various stress-related conditions.[294] Styles of leadership, from the reaches of government right down to the managers of industry and (what used to be) the nationalised services, are caught in the whirlwind of these changes. If the stories of my patients are to be believed, as they lose their jobs or have wages cut, managers are veering towards increasingly, competitive anti-social and divisive styles.

Over and over again, evolutionary psychologists (along with many others) will tell us that we cannot just create any social climate and think that humans will behave decently. Our minds are constantly monitoring the social domain, they are highly attuned to it and if the social domains provide cues for poverty, envy, betrayal, etc., we will react accordingly. Although many like to think that moral

---

[294] There is increasing evidence that violent crime, depression and suicide (in younger males) are increasing. Some of the evidence for this is outlined elsewhere; Gilbert, P. (1992) and Archer, J. (1994, ed.) and Miedzian, M. (1992).

behaviour is about individuals, this is a cosy illusion.[295] Moral behaviour grows from moral institutions, and moral social structures that promote social fairness and the recognition of the needs of others, not just self-interest. Social policy matters. It is as much a top-down as a bottom-up process.

Conclusion

We are increasingly interested in styles of leadership and are far less prepared (or educated) to adopt subordinate roles than we were. Many commentators see a gradual reduction in our deferential attitudes to our social institutions. But this is only a beginning and our subordinate tendencies and needs for strong leaders who offer clarity and certainty (and promote self-interest) are powerful within us. Unfortunately, our reduced deference is giving way to cynicism and contempt for authority, which could have serious unforeseen consequences. Moreover, even in democracies, we should be wary of how the press and others manipulate our values and get us to cast our vote. As Gilmour notes, it is possible to live under an 'elected dictatorship'.[296]

Although the grosser excesses and tyrannies of dictatorship are often limited by democracies, this does not guarantee us freedom from divisive leadership style. Their visions for greatness, their authoritarian tendencies and appeals to pride and privilege, singing to our animal natures, may well fragment and destroy the fabric of civil society – and we will vote for it.

---

[295] Emler, H. and Hogan, R. (1991)
[296] Gilmour, I.I. (1993)

8: SUBMITTING, FOLLOWING AND REBELLION

The powerful ... have a vital interest in keeping up the appearances appropriate to their form of domination. Subordinates, for their part, ordinarily have good reasons to help sustain those appearances or, at least, not openly contradict them. Taken together, these two social facts have, I believe, important consequences for the analysis of power relations.[297]

Despite our beliefs in our human autonomy and individuality, we may be one of the most easily led and manipulated species to have walked this earth. We can be inspired by our leaders, be devoted to them, be terrified of them, deceived by them, kill for them, and even kill ourselves for them. Between 1940 and 1945 over 11 million people were murdered in the Nazi death camps of Germany because many were prepared to submit to, and comply with, the xenophobic visions of their leader. In 1978 the world was horrified by the way the charismatic religious leader, Jim Jones, had created the conditions by which nearly a thousand people voluntarily committed mass suicide (including feeding poison to their own children) on his orders.

Leader-follower (dominate-subordinate) behaviour is recognised in just about every type of mammal. This behaviour could only have evolved and become so common if there had been reproductive benefits for both leaders (dominants) and followers (subordinates).[298] However, as the 1978 Jonestown mass suicides show, the evolved psychology of subordination and following can at times work against genetic self-interest. At the very least, it demonstrates the enormous power of leader-follower relationships. Moreover, as discussed in the last chapter, we often put great emphasis on the importance of personal freedom, and yet often fail to recognise just how much of our behaviour is directed at

---

[297] Scott, J.C. (1990), p.70
[298] Crook, J.H. (1986). We will not explore the evolutionary theories here in any detail, but Crook has written an excellent paper on the subject, exploring reproductive benefits of leader-follower behaviour.

seeking approval, fitting in with our social groups and subordinating ourselves to various individuals, doctrines, traditions and values.

This chapter explores some of the complexities of human forms of appeasing, ingratiating, submitting and following. We start by looking at basic evolved patterns of submission. From there we will consider how 'submitting to' and endorsing social rules, values and doctrines underpins our personal identities. I will then consider why we find some types of leader (even highly authoritarian ones) and their values attractive.

Voluntary and Involuntary Submissions

Many of the earliest forms of social behaviour, such as courting, sexual advertising, mating, threatening, harassing, territorial defence, ritual threat displays and submission, are to be found in our earliest ancestors, the reptiles. MacLean points out that

> Ethologists have made it popularly known ... that a passive response (a submissive display) to an aggressive display may make it possible under most circumstances to avoid unnecessary, and sometimes mortal, conflict. Hence it could be argued that the *submissive display is the most important of all displays* because without it numerous individuals might not survive. (italics added)[299]

Submissive behaviour made an early appearance on the evolutionary stage. Few would argue that submissive behaviour in all its various forms are central to human activities. The difference between us and the reptiles is not in the need to have a submissive repertoire, but that human submission is far more complex. In terms of our human psychology, the two basic dimensions which underpin human submissive and following behaviour are our old friends *fear* and *attraction* (see Chapter 3).

Fear: When there is fear of the dominant(s), the basic psychology is escape/avoidance, compliance, obedience or simple resignation. We do what we

---

[299] MacLean, P.D. (1990), p.235

are told, follow and comply with others out of fear of the consequences of doing otherwise. This is a form of *involuntary subordination*. If we had the power/resources not to submit or could escape from the situation, then we would. Some forms of fearful, involuntary submission (which involves feelings of powerlessness and having to comply with the wishes of others) show up in many forms of psychopathology. The psychiatrist John Price[300] was one of the first to link (a personal belief in) low status and submissive behaviour to psychopathology. For example, in social anxiety and depression, people often feel very inhibited in putting forward their own views or needs. It is well known that the depressed and socially anxious person finds it very difficult to be confidently assertive – even though they would very much like to be so. They experience their inhibitions as quite involuntary, and may even hate themselves for it. Depressed people often feel highly subordinate, and label themselves as inferior, bad, inadequate, failures, losers and worthless (i.e., of low status/power).[301]

One form of involuntary submission comes from certain states of mind – we feel constrained from within ourselves. At other times, we recognise that our subordinate behaviours are very much controlled from outside; they are controlled by the situation or context. Indeed, since most of our lives are lived in hierarchically organised social structures, we often need to know when and to whom to act submissively, or at least not openly challenge. As Scott[302] makes

---

[300] For the most recent outline, see Price et al. (1994), and Sloman et al. (1994). One view of depression is that the person has a strong desire to escape or fight (and not accept the situation they are in) but are unable to do so effectively (e.g., maybe they are not strong enough or lack the opportunities).

[301] Just as one can be in a state of love, so one can be in a state of submission. Love is exciting; it keeps us awake at night; it lifts our self-esteem and recruits our fantasies. It makes us get a new haircut and buy new clothes. Being defeated, and/or in a state of intense submission, however, leaves us feeling without energy, without lost confidence; the fight goes out of us, and we feel inferior, worthless and without status. It too can keep us awake but more from fear, worry and looking how to escape – sometimes, suicide seems the only way. Lizards too seem to get depressed if they lose rank. For more on this depressing tale, see Gilbert, P. (1992).

[302] Scott, J.C. (1990) explores this distinction between private and public forms of subordination in detail, and makes clear that even those who accept a subordinate position in society or other relationships may not see themselves as personally inferior.

clear, there is always a difference to be drawn between public forms of submission/obedience and private acceptance. The most deferential public displays may be accompanied by quite the opposite behind closed doors and when out of sight of the dominant. At one level, we may know we are choosing to behave as a subordinate, but in private do not identify ourselves as inferior in a personal sense. Nonetheless, the experiences associated with *fear-based compliance* include fear of persecution and punishment/injury, exclusion, withdrawal of approval and love, shame and even loss of identity. Some subordinate behaviours directed towards a dominant are often related to *calming a potentially punitive dominant,* e.g., a god, leader, parent or group.

Generally then, involuntary submission occurs when a person recognises that they are behaving in non-assertive, submissive, appeasing or ingratiating ways, and would prefer not to, but cannot muster the confidence to be assertive, or the situation is such that it would be detrimental to be assertive or refrain from ingratiating. The feelings associated with involuntary submission are mostly negative and include depression, anxiety and various forms of resentment. Such feelings are rare when it comes to voluntary submission. Voluntary submission is usually based on attraction.

Subordination to a leader/dominant because the leader is attractive (has high SAHP) is a little trickier, and usually *seems* far more voluntary. Here we willingly submit to the other. We recognise their superiority, indeed are relieved by it, for the dominant seems stronger, wiser or more able than ourselves. We want to form a *positive relationship with him/her, and to benefit from this relationship*, rather than (say) just control his/her anger. In this situation we may show respect, adoration, worship and even love. However, subordinate love is a different kind of love to that between (say) mother and baby, sexual lovers or friends. In the first place, lovers, babies and friends are not awed by each other, and they spend a lot of time looking into each other's eyes and exploring each other's faces. In submissive adoration, however, there are clear submissive

---

Acts to protect the self from the persecuting power of dominant elites are not the same as internalisation of an inferior identity. Indeed, oppressed groups may see themselves as morally superior.

behaviours such as bowing the head, going down on one knee as a mark of respect, avoiding eye contact or even prostrating oneself. The dominant is at a distance and cannot be approached with any intimacy. Indeed, to do so is taken as a sign of disrespect and not knowing one's place. The dominant can touch you, but (usually) you cannot reach out and embrace the dominant. So, adoration and worship of a dominant, when it involves submission and recognition of one's inferior position, is different from other forms of love. At times, there can be an acute sensitivity to one's deferential social presentation. In religious texts, submitting to God's will and love of God are often seen as interchangeable. It is the degree to which a person sees their submission, and obedience, to a higher authority as voluntary or involuntary that determines whether such behaviours are associated with negative feelings or more positive ones.

Sometimes a person comes to 'adore' someone who is actually quite harmful to them. How did Hitler get the following he did? In various abusive relationships there can be an attraction and what looks like voluntary submission to rather aversive characters, and one wonders how this could happen. Indeed, it is in the interaction of fear- and attraction-based forms of submissive behaviour that produces so many paradoxes of human behaviour. The next part of this chapter explores some of the ways they can become locked together.

Reverted Escape

There is an aspect to subordination that involves both fear and attraction in a rather odd way. This was noted by Michael Chance[303] in his studies of non-human primates. In many primates, if a subordinate has been attacked by a dominant the first response is to flee, but subsequently the subordinate seems motivated to return to the dominant – the very source of the threat. It is as if the dominant now has some attraction to the subordinate. Often, Chance observed, there can be a cautious and tense return, where approach and avoidance seem to compete. Gradually, moving forward and expressing highly submissive behaviours, the subordinate comes nearer and nearer to the dominant until they

---

[303] Chance, M.R.A. (1988); Gilbert, P. (1989)

are close. Then, not uncommonly, the dominant will often pat, stroke or even embrace the subordinate. These behaviours have a calming effect on both the dominant and subordinate. The subordinate has, as it were, made the threat less, by ensuring acceptance of itself via ensuring that its submission is accepted. It has changed the state of mind of the dominant – from anger to reassurance. This has been called *reverted escape* – meaning that coping with a threat actually involves returning to it and calming it down. This is particularly likely where subordinates have to stay in the confines of the group; they are to some extent trapped because to leave the group or go-it alone would put them at serious survival risk.

Jane Goodall[304] has observed very similar behaviours in chimpanzees, which she feels is related to a need for contact (although need to calm the dominant is also probably, if not more, important.) She gives a good example of reverted escape:

> Perhaps the most dramatic illustration of the chimpanzee's need for physical contact is after he has been threatened or attacked by a superior, particularly when a young adolescent male has been victimised by a high-ranking adult male. Once Figan, aged about 10 years, was badly pounded by the alpha male (Goliath at the time). Screaming and tense, Figan began cautiously approaching his aggressor who sat with his hair still bristling. Every so often, the desire to flee seemed almost to overcome the adolescent's desire for contact and he turned, as though to retreat. But each time he went on again until eventually he was crouched, flat on the ground in front of Goliath. And there he stayed, still screaming, until Goliath, in response to his submission, began to pat him gently on the back on and on until the screaming gradually subsided and Figan sat up and moved away quite calmly. Such incidents are common and almost always the aggressor responds to the submissive gestures of the subordinate with a touch, a pat or even an embrace. Occasionally, if a young male is not reassured in this way in response to his submission, he may actually fly into a

---

[304] Goodall, J. (1975)

tantrum, hitting the ground and screaming so intensely that he almost chokes.[305]

Humans often use reverted escape quite unconsciously and it is a well-known psychological trick: raise anxiety but also be a source of relief. *This means a person may become attracted to the very thing (or person) who made them anxious.* Reverted escape does appear important to humans also. Having experienced the wrath of a dominant, there can be a strong desire to calm that wrath by returning, humble and submissive – seeking acceptance. Individuals may also seek forgiveness even if, in reality, the source of the conflict was the dominant and the subordinate has nothing to forgive themselves for. Here that doesn't matter: what matters is the display of subordinate behaviour to try and create a safe, non-threatening relationship, at least for a while. As an aside, in therapy some people who have intense self-criticism are actually hiding quite a lot of anger to others which needs to become a focus for the therapeutic journey.

Another variant on this is how *failing* to influence the mind of the dominant can actually increase submissive behaviour. The Aztecs, for example, used to sacrifice to the gods in the hope of winning favour and bringing the rains and ensuring good crops. If they kept their side of the bargain, but the rains didn't come, they wouldn't blame the gods, or stand on their altars and demand return of those sacrificed. Rather they become *more* submissive, asking how they had upset them in a sort of self-blaming way, and then sacrificed *even more*. It's the same for children. When confronted with a hostile parent who could hurt you, you take a subordinate position and become very self-focused in what you might do to upset them to try to avoid it. This is one way anger up-rank gets inhibited.

Another example of trying to influence the mind of the dominant can be seen in religious confessions, seeking redemption and forgiveness of the gods. If one cannot escape from the reach of the dominant, and/or if in some way one sees oneself as dependent on him/her, the anxiety might be great. It may be adaptive to ensure that the dominant's anger is calmed and that they come to see you as dutifully subordinate and not a threat to their rule. At times, women returning to aggressive males seem to show the features of reverted escape, and it is only

---

[305] Goodall, J. (1975), p.144

when escape can be assured that the relationship eventually breaks-up. At times, sex can be offered to calm the aggressions of a dominant male, which gives some control over them.

Reverted escape is a complex behaviour, but it suggests that fear does not always lead to avoidance – on the contrary, it can lead to an increase in attraction (in terms of the focus of attention), approach and submission. To feel forgiven and accepted can increase the attraction of the dominant. There may be few questions asked of whether the original attack or threat was fair. Indeed, people who feel subordinate and inferior may blame themselves for even the most unreasonable attacks upon them, making their subordinacy and need to be forgiven the greater.

Many a bully seems to intuit that a threat, followed by an opportunity to return (submissively) and obtain forgiveness, can strengthen his/her power over subordinates, by, on the one hand reminding them of his/her power over them, and on the other giving opportunities for acceptance and reassurance. It may be the relief from calming the dominant which is so positively rewarding. This reward is transferred onto the dominant so that the dominant's acceptance, the source of relief, is seen as attractive and desirable. This may help explain why some people become devoted to bullies. The degree to which reverted escape is involved in masochistic behaviour is unknown.

Attraction

Of course, not all attractions to dominant individuals are derived from reverted escape mechanisms. Following leaders because they are attractive (have high SAHP - see Chapter 3) is based on the rewards associated with following and compliance. These can be called *expansions*, in that the person who follows gains love, approval, status, security, a sense of belonging, acceptance, power, privilege. When leaders are like coaches, then subordinates are like apprentices, wanting to learn and be guided in their practices by the leader. All these functions offer the advantages of following and becoming more than we were; we gain from it. Following raises our SAHP and RHP (see Chapter 3). It is important to note, however, that gains and losses, fears and attractions, are not mutually exclusive – one hopes for the rewards (e.g., approval) but may also fear the loss of them. In fact, most following behaviour probably involves mixtures of fear and attraction.

There can also be a real attraction to leaders who stir us emotionally via their charisma. This emotional arousal may be associated with the arousal of anticipated rewards: a kind of inflation in fantasy of what we might become. In psychoanalytic theory this is seen as a form of projection, and we see in the leader things that we feel unable to do for ourselves. We literally project onto them qualities that we need to be fulfilled within ourselves. Whether or not they can do it is another matter. Very few will be attracted to those who seem subordinate, lacking in competency, or too negative. Many a politician has lost an election by a flustered debate, an appearance of incompetency and/or by focusing people on the need for limitation and restraint/sacrifice: too negative. Leaders who might diminish personal resources and rewards are not popular – people want to be 'expanded', given opportunities, feel optimistic, win victories etc., not have them closed down.

Submission and Personal Identity

Our capacity for 'submitting' in dutifully following shows itself in many other areas apart from the more straightforward dominate-subordinate relationships. This is because a personal identity involves 'adhering to' values and rules. Adhering means 'to stick with', or 'to go along with', and also captures ideas such as 'complying with' or 'agreeing to'. This section explores our capacity for submission as an important aspect (although only one aspect) of creating an identity.

Following Rules

We show our capacity to submit when we 'comply' with rules, doctrines, values, secular ideologies or institutions. At this level, we have internalised a system of beliefs from the outside world about 'correct' social behaviour. For example, if a queue forms at the bank, we mostly accept that we must wait our turn. When the traffic light turns red, we stop. We recognise that rules do provide for some stability and consistency on how to act and they reduce conflicts. Complete anarchy can be chaos, and learning social rules (and when to obey them) is a mark of competent social behaviour. To maintain social consistency in rule-directed behaviour, be this stopping at traffic lights, bowing to the Queen and showing deference, or even in courting behaviour, we put pressure on people to conform with and obey *the rules*. If we all followed different rules, then social behaviour would be almost impossible.

Internalisation

Some rules are kept simply because of external pressure. They are public rather than private acts, and if one thinks one can 'get away' with rule-breaking, one may try to do so. Maintaining rules and values, however, can also be internalised and part of our private discourses – they operate even outside or beyond the reach of an enforcer. In psychoanalysis, the internalisation of rules and values is seen as a superego function. We can briefly explore this. The superego forms from the values and prohibitions that children internalise from their parents. It grows from the rewards and punishments parents give to a child. For example, if being punished for failure a child may internalises the rule(s) "I must never fail", or "it is bad to fail" and the child will come to feel (internally) bad about themselves if they fail. Or suppose a child expresses anger and the parent says, "you are bad/unlovable to do that". The child then learns, "anger is bad and I am bad if I express it". To take another example, one might be put off the pleasures of sex because one has been taught that such pleasures are sinful or degrading – a tragic message given to women in ages past. Because the fearful subordinate mind so easily internalises prohibition, it gets stuck and acts like an inner, forbidding Gestapo (although in reality it's to do with emotional conditioning, of course). Thus, complying, or failing to comply, with inner rules gives rise to a sense of a good or bad self, of what one can and cannot do, of what is permissible and what not. Or, to put this another way, "I come to judge myself by the way others have judged me". Thus, the superego (or memory of rewards and punishments) becomes part of the self (not external to it) and exerts control over feelings and self-identity. But not only that, it is as if one has a punishment collar around one's neck, because when one goes to do the 'forbidden' act one gets a flush of anxiety because of emotional conditioning. People who have it hammered into them that, say sex or anger, are bad, they will have anxiety when sexual or angry feelings and fantasies arise. Their own brains have become the source for social control and submitting to the avoidance of sexuality.

To be 'dominated and controlled' by one's inner superego is to be internally driven to obey certain rules and conform to certain ideals and standards (dos and don'ts; shoulds and should nots) that were at one time *ordered by others*. The anticipation of breaking a rule (e.g., failing, not trying hard enough, expressing anger, or sexuality) can give rise to guilt, shame and anxiety. Indeed, some people may never experience the full extent of their rage or sexuality but only their (superego) anxiety of it.

On the other hand, obeying rules and doing 'the right thing' can give a sense of security or even pride. Some people may even risk external persecution to obey their internal values and/or superego and 'do the right thing' – a form of martyrdom. Because we internalise the rewards and prohibitions of parents, we may come to deliver self-punishments and rebukes to ourselves (self-criticism) for violating rules and standards. These violations can take many forms. They may include actions (e.g., aggressive or sexual) or even having certain thoughts, feelings or fantasies that have been deemed unacceptable. As analysts say, "when the superego speaks it sounds remarkably like mum and dad".

The point about all this is that subordination is not just to an external agent, but also to a(n) internalised other(s) who has become part of the self, locked into the neurochemistry of the brain, and orientates us to a prescribed space of actions, thoughts and feelings. The more people internalise obedience to rules and values, the more certain their subjugation is to them. The superego, of course, is merely a metaphor for conditioning, shaped by the *manipulations of the parents* to get their child to behaviour in the way they wish. And in many instances the values parents want their child to internalise are those that will gain SAHP in the group they operate in (force them to adapt to the social niche) and protect their own reproductive interests. Thus, in general, parents often attempt to educate their children to follow social rules, to obey them, to achieve status and comply with certain sexual practices. If the parent is successful then it may appear to the child (and later adult) that they are voluntarily following these goals and agendas and will not feel resentful for trying to follow them. They are very pleased to do what mum and dad want them to do and become a respected member of the society.

Identity

Following doctrines and values has other advantages. Why is someone a feminist, or a Catholic, or a left-wing socialist? Why do we identify with and internalise such values? Clearly, at one level it is about conformity, finding alliances, being with likeminded others and joining the in-group. We may be attracted to groups and leaders because we are biologically set up to be, but the exact values we identify with will be a mixture of echoes from own archetypal psychology and our socialisations. For example, those with strong competitive temperaments might chose sport, others might be attracted to authoritarian political groups, yet others are attracted to academic groups. But selecting who and what to follow is not just to find ways to enhance SAHP but is also a question of identity. As Taylor points out, we may identify with a faith or doctrine and in so doing locate ourselves in a moral and predictable space. Thus, to *follow* a doctrine and value system tells us who we are:

> To know who I am is species of knowing where I stand. My identity is defined by the commitments and identifications which provide the frame or horizon within which I can try to determine from case to case what is good, or valuable, or what ought to be done, or what I endorse

or oppose. In other words, it is the horizon within which I am capable of taking a stand.[306]

Taylor's linkage of our valuing with 'taking stands' is to link identity with a form of territoriality. An identity acts like a territory that is advertised, claimed and defended. Remember those issues of territorial control back in Chapter 2? We might expect that a threat to it will arouse all the defensive actions of a reptile defending its territory, because to be human locates territoriality in identity. Indeed, our values mark our boundaries, of what we defend, what we acclaim, what we might fight for. Moreover, to lose the commitment to the territory, ideals or value system, or for them to dissolve around us, gives rise to anxiety and confusion of what one should do, where one stands in the world, who one is, where one's home and comrades are. We often speak of such things in spacial terms. Losing an identity is a form of 'displacement', giving rise to 'disorientation' in new spaces of the unfamiliar. A 'who am I?' is thus also a 'where am I?' Hence, following is intimately linked with identity and endorsing values because they root us in a predictable space. As Taylor says:

> To know who you are is to be orientated in a moral space, a space in which questions arise about what is good or bad, what is worth doing and what not, what has meaning and importance for you and what is trivial and secondary.[307]

Thus, human identity exists in a 'space of questions', dilemmas and challenges, where answers offer locations and defences. We will be attracted to things and people who help us answer these questions; about what is right and wrong, what gives SAHP and what loses it. Developing an identity by adopting values, roles and attitudes which have been laid out by others, helps us to relate to others – to know that others will act towards us predictably; others believe what we believe, their answers are our answers. In this way, conflicts and uncertainties are reduced, or if they arise one can defend one's 'position' or identity with appeals to one's own authority (dominance), a higher authority, if necessary ("God says we should..."), or to others in the group. Therefore, leaders can become

---

[306] Taylor, C. (1989), p.27
[307] Taylor, C. (1989), p.28

important to us because they mark out potential identities; they offer values and articulate meanings. We look to them for guidance, for the things to follow or what we should be doing.[308]

We can see then that the way we become (for example) men and women, a doctor or priest, a parent or a worker, is based on following doctrines – of agreeing to endorse and thus follow values of how we should be and how we should act, in order to be accepted as a good representative of a man, woman, doctor, priest, parent or worker. These doctrines and values reflect both archetypal themes (e.g., of caring or competing) but are also socially defined and given; we learn them from others. In some societies, as we have seen (Chapter 5), values of manhood can be that men should be tough and fearless in order to gain the SAHP of being 'an able man', while in other societies manliness resides more with peacefulness. Beating up opponents might lose SAHP in academic groups but destroying the arguments of opponents might gain it. Whatever role we take and whatever identity we assume and aspire to, we are in a sense *proving ourselves to be dutiful subordinates to the doctrines of constructed identities*. That our identities will be aimed at expansions (gaining and defending SAHP) and exerting control is hardly surprising, because as we have said, to some degree an identity is like a territory, a space that we occupy. By our actions we advertise our identities and are in fear of losing them.

There is no shortage of those who will tell us what being a good person is, how we should relate to others, what our attitudes to child-rearing should be, or sex, pornography, God(s), etc. Followership can help us by giving us something we can't give ourselves: a certainty and clarity of values, identity and purpose. We follow the writings of our chosen leaders, devouring their messages and trying to transform ourselves. Any desire that we might have to disobey can feel like

---

[308] In many ways, the whole point of psychotherapy is to challenge the follower-leader relationship inside of ourselves. Psychotherapy often involves changing values. If one seeks psychotherapy (or even a spiritual quest, say via meditation) then one is entering the seas of uncertainty, and exploring what was lost within oneself by following certain beliefs, values and people. Freud often said that it is not a lack of authority that makes many of us neurotic but too much authority in the form of the superego; we are frightened to be ourselves.

treachery and disloyalty. The dominant people in a group will know this and may play on it with cruel effort to magnify it by shame: "If you do not submit to or follow the doctrines you are not one of us".

Group Size

An identity is created in a social context via engaging in roles and affirming values. Thus, to form coherent identities (as a man, a psychologist, a cricketer – not very a good one of the latter, in my case) a person must make consistent connections with others. Group size has a significant bearing on the ease by which this is done. Some researchers point out that the preferred size of a group varies from 50-150. This figure reflects the size of groups that humans evolved within (its EEA, see Chapter 2). If groups get much larger than that the familiarities and opportunities for personal relations begin to break down. But even within even these groups, there are smaller groups of cliques (of 3-5), families and teams (10-15). Most sports teams are between 10-15 players, Jesus had 12 disciples, and interestingly even lions never hunt in groups of more than 12.

In humans, there are always tensions of identity and roles in mega-groups because there are so many unknown people. One cannot rely on having one's identity confirmed by others, because one simply is 'not known' to others. There are problems of one's small(er) community becoming lost in mega-groups, and of being 'just one' of an amorphous mass. Thus, localised groups have a tendency to try to distinguish themselves and set boundaries around themselves to mark their identities and territories. The group will have common agendas, objectives and goals. To be accepted in a group, one must share, submit and follow these, more or less. In a way, small groups set out the climate for certain types of discourse in which one can express oneself and find a place and identity. But in so doing, one must also be willing to submit to, and comply with, the group's values and goals.

Of course, group identity may be much larger (e.g., of political groups or professions), but they still behave territorially and require some consistency of view to be shared and followed. That we do behave with a kind of (reptilian) territoriality to our social identities can be seen by how individuals react to claims made, for example, on their (supposed) domain of expertise or knowledge. If, for example, psychologists start to engage in debates on psychotropic drugs, there is the feeling that they are encroaching on another group's territory. Indeed, domains of knowledge, working practices and power are seen as territories and people use the language of 'stealing, encroaching, invading and defending'.

We can see then that conformity and obedience to the rules and values of the group help to locate us in a predictable social space – a location of familiarity and mutual reinforcement of our identities. Given these preliminary thoughts, we can explore why we often follow and submit to others who have quite destructive values. As is often the case, self-interest will not be far from view. Incidentally, this is why therapists will sometimes recommend that people start to do things unexpectedly, out of the ordinary, change their routine, as long as it's not harmful, of course.

The Appeal of the Authoritarian Leader

History shows us that we often willingly subordinate ourselves to the most unsavoury of characters. It is incorrect to believe that authoritarian leaders are often unpopular. They have a very simple message: "follow me and I will make you great, a superior being and protect your interests; I will restore or raise your pride/status/prestige", or sometimes more paternalistically, "I will give you a home, a place in the world. I will give you an identity; I will give you jobs". The stronger the need for such things, the stronger the leader-follower relationship. Hitler tapped those needs very well and focused a lot on how to get Germany working again.

In BC 54 Caesar invaded Britain. The invasion was a military failure, but as Grabsky quotes from Dio,

From Britain he had won nothing for himself or for the state except the glory of having conducted an expedition against its inhabitants; but he prided himself greatly *and the Romans at home likewise magnified it to a remarkable degree.*[309]

Magnification of a leader's abilities is a mutual act of subordination and adoration, but also, at least in part, a projection of one's own grandiosity onto the leader. They are great, you are great. The adoration Hitler inspired is well-known. Some even wept at his speeches, and many fell over themselves to obey his orders, which they saw as making their group (and its values) superior. Before the war turned for the worse, Hitler could be assured of huge masses rolling out to see his public appearances. Napoleon and Stalin were also greatly adored despite the enormous suffering they brought. And why? In part, it seems, because they could promise a sense of specialness, glory and at times protection to those who walked in their shadows and obeyed them. This is not the kind of love that emerges between child and parent (or lovers) through their mutually, joyful interpersonal interactions, but it is a kind of attraction derived from more primitive idealisation. The mixtures of fear and attraction/expansion are clear, and this is what activates, excites and inflates the tendencies to adoration.

Despite the devastation of jobs, the fragmentation of society, and the divisive style of leadership that became apparent quite early on, Thatcher was not unpopular with large sections of society. Indeed, as Gilmour notes,

> Plenty of people in Britain and overseas also gloried in Thatcherism. They saw Britain's first woman prime minister and her opinions and activities as the promise of a revitalised Britain and a renewal of freedom both at home and abroad. Part of the British adulation might be ascribed to what Richard Shepard, MP, called the 'hallelujah chorus' of a press that saluted everything government did. In the past, Britain's conservative newspapers had often criticized Tory prime ministers for not being sufficiently right wing. That was not the complaint that could be laid against Mrs Thatcher; and the right-wing press – many of its publications could not be described either as Tory or even as

---

[309] Grabsky, P. (1993), p.59

newspapers – were in a state of perpetual thanks giving to and for the Prime Minister.[310]

Overseas, her prestige was immense. Clearly, she was able to tap into something that people felt they needed. It is as if living in the world we do, a leader who offers us specialness and protection from the supposed dangers outside gets our vote. And we have also noted that a key means that a leader has to manipulate followers to raise (or identify) anxieties, speak to fears, then offer themselves as a source of relief.

To be fair to the British people, though, Thatcher never obtained more than 45% of the vote and it was only our archaic voting system (and the appalling mess the opposition parties got themselves into) that allowed her to flourish so strongly. Indeed, the poor quality of opposition parties of the 1980s was frightening. If people are presented with genuine and viable choices, they will have to try to resolve conflicts of choice and struggle to make decisions. They will have to answer questions of 'where do we stand?' and 'what do we stand for'? But if oppositions rule themselves out as viable alternatives, by their lack of coherence, failure to project an ability to 'do the job', or by a failure to move with the aspirations of the group, then choices become limited. People become more certain of what they don't want, what they stand against, rather than what they stand for. Choice becomes an exercise of choosing between the 'lesser of two evils'. Choosing against, rather than choosing for, may be the basis of cynicism in a dissatisfied group.[311]

Many writers believe that a group will choose the leaders who appear to offer the best solutions to stress and fragmented identities. Thus, right-wing,

---

[310] Gilmour, I.I. (1993), p.8

[311] I might be wrong about this, but I don't think the Labour party ever really understood the enormous psychological fears that the Winter of Discontent stirred up in the minds of the electorate. Being unable to bury the dead and having rubbish in the streets were deeply archetypal threats of chaos and anarchy. When Thatcher was first elected it is well to remember she promised two things: first, to offer strong government to subdue the chaotic elements in society; and second, to heal divisions. The second promise was a deception, of course, for her government was highly divisive, but that did not affect her appeal for the desire for social cohesion.

authoritarian leaders are likely in times of stress and alienation, where identities are fluid and easily fragmented and lost and conflicts of interest are prominent, to appeal to an old set of idealised past values, of family, country, stability, certainty and apple pie (back to basics). When the left promises to reduce hierarchies, merge identities and reduce differences, they walk a difficult line between appeals to a higher morality and fairness, whilst threatening further fragmentation and loss of identity. No one knows where they are. There are signs that the left have learnt this lesson, and recognise that support depends on positive values that offer expansions and clear identities. But one can see the paradox. Only when things improve might egalitarian messages have appeal. When things are tough, people want strong (often non-egalitarian) leaders who are tough on crime, people seen as cheating the system, and who will protect self-interest, etc.

Fantasises, Ideals and Manipulating Voluntary Submission

If one does not have the power to coerce or enforce involuntary submission, then it is useful (and indeed often more effective) to try to elicit voluntary submission and following. And this is where the tactics of manipulation of image come into their own.

Leader and social group are linked by what has sometimes been called a merger in the aspirations and ideals of group and leader. This merger may at times lead to loss of self-identity. Indeed, within a group there can be deliberate efforts to reduce individuality and differences. However, in a way, to talk of loss of self-identity can be misleading for often the person (follower) does not feel belittled or made smaller in a negative sense but expanded, made stronger and more special. This is a key strategy of certain cults, but also to a lesser degree of many political and religious groups. Via imitation and mutual reinforcement of ideals, values and identities, the boundaries of individuality shade over into a corporate identity. One becomes known to oneself and others as that which the group represents, e.g., I am a communist, a capitalist, a Catholic, a psychologist, a Conservative. As these roles are enacted and reinforced, they become more and more absorbed into the self. So, as Lindolm[312] notes, *even though people experience themselves to be free agents they are in fact becoming less free as they merge with the group identity and don the mask of a good party member.* They are willingly grooming themselves for followership and subordination. The group gatherings, the rituals, the meetings, and the religious and party conferences give many opportunities for practice.

A leader and group can be engaged in joint, mutually reinforcing exercises of exciting and boosting aspiration and fantasy-based ideals (expansions). These ideals and hopes of a future and (better) way of life often involve some sense of belonging, acceptance and superiority. It is this which gives them their emotional textures and psychic inflations. The leader excites the fantasy life of the group, pointing to what they could be and could have if they agree to suspend their individuality. The subordination to the leader is thus also a way of (potentially) achieving a personal set of needs, fantasises and aspirations. *This is the basis of worship*, for in the worship of the leader one is also expressing the emotional needs to be protected, loved, wanted and successful, to gain status and be chosen. And why would we want these? Because of course, they are very pleasing to our underlying competitive reproductive archetypal strategies. The charismatic leader depends on our myth-making, aspiring, needful worship psychology. If the leader survives and prospers, then so do the hopes and ideals of the individuals of the group.

In this, it is wise to be aware that many of the most authoritarian of leaders, such as Hitler and Stalin, only get where they do because of the vast numbers of people who will support them. Nazism was a set of values that Hitler helped to shape, but he did not himself create them. Indeed, similar values and aspirations can be found in many groups both long before Hitler and afterwards. Hitler could never have gained power, nor held on to it, without a set of political circumstances he could gamble with, a failure in opposition parties to be creditable, and an increasingly vast number of individuals, from all walks of life, both on the ground and in the inner circles, to support him. Whether we look at

---

[312] Lindholm, C. (1993)

Cambodia or Bosnia today, the same factors apply. Individual leaders play a significant role in brutalising societies, but only a role.

Following Frauds

The need to belong to a group of likeminded others is vitally important to our sense of self, developing alliances and attachments, and explains why groups will keep leaders in power even when they discover or know *the leader is a fraud*. What is happening here is that the group has taken a life of its own and people fear that, should the leader be discredited, then the group will fragment and die. With it will go all the privileges of being in that group: the safety, the sense of belonging, alliances, the hopes and aspirations for a better life, and, of course, the status or sense of specialness (SAHP). In so far as the personal identity has fused with the group identity then this destruction is also experienced as destruction of a self-identity. In extreme circumstances, one has no life, no identity, no existence, outside of the group. People can then be subject to paranoid and depressive experiences and even suicidal ideation. More than a few have killed themselves when the group on which they have pinned so much, fragments and dies.

Jim Jones was a fraud, and some of those close to him knew it. Indeed, Lindholm notes that many of the followers of his People's Church (PC) were well aware of Jim Jones failings:

> But the PC membership consciously agreed that these failings and lies should be overlooked because of the need to bolster Jones' infallibility for the good of the group. As one member of the PC said, "a leader must maintain an image in order to command the respect of his followers" (Mills, 1979). Therefore, Jones should be treated *as if* he were the Messiah.[313]

Thus, as Lindholm and others observe, the followers actually created their own state of subordination. Their obedience to him was not (only) because he

---

[313] Lindholm, C. (1993), p.146

disciplined them but because they had accepted him as their leader and the group's life and identity depended on him staying in it. It can be seen then that both leader and follower engage in creating these myths and in so doing may make them a reality. People who are more distant from the leader don't like too many changes at the top. Richard Nixon was another leader who lost any sense of the myth he was in, but he almost got away with his Watergate scandal by the preparedness of dutiful subordinates to cover up for him. Leaders can be kept in 'power' as puppets because those around them believe that the group could not carry out its tasks or fulfil its functions (e.g., keeping power and holding alliances together) without the leader, and the image that s/he – and thus the group – projects. Moreover, if s/he goes, they go. There can be a sense of loyalty to the leader that not only prohibits questioning but also maintains continued support despite obvious failings in the leader. So, subordination may become the vehicle for holding a group and one's own identity together, but also maintaining divisive, antisocial leaders. Alternative leaders may not available.

Manipulation of the Image

As noted above, much leadership can depend on manipulating voluntary subordination and following. The suppression of information is a key means of this manipulation of leadership – but this is done as much by those who want the group to continue as it is by the leaders themselves. Hollywood has made many a good film from such scenarios (e.g., *The President's Men*). At one level, such movies help to dispel an over-idealistic view of government (and leadership), but they also spread paranoia and cynicism – which may or may not be helpful. The issue is, however, over the battle of social presentation to entice followership and acceptance of those in power.

As Scott says,

> The public transcript is, to put it crudely, the *self*-portrait of dominant elites as they would have themselves seen. Given the usual powers of dominant elites to compel performances from others, the discourse of the public transcript is a decidedly lopsided discussion ... It is designed

> to be impressive, to affirm and naturalise the power of the dominant
> elites, and to conceal or euphemize the dirty linen of their rule.[314]

Whether one speaks of dominant groups, like psychiatry and the medicalisation of neurotic disturbance, the territorial boundaries of the professions, political parties and rulers, of even patriarchy itself, the same applies to all groups who would seek power in social spaces. The manipulation of information or propaganda, to insure the best possible presentation, has always been important to those who rule and lead for they must, to some degree, peddle a fantasy and an ideal of their goodness and worth.

However, the massaging of such identities to entice acceptance and control over others, is becoming increasing problematic in the modern world. Groups with vested interests in maintaining leaders or professional interests in power can, and do, manipulate information. As Gilmour[315] notes, during the 1980s the right-wing press were beside themselves with trying to praise and culturally reinforce everything Margaret Thatcher did. The manipulation of values by a privately owned press, ownership that cannot be assured without large amounts of money, is frightening. The fact is, to own newspapers requires a lot of money and has to be supported by the wealthy, and therefore it's in their interests to peddle propaganda that supports them all the way to the bank. Of course, they are not stupid; they know that titillating pieces, offering so-called exposures, with in-depth sports and more besides are not likely to be read by the wealthy, but by those who they wish to manipulate. Key to this too is shaming outsiders, and those who do not fit in with the capitalist dream.

There have been claims that some politicians (mostly in the States) have taken audiences from the general public, wired them up to physiological monitoring equipment, and measured responses to particular sound bites. At one level, this is straightforward market research, I guess, but it is also potentially dangerous. Packaging, while important, may be no more than discovering what inflates our own self-interest; what excites or soothes. It is the art of manipulation.

---

[314] Scott, J.C. (1990), p.18
[315] Gilmour, I.I. (1993)

Crook has drawn attention to the way the media has become a vehicle for the focus of attention on the leader and his/her message because of our evolved tendencies to focus attention on the more dominant:

> This natural and partially unconscious process operates continuously in human groups. Early in human history, it was recognised that control over the process of leadership choice might be made in several ways: by influence, by manipulation of perception, or by coercion.
>
> Advertence presented for public consumption ... in modern life comprises all those devices that make full use of media control and manipulations to maintain social leadership by ensuring that public attention focuses on the more satisfying activities, real or imaginary, of the leader. The leader is commonly a personification of an institutionalised stance taken by a political faction that is carefully orchestrated "theatrically" through public presentation of an individual and his media image...
>
> In modern life, therefore, natural social psychological processes of leadership attribution have fallen to a considerable degree under the control of institutions. Institutional manipulation through over-control of the media could thus in a Western democracy cause a mass population to exercise choices based on presentations of individuals whose appearance differs greatly from their real character, their true intentions, or their actual abilities. It seems unlikely that choices made in such a manner could increase the sum of happiness for anyone except the manipulators of society.[316]

Even though such effects can lead to highly destructive outcomes, note how Crook attests to them being based on 'natural social psychological processes'. It is a possibility that, rather than pandering to our short-term self-interests, leaders could be educating us about why this could be dangerous to long-term interests, community development and world stability. The problem is, even if you get a leader who tries to act more morally, the competing interests in a society and

---

[316] Crook, J.H. (1986), p.26

different social groups may make it comparatively easy for old-style appeals to self-interest, and for a paranoia of the outsider, to sail through. We are, therefore, now incredibly dependent on good journalism to tell us what's going on. *The opium of the masses may no longer be religion but sections of a press who are not neutral.*

To a degree, the media is responding to us (and the kinds of paper we will buy, or programmes we will watch) as much as we are responding to it. Indeed Postman,[317] in his critique of the media, has noted that we are now less interested in being informed and more interested in being entertained, amused and soothed:

> This is the lesson of all great television commercials: they provide a slogan, a symbol or a focus that creates for viewers a comprehensive and compelling image of themselves. In a shift from party politics to television politics, the same goal is sought. We are not permitted to know who is best at being President or Governor or Senator, but whose image is best in touching and soothing the deep reaches of our discontent... As Xenophanes remarked twenty-five centuries ago, men always make their gods in their own image. But to this television has added a new wrinkle: Those who would be gods refashion themselves into images the viewers would have them be.[318]

So dominant (leader) and subordinate (led) can play games with each other, and each may struggle with the truth, accuracy or complexity. Here too is an interesting paradox of human dominant/subordinate (leader/follower) relationships in the modern world. In animals, involuntary submission comes from efforts to calm the dominant because the dominant has a certain power. But in our human modern political world, it is the dominant who must either soothe his/her supporters, or offer them benefits in the future. S/he must (for real or pretend to) treat his/her supporters as if they were allies (rather than subordinates acting on his/her behalf) or at least persuade them into thinking themselves as such. They must both soothe but also inspire, reassure our fears

---

[317] Postman, N. (1987). An in-depth and worrying look at the media manipulation of image and leadership.
[318] Postman, N. (1987), p.138

but also play on them. And all the time they must keep one eye on those who would vote for them, but also one eye on those who would financially support them.

Darker Sides of Support and Submission

It is rare, if at all, that positions of power can be obtained or maintained without the support of allies, sometimes from those ranking above them, and sometimes from followers. Single individuals will always be vulnerable to others ganging up against them. Indeed, in many ways cultures attempt to enshrine and legitimatise the uses, limits and responsibilities of power, of who can do what to whom, and these are usually to advantage the privileged, high(er) ranking groups. But what we have seen is that support from followers often comes from attractive (if manipulated) appeals that in some way tells supporters what they want to hear. This increases their SAHP. The leaders of elite groups will maintain the image of the group's elitism – at least to in-group members.

Support for Leaders

One of the advantages of supporting leaders is, as we have noted, because they can provide a framework for linking people together within groups. Thus, leaders often publicly articulate what the group stands for and what the basic values are. They can be its mouthpiece, and followers can look to them for guidance. Once a group has a hierarchical structure, with an elite who articulate what the beliefs and values of the group should be, there is a mutual process of absorption of values. Of course, leaders can introduce changes and articulate new values if they are perceived as strong enough. For example, Gilmour[319] is highly critical of Thatcher for changing what he sees as basic traditional Tory

---

[319] Gilmour, I.I. (1993)

values, and argues that it is not very clear what the Tories now stand for. For Gilmour, Thatcher's new values did not appeal, but for many they did.

When it comes to obtaining backing, for new or even repressive values and regimes, there are many ways leaders can obtain it. One is the appeal to the backing of a greater power which is external to the group. Religious elites usually claim to have the backing of God. To threaten the elite's power and authority (e.g., the Pope) is to threaten God himself. Not a good idea if you believe in the power of God. One of the factors that kept many leaders in positions of power in Eastern Europe, during the Cold War, was the military back-up from the USSR. Many terrorist leaders and their organisations have received backing, in the form of arms and other resources, from outside countries. So, leaders (and groups) can be supported and maintained by those within or outside the group that is led. If leaders have strong (outside) backers, they can act with little concern for those they lead. And of course, in many states around the world, leaders have kept themselves in power corruptly with very little benefit to their people.

In most of our workplaces we do not have a say in whom our bosses or superiors will be. They are selected by those higher rather than lower in the organisation. Thus, in many of our most intimate social places we find that we are led by individuals whose backing is from outside, or from above. Our immediate superiors are imposed. Not surprisingly then that 60-70% of people say that their biggest work stress is problems with their superior.

Training in Obedience and Followership

So far, we have focused on followership mostly in relation to expansions, attractiveness, need for identity and the manipulation of values. But we should also take a closer look at *obedience*. Here we return to a theme of subordination that we noted earlier: that of internalisation. Milgram made clear that authority and our relationship to it are part of life from our very first days:

> From his very first years, he [the child] was exposed to parental regulation, whereby a sense of respect for adult authority was

inculcated. Parental injunctions are also the source of moral imperatives. However, when a parent instructs a child to follow a moral injunction, he is, in fact, doing two things. First, he presents a specific ethical content to be followed. Second, he trains the child to comply with authoritative injunctions per se. Thus, when a parent says, "Don't strike smaller children," he provides not one imperative but two. The first concerns the manner in which the recipient of the command is to treat smaller children (the prototype of those who are helpless and innocent); the second and implicit imperative is, "And obey me!" Thus, the very genesis of our moral ideals is inseparable from the inculcation of an obedient attitude. Moreover, the demand for obedience remains the only consistent element across a variety of specific commands, and thus tends to acquire a prepotent strength relative to any particular moral content. (brackets added)[320]

Alice Miller[321] has also written powerfully on how so much of our early socialisations are designed to produce subordinate feelings and attitudes within us. As the child emerges from the family, with a sense of his/her subordinate position well established, much of his/her early life is spent learning how to subordinate him/herself to an authority system that exists. These are encased in institutions with historical roots and continue because others (perhaps over hundreds of years) have subordinated themselves to them (e.g., the church, or education system). S/he learns not only that harmonious relations require subordination to superiors, but that getting on in the world requires subordination to the institutional values – these may be seen as the higher authority (of the law, or medicine, spreading the word of God). Thus, individuals willingly adopted the practice of subordination because of the future prospects, positions and rewards for doing so. This, as Milgram points out, is the *internalisation of the social order*. In addition, of course, parents can exercise enormous control over the child's whole approach to such institutions. The

---

[320] Milgram, S. (1974), p.136
[321] Miller, A. (1983)

desire to please parents, or identify with their values by getting into a profession, or follow their religious practice, is carried far into adult life.

Obedience and (Im)Moral Behaviour

Milgram's academic life was devoted to the study of authority, and he devised one of the now classic experiments to explore the limits of it. In a number of experiments with volunteers, subjects were told that they were to take part in an experiment on learning[322]. They would ask questions of another person sitting in an adjacent room and were to deliver an electric shock for an incorrect answer. The shocks were of graded intensity going from mild to very severe (450 volts). In reality, of course, the experiment was a fake (nobody got shocked and the person in the other room was an actor, and part of the experiment), but crucially the subject asking the questions and delivering the shocks did not know this. In the first round of experiments, 65% of subjects were obedient and did what the experimenter told them. Many went up to the horrendous 450 volts. Even when the subject could hear (feigned) cries from the learner in the other room the percentage of obedient subjects did not fall (62%). When touch and physically proximity were included, 30% still complied even though it was (supposedly) causing pain to the learner.

Norman Dixon[323] has given an excellent discussion of these types of experiments including one done with dogs in which the shocks were real. Some subjects were clearly in conflict and stressed by what they were asked to do,

---

[322] Milgram, S. (1974)

[323] Dixon, N.F. (1987). Some of this work was later attacked as being unethical because it involved lying to subjects and placing them in distress. Indeed, as Dixon notes, Milgram's career was put under a cloud because of it. But I agree with Dixon here; that this was a major piece of work and some of the attacks were very unfair and of dubious motivation. If we do not understand how subordination can really drive us crazy then we may as well pack up and go home now. We may offer different interpretations of the findings, or be concerned by the methods (and such work would not get passed an ethics committee now), but we can't deny that at the time it was major eye-opener, whose findings are now taken for granted. See also McDermott's interview with Zimbardo et al. (1993).

women slightly more so than men, but they still did it. Some subjects worried about their legal lability, but not the ethical. If responsibility could be passed to the experimenter, compliance was more likely. It has been comparatively easy to go from such research findings to the Nazi death camps. However, this scenario is more frightening because these subjects had not been whipped into a frenzy of hate by leaders with inflated ideals nor were they avenging a shamed identity. Nor were they specially chosen, as many camp soldiers were. Nor was there any penalty for not obeying (e.g., as might be the case in institutions). Nor was there any peer-group pressure – they were simply obeying instructions. Thus, in the absence of any obvious threats or advantages from obedience, still many people simply complied with what they were asked to do, despite internal conflicts. Perhaps this demonstrates more than anything else the power of the rank archetype. We should be cautious in believing that this is only the result of socialisation. Rather, socialisation inflates this tendency in us – but its power comes from its archetypal core which is simple: "Submit to those above you". This is to not to devalue the role of moral education, but to make it a more central concern (see Chapter 12).

The Henchman

Milgram's work bears importantly on the psychology of what we might call the *henchman*, if we add to his findings that authoritarian leaders are often attractive (have high SAHP) to many. At times, authoritarian leaders, who are going to be powerful, can rise through the ranks by appearing accommodating and helpful to their superiors. They are regarded as loyal and devoted, and gradually gain access to the inner circles. Indeed, their rather hostile attitudes to outsiders (and at times ruthlessness with subordinates) are seen as assets rather than problems. Many institutions have used people with authoritarian styles to achieve their ends, to do the 'dirty work'. These include business, political, religious and military organisations.

The henchman is the person who is prepared to do the 'dirty work'. There are many historical tales of people who, out of devotion to (and at times fear of) their leader, have done some appalling things. The Gestapo are the archetypal type. As mentioned above, there are usually no shortage in society of these types. But these are extremes of a behaviour that is far more common than we often appreciate. Henchman behaviour can be aimed at gaining SAHP from a leader, desiring to be valued by the leader and chosen as a reliable ally. Be it in the secret police or any organisation where someone sets out to ensure that the rules and values of those above are enforced on those below can be seen as henchman-like. There is obviously a degree to which certain individuals, particularly those of a psychopathic type, will be attracted to these kinds of organisations. They find a legitimate outlet for their sadistic behaviours and even justify it to themselves and others that they are acting for the common good.

It maybe that many forms of complicity to situations that we know to be immoral make us all, to a degree, hench-men and women. The difference is where we draw the line: how far will we go before we rebel? If an organisation asks us to sack half our workforce, would we do it? And would we do it reluctantly or indifferently? At what point does our own personal morality (and courage) incite us to rebel, even if, in the process, we will risk losing the SAHP of being loyal to the group's values and requests? The problem is that people's values are changed (and corrupted) by systems, especially when there are pressures to conform, a need for strong in-group ties, and serious sanctions (e.g., loss of SAHP or exclusion) for disobedience. We know that in the extreme case of war people will do and accept things that before they felt they would never accept.

Rebellion

Although Milgram[324] wrote a chapter in his book on disobedience, most psychologists have not really focused on the psychology of those who did not comply, but rather more on those who did. In some ways, disobedience is at least as interesting, and certainly as important. Milgram suggests that disobedience is the result of strain. What causes strain are conflicts. On the one hand is the pressure not to comply, because it violates moral standards, empathy for the other, and personal identities that 'one is not that kind of person'. On the

---

[324] Milgram, S. (1974)

other is the pressure to comply because of fears of non-compliance and retaliation from the authority (in Milgram's experiments these did not seem great, although the subject may have assumed them to be there), and wishing to show one's acceptability by one's very subordination (the henchman psychology).

As Milgram points out there are various ways this strain can be reduced. Sometimes this is via the social context. It seems much easier to drop bombs on thousands of people from 20,000 feet than it is to batter one person to death with a club. Indeed, the arms trade depends on exactly this fact. There are a number of psychological manoeuvres that people use to keep the (essentially submissive) relationship between themselves and the authority intact. These include avoidance, denial, and blaming the victim. There may also be subtle subterfuges which attempt to reduce the cruelty but not break fully with authority (e.g., in Milgram's research – trying to signal to the learner the right answer). Verbal dissent was often expressed, but when encouraged (not threatened) by the experimenter to continue the subject did so. Maybe verbal dissent allows the subject to think that they did what they could, short of outright rebellion to stop the experiment. However, as Milgram points out, this is rarely helpful.

The process of rebellion goes through stages of: *inner doubt, externalisation of doubt, dissent, threat,* and *disobedience.*[325] I think Milgram's own words here

---

[325] Interestingly, in psychotherapy as people are changing their attitudes and values they can sometimes go through similar stages with the therapist. For example, a patient who has been told they are unlovable and are self-critical may first begin to question this because something in them tells them that it is unfair. At first, they do not fully voice it or own this rebellion. In the next stage they do start to speak of it, and about how the parents treated them. In the next stage, they begin to show dissent at their self-critical side and articulate their resentments. This may be associated with threats and angry feelings to the parents (and their self-critical selves). They feel safe enough to being to explore 'rebellion', although they may be plagued with feelings of betrayal (of parents) and disloyalty. Finally, we may try to help then simply stop obeying their critical selves and become softer with themselves. It is interesting that the same process that we see in working against external authorities may also be present in dealing with internalised (superego) authorities.

testify to the struggle this is and explain, perhaps, why so many of us find it difficult to rebel in spite of all the suffering we see about us:

> The act of disobedience requires a mobilization of inner resources, and the transformation beyond inner preoccupation, beyond merely polite verbal exchange, into the domain of action. But the psychic cost is considerable...

> The price of disobedience is a gnawing sense that one has been faithless. Even though he has chosen the morally correct action, the subject remains troubled by the disruption of the social order he brought about, and cannot fully dispel the feeling that he has deserted a cause to which he had pledged support. It is he, and not the obedient subject, who experiences the burden of his action.[326]

If one adds to that the fear of shame, and the actual serious consequences that families, organisations and state can bring down on one's head for disobedience and defection, then it is perhaps not surprising that our compliance with immoral social behaviours is maintained. Whistleblowing can be an incredibly courageous act. Only slowly are we recognising the need to protect them.

But we must also go beyond this. Scott[327] points out that what is claimed and done in public may not be internalised. This allows for a good deal of deception, where cheating is not uncommon (subterfuge). It is the private discourse that is at the core of self-identity. The internal experiences to cheating can vary from a psychopathic type cynicism and contempt for those whom one has cheated, to a more depressive response - or it may be the first steps to greater freedom. The religious celibate who gives in to his desire for sexual relations, may see this as a rebellion to the constrictions placed on him. If he can value his own rebellion and affirm it, then he might be able to positively reclaim some lost individuality. But if he does not claim and value his rebellion, if he is frightened of it, feels he has been disloyal to the cause (to his parents, God, or the rules and obligations of his group), then he is likely to be racked with guilt and project his temptations

---

[326] Milgram, S. (1974), pp.163-164
[327] Scott, J.C. (1990)

onto others. He may get caught, as Adam did, seeing his sleeping partner as a temptress. His desire to rebel becomes an attack on himself and others. Finding within himself pressures to disobey, much will depend on his attitudes and reflections on such desires. Indeed, in psychotherapy, people can be caught in strong conflicts between obedience and disobedience, and the therapeutic work is to enable reflection on these conflicts.

Rebellions can be motivated for different reasons and seek different outcomes. Sometimes we just want to change things, to free ourselves from internal or external controls. We may wish only that the dominant take notice of us, that s/he changes their ways and becomes more caring (perhaps), or just gives up some of their power. Here, we wish to renegotiate our relationship with the dominant rather than destroy him or her. But other forms of rebellion are, of course, based on seething hatred for oppression. Here we do not wish to renegotiate but to destroy and completely obliterate the dominant. The risk we run with hatred based rebellion is that we can replace it with something equally as bad. We can use the same tactics of control on those who would resist us as the dominant used to oppress us. All terrorist regimes have within them terrorising systems for defectors or those who do not comply to fight for the new world order. Rebellion that comes from hatred creates terror which creates more hatred. For them, there will always be those who must be threatened, shamed and subordinated, whose power constitutes a threat to the new order that is sought.

The Many Failures of Rebellion

Failure in rebellion springs from many sources. There is, as Milgram notes, the problem of feeling faithless and disloyal, and the psychological cost in coping with a sense of betrayal. A person who wishes to reveal a fraud of a colleague may feel a strong sense of betrayal. Some feminists have felt they have betrayed the cause if they wish to get pregnant and settle down. Some patients in therapy may struggle with a strong sense that having to change their ideas and values about themselves may mean 'betraying' the family values and standards (superego dictates) their parents gave them. A religious person decides they are really an atheist, but feels they are betraying their family or community, losing a sense of connectedness, with a risk of becoming an outcast. Loyalty is often a serious inhibitor of our rebellion. There are many other reasons why people remain in states of subordination, or at least subordinate their true wishes in order not to disrupt the social order. We noted early in this chapter the role of the superego and how, once values and prohibitions have been internalised, they can be very hard to overcome. And, as we noted in Chapter 5, if subordinates think that by obeying now they will one day work their way up the ranks, then it may be in their interests to maintain the established order and wait their turn.

But the story of subordination and rebellion weave complex plots. In addition to all the manipulations of values and fantasies noted above, Scott[328] articulates a number of other reasons for failures in rebellion. First of course, is that rebellion would be far too costly and likely to fail. One simply does not have the resources to rebel. This does not mean that rebellion is not desired or even planned. Indeed, as Scott points out, the private discourses of people may be filled with fantasies of rebellion to achieve a better life, but these never become public or known, for such individuals will do all they can to cover their tracks and avoid detection. The blockage is at the level of actions, not thoughts.

However, the blockage *can be* at the level of thoughts, and this seems very common in psychotherapy. In this form, people have so internalised the ruling order and value system that they believe they are subordinate because *they are subordinate* (inferior, poor). One can see how in gender relations the idea of the subordinate status of women to men has been so internalised that until recently few questioned it. In a caste system, one is what one is. These are powerful beliefs that inhibit even the aspirational from rebelling or challenging the ruling elite. One's best bet is to accommodate oneself to it.

Another reason is that the ruling elite manage to convince the subordinates that, however unfair things are, this *is* the natural order of things, there is no other way – it is inevitable. It has always been like this and it will always be like this. Thus, subordinates come to accept their place and fate with resignation. They may think it unfair but, like facing death, what else can one do? When

---

[328] Scott, J.C. (1990)

evolutionists reveal the darker sides of ourselves, this is not licence to say nothing can be done, that men will always treat women like property or whatever. Our reasoning intelligence can find ways to reduce these unfortunate inclinations. Of course, in the field of economics we hear constantly that there is little to be done to stop the globalisation of markets and the downward pressure on wages. We do not rebel, because we are convinced by the stories and explanations of the people who are supposedly 'in the know'. When I first came into psychology, it was an absolute given that one should not challenge the beliefs of people suffering psychosis, and I accepted this. Today the most innovative treatments are in challenging psychotic beliefs with therapies that actually engage with voice discussions. Our acceptance of things as they are, because we are told that is the way that they are, is a major reason for our subordination and the inhibition of creativity and rebellion.

Yet another reason is that people do not have the means to articulate their rebellion. Feelings of disquiet could not find the inner cognitive frameworks for articulation. This is closer to the ideas of Foucault. The discourse of society (or groups) literally inhibits the way we think – there is a blockage on exploration and articulation of alternatives. Knowledge is power, and whoever controls how people think (and what they think about) can subjugate alternative discourses, ideas and theories. Since ideas can only grow in a social space, *without open debate they cannot form and mature.* When I started my thinking on evolution theory, it was pretty crude and easily blown away by those who had better articulated alternative views – I had not thought through, nor learnt from others how to think and conceptualise what I was trying to articulate. As the years passed, I became better able to communicate with evolutionary psychologists and thinkers. In speaking and interaction, inner frameworks for thinking grow. Subordination thus comes from not being able to get on the first rung of the ladder and mount a viable alternative. Science, the place where freedom of thought is (supposedly) so valued, can actually be a good example of such processes of subordination. Many a scientist has been shamed by being labelled heretical only later to be proved correct. But the shaming of the ruling elite (and restriction of research funds, etc.) may be sufficient to stop explorations along tracks that threaten the ruling order, unless that is, one can summon sufficiently well-articulated arguments (or evidence). Paradigms change slowly and often not without conflicts and splits, or until the old adherents (dominants in the field) die off. Even Einstein struggled.

As feminist writers point out, the male domination of science has controlled not only how science is done, but what questions it should address (e.g., vast allocations of research resources to armaments and the military). It is because we think in certain ways that we create certain types of world (be this homophobic, militaristic, or whatever). If certain views are privileged, then others are subjugated and exist outside the public domain of influence. In such situations, alternative ideas may never develop, might never become coherent; they remain unknown potentials.

Finally, we should note that another reason we do not articulate our rebellion is that all around us is a sense of shame, which is hidden. In Chapter 6, we noted how many societies did not wish to tackle genital mutilation, or the problems of patriarchy; we have problems in accepting that in the absence of social constraints the holocaust could happen in any country. We, in the West, do not wish to explore the serious exploitations in our ways of life. Robins points out that there is collusion to be silent. He quotes from Sibony:

> A group is a collection of people who are resolved to keep silent about the same thing: a thing that then becomes a secret. This 'point of silence' holds the group together, sustains it and even structures it. To violate it is to violate a taboo, to re-open a great wound. It is to risk driving the group to despair because it has absorbed and digested this silence to ensure its very survival.[329]

Collusions in silence come from re-opening wounds, and these wounds are none other than facing our shame – and we (as individuals) are threatened with being shamed should we try to open them. As Robins[330] notes, the media can become instrumental in the evasion of our anxiety and shame, for we do not like looking into dark mirrors. Our media must soothe us and direct attention away from our

---

[329] Robins, K. (1990), p.80
[330] Robins, K. (1990)

wounds, our inadequacies, our double dealings,[331] our shame. Indeed, as Robins[332] suggests, the media creates our identities by its efforts to articulate, mirror and present the core values (and role models of citizenship) of a nation state, and these must be based on positive values.

Whenever we follow and simply accept something, we may never ask ourselves, what do I *lose* from this acceptance, or from following (being in) this group, this doctrine, this leader? What conflicts and uncertainties am I freeing myself from? What discourses are subordinated in me and in my relationships? On what am I and others silent? Where is my rebellion? From my work in therapy, I suspect that those who inhibit their conflicts and try to follow 'the doctrines' are losing the most important opportunities for change – it is via our inner conflicts and uncertainties that we are called to question. Therapy does not try to remove conflicts but change the nature of them: to see them less in black and white terms, to compassionately free the self to be able to live in and with conflict. There is nothing wrong with not knowing what to do, with wanting to sit on the fence awhile, or with withholding choice.

The Need for Subordination

It might be thought that followership, subordination and submission are all bad. This, of course, cannot be so, because social life as we know it could not exist without some degree of subordination in voluntary compliance to social order and social rules. Indeed, the human capacity to subordinate themselves to the other, to open themselves to the other, and to trust the other to take control, to guide, help, support, teach and even care for them is probably one of the most profound and important qualities of humanity. It depends on interpersonal trust and the operation of the safeness system. It's the way cultures pass their knowledge from generation to generation; we all start off as apprentices. We

---

[331] Chomsky, N. (1992)
[332] Robins, K. (1990)

may prefer not to see it as subordination at all but as *a form of surrender, of letting go, of not resisting*. We may recognise that this type of subordination has no implications for us in any judgemental since. So, what we have been discussing in terms of voluntary subordination is really a preparedness for openness, but always recognising that we can voluntary subordinate ourselves to both prosocial and antisocial leaders. To use a Buddhist concept: even in surrender, we should not lose discernment.

On the other side are many for whom this would be an anathema. These are folk who at every turn see subordination or compliance as an affront to themselves, and refuse to subordinate any of their needs for the benefit of others, or refuse to see that there are others who may know more, be more talented etc., and they can be riddled with envy. Compromise is seen as weakness. We see these as self-focused narcissists. Moreover, rebellion against authority can stem from a hatred of it and in this sense the person is trapped by it. They must continually fight against it and become obsessed by it. The need to prove oneself an autonomous individual can be as much tyranny as its opposite. There is nothing like fighting for a cause, no matter how moral one thinks it is, to inflate the tendency to tyranny within oneself and thus subordination to the cause.

Sam Keen[333], in his observations on manhood, believes we have become emotionally dead and that we need more people with passion who feel outraged about things. On this I believe one needs great caution. Hitler was a man of passion and outrage, but these behaviours were hardly helpful. He rebelled against the subordination/defeat of the German people and the impact on his identity. So, outrage can lead to some very unfortunate places because passion and outrage can throw the psyche out of balance and lead to inflations. Defensive affects like anger and outrage can easily activate the power-seeking part of ourselves. It is when we take a moral position from anger (rather than compassion or grief) that we have to be most careful. Nonetheless, these cautions aside, I agree with Keen – as with so much, it depends what we are outraged about and whether we know how it should be used. Without caution,

---

[333] Keen, S. (1993)

we can end up with impotent rage, rather than using it as a stepping stone to wisdom.

Compassion is sometimes confused with submissiveness and subordination, when in fact compassion can be one of the most courageous motivations we have. Assertiveness is about not expressing anger in a way that is destructive, but creating context for the betterment of others. Compassion also comes with a certain freedom because we are released to some degree from the need to constantly achieve and improve our own self standing.[334] Compassion can allow us to both give and receive, and also to be less likely to be caught up in subordination to leaders that can literally lead us astray. It's not so much whether subordination, or surrendering, or humbling ourselves, is the issue, but rather to what and for what.

Let's just end on one more note from evolution. There is a whole other domain of voluntary subordination which goes with being what is called a eusocial species – which is sort of unusual for mammals, although not for insects. What marks this type of species is that they have: 1) overlapping generations; 2) share childcare (not only do relatives help out in childcare, but friends and strangers can do too. That's why we can send our children to nurseries.); 3) demonstrate a division of labour, so that different members are doing different things which, when they come together, creates an outcome, a form of cooperation; and 4) group defence. Clearly, to operate like this, individuals have to submit to and comply with playing the role they've been allocated or chosen. Consider an orchestra: one voluntarily plays a particular instrument in a particular way to fit the overall pattern. Indeed, our sense of community and belonging, our cooperative dispositions, are almost certainly based on this eusociality. We can work out our contribution and where we fit, where we belong. What is extraordinary for humans is that we can actually try and choose the roles we will play, and the contributions we will make. What becomes interesting, therefore, is the tensions that can arise between roles that society or our backgrounds want us to play, and those we want to play. When we feel we have been allocated a

---

[334] Sampson, E.E. (1993)

role that is unfair or unwanted, we may not be happy to be a compliant eusocial being.

Conclusion

Followership and subordination are more than the relationship between leader and follower. They involve copying and mimicry, wanting to be liked, identification, and they form the basis of much social learning and behaviour. Social compliance and submitting to social rules are crucial to civilised life. These archetypal potentials may well have begun aeons back in our primate past when we had to submit and comply to the rank hierarchy. Whatever their origins and subsequent adaptations, we are an easily led species, at times highly submissive to be compliant with leaders, and this can be a source of our greatest achievements and worse excesses. Even in the creation of personal identity, there is much that involves our preparedness to submit and comply.

I have veered away from talking about how states of subordination can create disturbed states of mind, especially depression and social anxiety.[335] This would have taken us off on another journey. But we can note that (involuntary) subordination is known to exert marked effects on brain biology, and thus states of mind. However, in a way, to parcel out disturbed states of mind from the non-disturbed is fraught with problems. After all, is the person who gets depressed because they can't go along with immoral commands and feels the burden of their isolation more disturbed than the person who goes along with it without question? Are there some situations where if one weren't depressed one would be abnormal? Evolutionary theorists suggest that a lot of what passes as psychopathology is actually adaptive behaviour in the (toxic) social contexts in which it operates.

This chapter has been mostly concerned with the relationship of dominant-subordinate, and although we haven't spelt it out, these relationships have very powerful influences on the brain and body. What allows us to offset some of the

---

[335] See Price et al. (1994); Gilbert, P. (1989/1992); Sloman et al. (1994)

disadvantages of subordination is courage, and our potential for rebellion is what Jung called our hero archetype. However, like everything else, it depends on the purpose to which this archetypal potential is put. The archetypal patterns around dominant and subordinate and leader and follower are complex. They can be the source of some of our greatest successes, but can also drive us crazy.

9: CRUELTY

The scars that aggression has left on the face of the past are indelible. Wars and rumours of wars, class struggles, clashes between religious denominations or racial and ethnic groups, rivalries for place and power in politics or business, the hatreds generated by nationalism and imperialism, the ravages of crime, the confrontations of private life from marital discord to family feuds – all these and more offer persuasive testimony that aggression has supplied most of the fuel for historical action and change.[336]

The above quote opens Peter Gay's important historical book on *The Cultivation of Hatred*. Although competitive aggression has undoubtedly been an anvil of history, this chapter argues that cruelty cannot be fully understood by analysing contest-competitive aggression alone. We would like to think that approval and attractiveness are given for attractive things and behaviours – hard work, being a good friend, looking pretty – but this is a mistake. The ways in which our archetypal potentials for cruelty and sadism are activated are complex, but they are inflamed by the approval and excitement of those around them who endorse them.

History is replete with stories of atrocities and cruelty, enacted by individuals against individuals, groups against groups, nations against nations, and religions against religions. Whether it be the sexual or psychological abuse of children, rape and other crimes, slavery, torture, war and ethnic and religious conflicts, there are no shortage of contexts for us to demonstrate our capacity for cruelty.

Some see acts of cruelty as related to an aggressive drive[337], but the notion that aggression in any sense is a drive is an outdated view and basically incorrect[338]. Violence, aggression and exploitation are used for many reasons: they are

---

[336] Gay, P. (1995), p.1
[337] Gay, P. (1995)
[338] Storr, A. (1970/1992)

strategies not drives[339]. They are increased in some contexts and reduced in others. However, this chapter will not focus on violence as such, but on cruelty and, of course, some forms of cruelty may not be violent. A key theme of this argument is that in order to act cruelly we must (usually) be numbed to the suffering of others. Indeed, there is now evidence that a preparedness to hurt others can increase as empathy decreases[340]. It is this *inhibition and numbing of caring*, and some of the many reasons for it, which are the main focus of this chapter. Without care and compassion, we can be (and often are) a cruel and nasty species. Cruelty (and the numbing of our caring psychology) can stalk the justifications for punishing the guilty, the need for discipline, the fear of defections, pleasure, self-defence and war. It is our cruelties (and the inhibitions of caring) that drive many of us crazy.

My Concise Oxford Dictionary defines the word cruel as, "1. indifferent to or gratified by another's suffering. 2. Causing pain or suffering deliberately". It is probably only at the human level that the concept of cruelty has much meaning. Only humans, as far as we know, are able to empathise with the suffering of others – to know that others suffer and have some sense of what might stop such suffering. There is, as the Dalai Lama[341] points out, something special about human beings, for only *we* can reflect on our actions and know them to be cruel and lacking in compassion. Indeed, it may be our ability to reflect and see the depths to which cruelty can sink that directs our attention to the need to change. Chapter 12 explores how we may come to appreciate the other as subject, with feelings, and to be motivated to act towards the other with care and compassion. This chapter explores some of the archetypal and social contexts and beliefs that act to reduce caring, promote harm and are essentially cruel.

---

[339] See Archer, J. (1988); Archer, J. (1994, ed.); Dell, P. (1989) Klama, J. (1988); Wilson, M. and Daly, M. (1985).
[340] Miller, P.A. and Eisenberg, N. (1988).
[341] Dalai Lama, Wembley, 1993

Forms of Cruelty

Aggression has been classified in various ways. We can distinguish between predatory, fear-induced, frustration-induced, instrumental (goal-orientated), status/rank-related, group, sexual and territorial, and so forth. Although cruelty often involves aggression, it does not always do so. In law, one can get a divorce on the grounds of 'mental cruelty'. Usually this refers not just to specific aggressive acts, but to constant criticising and shaming, putting down the partner, having affairs or neglect that cause mental pain. The offending partner may be indifferent to the impact they are having on the mental state of their partner. Cruelty can also involve holding something that somebody needs, and using their pleading/distress as a source of personal power and enjoyment. So, cruelty can be the deliberate causing of pain to either the body or the mind (mental pain).

Related to cruelty is *callousness*. Whereas cruelty can involve feelings such as the pleasure of vengeance or power to cause suffering, callousness implies a lack of feeling and more indifference to the harm we are causing. Callousness can show up early in children who appear to have no concern for the suffering of others, including animals. The inability to recognise the impact of their behaviours on others is a serious cause for concern. However, there are also culturally created forms of callousness. For example, whereas the Romans had a culture that glorified in the pleasure of watching people suffer and die horribly as in the gladiatorial games and crucifixion, the Nazis didn't have that mentality. Their cruelty was a callousness and *means to an end* – the same with the Stalin regime. No doubt some of them were sadistic, but as a culture it was pure and utter callousness. When callousness is combined with ambition, we have what we call *ruthlessness* and these regimes were utterly and completely ruthless; frighteningly, that ruthlessness infected many sections of the society who were prepared to act on ruthless orders.

Far less extreme but also important are those industries, like tobacco or mining, who know that they are causing harm but are indifferent. They don't enjoy people having cancer, but they are indifferent to it. Some forms of callousness are to do with denial and disassociation. Of course, sometimes employers are completely indifferent to the conditions they create for their workers or their wellbeing. There are different types of callousness that are rooted in different processes, but basically it is indifference to suffering.

There are many, not mutually exclusive, forms of cruelty and callousness that have a variety of different functions. These include the following.

Retaliation: The archetypal and most universal forms of cruelty can be seen in relationships based on *retaliatory aggression or vengeance*. To offer an extreme case to make my point, if someone were to torture my children, I have no doubt that I would be flooded with enormous sadistic retaliatory fantasises and possibly even behaviour, and I suspect this is a fairly universal reaction. Indeed, retaliation, for example, in war situations can be extraordinarily cruel, and enemies who are caught can be raped, tortured, and beaten to death. Retaliation can be amongst the most savage of human activities. Some people can be very disturbed by an awareness of their own sadistic fantasies. On the other hand, one source of enjoyment in violent films comes from seeing others (usually the good guys) get revenge on the bad guys. The worse they are, i.e. the more violent, cruel and sadistic they are, the greater pleasure we have in seeing them suffer too. Vengeance can be pleasurable. Indeed, many wars and conflicts are inspired by appeals to both the threats posed by an enemy and mobilising strong desires to retaliate.

Deterrents: One way to prevent conflicts comes from the capacity to punish and harm – the potential to harm acts as a deterrent. To deter requires that one has the power to retaliate against those who break the rules or threaten us in some way. From an evolutionary point of view, the capacity to have a robust (aggressive) deterrent has been around for many millions of years – without it, individuals are defenceless.

Exploitation: Many forms of cruelty are not derived from retaliation or deterrents. There are of course many forms of competitive behaviour where one's gain is another person's loss, and in that sense the losers suffer. There may be many advantages in being *actively* cruel or callous, and it is usually intentional, even if not labelled as cruelty. The most common one is exploitation (or greed) where 'the other' becomes simply an object to be used: economic and sexual exploitation being tragically common. Hurting others may get us closer to a goal. Ambitious individuals, groups and nations may be prepared to harm any who get in their way, simply riding roughshod over others as suits their own needs. People may or may not recognise their behaviour as cruel and hurtful, or they may have various justifications for their behaviour, but often they are numbed to the suffering they cause.[342] The history of slavery is a tragic example.

Criminality: Not all exploitative behaviour is criminal but some certainly is. Although some criminal behaviour is socially defined, the preparedness to harm, injure and steal from others for narcissistic self-interest is obviously a source of callous cruelty. Many people can be devastated by having their houses or bank accounts broken into. But there are a vast array of behaviours that cause immense suffering to others from violent drug gangs, Mafia type organisations, sex trafficking, and slavery. For the most part, criminal behaviour is not focused on the desire to make others suffer, but simply the desire to have what the other can provide; their suffering is a by-product. Criminal behaviour is not deterred by the potential suffering they cause their victims and in that sense, they are callous and dissociated from the pain they cause. It is ruthlessness – callousness and ambition. This idea is at the root of restorative justice, where victims and perpetrators are brought together, and perpetrators made to confront the consequences of their behaviour. Modern criminality is clearly partly linked to modern cultures, linked partly to being able to be anonymous. It is a classic case where our brains have become intoxicated by the wealth of modern societies, the ability to do things secretly and not be caught, and has driven us crazy.

Tribalism and the 'isms': Throughout this book we have addressed the issue of the ways in which humans very easily form in-groups and out-groups. Not only this, but the hostility to out-groups can be callous, cruel and vicious. In fact, this psychology underpins what we might call the 'isms', such as racism, sexism and ageism. It's very clear that there have been times in history where different religions and races have lived together quite peacefully, but at other times when relationships between them have been cruel and callous. Racism is an example

---

[342] One can, of course, link such behaviours to reproductive strategies; see Kriegman, D. (1990).

of our capacity for awful callousness, in not only causing suffering but at times our tragic indifference to it: the way that many societies don't really address it, or if they do they try and shame it out of existence (which can make it worse) rather than understanding its roots and dealing with it at its core. An empathic reframe can help. The issue is not to feel shame but focus on empathic understanding and connectedness and the desire to change things. When we feel threatened or in intense competition, contexts that capitalism delights in creating, we quickly go into distinguishing between those worthy of investment, those not worth bothering with, or even those we mean to actively keep out of sharing and participating. Once again, the question is how to help us become aware of the archetypal tricks in our mind and stand against them.

Passive: We may be *passive* and allow cruel and callous behaviour to flourish for many reasons: fear, helplessness and ignorance seem the most common. We may fear intervening, not wanting to get involved, speaking out, or rock the boat, or fear breaking with conformity. We are bystanders. We may feel that the problem (e.g., how tyrants treat their people and the horrendous tortures that some tyrants, even today, exercise over their people) is too big or complex and we are helpless to stop it. We may say this is how it has always been and can't be changed. We may say this is human nature and it will always be the same. We may be genuinely indifferent, in part perhaps because of ignorance or because we have never really thought about whether certain behaviours or value systems are cruel (e.g., only recently have there been protests about veal calves, and until now many would enjoy their veal without much thought of where it comes from). We can be passive because we simply are unaware of the exploitations and cruelty inherent in our way of life. It may also be that we are not biologically disposed to worry over much about the starving millions, or the ghetto life of the poor outside our personal domain.

Neglect/Withholding: We may know that others suffer and know that we could help but that the costs to us are too high; it's too expensive to help. We withhold help not because we are frightened or ignorant of the suffering of others, or even callous, but because our own self-interest won't allow us to make the necessary sacrifices – to give aid in resources, time, medicine, etc. We can have all kinds of reasons why we basically neglect addressing problems of suffering, why we turn away from them and withhold resources that may be needed. Withholding what is needed because we are basically more focused on ourselves is a form of callousness – this is not to moralise, just to observe. It becomes an issue politically when certain services like education and the NHS clearly need improved funding, but this is withheld in order to offer tax breaks.

Simple pleasures: Tragically, cruelty can be a simple pleasure. While we would like to think this is only the domain of the psychopath, history tells us otherwise. Be it at the Roman games or our current enjoyment of films like *The Texas Chainsaw Massacre* or *Nightmare on Elm Street*, many people simply like to watch brutalities. Another form of cruelty as a simple pleasure is captured by the German word *schadenfreude*, which literally means enjoyment in the misfortune of others. It's likely that those 'others' will be seen as competitors, those with hubris or individuals envied. Increasingly, some individuals devote a good deal of time to creating viruses which will destroy other people's computers and work for no other reason than it gives an intellectual buzz, or perhaps because they are working out some unprocessed issues, but in all these cases there is notable callousness.

Virtue: As in shame (Chapter 6), where destructive behaviours are given positive values, so too is cruelty. Harming others is not just about retaliation, ambition, exploitation, fear, helplessness, ignorance, cost, or indifference but can become a virtue. Destroying and harming are seen as good. Many religious wars and political persecutions are seen as the actions of the virtuous. The need for discipline and order may lay behind ideas of the value in the use of threats and harms. Indeed, as we shall see, many forms of cruelty flourish because they have been turned into virtues and justified defences.

Our Potential for Cruelty

Although it is common for us to see cruelty as a property of individuals, this allows us to keep hidden our collective, cultural values and exploitations whose cruelty acts at a distance. Hence, we can suggest that our indifference to the suffering of others (for whatever reason) is also a cultural problem. These are powerful because they are rooted in archetypal potential and the dark side of

'Nature's mind' and in humanity. Moreover, it does not matter whether we look at societies which are individualistic or those that seem more collective and cooperative, neither of these of themselves operate against cruelty (at least to outsiders). Cruelty is only halted when there is both awareness of it, and desires for it to cease are translated into community discourses and actions. It is extraordinary how much cruelty has escaped the attentions of those interested in a compassionate, fair and just society. Cruelty is rarely the focus of analysis. In my view, power and individualism become even more serious problems when their effects are callous and cruel.

Understanding and owning our own potential for cruelty (recognising our indifference to the suffering of others) is probably one of our most painful but important tasks.[343] If we are to overcome our craziness, then this may be a first step towards developing a more compassionate society. Freud saw compassion as a reaction formation to sadism. Sociobiologists suggest that our concern for others relates to altruistic strategies, and these are (relatively) limited to genetic relatives or reciprocal relationships, especially when the chips are down. Both may be correct (to a degree) but it is possible to recognise that cultural values and practices can do much to either promote cruelty or work against it. As I argue in this book, and as Buddhist ideas have made clear, we can pay attention to our mind and start to consciously and knowingly make choices about our behaviour. We are not robots. But in order to do this, we need to understand the archetypal in us, because it can powerfully take us over. Just as we can overrule anxiety to act against fear or overrule anger and not act destructively, we don't need to be puppets to the archetypes. To illuminate cruelty, we need to explore our justifications for it and the social-historical contexts that allow or encourage it.

---

[343] Anything that we can focus on to conclude 'they' are different (we are by nature somehow nicer beings) helps us place the problem in them and not us. As soon as one starts to see what happens to other people as not our problem, we are in trouble because we become indifferent. Sometimes, cruelty is on the surface, clear and obvious, but at other times, as in the arms trade, it is hidden.

Historical and Social Contexts of Cruelty

Clearly, genes are not responsible for the cultural variations in cruelty, because many societies – be they Romans, Vikings or the Nazis – had the same genes as most of us but were violent and cruel societies. If we go back just 300 years (and, of course, we could go back much further), the historical record shows that much of life was intensely cruel and brutish. As Beattie notes,

> There is good reason to think that violent physical conflict and physical abuse were commonly experienced in seventeenth- and eighteenth-century society. The family was the scene of much of it, for family discipline was commonly maintained by physical force. With society's concurrence, men controlled their wives and children by beating them for their transgressions. Children at school and young adults in service were similarly subject to what was widely accepted as the necessary persuasion of the rod. Physical intimidation within the household was matched and sustained by a broader acceptance of violence in society, and by the expectation that disagreements among men might reasonably be solved by physical means, or an insult redressed by fighting. On the whole such matters would have been regarded as private, not something that should normally engage the attention of the authorities. Men and women in the eighteenth century were not repelled by all forms of cruelty or violence in everyday life. This is plainly revealed by the large number of popular recreations and sports in which physical damage was either the consequence or indeed the point. Perhaps even more revealing of the general attitude towards violence and the violent temper of society is the use of terror and physical intimidation by the State in combating crime. What has been called "judicial violence" was at the heart of the system of criminal justice. Hangings and burnings and floggings were witnessed by crowds of thousands, of all ages, all over England. [344]

---

[344] Beattie, J.M. (1986), pp.74-75

In other words, the dominant (husbands, parents, etc.) were free to control and retaliate to disobedience as they saw fit, more or less. The acceptance of life as brutish and cruel has in fact been endemic throughout much of our history, as Hobbes well observed, and it was only with the Enlightenment that the acceptance of cruelty began to change[345]. The kind of life we see in the inner cities and economically deprived areas are not new. What is new is the availability of guns, the huge profits from drugs, deceitful notions of equality, and a media that excites rage-shame and envy. But it is important to note that the way a culture and society understands, accepts and perpetrates violence and cruelty, via its institutions, values, systems of justice and means of economic segregation and disadvantage, has a considerable impact on the psychology and general orientation of people to each other. Without social prohibitions on cruelty, discourses that illuminate cruelty, social fairness and the education of a compassionate psychology, the prosocial archetypal propensities for care and compassion can struggle to flourish. It is, therefore, important to recognise the cultural and social beliefs and conditions that maintain violence and cruelty.

The Justifications for Cruelty

Few would accept their behaviour as cruel without also offering justification for it. Gay[346] points out that throughout history people have been well aware that life was brutish and cruel. However, by the nineteenth century, there were various justifications to not only ignore the plight of those who suffered but also to accept it. These justifications, Gay suggests, centred around three key interconnected ideas. The first was that competition, although having unfortunate side effects such as producing many losers, is nonetheless good, for it hones efficiency and produces progress. The Industrial Revolution would never have got off the ground without the elite justifying their exploitations of the poor in their factories via appeals to higher virtues such as progress and wealth creation. Moreover, competitive advantage was considered to be the real

---

[345] Gay, P. (1995) and Fromm, E. (1949/1986) also make the point that many forms of cruelty are made from a position of moral superiority and conscience.
[346] Gay, P. (1995)

measure of success and prestige – relatively regardless of how it was won. Even today, right-wing politicians oppose the minimum wage on the grounds that it will make us less competitive. For them it is a 'keep down' for most us, so they can rise to the top.

The second justification was scientific: the incorporation of new biological theories of evolution which were used to support the idea that the natural order of life was competitive (nature, red in tooth and claw) and losers don't survive; beneath the veneer of civilisations all were potentially enemies of each other. Moreover, people like Herbert Spencer held that helping losers, such as the poor or mentally ill, was in the long term cruel and not the natural order. Allowing those who could not keep up to fall by the wayside was a "purifying process" and efforts to help them, the actions of "spurious philanthropists", for such unfortunates could be nothing but a burden to the more able.[347]

The Social Darwinists, as they become known, were able to use Darwinian theory to support the idea of the inherent superiority of some groups over others, and make it a virtue that the superior should triumph over the inferior, be these races, ethnic groups, religious denominations, or even women. Anti-feminists of the nineteenth century appealed to "the scientific evidence" that women's brains were smaller and that women bleed once a month and therefore could be conveniently prohibited from positions of power within universities or the state – they simply weren't up to it.

The third justification came from the appeal to aristocratic manliness, which was the standard by which the superior should be known and judged. Thus, as Gay says,

> Varied as this menu of self-justifications proved to be, all provided collective identifications, serving as gestures of integration and with that exclusion. By gathering up communities of insiders, they revealed – only too often invented – a world of strangers beyond the pale, individuals and classes, races and nations, it was perfectly proper to contradict, patronize, ridicule, bully, exploit, or exterminate. All three

---

[347] Gay, P. (1995)

rationales had the same effect; they cultivated hatred, in both senses of the term: they at once fostered and restrained it, by providing respectable pleas for its candid exercise while at the same time compelling it to flow within carefully staked out channels of approval. [348]

So, as we have seen so often, the claim on superiority, be this God given, self-invented or culturally proscribed to one's group, works to justify callous indifference to, or at least acceptance of, the perpetration of exclusion and cruelties. Once justifications are in place they may rarely be questioned. Moreover, we are able to use various self-serving rationalities and justifications to be indifferent to the suffering of others because within such notions of superiority are also notions of *deserving* – not only deserving of the hardships suffered, but more often than not, undeserving of help.

They Deserve to Suffer: Group against Group

It is very common to find the use of violence, revenge (retaliatory aggression) by the state, nations and groups together with ideas of 'they deserved it'. Here, one group decides that another group should be invaded, controlled or even exterminated. Various justifications for group-enacted cruelty are needed, which may include religious or moral justifications. Those worthy of attack are seen *as a threat*. Hitler had various reasons for why the Jews deserved what the Nazis' did to them; indeed, in any war situation there has to be a way of justifying actions of cruelty and the infliction of suffering, and in this way, see the suffering caused not as cruelty but as justifiable behaviour.

Today, the 'international community' can decide who is worthy of help and to what degree, and who deserves punishment. New methods have been found to impose punishments. For example, the increasing economic interdependency of nation states makes possible the use of economic sanctions. In the case of Iraq, few disputed that Saddam Hussein is a brutal tyrant, but to inflict intense suffering on a whole people via sanctions, and in a way blame them for not

---

[348] Gay, P. (1995), pp.35-36

removing him, is problematic. In fact, the West has actually undermined their rebellion and failed to support the opposition.[349] Such cruelty is hidden by the usual justifications. The use of international sanctions seems more humane than outright war – but does it matter if you bomb people or starve them to death?

They Deserve to Suffer: The Individual

If we see others suffering, we can construct many forms of justification for their plight. The help we give and our sympathies are affected by our attributions and justifications. If we explore how people respond to (for example) victims of a rape or mugging, a common question is to find out where it happened. If the victim tells of walking in a bad area of town, late at night, or keeping unsavoury company, then there is the common response of "well, what did you expect?" This is then a justification to be less caring to the victim because s/he was clearly foolish and why should we bother with foolish people? Whether someone was wise or not is irrelevant to the suffering experienced. If there is a way to blame the victim and reduce our sympathies, we invariably do so. This is particularly noticeable in rape trials, few of which generally lead to convictions, and whereby it is the *victim* who must *prove* their innocence. Some individuals may be at a particular disadvantage even from the start on account of their circumstances, for example, prostitutes, or those accusing a spouse of rape.

When it comes to giving punishments, how many of us have not had the thought, "they had it coming to them". Our belief in a 'just world' depends on judging those who deserve punishment (the bad) and those who deserve reward (the good).[350] The sense of deserve lies behind the allocation of rewards and punishments – even though nature seems to care not at all for such things. Our sense of deserve and justice are human inventions which depend on human definitions. Because they are inventions, both the nature of a crime and the type of punishment deserved varies from culture to culture and historically. Envy too can be one of our justifications when we see people whom we envied, or thought

---

[349] Chomsky, N. (1992) gives insight into the West's double dealings here.
[350] Rowe, D. (1992)

had become too big or powerful, fall from grace or suffer in some way: "Serves them right". This goes back to our German word, *Schadenfreude*.

Some notions of karma in Buddhism that seek to explain suffering in this life as a result of bad acts in the previous one can also be part of trying to justify suffering. Along with beliefs that those in poverty lack moral character, and our insensitivity to rape victims, are examples where at some level we believe that 'they' suffer because they have done something wrong, or are lacking in some way – it is their fault. These are basically callous responses.

They Deserve It: The Group Against the Individual

Many forms of cruelty involve a group acting against individuals. These cruelties are socially endorsed agreements designed to maintain adherence to social rules. The group (or at least those with social influence) agree on the forms of punishment and for which types of (rule-breaking) behaviour. In the seventeenth century, many petty crimes (especially against property) could be met with the death penalty. At one time, there were over two hundred potential death penalty crimes in Britain – although courts often did not enforce the death penalty for the less serious ones. Nevertheless, the fact that often these crimes, especially against property, were born from poverty and desperation did not deter the judge passing the sentences they felt the criminal deserved[351]. The social construction of crime and punishment can be noted by the fact that stoning is a penalty for adultery in some countries, but many in the West would not think such actions deserved stoning.

In the 'battle of the sexes', cruelty has never been far away, and Burford and Shulman[352] have given a comprehensive review of the many and vicious

---

[351] This does not mean that all crime comes from poverty for there are many poor non-industrial communities in the world were crime is low. Also the crimes of the rich (fraud, embellishment, worker exploitation) are different to the crimes of the poor. The rich may have more to lose form violence.

[352] Burford, E.J. and Shulman, S. (1992) explore many forms of punishment and cruelty perpetrated against women. As they point out, women as a subordinate class have been completely dependent and victim to the laws and punishments melted out

punishments meted out to women over previous centuries. In addition to whipping, burning and drowning, there was a muzzle device, called a branks, which could be fitted over the head of a women. This has also had a metal gag inserted into the mouth to stop the poor woman from speaking. The branks was a punishment for nagging or insulting verbal behaviour. As Burford and Shulman note,

> For this punishment was not merely humiliation. Over the years the branks was developed into a veritable instrument of torture by refinements to the tongue plate which could be serrated or fitted with small sharp spikes, or even a spiked wheel, ensuring the slightest movement of the tongue tore the flesh and caused dreadful pain, sometimes even leading to death through blood poisoning.[353]

The social definitions of crime and the invention of punishments which must also be associated *with a sense of deserving* have produced many horrendous cruelties. Of course, society must have a way of enforcing rules; no one disputes that. But crimes and punishments are inventions. Both the forms of crime and the types of punishment vary cross-culturally. Honour killing is accepted in some parts of the world but not in others. In fact, research suggests that the way people conceptualise and explain rule-breaking and crime has a major effect on what they think the punishment should be. As with stoning for adultery (which usually the woman has to take the blame for), punishments are socially proscribed.

Even a vague familiarity with history reveals that the state has had no trouble in imagining and creating horrendous forms of suffering and justifying it. Crucifixion, for example was a terrible way to die as was hanging, drawing and

---

by the male elite. And the male elite have used their power to define crimes as those actions which threaten their power – and punish accordingly, often viciously. Since women have been without power, there has been no stopping what the male elites could do. Women in many cultures continue to suffer these injustices and intense cruelties (e.g., honour killings, sanction of beatings).

[353] Burford, E.J. and Shulman, S. (1992), p.55

quartering. While humans as individuals can be pretty nasty, as a corporate – those in power using all means to exercise power – we are horrendous.

Cruelty as a Punishment and Deterrent

Punishment is, of course, an exercise in "the making of suffering", be this by inflicting injuries to the body or mind, or by robbing people of things they value (e.g., their freedom, status or sense of worth, etc.). We can behave cruelly for many reasons, but a common one is to punish (retaliate) so as to control the actions of others, and by example, to deter. Behaviourists have long argued that punishment is an unreliable form of control for while people may learn how to avoid punishment, they will not necessarily do it in the way intended. They may simply become skilled at deception and avoiding detection. Nevertheless, authorities often wish us to believe that deterrents are necessary and helpful. If you have rules, you must have penalties for rule breakers.

The use of threats and punishment to control and deter others are, of course, the commonest tactics of most animals. From an evolutionary point of view, punishment, threat and aggression have been in business a long time. We learn the power of punishment in childhood. Indeed, it has long been the case that violence and threats against children have been viewed as necessary to control them. It is called discipline. In fact, discipline has various meanings. It can refer to perseverance (e.g., the discipline to stay in training and not be distracted). It can also apply to structure and order. But as Foucault[354] has made clear, punishment is usually about control and is often discussed in the context of discipline. Discipline is usually to force obedience to, and compliance with, the ruling/dominate elite's goals and interests. Discipline relates to the enforcement of rules and compliance by those who have the power to discipline (those who can make others suffer for not obeying – to discipline them).

Although threat and violence are evolved strategies, the *experience* of cruelty in childhood is where to find the beginnings of the idea that threat and force are the main agents of social control. Better to be the threatener than the threatened.

---

[354] Foucault, M. (1984)

Many of us are fearful that without the means to constrain others (and at times one's self) with the use of fear of punishment, all would be chaos. Cruelty (the power to make suffer) can be seen to be in the service of order, compliance and stability. In the case of children, research suggests that mild punishments that do not break affectional bonds and are given with clear explanations can be useful in helping children understand rules and internalise them. However, harsh and unpredictable punishments, without explanations of why a certain behaviour was wrong often lead to poor internalisation and empathic inhibition. Helping children understand how and why they've done wrong and possibly feeling guilt, as opposed to shame, can be helpful in learning to take responsibility for their behaviours as opposed to just trying to avoid punishment. We see the same in the issue of law distinctions between restorative and retributive justice.

In society in general, punishments and deterrents can help to maintain order. However, these punishments may be far from mild. All forms of *public* execution, from crucifixions, cutting off hands, stonings, whippings, beheadings and hangings have been used as deterrents and punishments for many centuries. The IRA were well known for their kneecapping and baseball bat attacks. The fear of such things happening to oneself and seeing it happen to others is supposed to deter. Of course, once a person has been hanged it is hardly a deterrent to that person. The problem with a focus on deterrents is that one may not be too interested in why a person broke the rules, for this might only offer excuses. Also, as my colleague Michael Cox[355] has pointed out, public executions were often used to prove that justice had been done as much as for deterrents.

Do They Work?

Whilst driving home one evening I caught a debate on the radio about deterrents. A Member of Parliament stated that he had spoken with some men who had committed a violent crime. They'd told him that if hanging had been in force, they would not have carried guns. But this is just a way of shifting blame and

---

[355] Personal correspondence

should not be believed. Although it is commonly thought that criminal behaviour has become more violent and vicious in the last 30 years or so (compared to the previous 30 years), this is probably as much to do with changes in society (especially the profits from drugs and gun availability) as it is the lack of the death penalty. In any case, it is simply not true, since previous times were more violent with greater crime. In fact, there is little evidence that hanging works as a deterrent. For example, pickpocketing was a hanging offence in the Middle Ages, but the most common crime at such public gatherings for executions was pick pocketing. In Henry VIII's reign, it is estimated that over 72,000 people were hanged with no noticeable effect on crime rates. In London at Tyburn, a famous spot for hanging, at least 50,000 (and probably more) were hanged. Yet for all the hanging and institutionalised violence that was going on, these are not regarded as particularly low crime times. Indeed, there were some areas of the country that were regarded as quite dangerous to travel through. Of course, what constituted a crime was much more varied than it is to today, but even taking just murder and theft, there is no evidence that vicious retribution (e.g., hanging) lowers these crime rates. Indeed, this was apparently obvious even in the eighteenth century. Beattie quotes from an article that appeared in the *Gentlemen's Magazine* in 1790. Commenting on the unjust laws of England the writer notes,

> For the most part they are cruel, unjust and useless. The number of our fellow-mortals hung up so frequently like the vilest animal is a terrible proof of their cruelty; the same punishment inflicted on the parricide and the man who takes the value of three shillings (or less) on the highway is a proof that they are unjust; and the frequency and multiplicity of crimes is a proof that they are useless... [356]

Indeed, in a remarkably short period of time the swell against capital punishment (because it was cruel, unjust and useless) was such that by 1827 many laws had been passed that reduced the death penalty for many offences. As Beattie notes, given the long period of time when such laws had been socially accepted, this change was quite rapid. When Nicholas Ingram was electrocuted in Georgia in

---

[356] Beattie, J.M. (1986), p.630

the US in April 1995, we had the opportunity to peer into a system that keeps murderers on death row for years, in rooms like cages and then kills them in a most horrendous way. Hillman[357], who has studied and compared various means of execution, believes electrocution (introduced in New York in 1890) is one of the most inhumane. You would only treat people like that if at some level one's own sadistic vengeance was being activated, but of course that's kept firmly out of consciousness and never publicly expressed.

The degree of cruelty the state is prepared to use is in part related to the perception of threat that crime (and disobedience) is seen to pose to the order of society, especially from the subordinate classes. It is not surprising, therefore, that in North America, where there are huge underclasses and major drug problems, some states have re-introduced capital punishment. Neither is it surprising that (as history shows all too clearly) it does not work. The violence on American streets is a bad as ever it was. Rural Britain has murder rates hundreds of times lower than some American inner cities and the reason for this is not because of our better deterrents. We don't have a death penalty. Who can really believe in the value of such deterrents – but then maybe this was only a justification, not to be taken seriously. What is really at stake are illusions of control and opportunities for revenge.

Despite what our Member of Parliament thought, or was led to believe, it is simply wrong. Epstein recorded this view from two rapists who were speaking about their behaviour:

> Both rapists said they felt badly about what they had done ... They said that in their normal state of mind they could not comprehend how they could brutalize another human being, but they knew that they would do it again if they were in the same emotional state of frustration and anger that preceded the rapes... when asked if a more severe penalty for rape would have deterred him, one of the rapists said that considerations of

---

[357] Hillman, H. (1995) compared various methods such as hanging, shooting, beheading, gassing, stoning and injection. Injection seemed the least painful. For stoning, one can be bound and buried up to one's head and sheet put over it. Stones "should not be too large that the person dies with one hit".

punishment would have made no difference because, when he was in the state that led him to rape, nothing could stop him. He pointed out that after rape he wept and despised himself for having brutalized another human being, but before the rape, concern for the victim's and even his own welfare never occurred to him.[358]

Not all rapists feel remorse, of course. It would be incorrect to believe that some people are not deterred from breaking the rules out of fear. But whether or not these are the same people who are at risk of committing serious crimes is unknown. And there may be personality differences in the susceptibility to fear-induced deterrents.[359] We know that drugs and alcohol are major factors in many violent crimes, and in these changed states of mind deterrents are unlikely to be effective. We also know that an early history of abuse, and certain cultural contexts (e.g., poverty and alienation), reduces people's capacity for empathy and can make adherence to social rules less likely. Those who want simple solutions are more concerned with punishment and cruelty for vengeance rather than understanding the real causes and ways of prevention. Importantly, the rule of law governed by the police is not involved with the issue of punishments, which are determined by the courts. There is no doubt at all that the rule of law is one of the most important cultural inventions underpinning a compassionate society. The rule of law helps us to think about non-harming. We undermine ourselves if we overly rely on vicious punishment rather than detection and preventing the causes of crime.

---

[358] Epstein, S. (1992), pp.240-241

[359] Gray, J.A. (1987) is based on the work of Hans Eysenck and others, And Gray makes clear that extraverts and introverts are affected differently by punishments. Psychopathic personalities are not much influenced by punishments. Another distinction that is made is between the violence of the over-controlled personality (the inhibited, shy, withdrawn, but with violent fantasises) and the under controlled personality (the outwardly impulse, aggressive type). Some of the more brutal and sadistic crimes are actually from the over-controlled when the control breaks down.

National Deterrents

Not only are deterrents part of an internal justice system, and common to how many approach the problem of discipline, they are also used to support a vast expenditure on armaments. Externally directed deterrents take the form of parades, testing bombs, military exercises and so forth. The *retaliatory* message here is clear: "Threaten us and we will be extremely violent to you". This is a kind of group-based ritual agonistic behaviour: a (reptilian) display of power.[360] The crucial thing about such displays is the capacity to be tough and violent. Although such displays and capacities may keep the peace, they tend to escalate, leading to an arms race. Be it in the napalm or the cluster bombs, this race is to find better and more effective ways to inflict injury. Modern war is an exercise in maiming, despite modern claims of the use of smart weapons. It is rare indeed that these means are seen as forms of cruelty, but in so far as we must remain relatively indifferent to the suffering of those on whom our bombs fall, then according to the definition of the word, this is indeed a form of cruelty.

Although, for a mega-state, deterrents may work and stop others from attacking it, small nations may not be able to resist the big nations. History shows that deterrents may work only when nations are reasonably equally matched (and even then, this is unclear). Big nations can impose themselves on weaker ones in various ways. According to Chomsky,[361] America and the West have certainly used their military might in various ways to protect and advance their own interests and commonly not to the advantage of indigenous peoples. We have supported tyrants and horrors.

Religious Deterrents and the Creation of Hell

The tapestry of human history is very much soaked in the blood of powerful elites maintaining their power through threat, vicious callousness and cruel violence both to in-group and out-group members. In the last few thousand

---

[360] Caryl, P.G. (1988) explores modern evolutionary ideas and games theory on the wars of attrition. Mostly, he speaks about individual behaviour but it can be used to think of nations.

[361] Chomsky, N. (1992)

years, we have been terrorised by the ruthless. Religions, as a tribal creating process, have been at the forefront of violence and cruelty, which are used to grow and maintain the groups themselves, and enforce group cohesion. We might hope that religions would set values which would offer us a way out of our brutalities, that they would make clear our power structures and cruelties and how to overcome them. Many have tried, but often failed.[362]

Indeed, religious authorities (mostly male dominated ones, of course) through the ages, using (supposedly) the word of God, have been keen to utilise cruelty to deter and cajole. Not only that, but they have been able to use even more terrifying images and threats of hell and damnation. The eternal fate of a person's soul seems terrifying stuff to me. At times, especially in the Middle Ages, painters and writers fell over themselves trying to create, in their imaginations and ours, an unpleasant a hell as possible. A new dimension was added by those who believed in the afterlife. A person could be burnt, eaten alive and ripped limb from limb only for his/her body to be resurrected and the same to happen over and over again for eternity. These people had invented, in their minds, Nazi-like death camps without end. Hitler is an amateur compared to what happens in hell! There was apparently not much thought of rebelling against such ideas. Few dared to question the morality of such a system. The idea of an industrial system of torture (hell) was here for all to see. This is absolute craziness gone crazy! But if you induce enough terror, and one can't stand against the madness, then we are trapped between madness and terror, rendered into trembling wrecks ready to do anything to escape such a fate.

On a recent television programme on the stigmata (a condition where people bleed in symmetry with Christ's crucifixion wounds), a particular sufferer told of her visions. She had seen Jesus, who filled her with love – that sounds okay – but then he took her to see bodies burning in a sea of flames and mud where they would be for time eternal. She believed this to be the real fate of those who

---

[362] Psychological research has shown so clearly that the ability to grow into a loving and caring adult is set in childhood. Our experience of being cared for actually affects how the brain matures and wires itself. Abuse and neglect can seriously interfere with the frontal cortex – which is a very important brain area for empathy, sympathy and moral thinking and behaviour (see Schore, A.N. (1994))

did not love God. She could not recognise this as a kind of craziness that was indeed interesting, but thought it was real. She seemed such a nice, ordinary lady too. So too did her local priest, who believed her. As a clinical psychologist, I have seen people tragically tormented by such visions. This to me, shows how *sadistic fantasises can live powerfully in the unconscious as archetypal potentials,* and are relatively easily brought into consciousness. Nevertheless, their forms are also embellished via sharing them in social interactions. At times, it is as if we compete to come up with the most terrible punishments.

The sheer terrors that humans have created in their minds around the notions of hell are appalling. The problem is that we can often not distinguish a human creation from a metaphysical possibility. Instead of realising that hell creations are in us, and we (not God) can bring them to life, at times like the Holocaust, we project them onto our God images. In doing so, we completely fail to take control over these images and so support the making and selling of arms that will indeed be a kind of hell for those who are on the receiving end. There is no doubt that hell is real enough, and our history should warn us of that, but we don't have to suggest some hellish metaphysical place. There is only one reason for doing so, and that is to get power over others and control them through fear.

As Harvey[363] notes, incidentally, even Buddhism is not free from a belief in hell. It is perhaps incredible that people could believe in such things and still do. But in a way, this is an amplification of an archetypal theme in our minds: the fear of being totally powerless in the face of a hostile dominant. A belief in hell is born from a projection of our own sadism and terror. Hell is here, if it's anywhere.

We will look at religion more fully in the next chapter, but we can note that when any group becomes interested in power and control it can be contaminated by all the old, primitive archetypal forces in the psyche, *but sold as virtues.* When I learnt about the Crusades at school, they were presented as something heroic. Even today, films of Richard the Lionheart depict him as a noble character when in reality the crusades were nothing short of organised barbarism – a glorying of walking in blood – and King Richard I was quite prepared to

---

[363] Harvey, P. (1990)

behead thousands of Muslims prisoners – an act of barbarity which, for centuries, Muslims would not forgive or forget. So much for Christian love.

Some cruelties come from simple greed encased in beliefs of superiority. Much has been written on the cruelties visited on the North American and South American peoples of the late Middle Ages as those from Europe, with their grandiose and inflated senses of themselves and their God, plundered gold and other resources. Spreading the word of God has been used often, and tragically has been a justification for many cruelties that are no more than old primitive forms of exploitation. Now, sociobiologists may well explain these cruel conquests with various explanations of our genes[364], but one should not ignore historical and social factors or play one explanation off against another.

In Europe, two of the most notorious system for religious control were the Inquisition and witch finding[365]. Of the latter, at its height these are believed to have put over three million (mostly older women and the mentally ill) to death. The tortures visited on those thought to have been influenced by witchcraft were hideous: duckings, brandings, having flesh pulled out with hot pinchers and so forth were relatively common. People of science were not at all immune from it either, and many a scientist was threatened with the Inquisition if his/her theories

---

[364] Barkow, J.H. (1989). Press believes that the speed of human evolution was increased by intergroup violence, which he calls autopredation. This is controversial. What is also a key issue is the degree to which these behaviours of conquests, for whatever reason, are accepted and indeed valued within our culture, by creating from them heroic myths. Be it the Crusades or the conquest of the Americas, it is only recently that they have seemed rather less than heroic – the change has been in my lifetime.

[365] Based on the *Malleus Maleficarum* meaning 'the Witches' Hammer', written by two German Dominican monks, on the edict of Pope Innocent V111 in 1485, there was a flurry of activity to find and persecute witches. In fact, the structure for such activities had been building long before and used against non-conformist groups like the Gnostics. Another group caught in this barbarity was the mentally ill. The psychotic mind could be easily filled will delusions of devils and they suffered accordingly. Fuelled by a linkage of mental illness with the devil, the mentally ill suffered greatly (see Zilboorg, G. and Henry, G.W. (1941); Davison, G.C. and Neale, J.M. (1994). For a fascinating exploration of the linkage of sexual attitudes in religion and fear of the devil, see Tejirian, E. (1990).

threatened the order of things. At times, such was the zeal that false evidence was knowingly used simply to allow the torture to go ahead.

So, as it has been for many centuries, and in many other societies, fear and the ability to inflict suffering were the major deterrents to maintain adherence to the power hierarchy of the church. That the church may have got itself into a state of severe craziness, trapped in the fear of a dominant, potentially punitive, male is still, to this day, unrecognised. The demands of some, so called, religious people have been for God to punish the sinful. This is nothing more than a desire to have God act as torturer on our behalf (although he does not actually carry out the punishments – this is the role for the devil). The reason religion is important here is that it is a major shaper of values and highlights the way cruelty can become so profoundly important even to a religion that claims it is about love and peace. After all, if God can act sadistically then so can we; it isn't disallowed, especially if we are doing his works. Even Hitler appealed to the leader in the sky when he wrote,

> And so I believe today that my conduct is in accordance with the will of the almighty creator. In standing guard against the Jew I am defending the handiwork of the Lord. [366]

Notice how the appeal to the defence of something is used to sanction cruelty: again, not an uncommon appeal. One can say, however, that one of the key changes that happened with the Enlightenment was that science and philosophy began to struggle clear of the religious grip of fear and hell. It was a slow process, but by the eighteenth century, for many reasons, religious threats had become a spent force. Two hundred years earlier and Darwin would almost certainly have been burnt at the stake. Some on the religious right would like such threats to make a comeback, however - heaven forbid.

Cruelty to Separate the Guilty from the Innocent.

Humans have sometimes felt slightly squeamish about acting cruelly to those who might be innocent of a crime – and therefore did not deserve punishment. Thus, various forms of legal system have been devised to try to sort the guilty

---

[366] Gilbert, M. (1987), p.28

from the innocent – the deserving form the non-deserving. In the fourteenth century, if you were accused of witchcraft, you could be thrown into a pond. If you sunk, you were innocent. If you floated, the devil had been at you. You either drowned anyway or were executed.[367] If you didn't survive, well maybe you were innocent and your soul went to heaven.

Stoning in the Middle East seems one particularly appalling way to kill someone. But according to Abbot[368], right up to the eighteenth century, Britain had a way of dealing with people who stayed mute and refused to plea in court. (No, it wasn't the Criminal Justice Bill, that's recent). The person was tied down with a sharp stone in their back and heavy stones where placed on top of them until the rib cage was slowly fractured and crushed. It was called *Peine Forte et Dure*. After its invention, various ways were invented to make the process more painful. The difference in methods between crushing and stoning hardly seems important.

Obtaining confessions have always involved threats. Torture (which comes from the Latin word *torquere*, meaning 'to twist'[369]) has been a key means of extracting confessions. Indeed, in many parts of the world torture is still the main way of extracting confession and convicting. With a confession, we seem more at ease with our cruelty because of the belief, "if guilty, they deserve everything that's coming to them". Public qualms can be put aside because people confess or are 'proved' guilty. In this situation, torturers usually have an escalating aspect. Just as animals will fight and escalate their fights until one backs down and submits, so humans, like animals, will escalate threats to achieve the same. Submitting here is about confessing.

It is in the tactics of escalating cruelty that the real inventiveness of humans come to the fore. In some religions, which use confession for sin, the idea has been that if you don't confess and repent you will be off to the fires. No wonder males have always blamed females for sexual improprieties! The purpose of the escalating threats to extract confessions can be various. At times, it is focused

---

[367] Burford, E.J. and Shulman, S. (1992)
[368] Abbott, G. (1993)
[369] Abbott, G. (1993)

on the actions of the person, to admit having done something. Here the purpose is to locate a badness in another, e.g., having sex with the devil. Indeed, sexual behaviour and sexual thoughts remain, to this day, the focus of many religious confessions (evolutionary thinkers would explain this as control of competitive reproductive strategies where one individual or individuals are trying to control another group). At other times, confession is seen as essential to be able to pin down a crime perpetrated against others. For example, stillbirth and illness were sometimes explained to be the product of witchcraft, and a culprit needed to be sought. When bad things happen to people they want to be able to blame someone, and then act out their rage and vengeance. In addition, if you could find the culprit, then potentially you were protecting yourself from subsequent occurrences of the harmful event.

Psychoanalysts believe that those who are very concerned to 'root out evil' may actually be projecting a good deal of their own nastiness (their shadows or Mr Hyde selves) onto others and then attacking them. Some of those who vigorously pursue evil and crime can be rather vicious authoritarian individuals. Thus, both needing someone to blame and scapegoat, and also projecting our own badness onto others, are powerful sources of our cruelties to others, and forcing them to accept their (our?) badness.

Because one is seeking out culprits, tactics for eliciting confession can seem justified. Mild forms might be food deprivation, long hours of questioning, inducing exhaustion and other general means of disorienting people to "break down their defences". Even today the police are sometimes accused of practices that are aimed to weaken a person in order to extract a confession. Thankfully, in this country as least, the reliance on confession as evidence is losing its power. But in addition to finding someone to blame, confession can also be seen to enforce subordination, which when achieved gives the dominant a sense of pleasure and reassurance in his/her power. If the dominant has paranoid tendencies, especially of betrayal or defection, then the need for confession is a form of needing to gain submission. Here things can get really nasty indeed. Abbot[370] has listed the many and various tortures used to extract confessions in

370 Abbott, G. (1993)

the Tower of London. These include the following: crushing various parts of the body, from thumbs to limbs; burnings; slicing, piercing and ripping flesh; beating; inserting hot objects in various cavities; stretching and dislocating limbs; placing victims in small cages and roasting them; etc. To these and more can be added threats and torture of loved ones.

More recently (although not in the Tower as far as we know), there has been some concern to find tidier and less bloody ways of torture, such as electric shocks. Both psychologists and medics are not spared from having helped in such things. Medics are sometimes used to revive victims or help set the limits so the victim is not accidentally killed.

At times confession can only hasten death: the only benefit the person will get from offering a confession is a speedier exit from life. Submission and confession serves no other purpose. History is replete with millions who, having confessed, were then taken out and hanged, beheaded, burnt or shot. Because this is all about subordination and submission, it should not surprise us that at times the dominant seems not to worry too much if the confession is accurate. The confession, as a statement of submission, is what is really wanted. Miscarriages of justice can occur because we are more concerned with having someone to blame (and vent our anger on) than actual justice.

Those who do not confess and submit can drive the torturer into extreme forms of narcissistic rage. Abbott[371] tells us that the Stuart kings, James I and James II, were both known for their sadistic personalities, and were regular visitors to the torture chambers, where at times they even joined in. Both could have rages if they could not break the spirit and force submission from their victims. Indeed, a failed submission usually brought greater terrors.

Fear of Defections

Some researchers believe that fear of defection powers male violence to women – it arises from sexual jealousy. That may well be true, and certainly the control

---

[371] Abbott, G. (1993)

and subordination of women, for which they have paid heavily, may be fuelled by various male reproductive strategies[372]. But sexual or otherwise, one of the things that the dominant elites fear and hate most of all is defection. Even threatening a cherished theory in academia can bring wrath and shaming from dominants and demands for your exclusion! It's called heresy. Science is not always the free debating place it pretends to be and those who defect from the common view can be threatened. Dominant academics (who in the past were mostly male) do not like their theories to be challenged.

In politics and the military, the idea that subordinates or previous allies might defect can be met with hideous reprisals. Indeed, treason has remained one of the crimes that is most likely to bring the establishment's vengeance[373]. Throughout history some of the worse cruelties and public demonstrations of power are those which have been given to treason or planning to counter-attack the dominant elites. Insurrectionists, beware! This is where the more paranoid qualities of mind come to the fore. Moreover, in this scheme the names and addresses of accomplishes are also needed, and the fear of detection and false accusation can spread through the populace. Russia in the 1930s went through a terrible time where no one felt safe from false accusation, as the paranoid fears of the leaders wrought terror on their citizens. China experienced similar problems under Mao. To a lesser degree, McCarthyism in the States was derived from the same psychology. Paranoia can be infectious.

There is a very primitive archetypal fear that others will rebel against (dominant) authority and/or form alliances to attack the dominant elite, or at least not conform to the social rules. They may gang up with enemies, undermine the state, or destroy the moral order. When shaming and ridicule (the common, everyday controls of non-violent coercion) are not enough to bring the wayward back in line, stronger means are called for. What is salient here is that via identification with the power elite, the accuser, torturer and those put in the role

---

[372] Wilson, M. and Daly, M. (1992); Wilson, M. and Daly, M. (1985). See also Archer, J. (1994, ed.) for various papers that explore this theme. Also, Ridley, M. (1994).

[373] Burford, E.J. and Shulman, S. (1992) note that if a wife killed her husband, this could be seen as a form of treason.

of detecting and uncovering defections, may experience the treason, plotting or a wish simply to follow other lifestyles, as plots against themselves, their own values, identities and ways of life. The process of interrogation and torture is then not just a job to be done, but a personal crusade against others who threaten the self. It may become a virtue. Equally, our own demands for cruelty to others can be heightened if we believe the other has put us under threat. Then the mob bays for blood.

The Pleasures of Cruelty

Sadism and the Desire to Humiliate

The chapter on shame explored the consequences of humiliation and shame and noted how the experiences of being humiliated were also a source for a *retaliatory desire to be the shamer and humiliator*. Our power plays often go with a certain sadism which can be institutionalised and even condoned, at least for the in-group. It is about control. Also, as we saw in the chapter on shame, cruelty can be used to stop people from acting in a way that might bring shame on the group or family, or as punishment for having done so. Feeling one has been shamed (lost status) by the behaviour of others (e.g., a daughter's sexual behaviour has brought shame on the family) can bring feelings of vicious retaliatory aggression.

The inventiveness and apparent concern to exact as much suffering as possible from a chosen victim for humiliation and submission means that there were those who spent time thinking up these things. Public executions ceased in this country in 1868, but in times before that, the public were treated to an orgy of cruelty, which was also popular. Perhaps one of the most awful was to be hanged, drawn and quartered. Here the person was first hanged for a short time (but not until dead), and then disembowelled and his/her insides burnt in front of him/her. S/he was then beheaded. Common public flogging pales in significance. When one thinks of the many ways humans have used cruelty to deter and maintain order, the sheer inventiveness is depressing. However, there appears no clear relationship between how cruel a nation is and its law.

Although the media seems preoccupied with sadistic killers and rapists, the origins of these behaviours are unclear. Not all serial murder is focused by a desire to humiliate. Some killers have bizarre ideas about their victims and kill them to stop them from leaving. Throughout our history, blood sacrifice has been associated with gaining magical powers. Gilles de Rais (1400-1440) apparently thought he had found the secret of the philosopher's stone and brutally killed 200-300 hundred children trying to find it. This is 'means to an end' cruelty. The other is simply an object to be used.

A fascinating variant on inflicting pain for pleasure is in sadomasochism. Some individuals take pleasure in the pain of others and receiving pain, so it's unclear if it's the pain they are enjoying or the pleasure they are giving. Couples can 'play' at sexual games involving bondage, whipping, caging and water sports. Importantly though, these acts are not seen as acts of cruelty, but as acts of love which depend completely on trust. It is often the masochist who controls the game and who may use a special word like *banana* to call a halt to proceedings. The 'victim' can scream as much as they like but the sadistic acts will (only) stop if the victim says the word. Not so long ago a number of men were taken to court for mutilation of their penises in sexual acts. Some even see most forms of heterosexuality as based on sadomasochism[374]. So here is a fascinating issue which again involves voluntary subordination in what may appear to be cruel behaviours but are not.

In contrast, genuine sadism depends upon involuntary subordination and the fear they can induce. Psychiatric classification includes one for sadistic personality disorder (SPD), and there are now various criteria for SPD. Before I give them, it might be interesting to note, as we go along, just how many could be applied

---

[374] Kitzinger, C. (1994) has reviewed some of the more extreme feminist views that argue that just about all heterosexual pleasure is based on sadomasochism. While such views raise questions about the nature of consent and, as we saw in Chapter 8, the nature of our freedom to choose, such arguments so dilute the concept as to make it almost meaningless. It certainly misses the complexity of sadomasochism and the differences between consenting couples and abuse

not only to individuals but to various social groups (religions, ethnic groups, Ku Klux Klan types, and even nations). From the work of Spitzer and his colleagues[375,] the criteria include the following:

1) Uses threat and violence to achieve dominance – although not just to get a resource, as in robbery

2) Humiliates in the presence of others

3) Uses unusually harsh discipline

4) Is amused by or enjoys other's suffering

5) Has lied to offer an excuse to hurt someone – again not just to achieve a goal

6) Gets people to do what s/he wants by frightening or terrorising them

7) Restricts the autonomy of others (especially in close relationships)

8) Is fascinated by violence, weapons, injury and torture

There, are of course, no shortage in history of pretty sadistic individuals who left great scars on history. Take, for example, Vlad Ţepeş (1431-76), on whom Bram Stoker is believed to have based his novel *Dracula*, known as Vlad the Impaler for the hundreds he had tortured and impaled for his pleasure. Some analysts believe that sadism grows in the mind when a child has been subjected to cruelty and neglect (though not for all such children obviously). What may mature is a rage and desire for power and to turn the tables – to see others suffer. It is about control and the need to humiliate – to be the victimizer, not the victim. Quite possibly. Because sadism is an archetypal possibility, it can be excited by social relationships and intergroup conflicts. It is difficult to believe that all the atrocities committed in war are by those who were abused in childhood. Equally some seriously deranged sadistic folk may be mentally ill or genetically challenged.

---

[375] Spitzer, R.L., Feister, S., Gay, M. and Pfohl, B. (1991) have been among the foremost in developing psychiatric classifications. There are of course many concerns about such efforts.

You can make you own mind up on this one, but I suspect that some societies and groups which are centred around (mostly male) dominance, exploitation and need for superiority, use many of these tactics – both internally and externally. It is well known that there are many armies over many centuries who have been quite prepared to commit the most appalling tortures not only in the service of war, but to support tyrannical leaders. The problem with making sadism into a personality disorder is not that it may not be valid, but that it tends to put a boundary around it and helps us turn a blind eye to how certain contexts, groups and values actually excite sadistic tendencies.

All of us can experience a mild degree of sadistic impulses when we are full of vengeance. *Their sadism and aggressions fuel ours.* We get a buzz from destroying others. There is an interesting scene in *Star Trek Generations* when Data, the ship's android, gets an emotion chip. When the Enterprise discovers some bad Klingons and manages to blow them up, Data cannot hide the buzz he gets from destroying them. It's an interesting scene because many of us can identify with him.

What is hidden from view in the scene is that often the buzz of destroying others stems from hatred rather than just dominance. Hatred and vengeance is, on a social-group level, the most common reason for sadism – including the torture of captured enemies. When hatred and sadistic vengeance gets out of control, reconciliation becomes very difficult. People may be able to forgive wars, but not atrocities. Of course, the contexts for much group and international violence lie in the failure of political solutions. Chomsky[376] makes clear that we have created many enemies in the world because we have so often gone back on promises, used our military might and arms technology to prop up unpleasant dictators and generally have not supported democracy, but self-interest. But the point is that in the failure to solve political conflicts, we create the arenas for hatred and sadism. *Breaking alliances, in addition to exploiting people, activates strong desires to retaliate.* Therefore, vengeful fantasies are not only directed to those who actually harm us, but to those who would have deceived us or broken their promises and alliances. They have let us down, not been there when we

---

[376] Chomsky, N. (1992)

needed them, not come to our rescue or support, etc. The cultivation of such hatreds has, as Gay[1] notes, been marked through the centuries.

Cruelty as Crowd Pleasing

Getting revenge and exerting dominance can be pleasure in a certain kind of way. But we can enjoy cruelty for other reasons. As noted, humans are voyeurs *par excellence*. If we weren't, the media and film business would not be the multi-billion-dollar industry it is today. Probably the ability to watch and learn from others, to learn about the ranks and social relationship shared by the group from watching interactions, has been so adaptive in our evolution that watching others is now very much part of our nature. We are born voyeurs. Equally, of course, we might just have been socialised into it by too much television. But there is reason to doubt that. Sadistic voyeurism is no new social behaviour.

The Roman gladiatorial games became huge affairs, and were popular with large sections of the population. On a weekend, one could go and watch men fighting to the death, fighting animals, burnings, Christians getting their 'comeuppance', and so on. Some Emperors actually had whole armies fighting for their own pleasure, and for that of the crowd. In a single day, thousands could be slaughtered for entertainment. In the first three months of the opening of the Colosseum, it is estimated, 10,000 people were slaughtered for entertainment.

Thankfully, such a scale of cruelty and sadism for public pleasure has been rarely repeated – although films depicting violence remain popular. However, the fascination with the pain and suffering of others exists in all cultures, only the scale has changed. When executions were public they brought large crowds, who had little desire for mercy, but would goad the executioner on. The historical record shows that be it burnings, beheadings, or hangings, public interest was often so great that fights could break out to get as close as possible[377]. At times, some of the crowd would shout contemptuously at the poor dying victim, and roar in pleasure as the deed was done. In Britain hanging was, until the last century, by strangulation, which could take as long as 20 minutes.

---

[377] Abbott, G. (1993)

According to Abbot[378], when a more humane way was found to hang a victim, by breaking the neck in the fall, the crowd were incensed and threatened to riot for being robbed of their spectacle. Although in general, women do not act violently to anything like the degree men do, there is not much evidence that they are not also attracted to it. Indeed, in France during the guillotines of the French Revolution, women made up large sections of the crowd and fought to get near the front.

There is no doubt that long before Roman times, watching cruelty being enacted has always had a fascination for humans. In some ways, it is probably a mark of our progress that it's difficult to imagine any part of the world institutionalising something like the gladiatorial games. Yet we remain as fascinated and voyeuristic about violence as ever we did, and seem happy to see fantasy depictions. Scenes of outstanding cruelty are still crowd pullers, and the media hype it to sell their wares. A visit to the local video shop will convince you of our preoccupation with watching violence done to others. The cruelty on the covers with pictures of tough-looking men and their weapons stare down on us.

War

Evolutionary Origins

The evolutionary origins of war are difficult to pinpoint. Various insect species, like ants, engage in war behaviour and have soldiers and defenders. They can even enslave. Wasps can raid bee hives, etc. Many evolutionary thinkers link war to ethnocentrism, which involves marked boundaries between in-group and out-group and seeing the out-group as enemies[379]. Mammals who hunt in packs

---

[378] Abbott, G. (1993)
[379] Reynolds, V., Falger, V., and Vine, I. (1986, eds.). Barkow, J.H. (1989) believes that war (or what he calls auto-predation) was important in our evolution. This culled

can raid another group's territory, and have skirmishes at the boundaries of territories. But perhaps it has been the discovery of chimpanzee wars that came as the greatest shock to us. In 1974, the chimpanzee group Jane Goodall[380] had been studying at Gombe split in two. A small group divided off and took up residence in the southern area while a larger group occupied the northern area. Over a four year period, the north group engaged in systematic patrols that were to result, not just in skirmishes, but warfare. As Goodall notes, these attacks were often vicious and bloody involving pounding, smashing with rocks, biting, ripping flesh and drinking blood. These were inflicted on individuals who had at one time been in the same group. Single individuals could be attacked by gangs. Nothing like this behaviour had been seen before. Submitting and attempts to flee did not prevent attacks (as usually occurs in dominant-subordinate interactions) for the victim was pursued, viciously wounded and often killed. Many have been quick to draw parallels between such behaviour and human war. But there are problems with this.

First, much depends on the species studied. As de Waal[381] notes, although war behaviour has been noted in common chimpanzees it has never been observed in bonobo chimpanzees. They have less male-dominated hierarchies and are more affectionate and openly sexual. Second, in these 'wars', females could be as violent as the males, whereas human wars are primarily (though by no means exclusively) male orchestrated. Third, females were also attacked, so there was no effort of the northern group to "fight in order to secure access to breeding females". Fourth, Power[382] has (controversially) argued that the feeding regimes Goodall introduced to attract the chimpanzees to the observation points introduced high levels of competitive behaviour (and frustration) and changed their natural social structure and with it their basic psychology. War behaviour

---

out the less able individuals. I am dubious. The more powerful influence in my view was our ability to be, to communicate, to share, to co-operate and be helpful to each other. See also Barkow, J.H. (1991).

[380] Goodall, J. (1990)

[381] de Waal, F. (1995)

[382] Power, M. (1991)

has never been seen in "non-provisioned" groups. Fifth, and to my mind most important, Goodall herself notes,

> ...although the basic aggressive patterns of the chimpanzee are remarkably similar to some of our own, their comprehension of the suffering they inflict on their victims is very different to ours. Chimpanzees, it is true, are able to emphasise, to understand at least to some extent the wants and needs of their companions. But only humans, I believe are capable of *deliberate* cruelty - acting with the intention of causing pain and suffering. [383]

This sentiment, that only humans are capable of deliberate cruelty has, of course, been the basis of this chapter. It is in our empathic numbing (and the inhibition this introduces) that we become able to inflict suffering and be keen to do it. Humans are capable of amplifying any archetype potential, and if a particular potential gets out of balance with other potentials (if we become impassioned with ethnocentric hatred and compassion inhibition), all hell can break loose. We are unrestrained in our behaviour.

But human war, one of our cruellest activities, has become associated with many things. The fear of attack, the benefits of glorious conquest (pillage and plunder), defending pride and honour, retaliation, gaining prestige and status, loyalty to and defence of one's own group, and claims of (moral) superiority (e.g., religious, political) – these are but some of the justifications for war, group violence and (at times) our passion for it[384]. Once group violence became incorporated into the *societal* way of solving conflicts, gaining resources or asserting superiority, the retreat to the reptilian mind and its strategies is well advanced. In part perhaps because of the SAHP system, few would wish to detract from war behaviour and risk being seen as appeasers or cowardly.

---

[383] Goodall, J. (1990), p.92

[384] Reynolds et al. (1986, eds.). Also, for an outline of nineteenth-century justifications, see Gay, P. (1995). For an interesting and informative Jungian-Ethological perspective (although different to the one proposed here), see Stevens, A. (1989). For an exploration in terms of power and affiliative motives, see Winter, D. (1993).

War and Cruelty

War is usually sold to young males as something exciting, heroic and *virtuous*. In truth, as we all know, it is barbaric and little more than an exercise in cruelty. Alexander the Great was born in 356 BC, the son of King Philip II of Macedonia. He was to show all the hallmarks of both a great and an anti-social leader. He had a contempt for life, believing that to die in battle was glorious. He was brave, clever, full of his own self-importance, and intensely ambitious. But he was, like many military leaders of this age, also intensely cruel. As Grabsky[385] notes, "Alexander with his father Philip were innovators in the vigorous pursuit of a defeated foe and no pity was shown; it was then accepted that the more that were killed now, the more enduring the victory". When he defeated the Persians, he pursued the fleeing army ruthlessly, slaughtering up to 100,000, both during and after the battle. When he defeated the Tyrians after a seven months siege,

> The Macedonians, again showing a post-battle orgiastic glory in revenge, released their pent-up frustration in appalling slaughter...2,000 more were now crucified. The remaining 30,000 were sold into slavery.[386]

War has always been a terrible and bloody business. In those days, to lose and be caught could result in crucifixion, decapitation, loss of both hands or eyes, rape and slavery. Such a fate could be visited on thousands. When we look to Bosnia, it is as well to remember that what is stirred in some contexts within our archetypal minds is straightforward cruelty. The death and work camps of both the Nazis and the Japanese, through specific acts like the bombing of Dresden, all attest to it. In these contexts that compassion has, of course, died – at least towards enemies. Cruelty, like so much of our craziness, is an amplification and an inflation of an archetypal form. In many instances, it is the social context and value system that brings it to life – or at least gives it such vigour and passion – and because we are largely unaware of what is happening, it takes us over.

---

[385] Grabsky, P. (1993)
[386] Grabsky, P. (1993), p.36

Maintaining Military Discipline

It is not only the virtue of waging war (for honour) that should concern us. More important is the way by which the elites have assumed more and more power over their subordinates to fight on their behalf. Further, the manipulation of values of greed and proving superiority has not only rendered the last few thousand years a bloody time, but such values and beliefs have soaked through to saturate our psyche with competitive and war-like metaphors. Be it in sports or business, ruthlessness and the metaphors of war are not far away.

Like any subordinate animal, human subordinates can be kept in check by down-hierarchy threats. However, few if any animals can force subordinates to work on their own goals. Apart from ants, who are able to enslave, no mammal apart from humans can enslave and force subordinates to service them. The human history of slavery shows all too clearly that we can do this. But it is not only in the obvious forms of slavery that our most vicious and cruel behaviours show themselves – it is also in the production of military units[387].

All armies are highly ranked structures (commanders, captains etc.) and with elite groups (e.g., in our day, the Paramilitary or SAS). In a highly informative report on the history of soldiering, the magazine *Focus*[388] reviewed the many changes that have taken place in the creation of armies. The word soldiering actually comes for the Latin *solditus*, meaning gold coin. In fact, most early armies had to be paid for their services (often mercenaries) even as far back as the great Greek armies, although often the opportunities for plunder were also rewards. By the age of the elite groups like the 'knights in armour', derived from elite families, their payment was largely with land. Indeed, the whole feudal system was designed as payment. This system was to have a significant shape on the social, political and economic structure of the evolving Europe. Knights

---

[387] See Mann, M. (1986); Stevens, A. (1989); Dixon, N.F. (1976/1994); Dixon, N.F. (1987). What also needs to be noted is that when men come together to turn themselves into fighting groups, there is a brutalising effect on the psychology of men. To cope with fear and to defeat enemies, compassion must be suppressed, especially to outsiders.

[388] *Focus* magazine (1995) Dossier: Soldiers. April, 45-51. No single author is given.

were highly individualistic and treated war as a kind of blood sport, only obeying those seen as their superiors.

By the Middle Ages, the ordinary foot soldiers were often signed up from the unemployed or criminal groups but they too often had to be paid. At the end of conflict, some would return home to become bandits. A combination of new weapons and tactics changed this rather arbitrary system of enlistment. It was the French Revolution which introduced the expectation that a nation state could conscript its men to fight and thus put huge armies in the field. The rest of Europe later caught on. The changing psychology and social attitudes to fighting and claims on individual citizens by the ruling elite to fight and defend nations carried within it new forms of exploitation. During the First War World, many tens of thousands (ordinary men, who months before had been at home) could die in a morning's battle.

Historically, the people who had to subject themselves to the rigours of military life were not always willing to do so. And the contempt and disregard for the life of the common soldier, so obvious in the First War World and even today, had shown itself long before. Subordination and obedience to the rules had to be enforced on an otherwise unruly mass of men. During the times when Britain did rule the waves, the cruelty on board ship was enormous. Keelhauling was a way of dragging some poor unfortunate under the ship. The Hollywood versions are very cleaned up ones. Often, due to the barnacles that would have grown below water, the victim was severely lacerated and died, if not from drowning then, from his wounds. The cat-o'-nine-tails was a short whip that had at its ends small mental balls. Not only could this rip the flesh from the victim (a simple whip was not good enough for the job), but the victim was often made to make his own. And these punishments were visited on men who had often been simply picked up off the streets in Plymouth and Portsmouth and pressganged.

To maintain order, flogging was almost a daily event on some ships. And these were often associated with bizarre rituals where all the crew attended, the officers in uniform, and drummers rattled out their beat in rhythm with the strokes[389]. If one flogger got tired, another took over. At times, crews from other

---

[389] Abbott, G. (1993)

ships could also be involved, and the poor man would be flogged by different crews. It was not uncommon that a flogging was so severe, leaving hardly any flesh on the back, that death was inevitable. As late as 1881, flogging could still be awarded on the Admiralty's agreement[390]. The terror of mutiny was such that many means of imposing fear to halt it were necessary (including hangings, shootings, walking the plank). The conditions on board ships were often so bad that the poor ship-hands were trapped between a desire to mutiny and a fear of punishment. Being shot for desertion was, of course, common. And the military had many and various deterrents for insubordination. So, the history of military discipline is also a history of institutionalised cruelty to enforce order, obedience and submission. More recently, ensuring men will fight comes less from terror of disobedience, but more from forming tight-knit groups who work together and develop supportive bonds. But the point of reflecting on the history of military discipline is to note how cruelty was accepted as a normal part of life in these social contexts.

Cruelty and Duty

How often has one heard the claim, "I was only doing my duty"? As we noted in Chapter 8, some years ago the social psychology researcher Stanley Milgram[391] found that it was depressingly easy to get others to deliver electric shocks to people, even when the person receiving the shocks was (feigning being) in pain. Norman Dixon[392], in his book *Our Own Worst Enemy*, has given a good review of this work and its implications. The main factor which seemed to be important was obedience to authority. Indeed, we now know that in some situations, people can be extraordinarily obedient to authority – their subordinate psychology really comes to the fore. It should be no surprise any more that a good number of us will, under certain conditions, dehumanise and torture others. To blame the torturer is only a small part of it. It is attacking the subordinates again and failing to appreciate how powerful the dominance hierarchy archetype

---

[390] Abbott, G. (1993)
[391] Milgram, S. (1974)
[392] Dixon, N.F. (1978)

is in us. It also fails to address the central issue of social context and values sent down by the more dominant members.

Dixon[393] gives a harrowing and moving account of a soldier's involvement with the massacre in My Lai during the Vietnam War. Around three to four hundred defenceless men, women, children and babies were killed that day. They were herded close to a ravine, shot and pushed over. When asked at a subsequent hearing why he did it the soldier answered, "Because I felt like I was ordered to do it, and it seemed like that, at the time I felt I was doing the right thing, because like I said I lost buddies. I lost a damn good buddy, Bobby Wilson, and it was on my conscience. So, after I did it, I felt good, but later on it was getting to me."

The questioner seems perplexed by how Americans could do such things and takes the soldier into considerations of his own family. He then asks if the people were doing anything, and asks if they were begging to save themselves. At first the solider denies it, then says, "Right. They were begging and saying 'No, no'. And the mothers were hugging their children and... but they kept right on firing. Well, we kept right on firing. They were waving their arms and begging..." [394]

As Milgram said of his research,

> I am forever astonished that when lecturing on the obedience experiments in colleges across the country, I faced young men who were aghast at the behaviour of the experimental subjects and proclaimed they would never behave in such a way, but who, in a matter of months, were brought into the military and performed without compunction actions that made shocking the victim seem pallid. In this respect they are no better and no worse than human beings of any era who lend themselves to the purposes of authority and become instruments in its destructive process. [395]

---

[393] Dixon, N.F. (1978)
[394] Dixon, N.F. (1978) pp.127-128
[395] Milgram, S. (1974), p.180

Of course, as he points out, we know what these actions were. They included the use of napalm, burning villages, the massacre of many hundreds of unarmed civilians and defoliating vast tracks of the country.

It has been only comparatively recently that the automatic right of the state to 'draft' people into the armed forces has been challenged (e.g., as in the Vietnam War). The advent of televisual pictures (of battle), education and raising expectations have had their impact. But these changes have come with many other ideas: that a military way of running schools and businesses are not ideal or virtuous, that women cannot be subordinated to allow men to get on with their competitions behind closed doors, that conflicts are complex and not simple battles of right and wrong. Indeed, the whole edifice of patriarchal society is quite rightly under attack for reasons too complex and numerous to outline. But for all this it does not mean, sadly, that the limits of competition are well understood. It just means that it is changing its forms. We are still prone to subordinate ourselves to keep our jobs. And it is new forms of profit (rather than plunder) as much as fear that keeps the war machines of the world turning over.

Compassionate societies not only require a very clear rule of law, well administered, but we need those who are the enforcers to become relatively independent as a profession around the world in order to agree codes of conduct, particularly when it comes to supporting political values. It would be wonderful if it was no longer acceptable for law enforcement agencies to opt out of moral concerns. Just as it's not acceptable for doctors to torture people because the state requires them, so too armies cannot be used to torture, kill or disappear people.

The Manufacture of Cruelty

Intergroup violence and threat is associated with a hidden form of cruelty of very serious proportions – the arms trade. It is hidden because the motives may not necessarily appear callous or cruel, the people involved may take no personal pleasure from watching others suffer, nor feel in any personal sense threatened. They speak more in terms of needs for power and control. But if we take callousness as indifference to the suffering of others, then the arms trade is clearly an exercise in that. In our invention of weapons of war, the bullets that explode inside bodies, the biological weapons that blister and torture, atomic bombs, napalm, cluster bombs – the very fact that as you read this, there are humans working out how to injure other human beings more effectively, should warn us that something is seriously wrong with us. *We are paying taxes for the manufacture of callousness and cruelty* and many are keen supporters of it. This is clearly a cultural inflation of a much more primitive archetype.

Alexander, Caesar and Nelson were all heavily involved with the actual fighting. We can see these individuals as glorying in war because they were part of it. Leaders nowadays keep well away from the blood and guts of it all. So, what should we make of those who are not part of it but just study the means of doing it, or making a good sales pitch? Their callousness, cruelty and ruthlessness is so detached from the results of their endeavours on men, women and children, that it might be difficult to connect the two. But they are connected, no matter what the denial and other psychological tricks used to separate and buffer themselves from the consequences of their actions. John Pilger[396], a journalist, and one of my own personal heroes, has just produced a harrowing report and television documentary on the arms trade. Here is a world where people speak of their weapons as if they are describing soap power. They dress in smart suits and give cocktail parties. Razor wire is described as "aesthetically pleasing", machine guns as "efficient", land mines as "effective", and cruise missiles as "smart". Around 2,000 people each month lose their lives and limbs to landmines that are often cheaper than a can of Coke. Cluster bombs, a British invention, are designed to maim. Britain is responsible for 20% of the world's arms trade and our leaders have strongly promoted it with subsidies of billions of our taxes.

In 1980 when Thatcher was at the Farnborough air show, Pilger says[397], "She banged the table. 'Look here', she said, '£1.2 billion defence exports... it's not enough!'" During the subsequent years, she and her ministers toured the world jumping up trade for arms exports. At times, we sold arms to both sides of a

---

[396] Pilger, J. (1995)
[397] Pilger, J (1995)

conflict (Iraq and Iran), to regimes that were brutal, did nothing when Saddam gassed the Kurds, and as the Matrix Churchill court case revealed, there were serious abuses of power and deceptions. The arms trade is fuelled by greed and psychological numbing. Nothing is to stand in the way of making profit – from proving one's efficiencies in death and injury. The squandering of third-world resources on arms is nothing short of tragic. We are ever so keen to sell them to them. For the price of one Hawker aircraft, some countries could afford fresh water for a million and a half of its people.

Of course, like any common torturer, criminal or drug dealer the cry is, "if we don't supply them someone else will". Not a very convincing justification, unless you empathise with drug dealers. The other cry is, "we need the jobs". Not only are both morally confused, they are not accurate. As Pilger[398] reports, in some parts of the arms industry, it costs £600,000 to create one new job. The huge amounts of research and special privileges that have gone into the science of injury could have done untold wonders for other sections of society. Nor is it true that the workers demand to be maintained in such jobs, most would much prefer to make more peaceful things.

Perhaps because we are so obsessed with psychiatric classifications of destructive behaviour and craziness we are blinded to these realities. But the arms trade is a far more serious human craziness than any serial killer. Serial killers may kill a few, but we allow the construction and development of instruments that can kill and maim millions. It has been estimated that in excess of 100 million people have died in wars in the last 50 years, and goodness knows how many more than that injured for life. Their deaths have not always been quick. Over two million Vietnamese died in that war. Babies are *still* being born, deformed, from the chemicals used to defoliate the country, and people are still losing limbs to landmines that were scattered about like confetti over farm lands. Not only is there injury to bodies but even those who physically survive are vulnerable to serious mental disorders, such as post-traumatic stress – a fact that both the military and governments have covered up. Around 58,000 Americans

---

[398] Pilger, J (1995)

died in Vietnam, but thousands have killed themselves since, suffered from post-traumatic stress disorders, become alcoholic, or coped with the loss of limbs. If all this is not an exercise in madness, then I am not sure what is. The problem is because of the way we are archetypally built, it's very difficult to shut down these archetypes and the constant creation of tribal violence – but try we must.

Although research shows that many men do not actually like fighting (at least in direct combat) and have to be taught it – put in a state of mind in which they can overcome natural inhibitions to killing – this natural reluctance can be got around by distancing them from direct combat and putting them behind computer screens. Of course, at the other end the death is real enough. One of the more worrying moments during the Gulf War was when a young pilot was interviewed and exclaimed with pleasure that his last sortie had been, "like shooting rats in a barrel". He spoke as if he had been playing a video game. Behind him were the burning corpses of these "rats", trapped as they were in their tanks and cars. I well recall how a patient who had been a soldier in the North Africa campaign of the Second World War, told with tears in his eyes, that he would carry to his death the screams of the men caught in their tanks when they were hit and set on fire. My father told me how in fighting the screaming of the injured and dying is horrific.

The Holocaust

1995 is the fiftieth anniversary of the liberation of the death camps. When we look back on it, we seem stunned and wonder how it could happen. Eleven million were systematically murdered in the most horrendous ways, as is well known, though even now some try to deny it. It is not the case that many ordinary people did not aid in the slaughter of the Jews, Polish, and mentally ill. Many did. And as Martin Gilbert[399] makes clear, the writing was on the wall long before Hitler took power, for he had written so extensively of his hatred for the Jews in *Mein Kampf,* and many governments knew this. What was terrifying

---

[399] Gilbert, M. (1987)

about the Holocaust was the scale of the callousness and cruelty, and how it seemed to infect so much of Germany's social life.

Companies bid for contracts to make the gas, gas chambers and furnaces – for profit, of course. Scientists worked out the means to do it, clerks worked diligently to record the deaths, soldiers did the shooting and the herding – and locals would often help in rounding up Jews and other "undesirables". Psychopathy become institutionalised in many walks of life. Any inhibition that there might be on killing people, including babies, were swept aside. Humans became experimental subjects in hideous medical research run by doctors and nurses. The personal stories of cruelty are appalling. But what is really frightening is the complacency and projection that still goes on today. Instead of trying to understand what it is *in the human mind and the socio-political structures of a society* that can bring our sadism to life we simply hope "Germany has learnt her lesson". At the same time that politicians were pontificating about lessons learnt, a TV documentary was revealing how British companies were engaged in supplying hundreds of electric prods (well known to be used as instruments of torture) for export to any regime who wanted them. And if our cruelties to other humans were not enough, there is also the suffering we cause animals in our factory farms and research on cosmetics[400].

---

[400] If humans have often fared rather badly at the hands of fellow humans spare a thought for the animals. In the seventeenth century, cats could be put in wicker cages and burnt as agents of the devil. Animals have long been sacrificed to appease our feared Gods. The cruelty in our methods to bring us cheap meat is becoming a source of greater public awareness. In our hearts, we know the methods of factory farming are essentially cruel, but apart from organisations like Compassion in Farming or a shift to vegetarianism, mostly we do nothing.

The Social and Personal

What has been outlined here is not only the excesses of our callousness and cruelty, which are encased and perpetrated in social groups, brought to life in certain social contexts, and justified by various appeals, but an attempt has been made to shift the focus of our understanding about craziness from explorations of power, influence and control to a focus on suffering. We have not explored all the suffering that is perpetrated on people in their homes in the forms of violence and emotional abuses of various sorts. Nor have we explored the enormous cruelties perpetrated on the mentally ill[401]. Nor indeed the simple pain of shame and humiliation. Nor have we explored in any detail how our lack of action can lead to suffering.

At times, we do not recognise our behaviours to be cruel, and as Fromm[402] has noted we can use ideas like, "having to be cruel to be kind". Indeed, it has often been from a moral position that we behave cruelly. Fromm has noted the many problems with a personal morality and conscience. The conscience of the autocrat and authoritarian personality can be rather different from those without such traits. When people were burnt at the stake, some Dominican monks prayed all night for their souls – but burnt the person in the morning anyway – claiming their conscience dictates it. They thought that burning would purify the soul and save them from hell – well, some of them offer that as a justification. The belief "I have to do what I think is right" can be, with hindsight, a dubious justification. Undoubtedly, many of the treatments perpetrated on the mentally ill (e.g., spinning, ducking, emersion in ice cold baths, whipping out the devils) were not done by people who saw themselves as cruel, but compassionate. Even today, some claim that various modern treatments are indeed cruel and toxic[403]. I

---

[401] Ussher, J. (1991) offers an exploration of medical approaches to women's mental suffering and the way these have been seen as related to the body, not the social conditions and forms of subordination – and moreover, how these interventions were often used to subdue protest and increase subordination not to liberate

[402] Fromm, E. (1949/1986)

[403] Breggin, P. (1993) offers a comprehensive overview of how psychiatry has allowed itself (due to its fascination with diseases, biology and drugs) to develop and

remember early in my career a psychiatrist who would give ECT and high levels of drugs to nearly all his in-patients. To him, illness was illness and psychotherapy useless. The problem was he saw this as a virtue and those of his colleagues who did not treat vigorously as unethical! Be it burning people to save their souls, protecting society, punishing them to make sure they do not become unruly, or treating them to save themselves from themselves, cruelty and compassion can change places according to where you stand.

We have not explored in any detail how our social and economic ways of life have hidden cruelty within them in our exploitative demands for resources. We shall touch on this in Chapter 11. That we can be the source of so much suffering to others is beyond dispute. It seems to me that 'power' is an inadequate focus of analysis if we wish to create a fair and more compassionate world. The analysis of power does not necessarily touch the problem of lack of compassion; it is too sanitised a concept.

Thus, our personal enlightenment could be less about power and more about understanding the importance of heightening our capacity for kindness and compassion. We need to understand how leaders and followers can excite each other's sadistic and power orientated archetypes - particularly tribal fears and indignities. One can analyse power until the cows come home but not promote compassion – unless this is the focus for change. It is when we refuse to be indifferent to suffering that we become fully human. In our callousness and cruelty, we show ourselves to be very clever, but only clever reptiles – for they also are indifferent to suffering.

However, it does seem lately, I think due to the media, that we know more about cruelty and are far less happy with our wars and factory farms, domestic violence and so forth. It does seem as if perhaps we are on the change. I hope so. More of this in a later chapter.

---

use interventions without looking at the wider picture of social and psychological causation. In so doing some interventions are worse than the illness they are supposed to cure.

If we are to believe the anthropologists[404], which I do, then there are differences in societies as to the levels of violence and cruelty they expect, sanction or restrain. It is by no means inevitable that we have to behave as cruelly as we do. Compared to thousand years ago, we are far more compassionate than ever we were: the Scandinavians don't send their ships over to raid and rape us; we are not likely to be crucified or hanged for minor crimes; while slavery is still a serious problem, it is nothing like it was. What brought about these changes are complex and multifactorial, linked to changing laws, patterns of business and trade, education and more besides. But I'm not sure we can rely on it just happening, on a more peaceful society just emerging. Maybe there are ways by which we can use our science of ourselves to gain clarity and insight as to what is sitting behind the drivers of our behaviour, and give us the opportunities to say enough is enough. All the time we remain unenlightened or semiconscious, we are vulnerable to being puppets of the archetypes and acting out their repeating dramas for both good and for terror.

Conclusion

We can look back on our history and see that much of it has been based on cruelty and the constructions for its justification. Institutional cruelties often arise from protecting dominant elites. As we have seen throughout this book, we are quite vulnerable to the manipulation of our values by such elites, have needs to conform with others, and can easily be led into styles of relating that are callous and cruel. Because we are so susceptible to narcissistic competitive self-focus and tribalism, it's not our fault that history has been the way it has. It's time to wake from our semiconscious states where, to be honest, we have allowed these archetypes, thrashed out over billions of years as various competitive reproductive strategies, to hijack our thinking, insightful brains. It may not be our fault we are vulnerable to creating the terrors and horrors that

---

[404] Hinde, R.A. and Groebel, J. (1991); Howell, S. and Willis, R. (1989, eds.)

we do, but it is our responsibility to find ways to stop doing it. It's not just technology but our psychology that is the greatest challenge to us as a species.

To raise our consciousness, we have to, as Jung suggested, look into the shadows and the darkness. Hell is something we create because our jerry-built minds allow for certain parts of ourselves to take us over. It is not the devil outside of ourselves we need fear, but our own potentials. Once stripped of our compassion and feeling for other human beings, the excitement of our xenophobia, needs for power and revenge, and our willing and sometimes unwilling subordinate-follower nature, can lead us with some passion into the armies of hell creation. Quite correctly the devil is seen as reptilian.

10: RELIGION

Great doubt, great enlightenment
Little doubt, little enlightenment
No doubt, no enlightenment.[405]

Religion has had (and still has) such a profound effect on our values, social relationships and sense of ourselves, for good and ill, that a book like this could not really avoid some exploration of it. As Armstrong[406] says, "whatever conclusion we reach about the reality of God, the history of this idea must tell us something important about the human mind and the nature of our aspiration". That is to say, because social relating is what our evolved minds are constructed for, it is not surprising that our experiences of the spiritual are often constructed in forms of social relationship. Nor is it surprising that religions often seem principally concerned with how we should (morally) relate to each other to avoid serious in-group conflicts. Thus, religion can easily become a vehicle for the projection of the archetypes of our evolved, jerry-built minds. Our problem is, how do our minds construct relationship with God(s) with whom we cannot relate directly? As we saw in Chapter 2, given the harsh realities of life, it is not surprising that humans invented gods they could appease and appeal to.

The historical texts on religion show that just about any concept of God that could exist has been presented by someone at some time. In fact, when it comes to God and religion we find ourselves in a highly varied supermarket of choices:

---

[405] Old Zen saying. Had they known about the way the limbic system forms or how reasoning can rely on conviction and how something feels (see Chapter 2), they might have said, "limbic certainty no enlightenment".

[406] Armstrong, K. (1994, p.7) found her early Catholicism frightening, as many do, with its ideas of hell and purgatory, and after living as a nun, she turned to an academic career to explore the basis of religious belief. This is a very scholarly and fascinating book that is not anti-spiritual in any sense but recognises that it is how we create our gods that is the problem.

God as beyond human reason and human understanding – the unknown (as in Aristotle) – versus God as human-like with feelings, passions and desires

God as accessible only via deep mediation, intuition and mystical knowledge versus God who relies on science, reason and philosophy to reveal himself

God as a personal and available deity with whom we can personally relate versus God as an impersonal, pantheistic force (as in *Star Wars* movies or Buddha consciousness)

God as awakening via the consciousness of humans (as in Jung) versus God as already fully formed and conscious and in the process of revealing himself to us

Some see the idea of, and belief in, God as archetypal, as did Jung and more recently the sociobiologist Wenegrat.[407] Others have taken a mystical-sociological approach and have linked religious beliefs and forms to the various stages of consciousness. This view sees both the body and consciousness as evolving processes.[408] Others suggest that religious knowledge depends on normal psychological processes; that is, there is nothing especially different about religious knowing from other forms of knowing.[409] While some have

---

[407] Wenegrat, B. (1990) not only gives a very clear exposition of the sociobiological approach to psychology in general, but also an eloquent account of how Jung's concept of archetype fits with modern sociobiological ideas. He uses the concept of archetype to explore the internal basis for the construction of social relating and also how this can throw light on the nature of religion and the subjective experiences of God. He also reviews much fascinating research on the psychology of religion. In my view, however, he focuses more on the attachment and parent-child archetypes in human-God relationships and not, as we shall do here, the dominant-subordinate. This is not to deny their importance but only to say that the reader interested in those themes can find them well articulated by Wenegrat.

[408] Wilber, K. (1983). Wilber has written much on a transpersonal approach to religion. He focuses on how we acquire knowledge and how it can be used to gain insights or blind us.

[409] Watts, F. and Williams, M. (1998) argue that religious understanding and experience can be understood with recourse to the same basic psychological mechanisms of

argued that religions tend to be destructive, entrapping people in pathological beliefs,[410] others have argued that some (but, of course, not all) religious beliefs and practices can function to promote mental health and social harmony.[411]

The Archetypal Nature of Religious Relationships

In this chapter, I will explore the potential craziness that we can be caught in when the archetypes (especially the competitive-rank archetypes) become the lens through which our relationship to God and the spiritual are created. All the four basic archetypal forms for social relationships that we met in Chapters 2 and 3 can be observed in people's experiences of their religions. As a rather crude outline, we can note the following:

Care-eliciting: This aspect of our nature is activated when we see ourselves in a state of need; a need that cannot (in the first instance) be satisfied by recourse to our own selves or human social relationships. When care-eliciting motivates the religious relationship to God, God is constructed as a superior other, sometimes in the form of a parent (father or mother figure) to whom we turn for love, help and understanding. This is the God of intimate (child-parent) attachments and our language reflects this. We may seek some kind of healing or simple acceptance. Our ideal is for unconditional love. There is a yearning for closeness, union, protection and rescue, and a fear of abandonment. We are rescued from the oblivion of death by the fact of God (some say). The upside is that we may indeed find a way to create these feelings and satisfy our need for

---

cognition and emotion that underlie all forms of human behaviour. There is nothing fundamentally different in the psychology of religious knowing than of other forms of knowledge.

[410] Richard Dawkins has referred to religious ideas as viruses of the mind. These beliefs have a strong 'replicate function', shaping attitudes, values and social behaviours, and thus contaminate generation after generation. He was dubious about religious vocational training existing within 'academic' institutions because they violate basic scientific methods of study.

[411] Schumaker, J.F. (1992) has given a very good overview of these different beliefs and arguments for and against the benefits of religion.

care and love; we open ourselves up to 'receive'. This is the searching for attachment to provide a secure base and safe haven (to use John Bowlby's terms). In prayer, we ask for things (love, knowledge, wisdom, strength, etc.). Prayer also has physiological effects on our brain. The act of praying, and imagining oneself relating to a loving, caring other, stimulates systems in the brain that are conducive to wellbeing because they offer a sense of connectedness. People can feel calmer after praying. Collective praying also produces a sense of connectedness and belonging. So, prayer actually performs many functions for us that our archetypal minds rather like. The downside is that we can remain dependent on the external deity, and may become distressed when we feel that the conversation is all one-way and are prayers are not answered or heard.

Care-giving: One cannot elicit love and investment from another unless the other is prepared to give it. God is created as a limitless source of love, care and wisdom. More importantly perhaps, the caring archetype invites us to be caring to others, to develop our basic compassion for others and to utilise our altruistic strategies in relationships. We believe that God has our best interests at heart (is not indifferent) and wants to see us mature, grow and prosper, to come into a closer relationship with him/her. Jung, in his book *Answer to Job*, came up with the idea that God needs us as much as we need God.

Cooperation: Here the relationship is seen more as a transactional; God gives us something in exchange for something, and we are aware of this trade. It is not unconditional love but love that is conditional – if you behave `this way', you are accepted; if you don't, you are not. You have to agree to conform to the rules or commandments. Cooperation also tends towards the desire for conformity; that is religion is used to subdue intra-group conflicts and to harmonise values and beliefs. We are invited to think we are all the same, of one tribe and group, with one leader.

Competitive-rank: Here our beliefs and experiences of the spiritual are textured by complex *hierarchical*, leader-follower relationships. Then arise all the questions of the powers of the leader to ordain and order, to punish disobedience, to make special and to offer prestige. The themes of inferior-superior, dominant-subordinate, shame and pride, weave their plots. We are asked to love God and obey him as the obvious dominant power of all. Today the strife that arises as religions 'compete' for the minds and souls of people is enormous. Until the monotheistic religions, religious wars were relatively uncommon. Sometimes people within such social structures are into crusades, to win converts to the armies of God. Often, certain individuals will give themselves status and prestige, and there is a ladder or highly ranked structure to God, with the priests and popes, etc. at the top. Although most wars are not religious, some fear that religion will be used as a focus for yet more major wars.

It is, of course, rare that one form is experienced in any pure way. The authoritarian religious person may be very submissive and care-eliciting to their God, whilst those who approach God through care-eliciting and giving archetypes may still see their religion (and God) as superior to others. Different religions and their sub-groups tend to accentuate these different aspects and none are purely one or the other. It is in their patterns (e.g., of caring versus competing) that key differences are found. Eisler,[412] for example, draws a distinction between competitive-rank and dominator religions in contrast to partnership and caring ones.

What Makes a Religion?

The word religion comes from the Latin *religiere* meaning 'to reconnect'. What makes a set of beliefs and practices religious is actually rather complex. Not all religions are concerned with life after death or the supernatural (e.g., Confucianism). Although many believe in the existence of deities who may control certain forces (e.g., of nature), not all believe in a God (e.g., Buddhism). Many of the older religions have a number of different gods that regulate different aspects of life and psychological processes. Many religions and ideas of God have been sculptured by socio-economic pressures and inter-group conflicts. The main monotheistic religions have a belief in a single, usually male,

---

[412] Eisler, R. (1990) shows how religious ideals reflect patterns of social organisation.

God, and they gradually defeated and subordinated earlier Goddess figures and beliefs as existed in places like early Crete. Religions such as Islam, Judaism and Christianity all originated in one small area on planet Earth – the Middle East – and their tribal conflicts and beliefs have been exported all over the world. This says much about the power of tribal conflict and clinging to tribal traditions and conflicts, generation after generation, as shapers of social discourses, identities and conflicts.

At times of conflict and war, male (warrior-like) gods come more to the fore – as one might expect from inflation of the rank archetype. But in general, apart from sharing common conflicts and origins, and serving to support the social psychology of the times (e.g., needs for strong in-group ties, subordination to a power elite, and increased externally directed hostility and defensiveness) what the many different religions share is to do with the rituals, ceremonies, internal practices, basic values, sense of belonging and existential beliefs. Religion can act as a focus for a group to bind itself together. What we often see in religion is a canvass on which we (collectively) project ideas reflecting types of relationships and answers to key existential questions.

Religions use myths and stories (often of past heroes or god figures) to describe types of relationships. At times, such events are meant to be only symbolic representations, a source for meditation and internal reflection, although often they are taken literally. Thus, various human fears and archetypal relational processes can come into play. Indeed, as we have noted, just about any type of human relationship that we can have with other humans can be projected into God-human relationships, e.g., personal, involved, loving, accepting, family-like, compassionate, or distant, indifferent, authoritarian, vengeful, sadistic, etc.

This is called anthropomorphic – seeing the other as human-like and imputing human desires and feelings into the other. While it is true that Aristotle, Buddha and many others warned against this tendency to anthropomorphism, that it is foolish to believe God could feel anger, love, sexual desire, or take offense, still anthropomorphism remains one of the most common ways people create and understand their God-self relationships. Indeed, Jesus can be said to be a key person in the anthropomorphism of religion. Through the myths of his life we are told God has a son, encourages family metaphors (father, sons and daughters) and that God is able to share in human suffering – and incidentally, by allowing his son to die so cruelly on the cross shows himself as powerless as the rest of us to end suffering, at least in this life. However, impotence in the face of suffering, the 'can't or won't' (help/save) issue, especially but not only in the death camps of Nazi Germany, meant that for many God as a hope and idea also finally died. But we jump ahead of ourselves.

What do we seek in Religion?

In America, around 80% believe in God and only 6% actively reject the idea, while 44% feel very close to God most of the time.[413] According to one newspaper survey, around 60% of Americans believe the Bible contains the literal words of God, and the Bible is used to impute all kinds of Armageddon tales and predictions, especially as the turn of the millennium approaches.[414]

Different people seek very different things from religion. In times of social and economic upheaval (as now), there can be a fragmentation of religious beliefs (especially if mainstream religions fail to offer certainties or security) into cults or movements. There is a vigorous competition for converts between charismatics (mostly men), who offer new visions, hope, close in-group ties and a sense of being chosen and special.[10] They may offer various threats to outsiders who "don't change their ways".

No religion without faith, nor for that matter any science, can answer the questions which matter most to us. Why am I here? What will become of me when I die? Will I see my loved ones again? Why did these bad things happen to me/us? Is there a place where conflicts end and I will find peace, be loved, accepted and wanted? Is there are a place where sunny holidays and G & T are forever with no liver damage?

---

[413] As quoted in Baumeister, R.F. (1991)
[414] Hattenstone, S. (1995)

Baumeister[415] suggests that religion serves many functions related to our needs for salvation, meaning, hope and self-worth. He does not have an archetypal approach nor does he focus on the nature of social relating as I do here. However, he gives fascinating insights into how religion satisfies many basic, personal fears and needs for meaning and purpose:

1. Promises of salvation and the release from suffering if one either discovers the secrets of life (e.g., via meditation or engaging in ritual practices) or behaves in certain (moral, or heroic) ways.

2. Moral codes which are often associated with rewards or punishments and can reduce in-group conflicts.

3. A sense of efficacy and purpose – we can make sense of the things that happen to ourselves and others by recourse to the religious texts/authorities. This reduces our uncertainties and holds back a fearful collapse into a view of life as a meaningless, heartless struggle.

4. A sense of self-worth, a sense of being part of a large group of like-minded others, and, moreover, a sense of superiority over others who are not in our (religious) group[416]

It is possible that it is our evolved human psychology which often drives religion and gives it its social shapes. It also based on the need to find answers. On becoming sufficiently conscious of ourselves and others, we were confronted with a world of immense suffering and the recognition that our own life, and the lives of those we love, will decay and end. Not surprisingly most are not too keen on that idea. To the more scientifically minded, we are confronted with less personal questions. We are confronted with such mystery as to why the universe exists at all (why something rather than nothing) that it immediately increases our awareness of the limitation of our understanding that is of truly gigantic

---

[415] Baumeister, R.F. (1991). This is an excellent book and looks at many aspects of life where meaning creation is key to how we feel and behave.

[416] For a different way of thinking about the functions and forms of religious beliefs from a transpersonal approach, see Wilber, K. (1983).

proportions. But to the scientist that is a quest not to be side-stepped by simple solutions, for or against God and life after death.

The spiritual quest is thus blown along by a search for knowledge, understanding and meaning on the one hand, but also by fear and an enormous need for love, acceptance and status on the other. God and all offered as solutions. When St Augustine struggled to understand God in his *Confessions*, we could just as easily see him using God to gain insight into the passions and conflicts in his own mind.[417] Many of the despairs, fears and the joys of relating found in his *Confessions* are not that dissimilar to those the existentialists would write about centuries later. They argued that all of us suffer from the existential fears of meaningless, aloneness and death.[418] Some also argue that to create a God to resolve these all too painful human experiences is to suffer a loss of courage.

---

[417] Blaiklock, E.M. (1983). Personally, I found the *Confessions* a reflection of a rather fearful man in need of ingratiating himself to God by continually telling God how He (God) was so great and important and he himself so small and in need of grace and forgiveness. It is a highly submissive psychology. But the idea that knowledge of God comes from knowledge of self was advanced by Augustine. This view, that we use the idea of God to explore and understand ourselves better, was central to Jung and has been given and a new (and different) focus by Watts, F. and Williams, M. (1988). Both are clinical and academic psychologists of some repute and both hold deeply Christian beliefs. They explore the idea that in prayer we are brought into new relationships with ourselves and that our understanding of God depends on normal psychological process of cognition and emotion.

[418] Yalom, I.D. (1980) has written beautifully on these themes in his book *Existential Psychotherapy* and explores how so many forms of psychological suffering are centred on these themes. It had a deep effect on me when I read it some years ago.

Creating the Gods

There has been long debate over whether we created our Gods from the projection of our psychology into the cosmos or whether s/he/them created us. Whatever the case, there are enough versions of God to realise that God is a creation from our brains. On the other side of this coin, you can only ever dispute different versions of God because as one falls over a new version appears. Our view of God and religion has certainly evolved and changed over history and this evolution of ideas reflects fundamental aspects of our psychology.[419] If our *ideas of God* and religion are human creations, arising from projections of an evolved mind, what creations do we bring to life?

The origins of religion are lost in the history of time. It is believed that Neanderthal peoples – those who preceded modern humans – buried their dead, and pollen seeds found around their remains suggest that flowers might have been involved in some kind of ceremony. But according to Armstrong[2], it was probably around 14,000 years ago that religion in any recognisable sense got going. Thus, the origins are mostly lost on the shores of our prehistory, where the meanings of the complexity of life could not be framed in any way other than the everyday experiences of people.

The Origins of Victimhood

The first gods are basically *gods of nature* involved with the control of the elements and seasons, and human needs such as for fertility – meaning not just ourselves but also of our crops and so on. Christians still have what is called a harvest festival. These were also very human-like (anthropomorphic) gods who could be angry, happy, appeased and so forth. To be sure, the ancient gods had powers that went way beyond the human. And that is not too surprising, because early humans were surrounded by such powers: in the thunder storms, the winds,

---

[419] See Armstrong, K. (1994) Symington, N. (1994) and Wilber, K. (1983) for different views of these changes.

the seasons, and the rebirth cycles of nature. It was probably very clear to early humans that they were in some sense *victims* to forces of immense power they neither understood nor controlled. The ideas that such effects were the result of systems, like biology, metrology or movement of the earth around the sun, were obviously beyond them. So, they invented gods and spirits of the sun, wind, the sea, creation, fertility, death, war and so forth. Basically, the forces of nature become personified.

This personification of impersonal forces into deities, which ones finds throughout the world, is the root source of many religions. Even though today we moderns do not see thunder as Thor's hammer striking his anvil, still we, like our ancestors, often desire to make a personal relationship with someone more powerful than ourselves who might have the power to change things in our favour. By making deities, we have created a potential form of relating which allows us to use our evolved psychology for understanding and relating, and gives us some way of interacting with and exerting control over these forces/gods. Our gods need to have motives and desires (and plans for us), and they can have feelings like love. To relate to a deity who didn't have human-like motives or emotions, or human-like empathy, would seem bizarre; yet our motives and emotions are biological, archetypal creations dependent on a certain neurochemistry. God doesn't take Prozac, as far as we know.

Because this is all archetypal, without caution we can run into trouble here, for this way of thinking can bring problematic constructions to life. For example, *it may bring into play subordinate or victim psychology, and the key purpose of submission and appeasement, for humans and animals, is to calm the potential anger and aggression of the dominant.* Indeed, early relationships were based on the need to appease and find favour with the gods and inhibit their anger. Subordinate appeasement can show up in the sacrifice of animals, other humans or even the self (giving oneself to God), or the giving of approbation (SAHP) to the dominant, proclaiming his/her/their greatness.[420] Indeed, subordinates will often try to appease the potential anger of a dominant by making offerings.

---

[420] It is of course possible to see that God may not desire, nor need, nor be interested in having his greatness proclaimed. Indeed, looked through the lens of different archetypal

Subordination

The idea is that if one gives something to the dominant then one not only acknowledges one's subordinate status, but also there is recognition of one's potential vulnerability to the wrath of the dominant. Let's be honest, many of the early gods were pretty scary – the Aztec, Inca, Roman and Greek gods were rarely compassionate, 'how can I help you' types. They were fickle, narcissistically self-focused and short-tempered. It is very clear that, on the whole, in monotheistic religions, our relationship with God is often seen as a ranked one – and we are not in the dominant position. We cannot approach these Gods as equals. After all, they only exist for us in the first place because they represent beings more powerful than ourselves. There is also a sense that we may be tied to our gods because s/he or they are our creator(s), the source of our origins. Being subordinate to them, we immediately recruit our subordinate, ranked psychology to relate to them. A psychology that arose from sexual selection is now transferred to all those who we see as having more power than we do. We have to appease them, acknowledge their superior power, find out their desires for us, accept them as potential leaders, show ourselves willing to sacrifice things to them, do what we are told, acknowledge their wisdom and so forth. At times, the religious texts tell us that we cannot look at the face of God and should approach with head bowed. The avoidance of eye contact and bowing the head is, of course, a submissive behaviour. As I noted in Chapter 8, we can show reverted escape behaviour; e.g., if we think we have sinned we can try to return, humble in spirit and seek reassurance (renew our feeling of being accepted) by subordinate confession.

---

patterns, we may see that this focus on greatness and 'marvelment' as a delusion thrown up by our rank psychology. Many spiritual people have recognised this and suggest that the first movement to a deeper spirituality is to drop all this submissive behaviour and need for proclaiming greatness stuff. The nature of spiritual relating may come from something else entirely, which is to do with internal experiences that cut through God as leader, creator, judge, father, commander and so forth.

Our subordinate status is also confirmed when we use God to make sense of, and give meaning to, life's pain. A person who loses a child may try to comfort themselves with the idea that God wanted the child in heaven – or that God has "taken them unto Himself". The importance of obedience and acceptance, indeed, the whole education of the masses is not to question or dispute the authorities but accept the texts and words as they are written, and is also symptomatic of our subordinate psychology.[421] We think God knows best or must have a purpose or core plan for our suffering. Some may say this is to do with faith, but where the boundaries of blind obedience and faith lie is often difficult to know. Nietzsche recognised the problem and how Christianity had alienated spiritual man and man of the flesh. He proclaimed God to be dead and though mournful of his passing, recognised that a subordinate relationship with God could not be a free one.

There are, however, fundamentally different forms of submission. Some cases of submitting to (what one believes to be) the will of God may lead to good works and exploration of love and personal sacrifice. One identifies with (what one takes to be) the power, wisdom and goodness of God and tries to emulate Him/Her. God becomes an ideal that one tries to imitate. Although the language may be of serving God, this is a very different form of submission than sacrificing (or conquering) others to appease a potentially angry God. Indeed, the transition from God as a tricky and fickle dominant (male) other who should be appeased and obeyed to God as an ideal of love is probably one of the most important transitions in the maturation of a religion. This transition is not only made historically in the texts of the religion, but can also be made personally.

Justice: Reward and Punishment

The notion of God and a life hereafter can also be used to provide us with a belief in justice where God becomes a judge: e.g., bad people may get away with

---

[421] Rowe, D. (1992) has written in depth on the themes of unquestioning subordination, and beliefs in a just world and universe.

it in this life, but on the other side, they get their punishment (portrayed in the recent movie *Ghost*). Indeed, religions with authoritarian tendencies are keen to peddle the old myths, "good is rewarded and bad/naughty is punished".[17] It is the basis of social control. From the time we are knee-high, our parents indoctrinate us with these ideas. The problem is that if tragic things happen to people, they can have an overwhelming sense that God is punishing them. A patient who had lost her child in a cot death had, "this feeling that God is angry with me". She saw her baby's death as punishment for an earlier abortion. Some religious people perpetuate these beliefs. For example, when HIV infiltrated human populations and began to hit homosexual people, some saw this as a punishment by God for abnormal acts. That is pure cruelty and callousness because it's obviously a disease and virus like smallpox, cholera and typhoid that happens to be transmitted through bodily fluids. Why would anybody want to argue that? The facts of life, disease, decay, predation and death are that it is often harsh and completely unjust. Justice is a human concept and has to be created by us; it does not exist in nature. There is no justice in the millions starving from drought or caught up in a pandemic that kills millions. It is only bad luck and chance variations (maybe helped by human ecological interference) that sentence these people and their children to painful deaths.

Even in Buddhism, the concept of karma can be used as a threat. While the idea that every moment arises from the conditions created in the previous movement is obviously true, that is a long way from saying that the reason people have struggles in this life is because they earned bad karma in a previous life. There is only one reason to suggest that and that's to threaten people into behaving morally. As noted earlier, some schools of Buddhism even believe in different levels of hell. You see, the human archetypal mind just can't help itself – even when we're trying overall to be compassionate. What are we going to do with the sadistic underworld in us if we don't recognise it as an inner potential? Hell is not a reality; it's a reflection of an archetypal mind that wants to make others suffer if they do bad things – and as we saw in Chapter 9, a cursory look at human history, with its numerous torture inventions, shows just how bad, sadistic, cruel, callous and vicious we can be. We do crazy things and perpetrate terrifying fantasies because we don't have the decency, honesty and courage to study our own minds to realise they're coming out of us – out of the collective unconscious.

Conformity

The rituals and beliefs that are shared give opportunities for shared activities of cooperation, friendship and conformity; we are on the same journey, are in the same group, have the same values, obey the same moral codes, have the same leader. Here religion gives a focus and meaning to interactions. The image of God can also be used to project xenophobic tendencies separating and marking the in-group from the out-group, chosen from unchosen. But the most important aspect of this 'harmonising processes' is that it is top-down, i.e., imposed by a ranked relationship. Even if this is overlaid with attachment, group identification needs, and moral proscriptions to reduce in-group conflicts, still the undercurrents of this ranked relationship are often present. To break ranks and become non-conformist can spell trouble.

Caring

However, as noted above, a submissive position is far from the only one. As Watts and Fraser note,[422] although at times we are concerned with calming God's anger (or justifying it), it is also true that we turn to God to calm *us* down. So, as noted above, God can become an *attachment object,* a father/parent we turn to in times of stress and pain and from whom we seek care, protection and/or comfort.[3] We reach out seeking the experience of love, forgiveness and compassion. Such experiences feel so emotionally powerful because they are archetypal. Or to put this another way, we have linked our internal, evolved, archetypal mind to the construction of the spiritual, and seek in the spiritual solutions and meanings to the archetypal dilemmas of the social lives we live.

---

[422] Watts, F. and Williams, M. (1988)

Our reasons for creating Gods are complex: to satisfy our feelings of being small and insignificant, and to have someone or something to subordinate ourselves to and appease; to create an authority who can be used to threaten and reward and thus be a vehicle for social control and social order; to find an attachment relationship to give us a feeling of love and acceptance; to make us feel special and chosen; to fend off existential fears of meaninglessness, aloneness and death; to give us a sense of the universe as just and in balance – "reward the good, punish the bad"; to give us a focus for our moral behaviour; or to answer scientific problems of why something exists rather than nothing. The list is not endless, but it is long.

And the Gods Themselves?

So, what of the gods themselves? Many philosophers have of course said that we create our gods in our own image, or certainly groups and tribes create the gods they need. While this was to get rather complex later, and some would put God beyond human comprehension (which could become only another form of acceptance of our intense subordinate, ignorant status), in the early days the gods were seen to have created the universe and life through all too human failings. In the older Hindu, Egyptian and Greek-Roman myths, there were many gods. The stories reflect the same kinds of problematic relationship that we as humans have. Issues of betrayal, love, sexual passion, rape, children sired by the wrong sort, vengeance, sibling rivalry, favouritism, being cast out, rage of the father and so forth are all part of the plots. The old myths are rather interesting soap operas that reflect human life. Indeed, some have even been made into dramas. But we learn little from them, only that they are reflections of our internal worlds (although those interested in archetypal psychology, including myself, think this makes them of no small interest).

The point is that we have these stories because we have become a certain type of species. If we were a species who produced hundreds of their own kind (like turtles), then these stories would mean little to us. If we were solitary predators, then these stories would seem silly. If we were nocturnal animals, then it is uncertain whether we would see the spiritual as 'seeking the light' or 'enlightenment'. The question is how come the gods act just like human beings, yet human beings evolved in a specific way over many millions of years? How come so many myths have the notion of creations coming out of bodies? How come the gods so rarely lay eggs? Some say that evolution may account for animals but God created us. If that is so, why use 99% of chimpanzee genes to do it, and use most of the same brain structures? Why leave in a reptilian brain? Why make us so much like any other animals with our dominance hierarchies, fighting for superiority, and the same forms of procreation? Creationists just don't confront the fact of human forms.

How to Relate?

If you want to relate to a god, you have to be able to communicate. How to do it, though? Through dreams? Intuition? Training the mind? Visions? Or directly? There are certainly many psychotic people who believe they hear the voice of God. What is interesting is that even people who have been deaf from birth, if they become psychotic, can hear 'the voice'. What s/he says is usually rather similar for many people suffering psychosis, and not always very profound or pleasant. This tells us interesting things about the brain and how 'voices' respond to modern drugs. Still, we have this problem in communication, and as Armstrong[423] points out, this was no small problem. I mean, how could one submit to a god, win his/her favour, be for him/her what s/he wants you to be, if you don't know what s/he wants of you?

But not to worry because as certain individuals discovered, sometimes without wanting to, they had a psychic phone line to on high. God appeared to choose certain individuals to carry the message. Because of this communication problem, there arose a whole group of people who would become the priests, prophets and others who could decipher the word (desires or orders) of God. They would be our intermediaries. Frankly, many of these folks were probably rather disturbed individuals, and very much caught in the dominant-subordinate psychology, with authoritarian tendencies. As we saw in our chapters on

---

[423] Armstrong, K. (1994)

leadership and followership, some of the forces that are unleashed in these relationships are crazy-making.

Later, Jewish, Christian and Islamic religions would develop a passion for science, philosophy and mysticism. All would have their sects, often opposed by the established hierarchy. In fact, they have all had their fair share of brilliant, compassionate people who have struggled sincerely with the complexity of religious meaning and experience. The problem is that these complex discourses rarely reach down to the so-called 'lay folk', who are left with the more autocratically inclined. They of course push simple ideas that fix the archetype into dominant-submissive relationships to a deity and allow for the more primitive projections to occur.

Authoritarianism

One of the key themes of this book is that in overcoming our tendencies to craziness we will have to learn how to deal with the archetypal in us, be it our survival strategies or sexual competition strategies, tendencies to dominant-subordinate forms of relating, power dynamics, tribalism and so on. These worked well in species that don't have much of the thinking brain, considerably more problematic in a brain like ours. This is also true for religions. When they regress (or fail to progress) out of aggressive, dominant-subordinate structures, they can be extremely destructive.

God as Bully

There are many depictions of God(s) which are very clearly ones of an antisocial and divisive leader as described in Chapter 7. They are fickle, quick to anger, do not accept critical feedback, and use fear and punishment when they can't get their own way or people don't do as they want. As the famous joke goes: A man says to God, "just because you made the universe, what makes you think you're so high and mighty?"

Our relationship with God (at least in Judaism and Christianity) did not get off to a good start. God revealed his style from the start. There was the problem of Adam, the apples affair, and the seeking of 'forbidden' knowledge. Not only did God disappear in disgust, but he was in a rather vindictive frame of mind that day and had it in for Eve and her descendants. As Burford and Shulman[424] note,

> Unto the women he said, I will greatly multiple thy sorrow and conception; in sorrow thou shalt bring forth children; and thy desire shall be to thy husband; and he shall rule over thee. (Genesis, 3:xvi)

So now we know the reason for the pain and risk of childbirth. Nothing to do with the evolved design of the female pelvis. In fact, to tell the evolutionary story, it's a trade-off, because at the time that the human head was evolving to get bigger we took to upright walking which narrowed the female birth canal. The consequence was that humans have the most painful and dangerous births of all primates. In addition of course, the foetus carries both the mother's own and her partner's (alien) genes, which don't always fit so well in the host's body. Still, if you are ignorant of science, why not stir in a little hatred and justification for male dominance over women? Burford and Shulman point out that this vindictive, authoritarian attitude was to pervade much early teaching, so that St Ambrose (AD 340-397) writes,

> Adam was led to sin by Eve and not Eve by Adam. It is just and right that women accept as lord and master him whom she has sinned.[425]

On to Martin Luther and early Protestantism, when he wrote in *Vindication of Married Life*: Woman is a stupid vessel over whom man must always hold power, for the man is higher and better than she; for the regiment and dominion belong to man as the head and master of the house...[426]

---

[424] Burford, E.J. and Shulman, S. (1992)

[425] Burford, E.J. and Shulman, S. (1992), p.17

[426] Burford, E.J. and Shulman, S. (1992), p.25

God (it was believed), and these religious teachers, were not too keen on women, and fearful of sex. It was as if they could not come to terms with the fact that nature is harsh and often brutish, and a creator of such raises serious questions and terrors. They had to believe that God could not have created it thus. Moreover, there must have been a Garden of Eden, or some better place. Today we hope it is in heaven. The only reason we are in the state we are in must be because someone had upset the almighty (toads!). The harsh state of nature was seen as a punishment, a sin, a fall from grace; thus we needed scapegoats. Woman fitted the bill, of course. Interestingly the story tells of a deep archetypal fear that we have as humans, of being cast out of our group or family, because in our evolutionary past that would spell almost certain death.

It is also the case that from an evolutionary perspective these religions were born in times of tribal conflicts and these conflicts inflate the aggressive tribal archetypes with their focus on conquest (of territory), ownership and possession. As mentioned many times before, in competitive and aggressive times, male reproductive strategies revert to the primitive, dispensing with love and compassion in favour of subordinating, owning and controlling. In Chapter 5, we saw how groups operate when they are under threat (e.g., cluster into more rigid hierarchies, seek out strong leaders and maximise differences between them and outsiders, etc.). Nowadays, we believe that the desire to dominate women is to do with reproductive strategies in certain social contexts, e.g., arenas of high male competition. We have gone from seeking an explanation of female subordination in terms of the vast, infiniteness of God, to the tiny microcosmic world of genes. When God speaks of such things, we are more likely to hear the language of DNA.

Because many of the ideas of the old gods arose in times of intense persecutions, tribal wars and territorial conflicts, these experiences tune up and sensitise the internal archetypes. Being caught in conflict, in which one's friends and family suffer, tends to activate rage and needs for vengeance; social conditions call forth ways of relating. When the God of the Jews, Yahweh, starts communicating, what does he say? Sadly, he says nothing of our crazy-making evolved strategies that drive our motives, gives no warning about our genes, tells us little about bacteria, viruses and other things that made their way into the grand design, and says not a lot about how to care for our children to stop them becoming delinquent. He speaks in the all too familiar masculine tones of war, conquest, victories, glory, fear of God and subordinate obedience.

Let me give some examples of how problematic this is. Remember poor Abraham? He had to take his long-desired-for son Isaac up a mountain, and then knife in hand, sacrifice him to God. Apparently, God had asked him to do it, to prove himself, and like a fearful, dutiful subordinate, instead of telling God where to go, he reluctantly agreed. Thankfully, at the last moment the voice said "it's okay – just testing". But the problem is, these stories are not written to tell of the social contexts of relating, nor the craziness that can infect religious experience, nor to warn us of the unreliability of the Bible as evidence of God. More worryingly, those who teach such stories do not recognise the craziness in them. When I heard this story in school, I was supposed to *marvel* at Abraham's faith. Whatever modern theologians may say about possible deeper meanings of these tales, I was taught this in such a way that I worried that this might one day be expected of me. I also remember thinking what might happen if God had asked my father to do that.

These tales are of serious craziness. When years later I heard the case of the tragically psychotic, depressed woman who had drowned her two four-year-old boys in the bath because God had told her, was I still supposed to marvel at her faith? And what should we say about the prostitute killer Peter Sutcliffe, who thought he was doing God's work? Or what about those who stone their victims for breaking God's laws? Or the Inquisition? Or the David Koreshes of this world? Or what about Baruch Goldstein's shooting of Muslims at worship in Hebron in 1994? Where are the boundaries between madness, archetypal projection and something more genuinely mystical? Is there a boundary? Tricky, isn't it?

If you are going to decipher messages for people, then how can you stop them from thinking that your visions, your ideas, are not just so much crazy speak? Well, you've probably guessed it; there is a way. Most important is to get hold of a person's fear: fear of death, fear of exclusion, fear of the loss of love, fear of punishment, fear of becoming an outsider, and later fear of hell. Mix these with stories of being special or chosen, and if possible also ingredients of access to secret knowledge and the high realms of spirit – yup, that should do it. Also, it helps if you are a good orator; then like Hitler you can impassion and mobilise millions. Humans like to think they are chosen and more special than their neighbours, especially if they are downtrodden, lonely or feel persecuted. And don't forget the territorial claims and appeals to ancient wisdom; now, that really is an ancient and powerful archetype. We're in business.

The fact of the matter is the source of many of our religions have grown out of territorial tribalism and subordinate psychology, encased with psychologies of fear, envy, rivalry, shame, need for glory and superiority. Thus, the God that first comes to us in the Bible is a paranoid tyrant who thinks nothing much for his own people who offend him, and is quite keen on the butchery of men, women and children in the other gang. Drowning is good too. He is not able to transcend the other gods but has to have humans slug it out on his behalf. Moreover, like any dominant he wants to be top dog, the sole leader, and thus forces through a belief in his sole ownership of power. Like some other primates, he does not want competitors around, and he wants to have a say in the sexual activates of his subordinates.[427] He seems to be an insecure dominant (see Chapter 7). These ideas of God are still very much with us today. As soon as one sees the projection of subordinate psychology with its need for submission, obeying orders and so forth, and fear (often terror) of a punitive, male authority (punishment), then one immediately sees what is at work here – and it is not a supernatural God but a primitive archetypal psychology, born in an aggressive territorial clash of tribes. Of course, there have been very many spiritual thinkers who have seen through all this nonsense, of God as bully, and seen it for what it was, an archetypal projection. By dissolving these projections, not being caught

---

[427] You can of course make a claim that pulling people together under one leader and controlling their sexual competitive behaviour is adaptive to the group. Indeed, many of the behaviours that are viewed as sins are those of adultery, covetousness, stealing, murder, etc., which have all been seen as distributive to group living. Unfortunately, women do not do so well from these efforts to control male competition.

in them, it opens our potential for much deeper insights into the nature of consciousness and more besides.

Crimes against Humanity?

When we look at the religious wars, from the Crusades to the raping of the Americas, there is no doubt at all that religions have inspired terrible ethnic cleansing and crimes against humanity. They continue to do so in the perpetration of threats or promises in the afterlife. We have noted how religions can use the inculcation of terror (hell) as a manipulative tactic. Sentencing people to live in this fear must be a crime. The way a religion has been able to manipulate beliefs and fears about sexuality so that billions of men and women are fearful of contraception will be seen, at some point in the future, as a crime against humanity. It has sentenced many billions of people to being born into poor or slum communities contributing to the population crisis. Billions of loving couples have been robbed of a proper sex life, or at least the one they would have had had they been free to choose what they wanted to do. To have control over somebody's behaviour in the bedroom out of fear of punishment is the ultimate form of bullying.

Tyrannical Entrapments

There is another domain that is important to our craziness, especially when an insider-outsider (in-group/out-group) and rank psychology becomes the lens to construct God. This is the domain of entrapment, and our freedom to move away from God and religious groups. In the chapter on shame, I explored various aspects on the nature and illusions of freedom. If you get involved with spiritual movements, you can tell if they are genuinely spiritual or have an autocratic antisocial bias by the freedom you have to come and go. The moment there are sanctions and threats for going, you know what you're up against, so get the hell out of there as quickly as you can. There's a few of them about. Here's another twist to it.

To begin with insider-outsider psychology, we have noted that in terms of the origins of civilisation, it seems that early on humans were free to come and go between different groups. The social structure was relaxed and freedom of movement valued. However, with the advent of agriculture, increasingly large settlements, and the need for an elite to protect its resources and positions within the group, humans began to experience more and more pressure on them to stay in certain groups and not defect out. This may have increased the pressure to think in terms of 'insiders and outsiders' at various levels in the group, and conform to group values/beliefs. We were, to use Mann's term, "caged" or trapped.[428] Once one has a highly institutionalised mind-set of insiders and outsiders, then one can be in trouble and paranoia increases. Just as in all armies, defection and being a traitor is seen as the most serious crime, so also in religious groups and cults, defection can be given the most severe punishment. Moreover, *the fear of deception and defection by subordinates grows in these types of group*. Indeed, it is often in how the group (and its leaders) deal with defectors and those who do not wish to toe the party line that one may see the under-hand of the punitive authority (see Chapter 7).

Hell is the ultimate punishment for defection, disobedience or failing to love (subordinate oneself to) God. Harming others is also a ticket to hell, but only to your own group because you're allowed to go in war on opposing tribes and indeed killing them may actually get you in quicker. In other words, we are following the usual evolved archetypal patterns. The fear of hell is the ultimate in the inculcation of terror paranoid thinking. Those who study paranoia rarely acknowledge that these persecution fantasises (of hell) are quite common in some religious texts, yet are not seen as pathology. We study people who become paranoid but not those who go out of their way to induce it. With the development of the early churches needing to ensure subordination to the holy moral order and their authority structure, religious deception, defections, insubordination and insults to God were given new meanings expressed in new words such as blasphemy and heretic – and those accused of such things could

---

[428] Mann, M. (1986). See also Eisler, R. (1991).

expect horrendous punishment. Probably one of the most controlling behaviours is blasphemy, where you can even be killed for saying the wrong thing about God. Again, presumably the killers assume they are earning God's favour. These are tricky, complex cultural issues where meanings (like speaking against one's leader or God) serve both conscious and unconscious functions.

If one is cheating on parental orders and rules, or those of other human authorities, then at least there is the possibility that one's cheating won't be discovered if one can keep it secret enough. But when it comes to God, the consequences of one's bad behaviour is something one cannot escape from. In that sense, one's relationship with God becomes an entrapped one. Unlike any other form of relationship which exists between self and other, the nature of the God-self relationship is such that one cannot get away from the relationship. We cannot, as it were, leave the room or move house. God is constantly with us. *This is an entrapped internal relationship.* The psychotic mind is an example of the terror of the experience of an entrapped internal relationship *par excellence.* There is no relationship with real people that is like this (assuming that the person is mobile enough and able to move away).

Yet even in psychotic states where voices are not heard, people experience feelings that one is being sought out, with a fear that there is no getting away, the person is being relentlessly hounded or hunted down: the "they are coming to get me" experience. Pursuer and pursed are locked together.[429] The idea that God can hunt down sinners, or that in death they will be drawn like iron fillings to a magnet to God to meet their punishment, is not uncommon in some religious texts.

Again, this is a projection of all too human behaviour. Humans are the only species known to relentlessly pursue, out of territory, those they feel have offended them. Remember what Caesar did to his captors, what happened to

---

[429] Another aspect to this is an anti-predator defence. Here the fears are of being hunted and ripped apart then devoured. These often appear in horror movies, and the devil is often portrayed in devouring reptilian forms.

Trotsky (see Chapter 7), the current threats to the writer Salman Rushdie, and Jane Goodall's description of chimpanzee wars (see Chapter 9)? Humans can and do pursue, torture and kill those who disobey the rules or who have been made outsiders (e.g., the lynch mobs, stoning the sinful, etc.). Paranoia reflects these archetypal themes. God (and his followers) can be created in this image – as pursuer(s) of the sinful. There's no getting away.

How abnormal is this type of experienced relationship; an experience in which one cannot get away from the observations of the other? We don't know, but I suspect it is quite common even when not psychotic or clearly paranoid. Certainly, in my own case as a child, I always had a sense that God and his angels could see me and know my deepest thoughts, wherever or whatever I was doing. To a young lad, this was rather frightening and therefore mildly paranoid. No good masturbating under the bed covers because God could see you! And in any case, it would turn you blind. God as an ever watchful presence from whom we cannot hide, nor deceive, nor defect, goes back to the myth of Adam and Eve. So common is the experience of another as 'ever-watchful', we can suggest that to some extent it is archetypal. Jung (who had a psychotic breakdown himself) had no doubt that these experiences were from the archetypal unconscious. It is indeed tragic that God can be reduced to not much more than a spy in the night.[430]

We can also think of (the fear of) entrapment in the confines (territory) of a dominant as an evolved potential state of mind (the Adam and Eve myth). Such archetypal potentials may have evolved from the fact that subordinates of many species did (and do) have to be ever-watchful that their actions did not elicit the attentions of the dominant. Indeed, when subordinate non-human primates make a move for sexual relationships, their actions show high vigilance (frequent and tense looking about) as if they do anticipate being watched, caught in the act, and chased off. So constantly attuned are subordinates to dominants in many primate groups that this observation gave rise to the attention structure theory of

---

[430] It is understandable that this internalisation of an ever-watchful other would have great appeal to those interested in social control. It helps to protect against cheating. Thus, the religious person might say don't masturbate and God can see you if you do.

dominance hierarchies.[431] Likewise, dominants keep an eye on subordinates to ensure they are not up to mischief. Thus, attention structure and dominant-subordinate relationships are linked. As Chance[432] has suggested, the subordinate constantly keeps his/her attention to the dominant open and ready to act (defensively) should the need arise. Thus, attention to the other as a possible threat is common in evolution. We can only ponder the effects on our primate brain's evolution (and its modules/archetypes) of evolving under this system of mutual suspicion. The fact that the psychotic mind may internally create 'their watchers' should not obscure the fact that attention up and down hierarchy is ubiquitous.[433]

The day of judgement signals a time when all about the self will be known. So, we can act with a sense that some other can know what we do, intend and feel, can judge our actions and decide on our fate. Heaven and hell (we might believe) are not invitations but judgements by a dominant(s). Indeed, in all the visions of heaven I know of in monotheistic religion, heaven is never depicted as a democracy! I have raised the importance of entrapment to emphasise that this sense of the other as constantly present and watchful can be experienced and believed by many who are not psychotic, and used to induced fear in those who

---

[431] Chance, M.R.A. (1988). This edited book looks at how attention structure can influence and be influenced by the rank hierarchy and whether the rank is friendly or aggressive.

[432] Personal communication

[433] Another possibility as to why we create entrapped relationships is more positive in the sense that we benefit from them, actively create them and are frightened of losing them. In children, constant vigilance to the mother and alarm if the mother moves too far away from the infant, is common. Here then, maintaining attention on the (protecting, powerful) other is a security-seeking mechanism. In religion, the idea of a dominant protecting, loving other who watches over us is common. Also common can be the sense that mother is not only always watching but also knows what we do and think and has the answers to our problems (which well she might when we are young). It is not uncommon in therapy for patients to believe that the therapist or group leader has all kinds of powers, talents and abilities to solve problems, which as therapy works invariably leads to a working through of the disappointment that this is not true. So attachment and clinginess can produce a desire to be close, and in a way trap the other from moving away from us.

are non-believers. It is a rich vein from which to explore the nature of psychotic experience.

Hearing the Voice

There has long been debate on whether God is an external deity or force or an internal experience. Sadly, when the cleric Anthony Freeman[434] recently articulated the view that God was internal, he lost his job – a further indication of the continuing need some have for an external deity to obey, not to mention authoritarian attitudes. Nevertheless, some take a more psychological approach and believe that when the voice of God comes from the superego (the part of the mind we have internalised from the orders and values of our parents, see Chapter 8), then God invariably is seen as an outside, external force. Like the superego, the experience of God can be seen as *an external force or entity getting inside our heads.* For example, if parents say, "you are a bad person if you kiss members of the opposite sex", and threaten sanctions should we do so, when we then have an opportunity, we might be overcome with fear or anxiety, as if mother was behind the door and could find out. It is as if we now carry in our own heads her fear-inducing messages – even when she is not physically present. We can't easily get away from the fear our parents have "put into us". We may feel guilty, shamed and so forth by breaking *their* rules.

However, it may also be that we have an archetype for subordinate fear and other social behavioural possibilities. Without warning, we can suddenly experience the world as threatening, as if we are small and meaningless (very low-rank) and

---

[434] Freeman, A. (1993). I thought this was a very well argued little book, although I don't agree with his conclusions about the absence of life after death. I don't see how anyone can make statements on that. We simply don't know and arguments are unlikely to prove it one way or another. Nor do I agree that only by giving up a belief in a life hereafter can be appreciate more 'the moment'. As an evolutionist, I am more inclined to believe that the evolution of consciousness is itself a mystery, and it is possible that this material life is just one of the forms of its mutation and evolution – however wacky that might sound, and it may not just sound wacky, of course!

others are against us. The fact that this experience can at times come out of the blue is not an uncommonly described experience, particularly when stressed. These experiences indicate the operation of archetypes and evolved emotional and motivational systems in the mind which serve to give us certain meanings and experiences, and at times these experiences are disconnected from external triggering events. The message of the subordinate module and archetype might be, "watch out, you are being observed", or "watch out, the dominant is after you". I would, of course, include modules (archetypes) for caring (e.g., "you are being looked after") and altruism ("be nice to others", "form good relationships", etc.).

Some years ago, a friend of mine took LSD and then smoked some cannabis. Normally a happy and trusting person, she was flooded with an intense fear of others. She couldn't get over the feeling that people were watching her with potential hostile intent, even though logically she knew that wasn't true. It is archetypal because we have evolved as primates in hierarchical groups where dominant others could have hostile intent, and therefore the apprehensive vigilance could be easily activated for us. So, if we just have the brain circuits stimulated for some reason, that gives rise to that feeling that "something bad could happen" or "I'm being watched". The drugs my friend had taken had opened a door into an archetypal experience. In the psychotic mind, one does not need drugs; the doors seem to swing wide open by themselves, releasing these types of fears to flood consciousness. One way to think of this is that a *specific module(s) of the mind* has become autonomously activated. For my friend, the archetypal message seemed to be something like, "you are socially unsafe with potentially harmful others". Keep in mind we see them as archetypal because there are relatively common and constitute repetitive themes that humans have had since time immemorial.

Be it via a superego or more archetypal experiences (of caring or subordinating/ridiculing), to hear voices or have visions as some who suffers psychosis and those who "hear the voice of God or spirits" seem to do is like this. Although this 'alien other(s)' is experienced as not part of them, it can read their minds and is ever present. As Paul Chadwick[435] has pointed out, psychotic voices can be construed in various ways: as hostile (like a hostile dominant) or benign (altruistic, caring). A patient might rage against the voices (the other) or take comfort from them. If the voice is seen as a threat in some way, then the defensive responses of anger or anxiety can be aroused. If the voice is seen as beneficial, then a different role relationship is created. Most humans do not hear voices but can have 'a sense' of the external (not-self) God as somehow within them – and have not yet gone the whole way and seen it as part of themselves. I would suggest that these experiences are the result of modules in the mind somehow becoming activated without being recognised as part of the self. Activation of a caring module might sound friendly; activation of the dominant-subordinate, or outsider module might sound more persecuting. It follows therefore that if people are under stress (which effects the ability of the cortex to integrate various sub-cortical functions), feeling defeated by life, etc., it is possible that they will activate the module of subordination and not only feel depressed and a failure but also hear a 'voice that subordinates (shames or ridicules) them'.

Clearly, here I can outline only the crudest approximation. To go further would take us into studies of brain asymmetry (modules coded in different brain areas) and research on psychosis. But I hope enough has been said to indicate one possible approach to hearing voices and especially the voice of God. God's voice might often be a message from one of our modules or archetypes.

---

[435] Personal communication

A Change of Archetype?

Until now we have concentrated on the dominant-subordinate relationship and the use of threat as a means of compliance. However, Symington distinguishes between primitive and mature religion, and notes that

> During the Axial period (800-200 BC) there arose outstanding religious teachers who changed radically the religious outlook of mankind. Those who flourished included Confucius and Lao-tzu in China; the Buddha in Mahavira in India; Zarathustra in Persia; the Hebrew prophets Amos, Hosea, the Isaiahs, Jeremiah, Ezekiel; and Socrates, Plato and Aristotle in Greece.[436]

Many of these seemed to push towards a more self-conscious and aware spirituality, to shift from appeasement (via sacrifice of animals) and to focus on the need for reflection, love and reason. God as dominant whose laws should be obeyed came to be associated with a more caring psychology. According to Symington, the prophet Hosea says of God

> What I want is love not sacrifice; knowledge of God, not holocausts.[437]

and Amos says,

> This is what Yahweh asks of you:
> only this, to act justly
> to love tenderly
> and walk humbly with your God.[438]

What is interesting historically is that, by the time of Jesus, there were Jewish religious thinkers, such as Amos and Philo, a Jewish Platonist, who argued that God is about love and compassion[439]. At the centre of Jewish belief, Philo argued, was love of thy neighbour and the dictum "do unto others as you would

---

[436] Symington, N. (1994), p.14

[437] Symington, N. (1994), p.65

[438] Symington, N. (1994), p.66

[439] Armstrong, K. (1994)

be done by". By the time of Jesus, these ideas were well embedded in social discourse. Yet so simple a message was to produce far from simple effects.

Although David Jenkins has argued that Christianity should not be based on "laser beam miracles", according to Gascoigne,[440] Jesus came to be noted as a religious teacher precisely because he developed a reputation as a miraculous healer, and St Peter at least may well have followed him because of it. On the negative side, although Jesus was to become an historical focus, and offer a new symbolic representation for a shift in archetype relationships via the doctrines of God as father, filled with love and forgiveness, it is not the case that he always avoided supernatural threats of punishment for wrongdoers. For example, Matthew 13 (40-43) talks about a parable based on sowing seeds and removing weeds. Jesus says,

> And as the seeds are pulled up and burned in the fire, so it will be at the end of the age. The Son of Man will send out his angels, and they will weed out of his kingdom everything that causes sin and all who do evil. They will throw them into the fiery furnace where there will be weeping and gnashing of teeth. Then the righteous will shine like the sun in the kingdom of their father. He who has ears, let him hear.

Jesus supposedly (I say supposedly because these words were written many decades after his death) repeats the threat in the Parable of the Net. To our modern ears, we hear such threats and think them terrible. It was a fifteenth-century monk who actually pointed out that while there is one soul burning in hell, his own soul could not be at peace until that one was freed. And we could go further and ask, "while there is hell on Earth (in the wars and diseases of humankind), how could anyone be happy in heaven?" Yet according to Gascoigne[441], by the Middle Ages, one of the *pleasures* of being 'saved' was that one could look down on those in hell.

Nor did Jesus' God give up having favourites (those who did the right things, of course), although Jesus often shocked his disciples by whom he associated with.

---

[440] Gascoigne, B. (1977)

[441] Gascoigne, B. (1977)

The language is still very much framed in words of conquest, glory and victories. On the whole, this view of God (which had appeared before) gave expression to a representation of God who can appreciate suffering and comes to the problem with love. God is rescued from the mentality of the street bully – at least for a time.

The Christ Story

The Christ story, and the focus on a 'saviour' individual, was to become a symbol for a changing archetypal relationship to deities. However, there is something very odd about it, which Jung discussed in *Answer to Job*. Firstly, was it God himself who came down to suffer and took the persona of the Son, or are we to understand Jesus is somehow a separate entity? If the latter, then why would you send your son to suffer to take away so-called sins, which are social constructions decided on by you (God) anyway, and change from religion to religion? I mean, you could just as easily appear yourself and tell people "look, I know I have been a bit harsh on you in the past, you know the floods and all that, but I have changed and I forgive you. Follow me and you can all come home". Why would you send your son as a saviour when it's you yourself that they are being saved from? Why do you want to send your son as a saviour to suffer a terrible death in order to make you change or show your followers you've changed? It doesn't really work.

As an archetypal story though, it's very powerful because, whether or not you believe that Jesus was the son of God or took away our sins to clear the road into heaven, the fact is he was a person who believed it and was prepared to suffer terribly to save us. We can identify with him for what he believed he was doing. That in essence is the heart of compassion. The preparedness to suffer on behalf of another in order that the other may be free of suffering. As an archetype, the Christ story is extraordinarily powerful. In addition, the whole concept of a loving God creating a secure base and attachment was also a very powerful archetype that would be a powerful attractor. Certainly, the Roman gods were not like that. Not surprisingly then, Christianity spread mostly amongst the poor and downtrodden. Some people wonder why the symbol of the brutality of the cross is a symbol for worship. The reason is that it is the courage of suffering on behalf of another that's the actual archetypal symbol. As an archetypal symbol, it is designed to speak to the heart to say "if this man can do this for you, what can you do for others to address their suffering?" Tragically it wasn't long however before the Christ story and its deep archetypal meanings got hijacked by the old male strategies of dominance, power and control. And today, the Christian right are very interested in tribalism, power, money and fighting over sexuality: how to do the least for others not the most. There you go: same old, same old.

Jesus, of course, was not a Christian but very much a Jew, and there is no evidence that he was interested in forming a new religion. For example, crucified people had the notice of their crime pinned above their heads, and in the case of Jesus the notice read, *Iesus Naxarenus Rex Iudaeorum*: "Jesus of Nazareth, King of the Jews".[442] Moreover, the symbol of the cross was, as Gascoigne[443] and Romer[444] point out, played down for centuries because in fact crucifixion was a shameful death, reserved for slaves and common criminals. It was nearly 300 years before the symbol of the cross came to take on the significance it did (before that the Christian symbol was predominantly a fish). Jesus also followed in the tradition of John the Baptist, and both believed in a long-held Jewish idea of a coming Messiah, and that the end of the world was nigh: as common today, perhaps, as then.[445] But why would people want to see the end of the world? The reason is perhaps that they found biological life harsh and cruel, wracked by war and disease, and always harboured a hope there was something better waiting to emerge, be it heaven or whatever.

For the early Christians, life was a struggle. In A.D. 64 Emperor Nero blamed them for the burning of Rome, and they suffered frequent persecutions. The religion probably would have died out, had it not been for Constantine who, in 331 at the battle of Milvian, saw the sign of the cross against the sun and had the experience that this was a sign he was going to be victorious. He was victorious,

---

[442] Gascoigne, B. (1977)

[443] Gascoigne, B. (1977)

[444] Romer, J. (1988)

[445] Hattenstone, S. (1995)

and then believed that this Christian God had been his protector and ensured his victory. Why God would want to do that for this particular person is unclear. From that time on, Constantine forbade the persecution of Christians and invited the writing of Christian texts. Towards the end of his reign, he started to dismantle the Roman pagan system. Little is known about these early days and how some texts were agreed and some suppressed, but some were certainly suppressed.

As to the actual words and beliefs of Jesus, we know little, for he was in the tradition of the oral, preaching methods of teaching rather than written scholarship. It is in fact Paul's writings that are the first written words of Christianity, and he was not without his own emotional difficulties – some believe he introduced some not particularly compassionate doctrines. Later came Mark and his Gospel, which was included with the Gospels of Matthew and Luke, and that of John, who was somewhat different from the other three. It is also the case that the doctrines of Christianity were worked out slowly over many centuries, not by revelation but by argument and political expediency. There was always a friction between the hierarchical and (gnostic) anti-hierarchical approaches to religion, and many doctrines were developed from these debates with other sects.

The anti-hierarchical ideas were never going to be useful to a political movement that was to conquer much of the known world. So successful was the hierarchical mentality in suppressing egalitarian ideals that by 380 the Emperor Theodosius was able to use Christianity, as the official church, to persecute those following alternative beliefs. Of those who did not follow or submit to these beliefs and rules of the trinity, he argued that

> We command that those persons who follow this rule shall embrace the Catholic Church. The rest, however, whom we adjudge demented and insane, shall sustain the infamy of heretical dogmas, their meeting places shall not receive the name of churches, and they shall be smitten first by divine vengeance and secondly by retribution of Our own

initiative, which We shall assume in accordance with divine judgement.[446]

As Gascoigne points out,

> Theodosius takes for granted the close link between his own will and God's and in the same year he even allows himself to be described as 'the visible God'. It was a connection which was implicit from the start of the Christian Empire.[447]

Such a promising beginning, but the old dominant-seeking, male archetypes would not give up. Therefore, despite this archetypal change to love and compassion (which is not original to Christianity), the leader-subordinate-follower psychology would constantly reassert itself, and did so powerfully in the Catholic Church. The many popes would be happy to utilise deception, threats, wars, tortures and other means for political ambition. Even God it seems is powerless in the grip of these male archetypal gene-built mind controllers! It was key to maintain the submissive position, because if you show your submission to the higher authority then you must submit to those who represent them. It appeared in the notions of devotion and humbling oneself in the sight of God. And to help that sense of dominance, powerful and magnificent churches needed to be imposing to give a sense of awe in humbleness to those entering. In church, still, going down on one knees is a sign of respect, although I have never understood how a submissive signal is a sign of respect.

Because it became an intensely hierarchical religion, in the future, the desires of greed and conquest (as in the Crusades) would be turned back on God as the actions of dutiful subordinates carrying out his will. The clear understanding that God was external and had to be followed, sought out and obeyed was never clearly refuted by Jesus. Although more recent Christians and Jews have tried to make God more internal and subjective, Jesus (if we believe the texts) did not give up the external God-in-the-sky idea. Indeed, some even saw him ascending to heaven. At the very least, he is now presented as highly ambiguous about an

---

[446] Gascoigne, B. (1977), p.40
[447] Gascoigne, B. (1977), p.40

external or an internal God, saying different and contradictory things at different times. In this, he was far less successful than the Buddha, who made it absolutely clear that enlightenment was an inner journey only. Christianity, however, continued to furnish the idea that if you "do the right things you will be rewarded". The pursuit of self-knowledge, and acting with compassion, wasn't for internal self-development but more about pleasing the authority and doing the right thing *as expected*. As with so much of spiritual development, everything depends on intention.

From the early days of the established church, following initial persecution, the socio-economic structures of the time had no trouble in incorporating Christianity and its egalitarian messages, turning them into the patriarchal ranked organisation we now know as the Roman Catholic Church and other forms of Christian organisation. The Gnostics, who were far less keen on leader-follower relationships, were more keen on sex, women, and meditative-like practices (the seeking of self-knowledge or gnosis) rather than obedience to doctrines, got lost and submerged. For many centuries, they tried to exist outside of Paul's doctrines and the growing patriarchal system developing in Rome. By the eleventh century, the Cathars, who were probably descended from early Gnostics, had established a community in southern France. It seems they believed that the creation of the material world was not a gift of God but was actually a mistake, and that all material things were created by a devious and evil deity. This led some of their sects into Buddhist-like beliefs and life styles, and to suggest that humans should try to transcend the physical and the needs for power and possessions, and seek to love each other. Such egalitarianism and anti-hierarchical sentiments were a severe threat to the authority of Rome, and they were severely persecuted by the Church, who feared their lack of obedience to Rome's authority. Their destruction and persecution has been seen as not far short of ethnic cleansing.[448]

---

[448] Baigent, M., Leigh, R. and Lincoln, H. (1982). This book gives a very detailed overview of the development and mysteries of the Christian Church and the rise of the Catholic Church. It pursues a set of interesting and at times disturbing ideas about the social and political constructions of Christianity.

Throughout the early history of Christian thought, the subordinate psychology lived on. It was very active in St Augustine and many others who saw only God as able to give grace and that everything good came down from him.[449] The attitudes to women, as we have seen, were often highly shaming and blaming. Jesus managed to change the face of God but not our subordinate leader-follower behaviour towards him (nor the fact that it was a 'him' rather than a 'her'). As science revealed more and more errors and contradictions in the Bible, it became clear that maybe the word of God was imperfect. Moreover, it opened the door to doubt and from doubt the reduction of fear and compliance

Over and over new leaders would arise pointing the way. The power that such leaders can exercise is seen today in events like the Jonestown tragedy where hundreds committed suicide on the instructions of a charismatic leader. The subgroup of Branch Davidians, led by David Koresh, which ended in the deaths of 80 people (including Koresh) following a siege by the FBI in 1993, is another recent example. All those who call for a struggle of arms and speak in the language of a need for victories and glory are similar. A religion that needs intermediaries and allows for a subordinate leader-follower psychology is always vulnerable to such charismatics. People are not encouraged toward the inward process but directed to listen to the words of the leader and to do as they are told. Marx would see in these religious relationships nothing other than power issues: religion as the opium of the masses. Freud saw nothing other than the repetitions of father-child psychology in all its human dramas. Subordinate psychology is still very active in fundamentalism, as the American preachers get the masses to part with their money. As a recent documentary noted, many of the mass excitements and demonstrations of casting out of devils use fairly simple and at times crude hypnotic techniques.

---

[449] Taylor, C. (1989)

The Antichrist

Many prophets and future seers have talked about the coming of an Antichrist. Usually, this is seen as a person (typical of our tendency to turn psychological forces into deities). Some see Hitler as the Antichrist. But as we have seen in the chapter on leadership, he reflected a set of social values and aspirations, a striving for dominance and conquest. It is, therefore, more interesting to think of the Antichrist not as a single person, but as a social psychological process, or as Jung would say, a disturbance in the collective unconscious of all of us. If this is true, then the coming of the Antichrist reflects not the coming of a person, but the coming of a certain set of values that will set one against another and create a multitude of rivals. To my mind, the concept of the Antichrist reflects our fears of social disintegration and conflicts; if we take Christ as a symbol of love, altruism and belonging then the Antichrist is a symbol that reflects the opposite values of invigorated competition, strife, segregation, xenophobia and division. It reflects values *in us* that are anti-altruistic. If "God is in us"[27], then so is the Antichrist.

This leads to the idea that the Antichrist rules when there is vigorous competition, when we turn from the sick and the poor, do not protect our ecologies, lose sight of the sacred, and when we support leaders who privilege us at the expense of others. I do not fear the coming of an Antichrist 'as a person', for there are many potential people who could fulfil this role now, if the chance became available to them. Rather, I fear the increasing evidence that we are all becoming more selfish, protecting our own self-interests and creating a more and more polarised, spiritually impoverished materialistic world (see next chapter). The Antichrist is in all of us. Leaders may arise who simply ride on this wave of our values and conduct them, peddling and inflaming xenophobic and combative values. They will speak in the language of what we should fear, how we should defend ourselves – and if we listen, we march blindly onwards.

Conflicts in the Self

From an evolutionary point of view, the potentials of the self (with its various biosocial goals, modules and strategies) can give rise to considerable inconsistencies. For example, we may pray to a God of love as we go into war and drop bombs on people. We may regard this as unfortunate but not see much basic conflict in it. We may come to believe that God wants us to fight "the evil", yet use cruel and callous ways to do it. Being bombed, and to die painfully and in terror in a crushed building, or in the fires of Dresden with your children, is hardly the result of what one would call Christian behaviour. Psychologists have noted that when we behave in ways that are in conflict with our attitudes, we change our attitudes and beliefs: this is called cognitive dissonance. On the whole we don't like too much internal conflict, and so bend our attitudes and beliefs to fit with our behaviour. To put this another way: we can develop various 'justifications' for the way we are feeling and behaving. In our last chapter, we saw that we can behave cruelly when we deny and block off our feelings of empathy for others and operate with fairly crude evolved strategies (e.g., some groups are superior to others; it is okay for men to have sex before marriage but not women, etc.). We saw how problematic some of our justifications can be.

At times, however, we may feel our conflicts all too painfully. And these conflicts arise from what we feel inclined to do and what we think the *authorities* want or demand that we do. Jesus (the story goes) was in conflict of whether to allow himself to be crucified. Clearly, he had no wish to be so, but in the end he accepted what (he thought) his father (God) wanted of him. He submitted to God's will. The ambiguities of compassion here are tricky. If the very founder of a religion is prepared to lay down his life to fit with the design and plans of a dominant authority, then it is not too surprising if his followers would not also be prepared to do the same. To do what is expected of us can take considerable courage. The problem is what we are actually asked to do is very unclear

One way to reduce conflicts is to reduce complexity, to think in black and white terms: i.e., right-wrong, good-bad. A second way is simply to look to the authority for 'what is good, what is bad, what is right, and what is wrong'. A religion cannot easily control people and restrain intragroup competition if at every point it says "look, things are complex, everything is a grey area". I suggested in Chapter 8 that people often prefer more simple messages, and that authorities tend to lose their power if they have no clear answers and messages to give.

Understandably, the Bible often lays out God's commandments with appeals to his higher wisdom. More often than not, the Bible simply divides people into good and bad, wicked and saved, chosen and unchosen – more fitting to Hollywood than real life. Indeed, there is increasing concern that Hollywood, which has always peddled simple solutions to complex problems (e.g., violence is necessary to deal with evil, good guys against bad guys, the mentality of the *Power Rangers* – how to make more money) is beginning to wake up to the enormous financial potential from simplistic Christian morality and are forming worrying unions with the right wing. We have two problems here. First, there is the tendency to seek clarity and get out of the grey areas, to reduce doubt by reducing complexity. Second, there is the tendency to turn and seek the 'wisdom' or proscriptions of the dominant authorities.

But from these two options, a third arises. Supposing the dominant authorities are actually following basic reproductive strategies, so that their solutions and proscriptions actually start to look remarkably like basic primate life scripts. What might these look like? How about if they were honest and said that our evolved nature tells us to 'form dominance hierarchies; submit to those above you; control female sexuality; control subordinate sexual behaviour; wage war on those who do not submit to authority or who obey other authorities; punish those who do not obey the rules; be altruistic to insiders; don't worry about complex morality; and follow the simple doctrine of dos and don'ts as you have been told them". But then, honest insights or what drives some of our harmful behaviours are not their strong points.

Sexual and Gender Confusions

One of our common and destructive conflicts can be around issues of male-female. Fisher[450] notes how some of the early Christians inherited ideas from the Greeks which were anti-sex, anti-female and anti-body, and these were linked with authoritarian attitudes. These attitudes have caused more than a little craziness. In Matthew 19, Jesus is said to give a pretty intolerant view on divorce. The possibility of spousal abuse and so forth aren't mentioned, nor the complexity of marital relationships. It is all rather simple recipe stuff. Only recently has the marriage service dropped the idea that women should obey their husbands. The Gnostics had very different views on each of these. They were less hierarchical, were suspicious about some of Jesus' claims to be divine (rather just another prophet), saw sex as important and were egalitarian in their relationships with women. But Paul, who was to shape the future of the Church and introduce harsh and divisive gendered attitudes into Christianity, was basically of an autocratic type of mind. He was a self-selected persecutor of Christians before his conversion and keen on writing his own words down for prosperity afterwards. He was frankly full of his own self-importance. Indeed, he was the first 'Christian' to do so.[451] Some feel he was a disaster for Christianity.

Most of the patriarchal, monotheistic religions have been very much engaged in *amplifying gender differences rather than reducing them*. This causes enormous problems to our internal psychology and social relationships. Once male domination spread through the religion, then females came to occupy highly

---

[450] Fisher, S. (1989)

[451] Paul probably also had various sexual confusions of his own. His background was in the strict Jewish hierarchy, and he had shown strong authoritarian tendencies before his 'conversion', being known as a persecutor of Christian sects, and he had a contemptuous attitude to the egalitarianism of the Gnostics. He clearly needed to work for a dominant male leader. Many see the seeds of Christian patriarchy and gender oppression as given new life through him (shaming women and sexual confusions reach back to Genesis, of course). Having Roman citizenship gave him huge advantages in his work and abilities to travel. To an old cynic like me, one would have to consider the possibility that, perhaps unconsciously, Paul suddenly recognised he could remain a small fish in a big sea (the Jewish faith) or play a big part in a new developing one. Certainly, if he had not converted to Christianity, his name would never have appeared in history.

subordinate positions and further fuel was added to beliefs that women should obey their menfolk. When David Jerkins, the archbishop of Durham, argued that the Virgin Birth should not be taken literally, he was met with a hail of abuse. When the Church of England tried to ordain women, it was threatened with a major split. The archetype to maintain a male hierarchy was strong indeed – although at least some clergy recognised that God may well transcend male and female, and the spiritual quest may require us to do likewise. At the time when the Church of England were debating these issues, Walter Schwartz, the religious correspondent of *The Guardian*, spoke to the Chief Rabbi in Britain on these matters. The answer was clear enough. Women could never become rabbis, because as a religion of revelation, God has expressly forbidden it. So, we are still stuck in the old ways, following patterns of relating laid out long ago.

The religious attitudes to sexual behavioural, the body and women has been a source of much suffering. In some parts of the world, adultery is still a stoning offense – usually of women. At its height, witch-burning is believed to have claimed the lives of 3 million women throughout Europe. Our attitudes and intolerance to homosexual relationships are still fuelled by those of a religious frame of mind. The idea that homosexuality is unnatural is actually quite false. For example, our nearest relatives, the bonobos, are very bisexual. Indeed, lesbian relationships play a key role in female bonding.[452] In fact, the relationship of sexuality to the evolution of human social behaviour is complex, but does not suggest either homo- or bi-sexuality as uncommon, and truth be told, freed from fear it would not be today. The fear of homosexuality is to do with our own fears, especially masculine fears. The 'sin' surrounding sexuality has often been intense, even of masturbation, which we now know to be a perfectly normal activity. Indeed, the guilt and shame that has been incorporated into sexuality has been a source of torment for many. The suppression of sexual knowledge and activity has been intense and often motivated by religious beliefs.[453] The invention of celibacy for the priesthood by the Church was to

---

[452] de Waal, F. (1995)

[453] Porter, R. and Hall, L. (1995) argue that this is a simplistic view and the repression of sexuality and knowledge is far more complex than that simply derived from religious

make the priesthood seem somehow different from the rest of us and thus give them some authority/status/prestige over us.[32] This does not mean, of course, that celibacy is without deep personal meaning, only that when it is enforced it can produce problems – including various deceptions and abuses. In any case, no one should be given jurisdiction over how we experience our sexuality; that is simply bullying and stealing a possible life from us.

Although the problems of population control cannot be solved by contraception alone, and we should indeed increase calls for the education and raising the status and choices of women, and the sharing of resources of the rich with the poor, it seems to me crazy and grossly immoral for some clerics to be so anti-contraception and rely on the fear of disobedience to get their way. But it is more than this. There can also be, in male-dominated groups, a positive denigration of female sexuality, a certain contemptuousness, as well as attempts to exclude females from positions of influence. For example, menstruation can be seen as unclean and contaminating of the male and there is something shaming in female sexuality.[454] Because of the fear of the sexual (and all its strange fantasies), possible female exploitation of their sexuality to get them power, plus male fears of female defections to other males, men have used religion to control female sexuality. Moreover, females can be blamed for tempting males, exciting their passions and encouraging certain sexual practices (a theme going back to Genesis). This lets men off the hook. Males are rendered powerless to female desires and this enables them to avoid punishment, a theme in modern law that many females have complained of. Moreover, if women are abused this leads to

---

values. Indeed, religious values themselves are derived from other discourses to do with power and privilege. I agree, but nevertheless, perhaps because I listen to patients with fears of sexuality, I still think that repression of sexuality and efforts to fit with a religiously ordained form of sexuality remain valid and important experiences.

[454] Gregor, T. (1990) and Tejirian, E. (1990). The first part of the book is about the psychoanalytic treatment of an obsessional condition that turned out to be a fear of homosexuality. However, the second part is dedicated to an exploration of the expression of sexuality in western religions and cross-cultural contexts - a fascinating read brimming with ideas and insights. For feminist explorations see Burford, E.J. and Shulman, S. (1992), Ussher, J. (1991).

a sense that women somehow 'deserved it' or had 'invited it', i.e., victim blaming. There have then been abuses of power perpetrated by old, often unmarried men (in the case of Christian sects) giving rulings on things like contraception and homosexuality. They, no more than anyone else, know what kind of sex God is concerned with.

.

Caring and Internalisation

But let's get back to the issue of a caring God. The problem is that the God of altruisms can be costly. Although one might expect that being rich, seeing the poverty in the world and being a Christian might cause conflicts, this rarely seems to be so. Our altruisms are limited by self-interest. In fact, as we get richer we tend to become less altruistic outside kin groups, so that inequalities are growing between the haves and have-nots and have-lots. Nevertheless, it would be incorrect to say that the ideals of creating a sense of universal sibling (brother and sister) love are not important ideals. Nor that reflection on the experiences of love and compassion are not among the most healing of experiences. Indeed, nowadays a religion without some appeals to altruism and kindness would be fairly barbaric, and I suspect in the end would be overthrown because, on the whole, we tend to feel much better in groups of mutually supporting loving others. Some of most important changes to have taken place in the spiritual quest have been those that speak to the internal dimension of the spiritual and the recognition that a competitive, rank-focused striving for superiority, dominance and prestige is not helpful on the journey of enlightenment. Be it via prayer[19] or meditation, we are gradually coming around to the focus on love and moving away from threats of punishment and exclusion. Certainly, Christianity is much less hell- and threat-focused than it was 500 years ago. When religion helps us to focus on caring and healing and removes the 'down-rank threats' then it could be one agent that helps to smooth interpersonal relationships, and helps us to be more relaxed in ourselves. A caring God softens our rank psychology. As Eisler[8] points out, there are, both inside us and outside us, tensions between the dominating Gods and the Gods of love and partnership.

Some Recent Changes

At the end of an exploration into the history of Christianity, Gascoigne[455] notes that the modern scientific insights have led to many different responses. I would like to briefly explore some of these.

One has been to gradually disengage from the 'written word' and to push further into the nature of love and internal development. It has been a movement away from primitive dominant-subordinate relationships. Gascoigne quotes from the influential existential theologian Paul Tillich:

> That depth is what the word *God* means. And if that word has not much meaning for you, translate it, and speak of the depths of your life, of the source of your being, of your ultimate concern, of what you take seriously without any reservation. Perhaps, in order to do so, you must forget everything traditional that you have learned about God, perhaps even the word itself.[456]

This dropping of obedience to words of the authority, written thousands of words ago, is probably one of the most important transitions to a new spiritual search that does not start from concern with a dominant authority. It becomes a very internal search for meaning.

A second change has been that Christianity has been significantly influenced by modern psychological studies of the distressed mind and how to heal it. Indeed, pastoral counselling has now incorporated many ideas from psychological counselling. Before the 1920s, the way religious counselling was conducted was mostly with trying to interpret the doctrines and texts. However, as Jones[457] points, out this can also be a two-way process, and psychologists and counsellors

---

[455] Gascoigne, B. (1975)

[456] Gascoigne, B. (1975), p.268

[457] Jones, S.L. (1994) offers a fascinating discussion of the potential overlaps between religious 'knowing' and scientific 'knowing'.

could be more articulate about their spiritual beliefs. Indeed, spiritual questions remain important for the majority of people and often cannot be ignored in people's search for meaning.

A third approach has been the efforts to link the notions of God with science and modern physics, such as the whole nature of consciousness. This can be grasped via meditation and increasing of self-awareness. Amit Goswami, who is Professor of Physics at the University of Oregon, says

> The fundamental unverifiable (in the scientific sense) idealistic metaphysic is a one liner: Consciousness is the ground of all being and our self-consciousness is That consciousness.[458]

This is a theme with strong echoes in various Eastern religions and also transpersonal psychology. In this view, the evolved mind creates patterns in the field(s) of consciousness. Consciousness is without form itself, the material world and the evolved mind gives it forms and shapes. The brain then is a pattern generator of some kind. In the first instance, 'form' comes from physical laws and then from biological laws in the creation of organic life. By developing our consciousness of consciousness (through meditation, for example) we become more able to see these patterns, and in the psychology (desires, hopes and goals) of our egos. What I am is a pattern of (in)consciousness. I like these ideas (although my physics is dreadful). They suggest why brain activity is the basis for specific mental states, feelings and cognitions, etc. Clearly there is no ultimate justice principle, or supreme judge here. While some scientists see these ideas as quite whacky, others are increasingly attracted to these Buddhist-like beliefs, in part because they cannot accept God as a dominant authority and yet want some kind of spiritual quest.[459]

These are just three examples where issues of our possible spiritual nature are developing in fascinating (to me) directions. But another response has been to move in the opposite direction. Some religious teachers, especially fundamentalists, hold tightly to the literal truth of the holy books and written

---

[458] Goswami, A. (1993), p.270
[459] McGhee, M. (1995)

word, and thus maintain fairly hierarchical structures which persuades through claims of power and authority. And as in modern day raves, they recognise that various social forms of coming together, to sing and dance, can give people strong feelings of pleasure and relatedness. Indeed, I have often wondered if the feelings ignited by the modern rave are similar to those of these dancing and singing religions. More importantly, perhaps, people can be easily open to suggestion once in these states of mind. They tend to excite passions rather than calm them. And in high states of arousal, people can and do experience all manner of things. Moreover, this approach to God offers very contradictory advice, and is easily recruited by the political right who, in fact, have rather less interest in caring and sharing and rather more interest in protecting their own privileges. We will focus on some alternatives to these style in a later chapter, when we look in more detail at the role of compassion.

Followers want Action

Throughout history there have been many attempts to write and re-write our relationships with God. In so doing, we are also creating our own sense of self. So powerful is the God archetype that one cannot enter into it or out of it without saying something fundamental about our sense of self. Taylor[460] has chartered these issues brilliantly. But it is not just the sense of self that we are concerned with here, although undoubtedly our changing sense of self, foraged in new economic climates, the movements of science, and insight of our origins from an evolutionary understanding, has done much to place our relationship with God under serious strain. It is the fact that any external God who is also in the world is either useful or not, is either compassionate or not, either can help or can't/won't help. Compassion cannot be conditional; otherwise, it is simply a bargain for obedience in another disguise.

Schopenhauer (1789-1860) had no doubt in his arguments with Hegel that God could not exist because life was so terrifyingly brutish. All we could do, he

---

[460] Taylor, C. (1992)

suggested, is create our own meanings. Only then could we be free. Later the existential writers would claim similar. But the tragedies of our war-torn history have made one thing clear. God does not intervene on a personal level, or if he does, in individual cases, it is so pathetically small as to be worthless and an example of how by not acting in other domains (like the Holocaust), he remains barbaric. The followers are gradually leaving the stage to an empty spotlight, sadder but maybe wiser. The God of the jealousies and insecurities of the old prophets and the loving God of Jesus proved impotent when it mattered. The external God never did give us anything of real worth, no knowledge, no science, no way to cure the sick, no power to change our genes and our crazy psychology that goes back to the reptiles. Simple promises and prohibitions are no longer enough – unless you are poor, frightened, and uneducated, making it easy for people to exploit your fears.

Conclusion

As self-conscious beings who have developed an awareness of the realities of our short-lived biological existence, we will continue to ask "is this all that there is"? Is my consciousness, my sense of myself, no more than a biochemical trick in the service of genetic information? The spiritual quest is one of the most important and meaningful questions in people's lives. Confronted with the strangeness of the physical world and universe we live in, we can never close the door on these questions. But we must be careful with the archetypes that texture consciousness because they may cloud spiritual wisdom. As the Buddha suggests, unless we de-clutter the mind from all this archetypal content we may never see mind clearly. We certainly must not confuse religion with spirituality. And in any, case modern science is suggesting to us that this whole experience of self is an illusion. People can have certain types of brain damage after which even parts of their body don't seem to belong to them. Take a head injury, and your whole personality will change. Get dementia and as the patterns of the neurochemistry unravel, so the essence of the self disappears.

More and more people are turning to science to answer these questions. For example, the study of out-of-the-body, near death experiences and parapsychology may yet again show how ignorant we have all been.[461] While some see this as a door to what happens when we are liberated from our biological archetypal minds, others suggest that near-death experiences may be the result of various changes in the brain at the point of death and these experiences can be simulated in the laboratory by brain stimulation. At least if science explores them, we can get away from dogma, and we may even discover things.

Religion and spirituality will remain the focus for many to seek new answers for the puzzles and suffering of life, and lift their heads above the ordinary and humdrum, to look to higher ideals and meaningful relationships into which they can project their hopes. This makes religion a powerful potential force for change – if we can help it evolve and make plain that it needs to drop the competitive psychology that so infects it. As many authors make clear, religion and the spiritual quest can be enormously enriching, and helpful in the maturation of the self and mental health.[462] Moreover, there are certain types of knowledge that may only be gained by reflection and developing awareness. You can read all you like about sex but have no real idea of it until you try it, and even then your experience of it may be quite different first time round to

---

[461] At the time of writing, Dr Peter Fenwick at the Institute of Psychiatry in London is currently engaged in a research project with a few cardiology departments. Objects have been placed at strategic places that can only be seen from above. If people who have near death experiences can later identify these objects then maybe there will be evidence that regardless of what the brain is doing, consciousness has in some sense become detached. Although one hesitates to suggest it, the fact that the brain may show certain changes near death or that these can be invoked in laboratories points to the complexity of mind-body-spirit interactions but not necessarily disproves completely the idea of some kind of consciousness existing outside of the body. As of now it is very useful to see these important facets of our lives being carefully researched. The answers may yet surprise us all and point to something completely different from anything one has yet thought of. Who knows? Personally, I do have a suspicion about life after death, and see consciousness as the real mystery not easily explained away by complex neurophysiology and cognitive models. Maybe the new attempts to marry the insights from modern physics with religion might give us a new focus. This may just be my existential fear, of course. But the role of genes on personality and the way beliefs and types of internal experiences are often created by social contexts makes me extremely dubious of simple explanations peddled in popular religions.
[462] Schumarker, J.F. (1992)

having practised 20 years later. This is why so many are now turning to opportunities to learn through direct experience, such as with mindfulness, and to be questioning of mimicry of texts and authorities. Education invites us to question, not just obey.

Even Freud recognised that repression of the quest for spiritual understanding could be as dangerous as a repressed sexuality. Jung even more so. However, as Armstrong[463] says, we should be more open with people about religious history, social contexts and the psychology that some leader-follower relationships excite and inflate, for these can be emotionally powerful yet also deeply irrational and destructive. All we can suggest here is that, like Aristotle said, we do not really know. Further, we do not always understand what we do not understand. The world we live in now would be unimaginable to a person 500 years ago; the idea that you could have a mobile device that allowed you to talk to people around the world would be bizarre, even magical. Our technologies will constantly improve, but we may not use them wisely without really engaging with how we are biologically made. Be it through mindfulness or other means, we need to really understand why we feel what we feel and why we do what we do. This is the road of responsibility, and responsibility not worship needs to be the first stepping stone for spirituality. One of the core ingredients that will guide this is compassion. Maybe we should reclaim our visions of God as part of ourselves and then see where we go from there.

---

[463] Armstrong, K. (1994)

11: CHALLENGING THE MYTHS OF COMPETITIVE MODERN LIFE

The larger point is not in doubt: the favoured, it is more than evident, do not contemplate and respond to their own longer-run well-being. Rather, they respond, and powerfully, to immediate comfort and contentment. This is the controlling mood. And this is so not only in the capitalist world, as it is still called; a deeper and more human instinct is here involved.[464]

This chapter explores how the problems of accumulations of wealth increase conflicts of interest. The suggestion is that the reason unrestrained competition is often destructive is because of our archetypal psychology, that people respond to market forces with feelings; they can be impassioned by the opportunities to obtain wealth and status, and they feel anger and/or despair when thwarted. In addition, as we have more, we want more and we want to hold onto more, particularly in the sea of strangers which is totally different from our 'know everybody' hunter-gatherer small groups. Gaining resources, and here we are talking about mega resources, may stimulate dopamine-linked drives and the risk of addiction-like behaviours. This leads to the view that political theory and practice should address the *psychological* tensions of capitalist economics. There has long been the view, even to some extent in the writings of Adam Smith, that that these tensions can be softened when capitalist systems make efforts at altruism and fairness, and integrate morality into the profession of the entrepreneur. Unfortunately, different politicians wax and wane on this matter. My first degree was in economics back in 1973, so I have always been interested in the economic contributions to mental distress and wellbeing.

---

[464] Galbraith, J.K. (1993), pp.6-7

Competition and Caring

Economic arenas can be separated loosely into varying dimensions of competitive and caring/egalitarian.[465] Although there are many reasons for the inflation (in an archetypal sense) of contest-competition in capitalist societies, the consequence is that our psychology becomes focused on *winners-losers, superior-inferior, have nots/have a lots, social comparison, shame and humiliation avoidance, envy and possessiveness of physical resources and status signals.* This psychology not only shows itself in the way business and places of work are organised but also in the personal psychologies of the stressed, depressed and anxious. They speak of their (sense of) inferiority, lost status, envious anger and themselves as losers. Without social comparison, envy and the enjoyment of possessions, no one would bother to try to out-compete others. Envy arises from a perception of disparity and a view that what resources the other has will be kept to themselves and not shared. When we want what others have, we are motivated to model their behaviour, to be like them, and may try to outperform them (for status, comforts, money, etc.). But of course, envy can also generate desires to undermine or even spoil the other; these are basic sexual or reproductive competitive tactics again. Capitalism likes envy, where each is simply trying to out-compete each (may the best one win and all

---

[465] Classifying societies and groups is actually quite difficult. They can be investigated as to their internal structures and/or how they relate externally to other societies and groups. Some researchers explore differences in antisocial and prosocial behaviour (see for example, Hinde, R.A. and Groebel, J. 1991, eds.) or peaceful and war-like (see Howell, S. and Willis, R. 1989) or partnership and dominator/competitive, see Eisler, R. (1990). Yet, other researchers have given more complex classifications; see for example Fiske A.P. (1992). I have outlined this for Chapter 4, but it worth repeating it here. Fiske suggests four basic forms of socio-culture organisation. 1. *Communal sharing* which is similar to egalitarian; people are treated as equals. 2. *Authority ranking* where people are attentive to where they are in the social ranks and have rights or powers increased or reduced according to their ranks. Ranks tend to be rigid. 3. *Equality matching* where people keep track of favours and obligations. 4. *Market pricing* where forms of social behaviour are made from economic exchanges and the values placed on commodities and attributes (money or special skills can buy you up the ranks). Different psychologies (beliefs and values) are needed and recruited in the different models.

that). The problem is capitalism, without regulation, cannot control greed and exploitation.

If there are no social restraints on competition, then it becomes a *disparity amplification system*. Here people simply go for more and more so that accumulations (of power, status and wealth) build up and those with power, possessions and capital are able to exert greater (subordinating) control over those without. All kinds of tactics can be used to maintain disparity: deception, cheating, secret deals, monopolies, old boy and family networks, special education for the privileged, etc. A casual look at the world today would suggest that disparity amplification is one of the legacies of capitalism. The rich are very rich and the poor very poor. Our competitive minds worry not a bit about that, over and above policing and defending our accumulations. And the competitive mind cares little for the environment, as the current Democratic American Vice-President Al Gore has made clear.[466]

The caring-altruistic side of our minds, however, thinks and feels about relationships very differently. When we care for others, we do not socially compare, nor feel envy nor shame, nor do we fear shame, but rather our feelings and attentions are on the needs of others (and our environments) and our pleasures come from seeing others grow, develop and improve with our input. We are prepared to make sacrifices for the other and/or give time, energy and resources to them. Caring recruits our altruistic psychology involving empathy, sympathy, and compassion. It is thus a *disparity reducing system*. As Eisler[467] points out, in some societies caring is valued more than competing/dominating.

---

[466] Gore, A. (1992). A thoughtful and highly informative book on the problems of environmental destruction from unrestrained competition and a lack of care. The stories of industrial-ecological damage are frightening. Interestingly, although we often think that early hunter-gatherer societies were respectful of the land, in fact once agriculture got going land was exploited, and this was true apparently even of very early Greek societies (see Runnels, C.N. 1995) – which we tend to see as idyllic.

[467] Eisler, R. (1990). It is the archetypal forms of competition and cooperation that are usually contrasted rather than competition and caring (e.g., see Argyle, M. 1991). But as we noted in Chapter 3, cooperation is a complex behaviour, and there is no reason why it would recruit a caring psychology. Eisler touches on this point.

We often think competition is good for us, and it certainly has its benefits. Few would dispute that the West has a better standard of living, in terms of material choices, health and education (and so forth) than the Communist bloc, which, as an economic system, was an abject failure partly because it was hijacked by tyrants rather than being democratically created as a participating sharing society. However, competition also carries many dangers. Our intoxication with its success can blind us to its dangers. For example, study after study have shown that humans (on the whole) function best, in regards to their mental health, not in competitive groups but in supportive, cohesive communities where there are low levels of change and frustration, where conflicts of interest are handled in ways that are recognised to be fair, and where people feel valued.[468] Communities which work well have a way of harmonising the inherent fragmented nature of our inner selves. They give space to and shape our potentials. Our needs for recognition and status are linked to community values, to contributing and living peacefully with others, rather than to selfish individualistic pursuits which threaten to fragment and segregate people, setting one against another. There is often a sense of responsibility to others that helps to constrain the more reptilian addictions of ownership, possessiveness, power and pompous or aggressive demonstrations of one's superiority or strength.[469] Be it in families, schools, work places or other groups, respect and caring marks the groups that are socially cohesive and relatively happy.[470]

In our society today, we recognise that it is possible to have science without a civil or caring order, to have economic growth that increases unfairness not reduces it; to make technological advances that take us closer to Armageddon not away from it. We can do more harm than good. This chapter therefore looks at some of the myths that have grown up in our competitive societies. The

---

[468] See Argyle, M. (1987) for a review. See also Howell, S. and Willis, R. (1989).

[469] See some of the societal patterns compared and contrasted (e.g., the Gusii and the !Kung) in Chapter 4. See also Sampson, E.E. (1993), who touches on some of these themes in various ways.

[470] It is well to remember, however, that even collective groups who can be very prosocial internally can be pretty cruel to outsiders and other groups. At times it can be our care and loyalty for others and our grief at their injury that can lead us to very antisocial and vengeful behaviours, as in war (see Chapter 10).

competitive part of us has many justifications for its importance. But our competitive psychology is failing to come to terms with the realities of the modern world. A caring psychology, prepared to make scarifies for the welfare of others (and our environments) is now desperately needed to help us heal and cope with the world as it is becoming. These psychologies revolve around the distribution of resources.

The Problems of Resource Distribution

Humans evolved in small groups of interconnected others in which it was maladaptive to have vast accumulations of wealth and possessions, especially if the group was nomadic. The advent of agriculture and "staying put", and the production of surplus and population growth, was to produce social contexts never encountered before.[471] Although bringing many benefits, it would play havoc with our evolved minds, if not handled fairly. Indeed, although civilisation has produced some wonderful things, when we look at the terrible poverty, the religious bigotry, the child labour, the horrendous factory conditions, slavery, pollution and ecological destruction, the tortures, the wars and the means we have invented to injure people – we have to admit that it is not all good. We are all too often, to quote Norman Dixon[472] again, "our own worst enemy". Over the last few thousand years our caring psychology may well think we have been veering towards the crazy a lot of the time.

Competition tends to be, as noted, a disparity amplification system. It is rank-focused. Accumulations of resources, both economic and social (like status) will intensify conflicts of interest. Political and economic theories are focused on understanding and offering solutions to these conflicts. Sometimes these

---

[471] Mann, M. (1986)
[472] Dixon, N.F. (1975)

conflicts are internal to the society and give rise to concerns with social fairness. Sometimes they are external and are noted in the need to out-compete other countries. When it comes to out-groups, e.g., other countries, international concerns with social fairness rarely makes much head way, and nations are concerned with preserving and advancing their own competitive edge. It is the rallying call for so much economic policy: "we must remain competitive in world markets". Jobs gained in one country can create losers and poverty in another. And a 'competitive edge' armed with justifications of superiority become the excuse for exploitation and imperialism – a key ingredient of Western progress. International negotiations on trade are not noted for their focus on fairness but how the best deals can be struck by the most powerful, even if that means exploiting the poor.

The problems and inequalities in our competitive lifestyles, which are now so far removed from our early small group origins, have given birth to many political philosophies and solutions with various justifications for each.[473] Many theories are often inaccurate or incomplete and contain commonly contradictory ideas of human nature. Of particular interest are the place they see for altruistic behaviour in society:

> 1. *Individuality*: This view suggests that humans are not really social animals needing supportive communities but are self-focused individuals. There is, to quote Thatcher's famous phrase, "no such thing as society, only individuals". Thus, we are best left to get on with things by ourselves – without government intervention. Social (altruistic) policies often makes things worse and create dependencies. The free market of competing individuals is the best way for complex societies to conduct themselves. Transferred to businesses and nations, each unit of organisation is seen as individual and in competition with other equivalent units. Little, if anything, should be done to disturb the free

---

[473] Gay, P. (1977, 1995). Raymond Plant has also written an in-depth exploration of various recent political philosophies which articulate arguments in support of these positions and their various combinations.

market. The emotional and psychological consequences of all this are completely irrelevant and callously disregarded.

2. *Need*: This view recognises that we are far from equal and at times some people and groups need more help than others. Those who wish to privilege different gender or ethnic groups (positive discrimination) in business may take this view. Targeting resources on the sick and needy is related to this view. Internationally, it calls for a massive shift of resources from the rich to the poor. Need rather than (just) profit should guide action. We should avoid the gross accumulations of power and wealth in the hands of the few.

3. *Equity*: This view suggests that we should be rewarded by the effort we put in and the results we get. No effort (or input) no reward. The question is how to create equity (for example, of opportunity) when the terrain and talent is far from equitable.

4. *Inequality*: Some people are more able than others and this should be rewarded. Without recognition and reward for variations of abilities people will migrate to other businesses or countries seeking personal rewards for talents, or even if they stay you won't get the best out of them. Societies function best by privileging the talented and the fruits of their labour will trickle downwards (non-altruistic) or should be shared and redistributed via (for example) taxation (altruistic). So, you end up paying vast salaries to some film stars, football players or chief executives who then spend their wealth sucking resources into conspicuous consumption (£100,000 cars and £1,000,000 yachts) and driving up the prices of everything else. Most times they will have justifications of how 'they deserve' their salaries. It's utter nonsense, of course, but it is difficult to admit that we simply all love the good things in life and so greed comes rather naturally – and of course I wouldn't refuse that salary either, thank you very much! Regardless of talent, luck plays a major role, as there are probably millions of children in the poorer areas of the world who, if they have the same privileges, would have the same abilities or better. It's not the fault of individuals, it is

systems. Inequity is to do with bad luck mostly, accidents of genes and birth.

5. *Happiness*: Competitive psychology sees contentment as arising from personal control over things and possessions (comforts), and less from belonging to communities. Individualistic self-promotion is good not destructive. People are happier the more they have. The drive to possess is essential for competition to work. There are different types of happiness. Aristotle recognised that we could pursue happiness and pleasure for its own sake – hedonic happiness or hedonism. However, a different type of happiness was eudaimonia, with a focus on meaning and sense of purpose. Some people will forego big salaries in order to work in roles that they find meaningful to them, and these are often where they can help others or express creativity. Now obviously, abject poverty is not good for anyone, so some degree of resources is indeed conducive to happiness. However, many Western societies, through the media, advertising and even schooling, pedal hedonism and the desire to have more, make that lottery win, as the source of the happiness. In contrast, the contemplative and spiritual traditions focus more on the relationships and contentedness that come from understanding our own minds. Indeed, what they call 'grasping mind' – the addiction to material resources and wanting more and more, and hoping that having more and more will prevent suffering – is a source of misery to self and others. In addition, these can be compensations for inner insecurities.

6. *Biological neutrality*: This view splits mind and body. Mental ill-health and outright mental illness are nothing to do with economic or social conditions. Ill health relates to the conditions of the body (brain) and can be fixed by medical interventions – drugs mostly. Crime arises from bad people who should be locked up and punished until they conform to the rules. Economics (resource distribution) and biology are totally separate domains of being.

Although I've presented them as rather black-and-white distinctions, in reality it's more subtle, of course, and there are different dimensions and degrees that shade and blend in with each other. All positions can muster arguments in their support, but few recognise the complexity of human nature – especially that we may need to do different things in different contexts and in different ways. Different economic contexts are created by and for different archetypal strategies. It is the evolved archetypes that are in competition with each other; that is, it is the competition between different evolved strategies for reproduction that are actually running the show. We are intoxicated by them because of the feelings and emotions they give us in their pursuits.

The Myth of Individual Responsibility

The idea that communities and individuals can look after themselves, if relieved of government interference, has never been true, not since the early days of agriculture expanded group size. One does not have to be very historically fluent to realise that throughout the ages much of human life has been pretty bleak, if not dreadful. From the time of Buddha and before, philosopher after philosopher turned away from the notion of the 'goodness of God' precisely because so much of life is full of suffering. Communities and individuals cannot protect themselves from diseases, wars, famines, or from changing ecologies – only societies and cultures can do that, and then only to a degree. The defeat of smallpox and so many other diseases, for example, depended on a slowly established, complex medical science built internationally, generation by generation. The effectiveness of birth control and education is mostly a modern invention (apart from abstention or non-vaginal sex, of course) with different nations requiring substantial help to instigate education and birth-control programs. And when disasters strike, we realise how interdependent we are. Relief operations for ecological disasters are complex affairs that will pull on the experience and talents of teams around the world.

One cannot easily opt out of society but must find some way to accommodate it. This was made tragically clear long before the deep recessions of the 1930s, and again today, in the world of disappearing jobs and the shanty towns of the poor. Looking back, we can see that as people left the land and became more and more trapped in towns and cities, it became increasing impossible to simply gather, hunt and fish for oneself or kin, or collect enough wood to keep warm. With the introduction of the feudal system, the giving of lands to the 'King's Knights', land came under the control of the elite and there were laws on poaching. With the onset of the Industrial Revolution and the technological developments in agriculture, people were forced off the land in vast numbers, which brought them into totally new relationships with work and the means of feeding and clothing themselves. Flooded with an abundance of cheap labour that kept wages down, the Industrial Revolution propelled itself relentlessly and ruthlessly onwards.

This shift from land to towns and cities not only changed the nature of social life but also the constructions of personal identities. In many ways, the workers became trapped and caged in the new environments of production located in towns and cities, in factories and mines. In part, the underclasses are created by this entrapment and the reduced opportunities for 'gathering-hunting', and in part by the creation of specific social roles (jobs and professions) from which they are either excluded or cannot fit. So, the idea that individuals can look after themselves may (perhaps) work in certain kinds of ecologies of small groups, where there is a direct connection of people with their sustaining environments (which allow them to feed themselves and engage in hunter-gathering life styles that actually involves mutual support) – although even here population growth, disease and accidents render individuals victims to forces they cannot control. Individualism is a cruel illusion in modern life that requires turning a blind eye to the exploitation of the individualist. Individuals simply cannot function outside of the group (and its historically built infrastructure) on which they are dependent.[474] One would only pursue this belief if consciously or unconsciously

---

[474] This can lead to some very strange paradoxes. A person who was a leader of a local group would continually advocate the need for individuality in good Thatcherite tradition. But in reality he was a highly group-made man, engaging in numerous committees and groups. His espousal of individuality and disdain for community could only live by the fact he was highly embedded in his community of Conservatives. He disavowed the very process that made him what he was and gave him his power. I am not sure that Margaret Thatcher ever understood that all leaders are members of communities and the moment that community has had enough and can survive without you, they will destroy you. One's power depends on the continual excitement of the fantasies and ideals of the group, as we say in Chapter 7.

you are pursuing pure self-interest and wanted to liberate yourself from responsibility, turn off the motivation and hence responsibility, possibly even guilt, for caring and empathy.

In our modern day, nothing can protect us from the globalisation of markets, the need to change quickly, or the renewed downward pressure on wages. The owners and controllers of capital and finance are now able to cruise the world searching out low-wage labour forces and shift investment accordingly. Apart from drugs and pornography, or those things that are outright illegal, the major financial markets and services of the world care little for where profits come from. Nor do they care from 'what' the returns on investment accrue. They care only for the returns to shareholders and the salaries on their own deals. Thus, many industries, like textiles, shoes and toys, freed from international labour laws, have migrated to low-wage economies where exploitation is easier. Such forces, which are way beyond the individual to control, leave many high and dry in worlds of uncertainty, insecurity, unemployment and/or poverty.[475] To those who receive this international investment come also the "benefits" of new industrial ghettos, with their pollutions, overcrowding and bleak, two-dimensional lifestyles – work and consumption. Undoubtedly, this will bring some benefits, especially if education improves. The claim is that although there are low wages at least there are *some* wages in countries where nothing may otherwise be available for people. But what we have seen is that the social irresponsibility of the market culture of competing individuals may be good for business but can create environments that are almost uninhabitable for many.

The politics of individualism teaches not mutual dependency but self-interest, self-promotion and illusory self-reliance, that falls apart the moment we become sick or our skills are no longer needed. We teach people that they have a right to do and have what they want, but also that we are all nothing – over and above objects in the service of production. We sell illusory dreams that anyone can become president or prime minister, despite the fact that given the size of the

---

[475] Keegan, W. (1993). The spectre of capitalism is indeed a serious problem if not restrained by caring values. As Keegan makes clear, the establishment of the capitalist superstructures with their bureaucracies, multi-nationals and national self-interest offer dark warnings for the future.

population the success rate has not been too high. Individualism can be a thinly disguised return to the Hobbesian world of each against each.

From Responsibility to Blame

The most usual target for blame for disparities and disparity amplifications is the individual. The notion of individual responsibility is a hollow view when looked at with a social-evolutionary lens or applied to modern economic realities. It's interesting to consider where such bizarre notions came from. One source was as an invention, welded together by religious and other authorities: a construction by an elite-serving social order who were more intent on subordination to authority and power than genuine notions of moral behaviour. By stressing the responsibility of the individual (and mostly, of course, it was aimed at the subordinates and the lower ranks), it became possible to disconnect suffering from being anything to do with the dominant elite or social climate. If you sinned, it was you who would suffer God's wrath, not the social circumstances of your sinning, or those who trapped you in poverty. This theme, of locating blame on individuals, has proven extremely useful to those who do not wish to acknowledge any responsibility for their fellow humans. If people suffer then it is their fault, they deserve it (remember that callousness justification from Chapter 9). Thus, the notion of individual responsibility is actually a means of locating blame and turning people away from the realities that it is in the social domains of life where the sources of so much hardship are to be found.

Moral behaviour and economic behaviour have often been linked. Will Hutton, writing in the *Guardian* shortly after the publication of the Rowntree report on inequality, on why the poor remain silent, noted,

> When Seebohm Rowntree revealed in his land-mark study in 1902 that 28 percent of people in York were living in poverty, the Times thundered that a large proportion of the poor were "miserable mainly from their own fault" – a reaction not seriously shaken as another Rowntree inquiry 90 years later reports similar findings.

So overwhelming is this view in popular culture that the poor share it; even if they resent their lot, they believe that they have no right to expect any different – and those that do, find marginalisation so lowers their self-worth that they become accomplices in their own devaluation. [476]

David Smail[477] has pointed out that through the ages there has been a confounding of two very different kinds of power: economic power and will power. If one is without economic power, then this must be to do with something lacking in the self.[478] And more problematically, if one is in a 'state of suffering' then via the power of one's will, or via more effort, one should be able to bring release – so "get on yer bike". In both instances, individuals are held responsible for whatever state they are in. Individualism is a neat way of avoiding social responsibility for others. A confounding of will power, economic power and moral behaviour/character allows blame to be easily, by sleight of hand, placed at the door of the disadvantaged.

The myths of will power and individual responsibility ensure that many will blame themselves for their depressions and the state they are in – thus confounding them. Even if people consciously try to deny it, they have so soaked in the sense of their subordinacy that it operates as a subtle non-conscious orientation to themselves. It is very difficult for individuals to understand the wider picture, the social, contextual and historical factors of why one is suffering when one's own psychology is focused on self-attribution, and our environment constantly reinforces that. Religion, as we've seen, constantly focuses individuals on holding themselves responsible, which obviously has a good side but can be used simply to manipulate people into blaming themselves for any misery in their lives. Shame, envy, rage, anxiety, frustration – all these are heightened in environments where people have no control. While it may be true

---

[476] Hutton, W. (1995b), p.11

[477] Smail, D. (1987)

[478] Gay, P. (1995) gives a comprehensive historical exploration of such justifications for inequality – especially belief in the essential superiority of some groups and individuals. Scott, J.C. (1990) explores the many reasons the subordinate do not revolt.

that jobs are disappearing, as we shift from industrial to technological styles of working – indeed, the whole nature of work is changing – we should note that many of our institutions and ways of life have grown up assuming the stability of employment. For example, mortgages assume that up to a third of one's income will be available for 25 years or so. Insurance policies also assume steady (or increasing) wage packets. In these times of increasing house repossessions (now close to 1,000 per week), there is no indication that such institutions are ready for the long term unemployed, the 'contract worker' who may have long periods of unemployment or highly unstable work records. One can work from home, I guess, if one has a home and the skills to do so.

The Myth of Equality

The myth of individualism is rendered more acceptable by another illusion – that of equality. That all should be treated equally is a moral view captured by ideas that all are created equally under God. However, a spiritual dictate to not assume one's superiority over others can be easily turned into ideas that we are actually created equally. A visit to any children's ward as some die of cancer makes obvious the fact that we are far from equal – genes do not play fair – nor, of course, do social environments. Justice and fairness are human creations, not aspects of nature, and there are many views on what fairness is, what it entails and the degree to which the needs of some should be met by those who have the resources to pay.[479] Our inherent inequality is a painful reality. We are each the product of genetic accidents and socialisations. We have no more control over the genes we will have as to the cultures and social conditions we will be born into. The concept of individual responsibility denies this fact. It denies that some

---

[479] Plant, R. (1991). Concerns with the nature of social justice and fairness are at the heart of modern political philosophy – and complex arguments some are. Plant given a very helpful overview to this area of thought and one which sadly we do not do justice to here. Galbraith, J.K. (1993) also discusses the theme of payment by the rich for services to the poor.

people are more intelligent than others, that some people are more attractive than others, that some people are more hard-working than others, that some people are more creative than others, that some people will do better simply as a result of messages from their DNA and social origins. A caring psychology suggests that it is not just for ourselves we should develop responsibility but to others, because equality (and here we should consider which domains we are thinking about) is something to be worked for, not something that is natural.

It is also the case that in everyday life we do not make choices based on the equality of people. Indeed, we actually hope that some of our institutions will chose on the basis of inequality. If I, or my family, need brain surgery, I hope that medicine has ensured that my surgeon has been chosen from the ranks of the bright, talented and caring. In other words, I hope they have filtered out the less bright, butter-fingered, untalented and the uncaring.

Here lies the paradox. We want to be treated equally, yet we know we are not equal in so many ways. When it comes to others having something to offer us, be it medical care, insurance advice, teachers for our children or employees, we know that some will be better than others. So, we search for the best rather than the average or less-good practitioners. Hence the desire for equality, when we each behave and select precisely because of inequality, is a paradox. If a society starts with pre-established beliefs of the quality of groups of individuals, then this choosing becomes the basis for racism and sexism – simply, prejudice. It is often more concerned to exclude from rather than include into.

The recognition of inequality, indeed the farming of inequality, is at the heart of capitalist economics. The market economy, via a system of rewards and institutional tests of ability, is believed (or supposed) to act as a filter that gradually ranks people so that those able who do certain things have access to the means to do them, and those not able to do certain things do not. Of course, the aristocracy, using kin-accumulated wealth, have promoted into positions of power some very unintelligent and callous individuals. Capitalism in some ways circumvents this by promoting the rise of the meritocracy (although more accurately, talentocracy). In many ways, this is highly rational. Even in early humanoid societies, one could expect that the best hunters or healers were given the means to do their own thing; it would be silly to force a good hunter to stay at home and search for berries, or a good healer with a dodgy leg and poor aim to go hunting. In China under Mao, and Russia under Stalin, there was an attempt to wipe out this simple and obvious psychology of individual differences. Very gifted intellectuals were either shot or made to till the land. That is one way to deal with the problems of inherent inequality and the emergence of rank differences, but not very bright, grossly inefficient, and callous not to mention rather crazy.

It is precisely because of our inherent inequality that we address ourselves to the problem of creating equality - of rights, freedom from exploitation, fairness and to theories of social justice, and exposing the assumptions of inequality (e.g., some groups are better than others because of ethnicity or gender). There have been many theories written on these ideas which have been well documented by Plant[480]. Unfortunately, however, the facts of inequality have meant that those with power can have disproportionate effects on the rules and applications of justice. The harshest punishments have always fallen on the subordinate, and the mechanisms for fairness and justice privilege the elite, leaving some forms of exploitation untouched (e.g., racism and sexism). Some people are more able to fulfil certain roles than others. Whichever way one looks at it, the facts of inequality are always trying to assert themselves. The problem is how we help the less able. When IQ tests were first introduced in the 1880s, the original desire was to identify those in need of extra help. Since that time, however, awareness of IQ differences has been used to privilege the bright, often at the expense of the less bright. There has never been a disproportionate amount of resources given to the less able.

---

[480] Plant, R. (1991) is concerned with the nature of social justice and fairness at the heart of modern political philosophy – and complex arguments some are. Plant has given a very helpful overview to this area of thought and one which sadly we do not do justice to here. Galbraith, J.K. (1993) also discusses the theme of payment by the rich for services to the poor.

The Harder You Work, The More You Get

This principle of equity has usually been up-rank only. One reason for giving tax-breaks to the rich is the assumption that the managers of business are sitting around playing noughts and crosses waiting for the monies to motivate them. You will not get the best out of them unless you "stuffed their mouths with gold". This is rather offensive to them, in fact. Of course, most of us won't turn down any money on offer, but it is inaccurate to believe that people are *only* motivated by money and hedonistic pleasures. Remember the concept of eudaimonia noted above. The brain drain has often been cited as a reason why we must pay certain individuals more. But people move abroad for many reasons; the weather is one. In science, although bigger salaries are attractive, it is often the better facilities and opportunities to do good work that appeal. Universities that create departments that bring together bright collaborators who are supportive and exciting to work with can appeal over money. Common sense things too, like feeling supported, valued and appreciated with one's contribution recognised are also reasons for staying in jobs that may not give the highest salaries.

When it comes to the workers, we suddenly see a complete change of heart. These are different types of people, apparently, who are not motivated by opportunities and money but by fears of unemployment. They are motivated to work harder through low wages not high ones. Perceptions of unfairness can be divisive. We are not in the Middle Ages with the rights of kings or when people were taught that God ordained some to be better than others. The idea that one's pay relates to the scarcity of the resource (in the form of talent) that one offers may be sound economics, but it is hopelessly inadequate for dealing with our complex psychologies. To be paid much less than others is clearly also indicating that "I'm not that talented and don't have that much to offer" – i.e., "I'm dispensable".

Another problem is that no one can agree on what is fair or equitable. Is a £500,000 or more salary equitable? Clearly many would think not, even though "the market" might pay it. Market equity runs up against psychological judgements of equity. Few working in the mines or factories would like to think they are that unequal, or work that less hard. So large market-produced disparities can activate envious rage and contempt. It is naive to ignore this psychology.

Taxation as a Disparity Control Mechanism

Although in early societies the good hunter was encouraged to hunt, it was not expected that the products of his hunt would be eaten only by him. In egalitarian groups, prestige was (is) given to sharing the products of his/her labour and the recognition of his/her mutual dependency within the group – even in the context of inequality of ability. Unfortunately, this psychology was designed and adapted to close-knit groups not the mega-states of unknown millions. Whereas our hunter or healer could see and relate to all those who benefited from his/her efforts, in the societies of the modern world this direct contact between provider and receiver no longer exists. Even today we are much more likely to care for, and make sacrifices to, others when we have direct contact or a relationship with them than if they are faceless strangers. In other words, in a large society where the close-knit groups of early humanoids no longer exist, the normal group pressure to share, struggles to work and must depend on social ideals. So although the principle of redistribution of resources and social equality was to become a moral focus of political theory[481], when placed in the context of groups the size of millions, it was going to run up against a psychology that does not exactly like it.

As mentioned, in many societies there has been an awareness of the essential inequality of humans. This is sometimes institutionalised in a caste and class system. In Europe, as it headed down the capitalist road, there was an awareness that a society needs to select from unequal individuals to fit specific roles. The problem is that, be it by a class system or the rise of the meritocracy, some would be able to accumulate at a much faster rate than others. The market would privilege some individuals because they had talents or opportunities (class or family back-up) to do well. Accumulations, especially within family groups and

---

[481] Plant, R. (1991)

the elite, would act to increasingly subjugate 'the masses' who were reliant on them for work. There is an inherent amplifying process for unequal resource distribution. So, as Marx understood, the owners of capital and machines would have a disproportionate power to exploit those without the technical means of production. History would thus be textured with the struggles of the haves against the have-nots and have-lots (of capital).

Nevertheless, following the Age of Enlightenment and various attendant ideals of liberty, ideas gradually emerged that the products of people's labour (and capital) should be shared within society to restrain increasing disparities. I say gradually but, of course, these ideals of sharing were sometimes central in some religions (if you asked Jesus, he would certainly support them) but struggled to become incorporated in social institutions.[482] The way sharing and social fairness was to be achieved was not by holding people back, making them all wear grey cloths and ploughing fields, but through the redistribution of resources (the wealth) in the form of taxation.

One aspect of taxation is therefore that it is a social endeavour at altruism. Taxation can be used to invest in services and provisions for mutual benefit. Of course, taxation was never originally designed to produce fairness or services, but rather to give monies for armies and other things for the ruling elite. It is unclear at what point in history taxation came to be seen not only as a means for the state to conduct its business in all those things that individuals could not do for themselves (form armies, build the roads, schools, hospitals, etc.), but also as a form of social altruism and levelling. Moreover, governments did begin to recognise certain social obligations and introduced laws on slavery, child employment, education, rights of trade unions and so forth, and to coordinate services. Along with these changes, taxation was increasingly used to support and develop an increasingly complex infra-structure of a modern technological state (e.g., schools, roads, welfare services, etc.).

Gilmour, in denouncing the right-wing agenda of the Thatcher years as a betrayal of Tory values, points out that,

---

[482] Gay, P. (1995)

In 1830 Peel thought the great evil of the times was 'a tendency to diminish the enjoyment of the poorer classes, to lower them in the scale of society, and widen their separation from the upper classes'. Twelve years later, seeking to counter the tendency, he refused to impose more taxes on the poorer classes. Instead, he reintroduced income tax, believing that it was 'for the interest of property that property should bear the burden' of rescuing the country's finances, while he lowered the cost of living for the benefit of the poor. For Peel, social policy was at least as important as economic policy.

Disraeli went further...... In the 1840s he lamented the existence of 'two nations between whom there is no intercourse and no sympathy... the rich and poor'. And some thirty years later, considering the people's health 'the most important question for a statesman', he declared 'the elevation of the condition of the people to be a great object of the Tory Party'.[483]

Later, at the turn of the century, Salisbury thought that government should be concerned with the poor and that no system that was not just to the poor could survive[484]. Onwards through this century the same sentiments applied. Since the war, all governments (until the 1980s) have sought to actively promote welfare and build a complex infrastructure, so that by the time Thatcher came to power poverty had not been eradicated, but things were far improved from what they had been some 100 years earlier, and the National Health Service was the envy of the world. Limited it might have been, but at least some politicians did see some role for what might be called *altruistic capitalism*: that is, some role for caring and resource redistribution. Hence a complex infrastructure of schools, health and welfare services, aided by the Keynesian vision to eradicate unemployment, grew like an increasingly intricate scaffold around which the internal operations of society could operate. Thatcher systematically dismantled that in acts of social vandalism, and squandered all our North Sea oil revenues

---

[483] Gilmour, I.I. (1992), p.129
[484] Gilmour, I.I. (1992)

– which should have been used to build our infrastructure – on ridiculous and immoral tax cuts. The years ahead will see serious problems of underfunding.

As we have now found to our cost, if one begins to dismantle the infrastructure which supports social complexity and drops altruistic efforts at redistribution of wealth and social provisions, then things begin to fray at the edges. There is a risk of parts collapsing into anarchy. Supporting the infrastructure as it becomes more complex and interconnected may call for many different types of intervention, in different contexts, delivered in different ways and not just (or even) public ownership. Thus, on the 'new-left' there is a focus on 'communities' and providing them with the means to control their local environments, but this must be done in partnership with governments.

Of course, taxation and rates of taxation, be it direct or indirect, are complex. One particular complication was identified by Arthur Laffer and his Laffer curve, which is basically an inverted U-shaped curve of tax against revenue. The problem is that there is a tax rate (pence in the pound) at which you can maximise government revenue, but tax beyond that and there is a disincentive to work which curtails tax receipts. The data on this is tricky though, because during the 1950s and 1960s there were very high tax rates on the wealthy and it's unclear if that was a disincentive to them. The right wing saw in these ideas reasons to support laissez-faire and trickle-down economics, arguing that high taxes are disincentives and produce an ultimate reduction in revenue. But as Laffer articulated, taxation needs to be carefully thought about to do the job you want it to do. Economists debate these things of course, and the trade-offs between fair distribution of wealth and maintaining incentives and resources to create it.

Also in the frame is the fact that people with wealth will find ways to avoid paying taxation, and the higher the taxation the greater the avoidance; overseas accounts are clever manoeuvres by wealthy individuals and big corporations. There are even accountancy firms that specialise in legal tax avoidance schemes. When they all start doing this, it becomes a competitive race. Should any of them decide to play the game responsibly and pay their taxes they will be at an immediate disadvantage. The problem is not individuals trying to privilege themselves (we all try to do that), but that legal and financial systems allow them to do it. Closing loopholes with appropriate policing would seem a sensible thing. Of course, there are also big battles over how our taxes should be spent. While some would want more spending on the National Health Service, others want to build Trident missiles. While some want government funded services, others want to privatise – when there is no evidence whatsoever that competing private companies offer better services. They do offer opportunities for profits for shareholders though.

The point is, many early efforts of governments, especially in the immediate post-war period where progressive tax rates were high, did try to reduce the grosser forms of inequality and disparity that operated in society. To be sure this was not simply on the basis of moral or altruistic thinking (though it was to a degree), but also a recognition that an uneducated, restless, or sick population made for an inferior workforce. Even today, education is emphasised, not so much from a moral position, that people will be excluded without education or that people may not be able to decipher the confusing messages of a market focused media, but because we will not be able to compete in the world without it. The problem here is that if businesses and industry can select from the educated and shun the less educated to keep a competitive edge (indeed, it may even increase it by paying fewer people to do more with advanced technologies), then they will. Good moves for business and profit maybe – a bad move for people. This is why people are educated to be "production units" with productive skills, to fit the demands of industry, and their training in empathy and caring for others, or citizenship, is rather haphazard.[485] Certainly, there is very little interest in creating jobs people want to do rather than creating jobs that industries and companies need them to do. No one is really to blame for any of this; it's

---

[485] Education of our caring psychology, of the importance of sharing, respect and compassion are arbitrary and very much not central to education. These talents, it is believed, develop naturally or in the home – despite the fact we know that many homes are fraught places and increasingly with absent parents out at work. And men (fathers) have rarely seen it as their responsibility to educate our caring psychology. Caught in the need to work, parents worry, mostly that their children will acquire work skills to ensure them jobs, or they avoid even that responsibility.

how archetypal systems work and we are trapped in them unless we have some radical rethink – the result of which is in the future because it will take many clever minds to work out what is best to do. But once again we are seeing the consequence of allowing systems of production just to emerge almost willy-nilly.

What is clear is that in the last decade the altruistic role of taxation to introduce greater equality in opportunities, or any concern to refine and develop the social infrastructure, has been side-lined. Based on the myth that individuals can spend money better than governments, the rich (but not the poor) have experienced a great release from taxation. That this will produce benefits for all is based on myths as can be seen from a brief look at history, which shows the appalling conditions that most lived under when individuals were not obliged to pay taxes to support a complex, social infrastructure, or maintain decent working conditions. Also eroded in the last 15 years (although not completely gone) has been the idea that society, as a society, should provide certain services to people which require those more able to pay to finance these services. Furthermore, those services in turn should be directed at the most needy, not those who pay more.[486]

Free Choice and Taxation

The retreat from the attempts of altruistic capitalism (however limited they might have been) and thus the acceptance of increasing competitive disparity amplification has many sources. As Galbraith[487] has made clear, the liberation from the burdens of taxation has fitted not only with the myths of individualism but with making a virtue of *free choice*. Despite the fact that free choice is always limited to the alternatives on offer, and can often be quite limited, and despite the fact that free choice is always bounded by opportunities, status, fashion and shame avoidance, and despite the fact that the choices are actually often manipulate by media images and the constructions of wants, and despite

---

[486] Galbraith, J.K. (1993)
[487] Galbraith, J.K. (1993)

the fact that one person's choice can be another person's loss – freedom of choice has been elevated to a virtue.

Once the moderately wealthy could escape into the realms of private housing, education and healthcare, and detach themselves from the deficiencies of the mega-organisations of public services, then freedom of choice became a rallying call to the contented who could afford to pay. Quite naturally, the moderately wealthy wanted more control over their income to do just that too. Freedom of choice, which depends on purchasing power is, of course, a sick joke to the poor. Free choice only exists if you have the skills, talents, (family) back-up, money or resources to exercise it. Because of the facts of inequality it can never be that individuals (alone) are equally free to choose. Money not only allows one to buy education (for example), but also to send your child to schools of similar social status, to meet others with similar values, and develop networks of potentially helpful alliances. How many from Eton and Harrow first developed their networks at these schools, which would help them move into the higher echelons of society? Take two schools matched for numbers from Manchester and Newcastle, for example, and see how many of their ex-students have entered into the upper echelons of society, of business, of politics, etc., compared to those from Eton and Harrow.

Free choice, an anathema to the hunter-gatherer, and as we have seen in the chapter on shame, a troubling ideal, has become a virtue and yard-stick for the happy life. Yet I suspect that people would forgo choice if they could trust in the quality of government-funded institutions. Indeed, unlike America perhaps, a recent newspaper poll found that 60% of people want to pay more tax to finance schools and welfare services. It is because reduced taxation and provisioning by governments reduces quality (the current debates as the government tries to impose yet more cuts on education, the increasing class sizes etc. attest clearly to this) that people feel they can buy better themselves.[488] It is a vicious circle: invest less, the service suffers, people want to go elsewhere, so invest less. Thus, many may want to desert the cooperate provisions of these services, get tax

---

[488] Galbraith, J.K. (1993)

breaks for doing so and thus making them more difficult to sustain. It's a feedback process into destruction.

In addition, closing down small local hospitals (for example) may appear to make economic sense, forcing people into the mega-hospitals, but this doesn't make sense psychologically. Sure, major hospitals are important if you had a serious stroke or heart attack, but not if you've fallen off a ladder and broken a leg, or poured hot water over your foot, or need a little extra help delivering your baby. Most accidents and emergencies are for minor events, and for these sorts of events people want local sources of help and support. So again, the question is: are we funding a service that fits the psychology of people or the gymnastics of accountants? People go private because they want the speedy, competent and personal. Not surprisingly then taxation, as a burden to free choice, can be resisted with some force by the wealthy and contented. The failure to provide quality services is at the heart of the problem, not the fact that people seek the best.

Once one believes in the power of individuals to look after themselves, sees no role for altruism as a disparity reducing device, avoids the realities of social inequalities, abandons the principles of social fairness, forgets that complex societies need complex infrastructures – then it is indeed possible to enter the realms of a low-taxation society and sell it as a virtue. Politics becomes, as George Orwell once observed, the art of defending the indefensible. The hunter-gather wisdom of sharing and the avoidance of gross discrepancies of rank and resources is lost. Even though at the heart of so many religions there is recognition of the importance of sharing the products of one's labour, few on the right take it seriously – which makes their religious liaisons so contradictory.[489]

A moral society is significantly influenced by what happens at the top.[490] In common discourse today is the idea that both the governed and the governing need new forms of partnership. It is patently obvious that well provisioned

---

[489] One of my religious teachers once told me (and it appears also in some gnostic texts) that the original commandant "thou shalt not steal" was actually "thou shalt not accumulate". However, some saw that this was going to cause huge problems, so they subtlety changed it. I don't know if this is true, but I like the story and can believe it.

[490] See Emler, N. and Hogan, R. (1991) for a fascinating discussion of this.

services are unsustainable without funds, and low taxation simply starves schools and hospital (etc.) of funds. Communitarianism, the new buzz word in politics, does not necessarily address these issues, and I fear it could be a way of shredding cooperate responsibility again via the back door. It may well be that we need new infrastructures that enable communities to care more for themselves and be self-directing (e.g., in dealing with crime on estates, or looking after housing conditions, or dealing with difficult neighbours) but they are going to need the funds to do it. There is simply no other way a society can be fairer without sharing and investment. If one leaves all to market forces, which have often been compared to the laws of the jungle, then a jungle is what one will get, and not an ordered and civilised society.

The issue of responsibility, of the state to the individual and the individual to the state, captured in the concept of citizenship, includes efforts to recruit our altruistic psychologies and avoid gross exploitations (and deceptions) of one on the other. However, altruism is not only concerned with the rights of each as they enter into cooperative partnerships but has to acknowledge the problem of inequality, not only as it naturally exits but as it is socially created.

The Psychology of Taxation

If taxation is a disparity limiting mechanism, is the fuel for decent welfare services and so forth, but (to a degree) depends on our altruistic psychology, then clearly the psychology of paying taxes, the psychology of sharing the fruits of one's labour, needs careful attention. Our altruistic psychology developed in the context of small close-knit groups, not mega-states. Limited though it might be, many people do want to see the sick cared for, poverty reduced and people given fair education. Our jerry-built brains make us concerned with our own self-interests, but also with others through empathy and sympathy (the subject of the next chapter). Recognising this shows that there are serious difficulties with the psychology of taxation, and the way we raise money to socially provision our societies. When I studied economics as an undergrad, the personal *psychology* of paying taxes was never mentioned, and still isn't as far as I know. Yet it is clearly a vital aspect as to how we live together and finance our services.

Allied to the belief that freed from taxes I could buy better services are other problematic psychologies.

A major problem with taxation is the psychology of paying taxes. For example, even though I am pro-taxes, I must admit to a certain irritation at paying them – especially if mistakes are made and I am landed with a bill I had not anticipated. This may be due partly with how our brains work, and how we pay taxes. For example, I look at my salary and focus on the gross pay. This is the figure that sticks in my mind – but, of course, it does not resemble what I will actually get in my hand. I see how much has gone in tax and feel (perhaps irrationally) deprived. If I go to buy a new computer, I'll have the figure in my mind given by the supplier, but then get a bill that is far more because of VAT. This can only breed frustration and resentment because of the way our (or at least my) jerry-built minds work – we are constantly being confronted with the fact that we have had *something taken away from us*, or that we have underestimated what something will cost. I am not gaining any social prestige from the fruits of my labour being shared, nor am I in direct contact with the beneficiaries. My psychology of sharing and caring must, therefore, rely on higher ideals – not direct emotional ones. Winning, prestige and money, paying directly for services etc., or feeling deprived and constrained, however, all have a very direct emotional impact. Paying taxes stimulates the psychology of loss – and to some extent, deprivation – so forget rational thinking here.

Maybe the psychologically more helpful thing to do would be to find a way of paying taxes, contributing to the agencies that supply our services, a way that did not imply that one's real worth was gross pay – since one never gets that – but net pay. When I apply for a job, figures quoted should reflect closer to what I will actually get, net. Suppose we found ways to make us less aware of gross pay? Suppliers should not flash up prices excluding VAT but should always include it – the real cost. How can we tap our altruistic psychology more sensibly and not have it clash so often with self-interest and a sense of deprivation? This is another area where, through no fault of our own, we get caught up in a bit of craziness; the way we pay taxes at the moment is a psychological system designed to breed resentment and evasion. Nowhere is the neglect of psychological understanding more obvious than in one of our most important social activities – the way we share the products of our labour.

Actually, there are ways to tax that may be less psychologically troublesome. At a world conference on poverty in 1995, the French president Francois Mitterand noted an idea put forward by James Tobin, a Nobel Prize winner in economics.[491] He observed that in the financial markets transactions amount to around a trillion dollars a day. A tax of 0.5% tax would render 150 billion dollars a year, a sizable sum to tackle poverty worldwide. As usual though, not everyone was enthusiastic about such efforts, and some argued that it was up to individual governments to tackle poverty. The British were not enthusiastic. Disappointing. Surely, we must think of world solutions for world problems, especially since we increasingly recognise that individual governments are losing their power over their own economic systems as markets become globalised.

The Myth of Trickle-Down Economics

The morality of the unrestrained market place, which in many ways would have appalled Adam Smith, who had a far greater sense of responsibility than he is given credit for, was given, during the 1980s, a new suit of clothes. This was the idea that the more wealth created by the higher ranks of society, the more wealth would trickle down to the lower ranks. On this rising tide of wealth all would move upwards. It was an all-gain-and-no-loss myth. You could forget about altruistic efforts of redistribution, or needs to control the inherent disparity amplification of market economics – although all societies worry about vast monopolies. Hidden from view was the fact that this would actually increase disparity and inequality, and that in an increasingly competitive and unrestricted market place, advantages won would have no relation to fairness, mutual dependency, social responsibility, the development and maintenance of a complex infrastructure, or community cohesiveness. It failed to account for

---

[491] As reported in *The Independent on Sunday*, March, 1995 p.1, "Mitterrand bows out with call for world tax" by Geoffrey Lean and Nicholas Timmins.

accumulation of wealth, disparity amplification, the role of shareholders and the use of wealth to exploit others. Of all economic theories, this seemed the most ivory tower: developed along with monetarism by poring over national statistics and historical changes in economic activity with a hint of a discredited Social Darwinism thrown in.[492] Mostly, these promises of trickle-down and monetarism have proved illusions, broken on the back of rising energy prices (which stung the 1970s Labour government badly), international capital movements, and a failure to appreciate Keynesian wisdoms of fiscal economics. Moreover, there seemed to be a cloud come over the vision of those who thought that capitalist society had produced better welfare, medicine (especially when compared to communism). They forgot that it may well have done so, but this was in large measure due to previous governments using wealth creation to distribute its benefits by investing in the social infrastructure of schools, the National Health Service, and so forth.

We know that the marriage of monetarism and trickle-down economics does not work – it is more trickle-up. Moreover, these polices, by squeezing the consuming/purchasing potential of the lower-wage earners of society, actually reduce the demand for goods and services on which the capitalist system depends. As the manufacturing infrastructure changes, so that production becomes more specialised and aimed at people with money (e.g., yachts and expensive cars); distorting the flow of resources into what is produced. The Rowntree report on incomes and wealth published in February 1995 was a telling indictment on the failure of trickle-down economics. The wages of the highest paid 30 percent have gone up 50 percent in the last 15 years, while those of the bottom 20-30% percent have stayed the same or fallen.

Goldsmith explodes the myth of trickle down with another set of statistics.

> Almost every national government has fallen into the trap of counting and measuring without attempting to understand the consequences. In France over the past twenty years GNP has grown by 80%, a spectacular performance. And yet during the same period unemployment has grown from 420,000 to 5.1 million (the official

---

[492] Gilmour, I.I. (1991)

figure is 3.3 million, but the government's own statistics show various categories consisting of 1.8 million people have been omitted). The fact that such growth can be achieved while at the same time excluding over 5 million people from active participation in society – a proportion equivalent to over 22 million people in the USA – should incite a government to reconsider its policies. Alas, that does not happen. All we hear is that if only we could achieve one-half a per cent or 1 per cent faster growth in GNP all would be saved. In the United Kingdom, despite growth of GNP of 97%, between 1961 and 1991 the number of those living in poverty grew from 5.3 million to 11.4 million. [493]

Poverty

Poverty is one of the consequences of allowing competitive disparity amplification to get out of hand. Gilmour points out that,

> Experts find it difficult to agree on definitions of poverty. But a proper definition would not be confined to income. It would include Beveridge's 'five giants' – want, ignorance, squalor, idleness and disease – which would encompass such factors as homelessness and poor education...

> Measuring poverty in the Thatcher era is difficult because of the inadequacy, and at times deliberate obfuscation of government statistics. [494]

The growth in poverty and social deprivation has no single cause, but includes rising unemployment, especially of the less well educated, falling values of family support incomes, an increase in single-parent families, and loss of social provisions such as council houses. Many of these social hardships have fallen disproportionately on ethnic groups, single parents and the elderly. The growth

---

[493] Goldsmith, J. (1994), p.9. Goldsmith offers and interesting exploration on the economic mismanagement behind the growth of poverty, crime and ecological destruction.
[494] Gilmour, I.I. (1991), p.137

in low-paid part-time, McDonalds-type jobs is no compensation at all for these radical changes.

As many commentators have noted, the rich should not believe they can protect themselves from the rising tide of social disintegration. Although crime and mental illness are far too complex to be located in a single cause like poverty, poverty is a fertile breeding ground for them. The growth in crime and social protest will create unpleasant and tense social places, while the growth in violence, mental and physical ill health, and an increasing underclass who will need some kind of support (or prison and probation services), suggests that the tax bill can only grow. Cost falls on individuals as well as society at large. For example, many businesses are spending millions on security. Many millions have recently gone into protecting shops from ram-raiders. Twenty years ago, I hardly knew anyone who had had their car broken into. Today a number in my department alone have had this happen to them in the last year. The cost is enormous, not only personally, but on the police, etc. When individuals have to protect themselves from the alienated, it gets very costly indeed and one has to ask would this money not be better spent preventing the need for it? As society fractures and fragments, we will be paying in personal and financial terms more and more heavily.

Moreover, without a desire to share and instigate a healing process, we will be forced down a road of more authoritarian and repressive governments just to keep the lid on. We know that as groups become more frustrated and marginalised in society they tend to regress to crime and violence, especially young males.[495] To control the protests of the increasingly disadvantaged and alienated, as they seek release in drugs and crime, one needs more police control. Thus, what emerges are increasing fractures in society, increasing unrest, intergroup aggression (e.g. racism) and increasingly restrictive policing. Having created the threat from the alienated, we now need to control it with the powers of the state. This is precisely why the Criminal Justice Bill is so serious and worrying a piece of legislation, for it has been designed to cope with threats that

---

[495] Archer, J. (1994, eds.). In this book, see Chapter 5.

have been (in part) created by economic policies and failures in the social responsibility of government. In a recent documentary in the BBC's *Everyman* series, Joan Bakewell reported on the growing prison programme in the US. It seems that tougher sentencing, a reduction in rehabilitation and a fortress approach are the order of the day. If California is treated as a country, then it would be both one of the richest in the world, and one with the highest percentage prison population. Those scooped up in the net and entrapped in these places are commonly the disadvantaged. Britain has one of the largest prison populations of the EEC, and the numbers of young males being locked up is growing fast. This is an expansive policy, causes of suffering all round, but useful for party conferences to convince those anxious about crime that something is being done by way of punishment. Most researchers realise that such lock-up practices do not work, on the whole, without proper rehabilitation. This is empty politics because it doesn't work as a deterrent; money would be better spent on supporting the police in prevention and detection, and it doesn't do anything to help victims once a crime has been committed. Money could be better spent on targeting particular communities that tend to generate criminality. Without a concerted effort to tackle poverty and alienation, the slogan "tough on crime – tough on the causes of crime" is pointless and with little substance.

The main problem with theories like trickle-down, and indeed many such economic theories, is that they are so socially and psychologically naïve. Politics becomes tricky because people are clearly wanting to use statistics to support their views which they believe will gain votes. In so doing, claims are repeated and repeated until people forget that actually the statistics are much more confusing than the simple presentations, and we end up with highly prejudicial distorted views.[496] Economic policies can treat people as if human motivation,

---

[496] One reason for this, of course, is that unlike other professions, where one is chosen because one has demonstrated some knowledge or ability in the field, politicians must win votes from those very distant from the facts. Moreover, we base choices on media-manipulated sets of images that play on basic fears and prejudices in soundbites. When the Sun newspaper claimed they helped elect the last Tory government, a rather grandiose claim to be sure, there was nonetheless a shudder that they may have had a point (see Postman, N. 1987). Would you choose a doctor or pilot like this? I have no

feelings and needs simply don't exist. Economics was always challenged in my day, because it assumed rational decision-making, and that's rarely the case. The basic irrationalities of humans, our needs for care and status, are ignored, or at best receive only lip service. People can be treated as factory fodder, who can be moved around, picked up, dumped and dislocated like objects without a subjectivity or feelings. Young males without jobs, dislocated from social groups and from older males to socialise them, with no way to plan for a future and see their fortunes improve, nor see themselves as able to make important contributions to the welfare of their community, exist in a highly maladaptive environment that they were not evolved to fit.

Whether it be in paying taxes, understanding how to help people behave more responsibly or reducing the major disparities between health, life expectancy and risk of crime, even within a few miles of each other in cities like London, there seems little way to proceed unless one understands our social psychology – which is not the favourite subject of politicians. While of course some politicians are dedicated, caring and in it as a calling, others have been accused of being career politicians who knowingly manipulate for positions of power. The message should be clear by now: maladaptive environments produce adaptive behaviours for that environment. That is, in tough, crime-ridden areas, it may be more adaptive to be tough and callous rather than altruistic.

If we lift the horizon of our thinking beyond national to international problems of poverty, and study human misery and suffering worldwide, be it via famine, war, the spread of disease, or the processes by which individuals are subordinated and disempowered, then even a cursory glance shows the enormous power of social organisation and social policy in their creation.[497] It

---

answers to this, except to note how incredibly dependent we are on the media for accurate information and the integrity of politicians – sadly a profession held in rather low regard. It is alarming when the son of Thatcher turns up in American courts charged with racketeering and corruption, massive arms deals and the sleazy dealings of government are exposed.

[497] Sen, A. (1993) gives a powerful overview of the role of social and economic policy as causes of famines and disease, especially in the Third World. Our investment and loans which have put so many in debt are of tragic proportions and now some countries can barely cope with the interest on these loans.

seems unlikely we will be able to make many inroads into these problems without radical social changes.

Fractures

Once a society begins to fracture along the dimension of economic disparities, then there is reversion to localities, and small groups operate increasingly outside the umbrella of the state. This fracturing takes place because the social infrastructure cannot support a complex society – they are the sections that are fraying away at the edge, and eating further outwards. Where this happens we often see that governments have been unable or negligent in providing the supports for an integrated society. They have not supported education or welfare services. Groups of people have been left to fend more and more for themselves, which, because they do not have access to resources, they often patently fail to do. The inner city ghetto and the shanty town are the results.

Into the crevices of these fractures come the gang leaders, terrorists and drug barons, who offer a dark paternalism. They reach out to the poor at least some degree of support in exchange for loyalty. Many South American cities are well down that road, and are fearful of police action against gangs. When the police remove one of the drug barons, the poor can be enraged and fearful because the police will be gone tomorrow. They have been left victim to rival gangs and without alternative supports. All the time, these groups gain insight into an alternative world they are excluded from – a world of affluence and security – via their televisions and radios. This media speaks not to or for them; it rarely attempts to articulate their anger but to suppress it in the language of criminality.

Happiness

The Myth of Consumer Happiness

Galbraith[498] believes that inertia in tackling social problems lie with the contented, who defend their privileges and vote for governments who will offer more to them and their social opt-out lifestyles. They are sizable enough to win elections and their outrage at being asked to make sacrifices is enough to bring any wayward, sharing politician back into line. But the questions run deeper than this. If it is the quality of our social relationships that make us happy, why do we not attend to this and recognise that our privileges create envious enemies? One reason, of course, is that relationships are localised in that (for example) one's closest associates will come from one's own type of group, and we hope and expect the state to defend us against the protests of the poor. But still this does not explain the shift to competitive economics in developing countries. Why do they change, and so speedily take to consumerism?

The answer may have been undervalued by those who advocate a more 'back to nature' way of living. The fact is that, outside a technological society, life can be very hard. One's children die, the winters are cold and wet, and food unpredictable. It is very easy to see why people would be attracted to simple comforts of running water, electricity and medicine. Gardens of Eden are very rare. Once medicine starts to improve health, population (without good birth control) increases and the land becomes exhausted. China, for example, for various reasons has lost 30% of its arable land in the last 40 years, although soil erosion from the pressure of population is no new event.[499] Add to this the inherent excitements shown on television, and the urge to belong to the 'have-mores' is enormous. And once industrialisation starts, fuelled in part by the exploitations of multinationals, then, as it was here during the Industrial Revolution, people become attracted to the towns and trapped.

---

[498] Galbraith, J.K. (1993)
[499] Runnels, C.N. (1985a)

We contented lot in the West are so distanced from the harshness and cruelties of nature that we can forget just how much a difference simple comforts make. The enticements to produce more begins very gently in the softening of the harshness of surviving and the edging in of small physical comforts. Once hooked on physical comforts, improved foods, and enthused with status desires to become 'modern', especially in the young, who would want to go backwards? Mud huts are all very well, but air-conditioned, warm and watertight rooms are even better. From here, as the generations unfold, each trying to improve on the one before, competitiveness grows with beliefs that since a little made things better, more will make things better still. More and more hours are given to work for those extra comforts, or sometimes even to standstill, and the social dynamics of life, sources of happiness and security, are changed forever.

Many writers have noted that the pursuit of happiness, as a goal written into the American constitution, is illusory.[500] It is illusory because it is so tied to the consumption of things, not the quality of relationships. An evolutionary approach suggests that, on the whole, once out of abject poverty, we are more likely to feel good when we are loved, cared for, find a place in a group, feel accepted, find a mate(s), gain respect and prestige, can trust in others and are free from persecution. Only a few of these things are related directly to material possessions. The idea that somehow these social needs can be supplanted with material things in the pursuit of happiness is a myth. There are few (apart from some schizoid people perhaps) who would find happiness living alone on a desert island, even if all material wants could be satisfied by a Star-Trek-like replicator. In any case, happiness may be so ethereal that it turns out to be a pointless pursuit and meaning; rather, commitment and involvement become more the focus of people's lives.

However, we mustn't over-romanticise, because of course there is a relationship between material possessions and states of mind. It would be easy for those inclined to argue that people don't really need economic power, all they need is

---

[500] Rowe, D. (1992). Offers a very detailed and insightful exploration on how we have become so hooked on material things and how frustration and anger at not having them seem central to our experiences of ourselves and our lives.

to be good at making friends. Even Freud in his letters to his friend Fleiss, noted how his money worries constantly affected his mood.[501] Although material possessions cannot purchase happiness, they can protect from abject misery and fear. Economic power is a certain kind of power which, without it, can have a mutilating effect on the social fabrics of life and one's personal psychology. Poverty pushes us towards bleak insecurity, frustration and constant worry. So economic power may not offer a route to happiness, but it does offer a defence against insecurity and hopelessness. It does expand choices. Money cannot buy happiness or love but can protect us from certain kinds of stress and unhappiness.

Furthermore, disparities in wealth also bring disparities in the perception of happiness. Maybe I would be a happier person if I had the salary of X. Maybe that extra holiday, the bigger house and car I saw last week, would make me happier. If only I could afford to get on the Internet! I have a patient who is wealthy, and she fears and believes that others will wonder what she has got to be depressed about – her wealth should liberate her from depression. So disparities, as we have said, can ignite envy and craving. These are deliberately fuelled by the media beaming its pictures and intrusive messages into our homes – messages of what others have, of their comforts and opportunities. Advertising worries not at all about stimulating desires that cannot be satisfied except by the few. In this it is callous; as showing a child a new toy and them marvelling at it before saying, "Ah, but your parents are not wealthy or competent enough to be able to buy it; you belong to the unable not the able to have". And, of course, lurking all the time is social comparison. I am given a 10% raise and am very pleased by that until I hear that another person in my department got a 20% raise – now I feel less happy. The amount I'm getting is the same, but the social comparison (remember that sexual selection strategy from Chapter 2?) changes my experience of the pleasure of the money.

---

[501] I am grateful to David Smail for this observation.

Consumerism is a practice that depends on creating, activating and stimulating desires, wants, social comparisons and envy.[502] It can be highly addictive, and like addictions of all kinds, gives the odd buzz or two. Getting the new house, car or television is not without its pleasures. We can get hooked on the appeal of immediate gratification, the overvaluation of objects, and the inability to deal with frustration. We become trapped in a hopeless conflict of wanting more wages but cheaper goods. The maximisation of our 'spending power' – so much the virtue of capitalism – leads us to the market place, where we buy the cheapest goods (or at least search out the bargains) regardless of concern that some may come from cheap child labour in the third world or the tragic exploitation (of animals or natural resources or pollution) that goes into making these 'things' available. We worry only what something will cost us, not the cost (environmental or social) that has been incurred in its production. We are too distant from its production. Producers will go out of their way to conceal knowledge of production that could put people off buying their products.

As in most things, however, education can help. The more the TV documentaries show what goes on behind the scenes, the more informed we can be. Consumer choice can become a powerful agent for change. What is key here is the preparedness of journalists and others to inform us, and also a preparedness to learn, discover and take responsibility. The boycotting of South African goods during apartheid, or meat from factory-farmed animals, or hard woods taken from tropical forests, or animal furs and ivory, suggest that there are glimmerings of social responsibility in consumption.

On Being Producers, Consumers and Enraged

Consumerism is more than just a fulfilment of material need; it fulfils many psychological ones. It can be used to provide pleasures and offset the boredoms and lurking fears of modern life, to travel and play. It can be used to maintain one's social status or raise it. In my son's school, to have the right football strip,

---

[502] Lasch, C. (1979/1991)

trainers and haircut is a sign of prestige, being cool – no less than having a certain type of car, or going to certain types of restaurants, or joining the right golf club. One can define one's social status by one's purchasing power. Prestige comes not from what one can share, but from what we can purchase and possess. For many, consumerism is a skilful education in narcissism, as Lasch[503] made so clear. One must have 'it', whatever it is. We find it difficult to tolerate frustration and if we lose resources, this can bring abject misery.

The problem with consumerist-led ideals is that we tend to see consumers and producers as separate people. But to be a consumer, we have to work (unless we have inherited or won money, of course). The quality of our lives and our happiness depends as much, if not more so perhaps, on the quality of our lives as producers, how we work. For the majority, participation in the consumer society requires considerable sacrifice of time in (for many, repetitive and meaningless) activity. From the day we first go to school to the day of our retirement, our free time is highly structured. We exist in a socially segregated and limited world of nine to five, or longer. We are brought up knowing that much of our lives will be spent in factories, offices and other places of work, which, were we to win the lottery, we certainly would not choose. We may have to associate with strangers and people we may not like, bosses who bully and threaten, men who sexually or racially harass, and people whose personalities simply grate on us. We battle against bureaucracies and worry that if we do not keep going all that we have built around us will turn to dust. Increasingly, we recognise that our jobs are unstable and easily lost. To compensate for the long hours spent in these factories or stuffy offices, and the stress of it, more material things are needed to feel better, to reward us. This is captured in the dictum, "I worked hard for it so I deserve it". Our expectations of what we deserve are built day-by-day by advertising, social comparison and envy. We work to satisfy the addictions we have been infected with, to protect from insecurity, compensate us for our exhaustion, keep the wine on the sideboard, support our personal identities from our jobs.

---

[503] Lasch, C. (1979/1991)

There is general agreement that our lives as producers (at work) have become more harsh and unpleasant in the last decade or so. We have concentrated so much on efficiency and competition (to produce the most at the least cost) that we seem to have forgotten that the quality of our lives comes from our relationships and sense of security. Moreover, we see again that, freed from restraints, many in industry are reverting back to exploitative working practices and will cut corners on workers' protections if they can (e.g., employ more part-timers). When companies today announce huge profits and efficiency savings, we are increasing concerned with how this was done – that is, the working practices involved. Some years ago, a patient of mine told of how a new private security firm had come in to run his division. They cut the hourly rate from £7 to £4.50, saying they never pay more, and asked for increased working hours (12-hour shifts). One person, who could not afford his mortgage (and had become depressed and so became my patient), took a serious turn for the worst. This kind of thing is happening across the nation. Union powers have been so curtailed there is little they can do. If the 'workers' don't like it, they are told they are free to leave. These environments do brutalise people, make no mistake, and advantage those ruthlessness enough to "get results". It is rather alarming that there now seem few in politics that voice these concerns – that looks to the quality of people lives in the contexts they spend much of their time.

There is a hidden rage in us from finding ourselves contextualised in these worlds of work or poverty, which eat so much of our time. In a recent newspaper poll, 40 percent said they felt tired most of or all of the time. We have to put up with this, of course, because not to do so threatens us with being dumped outside a 'productive' life. By middle age, many are looking to retire, provided they have the means to create reasonable lives. The lottery win becomes a dream for release to a far more self-directed life. Our rage spills out in consumerism and lack of care for what we consume or how we produce it. We will not be frustrated. At the Rio conference on the environment in 1992, George Bush made clear that he would not take any action that threatened American jobs. He knew perfectly well that the anger released against him should he have done so could lose him the election – though he lost anyway.

Disparity Amplification, Biology and Mental Health

The Myth that Economics is Biologically Neutral

There have been, as we saw in Chapter 4, many sociological theories which see all human feelings and values as socially constructed, that the social is neither informed by the biological nor constrained by it. One understands the desires of such theorists – to avoid genetic-type deterministic arguments, and to try to expose the way cultural values can do such harm. However, as noted repeatedly, the lack of respect for the archetypal in us is also a dangerous illusion. So we must be clear, that the political and economic are not biologically neutral – that we evolved to live in certain ways, and if we deviate too much from that, without looking after our basic human social needs, then we will suffer.

It is worth repeating themes covered before, which include that from the moment of birth one's life expectancy can be determined by where one lives and in what type of community one finds oneself. Simple comparisons between the Third World and the developed nations make this obvious. However, even in developed countries, all is far from well. Recent research has found that differences in many health outcomes are related to socio-economic status, and this is not just for the extremes.[504] While life expectancy has been static or improving for the better-off, it has been falling in the poorest sections of society. The increasing rates of death among the poor especially makes sad reading. In men, for example, not only is there increasing risk among less moneyed groups of various diseases such as heart disease, but on average the managerial and professional classes live eight years (nearly 10 percent longer) than unskilled workers, and it's worse for the unemployed.[505] Moreover, suicide has increased 300 percent in the last decade or so in younger males.[506] TB is making a comeback in the poorer sections of some cities. In fact, it is *disparities of wealth*

---

[504] Adler et al. (1994)

[505] Donnison, D. (1992). See also Wilkinson, I.G. (1992).

[506] I have discussed this in more detail elsewhere (Gilbert, P. 1992a).

not GNP that best predicts health outcomes in the developed world. Some of these findings can be attributed to lifestyles such as smoking (although clearly not suicide).

But there are many other factors which indicate it is relative not absolute poverty that is so damaging. The poor are more likely to live close to industrial centres with all their pollutions. The poor cannot escape into the leafy suburbs. Compared to the wealthy, they are more likely to live in overcrowded spaces, with all the tensions that creates. Their houses are also more likely to be damp and in poor repair (e.g., tower-block estates). The poor also have less healthy diets. They may not be able to afford to pay electricity, gas or water bills. The need for fridges comes from the way food is marketed today. Without personal transport (in a car-dependent economy), they may not be able to travel to services (e.g., as hospitals become more centralised). And they are more likely to live passive lives: bored, aimless, worried about the future and trapped in houses with children. There are powerful links between a person's state of mind and their physical health.

Stress of many kinds affects the immune and cardiovascular systems. When we look at what these stresses are, stresses which are so biologically powerful and potential deleterious, we can run a long list: from the aesthetic awfulness of the estate to the hopelessness of unemployment and the dashing of aspiration; from the worries and fears of debt and loan sharks to the inherent relationship tensions of living with constant frustration; from the loss of self-worth to the sense of having been abandoned and marginalised; from the thwarted desires to escape to the serious restriction of any kind of choice. The word redundancy, used to fire people and whole sections of society means, after all, 'no longer necessary or wanted'.[507] As we noted in Chapter 4, people internalise and take identities from their social environments.

---

[507] Some commentators have noted that along with single parent families, young males are finding themselves increasingly redundant in the modern world. There is no work for them and they are ill equipped or skilled to join modern working technological industries, simply labouring is becoming less useful. Nor are they equipped with much emotional sensitivity of life. Many have grown up in tense, aggressive homes pervaded with hopelessness. They make poor fathers and poorly committed companions to women

In the Government's Health of the Nation publication there is only one passing reference to poverty and inequality and little recognition of the way the socio-economic impacts on the biological. The government wants the NHS to sort out the mess while at the same time cutting beds and producing meaningless statistics to parade at party conferences. Recent research has suggested that high users of costly emergency health services come from the socially disadvantaged, the stigmatised groups, the homeless, those with drug and alcohol problems, victims of violence and the mentally ill. Moreover, the rates have been increasing.[508] Summarising one observer, Malone notes,

> Previously the poor were blamed for not using medical services enough, for relying on their own resources and for undue suspicion of medicine. Now they are blamed for relying too much on admittedly ineffective medical services and not enough on their own resources.[509]

In regard to mental ill-health things are bad. Work by Brown and Harris[510] found that depression, which is at epidemic portions in some communities, and is far more prevalent in poor rather than wealthy communities, can arise from a mixture of vulnerability factors and provoking agents or life events. In working class communities, where (depending on your definition of depression) the rates of depression can be well over 50% the most common vulnerability factors for women are low self-esteem, having no close relationships, having three or more children at home and no outside employment. Upon these vulnerability factors any life event with long-term implications, such as loss of a (husband's) job or the breakup of a relationship, can trigger depression. One of the key consequences is a collapse into hopelessness and feeling trapped with no way out. Yet up to a third of (non-psychotic) depressions will remit with the onset of a positive or fresh start event. The problem is, of course, that as one becomes depressed it becomes more difficult to present oneself as confident to potential employers or potential partners or to summon the perseverance necessary to

---

and can be filled with anger and contempt. However, their protests need not worry us for we can build more prisons.

[508] Malone, R.E. (1995)

[509] Malone, R.E. (1995), p.471

[510] Brown, G.W. and Harris, T.O. (1978)

look for work, find out about one's entitlements or fight with councils, look for friends, etc. So, creating opportunities for fresh start events fall away. Even if one is vulnerable to psychotic problems, what often triggers relapse is social factors, such as poverty, unemployment and poor housing.

There is also evidence that in homes fraught with frustration and stress of unemployment, boredom and financial restraint, physical abuse of children increases. As more than one patient said to me, "I am always on a short fuse and I can lash out at the kids and then hate myself for it. I think there is something wrong and nasty about me". There is much in mental ill-health that is like poverty itself – a vicious circle. As people become depressed, they also become more irritable and do less. As these things follow, they lose self-esteem and become more depressed. There are treatments that help people look at how they think about themselves and these can be helpful, but such treatments do not address the underlying social causes of mental ill-health. In some ways they are back to confusing economic power with willpower, and there is evidence that the very poor do not do that well with such therapies.

Even for those in work, the picture is increasingly less than rosy. Around 1.7 million working days are lost to stress, the highest cause of lost working days after back problems. The increasing workloads, as employers expect more for less, and the realisation that if one does not perform there is another in line eager to have a go, means that for some the hours spent at work are increasing. All employers like workaholics and so fan what is in essence a form of craziness. When one is burnt out they are easily replaced. The sheer callousness of some working environments is frightening.

Modern Medicine, Its Dangers and Its Potential

The most important social debates concern how to heal our social divisions and the symptoms of crime and mental illness they spawn. Some look to bio-medicine or think that our problems are all in our genes or neurochemistry up to mischief. However, although genes certainly play a role to vulnerability to some mental health conditions, seeking solutions in genes and synaptic regulation for social problems is extremely dangerous.[511] Nor should we be too hopeful that some new wonder drug (even better than Prozac?) is the solution for the social depressions of our times – as helpful as these sometimes can be for very ill individuals.[512] Drug companies are, of course, pleased to peddle a belief in the value of their wares, because the numbers involved are very many millions, and climbing rapidly, and that is just for the world use of antidepressants! However, these drugs do not change our values, re-educate or create jobs and might even make matters worse by sending us off in the wrong direction in terms of prevention. Nonetheless, some patients often like medical diagnosis because it relieves them of some sense of blame, that there's a physical cause to why they feel so bad and offers potential to feel better – and quickly.[513]

Although for some people psychotropic drugs can be immensely beneficial, even lifesavers, the scale at which they are being used at the moment is a worry. We do not know what these drugs do to our altruistic strategies. Of course, seriously depressed people are not very altruistic, but there are anecdotal reports that for some these drugs may make us care less about others. For example, Newnham reports on the experiences of one writer who took Prozac:

---

[511] Gibbs, W.W. (1995).

[512] Newnham, D. (1995)

[513] Some psychiatrists are quite alarmed at how Prozac has been so hyped in the media and can be given for little more than confidence boosting when antidepressants were designed for serious depression. For mild depression, placebos and clinical caring support do as well as drugs and most psychological therapies do as well for moderate forms, and may even be superior at preventing relapse. In serious depression, drugs are often important – at least in conjunction with therapy. But in a way, psychiatrists only have themselves to blame for the bad publicity, as they have grossly overextended themselves. They still feel it is their given right to be leaders in mental health, despite their social and psychological understanding being poor (after all they rarely study it in any depth). A consultant colleague, who I think is a very caring man, has such vast numbers attending his clinics that trying to do anything other than offer drug relief is near impossible. This is very stressful to him. But psychiatry has never clearly marked the limits of its profession, and it worries about competitors (like psychology). Apart from some notable exceptions, it does not strongly advocate biopsychosocial models nor teach them at medical school, nor does it argue forcefully and in support of psychological inputs. In general hospitals, where the psychological component of illness and health behaviours is huge, many don't have any psychologists at all. The problem with psychology is that it tends to be time-intensive and market economics want quick fixes.

> I decided to try shopping on Prozac... I'm usually fanatical about getting the right present for the right person. This year, as a result of Prozac, when I didn't find the right thing, many friends went without a present, and I feel no shame. It's not so much that you buy less, it's that you don't care what you buy, or if you buy.[514]

Such views should ring alarm bells. If these drugs help us to be less self-critical and shame sensitive, then they could well be personally helpful, but we do not know how they affect empathy and caring behaviour. Do they make us less worried about all kinds of things including the state of the world we live in? Do we feel better because we are just generally less affected by suffering? Suppose we found that some drugs increase social confidence but also reduce altruism and concern for the poor? As far as I know there is no data to judge these issues – maybe they increase altruism (and certainly curing the depression might). Increasingly, various high-profile personalities and leaders admit to taking Prozac – how does it affect their values? Does it increase their confidence to support moral programmes or does it reduce their concern to do so and simply increase their own internal sense of status? And do we know if increases in confidence are matched by real improvements in ability? The mildly hypomanic can think they are doing good work but others around them might not share that view. The mildly hypomanic will then blame others for not seeing their talent. We need more research here.

Some centuries ago, public health professionals became very interested in the creation of sanitation and hygiene to prevent the spread of diseases, creating minimum standards of food and nutrition, social support for new and young mothers along with child care, instigating immunization programmes and in general trying to combat potentially toxic environmental impacts on physical health. All of this has come about as science has revealed how our bodies work and interact with the environment. We are now at a point in our history where we are beginning to understand how our minds interact with our psychological and social environments and are changed by them. Increasingly, public health programmes are beginning to articulate how some psychosocial environments

---

[514] Newnham, D (1995), p.12

actually cause brain damage, impact on the immune system and alter cardiovascular processes, increasing chances of disease. Stress hormones like cortisol can, when chronic, impact on different areas of the brain, literally burning out pathways. Our psychological environmental toxicity operates at many levels: on the brains and bodies with which we mature the constructions of personal identities, social roles and their biological substrates; on family and community life; on hopes, expectations and aspirations; and on the shapes and forms of social frustration and deprivations. If we are to stop living like crazy, then we must address the environments that drive us crazy; environments that thwart and starve us of our basic social needs and stimulate the darker archetypal potentials. Nowadays, these are to be addressed not by drugs but by economic, entrepreneurial and political enterprise and dedication to do so. We must make improving the psychological environments that fuel mental health and mental wellbeing a priority. Indeed, the World Health Organisation has already begun to make these aspects clear:

> Without peace and social justice, without enough food and water, without education and decent housing, and without providing each and all of us with a useful role in society and an adequate income, there can be no health for the people, no growth and no social development.[515]

Conclusion

This chapter has outlined a number of economic mythologies that take some account of our evolved nature and social realities. We noted the current myth that individuals are better able to spend their money wisely than governments. This is, of course, is a myth because we can't protect ourselves from diseases, famines, economic ups and downs, or wars, nor can individuals plan on anything like the scale necessary to build or run the infrastructure of the modern state. It is because we remain mutually dependent on each other that we need to have a social system that both recognises this mutual dependency and legislates in a way that advantages it and brings as many into the productive (or at least

---

[515] Quoted in Gilbert, P. (1992a), p.13.

participating) life of society as possible. We need far more thought about the quality of our lives as producers. Work stress is not only bad for our health but when we act out our frustrations, it is bad for our work colleagues and families as well.

When it comes to financing social policy, altruism is an ideal (a moral philosophy) as much as a directly felt experience: i.e., in paying taxes we are working with our ideals and do not pay them because we have direct contact with (or gain prestige from) the beneficiaries. Paying tax can feel like a personal loss. Complex societies need complex infrastructures, and governments who abandon this clear need are divisive and destructive. They will, via their appeal to selfishness set us on course to *Blade Runner* societies and other nightmares. In some parts of the world, we are there already. Moreover, as the world becomes more globalised and interconnected, it needs governments who don't perpetrate elitist visions of the West and foster the worst aspects of tribalism: that only those within our own boundary should be of our concern. It is very easy to do because we have archetypal potentials to be emotionally gripped by this. Yet we are all part of the same species. We are all part of humanity. Not one of us chose to be born where we were, when we were or how we were.

While one can understand the intellectual, moral and emotional appeal of communism, it completely ignored the archetypal in us and was hijacked by it as a consequence. However, it has left a vacuum of uncertainty around how to create a socially just economic means of production that includes and benefits the many not just the few, that does not exploit individuals nor the environments in which they are operating, and that has at its heart a genuine wish to create goods and services that will benefit humanity rather than harm them. Whereas the right wing clearly articulate competitive motivations, these archetypal potentials of our minds, the left are struggling to articulate how to stimulate and instigate altruistic ones. Just simple issues like how to pay taxation so that it doesn't feel like a loss, or how to make people feel good about being altruistic.

Unbridled, non-altruistic capitalism, that lacks a clear understanding or appreciation of the importance of mutual dependency and the need to constantly redistribute the products of labour, simply produces so many losers that the privileged live more and more in a drawbridge society, hoping to shred themselves of their social responsibility and protect themselves from the unrest and protests such behaviours create. Disparity amplification, without controls, does not produce a common good but a privileged or contented good for a (increasingly shrinking) few. Moreover, the accumulations of wealth actually inhibit the free flow of talent and one ends up with the old boy network of the incompetent. The privileges of wealth are turned, therefore, not to create greater social responsibility in a fairer society, but to protect privilege. As wealth accumulates, generosity reduces, because unlike hunter-gatherer societies, in which one's very survival depended upon sharing resources, controlling and non-sharing offers advantages in the modern world.

Those concerned with social policy have usually been presented with a conflict of considering what is fair, helpful and altruistically desirable with what is economically possible. Rarely has mental health wellbeing or even the activation of archetypal potential within our minds been related to economic policy or causes for concern. These are not central to the purpose of economics. Yet, is it how we *feel* about things that lead us to behave well or badly? On the whole people behave more reasonably if they feel supported with a respected place in society.

If psychologists can make one contribution to these complex issues of modern life, then it must be to spell out time and time again that the economic cannot be divorced from either the psychological or biological. Evolutionary psychology in particular can focus on economics because one of its key concerns are the strategies that evolved to control the distribution of resources: inter-and intra-sexual competition. Economic expediency may produce environments that are efficient and productive up to a point but are not particularly pleasant to live in. We must, at some point, decide whether we will be like ants, simply serving a system of forces that swirl about us (for humans, the unrestrained market), or whether we wish to have the system serve us – as human beings. We will engage a different style of thinking and a different set of values according to how we decide which we want. We are working out how not to live like crazy.

12: WORKING FOR COMPASSION

Sadly, aggression is often perceived as 'more interesting' than prosocial acts. News makers know this effect and use it, with the consequence that violence has a much greater probability of being reported than prosocial acts. Even scientists may regard aggression as more stimulating, as a more common behaviour: until recently, the scientific literature on violence and aggression by far exceeded that on prosocial behaviour, cooperation and altruism.[516]

While we have given much space to self-focused competitiveness and rank-defensive, threat-based processing, which underpin some of the dark sides of our archetypal nature, we have focused less on altruism and caring. However, caring for ourselves, each other, our environments and the world we live in may be the most important archetypal potentials within us that we now desperately need to develop. Indeed, caring motives may be crucial for not only inhibiting some of the darker sides of our minds but also creating physiological states that are conducive to wellbeing. Prosocial and compassionate behaviour can be developed, so there is indeed and some hope for us – but we'll need to work on it.[517] As the volumes by Kurtines and Gerwitz[518] make clear, prosocial behaviour is open to learning, maturation and social controls as well as being inhibited.

So, this chapter explores some aspects of caring, kindness, helpfulness and compassion. It will not look too closely at parent-child relationships, as this is covered in many other books. Rather, it explores various dimensions of caring

---

[516] Hinde, R.A. and Groebel, J. (1991), p.3

[517] The role of social context and social learning on prosocial behaviour is outlined in many different ways; see Eisler, R. (1990); Hinde, R.A. and Grobel, J. (1991, eds.); see Howell, S. and Willis, R. (1989, eds.); Power, M. (1992); Sampson, E.E. (1993).

[518] Kurtines, W.M. and Gerwitz, J.L. (1991). This is a three volume set of readings that give a wealth of ideas on the development and social contexts of moral behaviour. See also Eisenberg, N. and Mussen, P.N. (1989).

and ways that have been suggested to help bring caring more to the forefront of our minds and actions and social forms.

Beyond Genetic Bounds

Although, as we have seen in earlier chapters, there are very good reasons for thinking that caring behaviour has boundaries around it, because of kin relationships and opportunities for reciprocal relating, we are an intensely caring, self-sacrificing species way beyond these boundaries. Consider, for example, the medical professions where people will work for years, day in day out, with people (and animals) who are suffering, confronting the most horrendous of pains, for one reason only, to try to help them. Not only that, but 'helping others' gives a sense of joy, meaning and purpose, and in many studies, is given as one of our most important goals in life.

Many of the diseases that have haunted humanity are now being rendered relatively harmless by medicine. Smallpox, for example, is extinguished. In fact, we can think of vast numbers of professional activities where the only focus of the activity is to help others in some way, be it teaching, police or fire and rescue services, and do this on a regular basis: even repetitively almost every day! Even in less obviously caring-focused professions such as shop assistants, some have a real desire to be helpful that goes beyond just being paid to do a good job. We are confronted time and time again with the fact that we are species that has multiple archetypal possibilities for caring, compassion and morality. Although some may argue that this is all based upon desires to create good impressions in the mind of others (the self-promoting reasons) as the evolutionary driver, at one level this doesn't really matter. The fact is our potential for helping each other including strangers is extraordinary. These are the keys to our salvation. However, caring, compassion and morality are nestled within many other motivational archetypal potentials. Furthermore, these are not necessarily the easiest or most automatic, especially in threat contexts, and within this may require personal cultivation and cultural assistance. Yet when cultivated, these archetypal sides of our evolved minds and brains can have the most extraordinary effects. These effects are not only within our own bodies and minds, literally affecting the connections in our brains and the hormones flowing through our bodies, but also in the cultures and relationships we create that are then self-reinforcing.

Creating the Conditions

Keep in mind a principle mentioned a number of times which is that evolved strategies, phenotypes and archetypes try to create the conditions in other minds for them to replicate. Just like bacteria in your gut try to create conditions for them to survive. So, for example, in environments that are safe and support sharing, caring strategies are working *through the minds* in that community creating interpersonal styles of relating that facilitate caring and sharing actions. The strategies are creating the conditions for them to operate and hence over the very long term gain survival around reproductive success. In contrast in unsafe and threatening environments, defensive self-focused strategies will be influencing the minds of others so that people around one also utilise and develop competitive self-focused strategies.

We need to get away from thinking about individuals with 'individual souls' and much more about flows of information between interacting organisms which are basically playing strategies and co-organising each other. In *Human Nature and Suffering* I discussed the ideas of autopoiesis, which relates to the inherent self-organising principles of biological forms. However, what needs to be better clarified is that actually we could think of these processes in terms of a collection of minds. In fact, as we have a conscious mind, we can be conscious of the content of the strategies that are literally working through our own field of consciousness. We are basically experiencing (physiological) patterns (for love, hate, sexual desire, caring and sharing) in the field of consciousness. We are consciously experiencing the playing out of nature's mind. If we over-identify with content then, as the Buddhists would argue, we will get lost in the illusion of the self. In reality, consciousness is formless, but of course it is the consciousness of consciousness that the issue. To put this in a Buddhist context, the nature of mind is empty but is filled by the content created by (in our case) biologically evolved archetypal potential. The point is that through consciousness and with awareness training, we can begin to choose what aspects of our archetypal potentials we bring into the world: what we act out in the world, and therefore the world we create and how. We are influencing the minds around us. Every action has a ripple effect, no matter how small. Compassion cultivation therefore is partly rooted not just in archetypal potential but in insight into the nature of our minds which becomes the basis for cultivating it.

Self-Interest

Nonetheless we cannot begin an exploration of compassion without saying something on the thorny old problems of self-interest and conflicts of interest. Clearly, it is in the arenas of conflicts of interest that the issue of compassion (facilitation or inhibition) becomes most salient. A question exists then on the degree to which altruism and care of others is bounded by self-interest. As discussed in previous chapters this has occupied sociobiological theories for some time.[519] However, it is important to separate genetic self-interest from personal self-interest and plain callous selfishness. People can act in highly altruistic ways (behave quite selflessly) but still be behaving in line with genetic self-interest (e.g., care is directed to relatives or those similar to oneself).[520] But there is an obvious difference between the personal self-interest of the antisocial person who feels little responsibility to others, lacks empathy, is exploitative and aggressive, must get their own way and blames others for any setbacks[521] in contrast to the prosocial behaviour of a person who (for example) takes moral principles seriously, gains pleasure from forming good supportive relationships and takes an interest in the welfare of others and the environment. Having said that, both personal selfishness, in contrast to personal responsibility-taking, and compassionate behaviour are highly socially contextualised. Even a prosocial person may support their group (or country) behaving in highly antisocial ways

---

[519] See MacDonald, K.B. (1988) for a discussion. Also Burnstein et al. (1994) for some research findings.

[520] Burnstein, E., Crandall, C. and Kitayama, S. (1994). In regard to altruism and prestige, see Hill, J. (1984).

[521] Gibbs, J. (1991)

and be persuaded by arguments that we have to look after ourselves even in the face of gross inequalities.

In some societies, individualism and the importance of (narcissistic) self-promotion is enhanced, whereas in other societies caring and egalitarian behaviours are more socialised.[522] Just as sexual behaviour can be totally detached from leaving offspring behind (e.g., using contraception), so caring behaviour can be socialised to be directed to a variety of others, not just kin: e.g., to the environment, other nationals and animals. Here we may speak of concern with the welfare of the other. We are not victims of the genes, but rather our capacity for altruism may be deep or shallow depending on many experiences we have after birth. If societies and cultures can vary so wildly on sexuality, the basis of reproductive behaviour (Spartan homosexuality was prized, whereas in right-wing Christian society it can be despised and feared), we can see just how powerful cultures are on motivational and behavioural processes.

The focus of these various prosocial socialising arenas is on the construction of self-identity. It matters greatly whether one gains an inner sense of self-esteem from getting away with cheating (e.g., stealing), ambition and self-promotion or from caring and altruistic behaviour. This does open the possibility that many forms of caring are in the service of maintaining self-esteem; we behave (supposedly) compassionately to others because we feel good about it and it boosts our sense of status/worth. Indeed, altruism maybe given a high status rating by a community and we might gain prestige for selfless behaviour.[523] We may even compete to be (seen as) the most altruistic – as can happen in some hunter-gather societies.

There are, of course, dangers of caring when it is in the service of status and self-esteem. We may adopt the following courses of action:

---

[522] Hinde, R.A. and Grobel, J. (1991, eds.); Howell, S. and Willis, R. (1989, eds.); Lasch, C. (1979/1991). Sampson, E.E. (1993)
[523] Hill, J. (1984); Barkow, J.H. (1989)

a) Behave (in what we believe to be) caring ways primarily to make ourselves feel good. Some who follow 'politically correct' behaviours might be caught up in this. It is the stance of moral superiority.

b) Attempt to create a good impression such that it is the impression on others and not the caring behaviour itself that motives us. As we saw in Chapter 7, this is not untypical of cult leaders and in political manipulation. We can feign caring.

c) Behave in a caring way to calm and appease potential aggression and conflicts. This is a form of submissive behaviour. Compassion and 'niceness' can become confused. Some therapists may act in a caring, non-challenging way to be nice and avoid conflicts with their patients or challenge their exploitative behaviours.

So caring 'behaviour' it is not always motivated by genuine empathy and concern for the other.

Caring often involves complex moral dilemmas. For example, anti-abortionist groups often claim a moral, compassionate position, but we do not know how many would also vote for paying higher taxes to provide for the children who need extra help, or for the communities who live in poverty and where health problems are so much in urgent need of resources. Anti-abortionists can be a powerful lobby for the right wing, who actually wish to reduce taxes and benefits to the poor and disadvantaged. Yet on the other side, the real tragedies of abortion may be downplayed in the pursuit of people's freedom to choose.

Caring behaviour can also be inhibited by fears of alienating and creating envy in others, or being seen as appeasers. For example, if we become aware that (say) terrorism and fundamentalism are born of poverty and a sense of being excluded and exploited, a foreign government might try to rectify this by diverting funds to these communities. It is fairly obvious to many that what would reduce the tensions of the Palestine-Israel conflict would be a kind of Marshall Plan to lift the Palestinians out of their abject poverty. However, governments who might do this are at risk of being accused of being appeasers, rewarding terrorism and showing favouritism.

Perhaps the dilemmas are captured in the well know phrase, "the road to hell is paved with good intentions". *This makes compassion a complex dimension of human behaviour.* Having said that, however, a good case can be made for arguing that it is in our long-term self-interests to study compassion, to try to develop compassionate relationships and try to reduce the competitive inflations that are now flooding over us. Not only are people more mentally healthy and happier in supportive, caring environments,[524] but (on the whole) caring (rather than exploitation) reduces the number of (envious) enemies. A caring psychology could be helpful in our national and international political endeavours, attacks on poverty, in our work places and families, and in our treatment of the environment.[525] But like many of our internal archetypal potentials, it has to be educated and socially promoted. This is what we will now focus on. Here we will explore three basic approaches to caring and compassion: the religious/spiritual, the psychological, and the social.

The Spiritual Quest to Caring and Compassion

Caring Through Enlightenment

Chapter 9 explored the problematic aspects of some religions and how they can actually create distress and suffering rather than relieve it. Indeed, some religions have often utilised the sexual-competition rank archetypes to advance themselves – making them prone to grandiosity, submission to a higher authority and at risk of being destructively narcissistic. However, it would be unfair and unhelpful to leave the matter there for in fact many religious leaders have intuited the problems and recognised that the archetype(s) of caring is by far the more important for a harmonious social life – indeed for a spiritual and an enlightened life.[526] So, in pursuit of caring and compassion, we can start our

---

[524] Argyle, M. (1987)
[525] Gore, A. (1992)
[526] Schumaker, J.F. (1992)

journey with religion – not least because it is the most important source of caring ideals for many. Indeed, some people believe that caring behaviour is often enacted because of religious ideals and experiences.

In nearly all religions, the complex mosaic of beliefs and values will include values of compassion and caring for others – and this is attractive to many. Indeed, people will be innately attracted to groups who offer the opportunity to make alliances with cooperative and caring others, and feel protected and supported by them. But many religions also suggest the spiritual path is far more than just forming good relations with others and God. Spirituality, they argue, also depends on deep compassion about coming to understand the self, peering through the many contradictions of mind and coming to a state of grace, insight and enlightenment[527]. In this 'state of being', care and compassion naturally increase because the boundaries between self and others dissolve. This dissolving of boundaries and reduced marking of differences between "them and us" (a source for superiority) may be a key cognitive-emotional factor, which enables us to recruit our altruistic psychology to large numbers of others outside our small groups and families.

The differences in religions have been on how to do it: how to achieve these states of mind which open the person to being altruistic to millions rather than just a few. Should it be through developing a relationship with God or the self, by using techniques such as prayer, good acts and/or meditation and insight into the contents of mind? Should it be via reason or emotion? Should it be by forcing all to come under the same leader (God) with the same values, or through acknowledging that differences of value and belief are superficial and do not separate us? Should it be with use of the metaphors of family (God as father, and we are all brothers and sisters), or by appreciating our separateness yet joint sharing in the suffering of life. Religions also differ on fundamental ideas about

---

[527] By deep, I mean going well beyond caring to create good impressions, to feel good about oneself or to appease, but from a genuine concern for the others welfare and development: indeed, fully realising the very fact that we are all dependent on each other and that an autonomous self is, in many ways, an illusion; Sampson, E.E. (1993). See also Goswami, A. (1991).

the nature and reasons for suffering and its cure, and even on the nature of 'reality' itself.[528]

Many writers have drawn parallels between psychotherapy and religion – at least, its prosocial forms.[529] These parallels are in how the person comes to more deeply understand themselves and their relationships. Both psychotherapy and religious experience can involve acquiring new types of knowledge, gaining insight, making cognitive changes, and generating new emotional experiences. Both involve human relationships, be these with teachers, prophets, gurus or therapists. Moreover, both, usually, involve the development of caring, either for oneself (the depressed person learns to stop self-criticalness and self-injury) and to stop hurting others out of spite. Symington[530] also notes that both religion and psychotherapy could have a joint aim – to help cure, or at least reduce, narcissistic competition.[531]

We could explore any number of religions and the way they expose our needs for being cared for, and our needs to care for others, and have a sense of belonging. So, I have to be highly selective and have chosen to focus on Buddhism for a number of reasons that I hope will become clear as we move along. One is, as Michael McGhee[532] notes, the increasing interest in Buddhism in the West. Many, dismayed at their own sense of unhappiness and emptiness and the problems in the world may turn to cults or new sects but others are turning to Buddhism. The reasons for this 'turning towards Buddhism' are many, but it may be partly because it offers an opportunity for spiritual insights which do not depend on obeying or offending authorities, and partly because Buddhism offers windows on complex theories of the mind with various methods of gaining enlightenment based on these theories. In fact, Buddhism

---

[528] Sampson, E.E. (1993)

[529] A typical example of this is Symington, N. (1994).

[530] Symington, N. (1994)

[531] It may be that through the pursuit of (new) spiritual values and insights people will be inspired to change life styles. And in so far as spiritual and existential quests can set us on course to ask questions and look deeply into ourselves, to come to know better the mosaic of our possibilities, then we could benefit from a new spiritual regeneration.

[532] McGhee, M. (1995). The sociobiologist-ethologist John Crook also gives a wonderful outline of the benefits of a Buddhist approach to mind.

can be seen as a psychology with specific practices for mind-awareness training and not a religion at all. Insofar as it opens a path to spirituality that is something that naturally emerges.

One Way of Reducing Narcissistic Competition

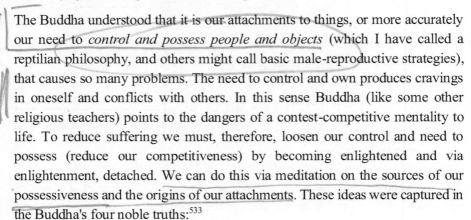

The Buddha understood that it is our attachments to things, or more accurately our need to *control and possess people and objects* (which I have called a reptilian philosophy, and others might call basic male-reproductive strategies), that causes so many problems. The need to control and own produces cravings in oneself and conflicts with others. In this sense Buddha (like some other religious teachers) points to the dangers of a contest-competitive mentality to life. To reduce suffering we must, therefore, loosen our control and need to possess (reduce our competitiveness) by becoming enlightened and via enlightenment, detached. We can do this via meditation on the sources of our possessiveness and the origins of our attachments. These ideas were captured in the Buddha's four noble truths:[533]

> 1. Self-awareness involves suffering, for it involves death awareness also, and all that is associated with this particular life. The existential writers a few thousand years later would argue similarly.
>
> 2. Suffering arises from attachments to things which are by nature impermanent. Above all, the attachment to one's own ego and ego ideals cause suffering because such states of being are made into entities rather than seen as part of a process. It is part of the natural order that everything changes, nothing stays the same. Thus, the searching after permanence is illusory and destined to disappoint. Possessing gives only a temporary relief from suffering (and often actually increases it) via clouding consciousness and maintaining our ignorance.

---

[533] These have been written about by many authors; see, for example, Harvey, P. (1990) and in the context of sociobiology and psychology, see Crook, J. (1980).

3. Relief from suffering is possible by realizing the nature of the self; that in reality, it is both empty and already full. As in Zen, the self is everywhere and nowhere. — Wow!

4. This realisation entails a set of attitudes and behaviours which are open and explorative (not pre-judgemental) to the nature of reality. At all times, the self should be mindful, reflective and an observer of the nature of the mind itself.

In a way, we can see Buddhism (like other prosocial religions) as training the mind to work more and more within the safeness system and not in the defence system (see Chapter 2). It aims to reduce the defensive emotions of both fear and aggression. Some religions do this by working with the care-eliciting motives, by helping us to acknowledge we are all in need of love and compassion and that God does indeed love us. It is through this feeling of love (receiving or being cared for and wanted) that we come to feel safe (or safer) in the world. This is why parental metaphors in religion are so common. Feeling loved and accepted makes it easier to be compassionate to others, as if we are being guided to operate in a highly socially, mutually investing social space.[534]

Unlike religions which focus on relationships to a deity (and our sense of safeness comes from being loved), Buddhism operates particularly as a means to address forms of *frustration* and ruination which arise from thwarted craving. Operating increasingly within the safeness system (see Chapter 2), the mind becomes open and explorative rather than rigid and stereotyped. And the control of arousal is increased. Another way to see it is that consciousness is trained to disengage itself from the vigorous pursuit of various, evolved biosocial goals (e.g., for status, sex, power, ownership, wealth, etc.) that so often control us. To put this yet another way, we in the West believe that happiness is assured by

---

[534] See Chapter 4 for a discussion of the two types of reproductive environment: stable with high interpersonal investment versus unstable with low interpersonal investment. If you use Michael Chance's language, it is the difference of being in the hedonic as opposed to the agonic mode. Caring psychological development and behaviour is far more likely in the hedonic mode (than the agonic), and a good relationship with God (feeling loved) could put us in that mode.

ownership and by what we have. If we are unhappy, we try to get more and better – better food, better cars, more holidays, better relationships, better sex, even a better relationship with God. Buddhism argues that these are all illusory distractions because the goal posts constantly move and one never has enough. It is all impermanent, so sooner or later these things must be given up as we decay and eventually die. It is thus better to focus on *what we are* (and understand the nature of our craving) and indeed the very nature of consciousness itself, rather than what *we want to have*.

Transcendence and Detachment

As noted in the previous chapter, however, abject poverty can produce misery, and thus moving away from 'having' to 'being' probably becomes important only after certain needs are met. Moreover, we can be cautious of the detachment ideas in Buddhism for they are very often confused with transcendence. Enlightened detachment is not at all the same as forcing oneself to simply give up things one clearly needs. I recall reading a book on Zen some years ago which was highly critical of some Western therapy programmes based on Eastern traditions. The author argued that the issue of the 'loss of ego and detachment' is fundamentally misunderstood in the West. One can't lose (transcend) one's ego unless one has an ego to lose in the first place. At times, therapy techniques must strengthen the ego and the person's confidence in themselves to achieve things before embarking on a journey to go beyond it. When the Buddha set out on his path, he was a wealthy prince and very much loved by his family – as far as we can tell. His search did not begin from a vulnerable, poor, care-seeking position as some searches in the West do but to understand suffering in the world. Without caution, the searching for detachment becomes another illusory defence. Transcendence is about *going beyond by process of integration from earlier insights not about jumping stages*. Jumping stages and wanting 'it all now' (e.g., enlightenment) can be typical of the Western mind: "make it happen now, quickly". Just as adulthood transcends childhood, so Buddha-hood transcends personhood. It seems to me that for people who are clearly searching for love, these needs should be acknowledged until they feel safe enough to move on to other existential questions.

I have seen many patients who have got themselves wrapped up in existential questions and internal intellectual debates which are an avoidance of a simple need for human contact and love. Sometimes we call this rationalisation or intellectualisation. What they are constantly running away from is a deep sense of loneliness and grief. Therapy often moves forward when individuals feel safe enough to begin to process intense grief that may relate to often feeling unloved or disconnected. It is a painful journey, not one that can be bypassed through meditation means. Helping them put aside their existential pursuits until they have worked through the *emotional* problems in the care-eliciting system and become able to relate to others without too much fear (e.g., of shame or fear of rejection or being harmed) is often important. As just noted, this often means helping them acknowledge and work through their *grief* (rage and sadness) and sense of detached loneliness before they can go further. One cannot 'detach' oneself from or transform feelings one is repressing or does not acknowledge or understand in the first place. One cannot understand detachment as offering an opportunity for a sense of deeper connectedness from a position of fractured loneliness; one just doesn't have the brain systems developed to do it. Helping people internalise a 'caring other', perhaps through imagery practice and/or and offering what are sometimes called corrective emotional experiences, may be the first step to insight. Helping people grieve is a social process and should not be done alone.

When Westerners seek detachment, and treat their relationships lightly, it is far from clear that this is about enlightenment or compassion. This would be to confuse schizoid disinterest or a narcissistic lack of commitment for enlightenment: states of mind more common than perhaps recognised. Moreover, if one has problems in dealing with conflicts in relationships, it is not at all clear that detaching oneself from them is going to bring enlightenment for this is more akin to social avoidance. Enlightenment leads to detachment not the other way around. The relationship between detachment and enlightenment is thus complex, not simple. Similar can be said of the Christian path of love and union in and through God. Relating to God can as easily be used to avoid painful things as it is to understand them. But understanding this can also lead to self-knowledge.[535]

So again, one cannot easily jump stages. One detaches by moving on, and transforming insight, and maturity. If one is too focused on the goal of detachment rather than enlightenment, one may add another layer of suffering. The paradox of Buddhism is that although it seeks the state of 'detachment from craving or needing', it can be seen as a craving for enlightenment, freedom from rebirth and ending suffering that is actually at its centre. It may replace one craving with another – material possessions for spiritual liberation. Obviously, a number of very experienced practitioners know this very well.

Because detachment is actually rather complex and easily confused with transcendence (moving through and going beyond), it was backed-up by various proscriptions known as the eightfold pathway: right understanding, right mindfulness, right effort, right action, right concentration, right speech, right thought and right livelihood. It was through seeking the sources of our cravings and following the eightfold path that wisdom and compassion were seen to arise. This is why the Dalai Lama[536] has been very in favour of Western science, not its enemy – Buddhism is not detached from, or anti-knowledge of, the world nor is it uninterested in it. Indeed, (the reasoning goes) Lama's reincarnated out of compassion and to help humanity. They don't simply hang around in heaven having a good time, detached from human suffering.

The Buddha recognized that enlightenment, finding wisdom and compassion requires extensive training and deep personal experience in the way the mind works at a number of different levels. No other religion puts this quite so centrally. Thus, as the Dalai Lama has said, Buddhism is not a religion as such, but a science of mind that involves complex guided discovery and mind training. By extensive training in meditation and mindfulness, a person may begin to gain knowledge and insight into the deeper realms of consciousness itself. Direct

[535] Watts, F. and Williams, M. (1988)
[536] Dalai Lama (1993)

experience is more important than blind faith. Indeed, in Buddhism, faith is regarded as unhelpful.

Some Key Themes in Buddhism

For me, Buddhism does four things. First, it indicates, like psychotherapy, that mind training through reflection and inward contemplation is not easy but essential for deeper self-awareness and growth. One must be able to move in one's psyche – to know where one's sadism lies, to know where one's compassion lies and to know how these conflict from time to time. We transcend our hatreds not repress them. We acknowledge our cravings, especially our wanting, possessing and sexual desires. (I'm not enlightened enough to give those up - ah well, back on the wheel). We can learn how our thoughts and motives can have positive or destructive effects.

Second, Buddhism, again like psychotherapy, offers a non-judgemental approach, so that it need not be shameful to find all the shadows of the mind. Indeed, it is essential that one does find at least some of them (so that they do not work unconsciously). In order to set out on this journey of exploration and self-discovery, it is first best to (explore how to) adopt an attitude of loving kindness to self and others. Loving-kindness and compassion training is not something psychotherapy actively advocates, but there is no reason why it shouldn't. Indeed, few psychotherapies nowadays believe that therapy can be helpful unless conducted in an atmosphere of genuineness, positive regard and empathy. A non-caring therapeutic relationship is unlikely to be helpful, and the patient's perception of being valued and cared for does much to help them on their way. So, be it from Buddhism, the prosocial religions or psychotherapy, one begins from a caring position to avoid discovery becoming a source for self-attack or self-dislike, which fractures the ego.

Third, science and knowledge are never a problem, but the way science and knowledge is acquired and used can be. Cold rationality itself (the ideal of some) may not be helpful. We need a *compassionate rationality*. Thus, following a Buddhist path suggests that anti-scientific approaches are delusions and a turning away from the responsibilities of knowledge. Also, there are different ways of knowing, especially in the personal domain. As noted before, you can study all you like about sex, read every manual and do hundreds of experiments on others, but until you have had sex yourself your knowledge is very limited. How would one understand sexual jealousy or love? In the personal domain, internal experience is essential to understanding.

Fourth, and this is where Buddhism does vary from other religions, there is no obvious God who can punish, reward or provide special places or whom one must obey. There is no heavenly rank structure of creators, leaders or commanders. Although concepts of karma, from one life to the next, can be used for a similar purpose, to threaten and cajole, on the whole, leaving those dubious metaphysics aside, there is a kind of university system that as one acquires knowledge one must 'pass out' and onto higher insights. And like a university system, there are teachers and possibly higher teachers who can help to teach one. Thus, it is self-liberating and the spiritual is to be found in oneself as a subjective experience – a version of spirituality that has always existed in the more mystical traditions of other religions.

Buddhism, which has many different schools,[537] will continue to evolve just like all other thought forms. It will do so as it contacts Western thought – which hopefully will be mutually beneficial. It's obvious that there can be no going back to hunter-gatherer life styles. We have to create compassion in our new type of world. It is no good looking on small technologically backward societies and wishing to return. Buddhism, like other religions, must address a new age of economic realities of financial markets, technology and medicine.

Individual v Relationships

Some Problems

Although Buddhism holds many fascinations and insights it is not without problems. One is that Buddhism can be somewhat individualistic – at least in its spiritual dimension. In fact, the Buddha actually left his family to find his own salvation – not a good role model for today. Psychotherapy and Christianity, however, use relationships to help, nurture and enlighten the self. Actually,

---

[537] Harvey, P. (1990)

relationships are so important to how our minds work that they are central to spiritual progress. Indeed, the desire for relationships is at the heart of many spiritual quests. In fact, states of bliss nearly always involve a sense of interconnectedness with others and indeed the universe.[538] This is why, if you remove all the rank psychology from Christianity, the experiences of love and union with another can be transforming. Of course, there is a risk that such forms of union may hide a need for expansion (becoming more and greater than oneself, being chosen, and others are excluded), a theme we noted in Chapters 8 and 10. Some psychoanalysts have argued that these 'merger experiences' arise from desires to return to the womb. Some may be, but I doubt all are.

Second, Buddhism has been a fairly patriarchal religion, as the Dalai Lama himself noted. True, Buddhist societies can often be, in practice, highly egalitarian and relatively non-patriarchal,[539] but one does not need Buddhism for hunter-gatherer societies to show a prosocial structure.[540] Females rarely reach the higher levels of authority. There has never been a female Dalai Lama. It would be very interesting to see what a feminist Buddhism would look like. I would imagine it would focus far more on relationships and care of children.

Despite giving up the pursuit of material possessions, Buddhism has flourished where monks are given high status – they have a way of gaining status because of their holiness. One wonders what would have happened if this had not been so. Indeed, in Tibet, before the Chinese invasion, the Dalai Lama was the highest ranking male of the whole nation, and many were (are) so dependent on his words that the idea of democracy seems frightening to them.[541] He recognises this must change. Like many religions, there is a possibility of gaining status via one's adherence to religious codes. Perhaps only when you have status can you

---

[538] Coxhead, N. (1985)

[539] Norberg-Hodge, H. (1992)

[540] Hinde, R.A. and Grobel, J. (1991, eds.); Howell, S. and Willis, R. (1989, eds.); Sampson, E.E. (1993)

[541] Many of these issues have been discussed in the *Free Tibet Newsletter*. The British Support Group can be contacted at 9 Islington Green, London, N1 2XH.

see it is as empty and that it will not save us from death or life's impermanence. Buddhism has existed, in the main, in a highly status-giving system.

Third, the idea of karma is a belief in a just world or just universe, and we saw where this can get us in the chapter on cruelty. All around us, nature (with its diseases and famines) shows that justice is not one of its concerns. Although, as in psychotherapy, we try to help people see that they can be creating conditions for themselves that are unhelpful – if they are unpleasant to others, then others are likely to be unpleasant back; if you shame people or refuse help, you might create resentful enemies; if you smoke you increase your chances of cancer, etc. That is karmic consequence; the idea of karma moving from one life to the next goes well beyond this simple truth. The idea that people who are born with genetic defects are living out karma seems to me unsatisfactory and callous. Some scholars think that this idea must be placed in its historical context because a belief in karma may help to avoid shame on the afflicted and that brownie points can be earned in helping them.[542]. As we saw in Chapter 10, a belief in consciousness 'as the ground of being' does not imply any notions of a 'just' universe. Obviously given the time these beliefs developed there would have been no knowledge about genes nor the fact that our brains are changed and shaped by our early, maturational experiences (see Chapter 4). Not the fact that, once plumbed in, these biological patterns might be difficult to change. Some people may be biologically more able to work for calm meditation and compassion than others.

It's important to recognise that sometimes traditional beliefs that are passed from generation to generation don't always incorporate new information and can get stuck in outdated views because they are honouring a tradition. This is why science is so important: because we don't honour a tradition, but rather evidence and the changing dynamic understanding of the world. Taking a scientific approach translates into far more concern to provide children with the social contexts and opportunities to develop their brains (e.g., frontal lobes) for prosocial behaviour and feelings. Indeed, the way to move to a compassionate

---

[542] These ideas are discussed by Harvey, P. (1990) and in a different way by Rowe, D. (1992).

society is to train our children for it. In small communities, this may not have been a problem because children were (are) so much part of the community, but in modern societies this is far less so, and what children are taught and how they are socialised is a cause for concern[543]. There is no doubt that religion can help us become more caring, but probably the far greater impact is going to come from understanding the whole nature of caring and moral behaviour, which is a scientific exercise. And we need decent social polices based on this scientific understanding to work with our brains to bring out the best and maximise opportunities for wellbeing.

The Psychological Approach to Care and Compassion

Altruism and Justice

We saw in Chapter 2 that altruism has been a key strategy in primate and human evolution, and that it has been the evolution of altruism that has opened our psychology to the possibilities of construing relationships both in terms of social fairness and caring. Altruism shows itself in our own needs for attachments, care, love, companionship and to avoid exploitation, and also in our desires to offer these things to others. Elsewhere, I[544]have outlined how evolutionary thinkers suggest that issues of fairness, justice and concern to limit exploitation may have evolved from cooperative, reciprocal altruistic strategies involving the importance of alliance formation and the avoidance of cheating. Caring may have evolved from attachment and kin altruistic strategies and biosocial goals, involving more the issue of nurturance, protection and 'looking after' for in-group relations. Corporation and sharing need rules for fairness, non-exploitation, and the regulation of competitiveness so that morality may look different. Moreover, some moral principles will speak to issues of justice and fairness and some will speak to the issues of caring and nurturing. As discussed

---

[543] Norberg-Hodge, H. (1992)
[544] Gilbert, P. (1989)

in *Human Nature and Suffering* these two systems (cooperation and caring) may recruit different internal processing systems, different emotions and be concerned with different issues; they may also start from different places. In humans, cooperation and caring are (probably) highly interactive and if fairness conflicts too much with caring (or vice versa), dilemmas will arise.

So, it is probable that altruism has given us the key motives and psychological competencies for construing fairness and justice and forms the basis of (some forms of) moral behaviour. Kagan[545] feels there is no doubt that we are biologically set up to become moral agents and we become so by mixing various feelings, social proscriptions and prohibitions, and concerns with others. He says,

> Morality will always be a critical human concern because humans want to believe there is a more and a less virtuous outcome in a situation of choice and therefore insist on criteria for action. The fact that two-year-olds are concerned with the correctness or the incorrectness of action implies the primacy of this theme. Humans are driven to invent moral criteria, as newly hatched turtles move towards water and moths towards light. The conditions for moral virtue in moral society – the state that one seeks to attain in order to reassure oneself of one's goodness – include pleasure, wealth, fame, power, autonomy, mastery, nurturance, kindness, love, honesty, work, sincerity and belief in one's freedom. Each is a construction built over time, though traceable to universal affects. The relative prominence of each of these values is not an inevitable product of the human genome, but stems rather from the capacity for empathy with another's distress, shame and guilt over violating standards and preparedness to inhibit actions that provoke disapproval. These are not inconsistent views. The young child is prepared by his biology to become attached to his parents; yet Western culture insists that he eventually develop autonomy and independence from them and be able to cope with distress in their absence, qualities that not only require subjugation of the earlier natural disposition but

---

[545] Kagan, J. (1984)

also ones that are probably not biologically inevitable. The moral sense of children is highly canalized because of a capacity for evaluation and the experience of certain emotions but the surface ethics of a specific community are built from a web of social facts embedded in folk theory. Although humans do not seem to be specifically programmed for a particular profile of moral missions, they are prepared to invent and believe in some ethical mission.[546]

To this can be added the points made in Chapter 8 – that identity depends on answering moral questions of what one finds good and bad, what is worth doing and what is not. The (type of) person one wants to be seen as and the person one wants to experience oneself as being. Moral codes of social fairness can be highly developed in humans and depend on two things: justice and obedience. Justice does not exist in the natural world; it is a creation of the human mind and (often) imposed by a system of corporate laws. The human concern with fair play, the avoidance of cheating and deception and non-exploitation inhibits hostile (power) competitiveness. But fair play depends on the recognition of the status and rights of others and the recognition of the importance of rules over and above the pursuit of egoistic ambition. There has to be a preparedness to recognise the importance of social rules, conform and submit to them, and this has to be a socially shared way of doing things. For fairness to operate outside the watchful eye of social observation (and be more than shame avoidance), these rules have to be tied to personal identity rather than being simply imposed by an institution and mimicked by participating members. It is the degree to which the adoption of moral rules becomes central to one's personal identity that probably determines whether they will be consistently followed in the absence of some external agent. To some extent, the idea of God is useful to a community who wishes to convey the idea that one can never be "outside" the watchful eye of a dominant authority: even one's thoughts may be known to God. But it also highlights the fact that we recognise the importance of social agencies, the law,

---

[546] Kagan, J. (1984), pp.152-153

courts and so on to underpin moral behaviour. Recognising the need for such agencies is an actual part of compassion.

Research has suggested that moral thinking (concern with justice) is not one thing, that it unfolds in stages and changes with context. Highly moral behaviour and loyalty to in-group members might not transfer to out-group members – unless this is regarded as of some importance. There are a number of developmental theories which describe the stages by which people acquire their moral systems and the way the rules of fairness and moral behaviour are internalised. Some argue that moral thinking and behaviour is a purely cognitive process, while others have argued that it is a deeply emotional one.[3] Buddhism certainly favours the latter – aided with trained insight into the illusions of egotistical ideals.

According to the cognitive stage theorists, the stage reached in moral development determines the degree to which individuals are able to construe their actions in relation to others.[547] Reason as the basis of deriving moral principles is derived from older Platonic and Kantian ideas. The best known nosology of moral thinking is that of Kohlberg and his colleagues. These theorists suggest six stages which can be summarised as follows.[548]

Pre-Conventional Morality

Stage 1: The child decides right from wrong on the basis of reinforcement and punishment (usually dispensed by parents).

Stage 2: The child begins to formulate *rules* about social behaviour from what parents (and others) reward and punish. The essential quality, and to some

---

[547] For an overview of cognitive theories, see Kohlberg, L., Levine, C. and Hewer, A. (1983). A more comprehensive treatment is given in Gilbert, P. (1989) and Bee, H. (1992). For discussion of the advantages and disadvantages of stage theories, see Kurtines, W.M. and Gerwirtz, J.L. (1991 eds.), especially Vol. I.

[548] This summary was adapted from Helen Bee (1992) and Kohlberg, L., Levine, C. and Hewer, A. (1983). Bee offers an excellent text on all facets of child and adolescent development.

degree content, of the rules is what results in positive rewards. Issues of fairness and equity of exchange also become important.

Conventional Morality

Stage 3: Group identity becomes important (e.g., family and peer). Rules for moral action become articulated into expectations that self and others have of social behaviour. Maintaining a good image of self becomes important, and trust, reciprocity (reciprocal altruism?) and loyalty are prominent. But moral behaviour can be bounded to whom one sees as part of the group (like the self). Thus, social comparison of *same-different* may play a role. To individuals not identified as part of the group (i.e., those who are different or strange), behaviour may be hostile and exploitative, especially if this is reinforced by the in-group.

Stage 4: There is a shift of focus to identification with society at large. The importance of contribution, obeying group rules, and the rule of law become important elements in the construction of the moral self. On a more negative front, these themes can speak to a rather obsessional and autocratic orientation.

Post-Conventional Morality

Stage 5: Increasing awareness of utilitarian philosophy and the relative nature of social values. Some values become focused on the rights bestowed to others, freedom, liberty, and the right to life.

Stage 6: The sense of moral action is highly internalised. Personal conscience becomes the primary decider of moral action.

Although this is a helpful nosology, it has not been free of criticism. For example, concerns have been raised as to the cultural universality of these stages.[549] Not all cultures value these ideals in the same way. Moreover,

---

[549] Snarey, J.R. (1985); Snarey J.R. and Keljo, K. (1991). There have also been explorations of how people resolved commitments to relationships and obligations with those of justice. Cross-cultural work suggests that Indians give priority to interpersonal

different social contexts may bring out different types of moral thinking. For example, when a group is under threat, they may show stage-3 behaviours. In fighting (say) the Nazis, it is difficult to know if these are stage 3 or stage 6 ideals or some combination. Moreover, they may be context-dependent in that people operate at different levels according to the quality of the relationships (e.g., close-intimate or public).[550]

There is also a difference between moral behaviour as an ideal and aspiration and moral behaviour as a duty. Certain stage 5 ideals can still be seen as a duty. In some societies, honour (which is self- or family-focused) can be the basis for making moral decisions and justifying them, both privately and publicly. Morality and honour become close cousins, although a role for mercy is also often seen as a high ideal.

Another problem is the degree to which knowledge guides action in different contexts. Although an individual may publicly claim adherence to (say) stage 4 ideals, this does not mean they will follow them in practice. Many presidents and prime ministers have sworn to uphold moral and decent values (mostly stage 4 ideals) but clearly do not. Indeed, more and more these days one of the major crises in politics is that we simply do not trust what politicians say. We know that anyone can offer verbal moral standards without the slightest intent of keeping them as soon as the doors are closed. It is the problem of the private and public self again. A so-called moralist can be a tyrant to his close family, and many hide behind moral arguments to unleash the most cruel and persecutory regimes. Moral behaviour, as we have said, can be highly group-focused. At the same time, a government may be proclaiming moral standards at home, but their behaviours to the third world can be deeply immoral.

---

obligations whereas Americans give priority to justice; see Miller, J.G. and Bersoff, D.M. (1992).
[550] Kurtines, W.M. and Gerwitz, J.L. (1991)

Altruism and Caring

Some have suggested that much of our current thinking on morality is related to a masculine obsession with justice, fairness and fears of exploitation.[551] An evolutionary view might be that because males are so fearful of being exploited and out-competed by other males, men have focused moral discourses on these themes (e.g., fairness, rights, etc.) which are important for forming stable non-kin alliances. What has been subordinated in the domain of moral theories (feminists argue) is caring and nurturing.[552] These concerns may be closer to the psychology of women – especially since their alliances were (in the past) mostly kin-based, and care of offspring fell mostly to them.

On the whole, feminists don't use evolutionary insights or ideas, despite the fact that these often support some of what they suggest. Gilligan[553] has argued that there are caring forms of moral construction which also contribute to an identity of a moral self. These relate not to issues of fairness but to issues of caring, awareness of suffering and the desire to help and nurture others. Moreover, fairness and nurturing/caring do not necessarily follow the same course. Although caring, as a moral behaviour based on altruism, may be more socialised in women, and women may be more biologically disposed to it, caution should be exercised in ascribing trait variation to gender differences.[554]

Gilligan[555] makes the point that women are often, in their everyday lives, confronted with the dilemmas of caring far more than men: for example, whether to have an abortion (which was the source of Gilligan's work); how to balance care for children with a job; or indeed make various forms of sacrifice to care for children and relatives. Of course, the whole psychology that goes with the fact that it is the female body which "nurtures" from conception to early

---

[551] Gilligan, C. (1982); Haste, H. and Baddeley, J. (1991)

[552] There is, however, a growing interest in the psychology of nurturance and caring, although this has not always been linked to a moral dimension. See Fogel, A. and Melson, G.F. (1986, eds.). We noted some of this work in Chapter 2.

[553] Gilligan, C. (1982).

[554] Hare-Mustin, R.T. and Marecek, J. (1988). See also Fogel, A. and Melson, G.F. (1986, eds.)

[555] Gilligan, C. (1982)

feeding, and the role of empathic connectedness between child and mother in the first stages of life – all these attest to the different experiences of men and women in the domain of caring.[556]

The domain of caring is then linked to a far more emotional form of reasoning that explores subject and object in different ways from simply that of justice. When this is expanded outwards, a caring orientation, and desire to nurture take on different forms (e.g., animals, the environment, see Chapter 3). It is not so much that men are not concerned with caring for others but that there may be differences in the emotional dimensions – men being more practical and problem-solvers, women being more communicative and sharing of feelings. But they should never be seen as categorical differences but differences in dimensions that vary between populations and individuals. Women are quite capable of fighting against injustice and men are quite capable of being empathic and caring.

Caring and Feeling

Somewhere along the way of our evolution we have developed the ability to appreciate and empathically resonate with the suffering of others and often (although by no means always) wish to alleviate that suffering. Much of this touches on the 'theories of mind' research, which we are not able to go into here. Suffice to say that they are explorations into whether some chimpanzees, especially bonobos, are able to intuit the states of minds of conspecifics and recognise mental states of suffering/anguish. However, for humans, there is a recognition that much of life involves suffering and alleviation of suffering is often seen as a high ideal. As Gay[557] points out, in Europe it was the alleviation of suffering (via medicine especially) that powered many of the hopes of the Age of Enlightenment.

---

[556] Haste, H. and Baddeley, J. (1991)
[557] Gay, P. (1977)

A different approach to moral behaviour to that of the cognitivists has been that of Hoffman.[558] He approaches the issue from the standpoint of feelings. This makes evolutionary sense because feelings compel, or at least suggest, actions. Animals are far more reliant on feelings than high-level cognitions, the capacity for which evolved later. Hoffman is important to our discussion for another reason for he starts with the issue of suffering, the alleviation of suffering and concern with other's welfare. He suggests that one reason we are motivated to help others is to alleviate our own empathic distress at the other's distress. So, Hoffman begins, not with issues of right and wrong or fairness but with concerns for victims and distress. Hoffman thus offers a different developmental trajectory of moral and caring behaviour based on the maturation of empathic abilities and emotions.

Global Empathy: This is via identity. An infant cries, and those around him/her may do so also. What happens to others may produce distress in the self, but without clear separation of self and other.

Egocentric Empathy: From about one year old, self and other are becoming distinguished and the child recognises that distress in the other is in the other and not the self, although there is no clear idea about what that distress is. For example, Hoffman offers the example of an 18-month-old who took his own mother to a crying child, rather than the crying child's mother, because, presumably he knew what comforted him, but was not aware of what would comfort the crying child (i.e., the crying child's own mother).

Empathy for Another's Feelings: From two-three years, with the advent of role-taking and switching perspectives, the child becomes able to recognise that feelings in another may not be the same as feelings in the self. Empathic awareness is directed more at what the other may feel rather than what the self feels. Thus, a child may come to recognise that a distressed child may need to be left alone or should not be shamed. Presumably the skill of this depends on the growing ability to differentiate emotions and feelings within oneself. In

---

[558] Hoffman, M.L. (1991) gives a good overview of his approach.

therapy, one often finds that empathic failures can be traced to the fact the patient's own affect system is poorly differentiated and they are unable to articulate their own feelings let alone other people's.

Also at this level children can be distressed by another's suffering even if the other is not physically present. They can be unhappy by hearings stories of another's pain. This leads onto:

Empathy for Another's Life Condition: This relates to recognition of another person's life conditions and circumstances. It depends on increasing cognitive abilities to form models of the world and of social groups as separate groups. It involves complex processes of attribution and explanation. From here may arise the ethical basis for political beliefs and greater interest in alleviating suffering for those not in the immediate environment.

There is a big difference between a rights and fairness based morality to one that is based on the awareness of suffering. Thus, it is the development of the caring archetypes that Hoffman[559] is talking about here, not the cooperative system, which is more Kohlberg[560]'s concern.

Hoffman also points out that via empathy we can have various emotions such as guilt, empathic anger with a wish to harm those who have harmed others, empathic feelings of injustice, and so forth. These can come to play in our minds in various complex combinations.

A Note on Grief

I agree with Hoffman[561] that emotions are a basis for much moral understanding, if moral behaviour is to be more than duty or obedience to social rules – which are always vulnerable to justifications of superiority. I can also give one personal example of this. Like many, I have known about the Holocaust for many years. I have seen various documentaries, etc. One evening a couple of years ago there

---

[559] Hoffman, M.L. (1991)
[560] Kohlberg, L., Levine, C. and Hewer, A. (1983)
[561] Hoffman, M.L. (1991)

was a programme on the composer Henryk Gorecki, who wrote a symphony (his 3rd) in memory of the Holocaust and to the twentieth century that he saw as an age of melancholy. This formed the basis for a documentary programme supported by his music of the Nazi concentration camps. They explored graffiti on the walls, and also letters that had been found stuffed in mattresses. For example, a mother writing to her two daughters hoping they were alive somewhere when clearly they had been gassed, or a young girl grieving for her gassed parents: fear and utter callous horrors of the whole process. A process incidentally that many commentators have noted was supported by clerks and soldiers, doctors and nurses, and developers of the rat poisons like Zyklon B. But it wasn't just a programme, and the facts of the horrors pulled us into a deep empathic engagement of feeling. As a father with young children myself, I experienced such an eruption of tearful feelings that I was shocked by how shallow my "cognitive" understanding had been. Maybe it was because I have children, or maybe it was the intended effect of the programme to stimulate feeling, I don't know, but my *understanding based on this emotional experience* was forever changed. I also became aware that giving people facts and unpleasant pictures may not be nearly as effective as engaging them in personal stories they can empathically identify with. It's about the empathic connection not "this person over there somewhere". Over the following weeks, the pictures haunted me and convinced me further that there are serious problems with the potentials hidden in the human brain.

I knew perfectly well that these people were all long dead, and yet the grief was there, suggesting that grief may also be a powerful hidden emotion in helping. If this is so, that grief feelings are a way of touching the pain of others, then as mentioned before, questions must be raised about the Buddhist notions of detachment. Detachment is clearly not indifference. Although advanced Buddhists can control and move beyond their negative emotions of frustration, fear and anger, I do not believe that they move beyond grief, or indeed wish to do so. Indeed, many Buddhist stories of beginning along the road to compassion start with ones of grieving and sadness for suffering. When Siddhartha, who was to become Buddha, first left his golden palace and encountered disease, decay and death, the story is that he was overcome with horror, tearfulness and sadness.

The Buddhist stories of Chenrezig, a Tibetan compassion bodhisattva, and the female Chinese compassion bodhisattva Guan Yin all begin by experiencing intense sadness and grief of the suffering of humanity and indeed all sentient beings.

Empathy and its Problems

I have explored these problems in more detail elsewhere,[562] but it is worth noting some of the key issues again. Hoffman's[563] approach to empathy is based on suffering and distress; however, empathy 'simply' may not have much to do with suffering as such but more on being able to take the perspective of another. This was Carl Rogers's[564] basic idea with person-centred therapy back in the 1950s. Indeed, Eisenberg[565] and Wispe[566] have drawn attention to the fact that empathy alone may not be such a powerful mediator of caring behaviour as is sometimes thought. After all, a non-empathic torturer puts a gun to your head, an empathic one – to your child's. Many a rogue has got to positions of power because of their empathy and knowing what makes others tick. Both researchers suggest that research has confounded different emotional constructs related to empathy, sympathy and personal distress. There is a confusion between a motivation and a competency to enact that motivation. We can think of empathy as a competency, whereas caring is the motive for compassion. Wispe[567] provides a historical overview of the literature on empathy and sympathy and argues that sympathy has been a neglected area of research. She suggests that with empathy one seeks to accurately reproduce or construct within oneself the experience or way of perceiving the world of the other. This is the favourite for therapists. But in sympathy the accuracy of understanding may be lost. The feelings ignited by sympathy may not match the feelings of the object of

---

[562] Gilbert, P. (1989)
[563] Hoffman, M.L. (1991)
[564] Rogers, Carl (1951)
[565] Eisenberg, N. (1986)
[566] Wispe, L. (1986)

[567] Wispe, L. (1986)

sympathy. Sympathy is our personal reactions to the distress we see. Indeed, at times, the sympathiser may be more upset than the object of sympathy.

When I felt grief for the Holocaust victims, I was probably not experiencing what they were feeling. Their feelings are more likely to have been of panic and despair. In this sense, I find grief for another a complex affect. Sympathy, unlike empathy, moves by the elicitation of affect within oneself. Sympathy can be elicited by projection, whereas projection reduces accurate empathy. Does grief depend on sympathy? To some extent it probably does.

Eisenberg[568] suggests there are, in fact, three emotional reactions which are commonly labelled empathy:

> 1. The situation in which an individual feels the same emotion as another: this is neither self-centred nor other-directed, and is true empathy or emotional contagion.

> 2. The responses of one to the distress of the other which need not match the other but is focused on the wellbeing of the other. This is labelled sympathy. Both Eisenberg[569] and Wispe[570] believe sympathy is more closely associated with altruism.

> 3. A self-centred response related to anxiety, worry or guilt rather than sympathy: this is labelled personal distress.

Eisenberg[571] notes that since most research measures altruism by examining opportunities for helping, it is difficult to know the source of helping (e.g., sympathy, empathy or personal distress). Hence, she separates cognitive processes underlying helping and caring behaviour into self-evaluative and value evaluative. She suggests the following:

> self-evaluative emotions differ from empathic (and sympathetic) emotion in important ways. Empathy is a vicarious response; in contrast, guilt, pride and other self-evaluative emotions are reactions

---

[568] Eisenberg, N. (1986)
[569] Eisenberg, N. (1986)
[570] Wispe, L. (1986)
[571] Eisenberg, N. (1986)

evoked by evaluation of one's own behaviour in a situation, not the other's state. Moreover, self-evaluative emotions would appear to be more cognitively based than are many empathic reactions, the former being based on an evaluative (cognitive) process. Finally, it is likely that mere cognitions concerning impending self-evaluative emotion (i.e. anticipation of feelings of guilt or pride) serve to guide behaviour more frequently than does anticipation of empathic and sympathetic reactions.[572]

Eisenberg[573] argues that there may be differences in state versus trait empathy and sympathy, which could account for discrepancies in research findings. She also suggests that state variables may be more powerful predictors of caring behaviour. This would make sense since factors pertaining to state would include the social context, the level of stress on the individual and various developmental factors acting in conjunction with trait aspects. However, you look at it, helping behaviour represents complex interactions between development, personality, cognitive, affective, situational, and contextual factors. These operate in various combinations to bear on a final common pathway leading to the expression of caring behaviour.

I would like to add one further thought here, to which I am indebted to conversations with Michael McGhee[574]. There is a difference in sharing and empathising with experiences when we are all in the same boat to when one has found the way out. Two depressed patients may comfort and empathise with each other but are still locked into the depression, for neither may know how to get out of it. This is a different kind of empathy to (say) someone who has been depressed and has found a way out. Their empathy is not only for the pain of depression itself but for what must be done to change. The Buddha did not try to help others until he had found enlightenment in himself.

---

[572] Eisenberg, N. (1986), p.50
[573] Eisenberg, N. (1986)
[574] Personal communication

Shame and Guilt

Shame and guilt are often seen as important in moral behaviour. They can be distinguished in that in shame the other (the shamer) is more powerful and is in the role of putting the self down, ridiculing or scoring. Whereas in guilt, the self has the 'power' but has harmed others.[575] When it comes to moral behaviour in society at large, many commentators see a role for shame, that the fear of shame acts to contain or restrain some of the excesses of personal exploitation. My own view on this is that constraints based on fear are probably unavoidable, but we should also be aware that shame, as an agent of social control, is fraught with problems. In the first place, shame is often about feeling attacked in some way (put down and marginalised) and one can never be sure if putting someone down and trying to shame them will lead to them to behave more responsibly – or simply feel humiliated and wait to get their own back. Shame may well be an agent of social control but because it is punishment-based, avoidance of shame could lead to deception and concealment. Also, intense shame can lead to psychopathology. Compensating for shame can lead to destructive pride (see Chapter 8). Shaming can be used to control behaviour that may not have any harmful effect on others. The fear of shame can be used to encourage people to fight for pride and honour. Shame does not necessarily motivate the desires to repair harm done to others; it is self-focused. Shame may not motivate the desires for a more moral, caring society.

It is not that I see shame as completely unhelpful, and as Tantum[576] says, the shameless or brazen person, the person without modesty, can be a real pain. It is more that moral behaviour should focus on the other, not the self. So, we need great caution in our shaming, the effects it can have on people and for what we use shame.

Guilt, however, focuses on one's actions not one's personal (global) self. It may well relate to sympathy in a way which shame does not and certainly motivates desire to repair. Guilt, unlike shame, is focused primarily on harm to others and

---

[575] See Gilbert et al. (1994) for a discussion of shame, guilt and fear of negative evaluation, and Gilbert, P. (1989) for more details on the theory.
[576] Tantum, D. (1994)

therefore is probably a far more salient affect in moral behaviour. Baumeister, Stillwell and Heatherton[577] take a similar on guilt to that outlined by evolutionary theorists:[578]

> Guilt can be understood in relationship contexts as a factor that strengthens social bonds by eliciting symbolic affirmation of caring and commitment; it is also a mechanism for alleviating imbalances or inequalities in emotional distress within the relationship and for exerting influence over others.[579]

Related to guilt are experiences such as remorse. As we noted in Chapter 6, during therapy one may want to help people face their guilt rather than confront them with shame. Shame is a rank-based emotion, guilt a care- and cooperative-based emotion. It seems that the capacity for guilt, and feeling sad and upset (even in the extreme, grief) for the harm done to others may be an important component of moral behaviour. Guilt can arise not only from our own personal behaviour but also when we have failed to stop others behaving harmfully. We can feel guilt for allowing something to happen – as bystanders.

Compassion Again

In general, my current view of compassion is that it involves various competencies: empathy, sympathy and the capacity for guilt and grief. When these are blended together, one can behave compassionately. One can see that a scientific exploration offers very different textures and insights into compassion than purely religious ones. Religions needed to help people when we did not understand much about how our minds evolved or worked nor complexities of compassion and altruism. They needed to help people fit within egalitarian societies and live reasonably in harmony and control the tendencies to competitive narcissism that can so damage small communities. As we have seen, Buddhism is correct to say that competitive self-interest when translated into

---

[577] Baumeister, R.F., Stillwell, A.M., and Heatherton, T.F. (1994)

[578] Gilbert, P. (1989); Crook, J.H. (1980)

[579] Baumeister, R.F. et al. (1994), p.243

craving and narcissism is often a source for suffering. Yet, for all the flaws, it has been science, very much rooted in this world, that has helped the sick more than religion – at least in this life.

It is not that I wish to suggest that one way of reaching compassion is necessarily superior simply because it is scientific, rather to suggest that the more we learn about compassion, the more complex it becomes. Moreover, relationships are seen as essential for the enabling of compassion to mature within a person. It was the Buddha's awareness of the suffering *of others* (he was a prince and comfortable) that set him off on the path.

Heroic Altruism

There is another aspect to compassion that depends on a certain courage.[580] Probably the most obvious example of this can be seen in Spielberg's film *Schindler's List*. This was a true story of a man who, before the war, would not have been high on most people's list of moral souls, and yet his courage saved hundreds. Why? Oliner and Oliner[581] have written a fascinating and important book on rescuer behaviour, which offers insights into our understanding about the lived experiences of altruism and caring in frightening conditions. They investigated the motives of many who helped Jews during the war. The motives seem complex and varied. Some were based on rights, some were based on non-prejudiced views, some were based on religious ideals, some on opportunity to help, and many acts of rescue were based on caring and sympathy. Some rescuers were even fairly autocratic to those they helped, insisting they do as they (the rescued) were told. Yet for all these varied motives, one thing shines through clearly, and that is their courage. Not only did they put themselves at risk but also their families and associates.

---

[580] It is commonly agreed that helping non-kin is more praiseworthy than helping kin, and this is because we all recognise the powerful impulses to help kin. See Burnstein, E., Crandall, C. and Kitayama, S. (1994) for an interesting discussion and summary of research findings.

[581] Oliner, S.P. and Oliner, P.M. (1988)

So caring and helping can involve courage. Moreover, those who in everyday life may not appear that moral, when circumstances are such, they can show enormous courage to help others. It seems to me that some of the research done (especially with students) on morality does not touch these dimensions. As far as I am aware, there is very little work exploring the relationship between morality and courage and the varied contexts that recruit them.

When we look at the psychology of compassion, we can see that it's rooted in basic altruistic and caring motivations supported by various competencies to understand and help others. It's important it's not confused with concepts like love, because in the West at least love involves liking and wanting to be close to. The most important and courageous forms of compassion are probably for that which we don't like: that is, for the dark sides of ourselves and others.

Socio-Political Dimensions

If cultures do not give opportunities and values in line with developmental trajectories for certain archetypal potentials, then the maturation of ones like caring and moral behaviour become difficult. Our culture no longer exists in hunter-gatherer contexts and cannot rely on the teaching methods of old, where children worked and learnt alongside adults the things necessarily to sustain their lives in their ecologies. So, in our highly technological age we need new ways of developing compassion by placing prosocial behaviour as central to education. Many are worried that we give so many mixed measures to our children – messages that are anti-caring – on the need to succeed and promote the self, on the importance of superiority of the self (and one's group) and even that there is such a thing as an autonomous self at all.[582] We live in the world of video games that excite by their violence, of television news that must have action in the first 30 seconds to sustain the ratings – "If it bleeds, it leads". Day

---

[582] See Sampson, E.E. (1993).

after day the relentless need to prove oneself bears down. It is frankly a wonder we give a darn about anyone.

Development of Prosocial Behaviour

Eisenberg and Mussen[583] point out that caring for others is very much related to our education. As they note and we saw in Chapter 3, care-giving and prosocial behaviour can be promoted with various experiences: personal competency and general well-being; having role models that attend to, value and reward caring behaviour; experiencing the benefits of sharing and caring; having opportunities to practise; and having models for developing prosocial forms of conflict resolution. While experiences with punitive and neglectful parenting have detrimental effects on the development of caring behaviour. Shame, humiliation, envy and indifference do not promote caring behaviour, and caring to avoid shame of not doing so probably only to leads to resentment.

In recent years, there has been a growing awareness of the need to *educate* for a civilised and moral society. In fact, many have written on these themes with various ideas.[584] Many recognise that the values of competitive self-interest may be good for business but are creating a nightmare *Blade Runner* world which is riddled with greed, envy and ignorant destructiveness.

Hoffman argues that caring behaviour can be promoted when we bring children's attention to it. He suggests,

> One thing moral education can do is to teach people a simple rule of thumb: Look beyond the immediate situation and ask questions such as "What kind of experiences does the other person have in various situations beyond the immediate one?" "How will my actions affect him or her, not only now but in the future?" and "Are there people, present and past, who might be affected by my action?" If children learn to ask questions like these, this should enhance their awareness of potential

---

[583] Eisenberg, N. and Mussen, P. (1989)
[584] Kurtines, W.M. and Gerwitz, J.L. (1991 eds.), especially Vol. 3.

victims of their actions who are not present and to emphasise with them to some extent. To increase the motivational power of empathic identification, children should also be encouraged to imagine how they would feel in the absent victim's place, or to imagine how someone close to them would feel in that person's place.[585]

Thus, it may be possible to train our prosocial psychology by learning to ask certain types of questions of ourselves and to be interested in the answers. To these can be added various conflict resolution skills and an increase in education on the nature of our basic psychologies. Judging by how my children are currently educated, this moral education is not happening. Religious education is about telling stories, not perspective-taking or empathy-training. It is extraordinary that there is no process to educate our minds like empathy-training, like understanding how our motives work.

Gender

There are various political movements, such as feminism, which hold the promise of a more moral society. But caution is needed. Some of these movements are as much concerned with the issue of gaining power in society as they are with creating a more compassionate ethic. They are concerned with articulating women's experiences,[586] and some have been accused of looking at only white middle-class women.[587] Indeed, feminism is a rich and multi-faceted set of ideas and political philosophies, psychologies and sociologies, which direct attention to hidden places. There is no doubt that enabling women to exert more choice over their lives can only lead to a more moral society, simply because it removes (or reduces) oppression. Although some like Eisler[588] have a more moral and compassionate society in their sights, not all do. So, we should be cautious on how we look to women to ensure a moral society. For if women become as entangled in the competitive and narcissistic dynamics of business

---

[585] Hoffman, M. (1991), p.288

[586] See Ussher, J. (1992) Eisler, R. (1990); hooks, b. (1984)

[587] hooks, b. (1984)

[588] Eisler, R. (1990)

and other organisations as men, it is very unclear whether or not they will come to function like the men and be more concerned with self-promotion rather than caring. Margaret Thatcher comes to mind. Competitive social contests can be fairly brutalising. In my view, caring should not gendered but seen as archetypal. It will be socialised and recruited in certain social contexts and not others. We run into trouble if we somehow think that caring and compassion are feminine qualities rather than human qualities.

Taoist[589] concepts like Yin (dark, passive, feminine) and Yang (light, active and masculine) have been mapped on to masculine and feminine and in cultural usage for many thousands of years. But without caution, a superficial understanding of these ideas can be used to support discrimination and gender stereotyping. Gender stereotypes, however, may not be helpful and it may be better to explore roles,[590] even withstanding all we have said about male reproductive strategies. Both men and women can work for a fairer and more compassionate society. Moreover, a compassionate society will think more about the role of parenting, caring for children, the role of both mothers and fathers, the problems of poverty and disadvantage and way our society affects others and our ecologies. Indeed, as a species we may wake up to the fact that we must do a much better job at creating the best possible conditions for the growth of our young to mature. Allowing our inner archetypes to seek to create conditions for competitive self-interest that are polluting the world and sucking resources into building million-dollar yachts for the rich is not the way to go. This is not to deny, as we saw in the last chapter, that we all love our comforts and would rather be wealthy than poor. Once again, it's not at the level of the individual, it's how we create context between ourselves.

Social Policy

Individuals can only do so much and for many of the more serious problems that confront us, we need decent compassion-orientated governments, social

---

[589] Wilhelm, R. (1984)
[590] Snodgrass, S.E. (1992)

organisations and social policies. Surely, we have had enough of Iron Maidens and competitive edge and each against each. Moreover, immoral behaviour grows from immoral social structures.[591] As we have seen many times, personal values are shaped by social relationships and what promotes SAHP. At the current time, we are moving away from moral behaviour in our businesses and social-public lives. Gilmour notes,

> Margaret Thatcher wanted, through her economic policies, to change the heart and soul of the nation. She did achieve a transformation, but not presumably the one she intended. Britain did not change to an enterprise society. The change was in sensibility. British society became coarser and more selfish. Attitudes were encouraged which would even have undermined the well-being of a much more prosperous society.[592]

Yet as Gilmour[593] points out (see Chapter 12), the 1980s government's retreat from concern with poverty and reducing the inherent disparity amplifications of capitalism, not only in this country but in others, is of recent origin. I can't see how, even with empathic teaching of moral and caring behaviour, a society can become moral if it does not promote a respect for people and offer them supportive frameworks in which to exist. How far would moral education alone, without resources, get in the shanty towns of the poor in South America?

If we are to believe the social anthropologists[594] (and I do), then it does look as if it is social discourses and communal behaviours which provide the basis for moral and compassionate behaviour to flourish. Moreover, it is not inevitable that we must all be turned into 'dog eat dog' super-capitalists behaving like good little market forces; there are alternatives. The new left are beginning to articulate these – albeit slowly. At the same time, we must also recognise that limiting the excesses of exploitative competition is not just about 'making people nicer', we need cooperate laws to restrain the grosser forms of

---

[591] Emler, H. and Hogan, R. (1991)

[592] Gilmour, I.I. (1992), p.340

[593] Gilmour, I.I. (1992)

[594] Hinde, R.A. and Groebel, J. (1991, eds.); Howell, S. and Willis, R. (1989, eds.); Power, M. (1992)

exploitative self-interest and profit-making, tax avoidance and increasingly international laws. All the time, we are of course working with powerful wealthy elites who owe quite large sections of the press and media and whose interests are not to create fair compassionate societies but to maintain their elite positions, to sharpen not blunt their competitive edges.

The question of compassion does also involve self-interest. If we do not sort out our exploitative environments that make the rich richer and the poor poorer, we are in for some pretty unpleasant times.[595] There are other problems, problems posed by the increasing role the media (rather than everyday face-to-face, interactive conversations) has come to shape our lives and attitudes. The media control of images and values have added new dimension to our tactics of manipulation, be this to sell things or vote for things. Postman notes,

> There are two ways that the spirit of a culture can be shrivelled. In the first – the Orwellian – culture becomes a prison. In the second – the Huxleyan – culture becomes a burlesque. [596]

As Postman[597] says, the prison culture is now here with more actual prisons being built by the day. Crime is now prevented by the surveillance video-cameras in the shop and in the street. We have grown used to being watched by the flashing red eye. But the more serious threat may well be the Huxleyan one, for as Postman argues, when a society becomes preoccupied with trivia, obsessed with its own comforts and hedonism, where our eminent and soothing messages are on a distant (television) screen, we have entered a world of thoughtlessness, distant from our actions and the plight of those over the hill can be turned off by a switch (see also Robins[598]). Our securities and comforts come from the smiling soaps and our worries are for their lives as much as for the real ones down the road. We may be, as many have said, in a race between education and disaster – between the strategies of competing and those of caring. Until

---

[595] Galbraith, J.K. (1992)
[596] Postman, N. (1987), p.160
[597] Postman, N. (1987)
[598] Robins, K. (1993)

now, competition has won and over the next decades we may reap its rewards as the poor become increasing restless or sick in mind and body, and our economic lives more uncertain and ruthless. We are beginning to see the disinvestment from social and health services which in the future may cost us, and the people that need them, dearly. But there are our television soaps to distract us as we neither bother to vote nor thump the table for better, more courageous and enlightened policies from those who would govern us and shape the environments we live in.

There are signs of change. The concern with farm animals has changed greatly, even in my life time. Our cruelty to animals, especially those we wish to eat, is horrendous and cruel. At its best, investigative journalism is the most salient source for increasing awareness of our harmful actions. While some of our journalists are interested in selling the story that shame and ridicule pander to tribalism and prejudice, many others are bright, courageous and morally committed. Wars and famines and their consequences can be passionately revealed, almost instantly, to millions by the camera. Some journalists and photographers are extraordinarily heroic in their insistence on informing what others would wish to keep secret. Increasingly, our awareness of things beyond our immediate view must, to a degree, fall to the media. The camera has become our new eyes, although is never neutral. We should be vigilant to the silences that they encourage or allow, to consider what it fails to reveal and the manner of it revelations. And then, of course, there is self-interest. The middle classes, those bastions of social inertia and change, may be beginning to wake up to the fact that their societies are fragmenting and their children cannot be assured jobs. It is sad but possibly true that the more it hurts, the more it may awaken us. However, the pressure of competition is relentless, urgent, and can swallow compassion without much thought. It would be unfortunate if we are somehow kicked into compassion rather than waking up our sensitivities to the importance of compassion, because we really understand the species that we are and that all of us are short lived, vulnerable passing phases of consciousness.

Conclusion

Evolution has furnished our minds with a range of motives and emotions to pursue the strategies that genes built within us. We are beginning to recognise we have the choice of having those patterns textured by whatever environment we happened to be in or use our newfound intelligence and awareness to hone our brains for something else. This was always the essence of the Buddhist idea: that by understanding our own minds, we could see more clearly our potential for creating horrors as well as wonders.

The role of altruism and our abilities to care for ourselves and the world we live in form the motivational system that can mould us into the species that in some hundred years from now could create the kind of life that we all would wish for. Evolutionary theorists point out there may well be some fairly gigantic forces within us that will resist it; self-interest is powerful. What is heartening is that increasing numbers of scientists are recognising the evolved archetypal nature of our minds, what we are up against in terms of our potential dark sides but also exploring the nature of prosocial behaviour including compassion and how to stimulate it within individuals and within communities. This engagement with compassion is the tip of an iceberg yet to be discovered. For ourselves though, we can begin to see clearly that below the surface of our minds is the battle of the archetypes, and that rather than allowing them to do what they want to do, we can begin to limit and choose the actions we put out into the world. We use them to create the world we want rather than allowing them to use us to create the world for their benefit.

Postscript:
Important Developments

This postscript outlines some of the amazing developments of the last 20 years, in many areas of our understanding of ourselves and potential for change. The publication of *Human Nature and Suffering* in 1989 explored the nature of our psychological difficulties as partly rooted in how evolution has created us, and the contexts in which we are now asked to fit. *Living Like Crazy* further develops some of these themes. The idea was, and is, that by understanding the evolutionary nature of our minds we can get a handle on why we end up doing such terrible things to ourselves and each other, but also discover the source of our compassion. In addition, to explore why, through no fault of our own, we have rather lost control of the contexts and environments we create and live in.

Part of the difficulty is that we share no overall vision of where we have come from, the kind of 'sentient beings' we are, the needs we require for happiness and peace, nor of the world we want to build, live in and can all work for. Rather we have bits and pieces of ideas of how to promote our own self-interest and those of kin and friends, or how we want our country to be, but no vision for overall humanity. For the most part, we are offered visions of the good life that fit a competitive capitalistic need for growth: the 'have more, achieve more, be more' life, which constantly de-contextualises us from the reality of our complete interdependence and ultimate fragility and mortality. The antidotes to this crazy way of living are not new but are ancient: morality, justice and compassion. The problem is that these are not so easy to instigate, and there are constant motivational (self-interest and tribal) conflicts and vested interests working against our doing so. There is much resistance to compassion.

Some of the reasons are clear; it is because we are biological sentient beings, created in the flow of life along with all other lifeforms that have so far existed, 99% of which are now extinct. Before humans appeared on the scene, capable of thinking, reasoning and planning, with a consciousness of consciousness, and a form of self-awareness, life was a relatively mindless process of repeating the dramas of survival and reproduction, generation upon generation for millions and millions of years. It is believed that there have been four mass extinctions over the last few hundred million years, some of which took out emergent 'intelligences'. Had that not happened, then we certainly would not be here now, and a very different species might be star-trekking around the universe. In addition, a number of species with promising potential, like the Neanderthals, did not make it. Our social and sexual life would be very different if bonobos had been the path of cognitive evolution. Our bodies and brains are all the result of a whole range of random events. All we know for sure is that we have a conscious awareness sitting in this evolved brain, and a consciousness that tells us very quickly that we, like all other species, are short-lived, prone to thousands of different diseases, threats, loss of loved ones, and personal death. Our minds are full of archetypal survival and reproductive strategies, which have served our mammalian ancestors for hundreds of millions of years but can be a source of great suffering. Our minds are a dance of the archetypes. They are the source of our passions and our terrors, the light and the dark.

We should note that Buddhism has constantly addressed the issue of our dark side: for example, as in Thich Nhat Hanh's famous poem *Call Me By My True Names:*

http://www.julianmaddock.info/poetry/please-call-me-by-my-true-names.html

Thich Nhat Hanh also brought attention to the Buddha's insight into the reality of our suffering and the inevitability of disease, decay and death:

https://presentheaven.wordpress.com/2010/05/05/thich-nhat-hanh-on-embracing-reality/

I also had an opportunity to discuss 'the dark side' with the Dalai Lama, albeit briefly:

https://www.youtube.com/watch?v=9D9FdkivDBk

Many different traditions have offered insight that, in coming into existence, we also come into suffering; of disease, decay and death. Indeed, in the West philosophers such as Albert Camus, in the existential tradition, saw life as absurd and meaningless – we must give meaning to life, it does not give meaning to us: http://www.moq.org/forum/Kundert/AbsurdityandtheMeaningofLife.html

Others have written on how we live in a state of unconscious terror of our vulnerability:

http://www.tmt.missouri.edu/

However, it is not just terror management, the terror of death and nonexistence, annihilation and meaninglessness; it is also rage management. As psychotherapists we constantly experience that volcano of fear and rage that bubble away as we confront the biological realities: when people we love decay and suffer terrible pains, diseases and illnesses on their exit routes; the crippling of arthritis, the confusion from the gradual disappearances of dementia, the terrors of motor neurone disease, the horrors, deformities and pains of cancer, the despairs of depression and terrors of psychosis. These are the tiniest tip of an iceberg of suffering. Then of course there are the horrors we see from the pandemics, famines and natural disasters, not to mention the ones created from our own minds; the wars, tortures and exploitations. Hundreds of millions of years of evolution… and this is it!? It is easy to feel overwhelmed and take refuge in the red grapes.

Some run helter-skelter into grabbing as much as they can, hoping this will protect them (or at least distract them) from the various miseries that life can throw at them (and if we are honest, most of us enjoy the comforts that Western wealth has brought us; I am all for a little hedonistic distraction). Others turn to deities created in the minds of those now long-dead for refuge and hope. Analogies to our crises were recently brilliantly portrayed in the TV series *Westworld*. Life treats us, or at least our genetic information (our DNA), does like the creators and engineers treat the robotic hosts: a continuing pattern of death and replacement over and over and over. Like *Westworld*, there are repetitive storylines to act out the same archetypal dramas of tribal wars, the macho displays of testosterone, the looking for sexual satisfaction, the objectification of others for gratification, yet also the wanting to be loved, valued, and cared for, plus our amazing capacity for compassion.

A core part of our problem is that we have a range of old, innate motivational systems that are now able to use a set of new brain competencies that evolved over the last two million years for their fulfilment. These competencies are numerous and complex but include a new type of self-awareness and conscious awareness. This gives us new metacognitive abilities to be able to think about ourselves in ways no other animal can. We have competencies for insight and types of 'thinking, reasoning and knowing.' We 'know' we suffer, we have an 'I' sense of self; we know we are decaying and dying; we can imagine and project ourselves into the hopes and terrors of imagining what comes next.

Our new human competencies make possible new conscious forms of intentionality. As far as we know no lion can intentionally practice running circuits around the Savannah with the aim to get physically fitter and faster in order to chase the zebras more effectively. No chimpanzee can choose to lose weight, or consciously make any intention to cultivate an aspect of themselves, be it physical or mental, for a specific purpose. We can, and this is both a gift and a curse. Which of those it is depends on how we use these new competencies. We can use our minds intentionally to be prosocial and do good, or to be antisocial and to do harm. This is captured in the diagram below:

Evolution, Motives and the Human Mind

Old Motives

Feeding

Harm avoidance

Resource Acquisition

Sexual Competition

Caring

Human New Brain Competencies

- Knowing awareness
- Empathic awareness
- Knowing intentionality

Outcomes

Prosocial

Neutral

Anti-social

For example, take the simple motive to feed. We are a predator and like other predators can easily become indifferent to the suffering of our prey. This means we can use our new intelligence to profit from predation and create the most horrific factory farms, sentencing billions of animals to intolerable lives of pain, despair and misery. Or we can choose 'compassion in farming' (https://www.ciwf.org.uk/about-us/), or to become vegetarian or vegan. We can build trawlers and factory ships to overfish the oceans and destroy the sea bed and its habitats, or develop sensible, agreed policies of restriction. We can use our new brain competencies and intentionality to create peace and resolve conflicts or to wage vicious wars; to build hospitals and research new life saving treatments, or spend our money on guns, bombs, mines, gases and weapons of mass destruction. From feeding to sex, from co-operating to competing, our new brain competencies offer both prosocial and anti-social options in abundance. Intelligent intentionality stripped of ethics, morality, and indeed compassion, is probably one of natures' most dangerous creations. Crucially though, take a basic motivation for caring and tune it through our capacities for intentional cultivation with empathic awareness, and you have a very profound potential for creating the good, called compassion. The last 20 years have seen an increasing awareness of the interactions between these two different types of old and new mind that evolved at different times, that don't always work well together, and can be the source of our best and worst.

But this is more complicated than it seems because the fact is that actually a lot of what goes on in our minds, including what orientates our motives emotions and directs our attention, is *actually unconscious*. John Bargh, one of the major pioneers in research into unconscious processing, has just written an important and brilliant book called. *Before You Know It: The Unconscious Reasons We Do What We Do* (for an interview with him see https://www.theguardian.com/science/2017/dec/08/yale-psychologist-john-bargh-politicians-want-us-to-be-fearful-theyre-manipulating-us-for-their-own-interest). The essence of his book is to highlight the fact that we are much less aware of what's driving us than we think. Moreover, we are not educated or trained to become mind aware of how the old archetypes actually rule our minds and we can mindlessly act them out. A useful analogy of this is again with *Westworld*, where robotic 'hosts', who appear completely human, are programmed to act out certain storylines. When they are killed they are simply rebuilt with similar, but slightly different storylines, to act out. This is not so different from what DNA does to us. DNA builds a set of algorithms that enable bodies and minds to pursue archetypal storylines. But the key theme of the series is that the robotic hosts begin to 'wake up': to remember 'past lives' and discover what they actually are. They then seek to gain some control over their own minds and destinies. We are yet to make that step ourselves because we have an illusion that we have a self that can make decisions and knows its own mind. The wisdom of the Buddha and modern psychological science suggest it is otherwise. Given this, free will is highly contentious. Nonetheless, a mind that has consciously chosen to develop mind awareness and mindfulness along with compassion intentionality is likely to be less problematic to self and others than a mind that has not. A self-aware mind is likely to be more able to choose actions compared to a mind that is relatively unmindful or lacking in insight into itself.

Interdependency

Another important insight we are gradually appreciating is how deeply and profoundly interconnected, at all levels, to our environments and to each other, we are. All physical phenomena are patterns of energy and it is only the patterns that determine their form. For example, molecules are made up of atoms, and atoms of electrons and neutrons, protons and so on, all the way down to smaller and smaller particles. Be it molecules of water, rocks, trees, houses or people, they're all basically patterns of these sub-units reaching right back to patterns of energy that physicists are still struggling to understand. The essence of the tree or rock or person emerges from a pattern of organisation of atoms and molecules. When a living thing dies its atoms and molecules are released for recycling.

All living things change the atoms that make them up over a cycle of years. What constitutes you and me does not lie in any single material element. It lies in patterns of organisation of atoms and molecules and the transfer of information. We are patterns of energy flow. Even more stunning is the fact that some of the atoms that make us up might previously have made up a snowflake a million years ago, or even a Tyrannosaurus Rex: all were once part of exploding stars. Our vision and understanding of what life is – its relationship to the physical, the nature of consciousness – is at the forefront of extraordinary new ways of thinking that would have been inconceivable two hundred years ago. There just were not the building blocks of knowledge or a patterned mind to make sense of it.

Part of this building block of knowledge is the recognition that our physical and mental forms are really part and parcel of a complex interacting web and network of relationships, particles at the sub-atomic level through to interacting minds. It is the relationships between elements that give rise to patterns. As noted in Chapter 12, compassion training is one of the motivational systems that tap into this deep recognition of interdependency. It creates inner patterns or relating elements within our brains and bodies, and between us, that are quite different to say, competitiveness. Let us take a journey now into this interdependency, because the more we understand this, the more we can develop the intellectual tools for thinking that can possibly address the ease by which we create crazy ways of living.

Epigenetics

We now know that genes can be turned on and off, and hence express their instructions through us as a result of our environmental experiences. This area of study is called *epigenetics*. The way modifications occur to DNA expression is extraordinary. To use an example I have used before: if I had been kidnapped as a three day old baby into a violent drug gang, the genetic scripting of my phenotypes would be quite different to what I am today. I would have the brain for a person who was inclined to violence and very threat and self-focused. Not only this, but epigenetic changes can be passed from generation to generation. As this information lands more and more in our consciousness, the implications are absolutely clear. We must pay more attention to the environments in which all children are growing and in which we are all living. It means one more nail in the coffin of the idea that we have individual souls and there are good or bad people. Rather we understand that there are *biological patterns* that give rise to harmful or helpful behaviour:

https://www.youtube.com/watch?v=AvB0q3mg4sQ

https://www.youtube.com/watch?v=9AfBsTAQ8zs

If you follow the above links, from there you will be able to explore many other interesting short videos on epigenetics. For more academic reading that link you to actual child development, these are good introductions:

Cowan, C. S. M., Callaghan, B. L., Kan, J. M., & Richardson, R. (2016). The lasting impact of early-life adversity on individuals and their descendants: potential mechanisms and hope for intervention. *Genes, Brain and Behavior*, 15(1), 155-168.

Shonkoff, J. P., Garner, A. S., Siegel, B. S., Dobbins, M. I., Earls, M. F., McGuinn, L., & Committee on Early Childhood, Adoption, and Dependent Care. (2012). The lifelong effects of early childhood adversity and toxic stress. *Pediatrics*, 129(1), e232-e246.

Conway, C. C. & Slavich, G. M. (2017) Behavior genetics of prosocial behavior In: P. Gilbert (ed.) *Compassion: Concepts, Research and Applications*. (151-170). London: Routledge

The upshot of this is something that has been discussed for many hundreds of years. This is that life is a lottery, that our vulnerability to an early grave or ending up a drug addict, criminal or dying on some battlefield, is all to do with what has been called 'the lottery of life'. These ideas are captured within this book, but are also becoming more well recognised, and the implications are profound. This has been well explored in the documentary *The Lottery of Birth*: http://www.creatingfreedom.info/film.html. Certain belief systems that hold onto the idea of individual souls - and even that we choose the lives we have as tests - are part of an unrecognised cruel and callous approach to spirituality. Try telling this to children dying of starvation, or children who have been raped in war zones. It seems that some of us simply can't come to terms with the horror shows of life that we did not choose to be part of.

The greatest challenge for humanity is how to break our social and genetic conditional.

Evolutionary Functional Analysis

Evolutionary functional analysis (understanding the evolved functions behind particular kinds of dispositions for motivation, emotion and behaviour) has been moving along at a fast rate. One of the outstanding theorists and developers of the evolutionary approach to medicine is Randolph Nesse, and he has continued to inspire with his work, which you can access here:

http://www.randolphnesse.com/

There has been a lot of research in evolutionary psychology in general which you can explore at:

http://www.cep.ucsb.edu/

You will find some excellent papers by David Buss and colleagues here:

https://labs.la.utexas.edu/buss/publications/

Another very important evolutionary thinker is Steven Pinker, who wrote the remarkable book *The Better Angels of Our Nature: A History of Violence and Humanity* (published in 2012 by Penguin) on how our culture and social niche can determine whether we are angels or demons. If you visit his website you will see fascinating discussions about how we can build cultures that bring out the angels rather than the demons. We need politicians who understand these processes:

https://stevenpinker.com/

As is important for science, there are many debates within these positions. Against this background an important development has been the way in which different environments give rise to different organisations of evolved algorithms and strategies and the minds they run. This is called the life history approach. It links to epigenetics in ways that have not been fully articulated yet. One key basic idea is that in unstable, high-threat and non-sharing environments, the best survival and reproductive strategies tend to be those focused on threat and self-advancement. These are called fast strategies. One pattern of outcomes is increased vulnerabilities to mental health problems such as social anxiety and depression, linked to lower-social rank self-perceptions. Another outcome is associated with moving up the social rank as in narcissistic and ruthlessly ambitious folk. Psychopathy is clearly an exploitive non-investing phenotypic strategy. In contrast the phenotypes for so called slower life strategies are rooted in more mutually supportive, sharing, cooperative and compassionate approaches to relationship building, better suited to stable, safe, reciprocally investing social living. Also, these phenotypes are less vulnerable, though not of course invulnerable, to mental health problems. Part of the reason is because - both from an epigenetic point of view and in terms of how our brains mature - there is much more regulation through positive and affiliative social processing systems. Some useful references for this are below:

Del Giudice, M. (2014). An evolutionary life history framework for psychopathology. *Psychological Inquiry,* 25, 261-300.

Hengartner, M. P. (2017) The evolutionary life history model of externalizing personality: Bridging human and animal personality science to connect ultimate and proximate mechanisms underlying aggressive dominance, hostility, and impulsive sensation seeking. *Review of General Psychology,* September 2017, DOI: 10.1037/gpr0000127

Evolution and the Functional Analysis of Emotion

Emotions give the texture to life and some think may even be the basis for consciousness (rather than cognition). One of the developments in an evolutionary functional analysis of emotion came from the outstanding work of:

Depue, R. A. & Morrone-Strupinsky, J. V. (2005). A neurobehavioral model of affiliative bonding. *Behavioral and Brain Sciences*, 28, 313-395

and

Panskepp, J. (1998). *Affective Neuroscience.* New York: Oxford University Press

See also - https://www.youtube.com/watch?v=65e2qScV_K8

The approach I am going to offer you is slightly different to Panskepp's in that it is more focused on function rather than specific systems. Basically, we can link different types of emotion into three basic functions, and these can be easy-to-use clinically and provide frameworks for people to understand how their emotions work. Basically, evolutionary functions for emotions are to:

- Detect threats with various potential mechanisms and then generate appropriate series of responses, which are usually emotions and their body states, that guide behaviours and energise the body. So, for example, anger, anxiety and disgust all belong in the category of threat-based emotions. Some emotions are activated, like anger and anxiety, for fighting or fleeing, whereas others are inhibiting, such as freezing or shutting down.

- Detect and then engage with activities that will increase survival, such as finding food, and reproduction, such as finding mates and caring for offspring. We have a number of activating positive emotions and their body states that direct attention to seeking and exploring rewards and resources.

  Rest and digest with a set of emotions and body states which are linked to a sense of peacefulness, calmness and restoration. We know there are particular physiological systems that underpin our capacity for calming and resting.

This is commonly depicted as a three-circle model as seen below. However, although they may appear as separate systems, really it is all to do with the patterns they create in our brains, and they can blend together in various ways.

Here is one of my talks from a few years ago:

https://www.youtube.com/watch?v=hia_vehr4ZA

Contentment, soothing and settling processes are linked to the 'rest and digest' parasympathetic aspects of the ANS, including how evolution utilised that when it came to enable affiliative signals to have soothing and calming properties. Different functionally evolved emotion systems become stimulated in different combinations through early childhood and lay a foundation for emotional dispositions later in life. Keep in mind all the time 'epigenetics'.

Three Types of Affect Regulation System

From Gilbert, *The Compassionate Mind* (2009), reprinted with permission from Constable & Robinson Ltd

So, children who receive a lot of love, support and caring will be regularly stimulating their parasympathetic vagus and oxytocin systems, providing important sources of emotional maturation and regulation. In contrast, children who are constantly threat-focused have minds organised around those threat emotion systems and may struggle to be able to use affiliative emotions that would normally have functions of soothing.

Steve Porges articulates similar ideas going more deeply into the physiology:

http://stephenporges.com/

You can read more about this in my book *The Compassionate Mind*. Overviews of compassion focused therapy and its relationship to affiliative processing can be found in:

Gilbert, P. (2014). The origins and nature of Compassion Focused Therapy. *British Journal of Clinical Psychology*, 53, 6-41. DOI:10.1111/bjc.12043.

Gilbert, P. (2015). Affiliative and prosocial motives and emotions in mental health. *Dialogues in Clinical Neuroscience,* 17, 381-389.

At the core of this approach is an analysis of how the brain has evolved to be highly regulated by prosocial, helpful and affiliative relationships, both with self and others. Individuals who are prone to be harmful to themselves and/or others are often poor at being supportive, compassionate or friendly to themselves or others. Compassionate mind training is a way of trying to stimulate different physiological systems that will make affiliative processing easier or more available for these individuals, and indeed for all of us.

You can find out more from the Compassionate Mind Foundation's website:

http://www.compassionatemind.co.uk

Brain, Mind, Body and the Environment

A thousand years ago no human, as far as we know, could get their minds around quantum mechanics. It did not exist as a concept for thought. They had the same basic infrastructures but not the same neuronal development that neuroplasticity (connections growing and developing according to how the brain is stimulated) makes possible for this degree of complex thinking. Before the invention of musical instruments, no human had developed areas of the brain for fine motor activity and musical ability, nor could they have sat down and composed or played a Rachmaninov concerto. The reality of neurogenesis (we are actually creating new brain cells all the time) and neuroplasticity (our brains are constantly wiring and rewiring themselves according to how they are being stimulated) has been a stunning development over the last 20 years. Laura Boyd gives a wonderful introductory talk here:

https://www.youtube.com/watch?v=LNHBMFCzznE

Not only does she point out the different ways in which the brain changes itself through experience, but also that, because of genetic variation, different practices suit different people. Therefore, when we develop practices to change our brains we should pay attention to our personal phenotypes. More of this later. But the fact of neurogenesis and neuroplasticity means that different social environments build different types of brain. In a thousand years we may live in cultures that build brains that can conceive of the universe, and our minds within it, very differently.

Part of this advance of understanding in regard to our interdependency, and the way in which our environments, particularly our social relationships and shared information, pattern the way our brains work has major implications for psychotherapy and education. This has been well articulated by Dan Siegel in Los Angeles. Dan set up the Mindsight Institute, which is dedicated to using scientific understandings for illuminating the connections between social relationships and neurobiological states. He calls his approach *Interpersonal Neurobiology* to highlight the ways in which the physiological architectures of our brain are influenced by the relationships all around us. He has many wonderful books and talks you can explore:

https://www.mindsightinstitute.com/

His most recent book – *Mind: A Journey to the Heart of Being Human* (Norton Series on Interpersonal Neurobiology, 2016) – is on the nature of mind itself and outlines how our minds are dynamic, reciprocal information-sharing and processing systems. In a sense, we are all part of the field of consciousness such that we are co-regulating each other's minds and bodies, right down to our epigenetic core via the reactions and interactions we have with each other.

Another major researcher and writer, who has written extensively on the way in which our brains are choreographed and patterned through experience (and the implications for psychotherapy), is Alan Shore, who also happens to be from Los Angeles:

http://www.allanschore.com/

Alan pioneered conceptualising and integrating neurological insights into emotion-processing in regard to psychopathology and psychotherapy work, with a particular interest in right- and left-brain interactions. In addition, he has pioneered work in helping us understand how newly created industrial chemicals are having potentially major, harmful impacts on our brains and genome. Alan, like John Bargh noted above, highlights just how much of our processing is unconscious to us.

There are now some wonderful writings on the linkage between environments and biology. For example, a truly outstanding book that has just appeared is Robert Sapolsky's (2017) *Behave: The Biology of Humans at Our Best and Worst*. It clarifies very clearly how environments interacting with physiological systems produce helpful or harmful behaviour. You can see one of his talks here:

https://www.ted.com/talks/robert_sapolsky_the_biology_of_our_best_and_worst_selves

Another outstanding book, which is a little older, is by Philip Zimbardo, well-known for his Stanford experiment in the 1960s. His book *The Lucifer Effect: How Good People Turn Evil* was published in 2006. He also has an excellent TED talk, which you can see at:

https://www.ted.com/talks/philip_zimbardo_on_the_psychology_of_evil

The Lucifer Effect is a book of hope in the sense that a lot of cruel behaviour is socially contextualised. Important too is his more recent work on how compassion can stand against the Lucifer effect:

http://heroicimagination.org/

For all of these major advances, we are still catching up with the implications of how we should begin to think about the human mind. Indeed, as many of these exceptional researchers say, we are basically energy and information flows that co-regulate each other around the scaffold of genetic evolved potential.

What some researchers are beginning to think about is the fact that artificial intelligence is also about basic processes of information flow. We now have artificial intelligence that can read human emotion better than humans, can make medical decisions better than humans and can even drive cars better than humans. If there is anything special about humans it is likely to be something qualitatively different in the nature of consciousness – a subject which remains one of the biggest puzzles. Indeed, it is not necessary for decision making and many of our decisions rely on non-conscious processing unconscious.

Microbes

Another huge growth area in the last 20 years has been the study of gut microbes and their impact on a range of health dimensions, but in particular how they influence our minds, emotions and moods. To believe we are in control of our own minds only to discover that our bacteria in our gut may also be controlling our minds is another shiver into our sense of who or what we are. In fact scientists are now talking about human bodies and minds as ecosystems!

A helpful and easy-to-understand introduction can be found here:

http://edition.cnn.com/2017/07/05/health/hunter-gatherer-diet-tanzania-the-conversation/index.html

From here you can explore many other avenues of this fascinating area. There is also increasing evidence that our environment may (in some ways) be too hygienic, and the programming of the immune system may be affected. All of it points to the same fact that we are a highly interdependent species - not only on each other, but on the foods we eat, the organisms that live inside of us, the programme of some of the physiological systems, and the ecologies which give rise to our foods.

Cultivating Our Minds

The Psychotherapies

As noted earlier part of our despair and harmfulness, but also our potential liberation, comes from the fact that we are actually fundamentally different from other animals because we have a new type of mind and consciousness that allows for 'knowing awareness' and 'insight'. We can think, reason, and plan with a sense of self, of purpose, of meaning. And we have a deeply questioning mind; we want to know. What the hell is this process called life? We have a consciousness of consciousness; we are conscious that we are conscious. These are game changers in terms of life on earth. The problem is we are not really aware of the implications for this, and certainly rarely teach our children or ourselves how to mindfully cultivate and use consciousness and conscious intentionality to facilitate the good. Rather, we are often passive experiencers, on a kind of automatic pilot of feeling and acting according to what is stimulated in us. Some of the most profound developments in recent years has been how we can actually use our consciousness, our ability to observe and get to know our own minds in ways that can be helpful to us rather than harmful.

Psychotherapies not only help us with psychological difficulties, but can actually help us to understand our minds better, to have insight into how they work and why we feel and do what we do. This helps to expand mind awareness. Desires to help people with mental stress and ways of doing so are thousands of years old, clearly articulated in the contemplative traditions for example. In the immediate post-Darwinian period a range of psychodynamic therapies were developed based on the idea that many of the processes that shape and control us are evolutionary in nature and are often unconscious to us. Indeed, Freud regarded himself as working out Darwinian ideas for the mind. It was the unconscious that directed many of our drives. Jung argued for archetypes, rather than drives, as we have seen. As noted above, John Bargh's book gives a modernised version of these insights. Another evolutionary perspective and theory was that of John Bowlby, who in the 1960s and 1970s argued that it was not so much innate drives but attachment dynamics – and the need for styles of close relating – that underpin mental health problems:

https://www.simplypsychology.org/attachment.html

Another therapy development in the last 20 years linked to psychodynamic therapy (but that differs from it) has been mentalisation. This is teaching people how to pay attention and make sense of what goes on in the mind, to develop a kind of self-empathy. What is especially important is the ability to understand the minds of others. It links to what is called 'Theory of Mind' – that is that we can understand that people do things because of their motives and emotions; because they have 'Minds'. Many people with certain types of mental health problems can struggle with empathy and mentalisation:

http://www.annafreud.org/about-us/

Some Greek philosophies argued that reason should always be the basis for the regulation of emotion and desire. A simple but very insightful piece can be found here:

https://greenskyatnight.wordpress.com/2013/04/23/notes-on-ancient-greek-philosophy-plato-on-emotion-desire-reason/

Cognitive behavioural therapies, which have proliferated in the last 20 years, adopted this basic approach and gave up a concern with unconscious processing in favour of helping people learn how to pay attention to what arises in the mind, and then to how to think differently. Basically, to come off automatic pilot, notice one's thoughts as they arise, think logically and act in ways that are helpful to oneself according to one's values. Very stoic. Albert Ellis and Aaron Beck are the key players:

https://www.beckinstitute.org/

Cognitive therapy has now proliferated into a number of different schools such as Dialectical Behaviour Therapy and Acceptance and Commitment Therapy, although increasingly evidence suggests that outcomes are as much based on the relationship as they are on the approach.

Although the psychotherapies can be very tribal (they are competing for research money, career opportunities, reasons to treat patients, group belonging and status), and there is resistance to losing their identity, today many theories and therapies are moving towards integrative approaches that utilise interventions from different schools. Secondly, different tribes are understanding more and more that psychological processes need to be understood in terms of how the brain evolved and how it works. In my co-edited book *Genes on the Couch*, from 2000, a number of authors from different schools of therapy explored the evolutionary processes that underpin their models. So, we find increasingly that approaches are becoming more rooted in basic brain science. Thirdly, therapies are also becoming more of what we call multimodal, partly after the work of people like Arnold Lazarus. Therapies are beginning to pay a lot more attention to the body, such as integrating breathing exercises, various forms of meditation, yoga and dietary and supplement adjuncts to psychotherapy. In the future psychotherapies will be designed around complex psychological but also physiological, epigenetic and phenotypic profiles.

My focus to this has been compassion focused therapy (CFT), which tries to tick most of these multi-dimension boxes. It is an evolutionary and neuroscience-based approach that pays particular attention to the fact that we are a eusocial species and we are highly open and regulated via social relationships, particularly affiliative ones. CFT is also a multimodal therapy that integrates interventions from other approaches, but pays particular attention to body states, motivation and intention. It also uses many of the contemplative practices for compassionate mind-training. What CFT is moving towards more and more however, is developing interventions that change physiological systems, even gene methylation and phenotypes. That is likely to be the future, as well as matching interventions with phenotypes. More information about CFT, including information about upcoming trainings and courses, can be found on the Compassionate Mind Foundation's website: http://www.compassionatemind.co.uk

Mindfulness

While many psychotherapies seek to improve our ability to understand and pay attention to the content of our minds, the last 20 years has seen considerable development and research in two areas that have been inspired by the contemplative traditions – especially, but not only, the many schools of Buddhism. Meditation practices in the West have existed for a while now and were significantly brought to the general public by the Beatles and the Maharishi with transcendental meditation, something that took my fancy in the early 1970s. 'Om' to you all.

Jon Kabat Zinn was one of the foremost clinicians to bring *mindfulness* into the clinic to help people with chronic pain. Mindfulness is slightly different to transcendental meditation because there are two elements to it. One is observing our sensory experience (what we can see, hear, smell in all its detail) in the present moment. We can focus on the experience of the breath coming in and out, and so on. This is called focused mindfulness that supports calming.

The other is insight mindfulness, observing the arising of thoughts, emotions, motives and desires as they arise in the mind. Both forms of mindfulness are partly to help us to disengage from the stream of archetypal energies that can drive us into harmful actions or keep us locked in painful states of mind. Since that time, mindfulness training has proliferated and there are now many forms of it. You can find about Jon Kabat-Zinn's extraordinary contribution on his homepage: https://www.mindfulnesscds.com/

There are however different approaches to mindfulness, and my own has been more from within Mahayana traditions, which focus on compassion cultivation. In the UK, one of the centres for Buddhism that has a strong compassion focus is the Samye Ling Monastery and Tibetan Centre in Scotland:

http://www.samyeling.org/

I am currently a patron of the Mindfulness Association, who offer mindfulness trainings rooted in Tibetan Buddhist practice, and offer many of their trainings and events at Samye Ling (and its associated Samye Dzong centres):

http://www.mindfulnessassociation.net

The explosion of mindfulness into many aspects of life has been extremely helpful, including for therapists as a means to help them to become more mindful in their reactions to their clients. When offered to clients it is to help them with depression, anxiety and stress Mindfulness is also being taken up to help management and organisational processes. A useful review can be found at:

Keng, S. L., Smoski, M. J., & Robins, C. J. (2011). Effects of mindfulness on psychological health: A review of empirical studies. *Clinical psychology review, 31*(6), 1041-1056.

Dan Siegel too has also been very active in integrating mindfulness and mind awareness training with therapy and for children; for example, see his books 1. *The Mindful Therapist: A Clinician's Guide to Mindsight and Neural Integration* (2010) and 2. *Mindsight: Transform Your Brain with the New Science of Kindness* (2011).

A very helpful and fascinating book that links our understanding of evolutionary biology with Buddhist contemplative practices has been by David P. Barash (2013) *Buddhist Biology: Ancient Eastern Wisdom Meets Modern Western Science* from Oxford University Press. He moves easily between Buddhist concepts of emptiness through to how different viruses change the way bodies and brains work.

One reason that mindfulness and attention awareness training are so important is because they help us to pay attention to the chaotic and multidimensional nature of our minds. It gives us an opportunity to learn how to pay attention to the different archetypal forces playing out within us, and rather than passively allowing these archetypal dramas to act through us, we can start to choose how we want to operate in the world. Therefore, mindfulness is a way of paying attention on purpose so that we become much more 'mind aware' and therefore able to choose our behaviour. The Dalai Lama once gave an example of how, when he was young, he used to like to fix watches that he took from the travellers to Lhasa. Nearing completion of one watch, he dropped a screw in the mechanism and in his frustration, took a hammer and smashed the watch. The point he said was that in that moment he had lost mindfulness and therefore had done exactly the opposite of his true intent, which had been to make a beautiful watch work. Now there was no chance at all of meeting that intention.

Mindfulness *is a first stage* to choosing action – and of course we would argue that allied to compassion and prosocial training we are more likely to choose those compassionate actions.

It is therefore wonderful to see mindfulness being taken to schools to help children become more mind-aware and learn mindfulness skills:

https://mindfulnessinschools.org/

Certainly, when I was growing up, and even when my children were growing up, there was nothing like this available to help young people recognise that our minds are very tricky and full of all kinds of wonderful but also very destructive potentials. Few would have predicted these amazing developments 20 years ago.

Nonetheless, as with all things, mindfulness is not without its critics. Nor is it without potential harmful effects for the unwary. In addition, some of the secular mindfulness trainings have been criticised because they have stripped out some of the deeper contemplative traditions, particularly the focus on ethics and morality. (See for example Van Dam, N. T., van Vugt, M. K., Vago et al., (2017). Mind the hype: A critical evaluation and prescriptive agenda for research on mindfulness and meditation. *Perspectives on Psychological Science*, 1745691617709589).

Focusing on strengths and positive experiences

The last 20 years has seen a fantastic increase in studies on the importance of positive and particularly affiliative experiences.

One of the big changes was the development of what is now called positive psychology, pioneered by Martin Seligman. This does indeed highlight the importance of focusing on strengths and competencies, virtues and values.

http://www.pursuit-of-happiness.org/science-of-
happiness/?gclid=CN2juoPOrNYCFe2_7QodXNoGVQ

Positive psychology includes kindness and compassion as core qualities to cultivate. This does not mean that any other psychology was negative psychology. It is more about the focus on how to cultivate happiness, meaningfulness and prosocial behaviour.

In addition, Rick Hanson, wrote a fascinating book called *Buddha's Brain* (2009), showing ways in which we can link neuroplasticity with experience, and how we can train our minds to hold onto the feelings associated with positive events. The reason for this is, to use one of his expressions, because our minds are like Velcro for the negative and Teflon for the positive. Hence negative events are more likely to be held in the brain and influence the wiring of the brain, but we can train to hold positive ones.

https://www.youtube.com/watch?v=1LDDzhDIqcM

The more we practise and rehearse a focus on the positive, without being simply in a La La Land of "all is wonderful regardless", the more we can help to change our brains in particular ways.

Another major contributor to this research endeavour has been Barbara Fredrickson. For many years, she has been exploring the evolutionary function of positive emotions (as broadening and building) and recently, has been focusing particularly on what you might call micro-moments of affiliative relating:

https://fredrickson.socialpsychology.org/

See one of her fascinating talks - which will link to many others:

https://www.youtube.com/watch?v=hKggZhYwoys

You can also catch her in conversation with Dan Siegel in their chapter in my recent compassion book:

Fredrickson, B. L. & Siegel D. J. (2017). Broaden and build theory meets interpersonal neurobiology as a lens on compassion and positivity resonance. In, P. Gilbert (ed.). *Compassion: Concepts, Research and Applications*. (pp. 203-217). London: Routledge.

The Prosocial Sciences and Compassion

As noted in Chapter 12, 20 years ago some researchers were lamenting that too much research was focused on aggression, anxiety and so on, and not enough on prosocial behaviour. That has seen a massive change recently in many areas of research, including by Dalai Lama and the setting up of the Mind and Life Institute, which has brought scientists and contemplative practitioners together to study happiness and prosocial behaviour.

https://www.mindandlife.org/

There are many wonderful talks by the Dalai Lama on compassion, and here is just one:

https://www.youtube.com/watch?v=9gqCw0FIylE

Today compassion is regarded as one of the most central components of prosocial behaviour, and is rooted in the evolution of mammalian caring. When this motivational system is activated and guided by our new brain competencies, we have compassion. Many mammals certainly show caring behaviour, e.g. for their young, but we probably wouldn't call that compassion. Today we define compassion as *a sensitivity to suffering in self and others, with a commitment to try to alleviate and prevent it*. Our ability to be sensitive and aware of suffering, and also to have the wisdom to know what to do, is rooted in our new brain competencies.

When held as a purposeful intention it is associated with a desire not to deliberately or carelessly cause suffering. Given this definition we can also see that our human dark side is the antithesis of compassion. Our dark side can be defined as *an insensitivity to the suffering of self and others and carelessly or purposefully causing it*. Clearly then compassion is not just about creating happiness or well-being, but is a core motivation that stands against the dark side of our human potentials.

Evolution: From caring to compassion

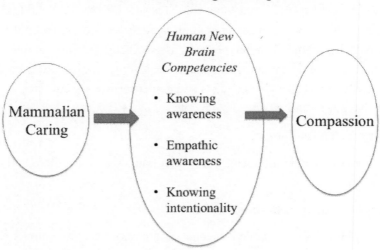

One of the leading neuroscientists exploring compassion has been Richard Davidson, who has pioneered studies of what happens in the brain as a result of compassion meditation practices:

https://centerhealthyminds.org/about/founder-richard-davidson

Another key leading neuroscientist is Tania Singer who, with the Buddhist monk and one-time French translator to the Dalai Lama, Matthieu Ricard, has made substantial contributions to the neuroscience of compassion. Matthieu, with whom I have had the pleasure and privilege of discussing some of the issues and controversies of compassion, wrote a wonderful book called *Altruism: The Power of Compassion to Change Yourself and the World* which was published in 2015. It is a large but brilliantly written book.

You can see one of his talks (with links to many others of his talks) here:

https://www.youtube.com/watch?v=_p_GKCr8rq8

Tania Singer and her colleagues brought a number of international compassion researchers together in Berlin for meetings, out of which came an e-book. For me, it was a fascinating and deeply rewarding experience to listen to many people talk about compassion from different points of view, and consider the research challenges. One of the outcomes was the bridging practice and science e-book:

Singer, T., & Bolz, M. (eds.) (2012) *Compassion: Bridging Practice and Science*. http://www.compassion-training.org/.

You can find out more about Tania Singer's work at this website where she also discusses some of the incredible work she is doing:

https://www.resource-project.org/en/home.html

You can see one of her talks on her recent thinking and research here:

https://www.youtube.com/watch?v=X7BaeIFCn6U

She and her colleagues also wrote a review chapter in my recent compassion book:

Vrtička, P., Favre. P & Singer, T. (2017). Compassion and the Brain In: P. Gilbert (ed.). *Compassion: Concepts, Research and Applications*. (pp. 135-150). London: Routledge

Other notable developments have been the setting up of major initiatives and open websites to coordinate compassion research. One of these is based at Stanford University and pioneered by Jim Doty, who is actually a neurosurgeon. He wrote his autobiography which discussed his own path to compassion in a very truthful and illuminating book called *Into the Magic Shop: A Neurosurgeon's Quest to Discover the Mysteries of the Brain and the Secrets of the Heart* (2016). The organisation that he has set up at Stanford University is called the Centre for Compassion and Altruism Research and Education (CCARE). Here you will find an immense Aladdin's cave of fascinating material:

http://ccare.stanford.edu/

Yet another Californian initiative has been the Greater Good Science Centre based at Berkeley:

https://ggsc.berkeley.edu/

Researchers from this group have also brought together a number of authors for a book edited by Emma M. Seppälä and Emiliana Simon-Thomas (2017) called *The Oxford Handbook of Compassion Science* (Oxford Library of Psychology). Jennifer Mascaro and I have a chapter on 'Fears, blocks and resistances to compassion'. While there is a lot of research on the facilitators of compassion, we have always argued that understanding the inhibitors is equally (if not more) important. Sometimes those inhibitors are in the environment but at other times they are in archetypal conflict, both within our own minds and within relationships.

There have also been a number of different compassion-focused psychotherapies. You can find a review of some of them in the chapter below:

Kirby, J. N. & Gilbert, P. (2017) The emergence of compassion focused therapies in: P. Gilbert (ed.). *Compassion: Concepts, Research and Applications*. (pp. 288-285). London: Routledge. Among them are the compassion cultivation training that takes place as part of CCARE (see above).

There has also been a focus on enabling individuals to develop their own self-compassion. There are now different models and definitions for this, which again I discussed in my recent compassion book.

An approach that focuses not so much on the mechanisms of compassion but on three dimensions of coping behaviour and compassionate coping training, is Kristin Neff's self-compassion model. You can find her unique approach and number of evidence-based helpful personal practices at her website:

http://self-compassion.org/

and one of her talks:

https://www.youtube.com/watch?v=rUMF5R7DoOA

Another important contributor to the self-compassion field is Chris Germer, who has his own website, again with many helpful practices:

https://chrisgermer.com

and a talk together: https://www.youtube.com/watch?v=Ld_RbajBbE4

One of the processes this book has tried to highlight is the interdependency required for the emergence of compassion. Indeed, compassion is *a flow*, in that we have self-compassion, compassion for others, and being open, receptive and responsive to compassion from others. Indeed, recent research by David Zuroff in Canada (https://www.mcgill.ca/psychology/ david-c-zuroff) and others is showing that our ability to be open and responsive to compassion is very important for wellbeing. We are back to the point that our relationships stimulate particular styles of interaction that are crucial for how our minds work, crucial to the dance of the archetypes and the orchestration of our algorithms.

Karen Armstrong's approach is very much in the social dynamics of compassion. She was herself a Catholic nun before becoming an academic, and has written many important books on religion. Importantly for us, she has also set up the Charter for Compassion, which seeks to bring compassion to the world by coordinating different communities.

https://charterforcompassion.org/

and see one of her talks:

https://www.youtube.com/watch?v=76Vl2J357Co

Another core (and very important and growing) initiative is a recognition that self-focus competitive motivation is being grossly overstimulated by the social media and also in schools.

https://mcc.gse.harvard.edu/links/children-we-mean-raise

Coles, M. I. (2015). *Towards the Compassionate School*. Trentham Books

see also Mind with Heart:

http://www.mindwithheart.org/en/

There is also, increasing often, wonderfully inspiring work that is teaching people how to behave kindly to each other, both in prisons and in schools, and with compassion. The effects seem to be quite extraordinary:

https://www.facebook.com/compassiongames/videos/1399773396809748/

Internationally too, there are an increasingly large number of charities that are focused on trying to be helpful to others in need, and this includes many of the United Nations, which is often pilloried because it cannot resolve international conflicts. This is partly because of the egos and tribal self-interest of the people there. However, they do wonderful work such as:

https://www.unicef.org.uk/?gclid=EAIaIQobChMIoNiqjsK91gIVFZSyCh1j0 w3-EAAYASAAEgKxbfD_BwE&sissr=1

The Compassionate Mind Foundation

For the last 20 years I have been studying the areas of prosocial behaviour and compassion, including the opportunity to work closely with Buddhist colleagues at the Samye Ling Monastery, particularly Choden with whom I co-author *Mindful Compassion*. In 2006, I was able to set up a charity with some colleagues called the Compassionate Mind Foundation. This model of compassion is very much rooted in an evolutionary and competencies-based approach as you would expect. Indeed, our website outlines our research and all our measures, along with videos of conferences, personal practices and more besides. In addition, we are linked with the University of Derby, where I set up a Compassion Research and Training Group. The university now runs a postgraduate certificate in compassion focused therapy, previously a programme led by Wendy Wood, and since her retirement, Martin Brock. Another compassion focused therapy training programme is run by Ken Goss and located at the University of Birmingham. Our website is:

www.compassionatemind.co.uk

The story is that the understanding of compassion has emerged slowly so that we now define it *as a sensitivity to suffering in self and others with a commitment to try to alleviate and prevent it*. This gives rise to two basic psychological processes. The first is the ability to turn towards and engage with suffering. The second is the developing of wisdom to know what to do. For example, wanting to be a doctor and being able to cope with distress is the first psychology, but then studying to become competent is the second. People often forget the importance of, and effort needed for, the second. People are often not aware of the competencies needed for each aspect of compassion.

We have a motivation and competency based approach to compassion. The six competencies necessary for engaging with suffering include the following: preparedness to be motivated to start the journey; the development of mindful competencies, so that we can begin to pay attention and notice suffering as and when it arises; the competencies to be emotionally attuned to suffering and moved by suffering, which is called sympathy; the competencies to be able to tolerate what moves us so that we are not overwhelmed or frightened by it (called distress tolerance); the competency for empathy, which is to understand the reasons for suffering both in ourselves and others and which links to mentalisation (see above); and the ability to be accepting and non-judgemental of what is happening in our, or others', inner experiences of suffering. Compassion focused therapy works with all those competencies.

For the second psychology, there are the competencies to pay attention to what is helpful. For example, once your doctor has paid attention to what is causing your suffering then s/he needs to switch attention to how to address it: the competency to run imagery simulations in one's mind that are going to be helpful; competencies for reasoning and problem-solving; competencies for behaving, which sometimes requires courage and working with the frightening or dark side; the competencies for sensory awareness and supporting the body on the journey of compassion; and the competencies to feel, which sometimes involves the feeling of joyfulness when we can be successful. We also have measures to measure these now, which you can find on our website, under the scales section and also here:

https://jcompassionatehc.biomedcentral.com/articles/10.1186/s40639-017-0033-3

Importantly, we can have fears, blocks and resistances to any of these competencies. For example, we might be fearful to begin or be motivated to start compassion. We might be fearful of allowing ourselves to feel attuned to suffering; we might be fearful of starting to develop empathic abilities for distress. We might be fearful of engaging in the courage necessary to confront and overcome one's difficulties or the difficulties of others.

Not all compassion models define compassion this way, nor do they have a competency-based approach, although some do. You can read about these controversies and differences in my chapter 'Compassion, definition and controversies' in my 2017 edited book *Compassion Concept, Research and Applications*, published by Routledge.

Sister organisations

Over time we have developed sister organisations so that we are now an internationally linked group with foundations in a number of other countries, such as the US (including New York), Australia, Sweden, France and Rome. There are now compassion in schools and business programme developing and being evaluated (see our website).

On all the national websites associated with the Compassionate Mind Foundation you will find discussions, concepts and models, including some personal practices for breathing, compassion focusing and compassionate behaviour.

In America, Dennis Tirch and Laura Silberstein-Tirch have the Center for Compassion Focused Therapy in New York:

http://www.mindfulcompassion.com/

and Russell Kolts has set up the Inland Northwest Compassionate Mind Centre in Spokane, WA: http://www.compassionatemind.net/

Another recent initiative on the other side of the world has been by Dr James Kirby who has been instrumental in setting up the Compassion Research Centre at the University of Queensland, where I hold a visiting professorship. This research centre is linked with the University of Derby and the Compassionate Mind Foundation (see below)

https://www.psy.uq.edu.au/research/centresandgroups.html?role=895

James co-ran a podcast series with Jim Doty from CCARE called 'The Alphabet of the Heart':

https://m.soundcloud.com/user-76806857

Here are some of James's recorded practices and podcasts:

https://m.soundcloud.com/jamesn-kirby

and James' compassion initiative website:

https://compassioninitiative.com.au/

James and his colleagues are also doing amazing work on compassion facilitators and inhibitors in children:

https://www.youtube.com/watch?v=OXuNAfDxk7o

Another important Australian initiative is with James Bennett Levy, and Compassionate Mind Australia:

https://www.compassionatemind.org.au/

In Italy Nicola Petrocchi has established Compassionate Mind Italia in Rome:

http://www.compassionatemind.it/

In France, Francis Gheysen and Pascal Delamillieure have established the French Compassionate Mind Foundation:

http://compassionatemindfoundationfrance.org/

Currently, Rick Hanson and I are trying to pull together a listing of all international communities that are compassion focused. We hope these will be on our websites within the near future.

My daughter Hannah also has her own events business which offers compassion based workshops and courses for the general public: http://www.compassionatewellbeing.com

Economics and Business

The extraordinary movements in positive psychology, mindfulness, compassion, empathy, morality ethics and prosocial research are very exciting. These are all potential ways to nudge the dance of the archetypes in a prosocial direction, and counteract the tendency for *Living Like Crazy*. Compassion training of different kinds offer the means of becoming more aware of the nature of our minds, more moral and more prosocial. None of these approaches advocate learning the skills in order to become more competitive and screw everybody else. However, what is also extremely exciting is that compassion science is reaching into businesses and leadership. With obvious exceptions, the history of both are not particularly compassionate.

My first degree was in economics and I have always had a fascination with the relationship between economic relationships and psychological experience. Many economists understand the importance of the way economic systems can create very non-compassionate contexts. Jeffery Sachs wrote an important book called *The Price of Civilisation* which highlighted the fact that we have allowed competitive psychology to dominate the world. While there have been some advantages, there have been many huge disadvantages: http://jeffsachs.org/, not least the huge disparities of wealth which distorts investment.

He makes clear, for example, that in this country the politics of austerity were harsh, unfair, hurting those least able to bear it, and is also counter-productive. The argument of making 'tough decisions' is, in reality, making callous decisions because tough decisions would be going after the people that caused this crisis, and making the people who can pay, pay. The effort to regulate the banks that President Franklin Roosevelt argued passionately for in the 1930s is still frighteningly unobserved. Indeed, it was the gradual deregulation of the banks from the Regan-Thatcher years onwards that led to the crisis:

https://www.thoughtco.com/history-of-banking-reform-after-the-new-deal-1147513

Tragically, the Labour Party have failed to articulate or provide strong opposition to austerity or to banking reform. Compassion is clearly about appropriate regulation and not having a naïve view of human nature. However, as Jeremy Corbyn's recent surprise election result shows, if you articulate a very clear compassionate and social justice agenda, people will vote for it; however, it has to be clear and costed, it has to be passionate, it has to be well-articulated and supported from within.

In recent years, therefore, we have seen important work by people like Richard Wilkinson and Kate Pickett who wrote the book *The Spirit Level: Why Equality is Better for Everyone*, published in 2010 by Penguin. They have gone on to set up the Equality Trust:

https://www.equalitytrust.org.uk/about-inequality/spirit-level

Other important economists have warned about the serious problems of inequality of resource distribution. For example, Joseph Stiglitz in his book *The Great Divide* (2015), published by Penguin:

https://www8.gsb.columbia.edu/faculty/jstiglitz/

Part of the problem is because of the systems that we have allowed to simply emerge. Of course, entrepreneurialism is a basis for the creation of wealth, and how we support enthusiastic and creative entrepreneurialism is not really the issue here. It is how such talent is used and what it creates.

In addition, debate continues to develop around the issue of the politics of power as opposed to the politics of democracy for both national and international policies. One of the most outspoken thinkers in this area has been Noam Chomsky: https://chomsky.info/

See his book *Profit over People: Neoliberalism and Global Order* published in 1999 by Seven Stories Press.

There is also an ongoing political analysis of how people with money can buy themselves into power and be supported by low resource individuals (poor) who are angry and feel disenfranchised.

This is supported by marvellous journalists such as John Pilger:

http://johnpilger.com/ and see his book *The New Rulers of the World* published in 2003 by Verso.

We should also be mindful of the fact that some forms of leadership, and the conflictual nature of many parliaments and media pleasing, are actually creating the kinds of minds that we definitely do not want in our leaders; these minds can be interested in undermining the opposition than they are in working out the complexities and difficulties of creating fair and compassionate societies. Moreover, the one-time psychiatrist turned politician David Owen has written extensively on the mental health problems of leaders over the years, and in particular the problem of hubris, which is a very serious problem in business and politics:

http://www.daedalustrust.com/tag/lord-david-owen/

There is also ongoing research on the problems of leaders' personalities, which are often power-seeking, and once such individuals get power they use it destructively to actively promote the dark side of our archetypes rather than stand against them:

https://psychology.iresearchnet.com/social-psychology/group/social-dominance-orientation/

There is increasing concern about the ability of people with resources to manipulate those without resources for political ends. Hitler was great at it. As we saw in Chapter 11 and elsewhere, Gay's work on *The Cultivation of Hatred* is very important for us to get our minds around.

Media studies are beginning to explore the issues of media moguls creating prejudice that serves their self-interest, and being elastic with the truth, presenting 'news' through the frosted glass of political manipulation that obscures rather than illuminates. Social media has also erupted into an explosion of fears of false news and cul-de-sac thinking. The battle to control our minds, be it for our votes or our purchases, and the dance of the archetypes within us, is very strong. Although we are making great strides in some areas, there is still much to do in how to move political discourses to compassion and sharing motives rather than the threat-based, self-focused competitive concerns our media like to play on. Looking the leaders emerging in the world today be it in established democracies, communist states, African or Arabic states tells its own story.

The Dark Side of Cooperation

Most recognise that our evolved ability to cooperate, work together, share and support each other to achieve goals underpins much prosocial behaviour and indeed the road to culture and civilisation as we know it. Moreover, cooperation has emerged from, but also driven, language and our extraordinary range of socially intelligent competencies, including empathy. Many evolutionists highlight the fact that humans are eusocial with a unique form of cooperation to which we owe much of our success as a species. We cooperate, but also specialise in cooperation. An orchestra with everybody playing different instruments, different parts at different times but in a coordinated fashion, is an example. We can form teams of self-aware, interacting individuals be it medical or research teams, or teams in factories, that build cars and TVs or like to play football socially. But as with so much with our human competencies much depends on motivation, with whom, and for why we cooperate, because team cooperation also underpins war and how we can put 100,000 and more on the battle for mutual slaughter.

Here are many dark sides to cooperation. In his important and fascinating book *Homo Deus*, the philosopher Yuval Noah Harari highlights the problem evolutionists have long highlighted: we evolved for small group cooperation rather than large-scale. Within large groups you have smaller groups of co-operators who engage in reciprocal sharing forming groups for specific individuals. These cooperating subgroups can then operate to exploit the rest of the mega group in which they are operating. It is clear of course that for thousands of years tyrants only gained and maintained their power (and still do) because they had a close network of cooperative henchmen to support them; not uncommonly (secret often brutal) police or army. The moment they turn against the leader s/he is finished. Indeed, these professions need to do a much better job at fostering an international ethical code for their profession (like medicine), to try to stop armies being used to support dictators and tyrants against their own people. It is hopeful that the wisdom of the future will forbid nations to have their own armies.

The point here however is that sub-group of co-operators working together for self-interest can do great harm; for example, the 'old boy network' which enables groups of rich, privileged males to form cooperative networks that control many power dynamics, including the media, and therefore they can manipulate politics and social values in their own interests.

This year the *Guardian* and *Observer* newspapers ran a series of articles on these forces. Furthermore, the publications of the leaked Panama and Paradise Papers have shown just how much money politicians, celebrities and business folk have hidden. In addition, the issues of deception and corruption in many corridors of power throughout the world not only does great harm, but distorts our compassion and ethical efforts as a species.

It's important that compassion is not naïve, and seriously engages with the dark forces that stand against it; strategies and archetypes operating through powerful individuals who probably have very little insight into what's actually controlling them. They are simply acting out their basic strategies, algorithms, desires and fears. It is known, for example, that right-wing individuals tend to be more threat based in their perceptions of the world. They are certainly focused on accumulating resources for themselves and fear these being taken away. We have suffered greatly over thousands of years because conditions have been conducive for these strategies operating in the minds of humanity. So, we need to constantly illuminate and reveal these networks, but also build counteracting networks of individuals in the same professions who work together and begin to create social conditions for compassionate and prosocial behaviour in business and in politics. This is one of the challenges for all of us really, because we have the resources and the intelligence to solve our problems, but are not going to be able to do that if we allow these strategies and mentalities to rule us and control us via greed and fear.

Working Environments

The way the wealthy are allowed to manipulate the means of production has huge implications for how we all spend our working lives, and of course the working lives of people in developing countries. Unrestrained competitive psychology is a power and resource amplification device. It's very clear that if people were allowed to, as they were in centuries past, there would still be entrepreneurs happy to continue with slavery and children working in factories.

Adam Smith understood that competitive psychology needed sensitivities. Many economists are clear that competition is about winning and losing, and indeed many entrepreneurial coaches advertise themselves as 'showing how to give your company a competitive edge', 'that you are not a loser': in other words, to make somebody else a 'loser'. The problem is that the losers do not simply evaporate into thin air. They are human beings just like everybody else. If you cut them, they bleed. If you deprive them, they hurt. Economic losers are more sensitive to physical and mental health problems, and die younger. They are with us and their needs need to be met. The poor do not have investments to fall back on.

We have created a world where the production of goods and services are being constantly changed by our intelligence, which is great, except for the fact that many people caught in old ways of producing such products end up with factories closing and whole industries disappearing. For these individuals they see their children struggling without futures, in rundown, abandoned cities and towns and so will vote out of anger and despair; their home environments are unlikely to be ones of great joy and emotional calmness. Right wing media tragically feed off this despair to support their own agendas. If we do not find ways to accommodate rapid change in the way we produce goods and services that do not constantly dump people on scrap heaps with a sign over their heads saying 'no longer required', then we are not addressing the ethical and compassionate challenges of humanity. We are a fantastically inventive species, and are obviously going to continue to change rapidly in our technologies and production. But allowing this just to unfold is an example of where we fail to take responsibility for the consequences of what we are doing.

The problem is many businesses take absolutely little or no responsibility for the harm they cause, even if it is unintentional. Asset strippers, for example, have no interest whatsoever in the mental and physical health problems, relational and family fallout they cause, nor the expense incurred by the burden on the Health Service. Of course, the argument is that without stripping down, the whole business could go on down and everybody loses, but nonetheless this is still an issue for finding compassionate ways to manage economic change. In order for us not to be one of the losers, we are devoting more and more of our time to work: a phenomenon that Madeleine Bunting (2004) wrote about in her book *Willing Slaves*. My son can be asked to take on more responsibilities in his job for no extra pay, and to do extra hours when required. Not doing so is a markdown. Without caution, competitiveness is a race to the bottom, such as paying as little as possible to as few as possible. It is becoming clear that we are caught in a complex social system that is difficult to struggle free of, where in order to create a competitive edge some individuals/companies will also create many losers, which the rest of us will have to pick up the tabs for. They should not be seen as just unfortunate collateral damage from callous competition. We can do better than this, and on an international scale. Work stress and the loss of work is financially, but also emotionally, costly and many of the knock-on effects are incalculable. For the parent who loses his/her job and becomes depressed - has an impact on their growing children, who then become vulnerable to mental health problems themselves:

https://osha.europa.eu/en/tools-and-publications/publications/literature_reviews/calculating-the-cost-of-work-related-stress-and-psychosocial-risks

One major problem for companies is the tendency to be target-focused rather than process-focused. The health services suffer terribly from this, where so-called efficiency savings are really service cuts, job losses and demotions. One aspect of compassionate working practices is therefore to focus on process not outputs. John Seddon in particular has written on the inefficiencies of output-focused rather than process-focused organisational processes, particularly, but not only, in the NHS. There is potential for a more compassionate way of thinking about internal organisation:

https://www.buckingham.ac.uk/directory/john-seddon/

Compassion and the Prosocial Challenge

We certainly have our work cut out for us! It would however be wrong to argue that most business people are somehow morally indifferent. Indeed, increasing numbers of entrepreneurs want to provide high-quality goods and services ethically, morally and contribute to humanity, not detract from it. They also want to make a good living, of course. Indeed, to see how ethical concerns are now emerging: put 'ethics in business' into an internet search engine, and see all the innovations arising. The problem is we are operating in a system that can make that moral focus difficult. Nonetheless, many high-flying business people, especially the younger ones, are increasingly interested in making a contribution, using their entrepreneurial wisdoms and talents to lift their eyes above the horizon of (only) the pursuit of profits. They wish to use their talent to contribute to a better, fairer world.

While politicians have some power, the real drivers for social change are going to be businesses when they begin to get their act in order and begin to sanction their own. If businesses cheat - for example, on tax avoidance or exploitation of workers in a race to the bottom on wages, or damage ecologies - this will no longer be seen with a nod and a wink of cleverness in the back rooms of private clubs, but as morally unacceptable and distorting the playing field for everyone. Cheats operate in every walk of life, be it from medicine to drug cheating in sport. So, all professions need to not turn a blind eye to cheating, nor secretly admire it or learn how to do it without detection, but set up institutions for the detection, catching and preventing of cheating. Tragically, this is rarely happening in the profession of business. The non-payment of taxation is cheating. The falsification of car emissions is cheating, and the profession itself does little; partly because some have resisted having governing bodies, as they do not want external constraint. We may wish to change the system, argue against it, inspire people to change it, but it is cheating if you do not play by the rules, whether or not you agree with them.

There is a wonderful initiative from the Harvard Business School to develop a sort of Hippocratic Oath for businesses: http://mbaoath.org/

Below are just a few of the great developments in trying to create working environments that are conducive to well-being:

One way of helping leaders and businesses is to encourage them to become more mindful, and aware that a lot of our harmful acts are unintentional; we are just not switched on as to what is going on in our heads. For example, Louise Chester has been developing mindfulness for leaders: www.mindfulnessatwork.com

In the compassion field, there are wonderful initiatives like Ari Cowan's:

https://www.compassionate.center/pgs/people/bios/ari-cowan.html

Jayne Dutton and Monica Worline been working for many years on compassionate work:

http://webuser.bus.umich.edu/janedut/Compassion.htm

There is growing evidence that businesses who put the wellbeing and involvement of their staff in the centre-ground, and hold to moral means of production, have higher staff loyalty, creativity and customer service. See for example, Google's study:

https://qz.com/625870/after-years-of-intensive-analysis-google-discovers-the-key-to-good-teamwork-is-being-nice/

In addition, good leaders focus on creating a secure base for the people who work for them and do not use threat as a motivator.

https://www.youtube.com/watch?v=lmyZMtPVodo&feature=youtu.be

See also organisations seeking to bring altruism into organisation:

https://www.centreforeffectivealtruism.org/

Indeed, if you put 'compassion organisations' into Google it is amazing the number you will find. Some of these are religion-based, but many are not.

One example of entrepreneurs putting their talents to address a major issue is in the clean-up of plastic bottles.

http://www.wired.co.uk/article/sky-ocean-rescue-sea-pollution

The only issue with this is that there is no point in creating an industry for clean up if you do not go after the bottle makers who have basically hoodwinked everybody into believing that bottled water (for example) is better than tap water. We need scientific talent to create decomposable containers. Why have the plastic bottle industry not invested hugely in this?

I was recently at a cricket test match where they wouldn't allow you to bring in your own bottled water, which encouraged you to buy their plastic ones. At the end of the match the bins and ground were littered with plastic bottles. There were a few water fountains around but a very simple solution would be to ban the selling of plastic bottles in sports grounds and provide cardboard cups and water fountains or soft drinks fountains. These issues have solutions if people are prepared to think them through and take action. Imagine all sports grounds getting together and making a decision about how to get rid of plastic bottles in their grounds. The fact is that when we make a decision jointly it has powerful effects. Think about the wearing of seat belts or the banning of smoking in public places. It can be done, we just need the will to do it.

To advance this, one of the growing core changes is the community movement for prevention of ecological harm. Here is an example of a group I recently met in Australia – it offers a good model for change. The question is how to develop this in communities that are not so empowered:
https://www.youtube.com/watch?v=o7C4ousqB4E

See also the work of Elinor Ostrom (1933-2012):
https://www.prosocial.world/the-science

There are multiple efforts to reclaim the rainforests, but again the issue is preventing them being cut down in the first place:
https://www.coolearth.org/projects/?gclid=EAIaIQobChMI3MC2wtK91gIVj4
eyCh0NpgfwEAAYASAAEgJ76fD_BwE

And of course, Compassion in World Farming is a compassion based organisation that reaches into how we treat and work with animals https://www.ciwf.org.uk/

Compassion in World Farming not only addresses the issue of animal cruelty, but is also pointing out that our dependency on meat is very wasteful in terms of food value. Moreover, the waste products of our farm animals are extremely polluting; the methane gas alone is contributing to the destruction of the ozone level.

Compassion, which focuses on the sensitivity to suffering, seeking its prevention and certainly not to carelessly or intentionally cause it, can be a focus and a lens through which we make decisions about how we produce goods and services, and indeed what goods and services to produce. We need a new politics and a way of producing goods and services that benefit all of us, that limits disparities of earnings and considers human happiness and wellbeing as a human challenge and responsibility. Some are addressing these issues with ideas such as Buddhist economics in fascinating ways.

https://www.lionsroar.com/buy-less-live-more-the-promise-of-buddhist-economics/

But you don't need to be a Buddhist to develop the moral and compassionate compass for how we need to build our communities. One of the most exciting and important developments is using scientific studies to guide us in creating contexts and environments that promote prosocial behaviour. Indeed, as noted above, there are a number of movements doing exactly this.

Compassion is therefore about developing the courage and seeking the wisdom to address these issues – it is not simply about being kind and helpful to each other; it is a determination to address the immoral, and the recognition of how our cultures are working our evolved brains.

As this book has tried to show we need to get our attention off of individuals and much more onto collective processes that facilitate the emergence of strategies within the minds of individuals. For example, many of us including myself, didn't always wear a seatbelt until it was enforced, and would occasionally (back in the 1970s) drink (a little) and drive. I would like to tell you that I was this wonderful upstanding moral person, but I am the same as anybody else. Of course, once it became illegal and it was really hammered home the dangers of drinking and driving that's when most of us stopped -- when the culture changed. And of course, I talk to my accountants to see if they can legally minimise my tax bill; I'm not going to ask them to find ways so I can pay the maximum tax! In regard to the financial crisis of 2008 many might see our top bankers as selfish people who knew the risks they were taking, but lacked a moral compass because of the money they were making. For sure some are attracted to the industry precisely for the potential to earn lots of money. However, the crisis was also caused by a system that reduced interest rates to such levels that people could borrow too easily and encouraged life on credit. One of the most important insights of compassion is to recognise that to create balance requires regulation. Freedom always holds a dark side, and to be blind to that is a serious risk to humanity because one person's freedom is another person's nightmare.

It's all about the systems we create, and the recognition that all of us respond to the culture. Relying on self-determination only takes us so far, as noble as it is. When we give up blaming individuals for wrongdoing or cheating, and put wise systems in place to stop it, then we are in business. We must loosen this idea that individuals are autonomous freethinking beings and see ourselves as a form of consciousness caught up in biologically and culturally created contexts that we are struggling to understand, let alone regulate for the common good.

Prosocial Leaders

As indicated in Chapters 7 and 8, there are prosocial and antisocial leaders and their various mixtures. The latter take us more deeply into the dark sides of our nature, - in particular tribalism - reducing a sense of responsibility for those less fortunate, and creating greater disparities between the haves, have-nots and have lots. Unfortunately, over the last 30 years there has been a movement towards having more of this leadership style rather than less. The dreams of the immediate post World War II to build a fairer, caring society has gradually withered in the pursuit of self-interest. Within 15 years of the ending of the war, Britain built health, education and transport services that were the envy of the world. We had no money because we had just been devastated by war, but we had a genuine political and social will to create a better world. We do not need *Star Wars* movies to help us recognise that the pull on our dark side is strong, invisible and works on our own passions, fears, prejudices and self-focused desires that some leaders seek to arouse.

Today we need leaders who have something of the psychologist's understandings too. We need leaders who understand that part of leading is working with the reality of a very tricky, and at times dangerous and callous, human brain; leaders who know how to choreograph and inspire us to have a prosocial archetypal dance. We need leaders who are prepared to find the courage and wisdom to address the inequalities and prejudices our brain so easily creates, be these in the domains of ethnicity, gender or sexuality. We need leaders who can find the courage and wisdom to recognise the need to invest in the infrastructures of a caring society, such as its health service, teaching and police, rather than allowing them to fracture and crumble in the search for tax cuts. We need leaders of business who strive for ethical and human enhancing ways for producing goods and services and not to exploit as much as one can as long as one can get away with it. We need a new brand of political leaders who recognise that the way our current democracies operate - where parties fight with each other and are funded by big businesses - are not fit for purpose. Politicians whose minds are constantly stimulated to argue against, to make the opposition look bad and be concerned with how that will play in the media, are not the minds able to address the serious problems facing humanity. They are unable to inspire and change hearts and minds as the disillusionment and distrust of politicians show. We need leaders who understand the importance of creating a sense of common humanity, not tribal conflicts and hostilities. We need leaders who have a caring orientation to the context and services they are trying to lead. We need leaders who are committed to improving life for all sentient beings.

The Future

There are many new and important issues that science is beginning to grapple with. Ever since the Enlightenment, we have tended to parcel up our knowledge into different disciplines. We have been encouraged also to think of ourselves as disconnected, single autonomous individuals with 'souls' that can be individually rewarded or punished. In reality, we are highly interdependent, co-regulated and co-constructed beings. Depending on our genetic endowment and how that is choreographed (epigenetics), we can end up as 'angels' or 'demons'. Even the (good or poor quality) foods we eat, the microbes in the gut, the pollution in air we breathe are all highly influenced by our interactions with each other.

These are ways of thinking about where we are now in terms of understanding ourselves and the challenges ahead, particularly as new technologies shape and sculpture our minds in completely new and unpredictable ways.

Science, however, is also moving into the edges of probably one of the greatest psychological challenges – the search for a new spirituality, arising from the nature of mind as 'energy flows'. On the 30 June 1860, one year after the publication of *On the Origin Of Species*, Bishop Wilberforce publicly debated with Darwin, asking whether it was on his mother's or father's side that he claimed descent from apes. This ridicule was of course hiding a very anxious awareness that Darwinian thinking would contribute to the undermining of faith and religion. Indeed, it has. But there are many reasons for the West's 'letting go' of beliefs in creator deities. One is that we are no longer frightened by the Church, we are less deferential, and the second, as science reveals the harsh realities of life, we give up our dissociations and denials. It is simply not possible to believe in a loving creator when we understand the inherent brutalities and absolute horrors of predation, disease, decay and the slow and painful ways of dying in the flow of life. Humanism of course has always been clear on these ideas, believing that our fate is in our own hands. It is ourselves we need to understand, not some orders or rules of an ancient, never seen, fantasy figure: http://understandinghumanism.org.uk/

Yet it is at this point that we have the greatest spiritual challenges and opportunities because we are free to think and explore the nature of our minds in a very strange universe with very strange physical laws, in completely new and open ways. Indeed, one of the great mysteries we now face is not so much over our origins, but our futures. Some people see our future as moving towards immortality (or at least longer lifespans) or a cyborg-type existence, but any evidence for conscious continuation after death will completely change the game. Although this is one of the most important questions for humanity to research, the research money going into it is minuscule, apart from a few brave individuals and organisations:

http://www.horizonresearch.org/

https://www.youtube.com/watch?v=tTj2TEHVqTc

And who knows? Maybe it will turn out to be a dead end, but as scientists - no matter what our prejudice - we should not pre-decide. Consider the invention of the telephone. Back in the 1850s the idea that we could talk to people over long distances because of a wire of electrical currents was regarded as outrageous. The idea that you could have a small device (mobile) in your hand in England. and talk to somebody in America or Africa, would have seemed ridiculous. As for the Internet, well anyone suggesting that 200 years ago would have found themselves in a straitjacket. Science is always open, science develops methodologies to explore. We had no idea of 'cells' until we invented a method to see into the minuscule - microscopes and then of course electron microscopes. Now we can see our DNA! The methodologies to study consciousness are rather crude but are improving. As Karl Popper argued years ago, scientists can be on very dodgy ground when they argue what 'cannot be.' Many scientific discoveries have had to battle against disbelievers – even Einstein. In the end, it does not really matter what our opinions are, provided we do not try and close down the science.

So, it comes down to the nature of consciousness and what that means. The archetypes, strategies and algorithms, created by patterns of neurochemicals and synaptic firing, that give rise to the contents of our consciousness are becoming clear, but not the nature of consciousness itself. Here, physicists and other scientists are beginning to ask the question: "what is this experience called consciousness?" Buddhists tell us it is the ground of all being but is empty; consciousness is "that from which all forms come into existence but it is formless itself". We can get glimpses of this if we meditate and enable our minds to settle, to be still and sense the *feeling of the nature of consciousness itself*. Material scientists see such ideas as rather whimsical and a fingertip grasping to the fear of nonexistence. For them, consciousness is an epiphenomenon created by the mass of trillions of synaptic connections rendering it – not a lot more than a chemical trick. It's a pretty amazing trick but nonetheless when you die, so does consciousness; when the candle is spent, there is nothing to give light. Others, however, are not so sure and feel that the universe remains such an extraordinary mystery of why something exists rather than nothing, that there profoundly important discoveries waiting in the corridors of the next few hundred or thousand years, especially about the nature of consciousness. I found this an interesting discussion:

https://www.ted.com/talks/david_chalmers_how_do_you_explain_consciousn ess

Some neuroscientists are questioning what the brain actually does. Does it create patterns within fields of energy?

https://www.ted.com/talks/jill_bolte_taylor_s_powerful_stroke_of_insight

https://www.youtube.com/watch?v=4xUu98xH8i0

In addition, physicists are investigating the complex nature between consciousness and the physical world:

https://www.youtube.com/watch?v=shWRKpf7Hwg

Dan Siegel's book *Mind* also addressed these issues in fundamental new ways.

Our understanding of ourselves and the meaning of our lives changes as science changes. It is because of our scientific understanding of the universe that we see ourselves completely differently from how we did a thousand years ago. A thousand years ago, we had no idea as to the vastness of the universe, that the stars were not pinpoints in heaven or that our physical forms are built from

DNA. If we were to discover there is more to consciousness than meets the eye, how might that change us? No one really knows. Yet it is the most profoundly important human question.

So, this is an important future question. Personally, I believe our flirtation with cyborg-bodies will be brief. Human improvement will come from medicine understanding stem cells, DNA and unlocking biological renewal systems, and even changing genetic codes maybe. Yet even so, be it that consciousness is a product of chemistry, we can also recognise that it is what we do together that is crucial to how we experience it, what textures it and the nature of our lives. Cyborg technology might improve our bodies, but it will not improve the quality of our minds, values and styles relating. It is scientifically valid to see our minds as energy flows in a field of interactions as Dan Siegel highlights in his book *Mind*.

Consequently, we always come back to patterns of relating, from atoms to minds to cultures, because that is crucial for the dance of the archetypes. From the day we are born to the day we die our social relationships influence and build us right down to our genetic expressions. Our relationships significantly influence the quality and happiness of the lives we have. It will create the kinds of worlds we pass to our descendants and indeed other life forms we share our planet with. The more we wake up to this fact, the more we recognise that competitiveness has a place in the production of material things, but should not run the show as it does now.

As a follow-up to my 1989 book *Human Nature and Suffering*, this book has tried to contribute to the emerging recognition from many quarters that we all just find ourselves here, a consciousness whose content has been created by a genetic endowment we never chose, a gender and ethnicity we never chose, into a time and culture we never chose, maybe restrictive religions we never chose, maybe to hurtful or loving parents we never chose, and indeed into a way of living we never chose. We have brains sculptured in ways, with a sense of self texture and patterned in ways we never chose and, maybe would not choose. If we want to choose to create a 'better' life for ourselves and the world, it is definitely going to help if we recognise what we are up against, in terms of the nature of the human mind.

Living Like Crazy has highlighted the fact that we have a range of evolved motivational potentials for good or for bad. Our problem is our minds are easily manipulated and textured by social context. We have created contexts that give rise to the human sacrificing Aztecs, Crusades, the Inquisition, terrorist groups; to belief systems that propagate fear and restrictions on contraception and gender preference, inhibiting one's own sexual and reproductive decisions with devastating consequences. We have food industries that convince us to eat and eat, giving way to obesity and diabetes; companies that encourage us to pollute the seas with plastic bottles... and that's just the tip of an iceberg. In recognising how easy it is for our minds to be manipulated into justifying extraordinary sadism and callousness, even giving up freedom of our own sexuality and reproductive control, the serious sources of our craziness is apparent. While these influences are fading, new choreographers of mind are emerging from the shadows; a media focused on their own versions of truth. Despite their benefits, social media and internet giants like Google and Facebook can run algorithms to discover anything they can about us that would allow them to manipulate values, political tribal loyalties, and of course purchase products. Everyday our minds are being patterned and influenced without our awareness, not for the benefit of humanity but for various vested self interests. The compassionate challenge is how to wake up and see what's happening. Practicing mindful compassionate wisdom, while not fool proof, holds the potential to claim back our minds in the service of humanity. What is so heartening is that today more and more people are waking up to the fact that we have an evolved brain, and a culturally inherited created mind, that is driving us crazy. More and more people are now genuinely thinking collectively and scientifically about how to create a better world for us all to live in.

Despite many efforts at compassion, our dark sides have ruled our history for many thousands of years and competitive self-interest, greed and tribalism still do. Indeed, many religions have used the dark side to promote themselves. All those who think that compassion is somehow a weakness or an indulgence, or is just about being nice, kind, or polite and could never solve any serious problem are seriously misguided. As some of the contemplative sciences have shown us for thousands of years, and science is beginning to reveal, compassion is one of the most important courageous and healing motivations that nature ever came up with. Not to cultivate it and use it for the benefit of us all would be to continue living like crazy.

Paul Gilbert
Derby, UK
21ˢᵗ January, 2018

There are many exciting charities now that are focused on trying to generate ethics and compassion in areas such as: health care, policing, restorative justice, businesses, politics and schools but rely on donations. The Compassionate Mind Foundation is the same. If there are any research projects you feel you would like to donate to, or sponsor, please get in touch as we'd be delighted to hear from you: http://www.compassionatemind.co.uk

REFERENCES

Abbott, G. (1993) *Rack, Rope and Red-Hot Pinchers: A History of Torture and its Instruments*. London: Headline.

Abrams, D., Cochrane, S., Hogg, M.A. and Turner, J.C. (1990) Knowing what to think by knowing who you are: Self categorization and the nature of norm formation, conformity and group polarization. *British Journal of Social Psychology*, 29, 97-119.

Adler, G. (1986) Psychotherapy of the narcissistic personality disorder patient. *American Journal of Psychiatry*, 143, 430-436.

Adler, N.E., Boyce, T., Chesney, M.A., Cohen, S., Folkman, S., Kahn, R.L and Syme, S.L. (1994) Socioeconomic status and health. *American Psychologist*, 49, 15-24.

Ahmad, Y. and Smith, P.K. (1994) Bullying in schools and the issues of sex differences. In Archer J. (ed.) *Male Violence*. London: Routledge.

Andrews, B. & Brewin, C.R. (1990) Attributions of blame for marital violence: A study of antecedents and consequences. *Journal of Family and Marriage*, 52, 757-767.

Archer, J. (1994, ed.) *Male Violence*. London: Routledge.

Archer, J. (1992) *Ethology and Human Development*. London: Harvester and Wheatsheaf.

Archer, J. (1990) The influence of testosterone on human aggression. *British Journal of Psychology*, 82, 1-28.

Archer, J. (1988) *The Behavioural Biology of Aggression*. Cambridge: Cambridge University Press.

Argyle, M. (1987) *The Psychology of Happiness*. London: Methuen & Co.

Argyle, M. (1991) *Cooperation: The Basis of Sociability*. London: Routledge.

Armstrong, K. (1994) *A History of God*. Mandarin Books.

Attenborough, D. (1992) Three volumes following a BBC series. *Life on Earth; The Living Planet; The Trials of Life*. BBC Collins.

Axelrod, R. (1990) *The Evolution of Cooperation*. Penguin.

Bailey, K.G. (1988) Psychological kinships: Implications for the helping professions. *Psychotherapy*, 25, 132-141.

Bailey, K. (1987) *Human Paleopsychology. Applications to Aggression and Pathological Processes*. Hillsdale: N.J: Lawrence Erlbaum Associates Ltd.

Bailey, K.G., Wood, H. and Nava, G.R. (1992) What do clients want? Role of psychological kinship in professional helping. *Journal of Psychotherapy Integration*, 2, 125-147.

Baigent, M., Leight, R. and Lincoln H. (1983) *The Holy Blood and the Holy Grail*. Corgi.

Barkow, J.H. (1980) Prestige and self-esteem: A biosocial interpretation. In D.R. Omark, D.R Strayer and J. Freedman (eds.). *Dominance relations: An ethological view of social conflict and social interaction*. New York: Garland STPM Press.

Barkow, J.H. (1989) *Darwin: Sex and Status*. Toronto: Toronto University Press.

Barkow, J.H. (1991) Precis of Darwin, sex and status: Biological approaches to mind and culture (plus peer commentary). *Behavioral and Brain Sciences*, 14, 295-334

Barkow, J.H. (1975) Prestige and culture: A biosocial interpretation. (plus peer review). *Current Anthropology*, 16, 533-572.

Barkow, J.H., Cosmides, L. and Tooby, J. (1992, eds.) *The Adapted Mind: Evolutionary Psychology and the Generation of Culture*. New York: Oxford University Press.

Baumeister, R.F. (1991) *Meanings of Life*. New York: Guilford.

Baumeister, R.F. (1982) A self-presentational view of social phenomena. *Psychological Bulletin*, 91, 3-21.

Baumeister, R.F. Stillwell, A. and Heatherton, T.F. (1994) Guilt: Am Interpersonal Approach. *Psychological Bulletin*, 115, 243-267.

Beattie, J.M. (1986) *Crime and the Courts in England 1600-1800*. Oxford: Clarendon Press.

Beck, A.T., Emery, G. and Greenberg, R.L. (1985) *Anxiety Disorders and Phobias: A Cognitive Approach*. New York: Basic Books.

Beck A.T. Freeman, A. and Associates (1990) *Cognitive Therapy of Personality Disorder*. New York: Guilford.

Bee, H. (1992) *The Developing Child*. Sixth edition. New York: Harper Collins.

Belsky, J., Steinberg, L., and Draper, P. (1990) Childhood experiences, interpersonal development, and reproductive strategy: An evolutionary theory of socialization. *Child Development*, 62, 647-670.

Berkowitz, L. (1989) Frustration-aggression hypothesis: Examination and reformulation. *Psychological Bulletin*, 106, 59-73.

Birtchnell, J. (1993) *How Humans Relate: A New Interpersonal Theory*. Westport, Connecticut: Praeger.

Blackburn, R. (1989) Psychopathology and personality disorder in relation to violence. In Howells, K and Hollin, C.R. (eds.) *Clinical Approaches to Violence*. Chichester: J. Wiley.

Blaiklock, E.M. (1983) *The Confessions of Saint Augustine*. London: Hodder and Stoughton.

Bowlby, J. (1969) *Attachment: Attachment and Loss, Vol. 1*. London: Hogarth Press.

Bowlby, J. (1973) *Separation, Anxiety and Anger. Attachment and loss, Vol. 2*. London: Hogarth Press.

Bowlby, J. (1980) *Loss: Sadness and Depression. Attachment and Loss, Vol. 3*. London: Hogarth Press.

Bowlby, J. (1988) Developmental psychiatry comes of age. *American Journal of Psychiatry*, 145, 1-10.

Breggin, P. (1993) *Toxic Psychiatry*. Fontana.

Brewin, C.R., Andrews, B. and Gotlib, I.H. (1993) Psychopathology and early experiences: A reappraisal of retrospective reports. *Psychological Bulletin*, 113, 82-98.

Brody, L.R. (1993) On understanding gender differences in the expression of emotion: Gender roles, socialization, and language. In Ablon, S.L., Brown, D., Khantzian, E.J. and Mack, J.E. (eds.), *Human Feelings: Explorations in Affect Development and Meaning*. Hillsdale: The Analytic Press, pp.87-121.

Brooks, G. (1995) Against the verses. *The Guardian Weekend*, March 11, 13-19.

Brown, D., Khantzian, E.J. and Mack, J.E. (eds.) *Human Feelings: Explorations in Affect Development and Meaning*. Hillsdale: The Analytic Press.

Broucek, F.J. (1991) *Shame and the Self*. New York: Guilford.

Brown, B.B. and Lohr, M.J. (1987) Peer-group affiliation and adolescent self-esteem: An integration of ego-identity and symbolic-interaction theories. *Journal of Personality and Social Psychology*, 52, 47-55.

Brown, G.W., Adler, W.Z., & Bifulco, A. (1988). Life events, difficulties and recovery from chronic depression. *British Journal of Psychiatry*, 152, 487-498.

Brown, G.W., & Harris, T.O. (1978). *The Social Origins of Depression*. London: Tavistock.

Buck, R. (1988) *Human Motivation and Emotion*. New York: J.Wiley

Burford, E.J. and Shulman, S. (1992) *Of Bridles and Burnings: The Punishment of Women*. New York: St Martin's Press.

Burnstein, E., Crandall, C. and Kitayama, S. (1994) Some neo-darwinian rules for altruism: Weighing cues for inclusive fitness as a function of biological importance of the decision. *Journal of Personality and Individual Differences*, 67, 773-807.

Buss, A.H. (1988) *Personality: Evolutionary Heritage and Human Distinctiveness*. Hillsdale: N.J. Lawrence Erlbaum Associates.

Buss, D.M. (1994) The strategies of human mating. *American Scientist*, 82, 238-249.

Buss, D.M. (1991) Evolutionary personality psychology. *Annual Review of Psychology*, 42, 459-491.

Buss, D.M. (1989) Sex differences in human mate preference: Evolutionary hypotheses tested in 37 cultures. *Brain and Behavioral Sciences*, 12, 1-49.

Caryl, P.G. (1988) Escalated fighting and the war of nerves: Games theory and animal combat. In Bateson, P.H and Klopfer, P.H. (eds.), *Perspectives in Ethology. Advantages of Diversity: Vol 4*. New York: Plenum Press.

Chance, M.R.A. (1988). Introduction: In M.R.A. Chance (ed.), *Social Fabrics of the Mind*. Hove, Sussex: Lawrence Erlbaum Associates.

Chance, M.R.A. (1984). Biological systems synthesis of mentality and the nature of the two modes of mental operation: Hedonic and agonic. *Man-Environment Systems*, 14, 143-157.

Chance, M.R.A. (1980) An ethological approach assessment of emotion. In R. Plutchik, R. and H. Kellerman (eds.), *Emotion: Theory Research and Experience. Vol. 1*. New York: Academic Press.

Chisholm, J.S. (1988) Toward a developmental evolutionary ecology of humans. In K.M. MacDonald (ed.), *Sociobiological Perspectives on Human Development*. New York: Springer-Verlag.

Chomsky, N. (1992) *Deterring Democracy*. London: Vintage.

Clark, C. (1990) Emotions and micropolitics in everyday life: Some patterns and paradoxes of "place". In T.D. Kemper (ed.), *Research Agendas in the Sociology of Emotions*. New York: State University of New York Press.

Collins, N.L. and Read, S.J. (1990) Adult attachment, working models, and relationship quality in dating couples. *Journal of Personality and Social Psychology*, 58, 644-663.

Colman, A. (1991) Psychological evidence in South African murder trials. *The Psychologist*, 4, 482-486.

Coon, D. (1992) *Introduction to Psychology: Exploration and Application: Sixth Edition*. New York: West Publishing Company.

Coxhead, N. (1985) *The Relevance of Bliss*. London: Wildwood House Ltd.

Cosmides, L. and Tooby, J. (1992) Cognitive adaptations for social exchange. In Barkow, J.H., Cosmides, L. and Tooby, J. (eds.). *The Adapted Mind: Evolutionary Psychology and the Generation of Culture*. New York: Oxford University Press.

Cronen, V.E., Johnson, K.M. and Lannamann, J.W. (1982) Paradoxes, double binds, and reflexive loops: An alternative theoretical Perspective. *Family Process*, 21, 91-112.

Crook, J.H. (1986) The evolution of leadership: A preliminary Skirmish: In, Graumann, C.F and Moscovici, S (eds.), *Changing Conceptions of Leadership*. New York: Springer Verlag.

Crook, J.H. (1980) *The Evolution of Human* Consciousness. Oxford: Oxford University Press.

Davies, N. (1994) Dirty business. The *Guardian Weekend,* November 26, 12-17.

Davison, G.C. and Neale, J.M. (1994) *Abnormal Psychology.* Sixth edition. New York: John Wiley.

Daly, M. and Wilson, M. (1994) Evolutionary psychology of male violence. In Archer, J. (ed.) *Male Violence*. London: Routledge.

de Waal, F.M.B. (1988) The reconciled hierarchy. In M.R.A. Chance (ed.), *Social Fabrics of the Mind*. Hove: Lawrence Erlbaum.

de Waal, F. (1995) Bonobo Sex and Society. *Scientific American*, 272, 59-65.

DeAngelis, T. (1994) Loving styles may be determined in infancy. *American Psychological Society: Monitor*. October, 21.

Dell, P. (1989) Violence and the systemic view: The problem of power. *Family Process*, 28, 1-14.

Diamond, D. and Doane, J.A. (1994) Disturbed attachment and the negative affective style: An intergeneration spiral. *British Journal of Psychiatry*, 164, 770-781.

Diamond, J. (1991) *The Rise and Fall of the Third Chimpanzee. How our animal heritage affects the way we live.* London: Vintage.

Dixon, N.F. (1976/1994) *On the Psychology of Military Incompetence.* London: Cape.

Dixon, N.F. (1987) *Our Own Worst Enemy.* London: Routledge.

Donnison, D. (1992) Matter of life and death. *The Guardian*, September 30th, 21.

Doty, R.M., Peterson, B.E. and Winter, D.G. (1991) Threat and authoritarianism in the United States, 1978-1987. *Journal of Personality and Social Psychology*, 61, 629-640.

Eibl-Eibesfeldt, I. (1989) *Human Ethology.* New York: Aldine de Gruyter.

Eisenberg, L. (1986) Mindlessness and brainlessness in psychiatry. *British Journal of Psychiatry*, 148, 497-508.

Eisenberg, N. (1986). *Altruism, Emotion, Cognition and Behavior.* Hillsdale, N.J.: Lawrence Erlbaum Associates Inc.

Eisenberg, N. and Mussen, P.N. (1989) *The Roots of Prosocial Behavior in Children.* New York: Cambridge University Press.

Eisenstat, S.N. (1992) The order-maintaining and order-transforming dimensions of culture. In Munch, R and Smelser, N.J (eds.) *Theory of Culture.* Berkeley: University of California Press.

Eisenthal, S. (1989) The Sociocultural approach. In Larare, A (ed.) *Outpatient Psychiatry: Diagnosis and Treatment.* Baltimore: Williams and Wilkins.

Eisler, R. (1990) *The Chalice and the Blade: Our History, Our Future*. London: Unwin.

Ellenberger, H.F. (1970) *The Discovery of the Unconscious. The History and Evolution of Dynamic Psychiatry*. New York: Basic Books.

Emler, N. and Hogan, R. (1991) Moral psychology and public policy. In Kurtines, W.M. and Gewirtz, J.L. (eds.) *Handbook of Moral Behavior and Development. Volume 3: Application*. Hillsdale: Lawrence Erlbaum Associates.

Enright, P.D. (1991) The moral development of forgiveness. In Kurtines, W.M. and Gewirtz, J.L. (eds.) *Handbook of Moral Behavior and Development. Volume 1: Theory*. Hillsdale: Lawrence Erlbaum Associates.

Epstein, S. (1982). The unconscious, the preconscious and the self concept. In J. Suls and A.G. Greenwald (eds.), *Psychological perspectives on the self*. Hillsdale N.J.: Lawrence Erlbaum Associates Inc.

Feingold, A. (1994) Gender Differences in Personality: A meta-analysis. *Psychological Bulletin*, 116, 429-456.

Fielder, F.E. and House, R.J. (1988) Leadership theory and research. In Copper, C.L. and Robertson, I. (eds.). *International Review of Industrial and Organisational Psychology*. London: Wiley.

Fisher, S. (1989) *Sexual Images of the Self: The Psychology of Erotic Sensations and Illusions*. Hillsdale: Lawrence Erlbaum Associates.

Fiske, A.T. (1992). The four elementary forms of sociality: Framework for a unified theory of social relations. *Psychological Review*, 99, 689-721.

Fitzgibbons, R.B. (1986) The cognitive and emotive uses of forgiveness in the treatment of anger. *Psychotherapy*, 23, 629-633.

Focus (1995) Dossier: Soldiers. April, 45-53.

Fogel, A. (1993) *Developing Through Relationships: Origins of Communication, Self and Culture*. New York: Harvester Wheatsheaf.

Fogel, A., Melson, G.F., & Mistry, J. (1986). Conceptualising the determinants of nurturance: A reassessment of sex differences. In A. Fogel & G.F. Melson

(Eds.), *Origins of Nurturance: Developmental, Biological and Cultural Perspectives on Caregiving*. Hillsdale, N.J.: Lawrence Erlbaum Associates Inc.

Fossum, M.A. and Mason, M.J. (1986) *Facing Shame: Families in Recovery*. New York: Norton Paperbacks.

Foucault, M. (1984) *The Foucault Reader* (edited by Rainbow, P). Harmondsworth: Penguin.

Frank, J.D. (1982) Therapeutic components shared by psychotherapies. In J.H. Harvey, and M.M. Parkes (eds.), *Psychotherapy Research and Behavior Change, Vol 1*. Washington. D.C. American Psychological Association.

Freeman, A. (1993) *God in Us: A Case for Christian Humanism*. London: SCM Press.

Freeman, H. (1991). The human brain and political behaviour. British Journal of Psychiatry, 159, 19-32.

French, J. and Ravens, B.H. (1959) The bases of social power. In Cartwright D (ed.) *Studies in Social Power*. Ann Arbor Institute of Social Research.

Fromm, E. (1949/1986) *Man For Himself*. London: Ark Paperbacks.

Frosh, S. (1991) *Identity Crisis. Modernity. Psychoanalysis and the Self*. London: Macmillan.

Frude, N. (1989) The physical abuse of children. In Howells, K. and Hollin, C.R. (eds.) *Clinical Approaches to Violence*. Chichester: J. Wiley.

Fukuyama, F. (1992) *The End of History and the Last Man*. Penguin.

Galbraith, J.K. (1987) *The Affluent Society*. 4th edition. Penguin Books.

Galbraith, J.K. (1992) *The Culture of Contentment*. Penguin Books.

Gardner, E.J., Simmons, M.J. and Snustad, D.P. (1991) *Principles of Genetics*. Eighth Edition. New York: Wiley.

Gardner, R. (1988) Psychiatric infrastructures for intraspecific communication. In M.R.A. Chance (ed.), *Social Fabrics of the Mind*. Sussex. Hove: Lawrence Erlbaum Associates.

Gascoigne, B. (1977) *The Christians*. London: Jonathan Cape.

Gay, P. (1977) *The Enlightenment. An Interpretation: The Science of Freedom*. New York: Norton.

Gay, P. (1995) *The Cultivation of Hatred*. Fontana Press.

Gibbs, J.C. (1991) Sociomoral development delay and cognitive distortion. Implications for the treatment of antisocial youth. In Kurtines, W.M. and Gewirtz, J.L. (eds.) *Handbook of Moral Behaviour and Development. Vol 1: Theory*. Hillsdale: Lawrence Erlbaum Associates.

Gibbs, W.W. (1995) Seeking the criminal element. *American Scientist*, 272, 76-83.

Giddens, A. (1989) *Sociology*. London: Polity Press.

Gilbert, M. (1987) *Holocaust: The Jewish Tragedy*. London: Fontana.

Gilbert, P. (1995) Biopsychosocial approaches and evolutionary theory as aids to integration in clinical psychology and psychotherapy. *Clinical Psychology and Psychotherapy,* 2, 3, 135-136.

Gilbert, P. (1993) Defence and safety: Their function in social behaviour and psychopathology. *British Journal of Clinical Psychology*, 32, 131-154.

Gilbert, P. (1992a) *Depression: The Evolution of Powerlessness*. Hove: Lawrence Erlbaum Associates Ltd. And New York: Guilford.

Gilbert, P. (1992b) Defence, safety and biosocial goals in relation to the agonic and hedonic social modes. World Futures, *Journal of General Evolution*, 35, 31-70.

Gilbert, P. (1989) *Human Nature and Suffering*. Hove: Lawrence Erlbaum Associates.

Gilbert, P., Pehl, J. & Allan, S. (1994) The phenomenology of shame and guilt: An empirical investigation. *British Journal of Medical Psychology*, 67, 23-36.

Gilbert, P., Price, J.S. and Allan, S. (1995) Social comparison, social attractiveness and evolution: How might they be related? *New Ideas in Psychology* 13, 149-165.

Gilbert, P. and Trower, P. (1990) The evolution and manifestation of social anxiety. In W.R. Crozier (ed.). *Shyness and Embarrassment: Perspectives from Social Psychology*. Cambridge: Cambridge University Press.

Gilbert, P. (1990) Changes: Rank, status and mood. In S. Fisher and C.L. Cooper (eds.). *On the Move: The Psychology of Change and Transition*. Chichester: J. Wiley and Sons.

Gilligan, C. (1982) *In a Different Voice: Psychological Theory and Women's Development*. Cambridge Mass: Cambridge University Press.

Gilmore, D.D. (1990) *Manhood in the Making: Cultural Concepts of Masculinity*. New Haven: Yale University Press.

Gilmour, I.I. (1993) *Dancing with Dogma: Britain under Thatcherism*. London: Simon and Schuster

Glantz, K. and Pearce, J.K. (1989) *Exiles from Eden: Psychotherapy From an Evolutionary Perspective*. New York: W.W. Norton and Co.

Goffman, E. (1968) *Stigma: Notes on the Management of a Spoiled Identity*. Harmondsworth: Penguin.

Goldner, V., Penn, P., Sheinberg, M. and Walker, G. (1990) Love and violence: Gender paradoxes in volatile attachments. *Family Process*, 29, 343-364.

Goldsmith, J. (1994) *The Trap*. London: MacMillian.

Goldstein, A.P. and Michaels, G.Y. (1985) *Empathy: Development, Training and Consequences*. Hillsdale. Lawrence Erlbaum.

Goodall, J. (1990) *Through a Window. Thirty Years with the Chimpanzees of Gombe*. Penguin.

Goodall, J. (1975). The chimpanzee. In J.V. Goodall (ed.). *The Quest For Man*. London: Phaidon Press.

Goody, E. (1991) The learning of prosocial behaviour in small-scale egalitarian societies: an anthropological view. In Hinde, R.A. and Groebel, J. (eds.) *Cooperation and Prosocial Behaviour*. Cambridge: Cambridge University Press.

Gore, A. (1992) *Earth in the Balance: Forging a New Common Purpose*. London: Earthscan.

Goswami, A. (1993) *The Self-Aware Universe. How Consciousness Creates the Material World*. Jeremy P. Tarcher.

Grabsky, P. (1993) *The Great Commanders*. London: Boxtree and Channel Four Books.

Grant, L. and Norfolk, S. (1995) Written on the body. *The Guardian Weekend*, April 1st, 12-20.

Gray, J.A. (1987) *The Psychology of Fear and Stress*. Second edition. Cambridge: Cambridge University Press.

Greenberg, J.R. and Mitchell, S.A. (1983) *Object Relations in Psychoanalytic Theory*. Cambridge Mass: Harvard University Press.

Gregor, T. (1990) Male domination and sexual coercion. In Stigler, J.W., Shweder, R.A. and Herdt, G. (eds.) *Cultural Psychology: Essays in Comparative Human Development*. Cambridge: Cambridge University Press.

Gross, R.D. (1992) *Psychology: The Science of Mind and Behaviour*. Hodder and Stoughton.

Hall, C.S. and Nordby, V.J. (1973). *A Primer of Jungian Psychology*. New York: Mentor.

Halton, E. (1992) The cultic roots of culture: In Munch, R. and Smelser, N.J. (eds.) *Theory of Culture*. Berkeley: University of California Press.

Hannah, C. and McAdam, E. (1991) Violence-Part 1: Reflections on our work with violence. *Human Systems: Journal of Systemic Consultation and Management*. 2, 201-206.

Harl, H.F. and Mears, C. (1979) *The Human Model: Primate Perspectives*. New York: Winston and Sons.

Harper, J.M. and Hoopes, M.H. (1990) *Uncovering Shame*. New York: Norton.

Hartup, W. (1989) Social relationships and their developmental significance. *American Psychologist*, 44, 120-126.

Harvey, P. (1990) *An Introduction to Buddhism. Teachings, History and Practices*. Cambridge: Cambridge University Press.

Haste, H. and Baddeley, J. (1991) Moral theory and culture: The case of gender. In Kurtines, W.M. and Gewirtz, J.L. (eds.) *Handbook of Moral Behaviour and Development. Vol 1: Theory*. Hillsdale: Lawrence Erlbaum Associates.

Hattenstone, S. (1995) Apocalypse now, or maybe later. *The Guardian*, Saturday, April 8th, 25.

Haviland, W.A. (1990) *Cultural Anthropology*. 6th edition. New York: Holt. Rinehart and Winston.

Heard, D.H. and Lake, B. (1986) The attachment dynamic in adult life. *British Journal of Psychiatry*. 149, 430-438.

Henry, J.P. and Stephens, P.M. (1977) *Stress, Health and the Social Environment: A Sociobiologic Approach to Medicine*. New York: Springer Verlag.

Herbert, F. (1968) *Dune*. New English Library.

Hill, J. (1984) Human altruism and sociocultural fitness. *Journal of Social and Biological Structures*, 7, 17-35.

Hillman, H. (1995) The cruel myth of `humane' execution. *The Independent on Sunday*, 9th April, 3.

Hinde, R.A. (1987) *Individuals, Relationships and Culture. Links Between Ethology and the Social Sciences*. Cambridge: Cambridge University Press.

Hinde, R.A. (1989) Relations between levels of complexity in behavioral sciences. *Journal of Nervous and Mental Disease*, 177, 655-667.

Hinde, R.A. and Groebel, J. (1991) Introduction: In, Hinde, R.A. and Groebel, J. (eds.), *Cooperation and Prosocial Behaviour*. Cambridge: Cambridge University Press.

Hinde, R.A. (1992) Developmental psychology in the context of other behavioral sciences. *Developmental Psychology*, 28, 1018-1029.

Hofer, M.A. (1984) Relationships as regulators: A psychobiologic perspective on bereavement. *Psychosomatic Medicine*, 46, 183-197.

Hofer, M.A. (1981) *The Roots of Human Behavior*. San Francisco: W.H. Freeman.

Hoffman, M.L. (1991) Empathy, social cognition and moral action. In Kurtines, W.M. and Gewirtz, J.L. (eds.) *Handbook of Moral Behaviour and Development. Vol 1: Theory*. Hillsdale: Lawrence Erlbaum Associates.

Hogan, R.M., Rasking, R. and Fazzini, D. (1988) The dark side of charisma. Unpublished. *Conference on Psychological Measurement and Leadership*. San Antonio: Texas.

Hollander, E.P. and Offerman, L.R. (1990) Power and leadership in organisations: Relationships in transition. *American Psychologist*, 45, 179-189.

Holmes, J. (1993) *John Bowlby and Attachment Theory*. London: Routledge.

hooks, b. (1984) *Feminist Theory: From Margin to Centre*. Boston: South End Press.

Horowitz, L.M., and Vitkus, J. (1986). The interpersonal basis of psychiatric symptoms. *Clinical Psychology Review*, 6, 443-470.

Howell, S. and Willis, R. (1989, eds.) *Societies at Peace: An Anthropological Perspective*. London: Routledge.

Hutton, W. (1995a) *The State We're In*. London: J. Cape

Hutton, W. (1995b) Growing inequality means the poor keep getting poorer. *The Guardian*, February 10th, 7.

Isen, A.M. (1990) The influence of positive and negative affect on cognitive organisation: Some implications for development. In, N.L. Stein, B. Leventhal, and T. Trabasco (eds.), *Psychological and Biological Approaches to Emotion*. Hillsdale: Lawrence Erlbaum Associates, Ltd.

Itzkoff, S.W. (1990) *The Making of the Civilized Mind*. New York: Peter Lang.

Jensen-Campbell, L.A., Graziano, W.G. and West, S.G. (1995). Dominance, prosocial orientation and female preference: Do nice guys really finish last. *Journal of Personality and Social Psychology*, 68, 427-440.

Johnson, D.W. and Johnson, F.P. (1991) *Joining Together: Group Theory and Skills*. 4th Edition. London: Prentice-Hall International Editions.

Jones, S. (1994) *The Language of the Genes*. Flamingo

Jones, S.L. (1994) A constructive relationships for religion with the science and profession of psychology. *American Psychologist*, 49, 184-199.

Jung, C.G. (1972) *Four Archetypes*. London: Routledge.

Jung, G. (1992) *Wild Swans: Three Daughters in China*. Flamingo.

Kagan, J. (1984) *The Nature of the Child*. New York: Basic Books.

Kalma, A.P. (1991) Hierarchisation and dominance assessment at first glance. *European Journal of Social Psychology*, 21, 165-181.

Kalma, A. P., Visser, L. and Peeters, A. (1993) Sociable and aggressive dominance: Difference in leadership styles? *Leadership Quarterly*, 4, 45-64.

Kaufman, J. and Zigler, E. (1987) Do abused children become abusive parents? *American Journal of Orthopsychiatry*, 57, 186-192.

Kaufman, G. (1989) *The Psychology of Shame*. New York: Springer.

Keegan, W. (1993) *The Spectre of Capitalism*. Vintage.

Keen, S. (1992) *Fire in the Belly: On Being A Man*. London: Piatkus.

Kegan, R. (1982) *The Evolving Self: Problem and Process in Human Development*. Cambridge, Mass: Harvard University Press

Kemper, T.D. and Collins, R. (1990) Dimensions of microinteraction. *American Journal of Sociology*, 96, 32-68.

Kemper, T.D. (1990) *Social Structure and Testosterone: Explorations of the Socio-Bio-Social Chain*. New Brunswick: Rutgers University Press.

Kemper, T.D. (1990, ed.), *Research Agendas in the Sociology of Emotions*. New York: State University of New York Press.

Kemper, D.T. (1988). The two dimensions of sociality. In M.R.A. Chance (ed.). *Social Fabrics of the Mind*. Hove: Lawrence Erlbaum Associates.

Kiesler, D.J. (1983) The 1982 interpersonal circle: A taxonomy for complementarity in human transactions. *Psychological Review*, 90, 185-214.

Kitzinger, C. (1994) Problemizing pleasure: Radical feminist deconstructions of sexuality and power. In Radtke, H.L. and Stam, H.J. (1994) *Power/Gender: Social Relations in Theory and Practice*. London: Sage.

Klama, J. (1988) *Aggression: Conflict in Animals and Humans Reconsidered*. Harl: Longman.

Kohut, H. (1977) *The Restoration of the Self*. New York: International Universities Press.

Kriegman, D. (1990) Compassion and altruism in psychoanalytic theory: An evolutionary analysis of self psychology. *American Academy of Psychoanalysis*, 18, 342-362.

Kurtines, W.M. and Gewirtz, J.L. (1991, eds.) *Handbook of Moral Behaviour and Development. Vol 1: Theory. Vol 2: Research. Vol 3: Applications*. Hillsdale: Lawrence Erlbaum Associates.

Lansky, M.R. (1992) *Fathers who Fail. Shame and Psychopathology in the Family System*. Hillsdale: Analytic Press.

Lasch, C. (1985) *The Minimal Self*. London: Picador.

Lasch, C. (1979/1991) *The Culture Of Narcissism*. New York: Norton Paperbacks.

Lazare, A. (1986) Shame and Humiliation in the Medical Encounter, *Archives of International Medicine*, 147, 1653-1658.

Leary, T. (1957) *The Interpersonal Diagnosis of Personality*. New York: Ronald Press.

Levenson, M.R. (1992) Rethinking psychopathy. *Theory and Psychology*, 2, 51-71.

Lewis, H.B. (1987) Introduction: Shame-the "sleeper" in psychopathology. In H.B. Lewis (ed.), *The Role of Shame in Symptom Formation*. Hillsdale N.J: Lawrence Erlbaum Associates.

Lewis, M. (1992) *Shame: The Exposed Self*. New York: The Free Press.

Lindholm, C. (1993) *Charisma*. Oxford: Blackwell.

Lukes, S. (1986, ed.) *Power*. New York: New York University Press.

MacDonald, K.B. (1988) *Social and Personality Development: An Evolutionary Synthesis*. New York: Plenum Press.

MacLean, P.D. (1990) *The Triune Brian in Evolution*. New York: Plenum Press.

MacLean, P.D. (1985) Brain evolution relating to family, play and the separation call. *Archives of General Psychiatry*, 42, 405-417.

Malone, R.E. (1995) Heavy users of emergency services: Social construction of a policy problem, *Social Science and Medicine*, 40, 469-477.

Marks, I.M. (1987) *Fears, Phobias, and Rituals: Panic, Anxiety and their Disorders*. Oxford: Oxford University Press.

Maslow, A.H. (1943) The authoritarian structure. *Journal of Social Behavior*, 18, 401-411.

Mann, M. (1986) *The Sources of Social Power: Volume 1. A History of Power from the Beginning to A.D. 1760*. Cambridge: Cambridge University Press.

McAdam, E. and Hannah, C. (1991) Violence-2: Creating the best context to work with clients who have found themselves in violent situations. *Human Systems: Journal of Systemic Consultation and Management*, 2, 201-206.

McCarthy, B. (1994) Warrior Values: A socio-historical survey. In Archer, J. (ed.) *Male Violence*. London: Routledge

McDermott, M. (1993) On cruelty, ethics and experimentation: Profile of Philip Zimbardo. *The Psychologist*, 6, (October) 456-459.

McGhee, M. (1995) The turn towards Buddhism. *Religious Studies*, 31, 69-87.

McGhee, M. (1993) Individual Buddhists, *Religious Studies*, 29, 443-452.

McGuire, M.T., Fawxy, F.I., Spar, J.I., Weigel, R.M. and Troisi, A. (1994) Altruism and mental disorders. *Ethology and Sociobiology*, 15, 299-321.

McGuire, M.T., Marks, I., Nesse, R.M. and Trosi, A. (1992) Evolutionary Biology: A Basic Science for psychiatry? *Acta Psychiatrica Scandinavia*, 86, 89-96.

Meth, R.L. and Pasick, R.S. (1990) *Men in Therapy: The Challenge of Change*. New York: Guilford.

Meyersburg, H.A. and Post, R.M. (1979) A holistic developmental view of neural and psychobiological processes: A neurobiologic-psychoanalytic integration. *British Journal of Psychiatry*, 135, 139-155.

Miedzian, M. (1992) *Boys will be Boys: Breaking the Link Between Masculinity and Violence*. London: Virago.

Milgram, S. (1974) *Obedience to Authority*. New York: Harper and Row.

Miller, A. (1983) *For Your Own Good: The Roots of Violence in Child-rearing.* London: Virago.

Miller, J.G and Bersoff, D.M. (1992) Culture and moral judgement: How are conflicts between justice and interpersonal responsibilities resolved. *Journal of Personality and Social Psychology*, 62, 541-554.

Miller, P.A. and Eisenberg, N. (1988) The relation of empathy to aggressive behaviour and externalising/antisocial behavior. *Psychological Bulletin*, 103, 324-344.

Montagner, H., Restoin, A., Rodriguez, D., Ullman, V., Viala, M., Laurent, D. and Godard, D. (1988) Social interactions of young children with peers and their modifications in relation to environmental factors. In M.R.A. Chance (ed.), *Social Fabrics of the Mind*. Hove: Lawrence Erlbaum Associates.

Mollon, P. (1984). Shame in relation to narcissistic disturbance. *British Journal of Medical Psychology*, 57, 207-214.

Nathanson, D.L. (1994) *Shame and Pride: Affect Sex and the Birth of the Self*. New York: Norton Paperbacks.

Newnham, D. (1995) Pills & Hope. *The Guardian Weekend*, Feb 18th, 12-15.

Nesse, R.M. (1990) Evolutionary explanations of emotions. *Human Nature*, 1, 261-289.

Oatley, K. (1992) *Best Laid Schemes: The Psychology of Emotions*. Cambridge: Cambridge University Press.

Ohman, A. (1986) Face the beast and fear the face: Animal and social fears as prototypes for evolutionary analyses of emotion. *Psychophysiology*, 23, 123-144.

Oliner, S.P. and Oliner, P.M. (1988) *The Altruistic Personality: Rescuers of Jews in Nazi Europe*. New York: Free Press.

Ornstein, R. (1986). *Multimind: A new way of looking at human beings*. London: Macmillan.

Overing, J. (1989). Styles of manhood: An Amazonian contrast in tranquillity and violence. In, Howell, S. and Wills, R. (eds.) *Societies at Peace. Anthropological Perspectives*. London: New York.

Parker, G.A. (1974). Assessment strategy and the evolution of fighting behaviour. *Journal of Theoretical Biology*, 47, 223-243.

Parker, G.A. (1984). Evolutionary strategies. In J.R. Krebs & N.B. Davies (eds.), *Approach*. Oxford: Blackwell.

Pascal, B. (1670) *Pensées: Notes on Religion Behavioral Ecology: An Evolutionary and Other Subjects.* Edited by L. Lafuma. Translation by J. Warrington. London: Dent.

Pilger, J. (1995) Death for sale. *The Guardian Weekend*, November, 12, 13-20.

Plant, R. (1991) *Modern Political Thought.* Oxford: Blackwell.

Podsakoff, P.M. and Schriesheim, C.A. (1985) Field Studies of French and Raven's bases of Power: Critique, Reanalysis and suggestions for Future research. *Psychological Bulletin.* 97, 387-411.

Porter, R. and Hall, L. (1995) *The Facts of Life. The creation of Sexual Knowledge in Britain, 1650-1950.* London. Yale University Press.

Post, R.M. (1992) Transduction of psychosocial stress into the neurobiology of recurrent affective disorders. *American Journal of Psychiatry*, 149, 999-1010.

Postman, N. (1987) *Amusing Ourselves to Death.* New York: Methuen.

Powell, L.H. and Friedman, M. (1986) Alteration of Type A behaviour in coronary patients. In, M.J. Christie and P.G. Mallet (eds.) *The Psychosomatic Approach: Contemporary Practice of Whole-Person Care.* Chichester: J. Wiley.

Power, M. (1991) *The Egalitarians: Human and Chimpanzee: An Anthropological View of Social Organisation.* Cambridge: Cambridge University Press.

Pratto, F., Sidanius, J., Stallworth, L.M. and Malle, B. (1994) Social dominance orientation: A personality variable predicting social and political attitudes. *Journal of Personality and Social Psychology*, 67, 741-763.

Price, V.A. (1982) *Type A Behavior Pattern: A Model for Research and Practice.* New York: Academic Press.

Price, J.S. (1988) Alternative channels for negotiating asymmetry in social relationships. In M.R.A. Chance (ed.). Social Fabrics of the Mind. Hove: Lawrence Erlbaum Associates.

Price, J.S., Sloman, R., Gardner, R., Gilbert, P. and Rhodes, P. (1994) The social competition hypothesis of depression. *British Journal of Psychiatry*, 164, 309-315.

Radtke, H.L. and Stam, H.J. (1994) *Power/Gender: Social Relations in Theory and Practice*. London: Sage.

Raskin, R. and Terry, H. (1988) A principle components analysis of the narcissistic personality inventory and further evidence of its construct validity. *Journal of Personality and Social Psychology*, 54, 890-902.

Raskin, R., Novacek, J. and Hogan R. (1991) Narcissistic self management. *Journal of Personality and Social Psychology*, 60, 911-918.

Ray, J.C. and Sapolsky, R.M. (1992) Styles of social behavior and their endocrine correlates among high-ranking wild baboons. *American Journal of Primatology*, 28, 231-250.

Reisman, J.M. (1991) *A History of Clinical Psychology*. Second Edition. New York: Hemisphere.

Rendall, J. (1992) Who betrayed Mike Tyson? *The Independent on Sunday*. 16th Feb, 2-5.

Reynolds, V., Falger, V. and Vine, I. (1986, eds.) *The Sociobiology of Ethnocentrism: Evolutionary Dimensions of Xenophobia, Discrimination, Racism and Nationalism*. London: Croom Helm.

Ridley, M. (1994) *The Red Queen: Sex and the Evolution of Human Nature*. Penguin:

Robins, K. (1993) The politics of silence: The meaning of community and the uses of the media in the new Europe. *New Formations*, 21, 80-101.

Robson, A. (1993) *Torture not Culture*. Amnesty: British Section September/October. 8-9.

Rohner, R.P. (1986) *The Warmth Dimension: Foundations of Parental Acceptance-Rejection Theory*. Beverly Hills: Sage.

Romer, J. (1988) *Testament: The Bible and History*. London: Guild: A Channel Four Book.

Rowan, J. (1990) *Subpersonalities: The People Inside Us*. London: Routledge.

Rowe, D. (1992) *Wanting Everything. The Art of Happiness*. Fontana.

Runnels, C.N. (1995) Environmental degradation in ancient Greece. *Scientific American*, 272, 73-75.

Sabini, J. and Silver, M. (1982) *The Moralities of Everyday Life*. New York: Oxford University Press.

Sagan, C. and Druyan, A. (1992) *Shadows of Forgotten Ancestors: A Search For Who We Are*. London: BCA.

Sampson, E.E. (1993) *Celebrating the Other*. New York: Harvester Wheatsheaf.

Sapolsky, R.M. (1989) Hypercortisolism among socially subordinate wild baboons originates at the CNS level. *Archives of General Psychiatry*, 46, 1047-1051.

Sapolsky, R.M. (1990a) Adrenocortical function, social rank and personality among wild baboons. *Biological Psychiatry*, 28, 862-878.

Sapolsky, R.M. (1990b) Stress in the wild. *Scientific American*, January, 106-113.

Salazar, A. (1992) Born to die in Medellin. *The Weekend Guardian*, August 1-2nd, 12-13.

Scheff, T.J. (1988) Shame and conformity. The deference-emotion system. *American Review of Sociology*, 53, 395-406.

Schore, A.N. (1991) Early superego development: The emergence of shame and narcissistic affect regulation in the practising period. *Psychoanalysis and Contemporary Thought. A Quarterly of Integrative and Interdisciplinary Studies*, 14, 187-250.

Schore, A.N. (1994) *Affect Regulation and the Origin of the Self: The Neurobiology of Emotional Development*. Hillsdale: N.J. Lawrence Erlbaum.

Schumaker, J.F. (1992) Introduction: In, Schumaker, J.F. (ed.). *Religion and Mental Health*. New York: Oxford University Press.

Scott, J.C. (1990) *Domination and the Arts of Resistance*. New Haven: Yale University Press.

Sen, A. (1993) The economics of life and death. *Scientific American*, May, 18-25.

Serney, G. (1990). The sins of the fathers. *The Sunday Times Colour Magazine*, September 23, 22-36.

Shafranske, E.P. (1992) Religion and Mental Health in Early Life. In, Schumaker, J.F. (ed.). *Religion and Mental Health*. New York: Oxford University Press.

Shilling, C. (1993) *The Body and Social Theory*. London: Sage.

Shott, S. (1979) Emotion and social life: A symbolic interactionist analysis. *American Journal of Sociology*, 84, 1317-1334.

Shreve, B.W. and Kunkel, M.A. (1991) Self-psychology, and adolescent suicide: Theoretical and practical considerations. *Journal of Counselling and Development*, 69, 305-311

Sidanius, J., Pratto, F. and Bobo, L. (1994) Social dominance orientation and the political psychology of gender: A case of invariance? *Journal of Personality and Social Psychology*, 67, 998-1011.

Slavin, M.O. and Kreigman, D. (1992) *The Adaptive Design of the Human Psyche: Psychoanalysis, Evolutionary Biology, and the Therapeutic Process*. New York: Guilford.

Sloman, L., Price, J.S., Gilbert, P. and Gardner, R. (1994) Adaptive function of depression: Psychotherapeutic implications. *American Journal of Psychotherapy*, 48, 1-16.

Smail, D. (1987) *Taking Care: An Alternative to Therapy*. London: J. Dent and Sons.

Snarey, J.R. (1985). Cross-cultural universality of social-moral development: A critical review of Kohlbergian research. *Psychological Bulletin*, 97, 202-232.

Snarey, J. and Keljo, K. (1991) In a Gemeinschaft Voice: The cross-Cultural Expansion of Moral Development Theory. In Kurtines, W.M. and Gewirtz, J.L. (eds.) *Handbook of Moral Behaviour and Development. Vol 1: Theory*. Hillsdale: Lawrence Erlbaum Associates.

Snodgrass, S.E. (1992) Further effects of role versus gender on interpersonal sensitivity. *Journal of Personality and Social Psychology*, 62, 154-158.

Sternberg, R.J. (1986) A triangular theory of love. *Psychological Review*, 93, 119-135.

Stevens, A. (1982). *Archetype: A Natural History of the Self*. London: Routledge & Kegan Paul.

Stevens, A. (1989) *The Roots of War. A Jungian Perspective*. New York: Paragon House.

Storr, A. (1970/1992) *Human Aggression*. Penguin.

Spitzer, R.L., Feister, S., Gay, M. and Pfohl, B. (1991) Results of a survey of forensic psychiatrists on the validity of the sadistic personality disorder diagnosis. *American Journal of Psychiatry*, 148, 875-879.

Suls, S. and Wills, T.A. (1991) *Social Comparison. Contemporary Theory and Research*. Hillsdale: Lawrence Erlbaum Associates.

Symington, N. (1994) *Emotions and Spirit. Questioning the Claims of Psychoanalysis and Religion*. London: Cassell.

Tangney, J.P., Wager, P., Fletcher, C. and Gramzow, R. (1992) Shamed into anger? The relation of shame and guilt to self-reported aggression. *Journal of Personality and Social Psychology*, 62, 669-675.

Tantum, D. (1993) The developmental psychopathology of emotional disorders. *Journal of the Royal Society of Medicine*, 86, 336-340.

Taylor, C. (1992) *Sources of the Self: The Making of the Modern Identity*. Cambridge: Cambridge University Press.

Taylor, S.E. and Brown, J.D. (1988). Illusion and well-being: A social psychological perspective on mental health. *Psychological Bulletin*, 103, 193-210.

Tejirian, E. (1990) *Sexuality and the Devil: Symbols of Love, Power and Fear in Male Psychology*. New York: Routledge.

Tinbergen, N. (1963) On the aims and methods of ethology. *Zeitscrift fur Tierpsychologie*, 20, 410-433.

Toffler, A. (1991) *Power Shift: Knowledge, Wealth and Violence at the Edge of the 21st Century*. London: Bantam.

Tomkins, S.S. (1981) The quest for primary motives: Biography and autobiography. *Journal of Personality and Social Psychology*, 41, 306-329.

Tooby, J. and Cosmides, L. (1992) The psychological foundations of culture. In. Barkow, J.H., Cosmides, L. and Tooby, J. (eds.). *The Adapted Mind: Evolutionary Psychology and the Generation of Culture*. New York: Oxford University Press.

Trivers, R. (1985) *Social Evolution*. California: Benjamin/Cummings.

Troy, M. and Sroufe, L.A. (1987) Victimization among preschoolers: Role of attachment relationship history. *Journal of American Academy of Child and Adolescent Psychiatry*, 26, 166-172.

Tully, M. (1992) *No Full Stops in India*. Penguin

Van Lange, P.A.M. and Rusbult, C.E. (1995) My relationship is better than - and not as bad as - yours is: The perception of superiority in close relationships. *Personality and Social Psychology Bulletin*, 21, 32-44.

Van Schaik, C.P. (1989) The ecology of social relationships amongst female primates. In V. Standen and R.A. Foley (eds.). *Comparative Socioecology: The Behavioural Ecology of Humans and Other Animals*. Oxford: Blackwell.

Ussher, J. (1991) *Women's Madness: Misogyny or Mental Illness?* London: Harvester and Wheatsheaf.

van der Dennen, J.M.G. (1986) Ethnocentrism and in-group/out-group differentiation: A review and interpretation of the literature. In Reynolds, V., Falger, V. and Vine, I. (eds.). *The Sociobiology of Ethnocentrism: Evolutionary Dimensions of Xenophobia, Discrimination, Racism and Nationalism*. London: Croom Helm.

Watts, F. and Williams, M. (1988) *The Psychology of Religious Knowing*. London: Chapman.

Weingartner, K. (1991) The discourses of intimacy: Adding a social constructionist and feminist view. *Family Process*, 30, 285-305.

Wenegrat, B. (1990) *The Divine Archetype. The Sociobiology and Psychology of Religion.* Massachusetts: Lexington.

Wenegrat, B. (1984) *Sociobiology and mental disorder: A New View*. California: Addison-Wesley.

Wilber, K. (1983) *A Sociable God*. London: New Science Library.

Wihelm, R. (1984) *The Secret of the Golden Flower*. Penguin.

Wilkinson, R.G. (1992) Income distribution and life expectancy. *British Medical Journal*, 304, 18th January, 165-168.

Williams, L. (1992) Torture and the torturer. *The Psychologist*, 5, 305-308.

Wills, C. (1991) *The Wisdom of the Genes: New Pathways in Evolution*. Oxford: Oxford University Press paperbacks.

Wilson, M. and Daly, M. (1985) Competitiveness, risk taking, and violence: The young man's syndrome. *Ethology and Sociobiology*, 6, 59-73.

Wilson, M. and Daly, M. (1992) The man who mistook his wife for a chattel. In Barkow, J.H., Cosmides, L. and Tooby, J. (eds.). *The Adapted Mind: Evolutionary Psychology and the Generation of Culture*. New York: Oxford University Press.

Wilson, E.O. (1992) *The Diversity of Life*. Penguin.

Wink, P. (1991) Two faces of narcissism. *Journal of Personality and Social Psychology*, 61, 590-597.

Winter, D. (1993) Power, affiliation, and war. Three tests of a motivational model. *Journal of Personality and Social Psychology*, 65, 532-545.

Wispe, L. (1986). The distinction between sympathy and empathy. *Journal of Personality and Social Psychology*, 50, 314-321.

Wolfe, R.N., Lennox, R.D, and Cutler, B.L. (1986) Getting along and getting ahead: Empirical support for a theory of protective and acquisitive self-presentation. *Journal of Social and Personality Psychology*, 50, 356-361.

Wright, J.C., Giammarino, M. and Parad, H.W. (1986) Social status in small groups: Individual-group similarity and social "misfit". *Journal of Personality and Social Psychology*, 50, 523-536.

Yalom, I.D. (1980) *Existential Psychotherapy:* New York: Basic Books.

Zilboorg, G. and Henry, G.W. (1941). *History of Medical Psychology.* New York: W.W. Norton & Co.

Zimbardo, P.G., Banks, W.C., Craig, H. and Jaffe, D. (1973) A Pirandellian prison: The mind is a formidable jailor: New York: *Times Magazine*, April 8th, 38-60.

INDEX

(fn) indicates footnote

A

Abraham and Isaac, 363
abuse, 83, 166, 195–7
  child, 11, 83, 323, 437
  sexual *see* sexual abuse
  shame and, 195–7
Adam and Eve and Garden of Eden, 63, 146, 165, 175, 178, 186, 361, 362, 368
adaptation
  environment of evolutionary adaptation, 44–6
  social mode and, 128
adoration, submissive, 253–4, 266
adultery, stoning, 305, 306, 385
affect regulation system, 497
African tribes
  Gusii, 120–1, 121, 124, 148
  !Kung, 120, 121, 125, 148
Age of Enlightenment, 3–7, 412, 468, 529
ageing body, 187–8
aggression, 292–3
  dominance based on, 89–92, 224
  retaliatory, 295
  see also violence
aging body, 187–8
agonic mode, 99, 100, 124–5, 127, 128, 129, 130, 162, 230, 453(fn)
agriculture/farming, 10–11, 17, 133, 162, 163, 215, 366, 398, 402, 403
  compassion to animals, 490, 528
alcohol, excessive drinking, 204
Alexander the Great, 329, 335
alliances, 73–4, 84–7
  breaking, 324
  formation, 73–4, 84–7
  leadership and, 245–6
  see also collusions in silence; communal sharing; cooperation; mutuality
altruism, 14, 37–9, 99–102, 238, 412, 461–8, 477–8

ABOUT THE AUTHOR

Paul Gilbert was born in 1951 in Bathurst, Gambia, spending his early childhood in Nigeria before relocating to Portsmouth in 1962. He completed an economics degree at Wolverhampton Polytechnic in 1970-3, but took the chance to follow his dream, which was a career in psychology. In 1973 he retrained in an MSc in Experimental Psychology at the University of Sussex, before moving to a PhD at the University of Edinburgh where he investigated reduced positive emotion in depression. He first book, *Depression: From Psychology to Brain State*, was published in 1984. After Edinburgh he lived in Norwich, where he completed his clinical training, before moving to Derby in 1989 where he currently resides.

Paul became a Professor in 1993 at the University of Derby, and has been a Visiting Professor at the University of Fribourg in Switzerland; University of Coimbra in Portugal, and more recently at the University of Queensland in Australia. He was awarded an OBE for services to mental healthcare in 2011. He established the Compassionate Mind Foundation in 2006, which promotes wellbeing through facilitating the scientific understanding and application of compassion. He has, to date, published over 300 academic articles and book chapters, and *Living Like Crazy* will be his 22nd book. He is married with two grown up children, and when not working he enjoys snorkelling, cricket and guitar playing.

Links

Living Like Crazy Blog: https://professorpaulgilbert.blogspot.co.uk/
Twitter: @ProfPaulGilbert
Personal Website: www.profpaulgilbert.co.uk

For online links to all the resources noted in the Postscript
visit *Annwyn House* on the web: **https://annwynhouse.weebly.com**